CANADA

ONTARIO

QUÉBEC

ATLANTIC OCEAN

GULF OF MEXICO

BAHAMAS

CUBA

Canada Highway Map

0 mi 200 400
0 km 200 400 600

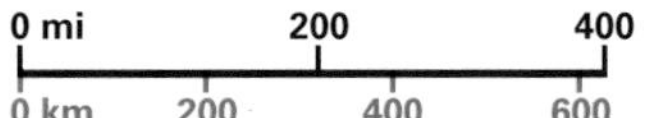

One inch equals 250 miles/Un pouce équivaut à 250 milles
One cm equals 159 km/Un cm équivaut à 159 km

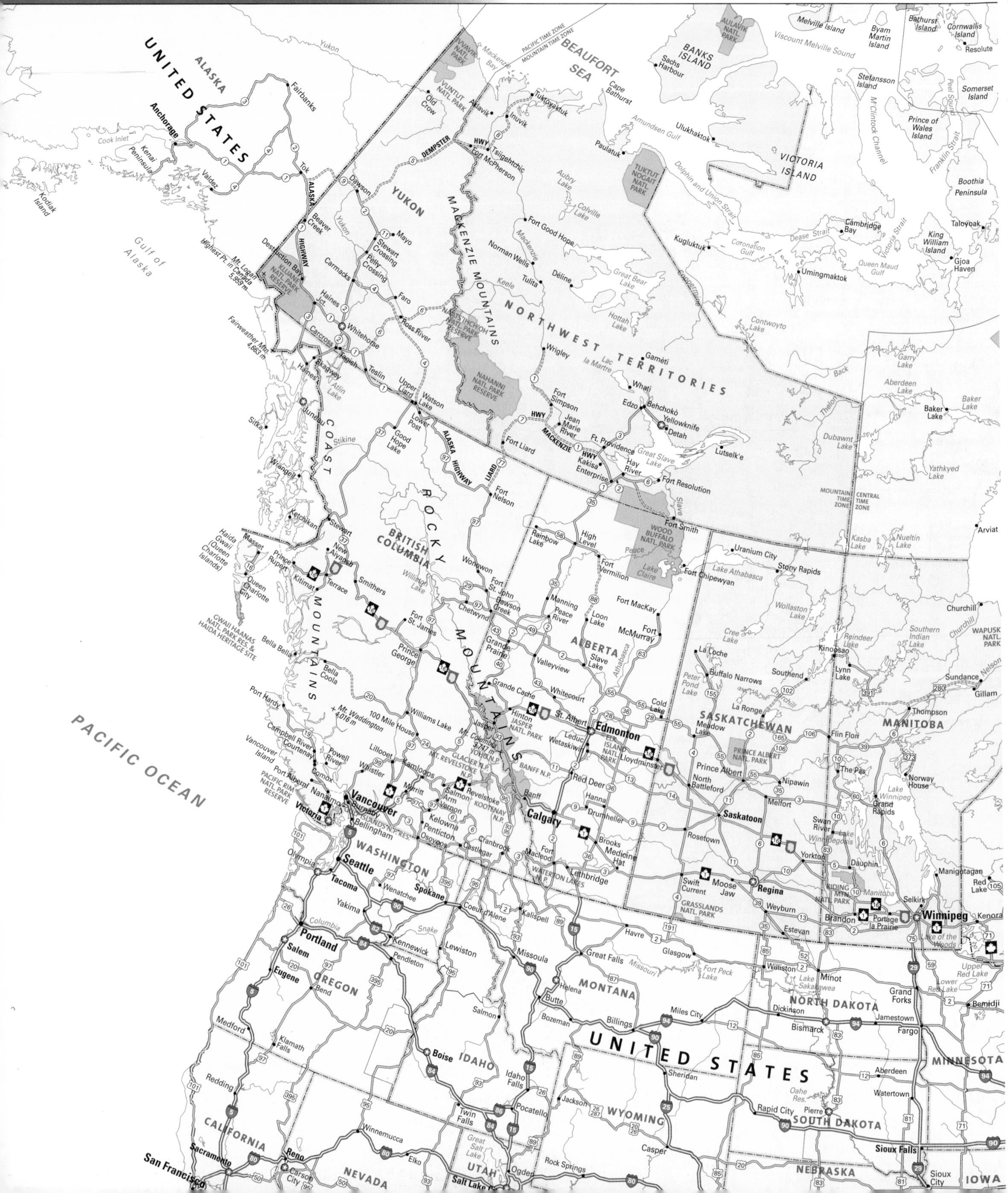

Road Atlas

USA CANADA MEXICO

ROAD MAPS are organized geographically. *United States, Canada, and Mexico road maps are organized in a grid layout, starting in the northwest of each country. To find your way, use either the* ***Key to Map Pages*** *inside the front cover, the* ***Listing of State and City Maps*** *on page 3, or the* ***index*** *in the back of the atlas.*

COUNTRY COLORS
Colors represent countries throughout the atlas.
Red → Canada
Green → Mexico
Blue → United States
Purple → United States (Northeast Corridor)

MAP SCALES
Scale bars are shown at a constant length throughout the atlas for quick and easy scale comparison between regions.

DRIVING DISTANCES
Use this chart to check driving distances between major cities within each map. Refer to distance and driving time information at the back of the atlas for travel over greater distances.

LOCATOR MAPS
A quick glance at this miniature map lets you check which states and/or provinces are shown on each page.

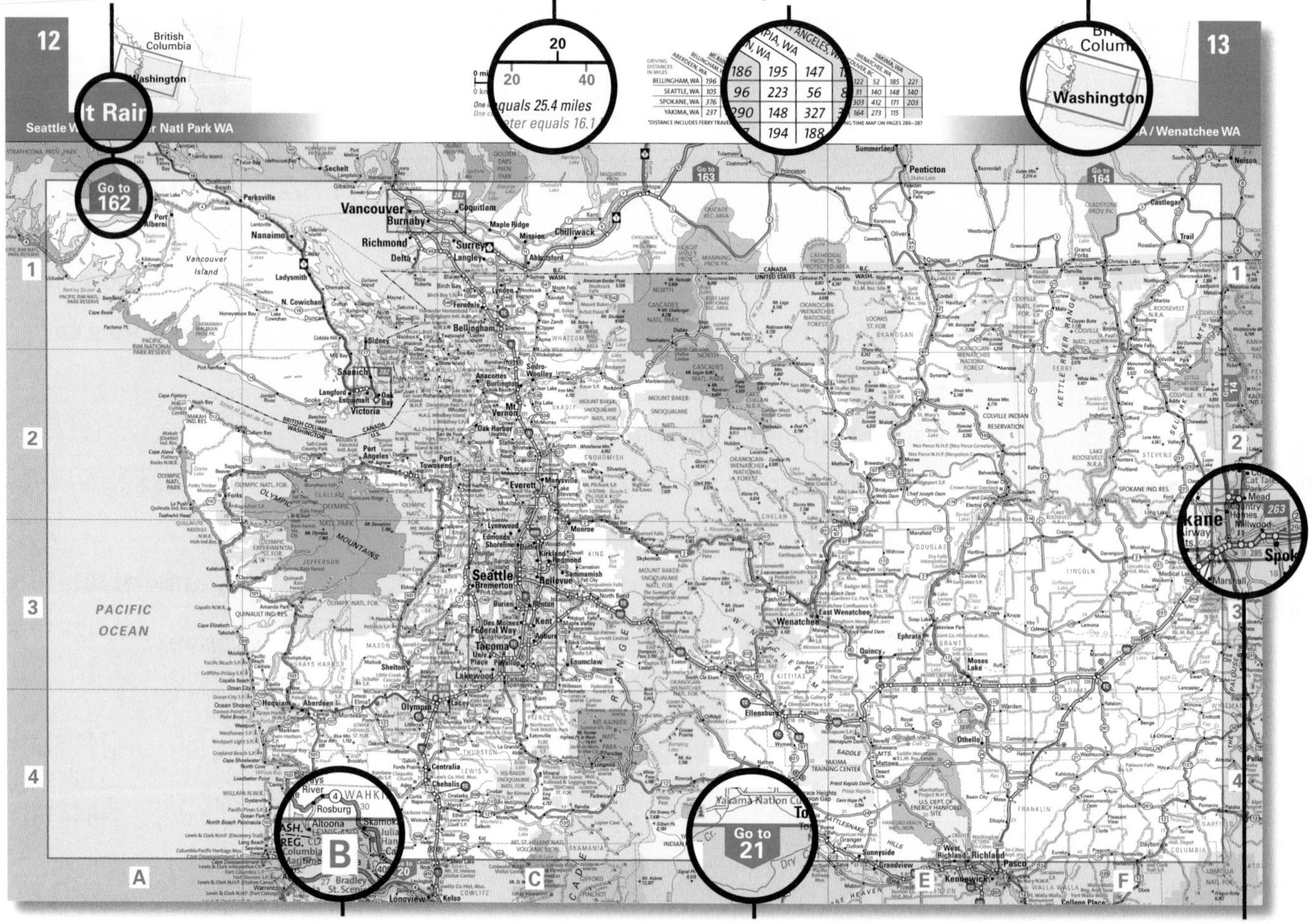

GRID REFERENCES
Use grid references to locate places listed in the index. For instance, Rosburg WA is listed in the index with "12" and "B4", indicating that the town may be found on page 12 in grid square B4.

"GO TO" POINTERS
Handy page tabs point the way to the next map, making navigation a breeze.

INSET MAP BOXES
These color-coded boxes outline areas that are featured in greater detail in the index section. The tab with "263" (above) indicates that a detailed map of Spokane may be found on page 263 (below).

HOW THE INDEX WORKS
Cities and towns are listed alphabetically, with separate indexes for the United States, Canada, and Mexico. Figures after entries indicate population, page number, and grid reference. Entries in bold color indicate cities with detailed inset maps. The U.S. index also includes counties and parishes, which are shown in bold black type.

INSET MAP INDEXES
Many inset maps have their own indexes. Metro area inset map indexes list cities and towns; downtown inset map indexes list points of interest.

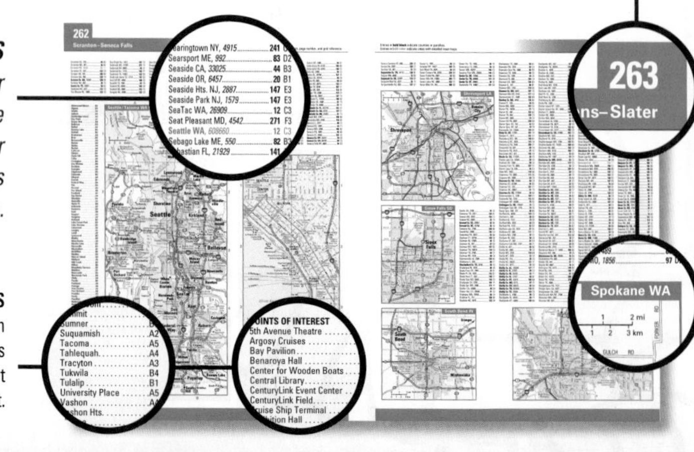

UNITED STATES pages 12–155

CANADA pages 155–183

MEXICO pages 184–187

United States Interstate Map

0 mi 125 250 375
0 km 125 250 375 500

One inch equals 217 miles
One centimeter equals 138 kilometers

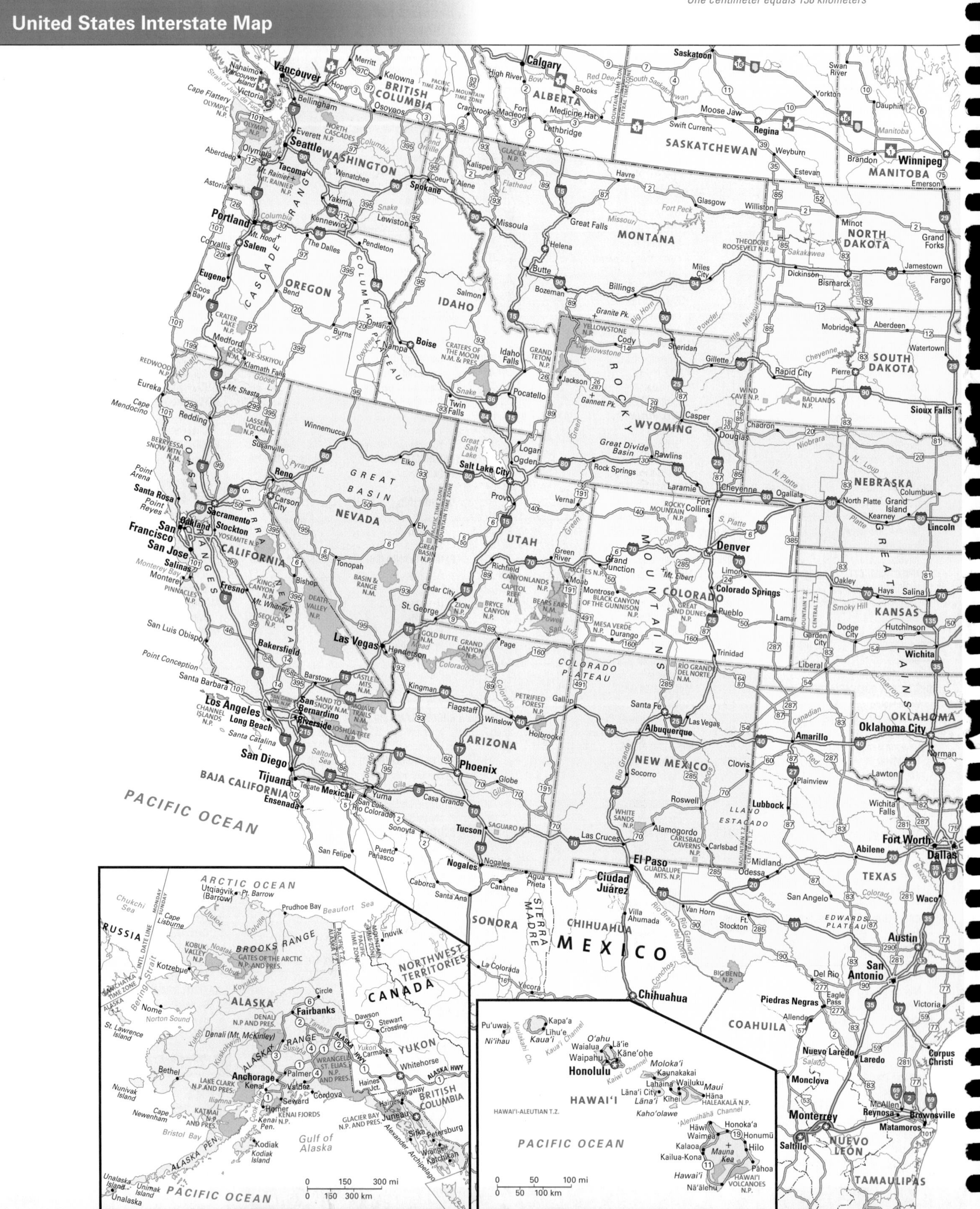

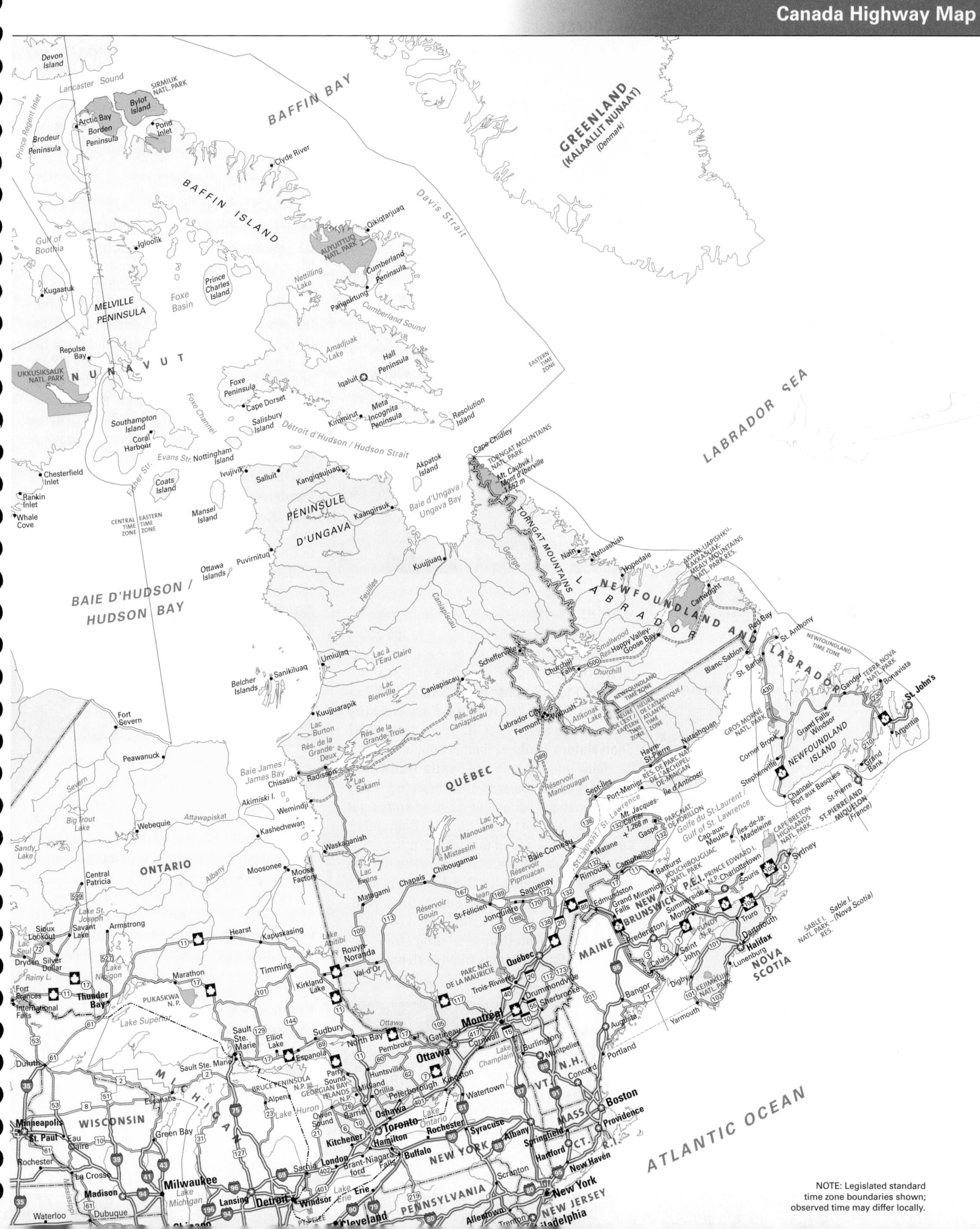
Devon Island
Lancaster Sound
SIRMILIK NATL. PARK
Bylot Island
Arctic Bay
Borden Peninsula
Pond Inlet
Prince Regent Inlet
Brodeur Peninsula
BAFFIN BAY
GREENLAND (KALAALLIT NUNAAT) (Denmark)
Clyde River
BAFFIN ISLAND
Davis Strait
Qikiqtarjuaq
AUYUITTUQ NATL. PARK
Gulf of Boothia
Igloolik
Kugaaruk
MELVILLE PENINSULA
Foxe Basin
Prince Charles Island
Nettilling Lake
Cumberland Peninsula
Pangnirtung
Cumberland Sound
Amadjuak Lake
Hall Peninsula
Repulse Bay
UKKUSIKSALIK NATL. PARK
NUNAVUT
EASTERN TIME ZONE
Iqaluit
Foxe Peninsula
Cape Dorset
Meta Incognita Peninsula
Kimmirut
Resolution Island
LABRADOR SEA
Foxe Channel
Southampton Island
Coral Harbour
Salisbury Island
Détroit d'Hudson / Hudson Strait
Cape Chidley
TORNGAT MOUNTAINS NATL. PARK
Mt. Caubvik / Mont d'Iberville 1,652 m
Nottingham Island
Evans Str.
Fisher Str.
Chesterfield Inlet
Rankin Inlet
Whale Cove
Coats Island
Ivujivik
Salluit
Kangiqsujuaq
Akpatok Island
Baie d'Ungava / Ungava Bay
Kangirsuk
PÉNINSULE D'UNGAVA
Mansel Island
CENTRAL TIME ZONE
EASTERN TIME ZONE
TORNGAT MOUNTAINS
Nain
Natuashish
Hopedale
Puvirnituq
Ottawa Islands
Kuujjuaq
BAIE D'HUDSON / HUDSON BAY
NEWFOUNDLAND AND LABRADOR
LABRADOR
Cartwright
Happy Valley-Goose Bay
Smallwood Res.
Red Bay
St. Anthony
NEWFOUNDLAND TIME ZONE
TERRA NOVA NATL. PARK
Schefferville
Churchill Falls
Churchill
Blanc-Sablon
St. Barbe
Umiujaq
Lac à l'Eau Claire
Belcher Islands
Sanikiluaq
Lac Bienville
Caniapiscau
Rés. de Caniapiscau
Labrador City
Wabush
Fermont
Gander
Bonavista
St. John's
Grand Falls-Windsor
NEWFOUNDLAND ISLAND
GROS MORNE NATL. PARK
Corner Brook
Argentia
Fort Severn
Kuujjuarapik
Lac Burton
Rés. de la Grande-Deux
Rés. de la Grande-Trois
Natashquan
Havre-St-Pierre
Île d'Anticosti
Stephenville
Channel-Port aux Basques
Grand Bank
St-Pierre
ST-PIERRE AND MIQUELON (France)
Peawanuck
Baie James / James Bay
Chisasibi
Radisson
Lac Sakami
QUÉBEC
Réservoir Manicouagan
Sept-Îles
Port-Menier
Akimiski I.
Wemindji
Attawapiskat
Big Trout Lake
Webequie
Kashechewan
Lac Mistassini
Lac Manouane
Mt. Jacques-Cartier 1,268 m
Gaspé
PARC NAT. DE FORILLON
Golfe du St-Laurent / Gulf of St. Lawrence
Cap-aux-Meules
Îles-de-la-Madeleine
CAPE BRETON HIGHLANDS NATL. PARK
Sydney
Sandy Lake
ONTARIO
Waskaganish
Moosonee
Moose Factory
Chibougamau
Baie-Comeau
Matane
Rimouski
Campbellton
Bathurst
Central Patricia
Chapais
Réservoir Pipmuacan
Saguenay
Jonquière
St-Félicien
Lac St-Jean
PRINCE EDWARD I.
Charlottetown
Souris
Edmundston
Grand Falls
Miramichi
NEW BRUNSWICK
P.E.I.
Summerside
Moncton
Truro
Lake St. Joseph
Savant Lake
Sioux Lookout
Armstrong
Hearst
Kapuskasing
Matagami
Réservoir Gouin
Rouyn-Noranda
Val-d'Or
Fredericton
Saint John
FUNDY N.P.
Halifax
Dartmouth
Lunenburg
NOVA SCOTIA
SABLE I. NATL. PARK RES.
Sable I. (Nova Scotia)
Dryden
Silver Dollar
Rainy L.
Nipigon
Marathon
Timmins
Kirkland Lake
PARC NAT. DE LA MAURICIE
Trois-Rivières
Québec
Drummondville
Sherbrooke
MAINE
Bangor
Calais
Digby
KEJIMKUJIK NATL. PARK
Yarmouth
Fort Frances
International Falls
Thunder Bay
PUKASKWA N.P.
Lake Superior
Sault Ste. Marie
Elliot Lake
Sudbury
North Bay
Pembroke
Gatineau
Montréal
Cornwall
Augusta
Duluth
Espanola
Ottawa
Lake Champlain
Burlington
Montpelier
N.H.
Portland
MICHIGAN
BRUCE PENINSULA N.P.
GEORGIAN BAY ISLANDS N.P.
Parry Sound
Huntsville
Midland
Orillia
Peterborough
Kingston
Watertown
VT.
Concord
Boston
Escanaba
Alpena
Lake Huron
Owen Sound
Barrie
Oshawa
Toronto
Lake Ontario
MASS.
Providence
ATLANTIC OCEAN
Minneapolis
St. Paul
WISCONSIN
Green Bay
Eau Claire
Kitchener
Hamilton
Rochester
Syracuse
Albany
Springfield
CT.
R.I.
Rochester
La Crosse
London
Brant-ford
Niagara Falls
Buffalo
NEW YORK
Hartford
New Haven
Madison
Milwaukee
Lake Michigan
Sarnia
Lansing
Detroit
Windsor
Lake Erie
Erie
Scranton
New York
NEW JERSEY
PENNSYLVANIA
Waterloo
Dubuque
Chicago
Cleveland
Allentown
Trenton
Philadelphia
NOTE: Legislated standard time zone boundaries shown; observed time may differ locally.

Experience the thrill of the open roads of North America with these great Scenic Drives from Michelin. The famous star ratings highlight natural and cultural attractions along the way.

- ★★★ **Worth a special journey**
- ★★ **Worth a detour**
- ★ **Interesting**

Michelin Scenic Drives are indicated by a green and yellow dashed line (▬▬▬▬) on corresponding atlas maps for easy reference. The following 17 drives are also plotted for your use.

ABBREVIATIONS

N	North	**NL**	National Lakeshore
E	East	**NM**	National Memorial/ National Monument
S	South	**NMP**	National Military Park
W	West	**NP**	National Park
NE	Northeast	**NPR**	National Park Reserve
NW	Northwest	**NRA**	National Recreation Area
SE	Southeast	**NWR**	National Wildlife Refuge
SW	Southwest	**PP**	Provincial Park
Hwy.	Highway	**SHP**	State Historical Park
Pkwy.	Parkway	**SHS**	State Historic Site
Rte.	Route	**SP**	State Park
Mi	Miles	**SR**	State Reserve
Km	Kilometers	**VC**	Visitor Center
Sq Ft	Square Feet		
NHS	National Historic Site		

For detailed coverage of the attractions, and for suggestions of places to dine and stay overnight, see Michelin's North America **Regional Atlas Series**, designed for the way you drive, and Michelin's **Green Guide Collection**, the ultimate guidebooks for the independent traveler.

NORTHWEST

Anchorage/Fairbanks/Denali★★★

892 miles/1,436 kilometers

Maps 189, 154, 155

From **Anchorage★**, Alaska's largest city, take Rte. 1 (Glenn Hwy. and Tok Cutoff) N and then E through the broad Matanuska Valley to the small town of **Tok**. The route passes agricultural communities, the **Matanuska Glacier** and the Wrangell Mountains before heading up the Copper River Basin. From Tok, take the Alaska Hwy. (Rte. 2) NW to **Fairbanks★**, a friendly town with a frontier feel. The road passes the **Trans-Alaska Pipeline** and **Big Delta SHP** then parallels the Tanana River. From Fairbanks, opt for Rte. 3 W that crosses the river at **Nenana**, then veers S to **Denali NP★★★**, home of spruce forests, grassy tundra, grizzlies,moose and North America's highest peak, **Mount McKinley** (20,310ft). Return S to Anchorage via Rtes. 3 and 1.

Alaska Range, Denali NP

Badlands★★

164 miles/264 kilometers Maps 253, 26

From **Rapid City★**, South Dakota, drive SE on Rte. 44 through Farmingdale and Scenic, then east to Interior to enter **Badlands NP★★**. Take Rte. 377 NE 2mi to Cedar Pass and stop at the park's Ben Reifel VC. From there, **Cliff Shelf Nature Trail★★**(.5mi) is popular for its shady junper trees and **Castle Trail★★★** (4.5mi) is spectacular in early morning when the moonscape valley and pointed spires get first light. Turn left onto Rte. 240, **Badlands Loop Road★★★**, along the northern rim, where prairie grasslands give way to buttes and hoodoos. **Pinnacles Overlook★★** is a sweeping viewpoint to the south. Drive N to I-90, and cross the Interstate N to Wall. On Main St. visit **Wall Drug★**, a "drug store" with more than 20 shops filled with historical photos, thousands of pairs of cowboy boots, wildlife exhibits and Western art displayed in five dining rooms. In the backyard a roaring, 80ft **Tyrannosaurus** sends toddlers running. Leave Wall on I-90, driving W. Take Exit 67 to Ellsworth Air Force Base, where the **South Dakota Air** and **Space Museum** displays stealth bombers and other aircraft. Continue W on I-90 back to Rapid City to conclude the tour.

Badlands NP

Black Hills★★

244 miles/393 kilometers Maps 253, 26, 25

From **Rapid City★**, drive S on US-16 then US-16A S past Keystone. Take Rte. 244 W to **Mount Rushmore NM★★★**. Continue W on Rte. 244 to the junction of US-16/385. Enroute S to Custer, **Crazy Horse Memorial★** honors the famous Sioux chief. From Custer, head S on US-385through Pringle to the junction of Rte. 87. Take Rte. 87 N through **Wind Cave NP★★** and into **Custer SP★★**. Follow **Wildlife Loop Road★★** (access S of Blue Bell, across from Rte. 342 junction) E and N to US-16A. Then travel W to join scenic **Needles Highway★★** (Rte. 87) NW to US-16/385 N. Where US-16 separates, continue N on US-385 to **Deadwood★★**, a former gold camp. Turn left onto US-14A, driving SW through **Lead★**, site of the former **Homestake Gold Mine★★**, to Cheyenne Crossing. Drive N on US-14A to I-90, turning SE back to Rapid City.

Mount Rushmore NM

Columbia River Gorge★★

123 miles/198 kilometers Maps 251, 20, 21

From **Portland★★**, Oregon's largest city, take I-84 E to Exit 17 in Troutdale. There, head E on the winding **Historic Columbia River Highway★★** (US-30), which skirts the steep cliffs above the river. For great **views★★**, stop at **Vista House at Crown Point**. You'll pass the 620ft **Multnomah Falls★★** and moss-draped **Oneonta Gorge**. At Ainsworth State Park (Exit 35), rejoin I-84 and travel E to Mosier (Exit 69), where US-30, with its hairpin turns, begins again. Continue E on US-30, stopping at **Rowena Crest Viewpoint★★** for grand vistas—and wildflowers. Just past the The Dalles, one of the oldest occupied places in Oregon, take US-197 N to conclude the tour at **The Dalles Lock** and **Dam VC★★**.

Grand Tetons/Yellowstone★★★

224 miles/361 kilometers Map 24

Note: parts of this tour are closed in winter.

From **Jackson★★**, drive N on US-26/191/89 to Moose. Turn left onto Teton Park Rd. to access **Grand Teton NP★★★** and **Jenny Lake Scenic Drive★★★**. From Teton Park Rd., drive N to the junction of US-89/191/287 (**John D. Rockefeller Jr. Memorial Pkwy.**) and follow the parkway N into **Yellowstone NP★★★** to **West Thumb**. Take Grand Loop Rd. W to **Old Faithful★★★**, the world's most famous geyser. Continue N on the Grand Loop Rd., passing **Norris Geyser Basin★★** en route to **Mammoth Hot Springs★★★**. Turn E on Grand Loop Rd. to Tower Junction, then S into **Grand Canyon of the Yellowstone★★★**. Continue S from Canyon Village through **Hayden Valley★★** to Lake. Head SW, back to West Thumb, to conclude to tour.

Grand Teton NP
© Jason Langley/Getty Images

Pacific Coast/Olympic Peninsula★★★

419 miles/675 kilometers Maps 245, 12

From the state capital of **Olympia**, drive N on US-101 to Discovery Bay. Detour on Rte. 20 NE to **Port Townsend★★**, a well-preserved Victorian seaport. From Discovery Bay, head W on US-101 through **Port Angeles** to the **Heart O' the Hills** park entrance for **Olympic NP★★★** to see **Hurricane Ridge★★★**. Back on US-101, head E then S to the park entrance that leads to **Hoh Rain Forest★★★**. Follow US-101 S, then E after Queets to **Lake Quinaulte**, home to bald eagles, trumpeter swans and loons. Continue S on US-101 to Aberdeen, taking Rte. 105 to the coast. At Raymond, return to US-101 heading S to **Long Beach**. Follow Rte. 103 N past the former cannery town of **Oysterville** to **Leadbetter Point★** on Willapa Bay, where oysters are still harvested. Backtrack S to **Ilwaco** and drive E and S on US-101 to Astoria, Oregon, to end the tour.

The Oregon Coast★★

368 miles/592 kilometers Maps 20, 28

Leave **Astoria★**, Oregon's first settlement, via US-101, heading SW. **Fort Clatsop National Memorial★★** recalls Lewis and Clark's historic stay. **Cannon Beach★** boasts a sandy beach and tall coastal rock. At the farming community of **Tillamook★**, go west on 3rd St. to **Cape Meares** to begin **Three Capes**

Cannon Beach, Oregon Coast
© Craig Tuttle/Getty Images

Scenic Drive★★. Continue S, rejoining US-101 just beyond Pacific City. Drive S on US-101 through **Newport★**, then **Yachats★**, which neighbors **Cape Perpetua Scenic Area★★**. From **Florence** to **Coos Bay★** stretches **Oregon Dunes National Recreation Area★★**. At Coos Bay, take Cape Arago Hwy. W to tour the gardens of **Shore Acres State Park★**. Drive S on the highway to rejoin US-101. Pass **Bandon★**, known for its cheese factory, and Port Orford, with its fishing fleet. Farther S, Samuel H. Boardman State Scenic Corridor★ shelters Sitka spruce, Douglas fir and **Natural Bridge Cove**. End the tour at **Brookings**.

SOUTHWEST

Big Bend Area★★

581 miles/935 kilometers

Maps 211, 56, 57, 62, 60

Head S from **El Paso★** via I-10, then E to Kent. Take Rte. 118 S to Alpine, passing **McDonald Observatory★** (telescope tours) and **Fort Davis NHS★★**. Continue S to Study Butte to enter **Big Bend NP★★★**, edged by the Rio Grande River and spanning 1,252sq mi of spectacular canyons, lush bottomlands, sprawling desert and mountain woodlands. The park has more species of migratory and resident birds than any other national park. Travel E to the main VC at Panther Junction in the heart of the park (US-385 and Rio Grande Village Dr.). Then take US-385 N to Marathon. Turn E on US-90 to Langtry, site of **Judge Roy Bean VC★**. Continue E to **Seminole Canyon SP★★**, with its 4,000-year-old pictographs. Farther E, **Amistad NRA★** is popular for water sports. Continue on US-90 to conclude the tour in Del Rio.

Canyonlands of Utah★★★

481 miles/774 kilometers Maps 39, 40

From **St. George★**, drive NE on I-15 to Exit 16. Take Rte. 9 E to Springdale, gateway to **Zion NP★★★**, with its sandstone canyon, waterfalls and hanging gardens. Continue E on Rte. 9 to Mt. Carmel Junction, turn left onto US-89 and head N to the junction with Rte. 12. Take Rte. 12 SE to **Bryce Canyon NP★★★**, with its colored rock formations. Continue SE on Rte. 12 to Cannonville, then S to **Kodachrome Basin SP★★**, where sandstone chimneys rise from the desert floor. Return to Cannonville, and drive NE on Rte. 12 through Boulder to Torrey. Take Rte. 24 E through **Capitol Reef NP★★**—with its unpaved driving roads and trails—then N to I-70. Travel E on I-70 to Exit 182, then S on US-191 to Rte. 313 into **Canyonlands NP★★★** to **Grand View Point Overlook**. Return to US-191, turning S to access **Arches NP★★★**—the greatest concentration of natural stone arches in the country. Continue S on US-191 to **Moab★** to end the tour.

Canyonlands NP
© Alan Copson/Getty Images

Central Coast/Big Sur★★★

118 miles/190 kilometers Maps 236, 44

From **Cannery Row★** in **Monterey★★**, take Prescott Ave. to Rte. 68. Turn right and continue to Pacific Grove Gate (on your left) to begin scenic **17-Mile Drive★★**, a private toll road. Exit at Carmel Gate to reach the upscale artists' colony of **Carmel★★**, site of Carmel **mission★★★**. The town's Scenic Road winds S along the beachfront. Leave Carmel by Hwy. 1 S. Short, easy trails at **Point Lobos SR★★** line the shore. Enjoy the wild beauty of the **Big Sur★★★** coastline en route to San Simeon, where **Hearst Castle★★★**, the magnificent estate of a former newspaper magnate, overlooks the Pacific Ocean. Continue S on Hwy. 1 to **Morro Bay**, where the tour ends.

Bixby Creek Bridge, Big Sur
© Michele Falzone/Getty Images

Colorado Rockies★★★

499 miles/803 kilometers

Maps 209, 41, 33, 40

Note: Rte. 82 S of Leadville to Aspen is closed mid-Oct to Memorial Day due to snow.

From **Golden★★, W of Denver★★★**, drive W on US-6 along Clear Creek to Rte. 119, heading N on the **Peak to Peak Highway★★** to **Nederland★**. Continue N on Rte. 72, then follow Rte. 7 N to the town of **Estes Park★★**. Take US-36 W to enter **Rocky Mountain NP★★★**. Drive **Trail Ridge Road★★★** (US-34) S to the town of **Grand Lake★**. Continue

Aspen, Colorado Rockies

S to Granby, turn left on US-40 to I-70 at Empire. Head W on I-70 past **Georgetown★** and through **Eisenhower Tunnel**. You'll pass ski areas Arapahoe Basin, **Keystone Resort★** and **Breckenridge★★**. At Exit 195 for **Copper Mountain Resort★**, take Rte. 91 S to **Leadville★★**, Colorado's former silver capital. Then travel S on US-24 to Rte. 82 W over **Independence Pass★★** to **Aspen★★★**. Head NW to I-70, passing **Glenwood Springs★★** with its **Hot Springs Pool★★**. Drive E on I-70 along **Glenwood Canyon★★** and the Colorado River to **Vail★★**. Continue E on I-70 to the old mining town of **Idaho Springs** to return to Golden via scenic Rte. 6.

Lake Tahoe Loop★★

71 miles/114 kilometers Map 37

Begin in **Tahoe City** at the intersection of Rtes. 89 and 28. Drive S on Rte. 89. **Ed Z'berg-Sugar Pine Point State Park★** encompasses a promontory topped by **Ehrman Mansion★** and other historic buildings. Farther S, **Emerald Bay State Park★★** surrounds beautiful **Emerald Bay★★**. At the bay's tip stands **Vikingsholm★★**, a mansion that resembles an ancient Nordic castle. At **Tallac Historic Site★★**, preserved summer estates recall Tahoe's turn-of-the-19C opulence. From Tahoe Valley, take Rte. 50 NE. **South Lake Tahoe**, the lake's largest town, offers lodging, dining and shopping. High-rise hotel-casinos characterize neighboring **Stateline** in Nevada. Continue N to Spooner Junction. Then follow Nevada Rte. 28 N to **Sand Harbor** (7mi), where picnic tables and a sandy beach fringe a sheltered cove. Continue through Kings Beach to end the tour at Tahoe City.

Emerald Bay, Lake Tahoe

Maui's Hana Highway★★

108 miles/174 kilometers Map 153

Leave **Kahului** on Rte. 36 E toward **Paia**, an old sugar-plantation town. Continue E on Rte. 36, which becomes Rte. 360, the **Hana Highway★★**. The road passes **Ho'okipa Beach Park**, famous for windsurfing, and **Puohokamoa Falls**, a good picnic stop, before arriving in **Hana**, a little village on an attractive bay. If adventurous, continue S on the Pulaui Highway to **Ohe'o Gulch★★** in **Haleakala NP★★★**, where small waterfalls tumble from the SE flank of the dormant volcano Haleakala. Past the gulch the grave of aviator **Charles Lindbergh** can be found in the churchyard at Palapala Hoomau Hawaiian Church. End the tour at **Kipahulu**.

Haleakala NP, Maui

Redwood Empire★★

182 miles/293 kilometers Maps 36, 28

In **Leggett**, S of the junction of Hwy. 1 and US-101, go N on US-101 to pass through a massive redwood trunk at **Chandelier Drive-Thru Tree Park**. To the N, see breathtaking groves along 31mi **Avenue of the Giants★★★**. **Humboldt Redwoods SP★★** contains Rockefeller Forest★★, the world's largest virgin redwood forest. From US-101, detour 4mi to **Ferndale★**, a quaint Victorian village. N. along US-101, **Eureka★** preserves a logging camp cookhouse and other historic sites. The sleepy fishing town of **Trinidad★** is home to a marine research lab. **Patrick's Point SP★★** offers dense forests, agate-strewn beaches and clifftop **view★★**. At **Orick**, enter the **Redwood National and State Parks★★**, which protect a 379ft-high, 750-year-old **tree★**. The tour ends in Crescent City.

Avenue of the Giants, Redwood Empire

Santa Fe Area★★★

267 miles/430 kilometers Maps 189, 48, 260, 49

From **Albuquerque★**, drive E on I-40 to Exit 175 and take Rte. 14, the **Turquoise Trail★★**, N to **Santa Fe★★★**. This 52mi back road runs along the scenic Sandia Mountains and passes dry washes, arroyos and a series of revived "ghost towns." Continue N on US-84/285, turning NE onto Rte. 76, the **High Road to Taos★★**. East of Vadito, take Rte. 518 N to Rte. 68 N into the rustic Spanish colonial

Taos Pueblo, Santa Fe Area

town of **Taos★★**, a center for the arts. Head N on US-64 to the junction of Rte. 522. Continue W on US-64 for an 18mi round-trip detour to see the 1,200ft-long, three-span **Rio Grande Gorge Bridge** over the river. Return to Rte. 522 and take this route, part of the **Enchanted Circle★★** Scenic Byway, N to **Questa**, starting point for white-water trips on the Rio Grande. Turn onto Rte. 38, heading E to the old mining town of **Eagle Nest**. There, detour 23mi E on US-64 to **Cimarron**, a Wild West haunt. Backtrack to Eagle Nest, then travel SW on US-64, detouring on Rte. 434 S to tiny **Angel Fire**. Return to Taos on US-64 W to end the tour.

Sedona/Grand Canyon NP★★★

482 miles/776 kilometers
Maps 249, 54, 47, 213

Drive N from **Phoenix★** on I-17 to Exit 298 and take Rte. 179 N toward **Sedona★★** in the heart of **Red Rock Country★★★**. The red-rock formations are best accessed by four-wheel-drive vehicle via 12mi **Schnebly Hill Road★** (off Rte. 179, across Oak Creek bridge from US-89A "Y" junction), which offers splendid **views★★★**. Then head N on Rte. 89A through Sedona to begin 14mi drive of **Oak Creek Canyon★★**. Continue N on Rte. 89A and I-17 to **Flagstaff★**, commercial hub for the region. Take US-180 NW to Rte. 64, which leads N to the **South Rim★★★** of **Grand Canyon NP★★★**. Take the shuttle (or drive, if permitted) along **West Rim Drive★★** to **Hermits Rest★**. Then travel **East Rim Drive★★★** (Rte. 64 E) to **Desert View Watchtower★** for **views★★★** of the canyon. Continue to the junction with US-89 at Cameron. Return S to Flagstaff, then S to Phoenix via I-17.

Grand Canyon NP

NORTHEAST

The Berkshires Loop★★★

57 miles/92 kilometers Map 94

From **Great Barrington**, take US-23 E to Monterey, turning left onto Tyringham Rd., which becomes Monterey Rd., to experience scenic **Tyringham Valley★**. Continue N on Main Rd. to Tyringham Rd., which leads to **Lee**, famous for its marble. Then go NW on US-20 to **Lenox★**, with its inviting inns and restaurants. Detour on Rte. 183 W to **Tanglewood★**, site of a popular summer music festival. Return to Lenox and drive N on US-7 to **Pittsfield**, the commercial capital of the region. Head W on US-20 to enjoy **Hancock Shaker Village★★★**, a museum village that relates the history of a Shaker community established here in 1790. Rte. 41 S passes West Stockbridge, then opt for Rte. 102 SE to **Stockbridge★★** and its picturesque **Main Street★**. Follow US-7 S to the junction with Rte. 23, passing **Monument Mountain★** en route. Return to Great Barrington.

Cape Cod★★★

164 miles/264 kilometers Maps 151, 95

At US-6 and Rte. 3, cross **Cape Cod Canal** via Sagamore Bridge and turn onto Rte. 6A to tour the Cape's **North Shore★★**. Bear right onto Rte. 130 to reach **Sandwich★**, famous for glass manufacture. Continue on Rte. 6A E to Orleans. Take US-6 N along **Cape Cod National Seashore★★★**, with its wooded and marshland trails, to reach **Provincetown★★**, a resort town offering **dune tours★★** and summer theater. Backtrack to Orleans and take Rte. 28 S through **Chatham★**, then W to Hyannis, where ferries depart for **Nantucket★★★**. Continue to quaint **Falmouth★**. Take Surf Dr., which becomes Oyster Pond Rd. to nearby **Woods Hole**, a world center for marine research and departure point for ferries to **Martha's Vineyard★★**. Take Woods Hole Rd. N to Rte. 28. Cross the canal via Bourne Bridge and head E on US-6 to end the tour at Rte. 3.

Brant Point Light, Nantucket, Cape Cod

Maine Coast★★

238 miles/383 kilometers Maps 82, 251, 83

From **Kittery**, drive N on US-1 to **York★**, then along US-1A to see the 18C colonial buildings of **York★★**. Continue N on coastal US-1A to **Ogunquit★**. Rejoin US-1 and head N to Rte. 9, turn right, and drive to **Kennebunkport**, with its colorful shops. Take Rte. 9A/35 to **Kennebunk**. Then travel N on US-1 to **Portland★★**, Maine's largest city, where the **Old Port★★** brims with galleries and boutiques. Take US-1 N through the outlet town of **Freeport**, then on to **Brunswick**, home of **Bowdoin College**. Turn NE through **Bath★**, **Wiscasset**, **Rockland**, **Camden★★**, **Searsport** and **Bucksport**. At Ellsworth, take Rt. 3 S to enter **Acadia NP★★★** on **Mount Desert Island★★★**, where **Park Loop Road★★★** (closed in winter) parallels open coast. From the top of **Cadillac Mountain★★★**, the **views★★★** are breathtaking. The tour ends at **Bar Harbor★**, a popular resort village.

Acadia NP, Maine Coast

Mohawk Valley★

114 miles/184 kilometers Maps 188, 94, 80

From the state capital of **Albany★**, take I-90 NW to Exit 25 for I-890 into **Schenectady**, founded by Dutch settlers in 1661. Then follow Rte. 5 W along the Mohawk River. In Fort Hunter, **Schoharie Crossing SHS★** stretches along a canal towpath. Near Little Falls, **Herkimer Home SHS** (Rte. 169 at Thruway Exit 29A) interprets colonial farm life. Rte. 5 continues W along the Erie Canal to Utica. From Utica, drive W on Rte. 49 to Rome, where the river turns N and peters out. The tour ends in Rome, site of **Fort Stanwix NM★**.

South Shore Lake Superior★

530 miles/853 kilometers

Maps 211, 64, 65, 69

From **Duluth★**, drive SE on I-535/US-53 to the junction of Rte. 13 at Parkland. Follow Rte. 13 E to quaint Bayfield, gateway to **Apostle Islands NL★★**, accessible by boat. Head S to the junction of US-2, and E through Ashland, Ironwood and Wakefield. There, turn left onto Rte. 28, heading NE to Bergland, and turning left onto Rte. 64. Drive N to Silver City and take Rte. M-107 W into **Porcupine Mountains Wilderness SP★**. Return to Rte. 64 and go E to Ontonagon. Take Rte. 38 SE to Greenland, then follow Rte. 26 NE to Houghton. Cross to Hancock on US-41 and continue NE to Phoenix. Turn left onto Rte. 26 to Eagle River and on to Copper Harbor via **Brockway Mountain Drive★★**. Backtrack S to Houghton via US-41, then travel S and E past Marquette, turning left onto Rte. 28. Head E to Munising, then take County Road H-58 E and N through **Pictured Rocks NL★**. End the tour at Grand Marais.

Villages of Southern Vermont★★

118 miles/190 kilometers Map 81

Head N from the resort town of **Manchester★** by Rte. 7A. At Manchester Center, take Rte. 11 E past **Bromley Mountain**, a popular ski area, to Peru. Turn left on the backroad to **Weston★**, a favorite tourist stop along Rte. 100. Continue to **Chester**, turning right onto Rte. 35 S to reach **Grafton★**, with its **Old Tavern**. Farther S, Rte. 30 S from Townshend leads to **Newfane** and its lovely **village green★**. Return to Townshend, then travel W, following Rte. 30 through West Townshend, passing **Stratton Mountain** en route to Manchester. S of Manchester by Rte. 7A, the crest of Mt. Equinox is accessible via **Equinox Skyline Drive** (fee). Then continue S on Rte. 7A to end the tour at **Arlington**, known for its trout fishing.

The White Mountains Loop★★★

127 miles/204 kilometers Map 81

From the all-season resort of **Conway**, drive N on Rte. 16 to **North Conway★**, abundant with tourist facilities. Continue N on US-302/ Rte. 16 through **Glen**, passing **Glen Ellis Falls★** and **Pinkham Notch★★** en route to Glen House. There, drive the Auto Road to the top of **Mount Washington★★★** (or take guided van tour). Head N on Rte. 16 to Gorham, near the Androscoggin River, then W on US-2 to Jefferson Highlands. Travel SW on Rte. 115 to Carroll, then S on US-3 to Twin Mountain. Go SW on US-3 to join I-93. Head S on I-93/ Rte.3, passing scenic **Franconia Notch★★★** and **Profile Lake★★**. Bear E on Rte. 3 where it separates from the interstate to visit **The Flume★★**, a natural gorge 90ft deep. Rejoin I-93 S to the intersection with Rte. 112. Head E on Rte. 112 through Lincoln on the **Kancamagus Highway★★★** until it joins Rte. 16 back to Conway.

White Mountain National Forest

Michelin Scenic Drives - continues on page 301

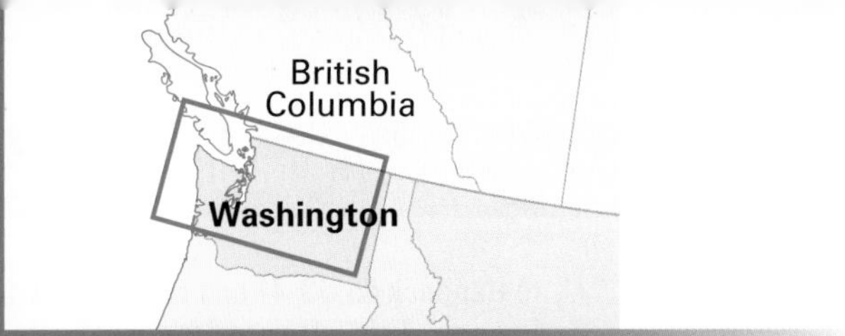

British Columbia
Washington

0 mi 20 40
0 km 20 40 60
One inch equals 25.4 miles
One centimeter equals 16.1 kilometers

Seattle WA / Mt Rainier Natl Park WA

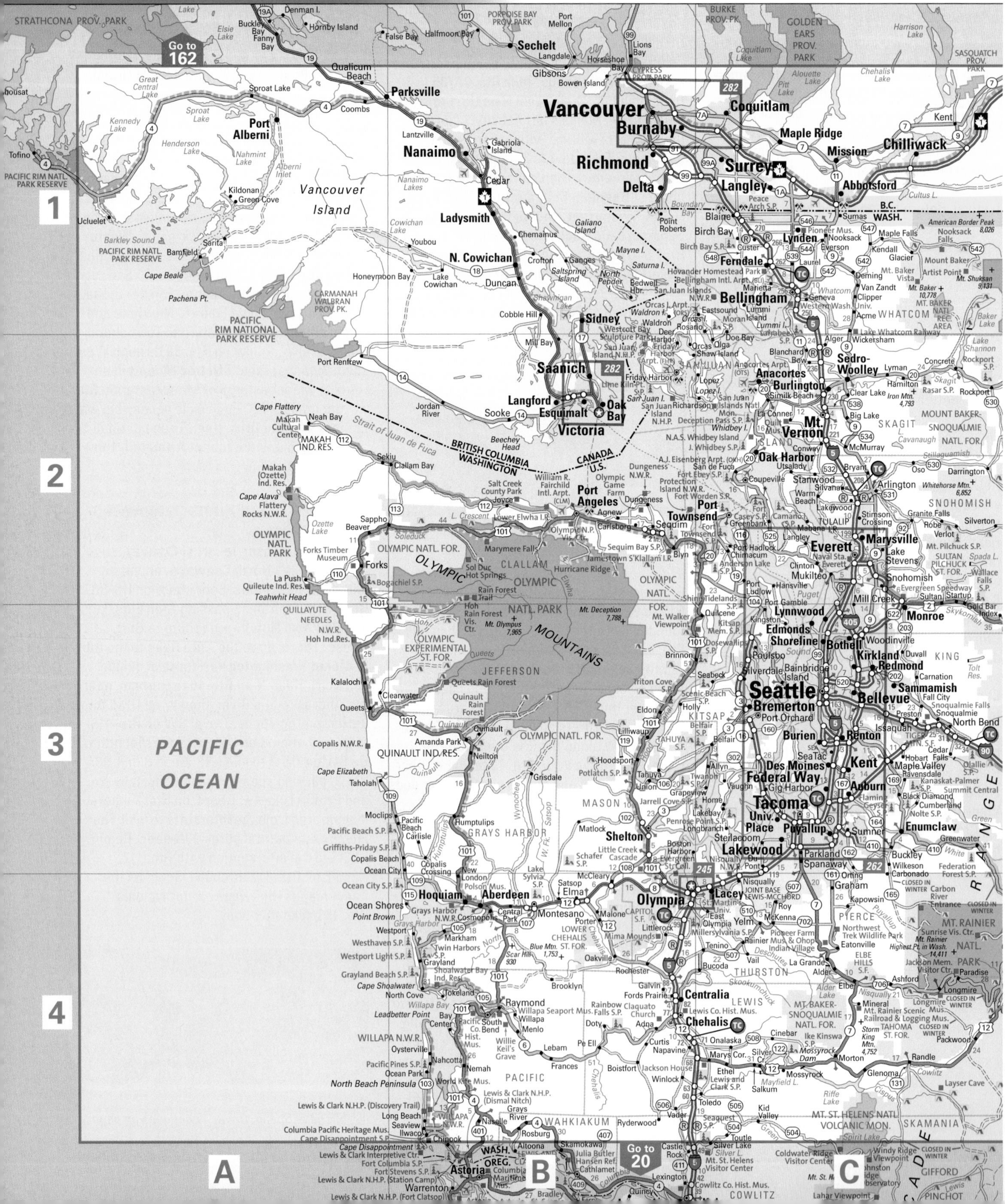

Go to 162

Go to 20

1
2
3
4

A B C

Vancouver
Burnaby
Coquitlam
Richmond
Surrey
Delta
Langley
Maple Ridge
Mission
Chilliwack
Abbotsford
Sechelt
Parksville
Port Alberni
Nanaimo
Ladysmith
N. Cowichan
Duncan
Sidney
Saanich
Langford
Esquimalt
Oak Bay
Victoria
Vancouver Island
PACIFIC RIM NATIONAL PARK RESERVE
BRITISH COLUMBIA
WASHINGTON
CANADA
U.S.
Strait of Juan de Fuca
Bellingham
Ferndale
Lynden
Anacortes
Burlington
Sedro-Woolley
Mt. Vernon
Oak Harbor
Arlington
Port Angeles
Port Townsend
Sequim
Everett
Marysville
Lynnwood
Edmonds
Shoreline
Bothell
Kirkland
Redmond
Sammamish
Bellevue
Seattle
Bremerton
Burien
Renton
Kent
Des Moines
Federal Way
Auburn
Tacoma
Univ. Place
Puyallup
Lakewood
Enumclaw
Monroe
Olympia
Lacey
Shelton
Hoquiam
Aberdeen
Centralia
Chehalis
Astoria
OLYMPIC NATL. PARK
OLYMPIC MOUNTAINS
OLYMPIC NATL. FOR.
MT. RAINIER NATL. PARK
PACIFIC OCEAN
WASH.
OREG.

DRIVING DISTANCES IN MILES

	ABERDEEN, WA	BELLINGHAM, WA	MT. RAINIER NP, WA	OKANOGAN, WA	OLYMPIA, WA	PORT ANGELES, WA	SEATTLE, WA	SPOKANE, WA	TACOMA, WA	VANCOUVER, BC	WENATCHEE, WA	YAKIMA, WA
BELLINGHAM, WA	196		186	195	147	127*	88	360	122	52	185	221
SEATTLE, WA	105	88	96	223	56	83*		278	31	140	148	140
SPOKANE, WA	376	360	290	148	327	362*	278		303	412	171	203
YAKIMA, WA	237	221	87	194	188	223*	140	203	164	273	115	

*DISTANCE INCLUDES FERRY TRAVEL

SEE ALSO DISTANCE AND DRIVING TIME MAP ON PAGES 286–287

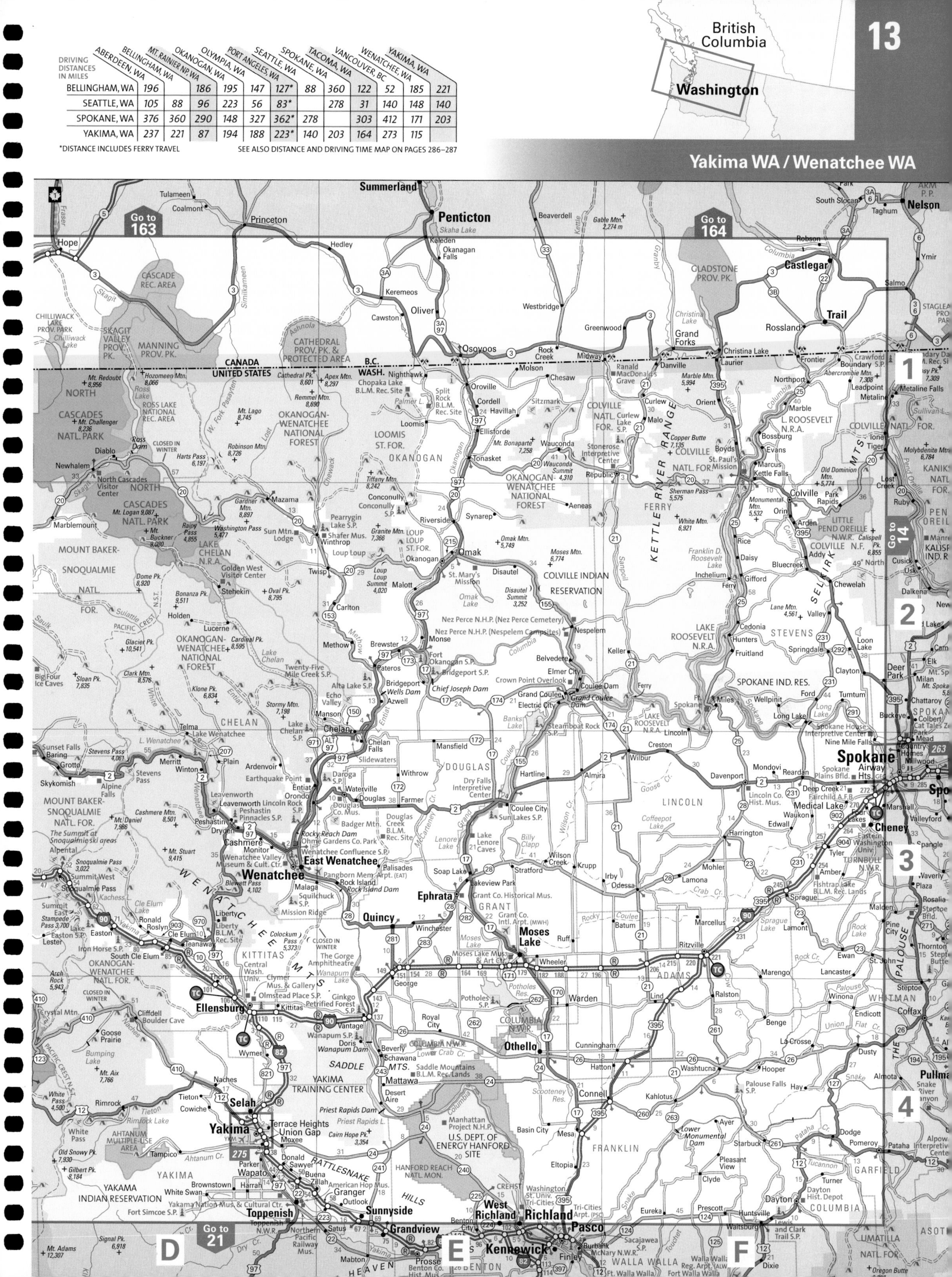

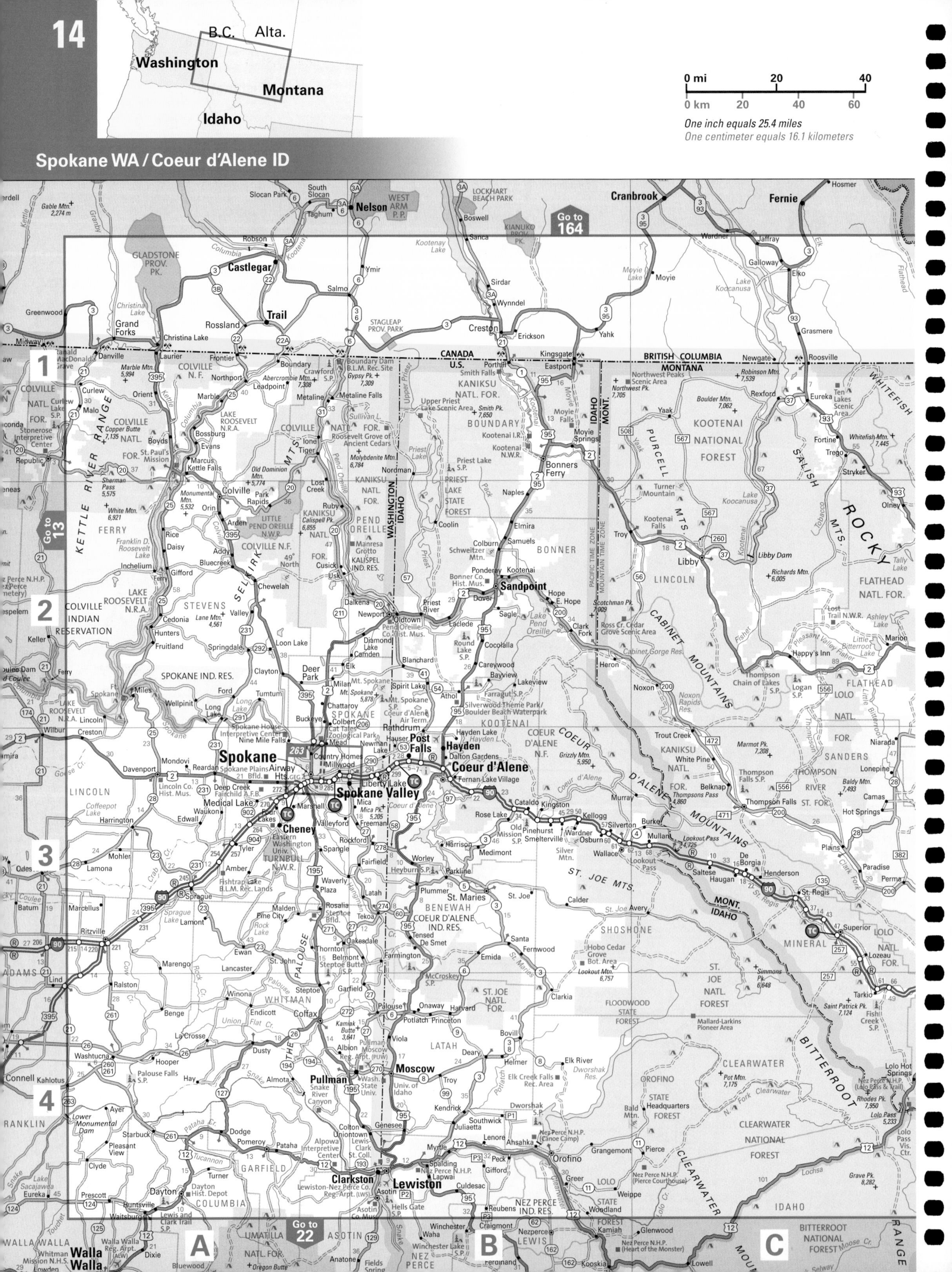

14
B.C.
Alta.
Washington
Montana
Idaho
Spokane WA / Coeur d'Alene ID
0 mi 20 40
0 km 20 40 60
One inch equals 25.4 miles
One centimeter equals 16.1 kilometers
Go to 164
Go to 13
Go to 22
Nelson
Cranbrook
Fernie
Castlegar
Trail
Rossland
Grand Forks
Greenwood
Christina Lake
Creston
Yahk
Kingsgate
Eastport
Porthill
BRITISH COLUMBIA
MONTANA
CANADA
U.S.
COLVILLE N.F.
KANIKSU NATL. FOR.
KOOTENAI NATIONAL FOREST
LAKE ROOSEVELT N.R.A.
COLVILLE INDIAN RESERVATION
SPOKANE IND. RES.
Bonners Ferry
Sandpoint
Newport
Colville
Kettle Falls
Chewelah
Deer Park
Spokane
Spokane Valley
Cheney
Post Falls
Hayden
Coeur d'Alene
Libby
Troy
Eureka
Kellogg
Wallace
St. Maries
Plummer
Davenport
Ritzville
Colfax
Pullman
Moscow
Lewiston
Clarkston
Orofino
Dayton
Walla Walla
KETTLE RIVER RANGE
SELKIRK MTS.
PURCELL MTS.
SALISH MTS.
CABINET MOUNTAINS
COEUR D'ALENE MOUNTAINS
ST. JOE MTS.
BITTERROOT RANGE
WASHINGTON
IDAHO
IDAHO
MONT.
STEVENS
LINCOLN
SPOKANE
KOOTENAI
BONNER
BOUNDARY
SHOSHONE
BENEWAH
LATAH
WHITMAN
GARFIELD
COLUMBIA
ASOTIN
NEZ PERCE
LEWIS
CLEARWATER
MINERAL
SANDERS
FLATHEAD NATL. FOR.
COEUR D'ALENE N.F.
ST. JOE NATL. FOREST
CLEARWATER NATIONAL FOREST
LOLO NATL. FOR.
NEZ PERCE IND. RES.
COEUR D'ALENE IND. RES.
1
2
3
4
A
B
C

DRIVING DISTANCES IN MILES	BONNERS FERRY, ID	BROWNING, MT	COEUR D'ALENE, ID	COLVILLE, WA	GREAT FALLS, MT	HELENA, MT	KALISPELL, MT	LEWISTON, ID	MISSOULA, MT	SHELBY, MT	SPOKANE, WA	WEST GLACIER, MT
GREAT FALLS, MT	369	124	364	471		85	222	420	199	82	398	192
LEWISTON, ID	196	413	118	176	420	334	315		221	448	103	348
MISSOULA, MT	244	201	167	274	199	114	116	221		227	201	136
SPOKANE, WA	110	336	34	73	398	313	238	103	201	426		271

SEE ALSO DISTANCE AND DRIVING TIME MAP ON PAGES 286–287

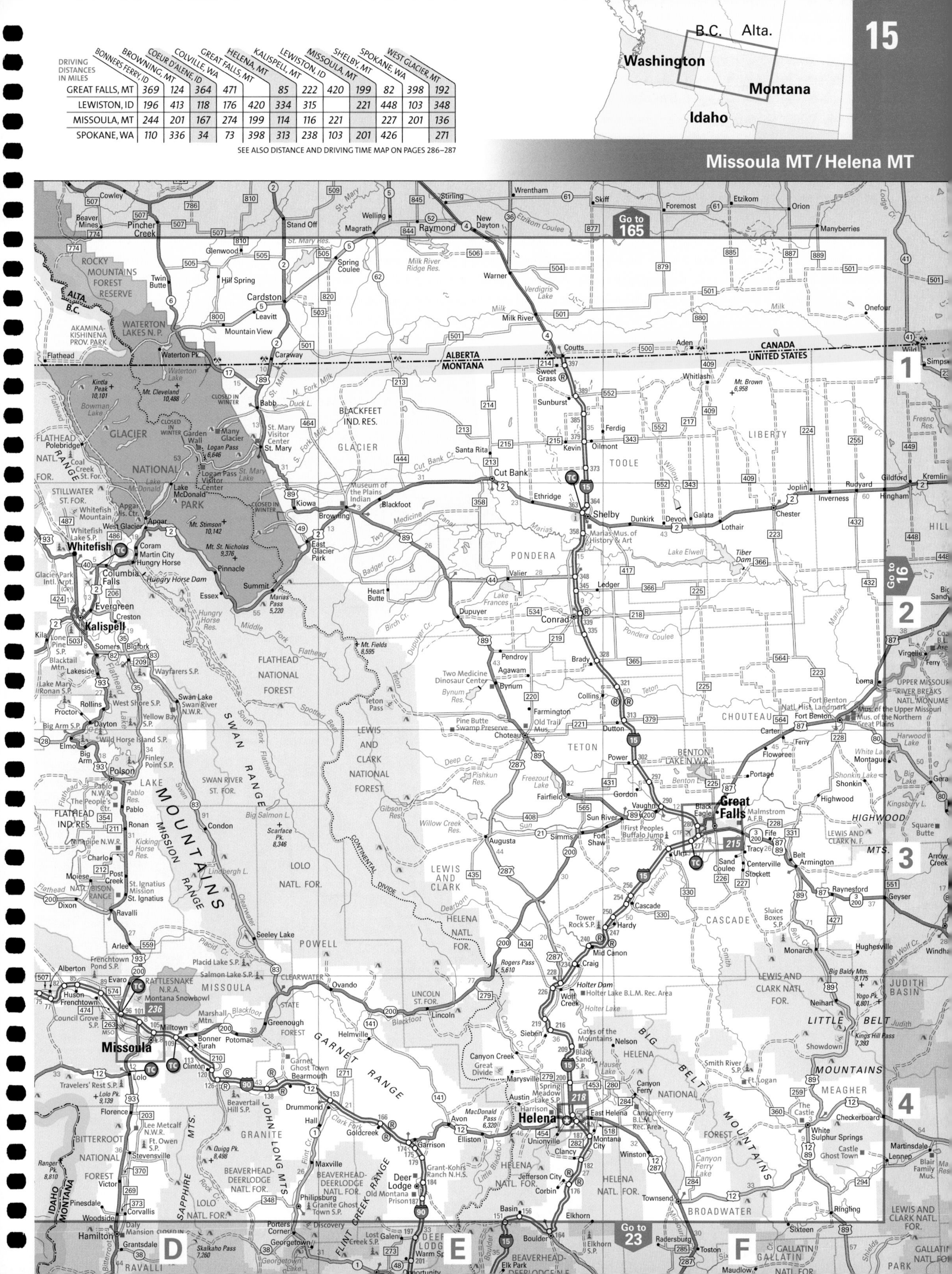

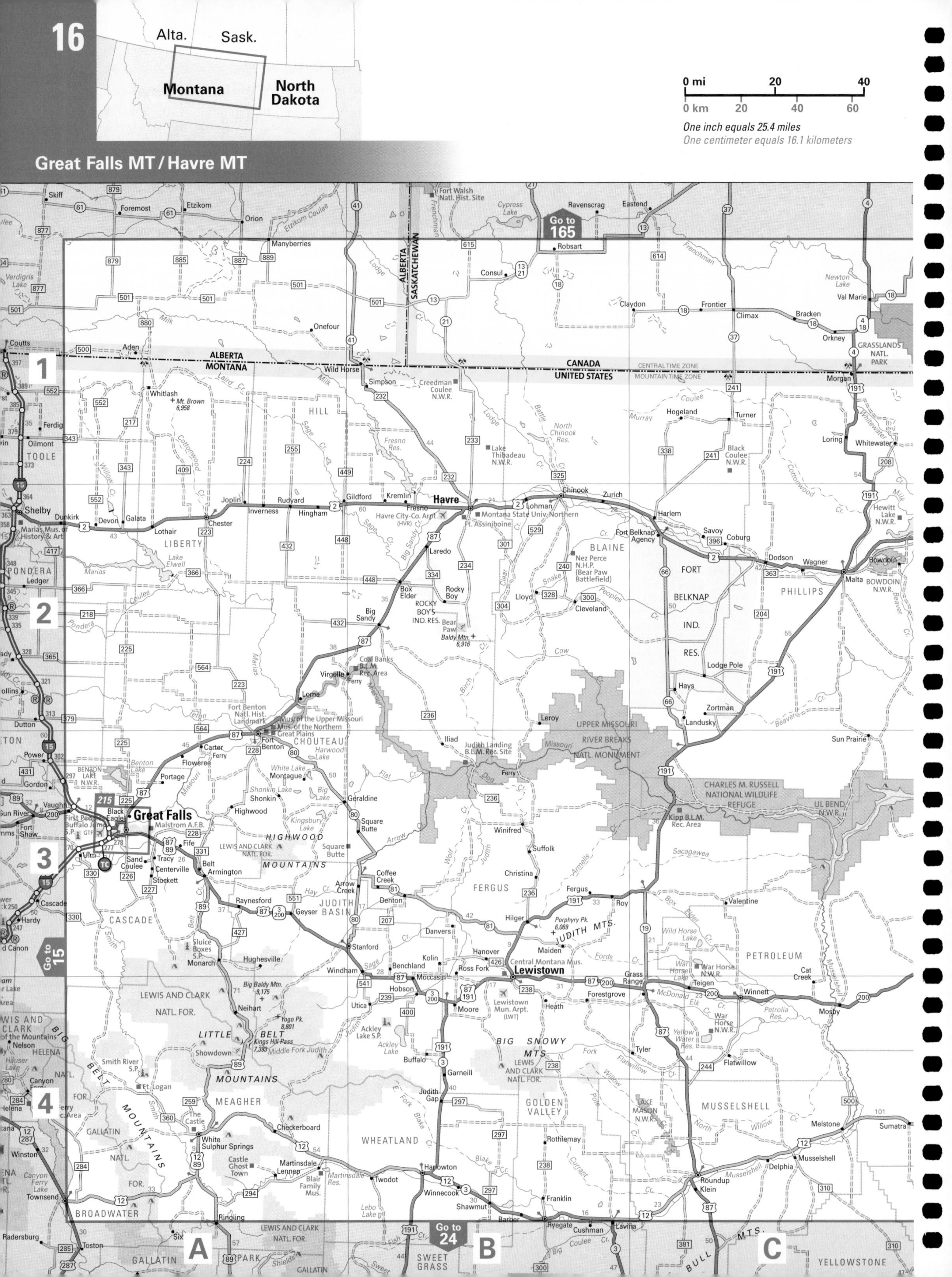
16
Alta.
Sask.
Montana
North Dakota
0 mi 20 40
0 km 20 40 60
One inch equals 25.4 miles
One centimeter equals 16.1 kilometers
Great Falls MT / Havre MT
Go to 165
Go to 15
Go to 24
ALBERTA
SASKATCHEWAN
ALBERTA
MONTANA
CANADA
UNITED STATES
CENTRAL TIME ZONE
MOUNTAIN TIME ZONE
Fort Walsh Natl. Hist. Site
GRASSLANDS NATL. PARK
Havre
Great Falls
Lewistown
Shelby
Chinook
Harlem
Malta
Fort Benton
Chester
Big Sandy
Stanford
Roundup
Harlowton
White Sulphur Springs
TOOLE
PONDERA
LIBERTY
HILL
BLAINE
PHILLIPS
CHOUTEAU
CASCADE
JUDITH BASIN
FERGUS
PETROLEUM
MUSSELSHELL
GOLDEN VALLEY
WHEATLAND
MEAGHER
BROADWATER
FORT BELKNAP IND. RES.
ROCKY BOY'S IND. RES.
UPPER MISSOURI RIVER BREAKS NATL. MONUMENT
CHARLES M. RUSSELL NATIONAL WILDLIFE REFUGE
UL BEND N.W.R.
HIGHWOOD MOUNTAINS
LITTLE BELT MOUNTAINS
BIG SNOWY MTS.
JUDITH MTS.
BIG BELT MOUNTAINS
LEWIS AND CLARK NATL. FOR.
GALLATIN NATL. FOR.
BULL MTS.
YELLOWSTONE
A
B
C
1
2
3
4

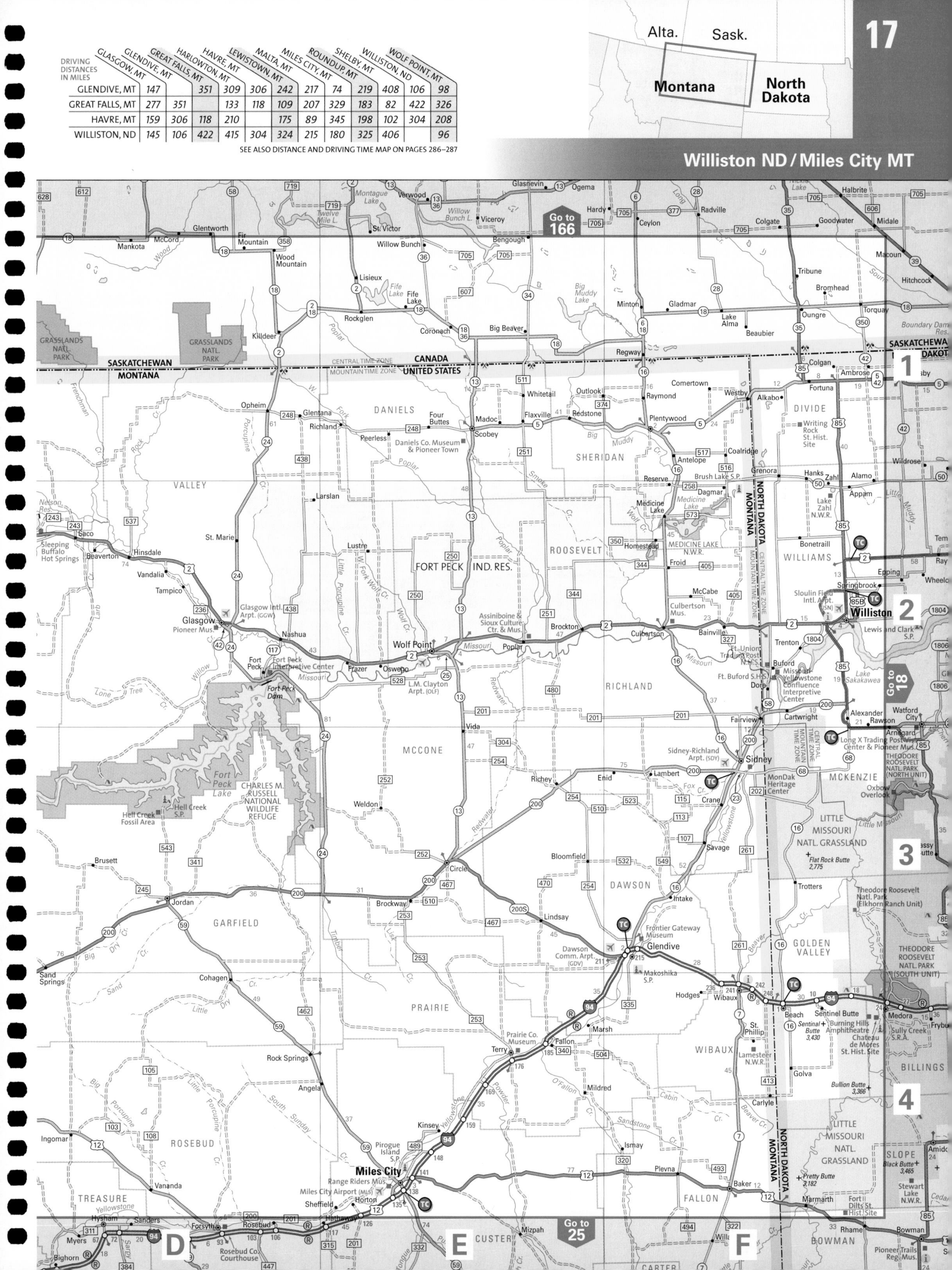

DRIVING DISTANCES IN MILES	GLASGOW, MT	GLENDIVE, MT	GREAT FALLS, MT	HARLOWTON, MT	HAVRE, MT	LEWISTOWN, MT	MALTA, MT	MILES CITY, MT	ROUNDUP, MT	SHELBY, MT	WILLISTON, ND	WOLF POINT, MT
GLENDIVE, MT	147		351	309	306	242	217	74	219	408	106	98
GREAT FALLS, MT	277	351		133	118	109	207	329	183	82	422	326
HAVRE, MT	159	306	118	210		175	89	345	198	102	304	208
WILLISTON, ND	145	106	422	415	304	324	215	180	325	406		96

SEE ALSO DISTANCE AND DRIVING TIME MAP ON PAGES 286–287

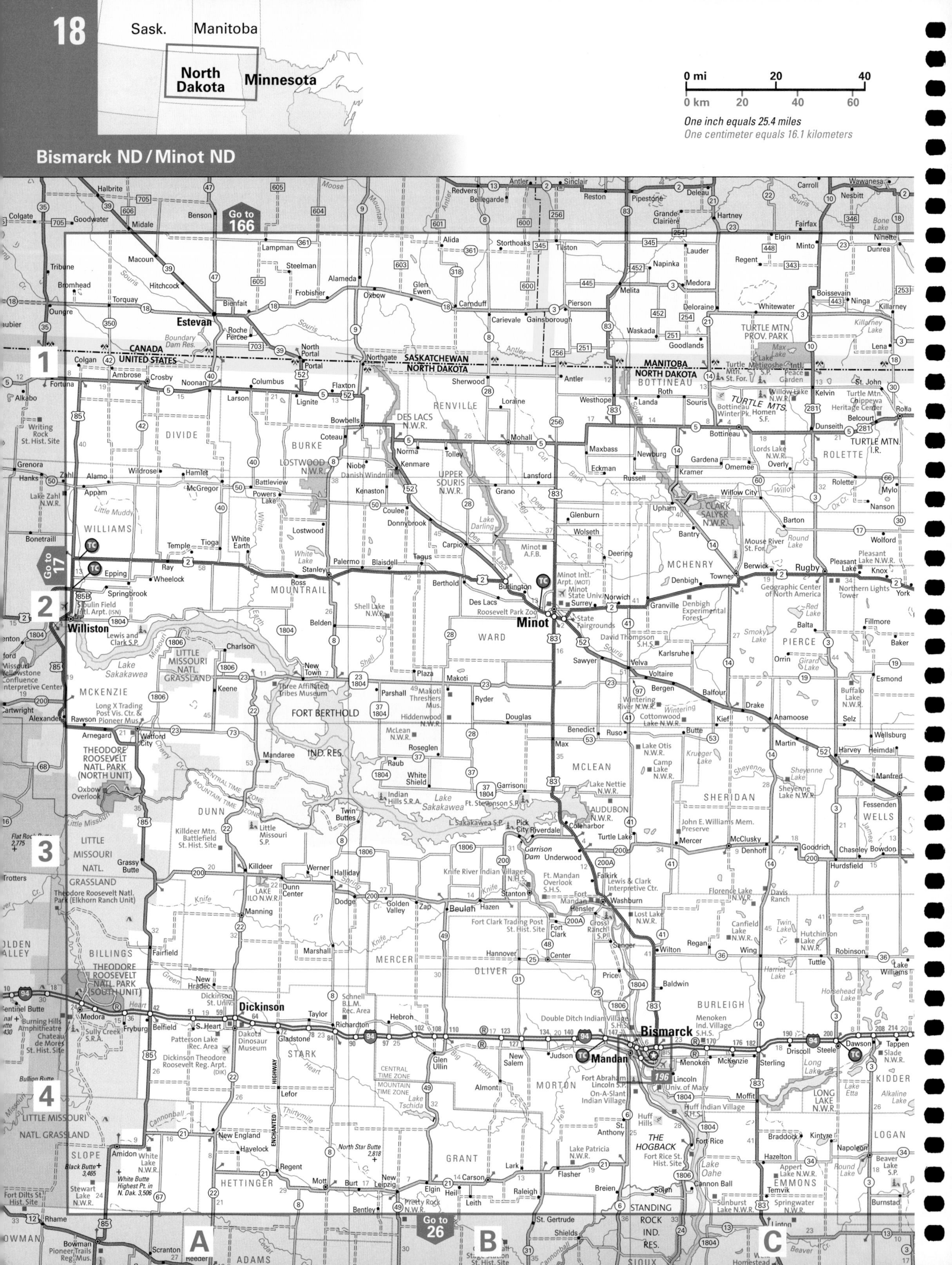
Sask.
Manitoba
North Dakota
Minnesota
0 mi 20 40
0 km 20 40 60
One inch equals 25.4 miles
One centimeter equals 16.1 kilometers
Go to 166
Go to 17
Go to 26
CANADA
UNITED STATES
SASKATCHEWAN
NORTH DAKOTA
MANITOBA
NORTH DAKOTA
Estevan
Williston
Minot
Dickinson
Bismarck
Mandan
DIVIDE
BURKE
RENVILLE
BOTTINEAU
ROLETTE
WILLIAMS
MOUNTRAIL
WARD
MCHENRY
PIERCE
MCKENZIE
MCLEAN
SHERIDAN
WELLS
DUNN
MERCER
OLIVER
BURLEIGH
KIDDER
BILLINGS
STARK
MORTON
GRANT
HETTINGER
SLOPE
LOGAN
EMMONS
ADAMS
SIOUX
FORT BERTHOLD
IND. RES.
STANDING ROCK IND. RES.
THEODORE ROOSEVELT NATL. PARK (NORTH UNIT)
THEODORE ROOSEVELT NATL. PARK (SOUTH UNIT)
LITTLE MISSOURI NATL. GRASSLAND
TURTLE MTN. PROV. PARK
Lake Sakakawea
Lake Oahe
CENTRAL TIME ZONE
MOUNTAIN TIME ZONE
1
2
3
4
A
B
C

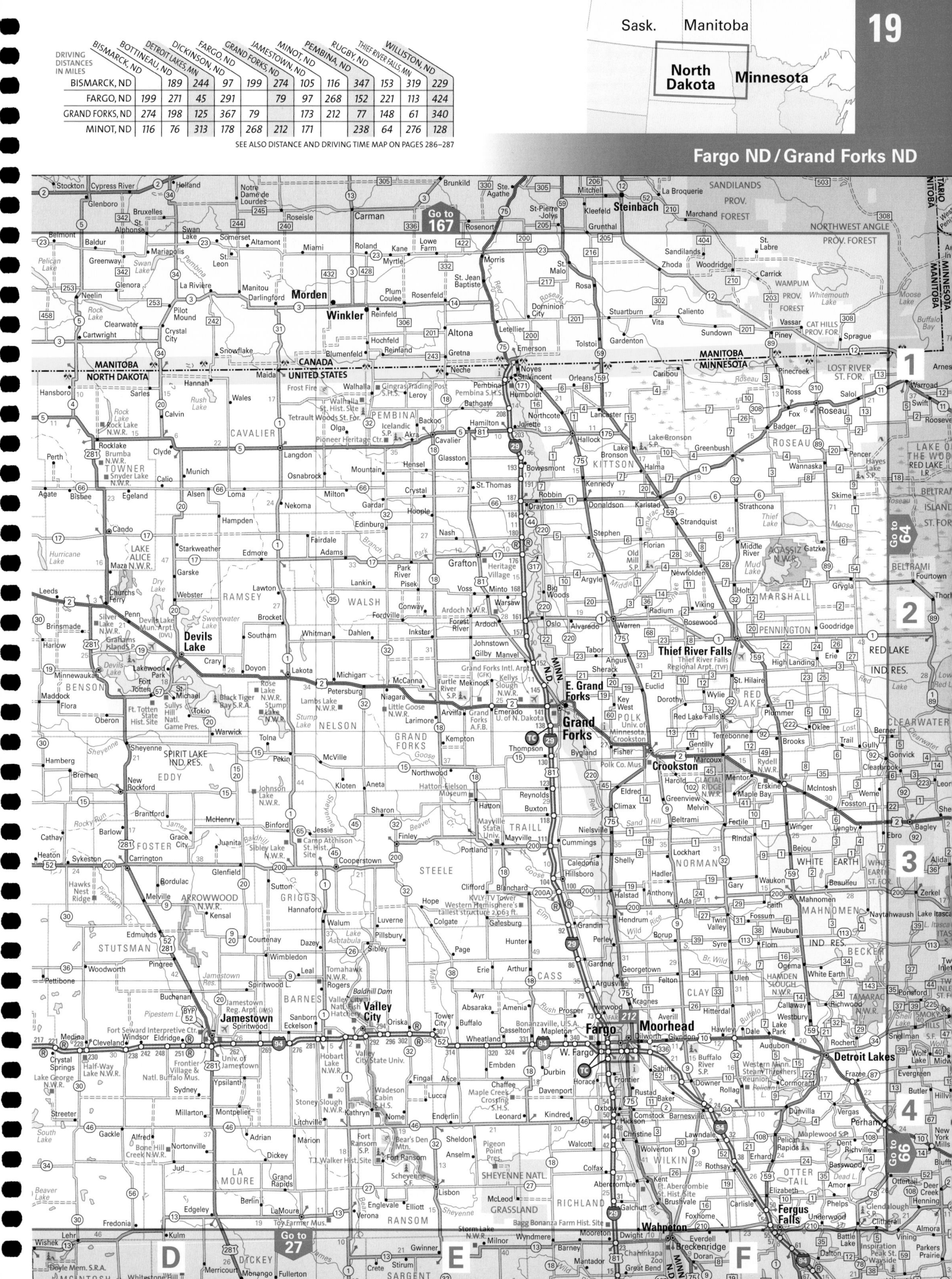

DRIVING DISTANCES IN MILES

	BISMARCK, ND	BOTTINEAU, ND	DETROIT LAKES, MN	DICKINSON, ND	FARGO, ND	GRAND FORKS, ND	JAMESTOWN, ND	MINOT, ND	PEMBINA, ND	RUGBY, ND	THIEF RIVER FALLS, MN	WILLISTON, ND
BISMARCK, ND		189	244	97	199	274	105	116	347	153	319	229
FARGO, ND	199	271	45	291		79	97	268	152	221	113	424
GRAND FORKS, ND	274	198	125	367	79		173	212	77	148	61	340
MINOT, ND	116	76	313	178	268	212	171		238	64	276	128

SEE ALSO DISTANCE AND DRIVING TIME MAP ON PAGES 286–287

Washington

Oregon

Portland OR / Eugene OR

One inch equals 25.4 miles

One centimeter equals 16.1 kilometers

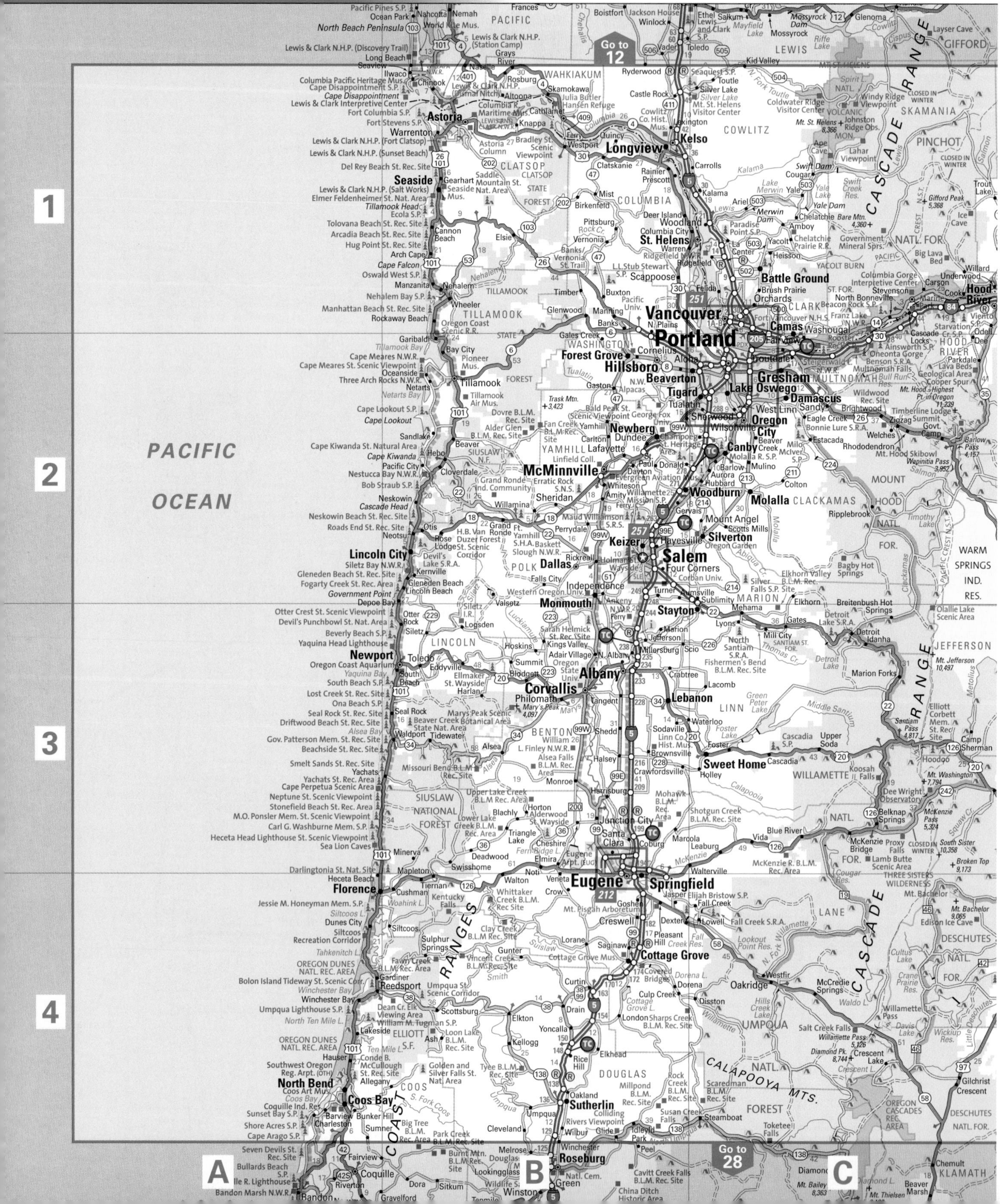

Go to 12

PACIFIC OCEAN

1

2

3

4

A

B

C

Go to 28

DRIVING DISTANCES IN MILES	ASTORIA, OR	BEND, OR	BURNS, OR	COOS BAY, OR	EUGENE, OR	KENNEWICK, WA	LA GRANDE, OR	NEWPORT, OR	PORTLAND, OR	SALEM, OR	THE DALLES, OR	WALLA WALLA, WA
BEND, OR	252		142	227	115	245	295	183	158	134	137	276
EUGENE, OR	216	115	257	105		328	377	101	112	65	198	359
KENNEWICK, WA	306	245	256	440	328		111	328	212	264	131	49
PORTLAND, OR	97	158	299	224	112	212	261	116		48	82	243

SEE ALSO DISTANCE AND DRIVING TIME MAP ON PAGES 286–287

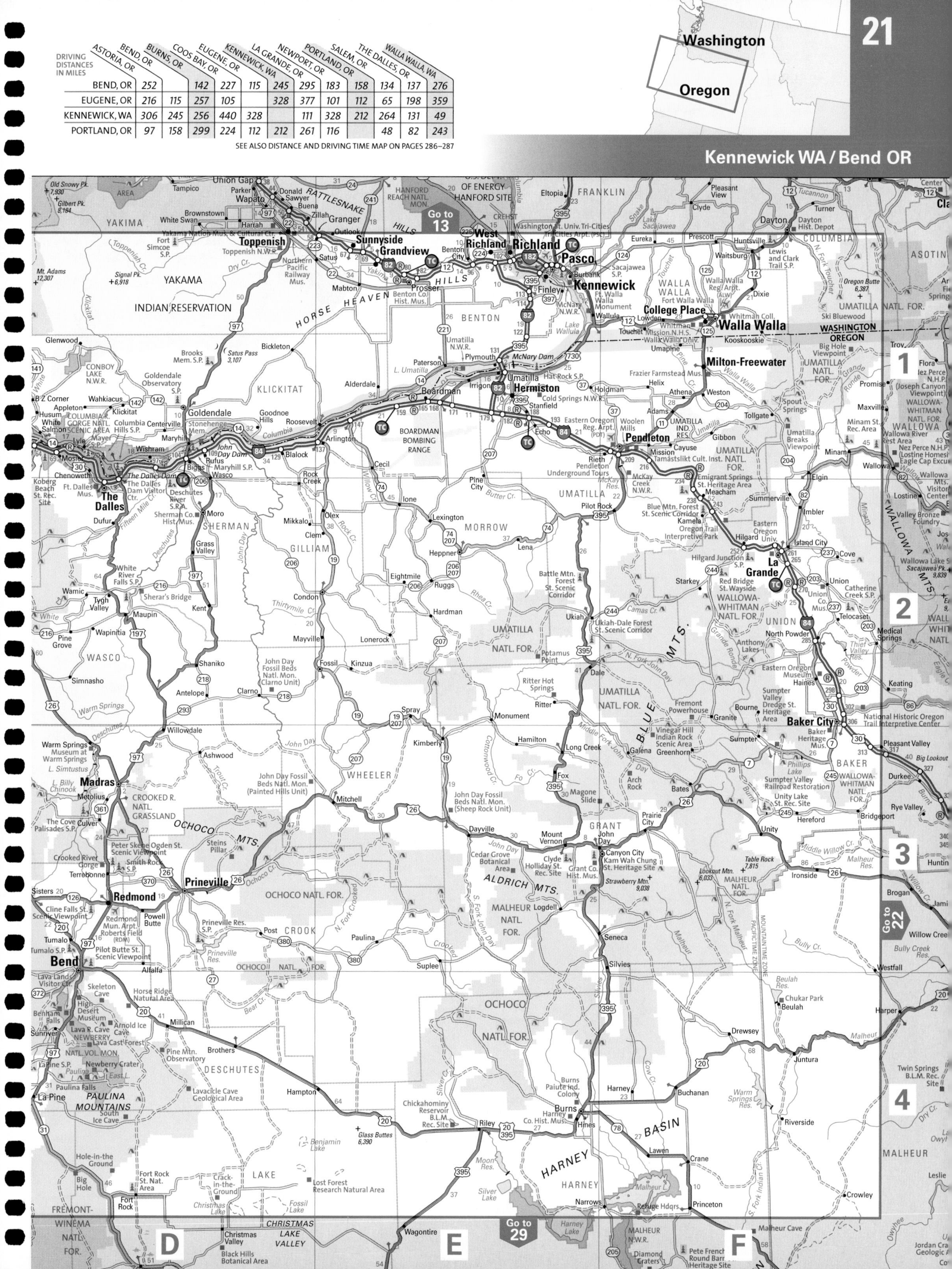

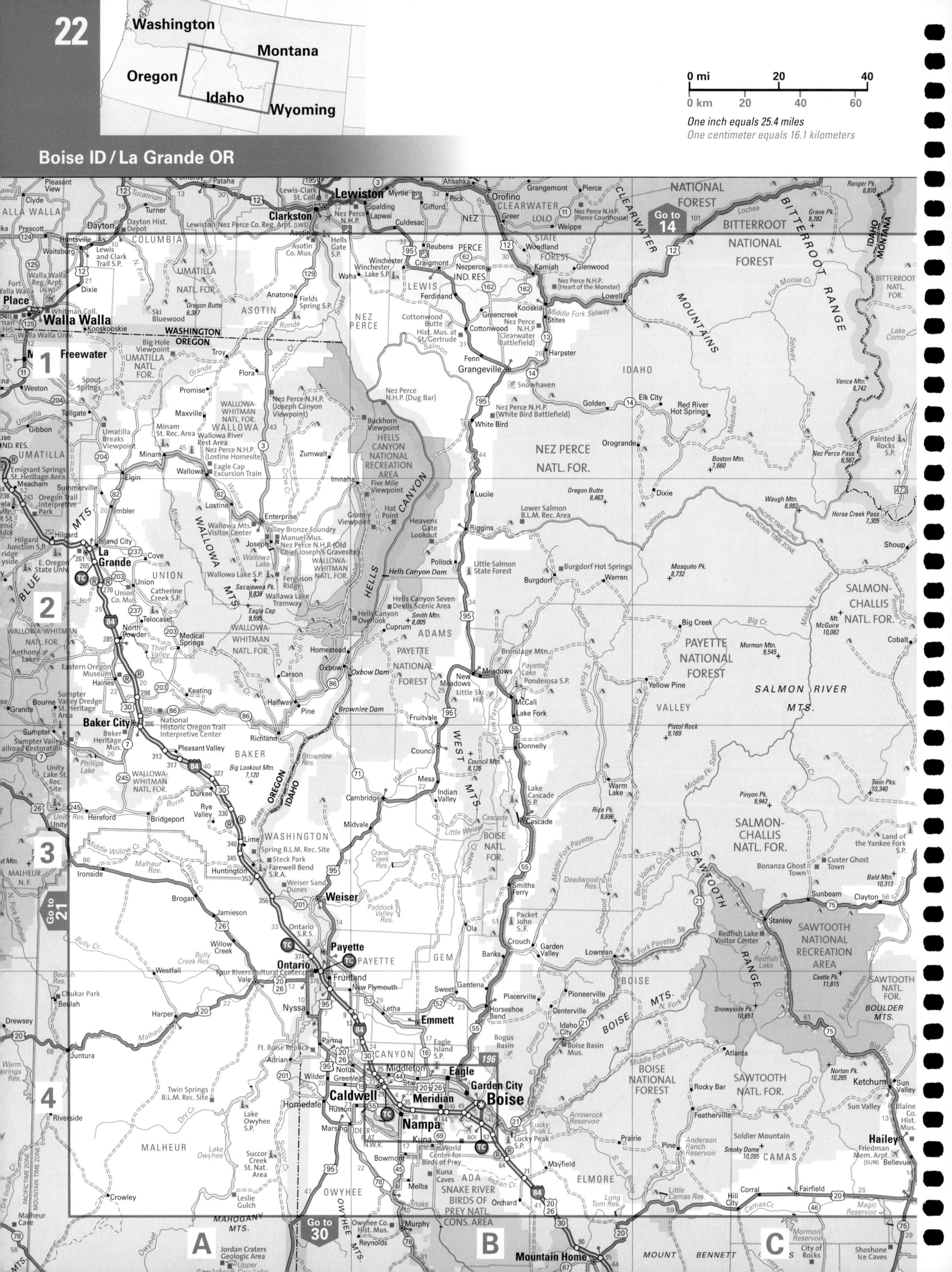

22
Washington
Montana
Oregon
Idaho
Wyoming
Boise ID / La Grande OR
0 mi 20 40
0 km 20 40 60
One inch equals 25.4 miles
One centimeter equals 16.1 kilometers
Go to 14
Go to 21
Go to 30
Lewiston
Clarkston
Walla Walla
Milton-Freewater
La Grande
Baker City
Ontario
Payette
Weiser
Caldwell
Nampa
Meridian
Boise
Garden City
Eagle
Emmett
Mountain Home
Hailey
Ketchum
Grangeville
Orofino
Cascade
McCall
WASHINGTON
OREGON
IDAHO
MONTANA
NEZ PERCE NATL. FOR.
PAYETTE NATIONAL FOREST
SALMON-CHALLIS NATL. FOR.
BOISE NATIONAL FOREST
SAWTOOTH NATIONAL RECREATION AREA
SAWTOOTH NATL. FOR.
WALLOWA-WHITMAN NATL. FOR.
UMATILLA NATL. FOR.
BITTERROOT NATIONAL FOREST
CLEARWATER NATIONAL FOREST
HELLS CANYON NATIONAL RECREATION AREA
SNAKE RIVER BIRDS OF PREY NATL. CONS. AREA
WALLOWA MTS.
BLUE MTS.
WEST MTS.
SALMON RIVER MTS.
BOISE MTS.
SAWTOOTH RANGE
BITTERROOT RANGE
HELLS CANYON
1
2
3
4
A
B
C

DRIVING DISTANCES IN MILES

	BOISE, ID	BOZEMAN, MT	BUTTE, MT	GRANGEVILLE, ID	HAMILTON, MT	IDAHO FALLS, ID	JACKSON, WY	LA GRANDE, OR	ONTARIO, OR	SALMON, ID	SUN VALLEY, ID	W. YELLOWSTONE, MT
BOISE, ID		485	486	202	339	288	378	170	58	247	163	395
BUTTE, MT	486	81		290	103	203	275	566	541	150	312	162
IDAHO FALLS, ID	288	199	203	483	272		92	455	342	168	153	109
W. YELLOWSTONE, MT	395	90	162	451	264	109	128	562	449	244	252	

SEE ALSO DISTANCE AND DRIVING TIME MAP ON PAGES 286–287

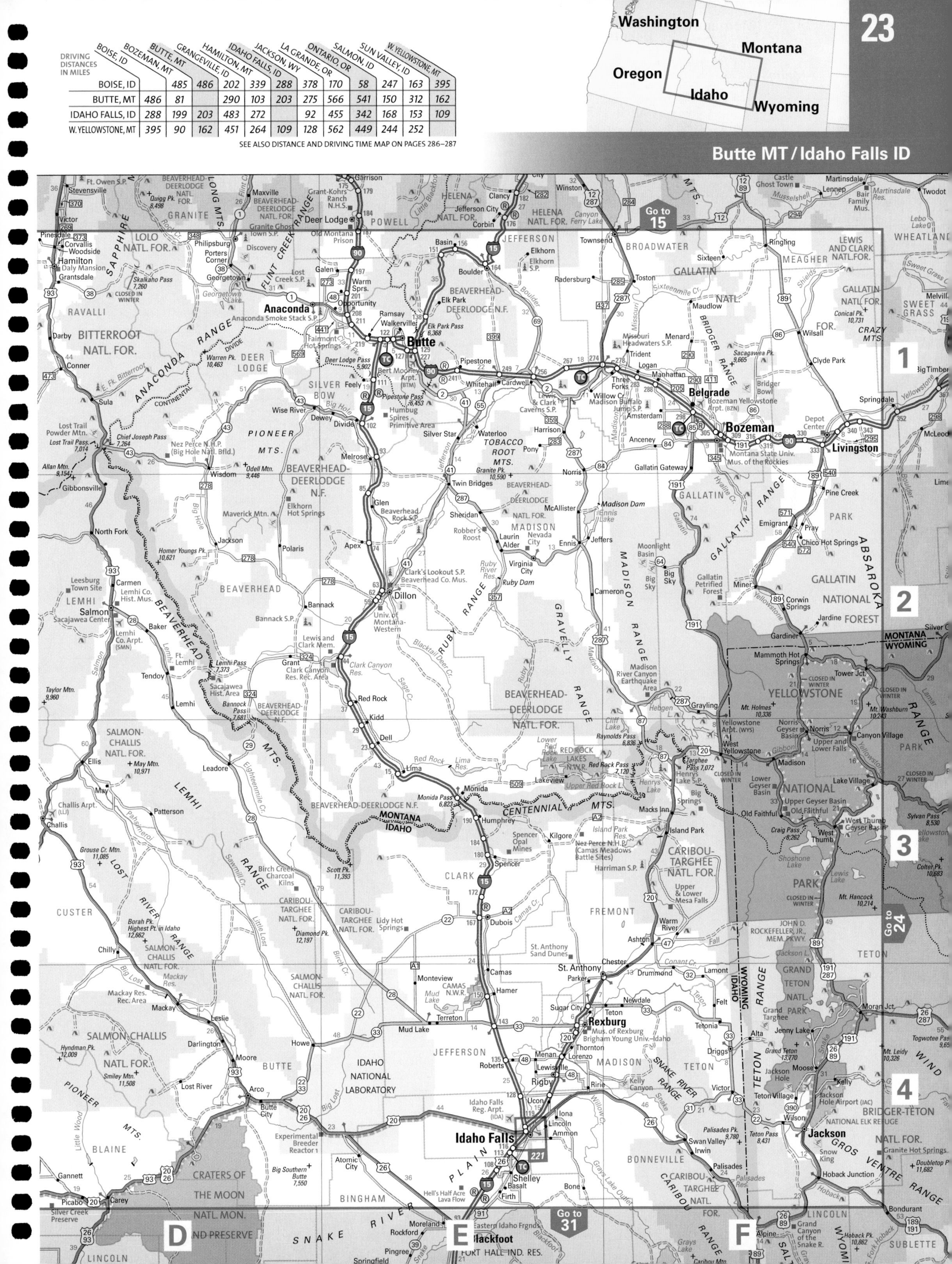

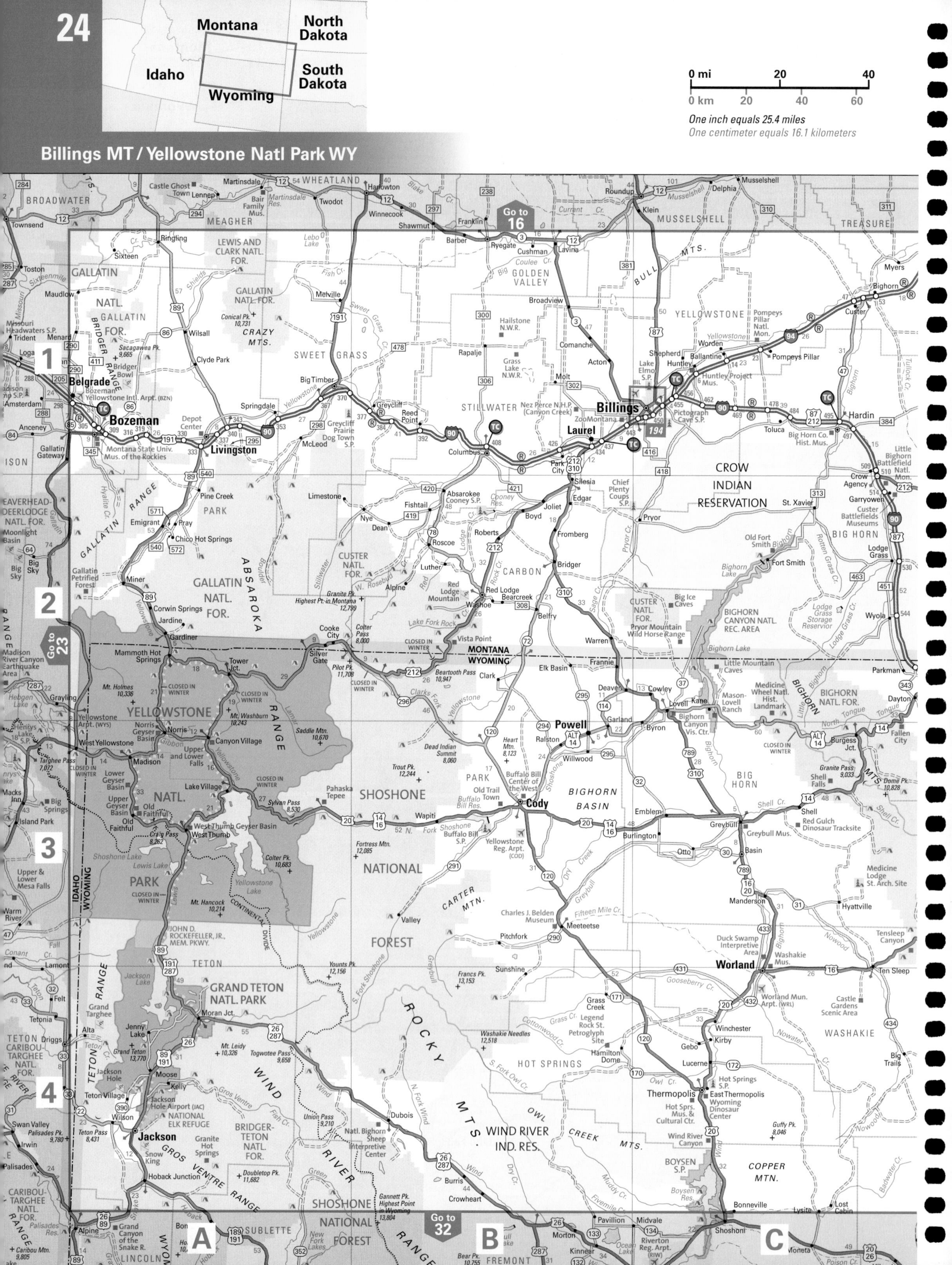
Montana
North Dakota
Idaho
South Dakota
Wyoming
0 mi 20 40
0 km 20 40 60
One inch equals 25.4 miles
One centimeter equals 16.1 kilometers
Go to 16
Go to 23
Go to 32
Billings
Bozeman
Belgrade
Livingston
Laurel
Columbus
Big Timber
Hardin
Crow Agency
Red Lodge
Gardiner
West Yellowstone
Cody
Powell
Lovell
Greybull
Basin
Worland
Thermopolis
Jackson
Shoshoni
YELLOWSTONE NATL. PARK
GRAND TETON NATL. PARK
CROW INDIAN RESERVATION
WIND RIVER IND. RES.
SHOSHONE NATIONAL FOREST
GALLATIN NATL. FOR.
CUSTER NATL. FOR.
BRIDGER-TETON NATL. FOR.
BIGHORN CANYON NATL. REC. AREA
BIGHORN BASIN
ABSAROKA RANGE
ROCKY MTS.
WIND RIVER RANGE
TETON RANGE
OWL CREEK MTS.
MONTANA
WYOMING
IDAHO
A
B
C
1
2
3
4

DRIVING DISTANCES IN MILES

	BILLINGS, MT	BOZEMAN, MT	BUFFALO, WY	CODY, WY	GILLETTE, WY	JACKSON, WY	MILES CITY, MT	RAPID CITY, SD	SHERIDAN, WY	SPEARFISH, SD	W. YELLOWSTONE, MT	WORLAND, WY
BILLINGS, MT		141	165	111	233	287	144	379	131	333	232	161
BUFFALO, WY	165	306		180	70	342	237	216	34	170	396	91
SPEARFISH, SD	333	474	170	350	100	512	186	53	202		564	261
W. YELLOWSTONE, MT	232	90	396	147	464	128	376	610	363	564		236

SEE ALSO DISTANCE AND DRIVING TIME MAP ON PAGES 286–287

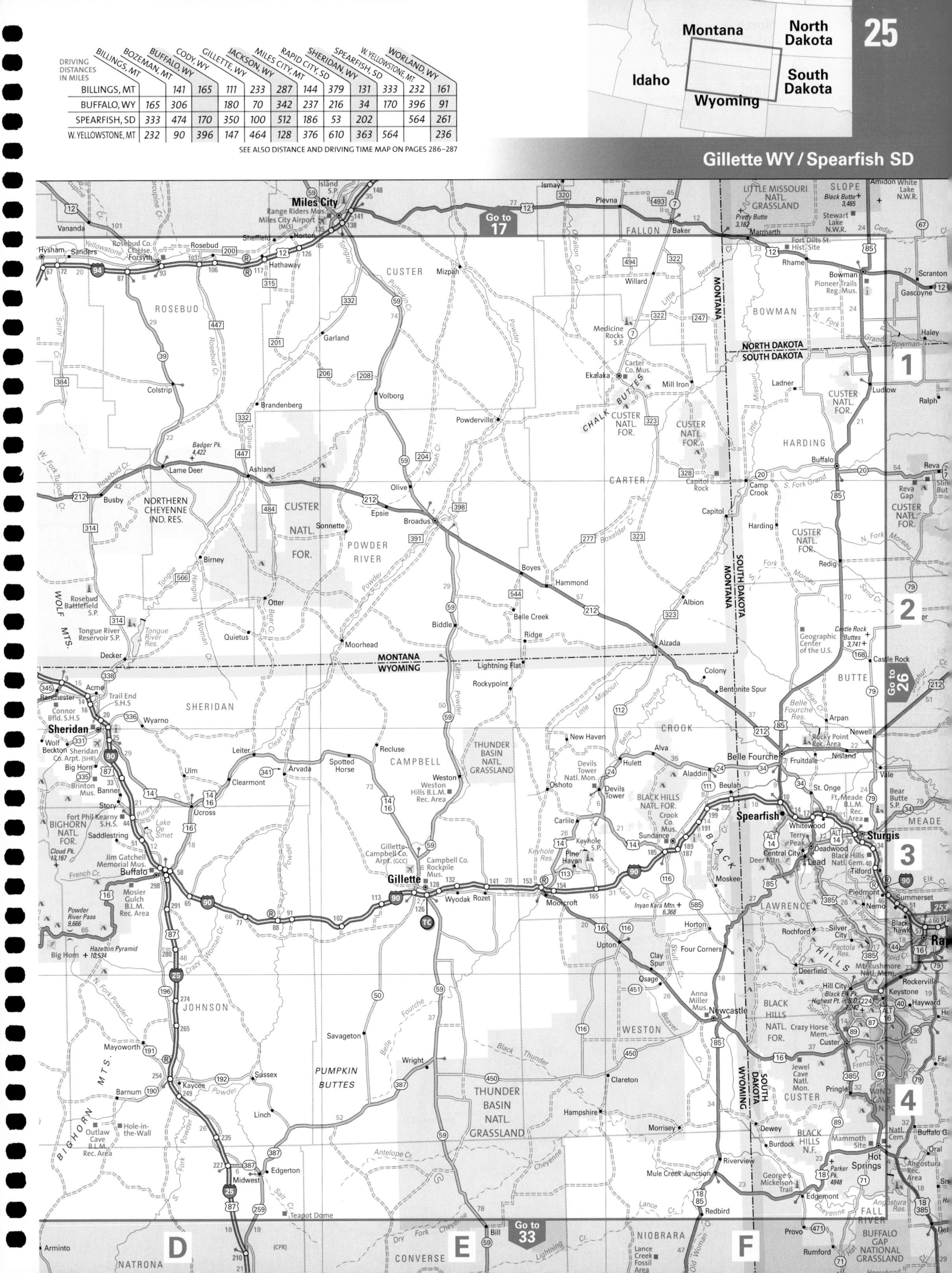

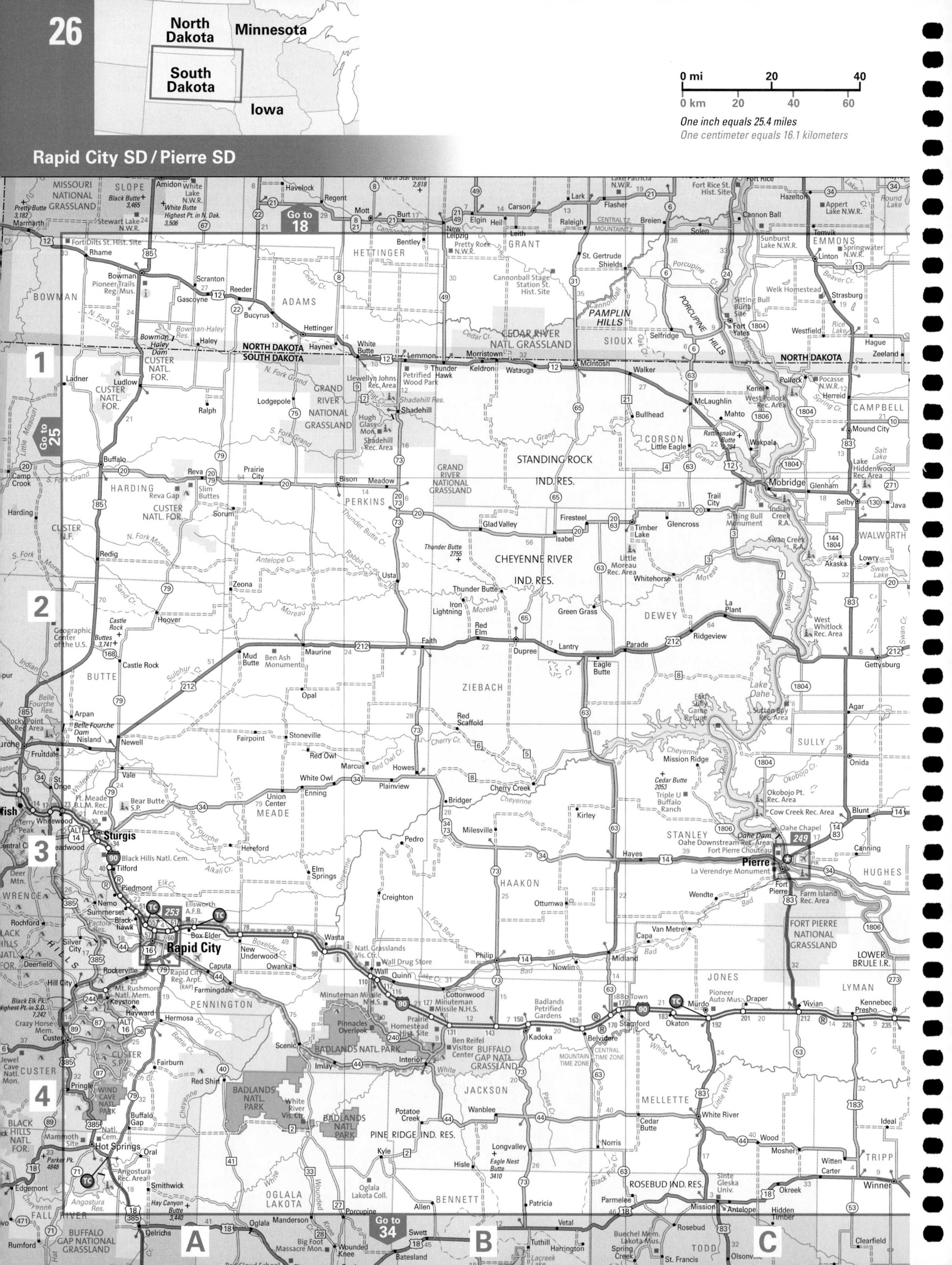
North Dakota
Minnesota
South Dakota
Iowa
0 mi 20 40
0 km 20 40 60
One inch equals 25.4 miles
One centimeter equals 16.1 kilometers
Go to 18
Go to 25
Go to 34
NORTH DAKOTA
SOUTH DAKOTA
MISSOURI NATIONAL GRASSLAND
SLOPE
BOWMAN
ADAMS
HETTINGER
GRANT
SIOUX
EMMONS
CAMPBELL
WALWORTH
HARDING
PERKINS
CORSON
DEWEY
BUTTE
ZIEBACH
MEADE
SULLY
STANLEY
HUGHES
HAAKON
PENNINGTON
JACKSON
JONES
LYMAN
MELLETTE
TRIPP
BENNETT
OGLALA LAKOTA
TODD
FALL RIVER
CUSTER
LAWRENCE
CEDAR RIVER NATL. GRASSLAND
GRAND RIVER NATIONAL GRASSLAND
STANDING ROCK IND. RES.
CHEYENNE RIVER IND. RES.
PINE RIDGE IND. RES.
ROSEBUD IND. RES.
LOWER BRULE I.R.
FORT PIERRE NATIONAL GRASSLAND
BUFFALO GAP NATL. GRASSLAND
BADLANDS NATL. PARK
CUSTER NATL. FOR.
BLACK HILLS NATL. FOR.
WIND CAVE NATL. PARK
PAMPLIN HILLS
PORCUPINE HILLS
Lake Oahe
Bowman
Rhame
Scranton
Reeder
Gascoyne
Bucyrus
Hettinger
Haynes
Lemmon
Thunder Hawk
Morristown
Keldron
Watauga
McIntosh
Walker
McLaughlin
Bullhead
Wakpala
Mobridge
Glenham
Selby
Java
Mound City
Herreid
Pollock
Strasburg
Linton
Fort Yates
Selfridge
Buffalo
Reva
Prairie City
Bison
Meadow
Lodgepole
Shadehill
Ralph
Ludlow
Ladner
Camp Crook
Redig
Sorum
Zeona
Hoover
Castle Rock
Mud Butte
Maurine
Opal
Faith
Dupree
Lantry
Red Elm
Parade
Ridgeview
La Plant
Isabel
Firesteel
Glad Valley
Timber Lake
Glencross
Trail City
Whitehorse
Green Grass
Eagle Butte
Gettysburg
Agar
Onida
Blunt
Canning
Pierre
Fort Pierre
Hayes
Newell
Nisland
Fruitdale
Vale
Stoneville
Fairpoint
Red Owl
Marcus
Howes
White Owl
Enning
Plainview
Union Center
Cherry Creek
Bridger
Milesville
Kirley
Sturgis
Tilford
Piedmont
Hereford
Elm Springs
Pedro
Creighton
Wasta
Wall
Quinn
Philip
Midland
Nowlin
Ottumwa
Wendte
Van Metre
Capa
Rapid City
Box Elder
New Underwood
Owanka
Caputa
Farmingdale
Keystone
Hill City
Hermosa
Custer
Fairburn
Scenic
Interior
Imlay
Cottonwood
Kadoka
Belvidere
Stamford
Okaton
Murdo
Draper
Vivian
Presho
Kennebec
Red Shirt
Pringle
Hot Springs
Oral
Smithwick
Edgemont
Oelrichs
Oglala
Manderson
Porcupine
Wounded Knee
Batesland
Allen
Kyle
Potato Creek
Wanblee
Longvalley
Hisle
Patricia
Vetal
Norris
Cedar Butte
White River
Wood
Mosher
Witten
Carter
Winner
Okreek
Mission
Antelope
Parmelee
Rosebud
St. Francis
Hidden Timber
Ideal
Clearfield
A
B
C
1
2
3
4

DRIVING DISTANCES IN MILES

	ABERDEEN, SD	BROOKINGS, SD	HOT SPRINGS, SD	HURON, SD	MITCHELL, SD	MOBRIDGE, SD	PIERRE, SD	RAPID CITY, SD	SIOUX FALLS, SD	WAHPETON, ND	WALL, SD	WATERTOWN, SD
ABERDEEN, SD		150	412	90	146	99	160	357	204	154	303	98
PIERRE, SD	160	188	247	115	155	107		193	226	301	138	189
RAPID CITY, SD	357	390	56	313	275	243	193		346	543	55	436
SIOUX FALLS, SD	204	57	401	127	73	303	226	346		210	292	103

SEE ALSO DISTANCE AND DRIVING TIME MAP ON PAGES 286–287

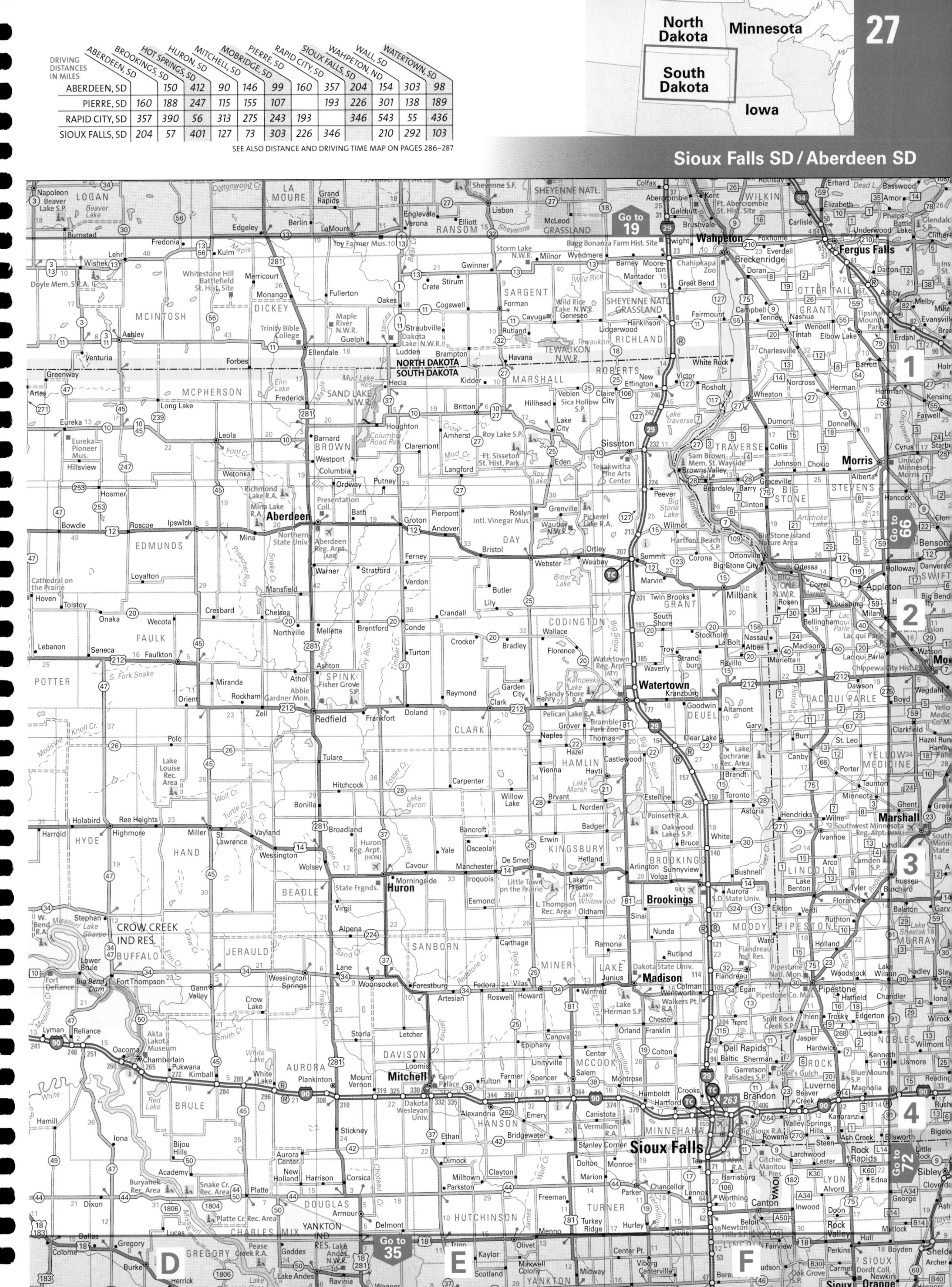

Oregon
California
Nevada

Medford OR / Redding CA

0 mi 20 40
0 km 20 40 60
One inch equals 25.4 miles
One centimeter equals 16.1 kilometers

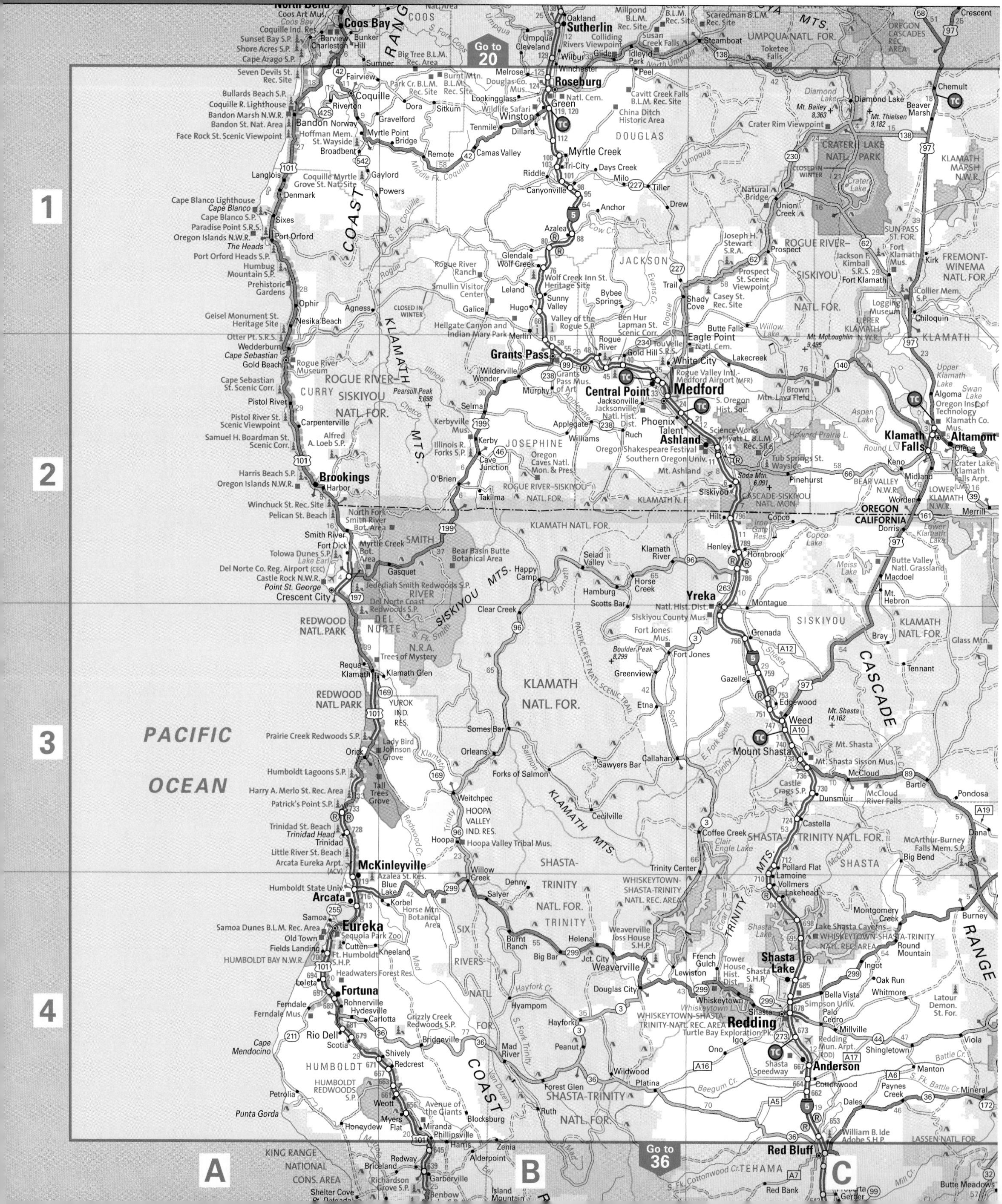

Go to 20

1
2
3
4
A
B
C

PACIFIC OCEAN

OREGON
CALIFORNIA

Coos Bay
Coos Art Mus.
Coquille Ind. Res.
Sunset Bay S.P.
Shore Acres S.P.
Cape Arago S.P.
Barview
Charleston
Bunker Hill
Sumner
Big Tree B.L.M. Rec. Area
COAST RANGE
Seven Devils St. Rec. Site
Bullards Beach S.P.
Coquille R. Lighthouse
Bandon Marsh N.W.R.
Bandon St. Nat. Area
Face Rock St. Scenic Viewpoint
Bandon
Norway
Riverton
Coquille
Fairview
Park Cr. B.L.M. Rec. Site
Burnt Mtn. B.L.M. Rec. Site
Dora
Sitkum
Gravelford
Myrtle Point
Bridge
Hoffman Mem. St. Wayside
Broadbent
Remote
Camas Valley
Tenmile
Langlois
Coquille Myrtle Grove St. Nat. Site
Gaylord
Powers
Denmark
Cape Blanco Lighthouse
Cape Blanco
Cape Blanco S.P.
Paradise Point S.R.S.
Oregon Islands N.W.R.
The Heads
Port Orford Heads S.P.
Humbug Mountain S.P.
Prehistoric Gardens
Sixes
Port Orford
Ophir
Geisel Monument St. Heritage Site
Nesika Beach
Otter Pt. S.R.S.
Wedderburn
Cape Sebastian
Gold Beach
Rogue River Museum
Cape Sebastian St. Scenic Corr.
Pistol River
Pistol River St. Scenic Viewpoint
Carpenterville
Samuel H. Boardman St. Scenic Corr.
Alfred A. Loeb S.P.
Harris Beach S.P.
Oregon Islands N.W.R.
Brookings
Harbor
Winchuck St. Rec. Site
Pelican St. Beach
Agness
KLAMATH MTS.
CURRY
ROGUE RIVER–SISKIYOU NATL. FOR.
Pearsoll Peak 5,098
Illinois R. Forks S.P.
Kerbyville Mus.
Kerby
Selma
Cave Junction
Oregon Caves Natl. Mon. & Pres.
O'Brien
Takilma
JOSEPHINE
Rogue River Ranch
Smullin Visitor Center
Galice
Hellgate Canyon and Indian Mary Park
Merlin
Grants Pass
Wilderville
Wonder
Murphy
Grants Pass Mus. of Art
Applegate
Williams
Ruch
Oakland
Sutherlin
Umpqua
Cleveland
Rivers Viewpoint
Colliding
Wilbur
Glide
Idleyld Park
Susan Creek Falls
Millpond B.L.M. Rec. Site
Scaredman B.L.M. Rec. Site
Steamboat
UMPQUA NATL. FOR.
Toketee Falls
Melrose
Douglas Co. Mus.
Winchester
Roseburg
Lookingglass
Wildlife Safari
Winston
Green
Dillard
Natl. Cem.
Cavitt Creek Falls B.L.M. Rec. Site
China Ditch Historic Area
DOUGLAS
Peel
Myrtle Creek
Tri-City
Riddle
Days Creek
Milo
Tiller
Canyonville
Drew
Anchor
Azalea
Glendale
Wolf Creek
Wolf Creek Inn St. Heritage Site
Leland
Sunny Valley
Hugo
Valley of the Rogue S.P.
Bybee Springs
Ben Hur Lampman St. Scenic Corr.
JACKSON
Rogue River
Gold Hill
Central Point
Jacksonville
Jacksonville Natl. Hist. Dist.
Medford
Rogue Valley Intl.-Medford Airport (MFR)
White City
Eagle Point
Butte Falls
Natl. Cem.
Lakecreek
Phoenix
Talent
Ashland
S. Oregon Hist. Soc.
Oregon Shakespeare Festival
Southern Oregon Univ.
ScienceWorks
Hyatt L. B.L.M. Rec. Site
Mt. Ashland
Soda Mtn. 6,091
CASCADE-SISKIYOU NATL. MON.
Siskiyou
Tub Springs St. Wayside
Pinehurst
Howard Prairie L.
Trail
Shady Cove
Casey St. Rec. Site
Joseph H. Stewart S.R.A.
Prospect
Prospect St. Scenic Viewpoint
ROGUE RIVER–SISKIYOU NATL. FOR.
Natural Bridge
Union Creek
Mt. McLoughlin 9,495
Diamond Lake
Mt. Bailey 8,363
Mt. Thielsen 9,182
Crater Rim Viewpoint
CRATER LAKE NATL. PARK
Crater Lake
Chemult
Beaver Marsh
KLAMATH MARSH N.W.R.
SUN PASS ST. FOR.
Fort Klamath Mus.
Jackson F. Kimball S.R.S.
Fort Klamath
Kirk
FREMONT-WINEMA NATL. FOR.
Collier Mem. S.P.
Logging Museum
Chiloquin
UPPER KLAMATH N.W.R.
KLAMATH
Upper Klamath Lake
Algoma
Oregon Inst. of Technology
Klamath Co. Mus.
Klamath Falls
Altamont
Olene
Keno
Midland
Crater Lake Klamath Falls Arpt.
BEAR VALLEY N.W.R.
Worden
LOWER KLAMATH N.W.R.
Merrill
Crescent
OREGON CASCADES REC. AREA
Hilt
Copco
Iron Gate Res.
Copco Lake
Dorris
Lower Klamath Lake
Butte Valley Natl. Grassland
Macdoel
Mt. Hebron
KLAMATH NATL. FOR.
Glass Mtn.
Tennant
Bray
Hornbrook
Henley
Klamath River
Seiad Valley
Happy Camp
Horse Creek
Hamburg
Scotts Bar
Yreka
Natl. Hist. Dist.
Siskiyou County Mus.
Montague
Grenada
Fort Jones Mus.
Fort Jones
Boulder Peak 8,299
Greenview
Etna
Gazelle
Edgewood
Weed
Mt. Shasta 14,162
Mount Shasta
Mt. Shasta Sisson Mus.
McCloud
Bartle
CASCADE RANGE
Pondosa
Dunsmuir
McCloud River Falls
Castle Crags S.P.
Castella
McArthur-Burney Falls Mem. S.P.
Dana
Big Bend
SHASTA
Callahan
Sawyers Bar
Cecilville
Forks of Salmon
Somes Bar
Orleans
KLAMATH NATL. FOR.
PACIFIC CREST NATL. SCENIC TRAIL
Smith River
Fort Dick
Tolowa Dunes S.P.
Lake Earl
Del Norte Co. Reg. Airport (CEC)
Castle Rock N.W.R.
Point St. George
Crescent City
North Fork Smith River Bot. Area
Myrtle Creek Bot. Area
SMITH RIVER N.R.A.
Gasquet
Jedediah Smith Redwoods S.P.
Bear Basin Butte Botanical Area
Del Norte Coast Redwoods S.P.
DEL NORTE
SISKIYOU MTS.
Clear Creek
REDWOOD NATL. PARK
Trees of Mystery
Requa
Klamath
Klamath Glen
YUROK IND. RES.
Prairie Creek Redwoods S.P.
Lady Bird Johnson Grove
Orick
Humboldt Lagoons S.P.
Harry A. Merlo St. Rec. Area
Patrick's Point S.P.
Tall Trees Grove
Trinidad St. Beach
Trinidad Head
Trinidad
Little River St. Beach
Arcata Eureka Arpt. (ACV)
McKinleyville
Weitchpec
HOOPA VALLEY IND. RES.
Hoopa
Hoopa Valley Tribal Mus.
Willow Creek
Coffee Creek
Clair Engle Lake
SHASTA-TRINITY NATL. FOR.
Trinity Center
WHISKEYTOWN-SHASTA-TRINITY NATL. REC. AREA
Humboldt State Univ.
Arcata
Azalea St. Res.
Blue Lake
Korbel
Horse Mtn. Botanical Area
Samoa
Samoa Dunes B.L.M. Rec. Area
Eureka
Sequoia Park Zoo
Old Town
Fields Landing
Cutten
Ft. Humboldt S.H.P.
Kneeland
HUMBOLDT BAY N.W.R.
Headwaters Forest Res.
Loleta
Fortuna
Ferndale
Ferndale Mus.
Rohnerville
Hydesville
Carlotta
Grizzly Creek Redwoods S.P.
Rio Dell
Scotia
Bridgeville
Cape Mendocino
Shively
Redcrest
HUMBOLDT
HUMBOLDT REDWOODS S.P.
Petrolia
Punta Gorda
Weott
Myers Flat
Avenue of the Giants
Honeydew
Miranda
Phillipsville
Blocksburg
SIX RIVERS NATL. FOR.
COAST RANGE
Denny
Salyer
Burnt Ranch
Big Bar
Helena
Jct. City
Weaverville
Weaverville Joss House S.H.P.
Hyampom
Hayfork
Peanut
Mad River
Forest Glen
Ruth
Douglas City
Lewiston
French Gulch
Tower House Hist. Dist.
Whiskeytown
Whiskeytown L.
Shasta
Shasta S.H.P.
Redding
Turtle Bay Exploration Pk.
Igo
Ono
Platina
Wildwood
Beegum Cr.
TRINITY MTS.
Pollard Flat
Lamoine
Vollmers
Lakehead
Shasta Lake
Lake Shasta Caverns
Montgomery Creek
Round Mountain
Burney
Ingot
Oak Run
Whitmore
Bella Vista
Simpson Univ.
Palo Cedro
Millville
Latour Demon. St. For.
Redding Mun. Arpt. (RDD)
Shingletown
Viola
Shasta Speedway
Anderson
Cottonwood
Manton
Paynes Creek
Mineral
Dales
William B. Ide Adobe S.H.P.
LASSEN NATL. FOR.
Red Bluff
TEHAMA
Red Bank
Gerber
Butte Meadows
Mill Cr.
KING RANGE NATIONAL CONS. AREA
Shelter Cove
Briceland
Redway
Richardson Grove S.P.
Garberville
Benbow
Harris
Zenia
Alderpoint
Island Mountain

Go to 36

DRIVING DISTANCES IN MILES

	ALTURAS, CA	CRATER LAKE NP, OR	CRESCENT CITY, CA	EUREKA, CA	KLAMATH FALLS, OR	LAKEVIEW, OR	LASSEN VOLCANIC NP, CA	MEDFORD, OR	REDDING, CA	ROSEBURG, OR	SUSANVILLE, CA	WINNEMUCCA, NV
LAKEVIEW, OR	56	153	282	332	98		192	171	199	265	161	212
MEDFORD, OR	176	80	111	192	76	171	208		148	94	221	383
REDDING, CA	143	198	189	133	141	199	63	148		242	114	364
SUSANVILLE, CA	105	226	303	247	170	161	74	221	114	315		250

SEE ALSO DISTANCE AND DRIVING TIME MAP ON PAGES 286–287

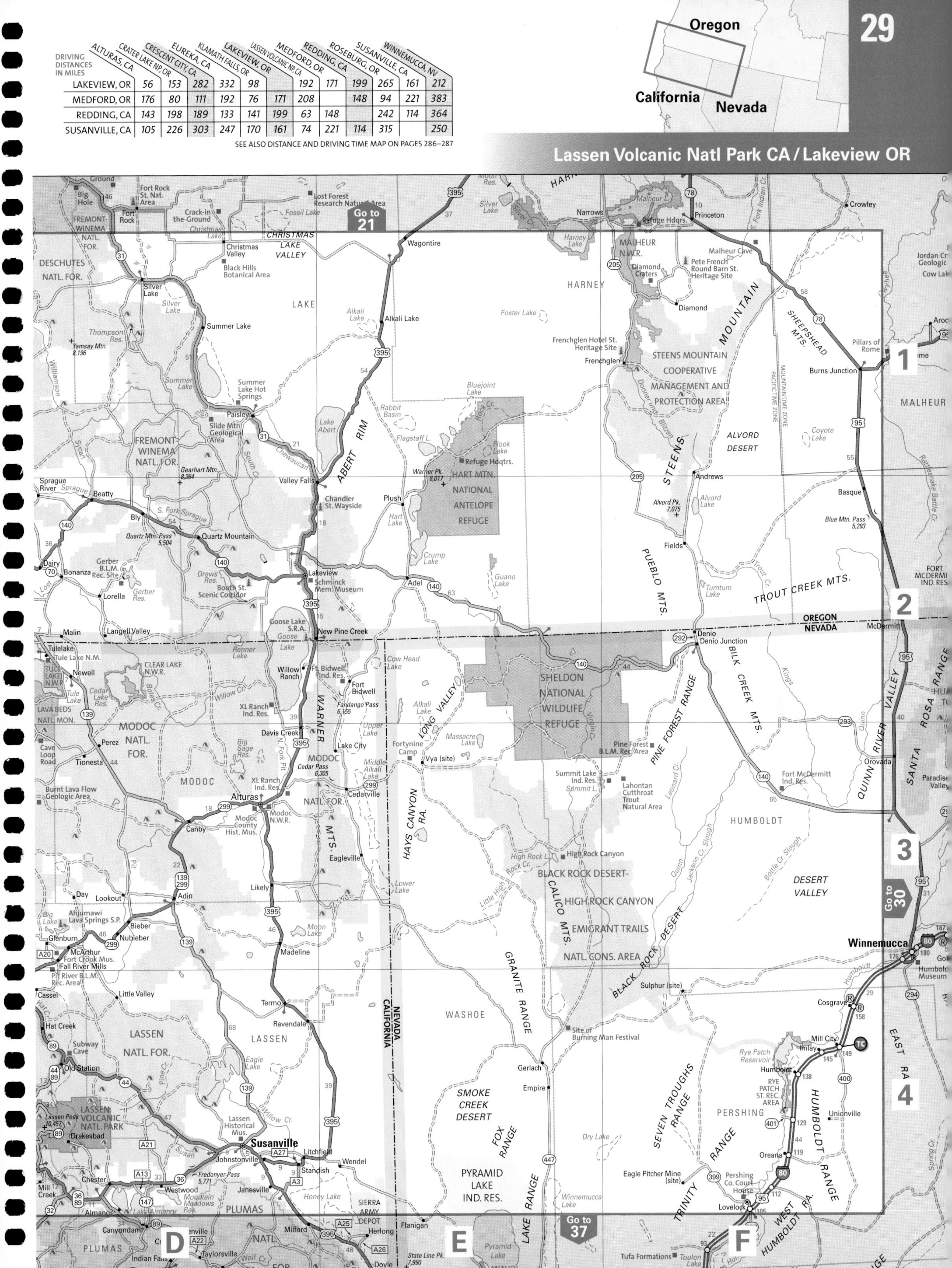

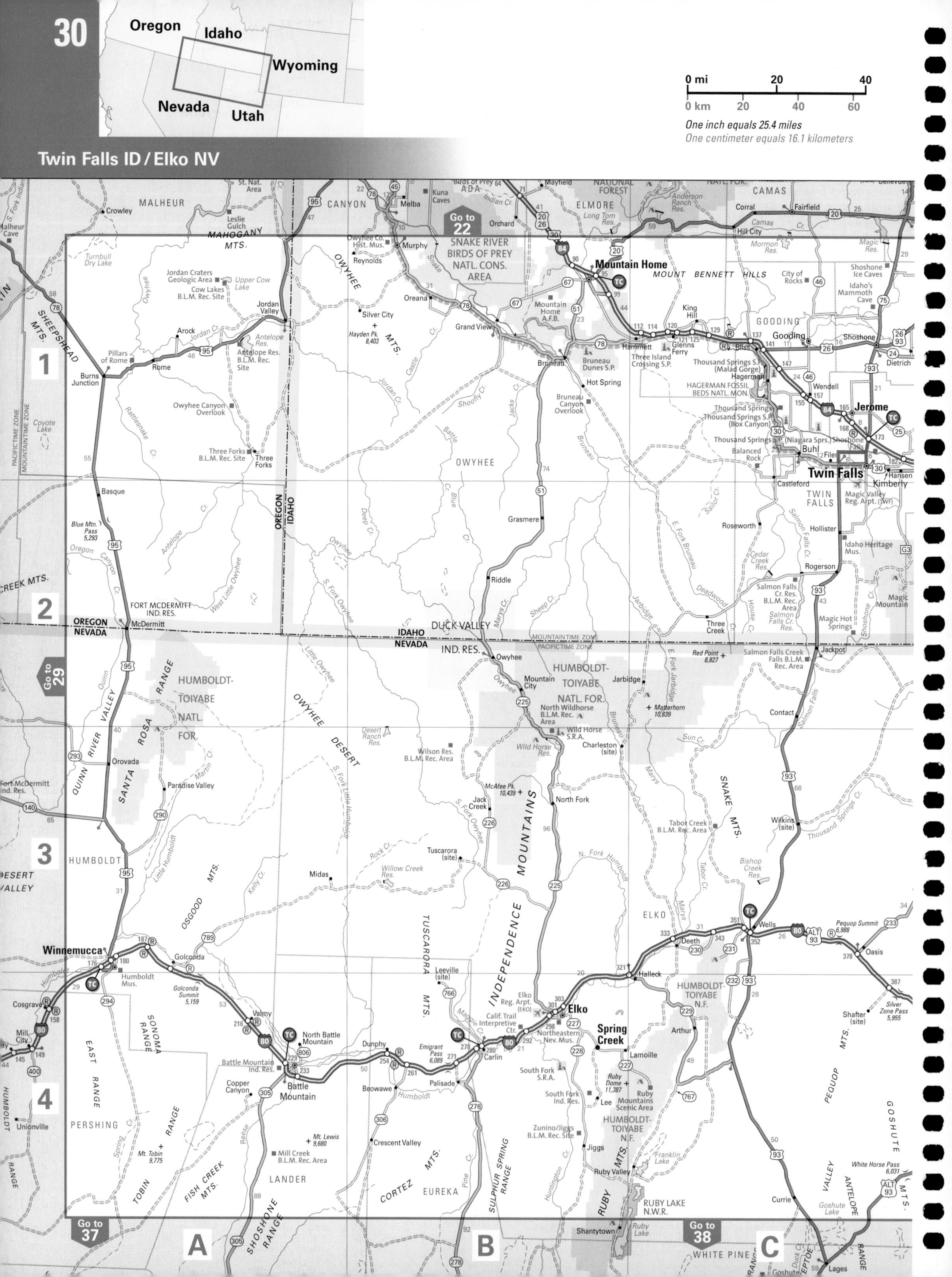
30
Oregon
Idaho
Wyoming
Nevada
Utah
Twin Falls ID / Elko NV
0 mi
20
40
0 km
20
40
60
One inch equals 25.4 miles
One centimeter equals 16.1 kilometers
Go to 22
Go to 29
Go to 37
Go to 38
A
B
C
1
2
3
4
OREGON
NEVADA
IDAHO
NEVADA
OREGON
IDAHO
MOUNTAIN TIME ZONE
PACIFIC TIME ZONE
MALHEUR
CANYON
ADA
ELMORE
CAMAS
GOODING
TWIN FALLS
OWYHEE
ELKO
HUMBOLDT
PERSHING
LANDER
EUREKA
Crowley
Leslie Gulch
MAHOGANY MTS.
SHEEPSHEAD MTS.
Jordan Craters Geologic Area
Cow Lakes B.L.M. Rec. Site
Upper Cow Lake
Jordan Valley
Arock
Antelope Res.
Antelope Res. B.L.M. Rec. Site
Pillars of Rome
Rome
Burns Junction
Owyhee Canyon Overlook
Three Forks B.L.M. Rec. Site
Three Forks
Basque
Blue Mtn. Pass 5,293
FORT MCDERMITT IND. RES.
McDermitt
Melba
Kuna Caves
Owyhee Co. Hist. Mus.
Murphy
Reynolds
SNAKE RIVER BIRDS OF PREY NATL. CONS. AREA
Orchard
Mountain Home
Mountain Home A.F.B.
Oreana
Silver City
Hayden Pk. 8,403
OWYHEE MTS.
Grand View
Bruneau
Bruneau Dunes S.P.
Hot Spring
Bruneau Canyon Overlook
Hammett
Three Island Crossing S.P.
Glenns Ferry
King Hill
MOUNT BENNETT HILLS
City of Rocks
Shoshone Ice Caves
Idaho's Mammoth Cave
Gooding
Shoshone
Dietrich
Bliss
Thousand Springs S.P. (Malad Gorge)
Hagerman
HAGERMAN FOSSIL BEDS NATL. MON.
Wendell
Jerome
Thousand Springs S.P. (Box Canyon)
Thousand Springs S.P. (Niagara Sprs.)
Shoshone Falls
Buhl
Filer
Balanced Rock
Twin Falls
Kimberly
Hansen
Castleford
Magic Valley Reg. Arpt. (TWF)
Fairfield
Corral
Hill City
Mormon Res.
Magic Res.
Roseworth
Hollister
Idaho Heritage Mus.
Rogerson
Cedar Creek Res.
Salmon Falls Cr. Res. B.L.M. Rec. Area
Magic Mountain
Magic Hot Springs
Three Creek
Grasmere
Riddle
DUCK VALLEY IND. RES.
Owyhee
Mountain City
HUMBOLDT-TOIYABE NATL. FOR.
North Wildhorse B.L.M. Rec. Area
Wild Horse S.R.A.
Wild Horse Res.
Jarbidge
Red Point 8,827
Matterhorn 10,839
Charleston (site)
Salmon Falls Creek B.L.M. Rec. Area
Jackpot
Contact
QUINN RIVER VALLEY
SANTA ROSA RANGE
Orovada
Paradise Valley
Fort McDermitt Ind. Res.
OWYHEE DESERT
Desert Ranch Res.
Wilson Res. B.L.M. Rec. Area
McAfee Pk. 10,439
Jack Creek
North Fork
INDEPENDENCE MOUNTAINS
SNAKE MTS.
Tabor Creek B.L.M. Rec. Area
Wilkins (site)
Bishop Creek Res.
Tuscarora (site)
Willow Creek Res.
Midas
OSGOOD MTS.
TUSCARORA MTS.
Winnemucca
Golconda
Golconda Summit 5,159
Humboldt Mus.
Cosgrave
Mill City
Valmy
North Battle Mountain
Battle Mountain
Battle Mountain Ind. Res.
Copper Canyon
SONOMA RANGE
EAST RANGE
Leeville (site)
Dunphy
Emigrant Pass 6,089
Carlin
Palisade
Beowawe
Elko Reg. Arpt. (EKO)
Calif. Trail Interpretive Ctr.
Northeastern Nev. Mus.
Elko
Spring Creek
Lamoille
Halleck
Deeth
Wells
Pequop Summit 6,988
Oasis
Silver Zone Pass 5,955
Shafter (site)
Arthur
HUMBOLDT-TOIYABE N.F.
PEQUOP MTS.
GOSHUTE
South Fork S.R.A.
South Fork Ind. Res.
Ruby Dome 11,387
Ruby Mountains Scenic Area
Lee
Zunino/Jiggs B.L.M. Rec. Site
Jiggs
Franklin Lake
RUBY MTS.
Ruby Valley
RUBY LAKE N.W.R.
Ruby Lake
Shantytown
Currie
White Horse Pass 6,031
ANTELOPE VALLEY
Goshute Lake
WHITE PINE
Lages
Unionville
Mt. Tobin 9,775
TOBIN RANGE
FISH CREEK MTS.
Mt. Lewis 9,680
Mill Creek B.L.M. Rec. Area
Crescent Valley
SHOSHONE RANGE
CORTEZ MTS.
SULPHUR SPRING RANGE

DRIVING DISTANCES IN MILES	BRIGHAM CITY, UT	ELKO, NV	EVANSTON, WY	MONTPELIER, ID	MOUNTAIN HOME, ID	OGDEN, UT	POCATELLO, ID	PROVO, UT	SALT LAKE CITY, UT	TWIN FALLS, ID	WELLS, NV	WINNEMUCCA, NV
ELKO, NV	286		314	375	194	267	283	279	232	167	50	127
POCATELLO, ID	107	283	200	87	193	127		205	159	116	233	410
SALT LAKE CITY, UT	56	232	82	145	295	37	159	47		217	182	359
TWIN FALLS, ID	165	167	259	204	86	185	116	264	217		117	294

SEE ALSO DISTANCE AND DRIVING TIME MAP ON PAGES 286–287

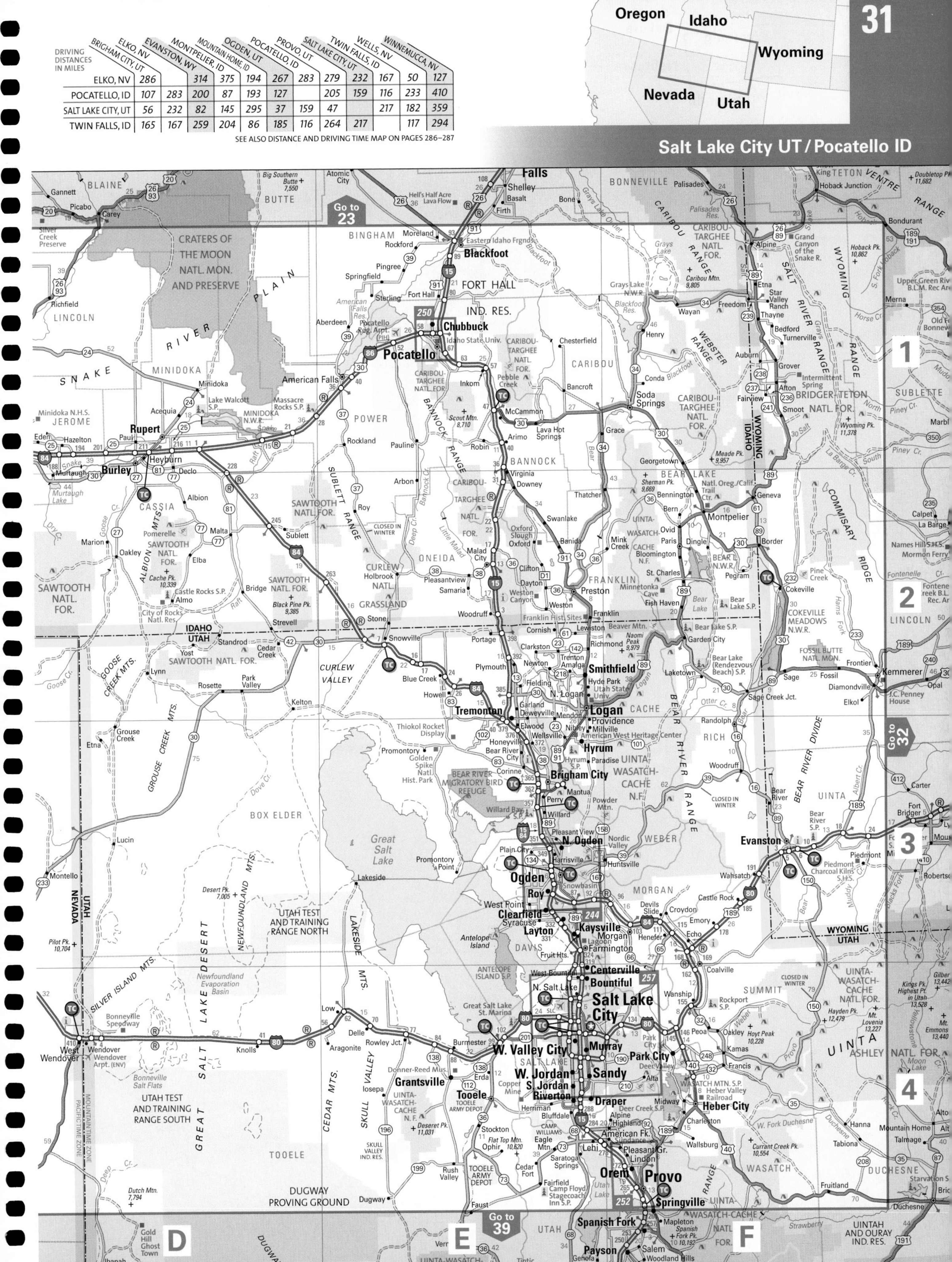

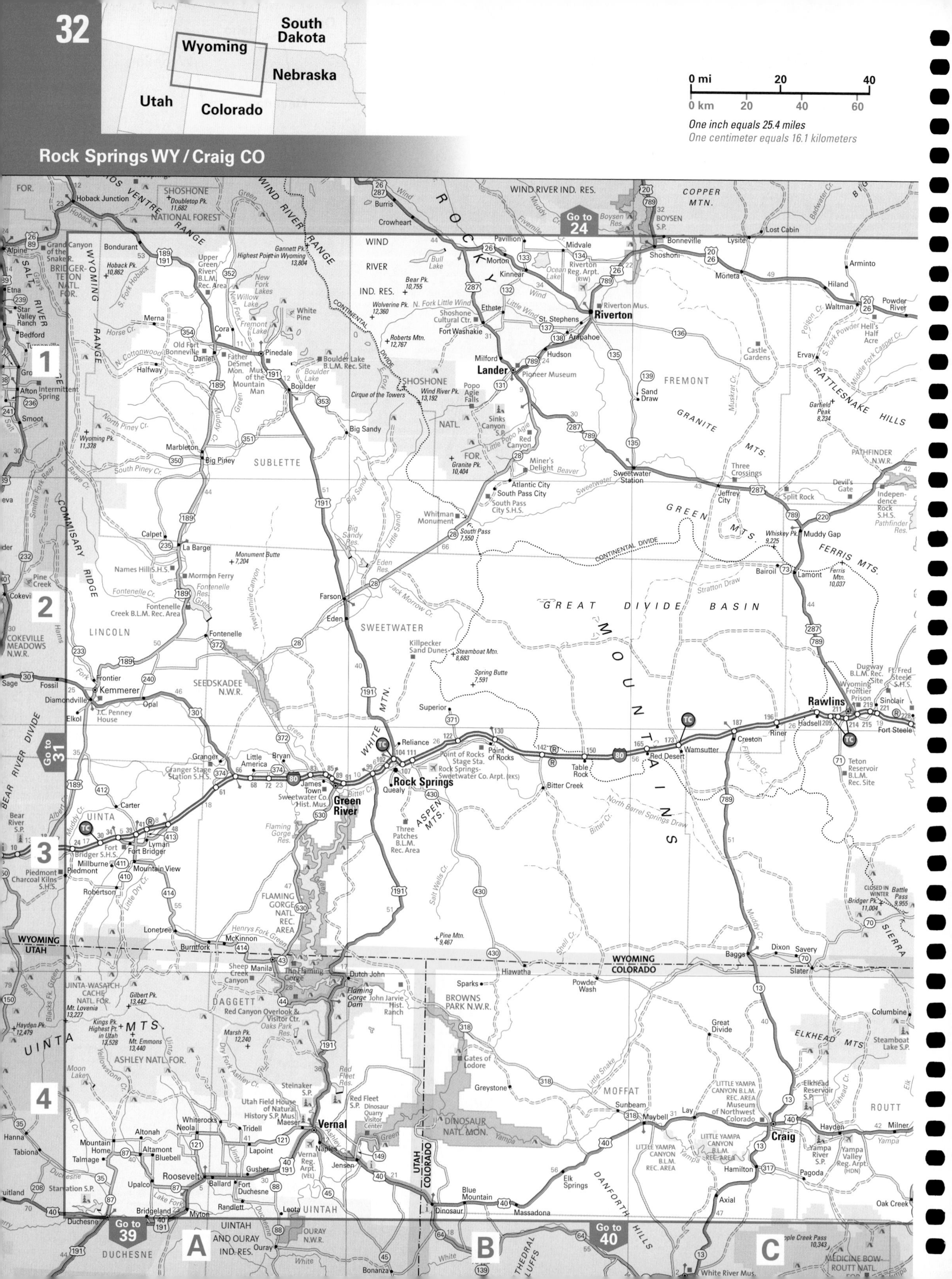
South Dakota
Wyoming
Nebraska
Utah
Colorado
0 mi 20 40
0 km 20 40 60
One inch equals 25.4 miles
One centimeter equals 16.1 kilometers
Go to 24
Go to 31
Go to 39
Go to 40
1
2
3
4
A
B
C
WIND RIVER IND. RES.
COPPER MTN.
BOYSEN S.P.
Hoback Junction
SHOSHONE NATIONAL FOREST
Doubletop Pk. 11,682
WIND RIVER RANGE
ROCKY MOUNTAINS
Burris
Crowheart
Pavillion
Midvale
Bonneville
Lysite
Lost Cabin
Shoshoni
Arminto
Moneta
Hiland
Waltman
Powder River
Bondurant
Grand Canyon of the Snake R.
Alpine
Etna
BRIDGER-TETON NATL. FOR.
Hoback Pk. 10,862
Upper Green River B.L.M. Rec. Area
Highest Point in Wyoming
Gannett Pk. 13,804
Bear Pk. 10,755
Wolverine Pk. 12,360
Morton
Kinnear
Riverton Reg. Arpt. (RIW)
Riverton Mus.
Riverton
St. Stephens
Arapahoe
Ethete
Shoshone Cultural Ctr.
Fort Washakie
Hudson
Milford
Lander
Pioneer Museum
Castle Gardens
Ervay
Hell's Half Acre
RATTLESNAKE HILLS
Garfield Peak 8,234
Star Valley Ranch
Bedford
Merna
Cora
Pinedale
Old Fort Bonneville
Daniel
Father DeSmet Mon.
Museum of the Mountain Man
Boulder Lake B.L.M. Rec. Site
Boulder
Roberts Mtn. 12,767
CONTINENTAL DIVIDE
Cirque of the Towers
Wind River Pk. 13,192
SHOSHONE NATL. FOR.
Popo Agie Falls
Sinks Canyon S.P.
Sand Draw
FREMONT
GRANITE MTS.
Halfway
Afton
Intermittent Spring
Smoot
Wyoming Pk. 11,378
Big Sandy
Red Canyon
Marbleton
Big Piney
SUBLETTE
Granite Pk. 10,404
Miner's Delight
Atlantic City
South Pass City
South Pass City S.H.S.
Sweetwater Station
Three Crossings
Jeffrey City
PATHFINDER N.W.R.
Devil's Gate
Split Rock
Independence Rock S.H.S.
Pathfinder Res.
Whitman Monument
South Pass 7,550
GREEN MTS.
Whiskey Pk. 9,225
Muddy Gap
FERRIS MTS.
Ferris Mtn. 10,037
Bairoil
Lamont
COMMISARY RIDGE
Calpet
La Barge
Monument Butte 7,204
Names Hill S.H.S.
Mormon Ferry
Pine Creek
Cokeville
Fontenelle Creek B.L.M. Rec. Area
Farson
Eden
GREAT DIVIDE BASIN
COKEVILLE MEADOWS N.W.R.
LINCOLN
Fontenelle
SWEETWATER
Killpecker Sand Dunes
Steamboat Mtn. 8,683
Spring Butte 7,591
Frontier
Kemmerer
Fossil
Sage
Diamondville
J.C. Penney House
Elkol
Opal
SEEDSKADEE N.W.R.
Dugway B.L.M. Rec. Site
Ft. Fred Steele S.H.S.
Wyoming Frontier Prison
Rawlins
Sinclair
Hadsell
Fort Steele
Superior
Reliance
WHITE MTN.
Creston
Riner
Wamsutter
Red Desert
Table Rock
Point of Rocks
Point of Rocks Stage Sta.
Rock Springs-Sweetwater Co. Arpt. (RKS)
Granger
Little America
Bryan
Granger Stage Station S.H.S.
James Town
Sweetwater Co. Hist. Mus.
Green River
Rock Springs
Quealy
Bitter Creek
Teton Reservoir B.L.M. Rec. Site
BEAR RIVER DIVIDE
Carter
UINTA
Bear River S.P.
Fort Bridger S.H.S.
Fort Bridger
Lyman
Millburne
Mountain View
Piedmont
Piedmont Charcoal Kilns S.H.S.
Flaming Gorge Res.
ASPEN MTS.
Three Patches B.L.M. Rec. Area
North Barrel Springs Draw
Robertson
FLAMING GORGE NATL. REC. AREA
Lonetree
McKinnon
Burntfork
Pine Mtn. 9,467
Battle Pass 9,955
Bridger Pk. 11,004
SIERRA
WYOMING
UTAH
COLORADO
Sheep Creek Canyon
Manila
Dutch John
Flaming Gorge Dam
John Jarvie Hist. Ranch
Hiawatha
Sparks
Powder Wash
Baggs
Dixon
Savery
Slater
UINTA-WASATCH-CACHE NATL. FOR.
Gilbert Pk. 13,442
Mt. Lovenia 13,227
DAGGETT
Red Canyon Overlook & Visitor Ctr.
BROWNS PARK N.W.R.
Columbine
Kings Pk. Highest Pt. in Utah 13,528
Hayden Pk. 12,479
UINTA MTS.
Mt. Emmons 13,440
Marsh Pk. 12,240
ASHLEY NATL. FOR.
Great Divide
ELKHEAD MTS.
Steamboat Lake S.P.
Gates of Lodore
Moon Lake
Steinaker S.P.
Red Fleet Res.
Greystone
Little Yampa Canyon B.L.M. Rec. Area
Museum of Northwest Colorado
Elkhead Reservoir S.P.
MOFFAT
ROUTT
Utah Field House of Natural History S.P. Mus.
Red Fleet S.P.
Dinosaur Quarry Visitor Center
DINOSAUR NATL. MON.
Sunbeam
Maybell
Lay
Craig
Hayden
Milner
Whiterocks
Neola
Tridell
Maeser
Vernal
Altonah
Mountain Home
Altamont
Bluebell
Lapoint
Talmage
Hanna
Tabiona
Naples
Vernal Reg. Arpt. (VEL)
Jensen
Yampa
Yampa River S.P.
Yampa Valley Reg. Arpt. (HDN)
Pagoda
Hamilton
Roosevelt
Ballard
Fort Duchesne
Gusher
Upalco
Starvation S.P.
Duchesne
Bridgeland
Myton
Randlett
Leota
UINTAH
Blue Mountain
Dinosaur
Massadona
Elk Springs
DANFORTH HILLS
Axial
Oak Creek
UINTAH AND OURAY IND. RES.
OURAY N.W.R.
Ouray
DUCHESNE
Bonanza
White River Mus.
Ripple Creek Pass 10,343
MEDICINE BOW-ROUTT NATL.

DRIVING DISTANCES IN MILES

	CASPER, WY	CHEYENNE, WY	CRAIG, CO	FORT COLLINS, CO	KEMMERER, WY	LANDER, WY	LARAMIE, WY	PINEDALE, WY	RAWLINS, WY	ROCK SPRINGS, WY	SCOTTSBLUFF, NE	VERNAL, UT
CASPER, WY		175	234	217	297	144	148	271	117	214	173	322
CHEYENNE, WY	175		221	44	342	276	52	355	151	260	111	367
CRAIG, CO	234	221		194	257	221	171	269	117	149	331	123
ROCK SPRINGS, WY	214	260	149	273	86	118	210	98	110		370	111

SEE ALSO DISTANCE AND DRIVING TIME MAP ON PAGES 286–287

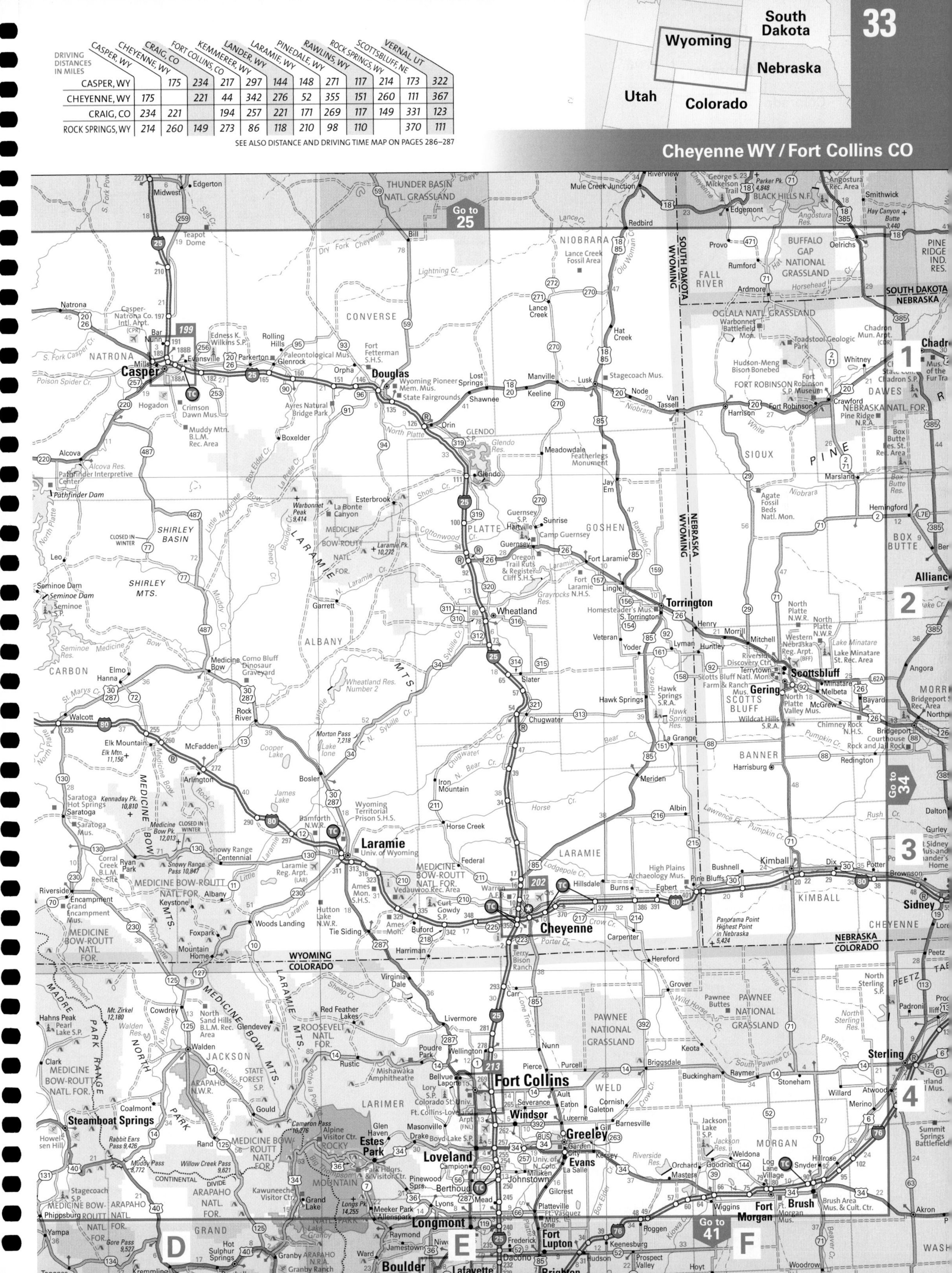

South Dakota
Nebraska
Iowa
Colorado

0 mi 20 40
0 km 20 40 60
One inch equals 25.4 miles
One centimeter equals 16.1 kilometers

North Platte NE / Chadron NE

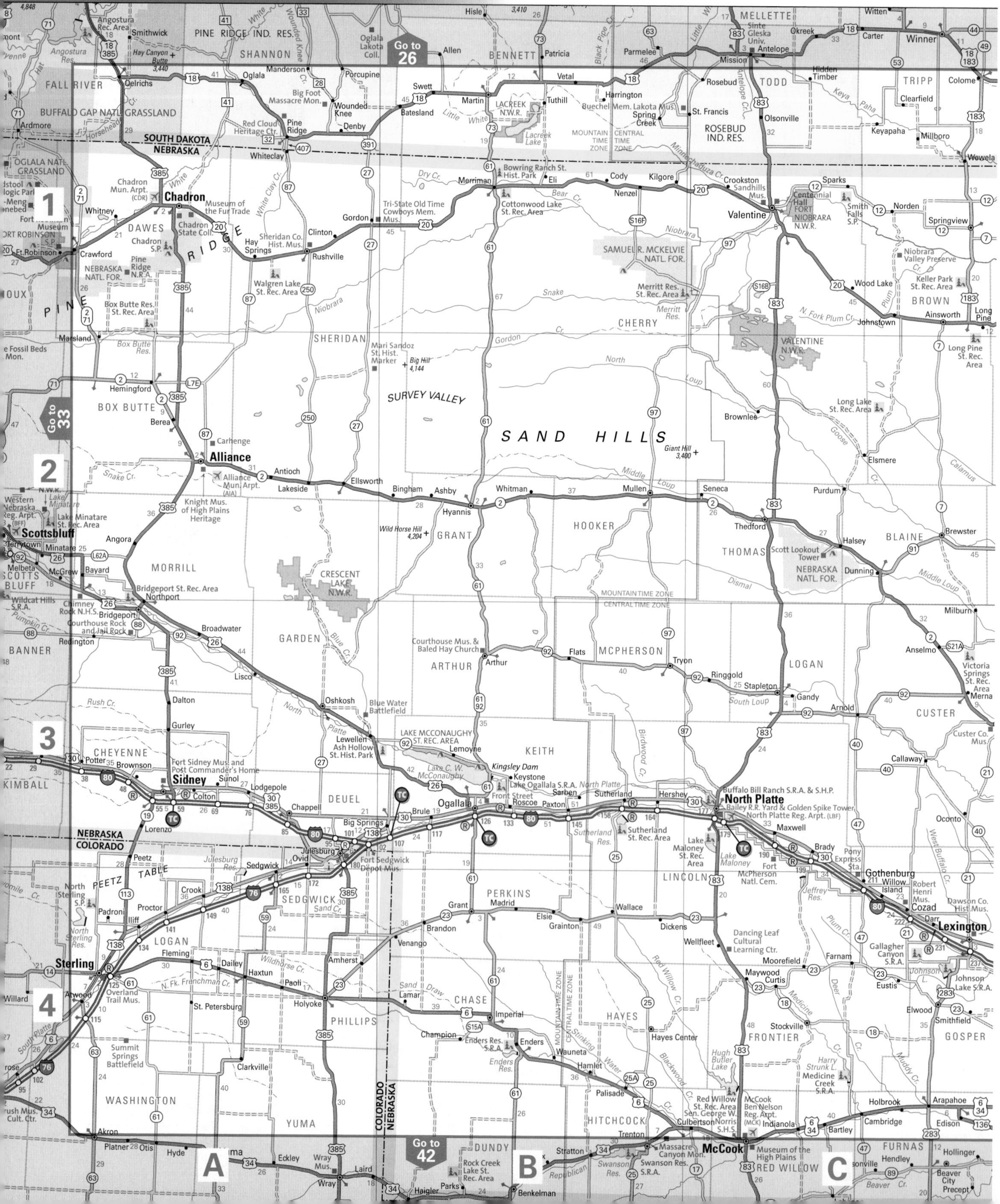

Go to 26
Go to 33
Go to 42

PINE RIDGE IND. RES.
SHANNON
BENNETT
MELLETTE
TODD
TRIPP
FALL RIVER
BUFFALO GAP NATL. GRASSLAND
OGLALA NATL. GRASSLAND
ROSEBUD IND. RES.
SOUTH DAKOTA
NEBRASKA
Hisle
Allen
Patricia
Parmelee
Sinte Gleska Univ.
Antelope
Mission
Okreek
Carter
Winner
Witten
Colome
Hidden Timber
Clearfield
Keyapaha
Millboro
Wewela
Angostura Rec. Area
Angostura Res.
Smithwick
Hay Canyon Butte 3,440
Oelrichs
Oglala
Manderson
Porcupine
Oglala Lakota Coll.
Big Foot Massacre Mon.
Wounded Knee
Pine Ridge
Red Cloud Heritage Ctr.
Denby
Swett
Batesland
Martin
Vetal
Harrington
Buechel Mem. Lakota Mus.
St. Francis
Rosebud
Olsonville
Spring Creek
LACREEK N.W.R.
Lacreek Lake
Tuthill
MOUNTAIN TIME ZONE
CENTRAL TIME ZONE
Ardmore
Whiteclay
Chadron Mun. Arpt. (CDR)
Chadron
Museum of the Fur Trade
Chadron State Coll.
Chadron S.P.
DAWES
PINE RIDGE
Whitney
Fort Robinson Museum
Ft. Robinson S.P.
Crawford
NEBRASKA NATL. FOR.
Pine Ridge N.R.A.
Hay Springs
Sheridan Co. Hist. Mus.
Clinton
Rushville
Gordon
Tri-State Old Time Cowboys Mem. Mus.
Walgren Lake St. Rec. Area
Merriman
Bowring Ranch St. Hist. Park
Eli
Cottonwood Lake St. Rec. Area
Cody
Nenzel
Kilgore
Crookston
Sandhills Mus.
Centennial Hall
FORT NIOBRARA N.W.R.
Valentine
Sparks
Smith Falls S.P.
Norden
Springview
SAMUEL R. MCKELVIE NATL. FOR.
Merritt Res. St. Rec. Area
Niobrara Valley Preserve
Keller Park St. Rec. Area
Wood Lake
BROWN
Johnstown
Ainsworth
Long Pine
Long Pine St. Rec. Area
CHERRY
VALENTINE N.W.R.
Box Butte Res. St. Rec. Area
Marsland
Fossil Beds Natl. Mon.
Hemingford
BOX BUTTE
Berea
Carhenge
Alliance
Alliance Mun. Arpt. (AIA)
Antioch
Lakeside
Ellsworth
SHERIDAN
Mari Sandoz St. Hist. Marker
Big Hill 4,144
SURVEY VALLEY
SAND HILLS
Giant Hill 3,400
Brownlee
Long Lake St. Rec. Area
Elsmere
Bingham
Ashby
Hyannis
Whitman
Mullen
Seneca
Thedford
Purdum
Western Nebraska Reg. Arpt. (BFF)
Lake Minatare St. Rec. Area
Scottsbluff
Terrytown
Minatare
Melbeta
McGrew
Bayard
SCOTTS BLUFF
Angora
Knight Mus. of High Plains Heritage
MORRILL
Wild Horse Hill 4,204
GRANT
HOOKER
THOMAS
Scott Lookout Tower
NEBRASKA NATL. FOR.
Halsey
Dunning
BLAINE
Brewster
CRESCENT LAKE N.W.R.
Bridgeport St. Rec. Area
Northport
Wildcat Hills S.R.A.
Chimney Rock N.H.S.
Bridgeport
Courthouse Rock and Jail Rock
Redington
BANNER
Broadwater
GARDEN
Courthouse Mus. & Baled Hay Church
Arthur
ARTHUR
Flats
MCPHERSON
Tryon
Ringgold
Stapleton
Gandy
LOGAN
Milburn
Anselmo
Victoria Springs St. Rec. Area
Merna
CUSTER
Arnold
Lisco
Dalton
Oshkosh
Blue Water Battlefield
Gurley
CHEYENNE
Potter
Brownson
Fort Sidney Mus. and Post Commander's Home
Sidney
Sunol
Lodgepole
KIMBALL
Colton
Chappell
DEUEL
Lake McConaughy St. Rec. Area
Lewellen
Ash Hollow St. Hist. Park
Lemoyne
Lake C. W. McConaughy
Kingsley Dam
Keystone
Lake Ogallala S.R.A.
KEITH
Front Street
Ogallala
Brule
Big Springs
Roscoe
Paxton
Sarben
Sutherland
Sutherland Res.
Sutherland St. Rec. Area
Hershey
North Platte
Buffalo Bill Ranch S.R.A. & S.H.P.
Bailey R.R. Yard & Golden Spike Tower
North Platte Reg. Arpt. (LBF)
Maxwell
Lake Maloney St. Rec. Area
Fort McPherson Natl. Cem.
Brady
Pony Express Sta.
Gothenburg
Callaway
Oconto
Custer Co. Mus.
Lorenzo
NEBRASKA
COLORADO
Julesburg
Ovid
Fort Sedgwick Depot Mus.
Peetz
PEETZ TABLE
Sedgwick
Crook
North Sterling S.P.
North Sterling Res.
SEDGWICK
Padroni
Iliff
Proctor
LOGAN
Fleming
Sterling
Atwood
Dailey
Haxtun
Paoli
Holyoke
PHILLIPS
Overland Trail Mus.
St. Petersburg
Summit Springs Battlefield
Clarkville
WASHINGTON
YUMA
Akron
Platner
Otis
Hyde
Eckley
Wray
Wray Mus.
Laird
Haigler
Parks
Benkelman
DUNDY
Rock Creek Lake St. Rec. Area
COLORADO NEBRASKA
PERKINS
Grant
Madrid
Elsie
Grainton
Venango
Brandon
Amherst
Lamar
CHASE
Imperial
Champion
Enders Res. S.R.A.
Enders
Wauneta
Hamlet
Palisade
HAYES
Hayes Center
Wallace
Dickens
Wellfleet
LINCOLN
Dancing Leaf Cultural Learning Ctr.
Moorefield
Maywood
Curtis
FRONTIER
Stockville
Hugh Butler Lake
Harry Strunk L.
Medicine Creek S.R.A.
Red Willow St. Rec. Area
Sen. George W. Norris S.H.S.
McCook Ben Nelson Reg. Arpt. (MCK)
HITCHCOCK
Culbertson
Trenton
Massacre Canyon Mon.
Swanson Res. S.R.A.
Stratton
McCook
Museum of the High Plains
RED WILLOW
Indianola
Bartley
Cambridge
Holbrook
Arapahoe
Edison
FURNAS
Hendley
Beaver City
Hollinger
Farnam
Eustis
Elwood
Smithfield
GOSPER
Johnson Lake S.R.A.
Gallagher Canyon S.R.A.
Lexington
Cozad
Darr
Willow Island
Robert Henri Mus.
Dawson Co. Hist. Mus.
Willard
Fort Sidney
A
B
C
1
2
3
4

DRIVING DISTANCES IN MILES

	CHADRON, NE	GRAND ISLAND, NE	LINCOLN, NE	MCCOOK, NE	NORFOLK, NE	NORTH PLATTE, NE	OGALLALA, NE	OMAHA, NE	SCOTTSBLUFF, NE	SIOUX CITY, IA	STERLING, CO	YANKTON, SD
GRAND ISLAND, NE	373		95	147	105	143	196	150	318	180	281	167
LINCOLN, NE	453	95		226	119	223	275	58	397	153	361	218
NORTH PLATTE, NE	230	143	223	67	248		53	278	175	373	138	310
OMAHA, NE	508	150	58	281	115	278	330		452	99	416	163

SEE ALSO DISTANCE AND DRIVING TIME MAP ON PAGES 286–287

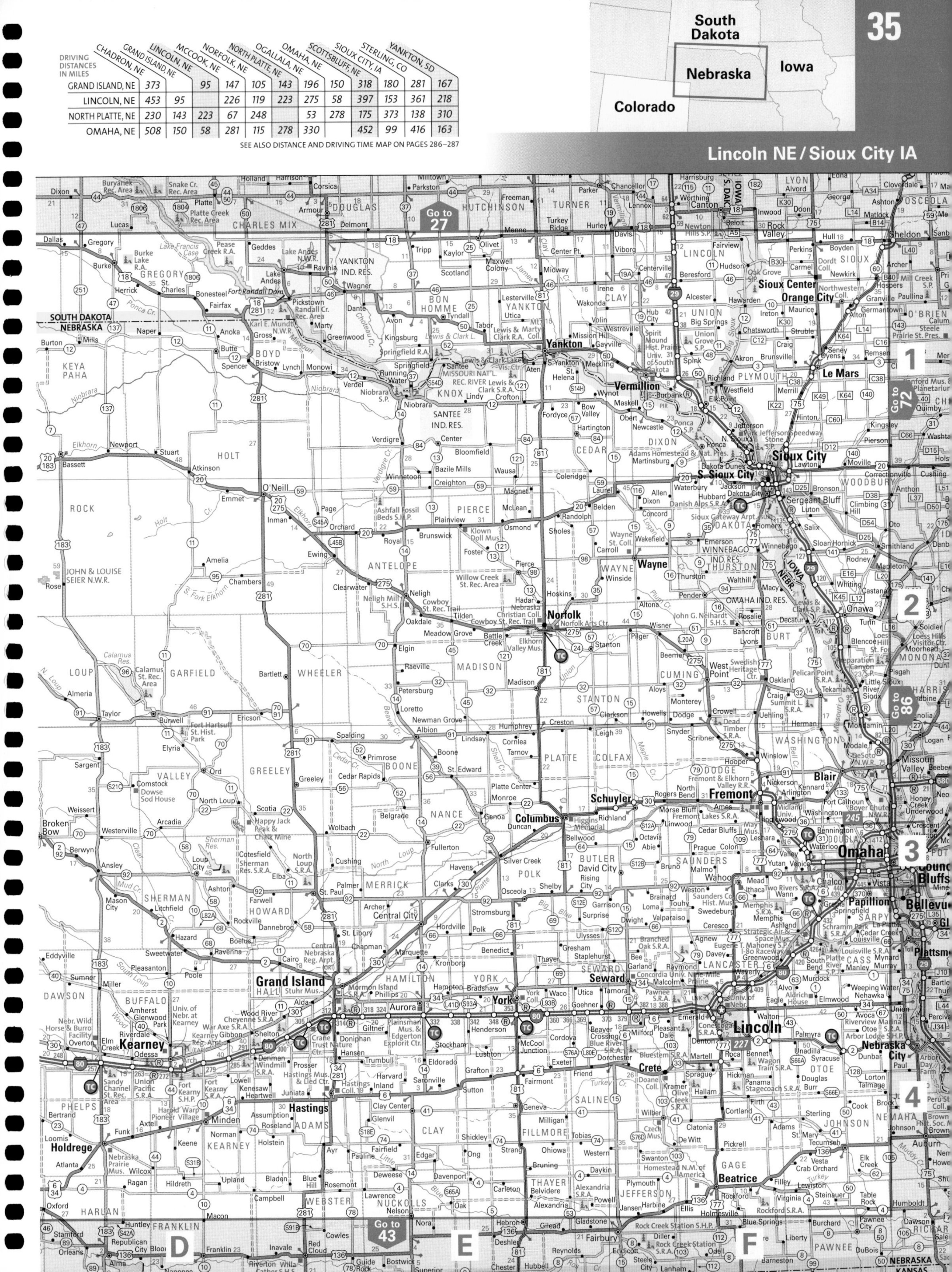

California
Nevada

0 mi 20 40
0 km 20 40 60
One inch equals 25.4 miles
One centimeter equals 16.1 kilometers

San Francisco CA / Sacramento CA

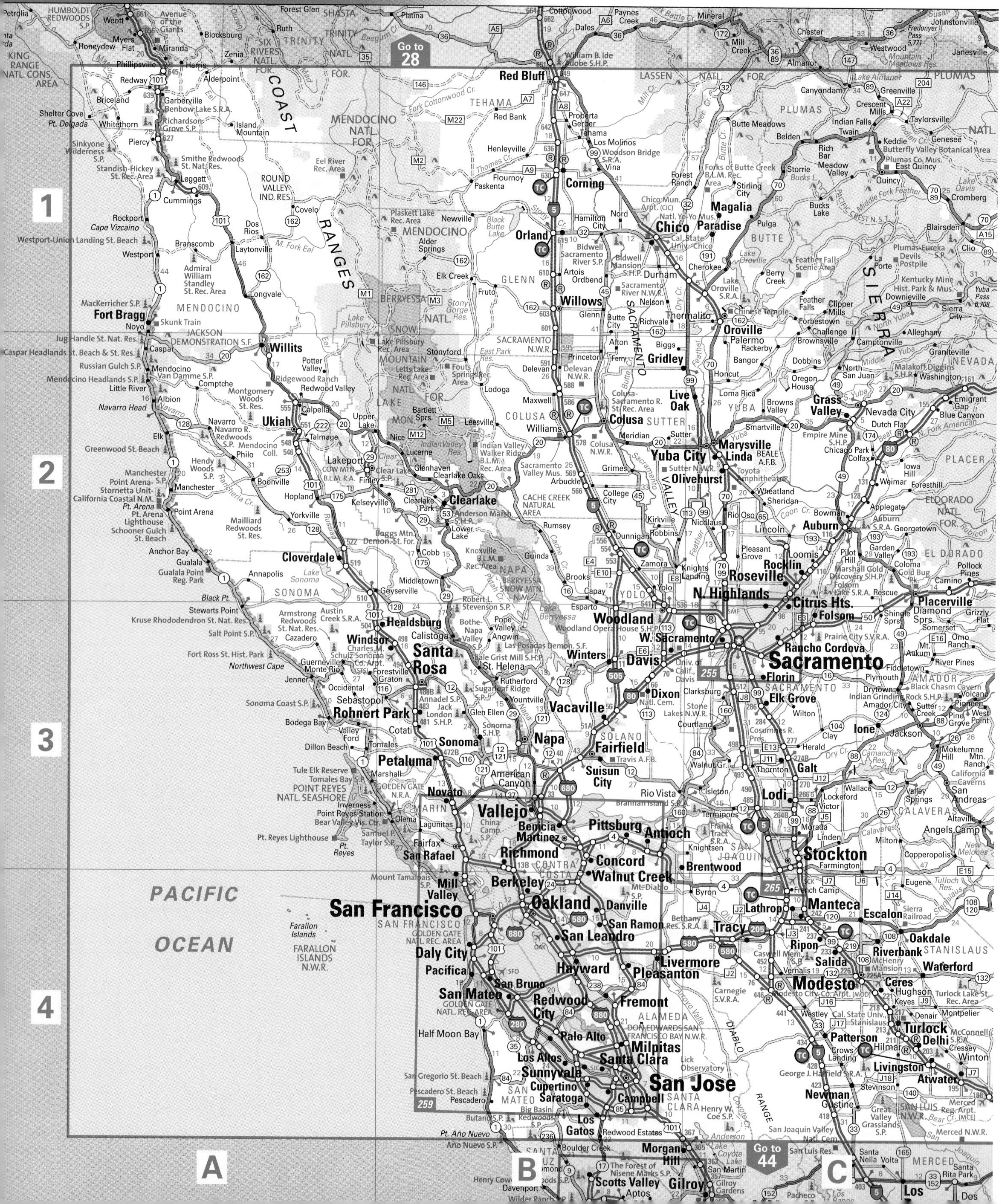

Go to 28

Go to 44

PACIFIC OCEAN

1
2
3
4

A B C

DRIVING DISTANCES IN MILES	AUSTIN, NV	CHICO, CA	MERCED, CA	RENO, NV	SACRAMENTO, CA	SAN FRANCISCO, CA	SAN JOSE, CA	S. LAKE TAHOE, CA	STOCKTON, CA	TONOPAH, NV	UKIAH, CA	YOSEMITE VIL., CA
RENO, NV	171	164	243		132	217	245	59	177	237	261	199
SACRAMENTO, CA	302	88	118	132		87	115	100	48	329	153	170
SAN FRANCISCO, CA	387	182	131	217	87		43	185	82	352	116	183
YOSEMITE VIL., CA	280	257	79	199	170	183	168	180	123	199	289	

SEE ALSO DISTANCE AND DRIVING TIME MAP ON PAGES 286–287

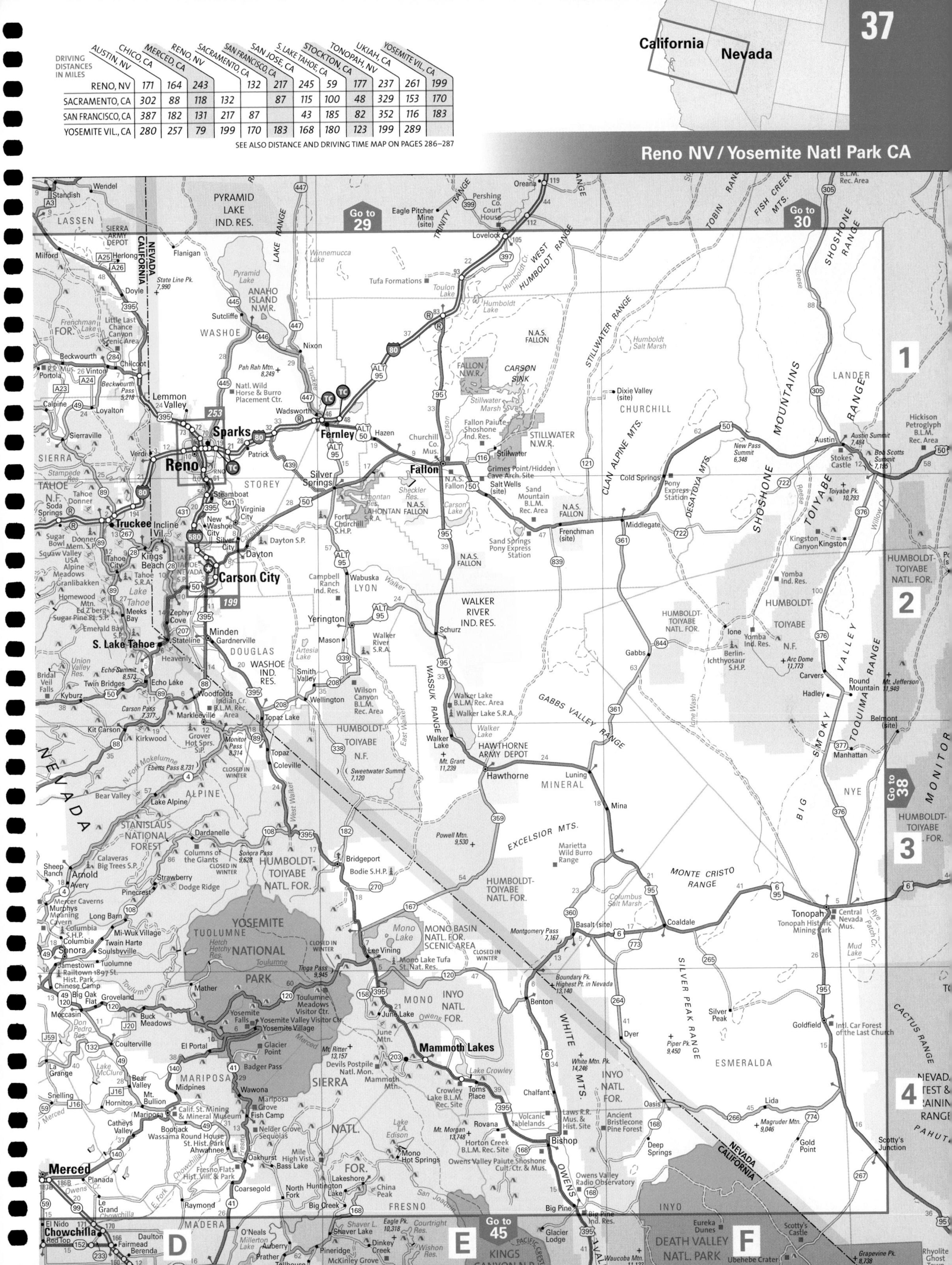

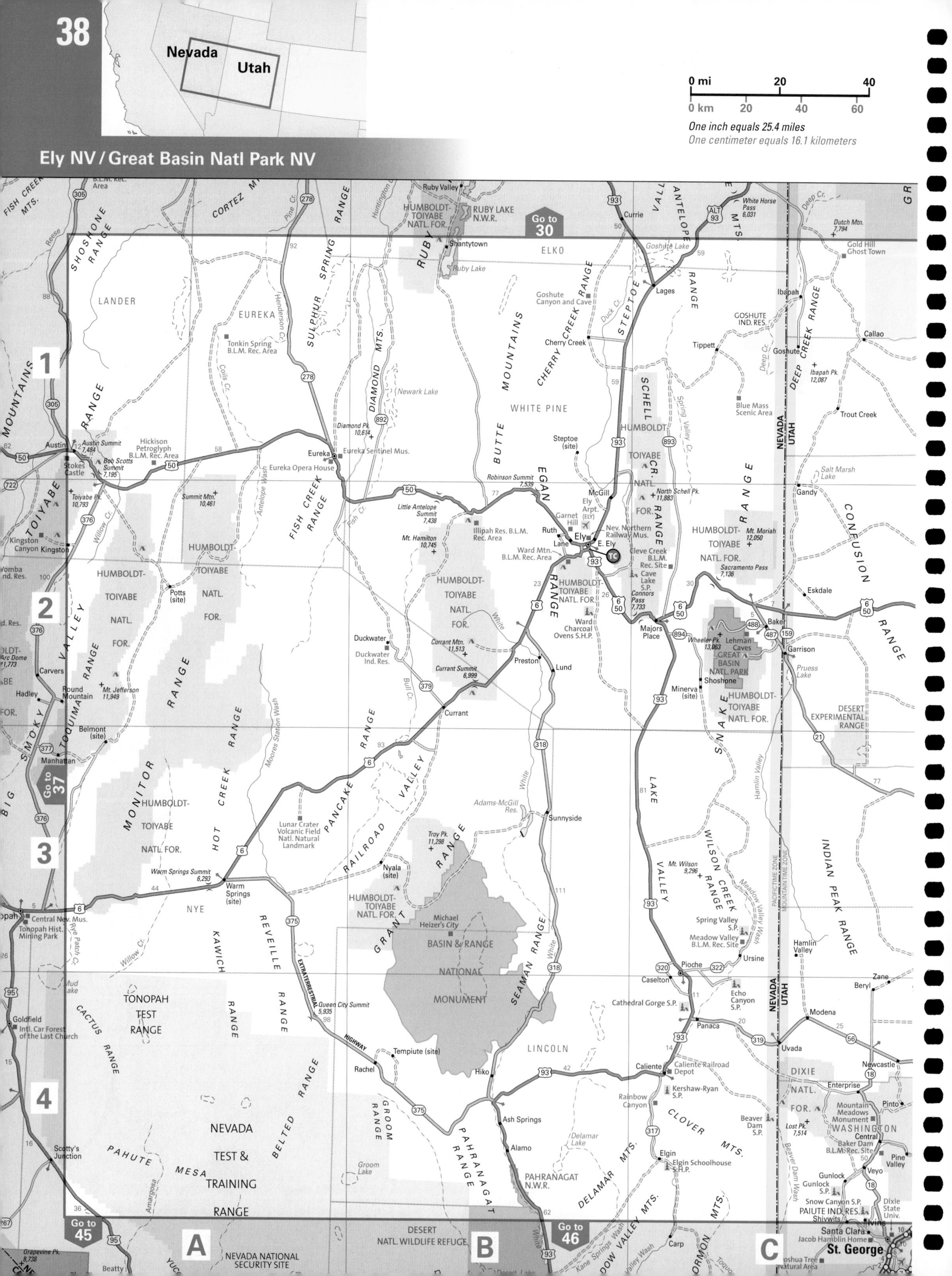
Nevada
Utah
0 mi 20 40
0 km 20 40 60
One inch equals 25.4 miles
One centimeter equals 16.1 kilometers
Go to 30
Go to 37
Go to 45
Go to 46
1
2
3
4
A
B
C
Ely
Eureka
Austin
Pioche
Caliente
Baker
Great Basin Natl. Park
Basin & Range National Monument
Nevada Test & Training Range
Tonopah Test Range
Humboldt-Toiyabe Natl. For.
Dixie Natl. For.
St. George

DRIVING DISTANCES IN MILES	AUSTIN, NV	BAKER, NV	CEDAR CITY, UT	DELTA, UT	ELY, NV	GREEN RIVER, UT	PROVO, UT	ST. GEORGE, UT	SALINA, UT	SPRINGDALE, UT	TONOPAH, NV	TORREY, UT
ELY, NV	147	68	198	156		332	243	216	224	261	167	307
PROVO, UT	426	193	204	88	243	137		256	94	266	410	172
SALINA, UT	371	187	128	68	224	108	94	180		190	411	78
SPRINGDALE (ZION), UT	408	193	64	205	261	297	266	45	190		339	191

SEE ALSO DISTANCE AND DRIVING TIME MAP ON PAGES 286–287

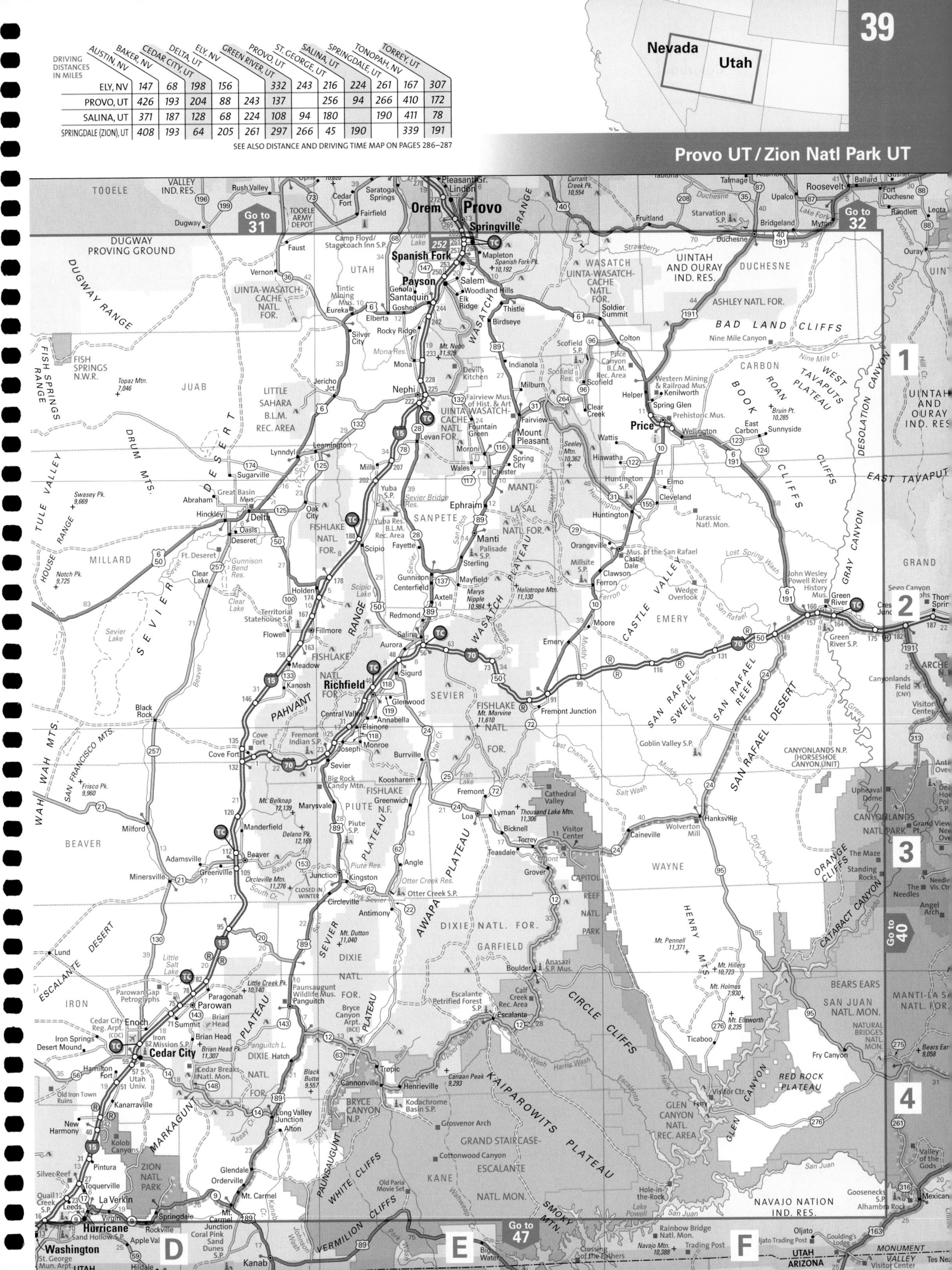

Utah
Colorado

0 mi 20 40
0 km 20 40 60
One inch equals 25.4 miles
One centimeter equals 16.1 kilometers

Grand Junction CO / Durango CO

Roosevelt
Ballard
Gusher
Upalco
Fort Duchesne
Myton
Randlett
Leota
Bridgeland
Lake Fork
Elk Springs
MOFFAT
Hamilton
Pagoda
ROUTT
Oak Creek
Phippsburg
Stagecoach S.P.
Muddy Pass 8,772
ARAPAHO NATL. FOR.
Blue Mountain
Dinosaur
Massadona
Go to 32
DANFORTH HILLS
Axial
OURAY N.W.R.
UINTAH
Ouray
UCHESNE
White
Bonanza
Rangely
CATHEDRAL BLUFFS
Canyon Pintado Natl. Hist. District
RIO BLANCO
White River Mus.
Meeker
MEDICINE BOW-ROUTT NATL. FOR.
Ripple Creek Pass 10,343
Yampa
Gore Pass 9,527
Devil's Causeway
Toponas
Buford
WHITE RIVER NATL. FOR.
Sheep Mtn. 12,241
Radium
McCoy
Burns
Bond
State Bridge
UPPER COLORADO RIVER B.L.M. REC. AREA
EAGLE
LAND CLIFFS
WEST TAVAPUTS PLATEAU
DESOLATION CANYON
UINTAH AND OURAY INDIAN RESERVATION
EAST TAVAPUTS PLATEAU
UTAH
COLORADO
Piceance Cr.
ROAN PLATEAU
Rio Blanco
Rifle Falls S.P.
THE FLAT TOPS
Deep Creek B.L.M. Rec. Area
Dotsero
Gypsum
Wolcott
Eagle
Edwards
Avon
Douglas Pass 8,268
Baxter Pass 8,422
GARFIELD
NAVAL OIL SHALE RES.
Rifle Gap S.P.
Harvey Gap S.P.
New Castle
Silt
Rifle
Glenwood Caverns Adventure Park
Glenwood Canyon
Eagle River B.L.M. Rec. Area
Eagle County Regional Arpt.
WHITE RIVER
Sylvan Lake S.P.
ROAN CLIFFS
Rulison
Parachute
Battlement Mesa
Cardiff
Glenwood Springs
Hot Springs Pool
Sunlight Mtn.
Carbondale
El Jebel
Basalt
Meredith
SAWATCH
Go to 39
ROAN CLIFFS
BOOK CLIFFS
Highline Lake S.P.
GRAND VALLEY B.L.M. REC. AREA
De Beque
BATTLEMENT MESA
THOMPSON CREEK B.L.M. REC. AREA
WHITE RIVER NATL. FOR.
Snowmass
Woody Creek
Aspen-Pitkin Co. Arpt.
Buttermilk Mtn.
PITKIN
Snowmass Village
Aspen
Aspen Mtn.
James M. Robb-Colorado River S.P. (Island Acres)
Dinosaur Journey Mus.
Mack
Loma
Fruita
Grand Jct. Reg. Arpt.
Colorado Mesa Univ.
Cameo
Mesa
Collbran
Vega S.P.
Molina
Redstone Castle & Coke Ovens
McClure Pass 8,755
Redstone
Aspen Highlands
Independence Pass 12,093
John Wesley Powell River History Mus.
Sego Canyon Petroglyphs
GRAND
Crescent Junction
Thompson Springs
Westwater
McINNIS CANYONS NATL. CONS. AREA
Grand Junction
Clifton
James M. Robb-Colorado River S.P. (Corn Lake)
Palisade
Powderhorn
Skyway
GRAND MESA
Grand Mesa Visitors Ctr.
Land's End Observatory
NATL. FOR.
Marble
Crystal Mill
Maroon Bells
Yule Marble Quarry
Paonia S.P.
Gothic Natural Area
Ashcroft Ghost Town
Independence Ghost Town
Castle Pk. 14,265
Green River S.P.
Cisco
COLORADO NATL. MON.
Mus. of the West
Glade Park
Orchard Mesa
Whitewater
GRAND MESA NATL. FOR.
MESA
BUCK MESA
Bowie
Paonia
Somerset
RUBY RANGE
Mount Crested Butte
Crested Butte
Natl. Hist. District
ARCHES NATL. PARK
Delicate Arch
Fisher Towers
Canyonlands Field
Cedaredge
Orchard City
DELTA
Hotchkiss
Mt. Gunnison 12,719
Kebler Pass 9,980
Ohio Pass 10,033
Taylor Park Res.
GATEWAY B.L.M. REC. AREA
DOMINGUEZ CANYON B.L.M. REC. AREA
Ft. Uncompahgre Living Hist. Mus.
Delta
Austin
Sweitzer Lake S.P.
Lazear
GUNNISON
WEST ELK MTS.
The Windows
Castle Valley
Castleton Tower
Visitor Center
Moab
Gateway
UNCOMPAHGRE PLATEAU
UNCOMPAHGRE NATL. FOR.
GUNNISON GORGE NATL. CONS. AREA
Crawford
Crawford S.P.
Maher
Olathe
Montrose Regional Arpt.
BLACK CANYON OF THE GUNNISON NATL. PARK
Western State Colorado University
Almont
Pitkin
Ohio
Gunnison
Parlin
Anticline Overlook
Upheaval Dome
Mt. Waas 12,311
MANTI-LA SAL NATL. FOR.
LA SAL MTS.
Hanging Flume
Columbine Pass 9,120
Ute Indian Museum
MONTROSE
Montrose
Blue Mesa Res.
Curecanti Needle
Cimarron
Sapinero
Gunnison-Crested Butte Reg. Arpt.
Doyleville
Mt. Peale 12,721
Dead Horse Point S.P.
Grand View Pt.
Paradox
Uravan
CURECANTI NATL. REC. AREA
Cochetopa Canyon B.L.M. Rec. Area
CANYONLANDS NATL. PARK
The Maze
Needles Overlook
CANYON RIMS B.L.M. REC. AREA
La Sal Junction
La Sal
Bedrock
Nucla
Colona
GUNNISON
Powderhorn
Standing Rocks
Looking Glass Rock
Wilson Arch
Vancorum
Naturita
Redvale
Ridgway S.P.
OURAY
North Pass 10,149
NATL. FOR.
CATARACT CANYON
Needles Vis. Ctr.
The Needles
DOLORES RIVER B.L.M. REC. AREA
Norwood
Ridgway
Owl Creek Pass 11,120
UNCOMPAHGRE NATL. FOR.
POWDERHORN B.L.M. REC. AREA
Cochetopa Pass 10,032
Church Rock
Angel Arch
Summit Point
Slick Rock
Gypsum Gap 6,100
UNCOMPAHGRE NATL. FOR.
SAN MIGUEL B.L.M. REC. AREA
Placerville
Sawpit
Dallas Divide 8,970
Ouray Hot Springs
Uncompahgre Pk. 14,309
Natl. Hist. District
Lake City
COCHETOPA
Ouray
GLEN CANYON NATL. REC. AREA
BEARS EARS NATL. MON.
Newspaper Rock St. Hist. Mon.
Shay Mtn. 9,988
SAN MIGUEL
Telluride Regional Arpt.
Mountain Village
Camp Bird
Box Canyon Falls
Pandora
Telluride
ALPINE TRIANGLE B.L.M. REC. AREA
Slumgullion Pass 11,361
San Luis Pk. 14,014
Monticello
Ucolo
Egnar
Bridal Veil Falls
Gladstone
Red Mtn. Pass 11,008
DIVIDE
Wheeler Geologic Area
LA GARITA
MANTI-LA SAL NATL. FOR.
Mt. Linnaeus 10,961
Abajo Pk. 11,360
Eastland
Disappointment Cr.
Lizard Head Pass 10,222
Mt. Wilson 14,246
Ophir
Spring Creek Pass 10,901
RIO GRANDE
Creede
CONTINENTAL
Dove Creek
DOLORES
Dunton
Silverton
Hist. Soc. Mus.
Natl. Hist. District
HINSDALE
Wagon Wheel Gap
Edge of the Cedars S.P.
Dinosaur Mus.
Molas Pass 10,910
Coal Bank Pass 10,640
Bears Ears 9,058
Blanding
Cahone
Rico
SAN JUAN
SAN JUAN MOUNTAINS
Spar City
MINERAL NATL. FOR.
NATURAL BRIDGES NATL. MON.
Purgatory Resort
WEMINUCHE WILDERNESS
Pleasant View
TAYLOR MESA
Stoner
Mt. Eolus 14,083
South Fork
Lowry Pueblo Ruins
Yellow Jacket
McPhee Res.
SAN JUAN NATL. FOR.
Anasazi Heritage Center
CANYONS OF THE ANCIENTS NATL. MON.
Lewis
Lebanon
Arriola
Dolores
Rockwood
Wolf Creek Pass Tunnel
SAN JUAN
Valley of the Gods
Hovenweep Natl. Mon.
Hermosa
Vallecito Res.
Wolf Creek
Summitville
Navajo Twin Rocks
Cortez
Mancos
LA PLATA MTS.
Trimble
Vallecito
LA PLATA
Montezuma Pk. 13,150
Platoro
Summit Peak 13,300
Bluff
Montezuma Creek
McElmo Cr.
Cortez Mun. Arpt.
MESA VERDE NATL. PARK
Mayday
Hesperus
Durango & Silverton Narrow Gauge RR
Durango
Fort Lewis Coll.
Grandview
Breen
Pagosa Springs
Goosenecks S.P.
Alhambra Rock
Mexican Hat
NAVAJO NATION IND. RES.
Aneth
Yucca House Natl. Mon.
Towaoc
UTE MOUNTAIN IND. RES.
MESA VERDE
Oxford
Bayfield
Gem Village
Chimney Rock
Chimney Rock Natl. Mon.
Nutria
Lonetree
ARCHULETA
Poncho House
Ute Mountain Tribal Park Visitor Center
Go to 48
Kline
Marvel
Durango-La Plata Co. Arpt.
Ignacio
SOUTHERN UTE IND. RES.
Navajo S.P.
Pagosa Junction
Chromo
Goulding's Trading Lodge
MONUMENT VALLEY
Visitor Center
Tes Nez Iah
UTAH
ARIZONA
Red Mesa
Four Corners Mon. & Navajo Tribal Park
MONTEZUMA
COLORADO
NEW MEXICO
Bondad
Tiffany
Allison
Arboles

1 2 3 4
A B C

DRIVING DISTANCES IN MILES

	ALAMOSA, CO	ASPEN, CO	COLORADO SPRS., CO	CORTEZ, CO	DENVER, CO	DURANGO, CO	GRAND JUNCTION, CO	GREEN RIVER, UT	MOAB, UT	MONTROSE, CO	PUEBLO, CO	TRINIDAD, CO
COLORADO SPRS., CO	162	157		359	70	314	318	418	404	236	43	127
DENVER, CO	230	164	70	452		337	250	350	337	277	111	196
DURANGO, CO	152	244	314	45	337		169	214	160	107	271	260
GRAND JUNCTION, CO	261	135	318	203	250	169		102	88	62	360	444

SEE ALSO DISTANCE AND DRIVING TIME MAP ON PAGES 286–287

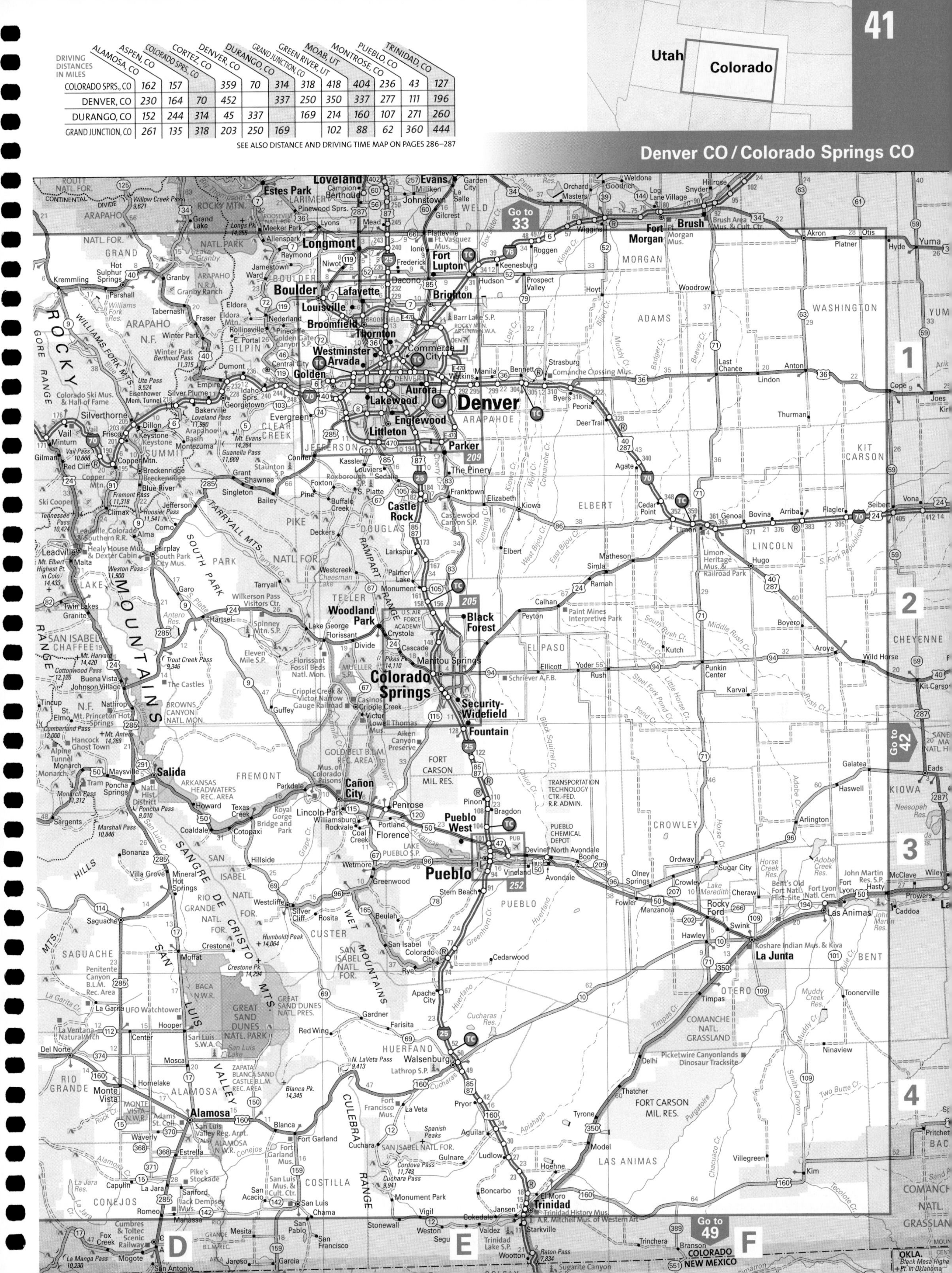

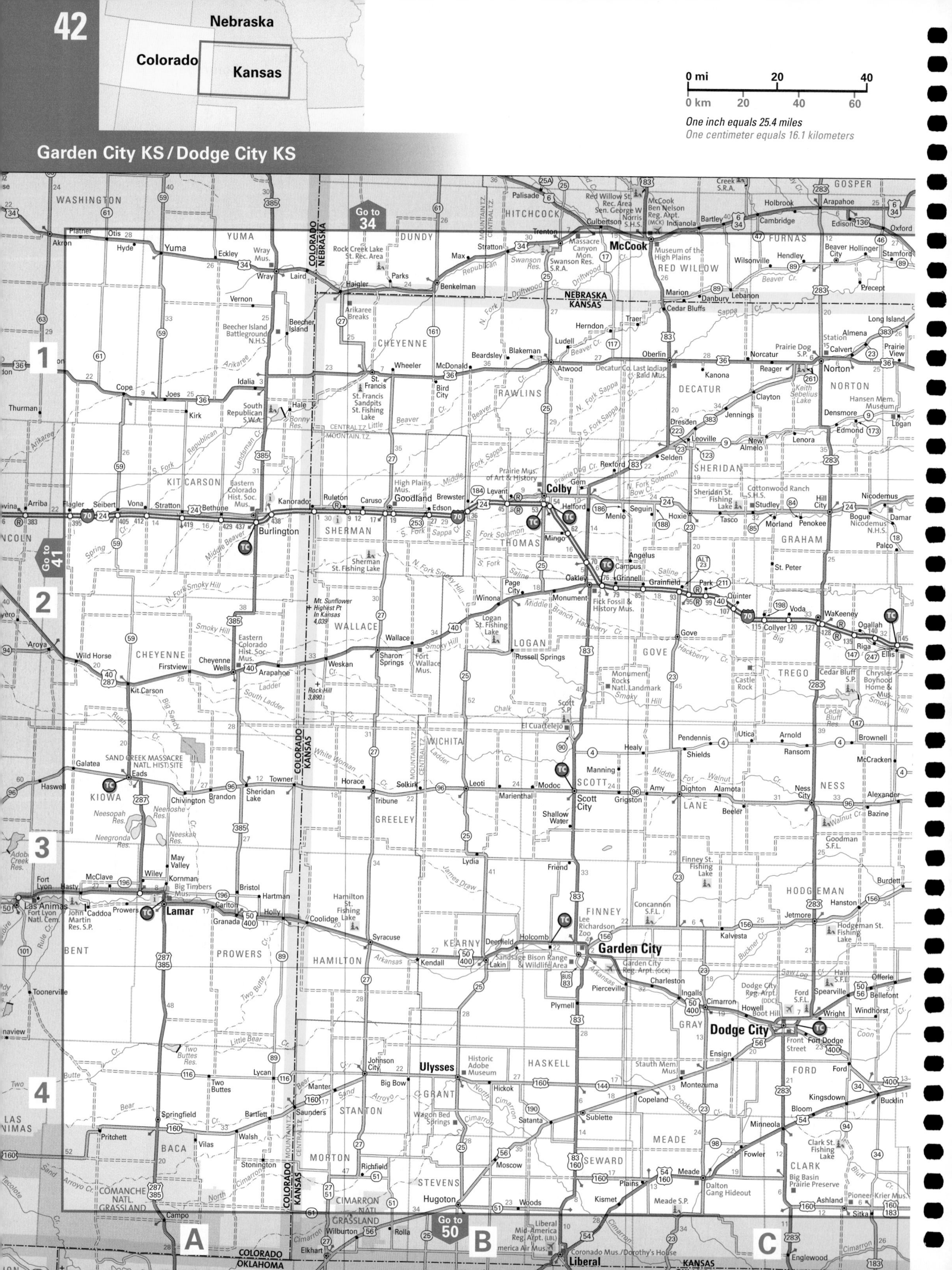
Nebraska
Colorado
Kansas
0 mi 20 40
0 km 20 40 60
One inch equals 25.4 miles
One centimeter equals 16.1 kilometers
Garden City KS / Dodge City KS
Go to 34
Go to 41
Go to 50
1
2
3
4
A
B
C
WASHINGTON
YUMA
DUNDY
HITCHCOCK
RED WILLOW
FURNAS
GOSPER
CHEYENNE
RAWLINS
DECATUR
NORTON
KIT CARSON
SHERMAN
THOMAS
SHERIDAN
GRAHAM
LOGAN
GOVE
TREGO
WALLACE
WICHITA
SCOTT
LANE
NESS
KIOWA
GREELEY
HODGEMAN
FINNEY
PROWERS
HAMILTON
KEARNY
BENT
GRAY
FORD
HASKELL
GRANT
STANTON
MEADE
SEWARD
BACA
MORTON
STEVENS
CLARK
LAS ANIMAS
COLORADO
NEBRASKA
KANSAS
OKLAHOMA
CENTRAL T.Z.
MOUNTAIN T.Z.
Akron
Yuma
Wray
McCook
Oberlin
Atwood
Norton
St. Francis
Burlington
Goodland
Colby
Oakley
Hoxie
Hill City
WaKeeney
Cheyenne Wells
Kit Carson
Eads
Lamar
Las Animas
Tribune
Leoti
Scott City
Dighton
Ness City
Syracuse
Lakin
Garden City
Cimarron
Dodge City
Jetmore
Johnson City
Ulysses
Sublette
Springfield
Elkhart
Hugoton
Liberal
Meade
Ashland
Mt. Sunflower Highest Pt in Kansas 4,039
Sand Creek Massacre Natl. Hist. Site
Monument Rocks Natl. Landmark
Cimarron Natl. Grassland
Comanche Natl. Grassland
Sandsage Bison Range & Wildlife Area
Garden City Reg. Arpt. (GCK)
Dodge City Reg. Arpt. (DDC)
Liberal Mid-America Reg. Arpt. (LBL)
Boot Hill
Fort Dodge
Lee Richardson Zoo
Dalton Gang Hideout
Meade S.P.
Scott S.P.
El Cuartelejo
Big Basin Prairie Preserve

DRIVING DISTANCES IN MILES

	BURLINGTON, CO	DODGE CITY, KS	EMPORIA, KS	GARDEN CITY, KS	HAYS, KS	LAMAR, CO	MANHATTAN, KS	MCCOOK, NE	OAKLEY, KS	SALINA, KS	TOPEKA, KS	WICHITA, KS
GARDEN CITY, KS	167	52	290		139	98	272	167	79	204	311	205
OAKLEY, KS	88	136	293	79	87	156	247	88		179	286	268
SALINA, KS	266	164	118	204	93	335	72	240	179		111	92
WICHITA, KS	354	153	85	205	181	303	131	329	268	92	137	

SEE ALSO DISTANCE AND DRIVING TIME MAP ON PAGES 286–287

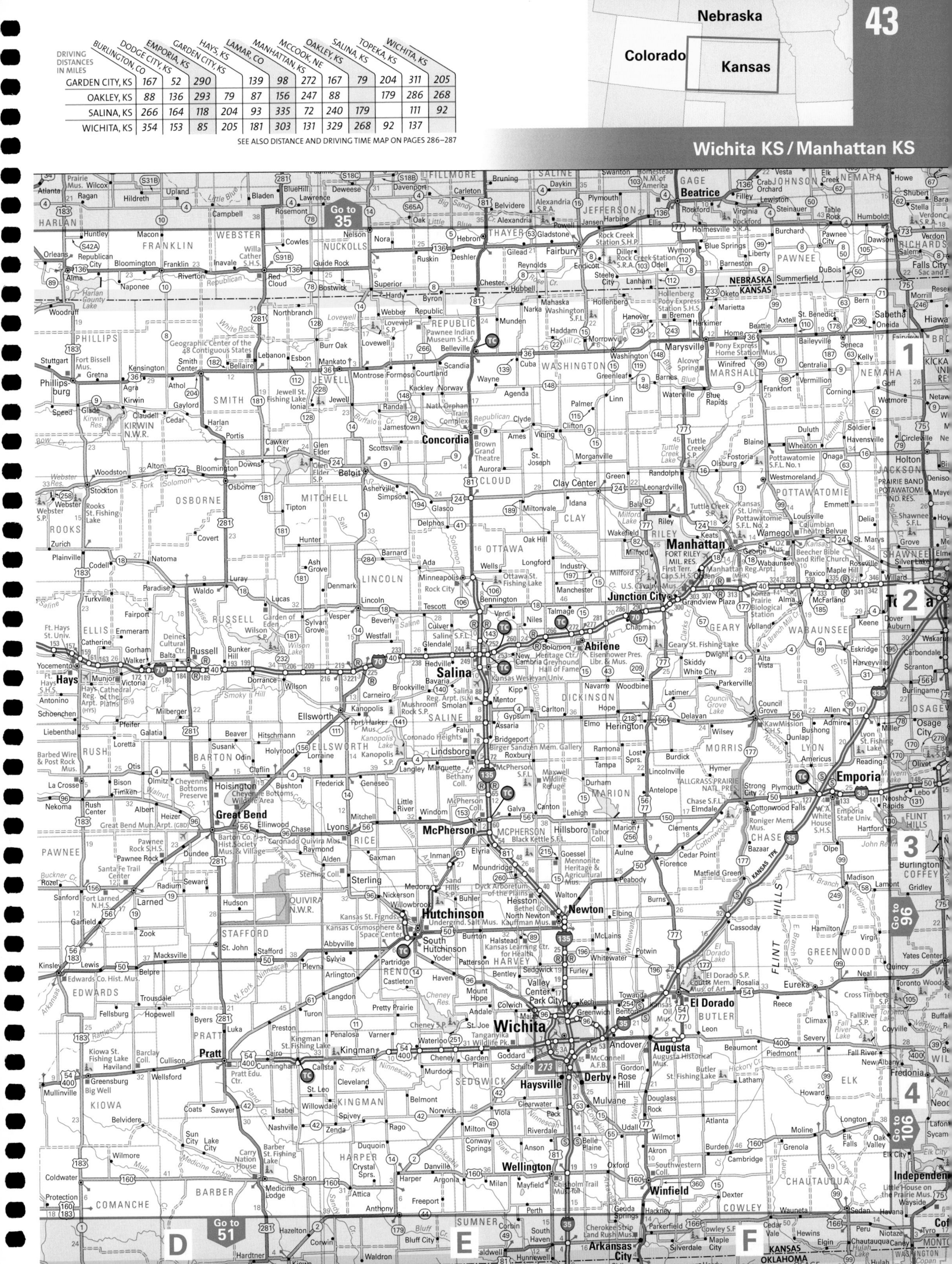

Nevada
California

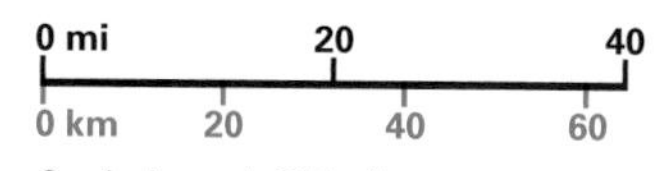

One inch equals 25.4 miles
One centimeter equals 16.1 kilometers

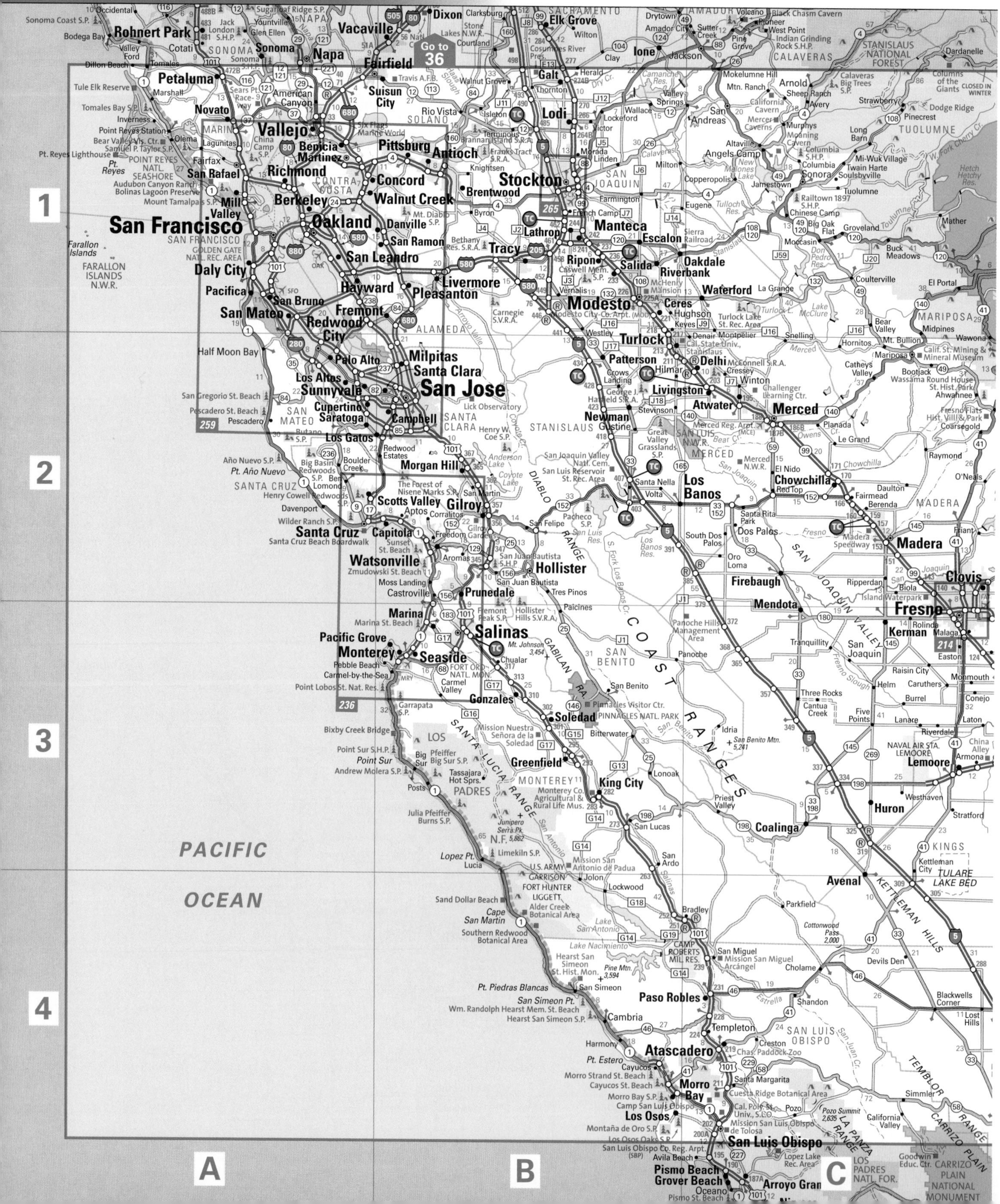

Go to 36

San Francisco
Oakland
San Jose
Stockton
Modesto
Merced
Fresno
Salinas
Monterey
Santa Cruz
San Luis Obispo
Paso Robles
Atascadero
Hollister
Gilroy
Madera
Coalinga
Lemoore
Huron
Vallejo
Fremont
Hayward
Tracy
Turlock
Los Banos
King City

PACIFIC OCEAN

COAST RANGES

1
2
3
4

A
B
C

DRIVING DISTANCES IN MILES

	BAKERSFIELD, CA	BISHOP, CA	DEATH VALLEY, CA	FRESNO, CA	RIDGECREST, CA	SALINAS, CA	SAN FRANCISCO, CA	SAN JOSE, CA	SAN LUIS OBISPO, CA	STOCKTON, CA	TONOPAH, NV	YOSEMITE VIL, CA
BAKERSFIELD, CA		215	236	111	99	209	287	245	119	243	318	200
BISHOP, CA	215		169	219	141	302	283	269	333	223	119	130
FRESNO, CA	111	219	333		196	145	190	153	134	130	288	90
SAN JOSE, CA	245	269	437	153	344	61	43		191	68	338	168

SEE ALSO DISTANCE AND DRIVING TIME MAP ON PAGES 286–287

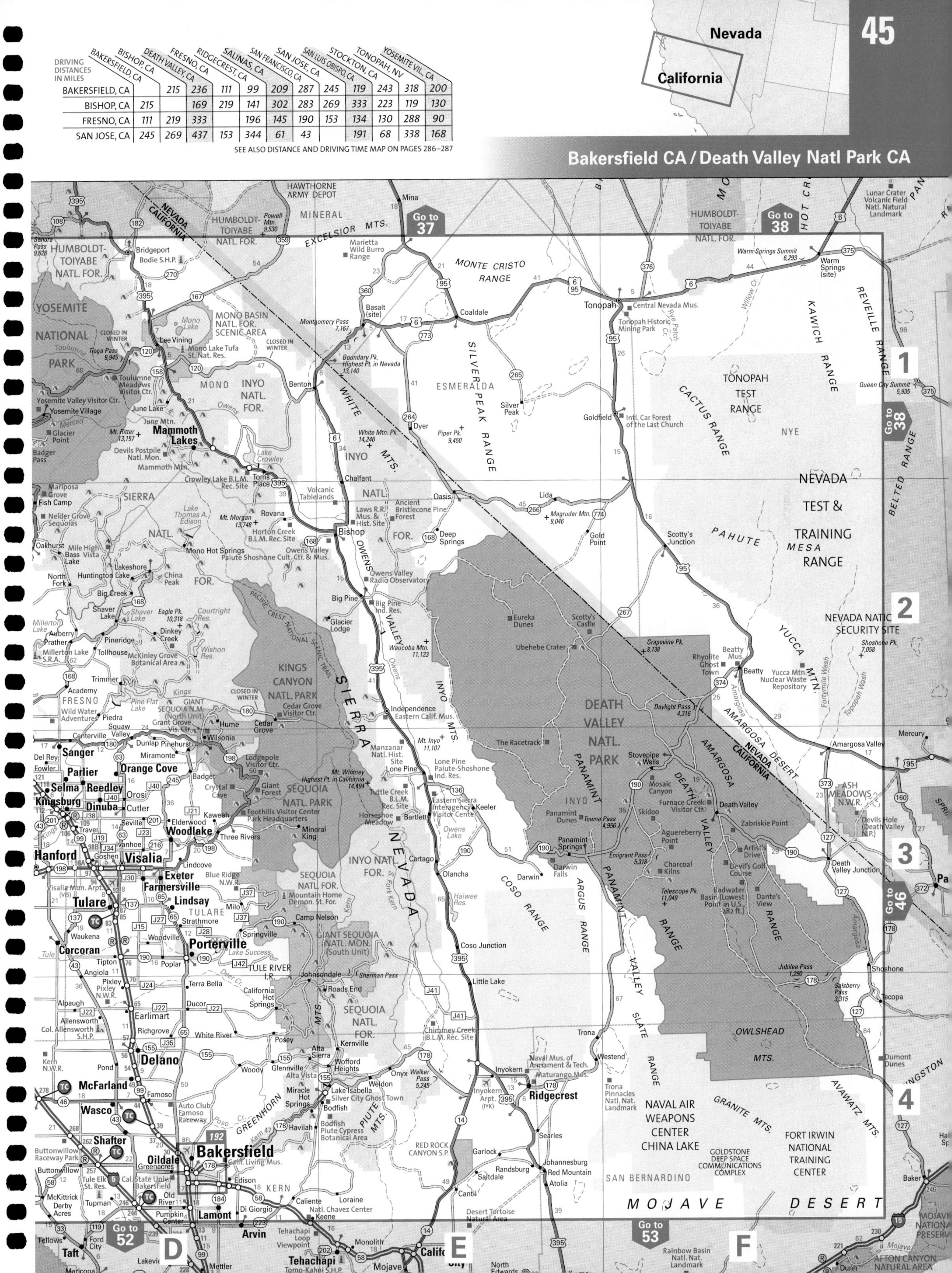

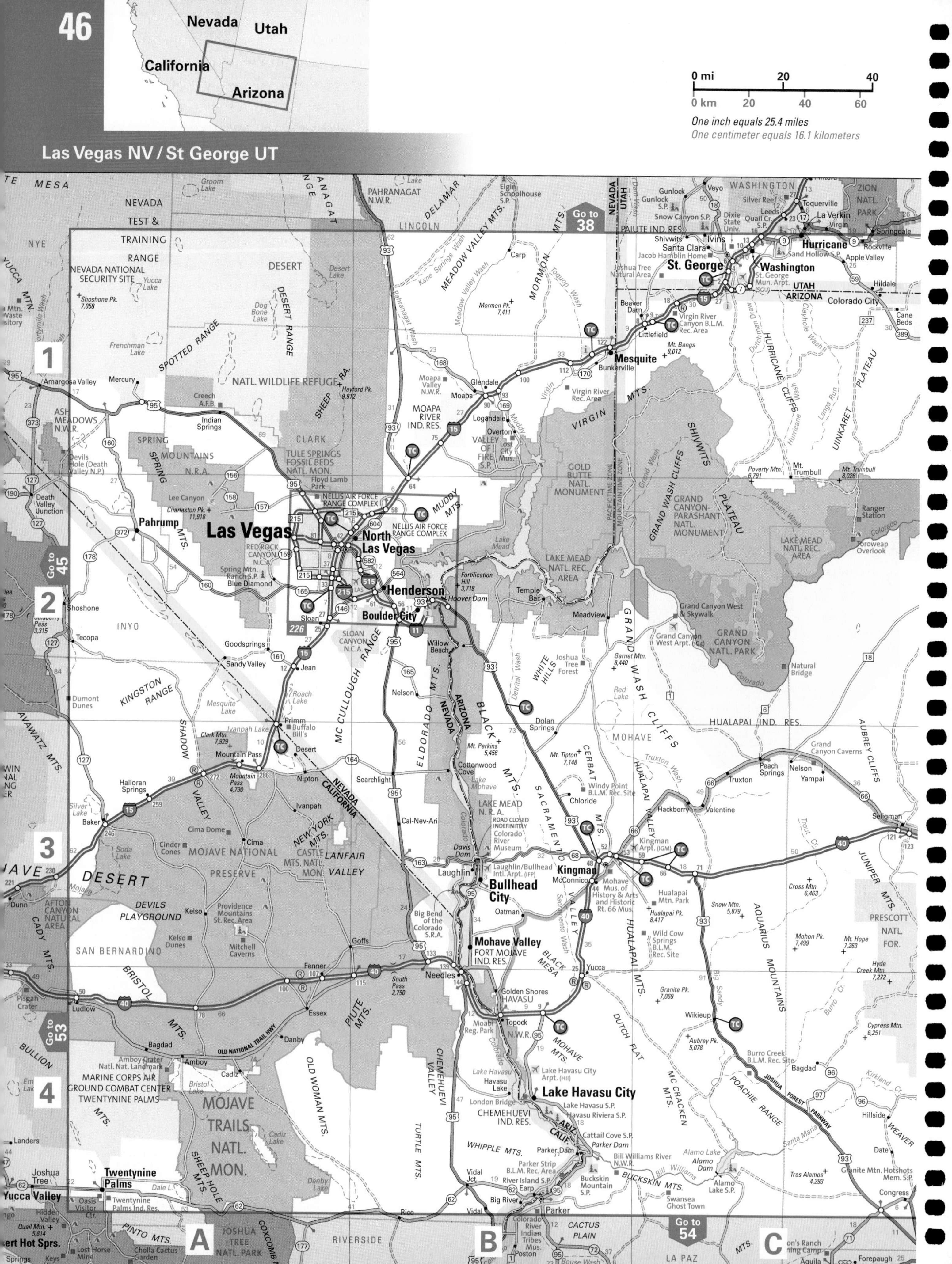
46
Nevada
Utah
California
Arizona
Las Vegas NV / St George UT
0 mi
20
40
0 km
20
40
60
One inch equals 25.4 miles
One centimeter equals 16.1 kilometers
Go to 38
Go to 45
Go to 53
Go to 54
1
2
3
4
A
B
C
226
NEVADA TEST & TRAINING RANGE
NEVADA NATIONAL SECURITY SITE
NYE
DESERT
DESERT RANGE
SPOTTED RANGE
NATL. WILDLIFE REFUGE
SHEEP RA.
PAHRANAGAT N.W.R.
DELAMAR
LINCOLN
MEADOW VALLEY MTS.
MORMON MTS.
CLARK
SPRING MOUNTAINS N.R.A.
TULE SPRINGS FOSSIL BEDS NATL. MON.
NELLIS AIR FORCE RANGE COMPLEX
Las Vegas
North Las Vegas
Henderson
Boulder City
Hoover Dam
Pahrump
Amargosa Valley
Mercury
Indian Springs
Creech A.F.B.
ASH MEADOWS N.W.R.
Death Valley Junction
Shoshone
Tecopa
INYO
Goodsprings
Sandy Valley
Jean
Primm
Buffalo Bill's
Desert
Nipton
Searchlight
Cal-Nev-Ari
KINGSTON RANGE
MC CULLOUGH RANGE
ELDORADO MTS.
SLOAN CANYON N.C.A.
RED ROCK CANYON N.C.A.
Spring Mtn. Ranch S.P.
Blue Diamond
Sloan
Willow Beach
Nelson
Mesquite
Bunkerville
Littlefield
Glendale
Moapa
Logandale
Overton
VALLEY OF FIRE S.P.
MOAPA RIVER IND. RES.
VIRGIN MTS.
GOLD BUTTE NATL. MONUMENT
LAKE MEAD NATL. REC. AREA
Lake Mead
Temple Bar
Meadview
Grand Canyon West & Skywalk
GRAND CANYON NATL. PARK
GRAND CANYON-PARASHANT NATL. MONUMENT
SHIVWITS PLATEAU
GRAND WASH CLIFFS
HURRICANE CLIFFS
UINKARET PLATEAU
HUALAPAI IND. RES.
St. George
Washington
Hurricane
Santa Clara
Ivins
Toquerville
La Verkin
Virgin
Springdale
Rockville
Apple Valley
Hildale
Colorado City
ZION NATL. PARK
Cane Beds
Gunlock
Veyo
Dixie State Univ.
Beaver Dam
UTAH
ARIZONA
NEVADA
BLACK MTS.
WHITE HILLS
CERBAT MTS.
HUALAPAI MTS.
SACRAMENTO VALLEY
Dolan Springs
Chloride
Kingman
McConnico
Hackberry
Valentine
Truxton
Peach Springs
Seligman
Grand Canyon Caverns
MOHAVE
AUBREY CLIFFS
JUNIPER MTS.
AQUARIUS MOUNTAINS
PRESCOTT NATL. FOR.
Laughlin
Bullhead City
Davis Dam
Oatman
Mohave Valley
FORT MOJAVE IND. RES.
Needles
Golden Shores
HAVASU
Topock
Yucca
Lake Havasu City
Lake Havasu S.P.
CHEMEHUEVI IND. RES.
Parker Dam
Parker
Big River
Vidal
Vidal Jct.
Wikieup
Bagdad
Hillside
Congress
Alamo Lake S.P.
BUCKSKIN MTS.
MC CRACKEN MTS.
POACHIE RANGE
DUTCH FLAT
MOHAVE MTS.
WHIPPLE MTS.
CHEMEHUEVI VALLEY
TURTLE MTS.
OLD WOMAN MTS.
PIUTE MTS.
SAN BERNARDINO
MOJAVE NATIONAL PRESERVE
NEW YORK MTS.
CASTLE MTS. NATL. MON.
LANFAIR VALLEY
DESERT
DEVILS PLAYGROUND
Baker
Halloran Springs
Mountain Pass
Cima
Kelso
Goffs
Fenner
Essex
Danby
Ludlow
Amboy
Cadiz
Bagdad
BRISTOL MTS.
MARINE CORPS AIR GROUND COMBAT CENTER TWENTYNINE PALMS
MOJAVE TRAILS NATL. MON.
SHEEP HOLE MTS.
Twentynine Palms
Joshua Tree
Yucca Valley
JOSHUA TREE NATL. PARK
PINTO MTS.
RIVERSIDE
CACTUS PLAIN
LA PAZ
Poston
Rice
OLD NATIONAL TRAIL HWY
JOSHUA FOREST PARKWAY
Landers

DRIVING DISTANCES IN MILES

	CHINLE, AZ	FLAGSTAFF, AZ	GRAND CANYON, AZ	HOLBROOK, AZ	KAYENTA, AZ	KINGMAN, AZ	LAKE HAVASU CITY, AZ	LAS VEGAS, NV	LAUGHLIN, NV	PAGE, AZ	PRESCOTT, AZ	ST. GEORGE, UT
FLAGSTAFF, AZ	216		89	93	152	148	209	249	182	135	89	271
GRAND CANYON, AZ	232	89		182	153	175	236	276	209	136	131	272
LAS VEGAS, NV	465	249	276	341	374	103	154		94	277	251	118
ST. GEORGE, UT	358	271	272	353	255	221	272	118	212	159	369	

SEE ALSO DISTANCE AND DRIVING TIME MAP ON PAGES 286–287

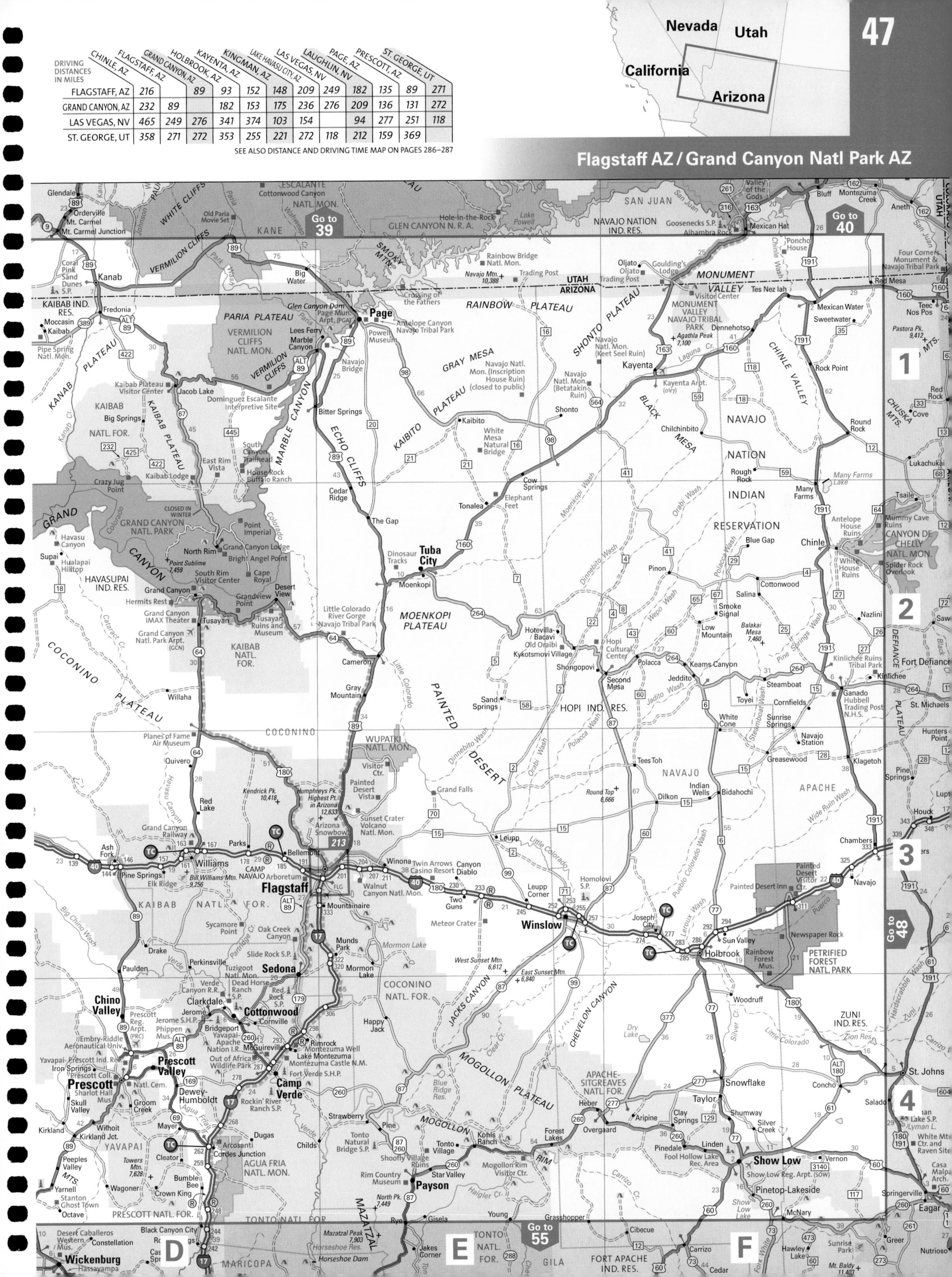

Albuquerque NM / Farmington NM

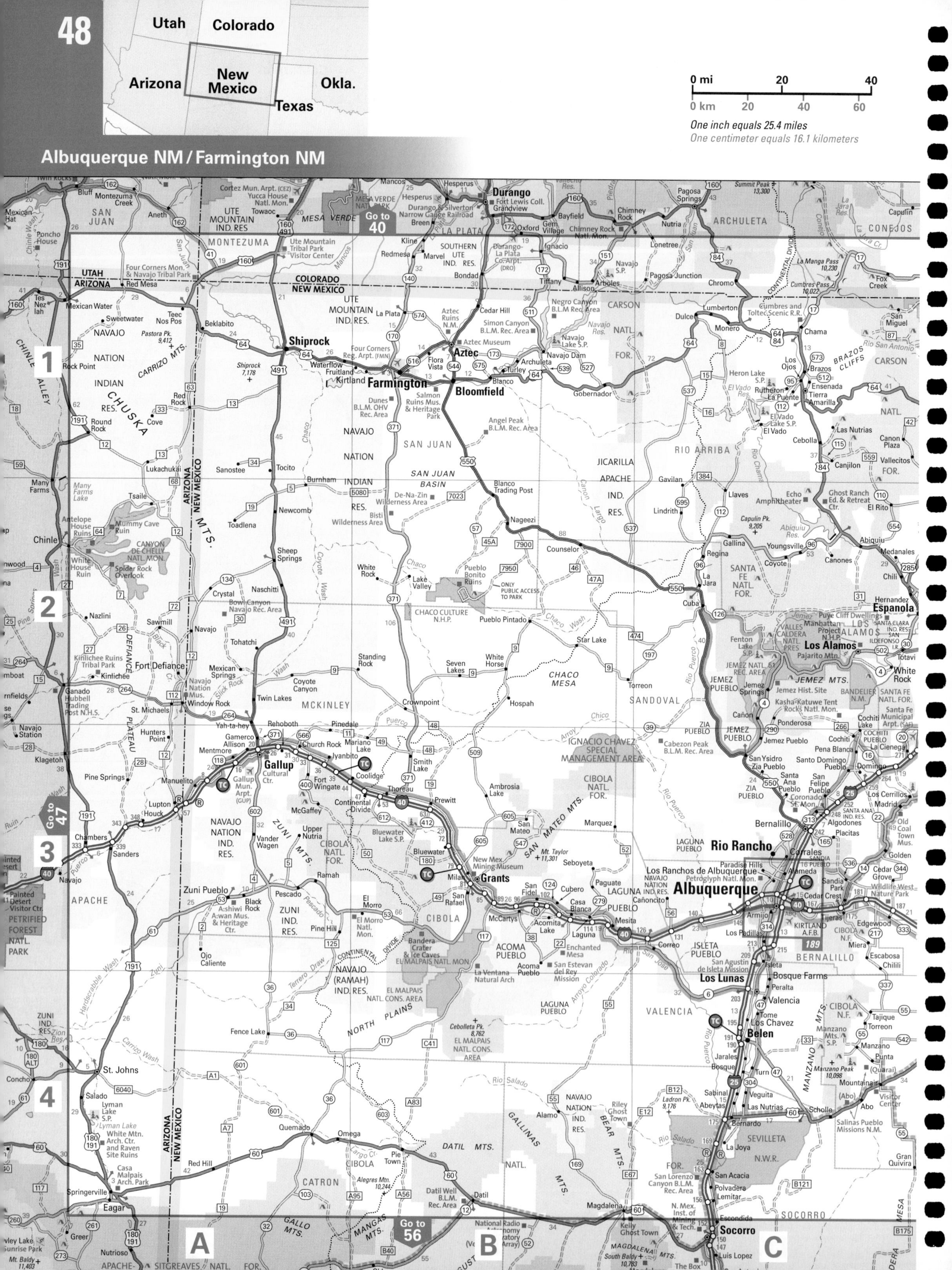

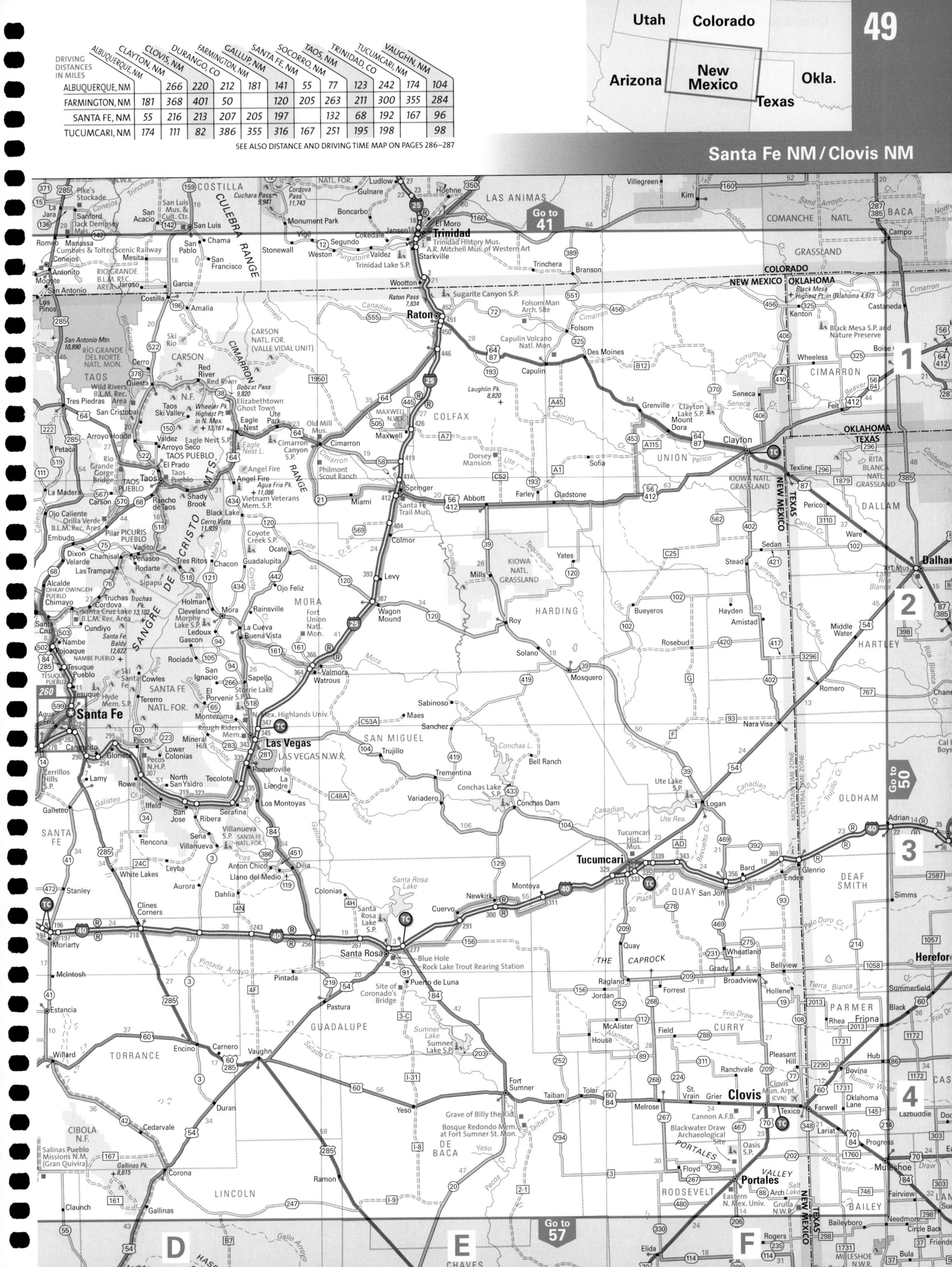

DRIVING DISTANCES IN MILES	ALBUQUERQUE, NM	CLAYTON, NM	CLOVIS, NM	DURANGO, CO	FARMINGTON, NM	GALLUP, NM	SANTA FE, NM	SOCORRO, NM	TAOS, NM	TRINIDAD, CO	TUCUMCARI, NM	VAUGHN, NM
ALBUQUERQUE, NM		266	220	212	181	141	55	77	123	242	174	104
FARMINGTON, NM	181	368	401	50		120	205	263	211	300	355	284
SANTA FE, NM	55	216	213	207	205	197		132	68	192	167	96
TUCUMCARI, NM	174	111	82	386	355	316	167	251	195	198		98

SEE ALSO DISTANCE AND DRIVING TIME MAP ON PAGES 286–287

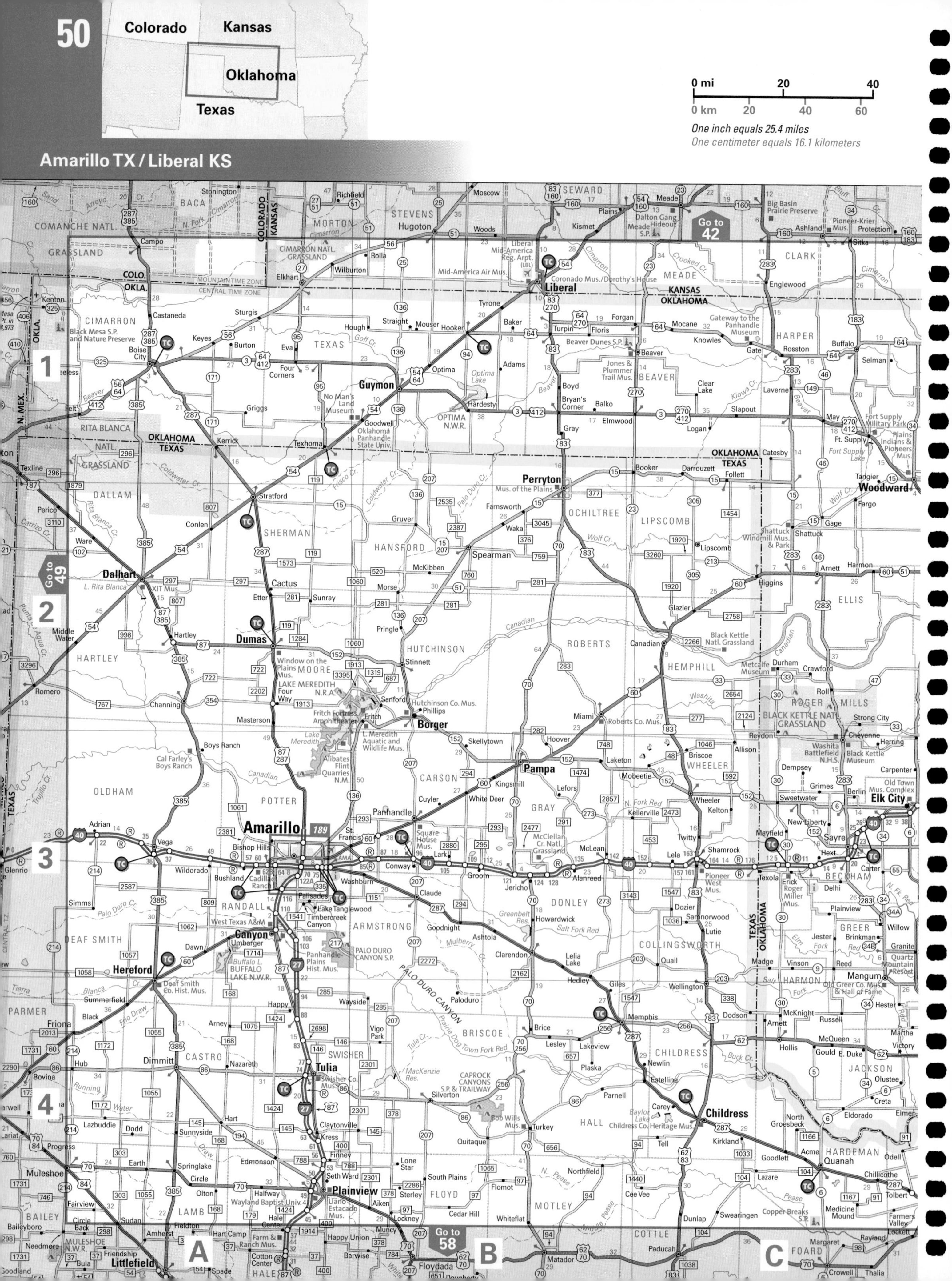
Colorado
Kansas
Oklahoma
Texas
0 mi
20
40
0 km
20
40
60
One inch equals 25.4 miles
One centimeter equals 16.1 kilometers
Go to 42
Go to 49
Go to 58
1
2
3
4
A
B
C
COMANCHE NATL. GRASSLAND
CIMARRON NATL. GRASSLAND
RITA BLANCA NATL. GRASSLAND
BLACK KETTLE NATL. GRASSLAND
MOUNTAIN TIME ZONE
CENTRAL TIME ZONE
COLO.
OKLA.
N. MEX.
KANSAS
OKLAHOMA
TEXAS
BACA
MORTON
STEVENS
SEWARD
MEADE
CLARK
CIMARRON
TEXAS
BEAVER
HARPER
DALLAM
SHERMAN
HANSFORD
OCHILTREE
LIPSCOMB
ELLIS
HARTLEY
MOORE
HUTCHINSON
ROBERTS
HEMPHILL
ROGER MILLS
OLDHAM
POTTER
CARSON
GRAY
WHEELER
BECKHAM
DEAF SMITH
RANDALL
ARMSTRONG
DONLEY
COLLINGSWORTH
GREER
HARMON
PARMER
CASTRO
SWISHER
BRISCOE
HALL
CHILDRESS
JACKSON
HARDEMAN
BAILEY
LAMB
HALE
FLOYD
MOTLEY
COTTLE
FOARD
Liberal
Guymon
Hugoton
Elkhart
Boise City
Dalhart
Stratford
Perryton
Spearman
Woodward
Dumas
Borger
Pampa
Canadian
Amarillo
Canyon
Hereford
Elk City
Sayre
Shamrock
Clarendon
Memphis
Childress
Mangum
Quanah
Tulia
Dimmitt
Plainview
Muleshoe
Littlefield
Floydada
Matador
Paducah
Palo Duro Canyon
Lake Meredith N.R.A.
Alibates Flint Quarries N.M.
Palo Duro Canyon S.P.
Buffalo Lake N.W.R.
Optima N.W.R.
Caprock Canyons S.P. & Trailway

DRIVING DISTANCES IN MILES

	AMARILLO, TX	ARDMORE, OK	BARTLESVILLE, OK	CHILDRESS, TX	CLINTON, OK	ENID, OK	LAWTON, OK	LIBERAL, KS	OKLAHOMA CITY, OK	STILLWATER, OK	TULSA, OK	WOODWARD, OK
AMARILLO, TX		361	419	118	177	298	240	165	262	329	371	177
LAWTON, OK	240	103	243	124	98	142		287	85	152	194	175
OKLAHOMA CITY, OK	262	99	157	225	85	84	85	259		67	109	143
TULSA, OK	371	206	48	334	194	117	194	321	109	71		205

SEE ALSO DISTANCE AND DRIVING TIME MAP ON PAGES 286–287

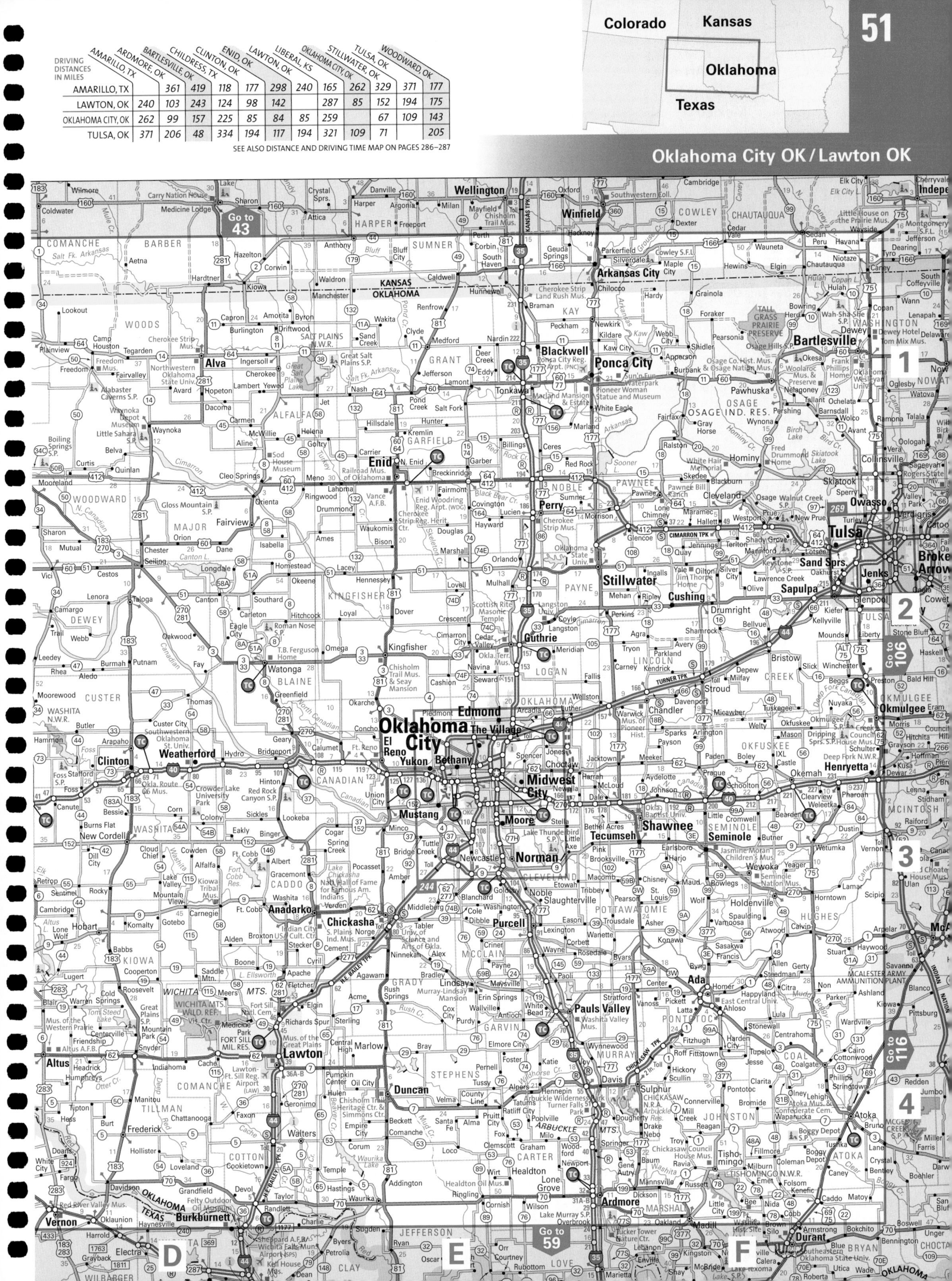

Nev.
California
Arizona
Mexico

Los Angeles CA / Santa Barbara CA

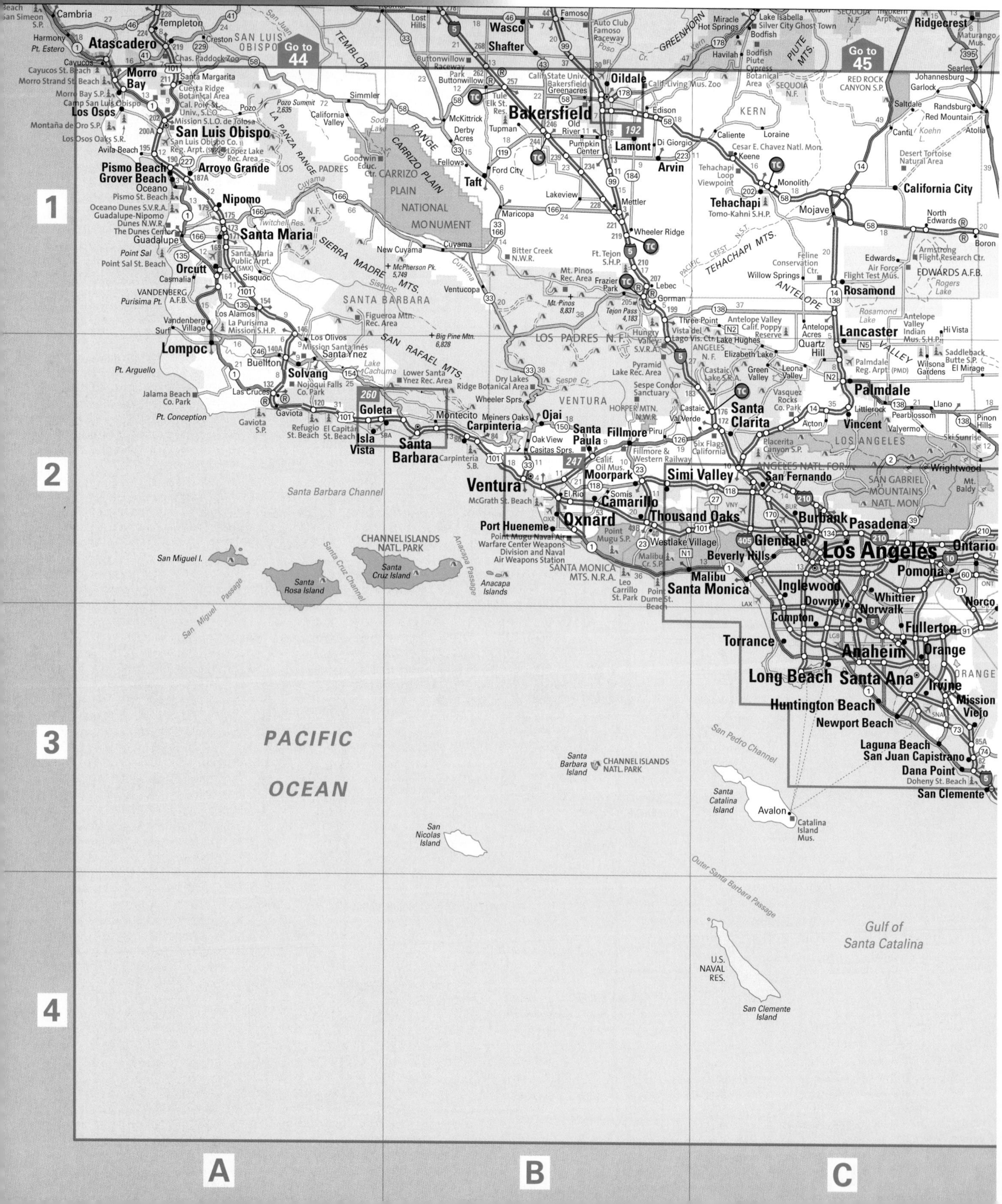

0 mi 20 40
0 km 20 40 60

One inch equals 25.4 miles
One centimeter equals 16.1 kilometers

Go to 44

Go to 45

PACIFIC OCEAN

1 2 3 4

A B C

DRIVING DISTANCES IN MILES

	BAKERSFIELD, CA	BARSTOW, CA	BLYTHE, CA	EL CENTRO, CA	LOS ANGELES, CA	NEEDLES, CA	PALM SPRINGS, CA	SAN BERNARDINO, CA	SAN DIEGO, CA	SAN LUIS OBISPO, CA	SANTA BARBARA, CA	YUMA, AZ
LOS ANGELES, CA	111	118	230	234		263	110	62	124	190	97	294
SAN DIEGO, CA	234	181	211	117	124	326	143	111		314	221	177
SANTA BARBARA, CA	150	213	325	330	97	358	205	157	221	93		391
YUMA, AZ	403	294	103	65	294	187	171	225	177	483	391	

SEE ALSO DISTANCE AND DRIVING TIME MAP ON PAGES 286–287

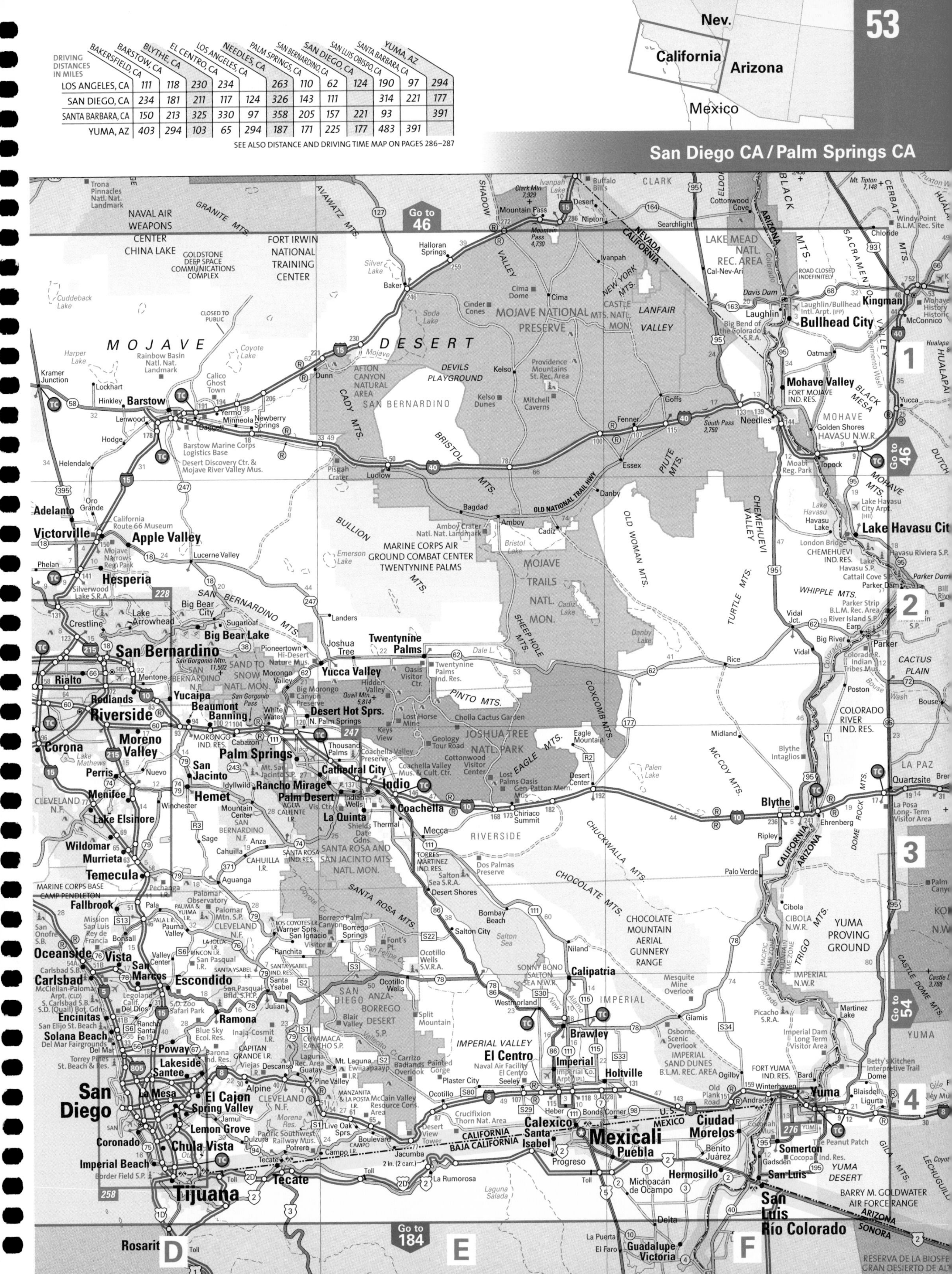

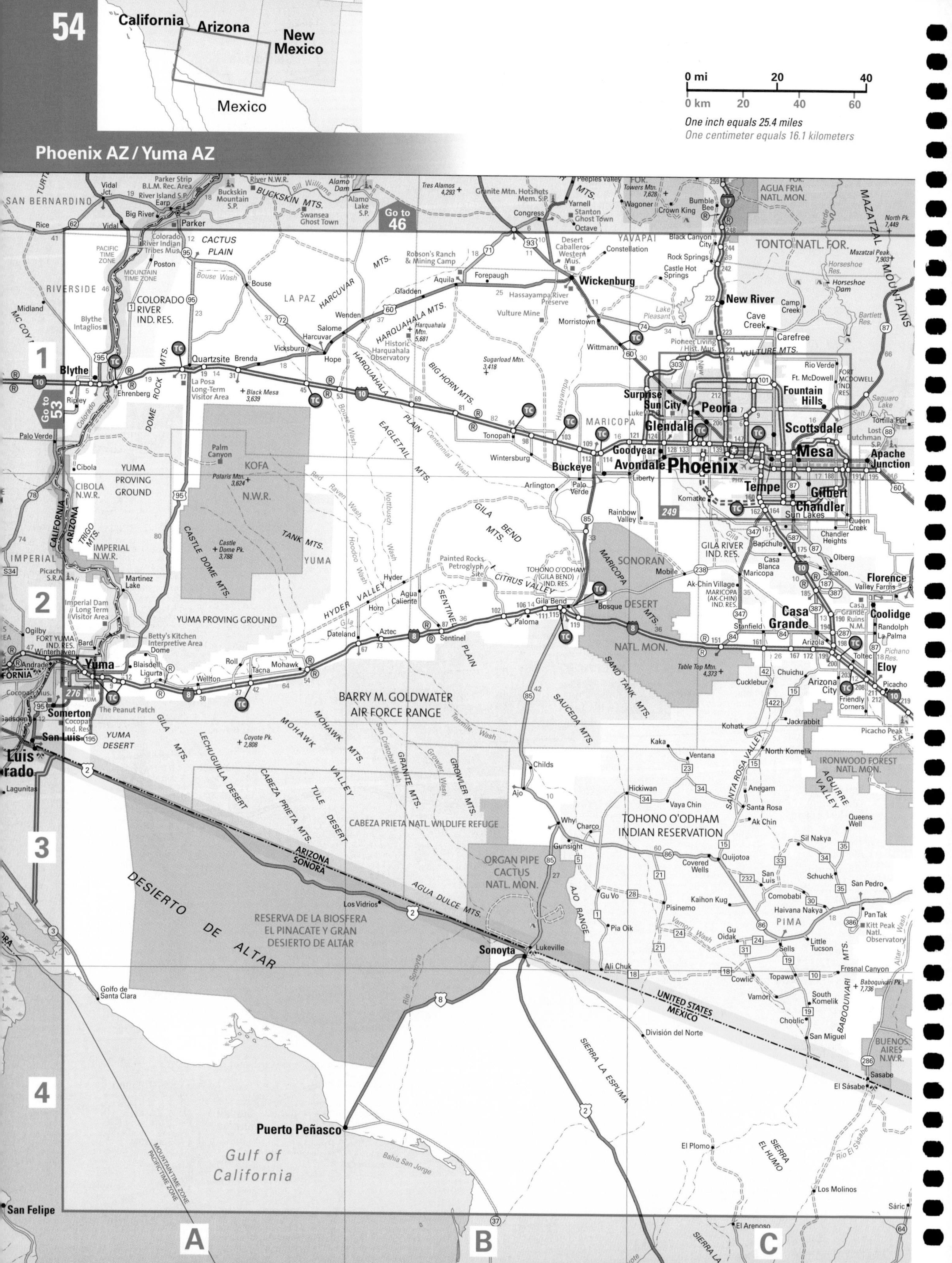

54
California
Arizona
New Mexico
Mexico
0 mi 20 40
0 km 20 40 60
One inch equals 25.4 miles
One centimeter equals 16.1 kilometers
Phoenix AZ / Yuma AZ
Go to 46
Go to 53
SAN BERNARDINO
RIVERSIDE
IMPERIAL
YAVAPAI
MARICOPA
LA PAZ
YUMA
PIMA
PACIFIC TIME ZONE
MOUNTAIN TIME ZONE
Vidal Jct.
Parker Strip B.L.M. Rec. Area
River Island S.P.
Earp
Parker
Buckskin Mountain S.P.
BUCKSKIN MTS.
Bill Williams River N.W.R.
Alamo Dam
Alamo Lake S.P.
Swansea Ghost Town
Tres Alamos 4,293
Granite Mtn. Hotshots Mem. S.P.
Peeples Valley
Yarnell
Stanton Ghost Town
Octave
Congress
Towers Mtn. 7,628
Wagoner
Crown King
Bumble Bee
AGUA FRIA NATL. MON.
MAZATZAL MOUNTAINS
North Pk. 7,449
Mazatzal Peak 7,903
TONTO NATL. FOR.
Horseshoe Res.
Horseshoe Dam
Bartlett Res.
Rice
Big River
Vidal
Colorado River Indian Tribes Mus.
CACTUS PLAIN
Poston
Bouse Wash
Bouse
Midland
Blythe Intaglios
COLORADO RIVER IND. RES.
HARCUVAR MTS.
Robson's Ranch & Mining Camp
Forepaugh
Aquila
Desert Caballeros Western Mus.
Constellation
Black Canyon City
Rock Springs
Castle Hot Springs
Wickenburg
Hassayampa River Preserve
Vulture Mine
Gladden
Wenden
Salome
Harcuvar
HARQUAHALA MTS.
Harquahala Mtn. 5,681
Historic Harquahala Observatory
Morristown
Lake Pleasant
New River
Cave Creek
Camp Creek
Carefree
Wittmann
Pioneer Living Hist. Mus.
VULTURE MTS.
Vicksburg
Hope
Blythe
Quartzsite
Brenda
Ehrenberg
Ripley
La Posa Long-Term Visitor Area
Black Mesa 3,639
DOME ROCK MTS.
BIG HORN MTS.
Sugarloaf Mtn. 3,418
Rio Verde
Ft. McDowell
FORT MCDOWELL IND. RES.
Fountain Hills
Saguaro Lake
Surprise
Sun City
Peoria
Luke
Glendale
Scottsdale
Tortilla Flat
Lost Dutchman S.P.
Tonopah
Wintersburg
EAGLETAIL MTS.
Centennial Wash
Goodyear
Avondale
Phoenix
Mesa
Apache Junction
Buckeye
Liberty
Tempe
Gilbert
Chandler
Arlington
Palo Verde
Komatke
Sun Lakes
Queen Creek
Palo Verde
Cibola
CIBOLA N.W.R.
YUMA PROVING GROUND
Palm Canyon
KOFA N.W.R.
Polaris Mtn. 3,624
Red Raven Wash
Nottbusch Wash
GILA BEND MTS.
Rainbow Valley
CASTLE DOME MTS.
Castle Dome Pk. 3,788
TANK MTS.
Hoodoo Wash
TRIGO MTS.
IMPERIAL N.W.R.
Picacho S.R.A.
Martinez Lake
Painted Rocks Petroglyph Site
TOHONO O'ODHAM (GILA BEND) IND. RES.
CITRUS VALLEY
SONORAN DESERT NATL. MON.
GILA RIVER IND. RES.
Bapchule
Chandler Heights
Olberg
Sacaton
Florence
Valley Farms
Casa Blanca
Maricopa
Mobile
Ak-Chin Village
MARICOPA (AK-CHIN) IND. RES.
Imperial Dam Long Term Visitor Area
HYDER VALLEY
Hyder
Agua Caliente
Horn
SENTINEL PLAIN
Gila Bend
Paloma
Bosque
Casa Grande
Casa Grande Ruins N.M.
Coolidge
Randolph
La Palma
Ogilby
FORT YUMA IND. RES.
Winterhaven
Andrade
Bard
Betty's Kitchen Interpretive Area
Dome
Dateland
Aztec
Sentinel
Stanfield
Arizola
Toltec
Eloy
Pichano
Yuma
Blaisdell
Ligurta
Roll
Wellton
Tacna
Mohawk
Table Top Mtn. 4,373
SAND TANK MTS.
Chuichu
Cucklebur
Arizona City
Picacho
Friendly Corners
Cocopah Mus.
The Peanut Patch
Somerton
Cocopah Ind. Res.
Gadsden
San Luis
BARRY M. GOLDWATER AIR FORCE RANGE
YUMA DESERT
GILA MTS.
Coyote Pk. 2,808
MOHAWK MTS.
MOHAWK VALLEY
San Cristobal Wash
Tenmile Wash
SAUCEDA MTS.
Kohatk
Jackrabbit
Picacho Peak S.P.
Kaka
Ventana
North Komelik
SANTA ROSA VALLEY
IRONWOOD FOREST NATL. MON.
AGUIRRE VALLEY
LECHUGUILLA DESERT
CABEZA PRIETA MTS.
TULE DESERT
GRANITE MTS.
Growler Wash
GROWLER MTS.
Childs
Ajo
Hickiwan
Vaya Chin
Anegam
Santa Rosa
Ak Chin
Queens Well
CABEZA PRIETA NATL. WILDLIFE REFUGE
Why
Charco
TOHONO O'ODHAM INDIAN RESERVATION
Gunsight
Sil Nakya
Quijotoa
Covered Wells
ARIZONA SONORA
DESIERTO DE ALTAR
ORGAN PIPE CACTUS NATL. MON.
AJO RANGE
San Luis
Schuchk
San Pedro
Gu Vo
Comobabi
Haivana Nakya
Kaihon Kug
Pisinemo
AGUA DULCE MTS.
Los Vidrios
RESERVA DE LA BIOSFERA EL PINACATE Y GRAN DESIERTO DE ALTAR
Pia Oik
Vamori Wash
Gu Oidak
Sells
Little Tucson
Pan Tak
Kitt Peak Natl. Observatory
Sonoyta
Lukeville
Ali Chuk
Cowlic
Topawa
Fresnal Canyon
Baboquivari Pk. 7,736
BABOQUIVARI MTS.
Vamori
South Komelik
Choulic
San Miguel
UNITED STATES MEXICO
División del Norte
Golfo de Santa Clara
Rio Sonoyta
SIERRA LA ESPUMA
BUENOS AIRES N.W.R.
Sasabe
El Sásabe
Puerto Peñasco
Gulf of California
Bahía San Jorge
El Plomo
SIERRA EL HUMO
Rio El Sásabe
MOUNTAIN TIME ZONE
PACIFIC TIME ZONE
Los Molinos
San Felipe
El Arenoso
Sáric
SIERRA LA
1
2
3
4
A
B
C

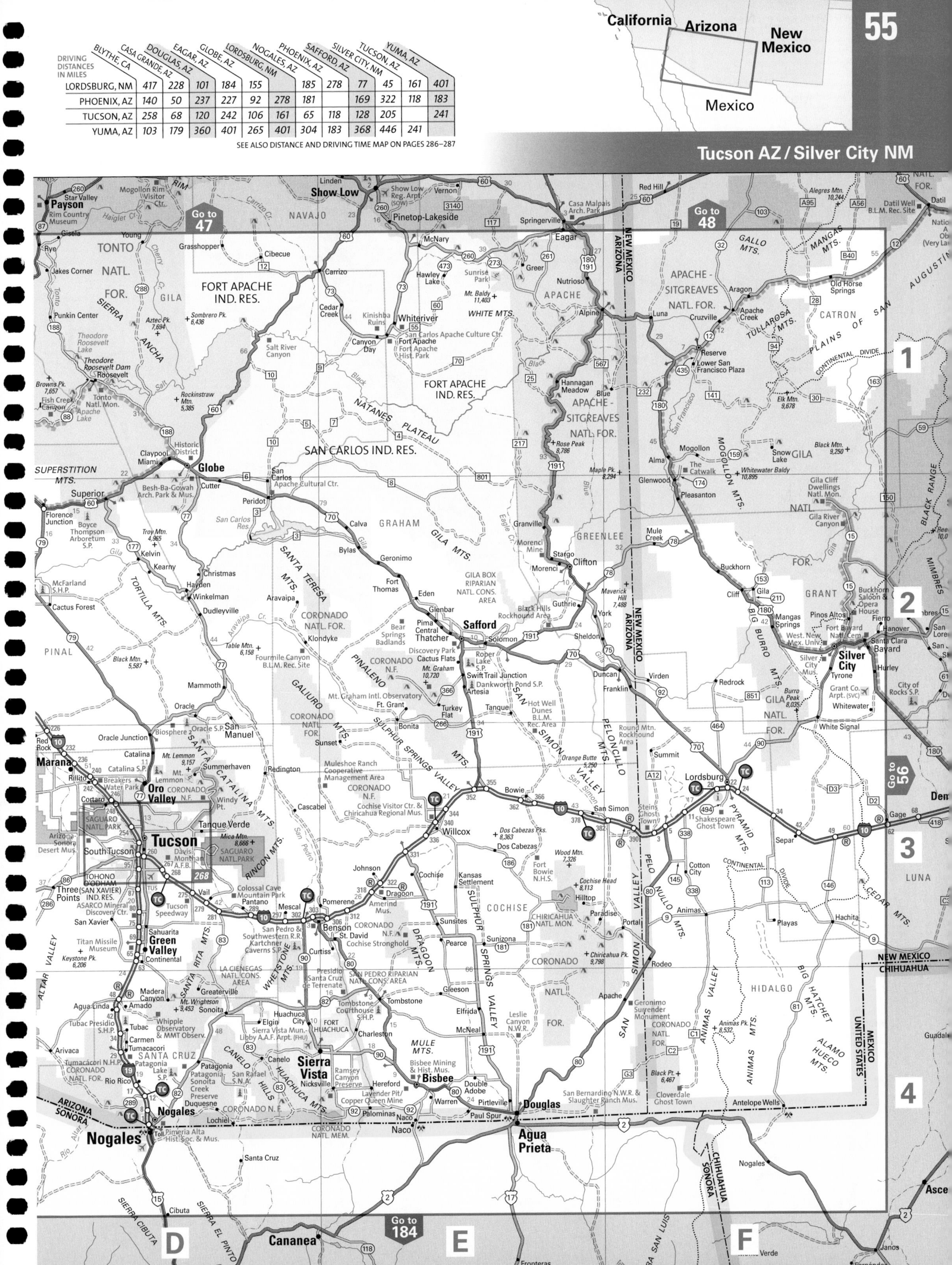

DRIVING DISTANCES IN MILES	BLYTHE, CA	CASA GRANDE, AZ	DOUGLAS, AZ	EAGAR, AZ	GLOBE, AZ	LORDSBURG, NM	NOGALES, AZ	PHOENIX, AZ	SAFFORD, AZ	SILVER CITY, NM	TUCSON, AZ	YUMA, AZ
LORDSBURG, NM	417	228	101	184	155		185	278	77	45	161	401
PHOENIX, AZ	140	50	237	227	92	278	181		169	322	118	183
TUCSON, AZ	258	68	120	242	106	161	65	118	128	205		241
YUMA, AZ	103	179	360	401	265	401	304	183	368	446	241	

SEE ALSO DISTANCE AND DRIVING TIME MAP ON PAGES 286–287

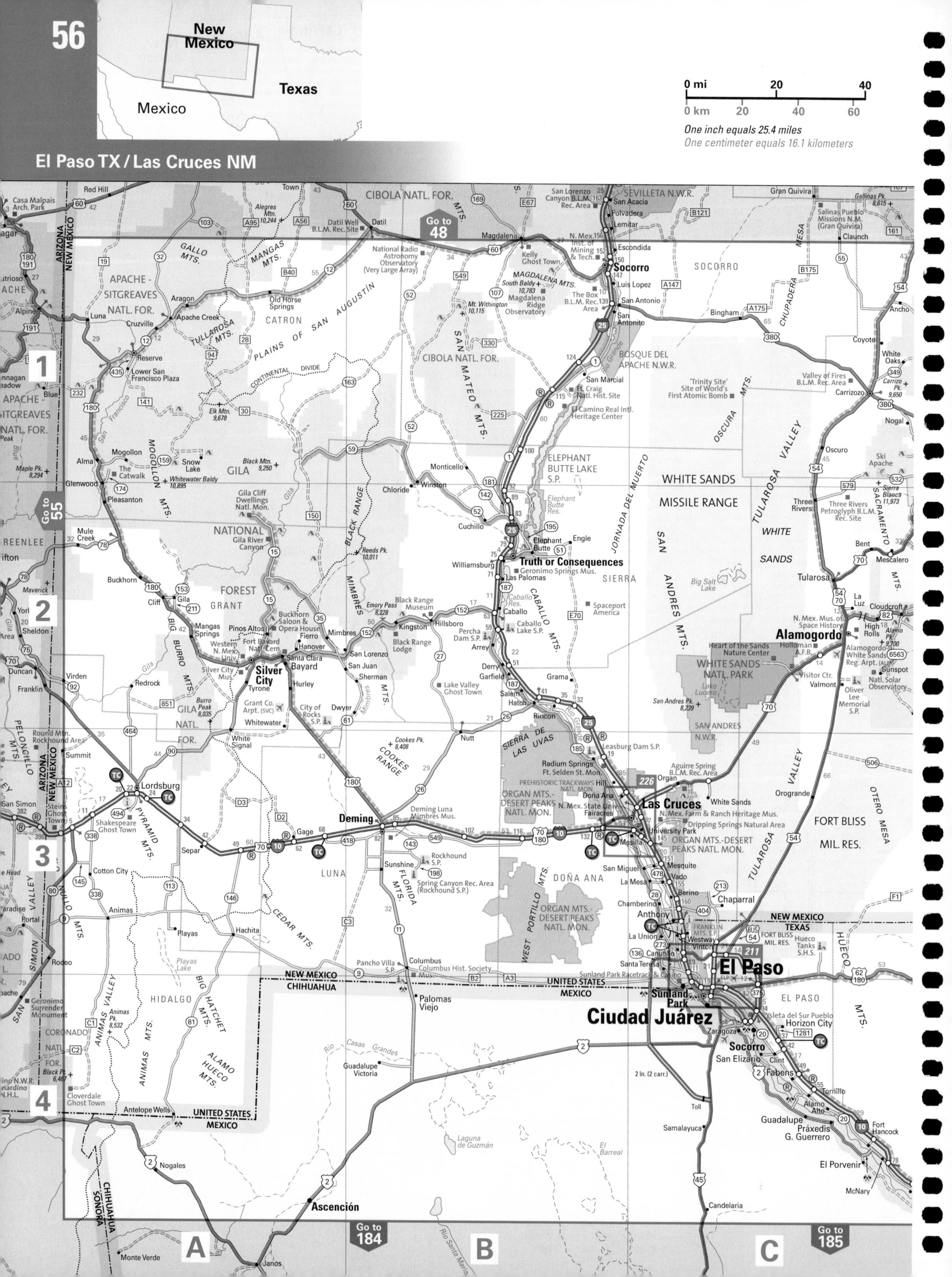
New Mexico
Texas
Mexico
0 mi 20 40
0 km 20 40 60
One inch equals 25.4 miles
One centimeter equals 16.1 kilometers
Go to 48
Go to 55
Go to 184
Go to 185
1
2
3
4
A
B
C
CIBOLA NATL. FOR.
SEVILLETA N.W.R.
Socorro
SOCORRO
APACHE - SITGREAVES NATL. FOR.
CATRON
PLAINS OF SAN AUGUSTIN
BOSQUE DEL APACHE N.W.R.
GILA NATIONAL FOREST
GRANT
Silver City
Truth or Consequences
ELEPHANT BUTTE LAKE S.P.
WHITE SANDS MISSILE RANGE
SIERRA
SAN ANDRES MTS.
Alamogordo
WHITE SANDS NATL. PARK
Las Cruces
ORGAN MTS.-DESERT PEAKS NATL. MON.
Deming
LUNA
DOÑA ANA
Lordsburg
HIDALGO
FORT BLISS MIL. RES.
OTERO MESA
El Paso
EL PASO
Ciudad Juárez
Sunland Park
NEW MEXICO
TEXAS
CHIHUAHUA
SONORA
UNITED STATES
MEXICO
Columbus
Palomas Viejo
Ascención
Janos
Nogales
Samalayuca
Guadalupe
Práxedis G. Guerrero
Tularosa
Carrizozo
Hatch
Anthony
Mesilla

DRIVING DISTANCES IN MILES

	ALAMOGORDO, NM	CARLSBAD, NM	EL PASO, TX	HOBBS, NM	LAS CRUCES, NM	LORDSBURG, NM	ODESSA, TX	PECOS, TX	PORTALES, NM	ROSWELL, NM	SILVER CITY, NM	SOCORRO, NM
CARLSBAD, NM	144		162	70	203	321	137	87	168	76	311	241
EL PASO, TX	86	162		232	42	160	285	209	295	203	150	190
LAS CRUCES, NM	65	203	42	250		122	325	250	274	182	111	146
ROSWELL, NM	117	76	203	117	182	304	201	163	92		293	164

SEE ALSO DISTANCE AND DRIVING TIME MAP ON PAGES 286–287

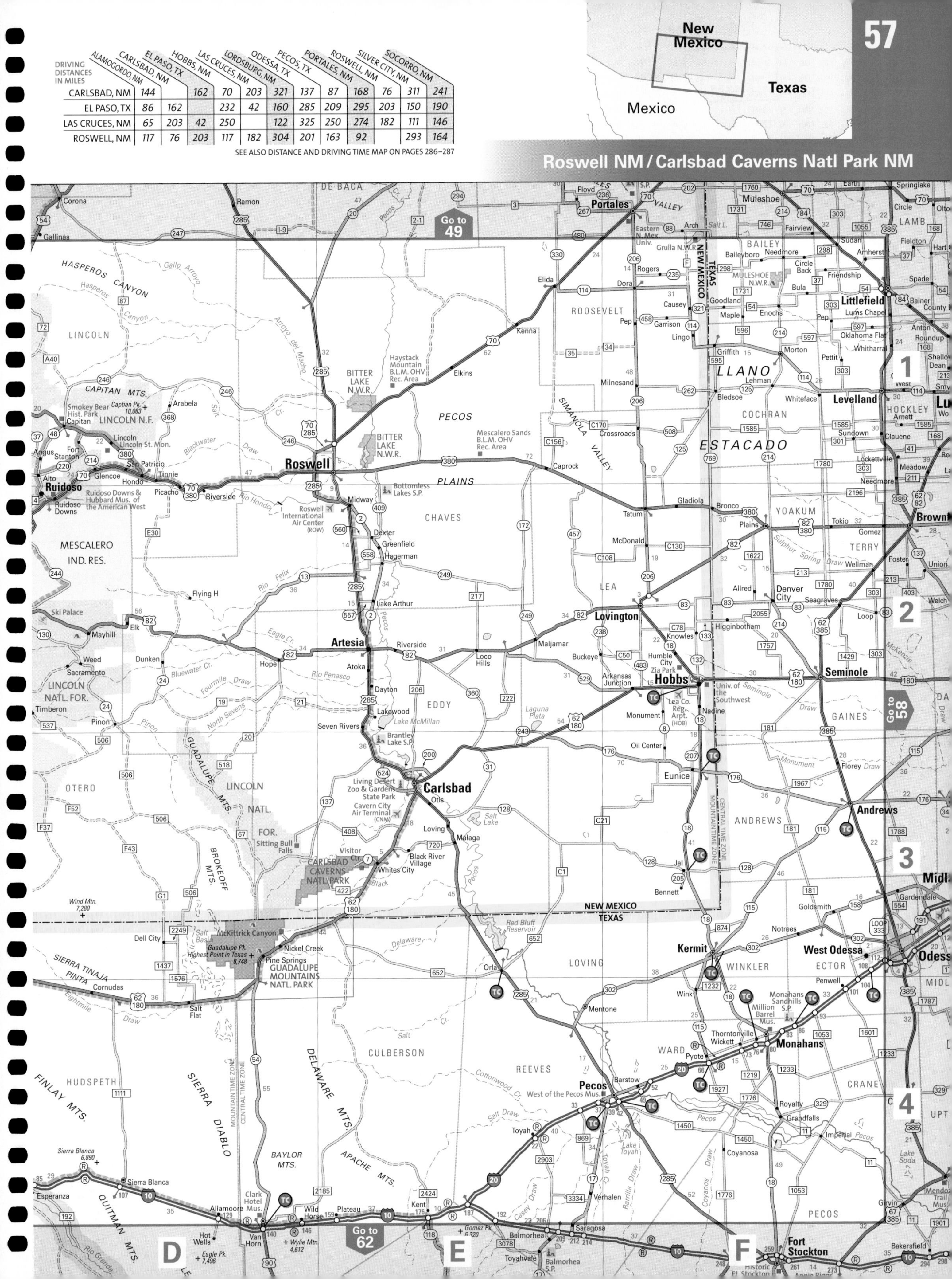

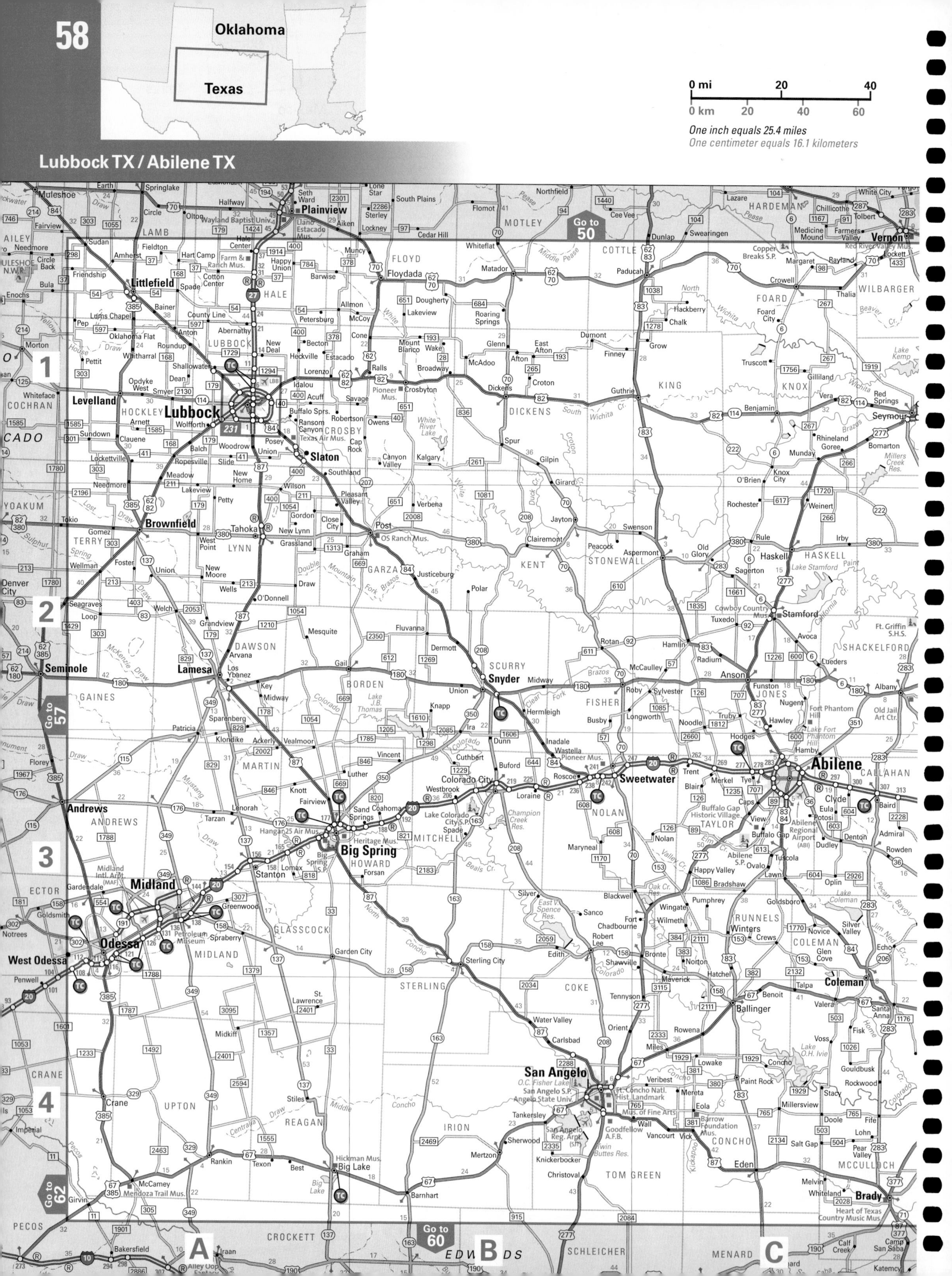

58
Oklahoma
Texas
Lubbock TX / Abilene TX
0 mi 20 40
0 km 20 40 60
One inch equals 25.4 miles
One centimeter equals 16.1 kilometers
Go to 50
Go to 57
Go to 62
Go to 60
LAMB
HALE
FLOYD
MOTLEY
COTTLE
HARDEMAN
WILBARGER
FOARD
KING
KNOX
HOCKLEY
LUBBOCK
CROSBY
DICKENS
COCHRAN
YOAKUM
TERRY
LYNN
GARZA
KENT
STONEWALL
HASKELL
GAINES
DAWSON
BORDEN
SCURRY
FISHER
JONES
SHACKELFORD
ANDREWS
MARTIN
HOWARD
MITCHELL
NOLAN
TAYLOR
CALLAHAN
ECTOR
MIDLAND
GLASSCOCK
STERLING
COKE
RUNNELS
COLEMAN
CRANE
UPTON
REAGAN
IRION
TOM GREEN
CONCHO
MCCULLOCH
PECOS
CROCKETT
SCHLEICHER
MENARD
Lubbock
Plainview
Littlefield
Levelland
Slaton
Brownfield
Tahoka
Post
Floydada
Crosbyton
Dickens
Matador
Paducah
Vernon
Seymour
Haskell
Stamford
Anson
Abilene
Snyder
Sweetwater
Colorado City
Big Spring
Lamesa
Seminole
Andrews
Midland
Odessa
West Odessa
Stanton
Sterling City
Robert Lee
Ballinger
Coleman
San Angelo
Eden
Brady
Big Lake
Rankin
Crane
McCamey
A
B
C
1
2
3
4

DRIVING DISTANCES IN MILES	ABILENE, TX	BIG SPRING, TX	BROWNWOOD, TX	DALLAS, TX	FORT WORTH, TX	LUBBOCK, TX	ODESSA, TX	SAN ANGELO, TX	SHERMAN, TX	TEMPLE, TX	WACO, TX	WICHITA FALLS, TX
ABILENE, TX		110	78	191	153	166	176	91	249	194	235	144
DALLAS, TX	191	298	190		32	354	364	265	64	130	94	141
LUBBOCK, TX	166	106	247	354	317		142	185	322	358	399	207
WACO, TX	235	343	124	94	87	399	409	219	159	40		201

SEE ALSO DISTANCE AND DRIVING TIME MAP ON PAGES 286–287

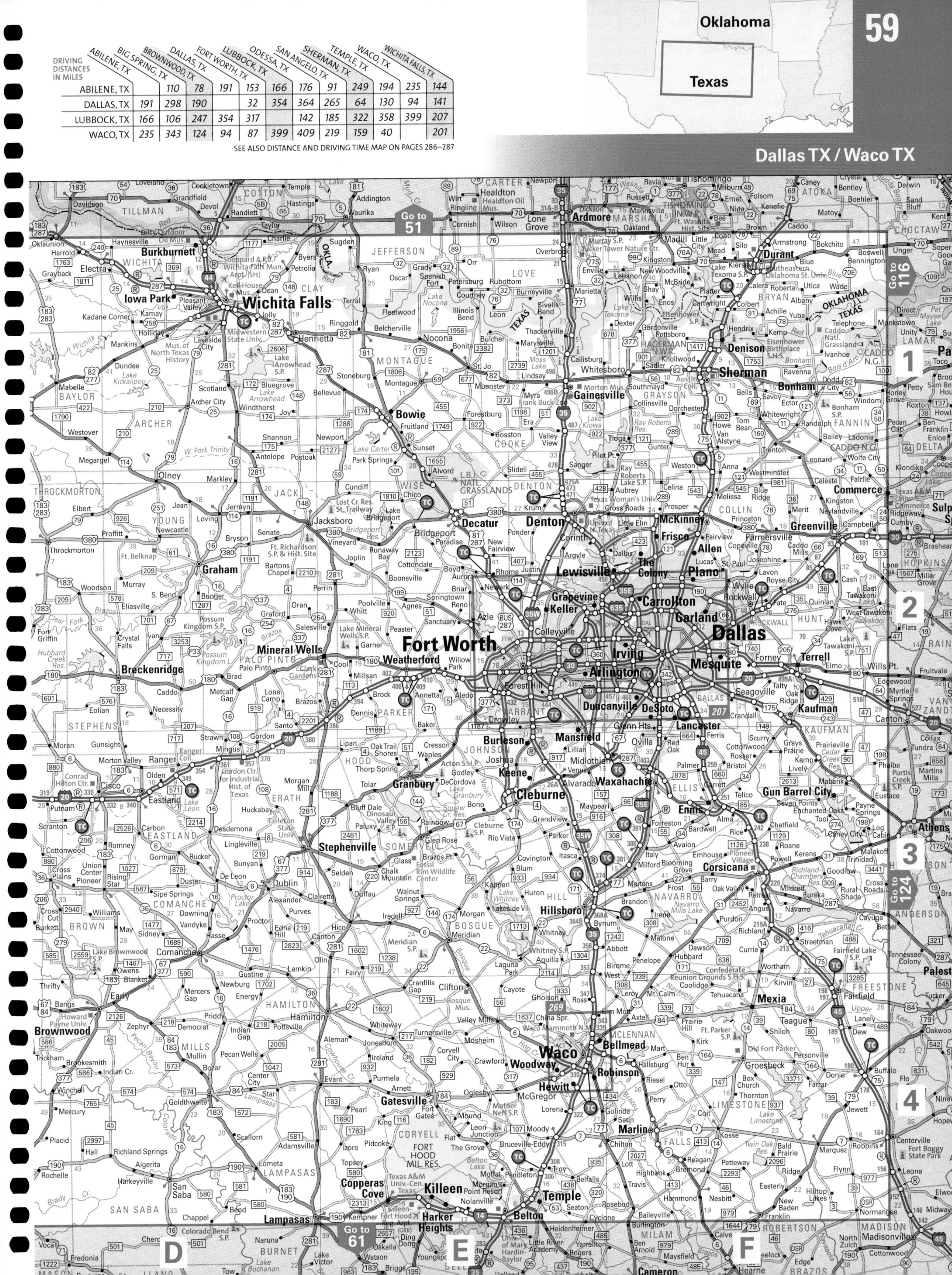

Del Rio TX / Eagle Pass TX

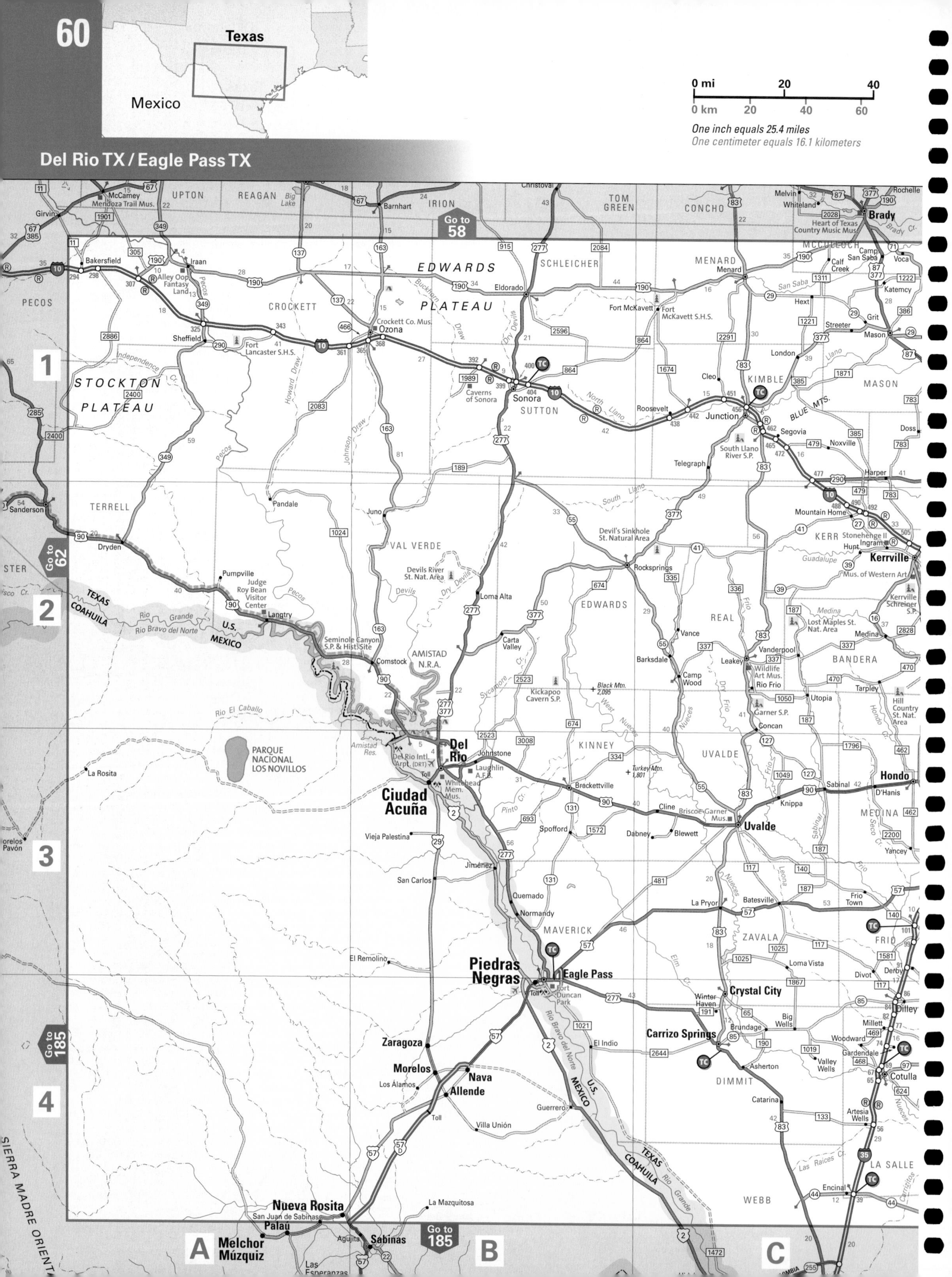

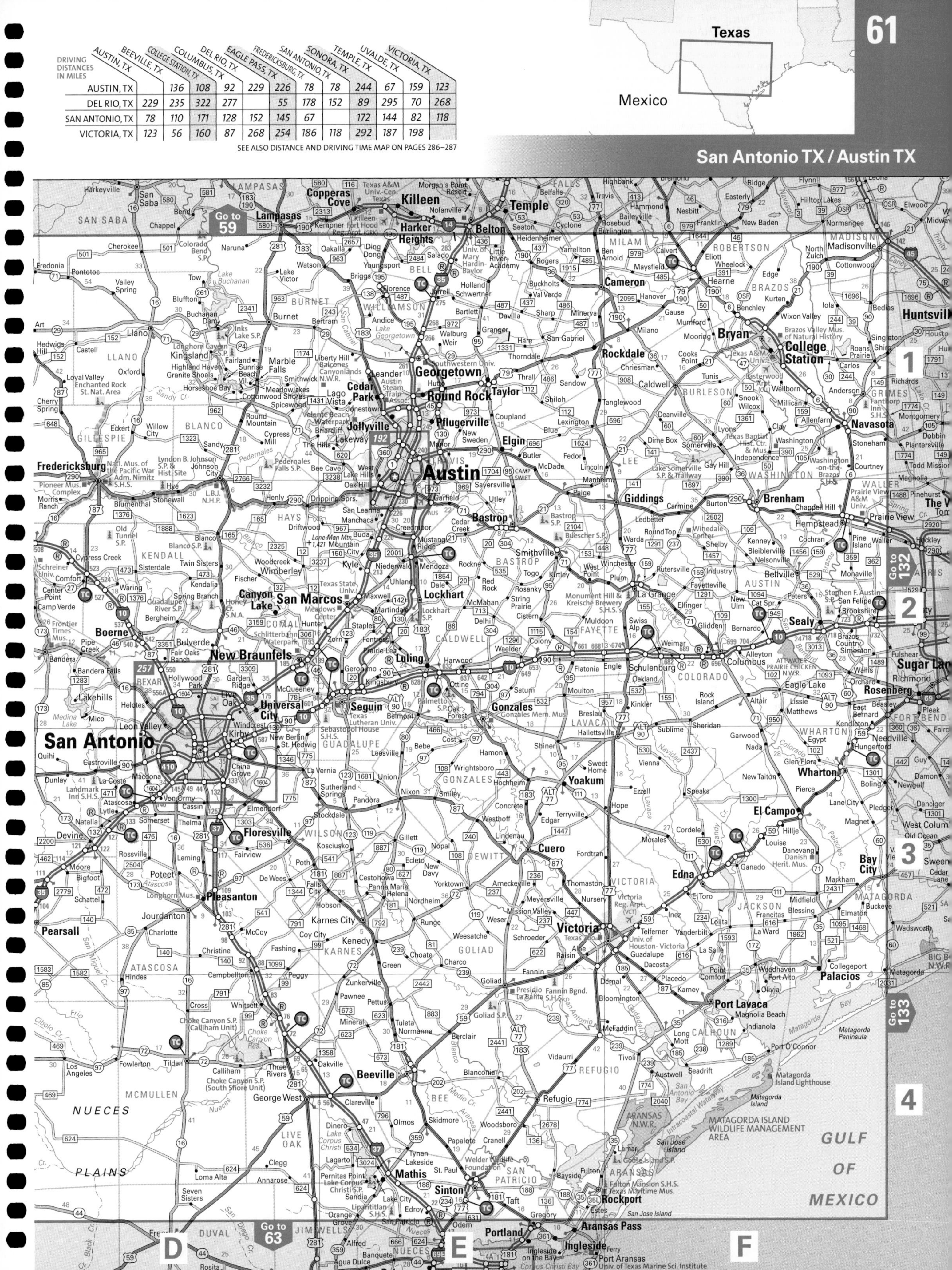

DRIVING DISTANCES IN MILES	AUSTIN, TX	BEEVILLE, TX	COLLEGE STATION, TX	COLUMBUS, TX	DEL RIO, TX	EAGLE PASS, TX	FREDERICKSBURG, TX	SAN ANTONIO, TX	SONORA, TX	TEMPLE, TX	UVALDE, TX	VICTORIA, TX
AUSTIN, TX		136	108	92	229	226	78	78	244	67	159	123
DEL RIO, TX	229	235	322	277		55	178	152	89	295	70	268
SAN ANTONIO, TX	78	110	171	128	152	145	67		172	144	82	118
VICTORIA, TX	123	56	160	87	268	254	186	118	292	187	198	

SEE ALSO DISTANCE AND DRIVING TIME MAP ON PAGES 286–287

Odessa TX / Big Bend Natl Park TX

DRIVING DISTANCES IN MILES	ALPINE, TX	BIG BEND NP, TX	FORT STOCKTON, TX	ODESSA, TX	PECOS, TX	VAN HORN, TX
ALPINE, TX		97	65	151	96	110
FORT STOCKTON, TX	65	123		86	58	119
ODESSA, TX	151	209	86		76	163
VAN HORN, TX	110	207	119	163	87	

SEE ALSO DISTANCE AND DRIVING TIME MAP ON PAGES 286–287

0 mi 10 20 30
0 km 20 40
One inch equals 25.4 miles
One centimeter equals 16.1 kilometers

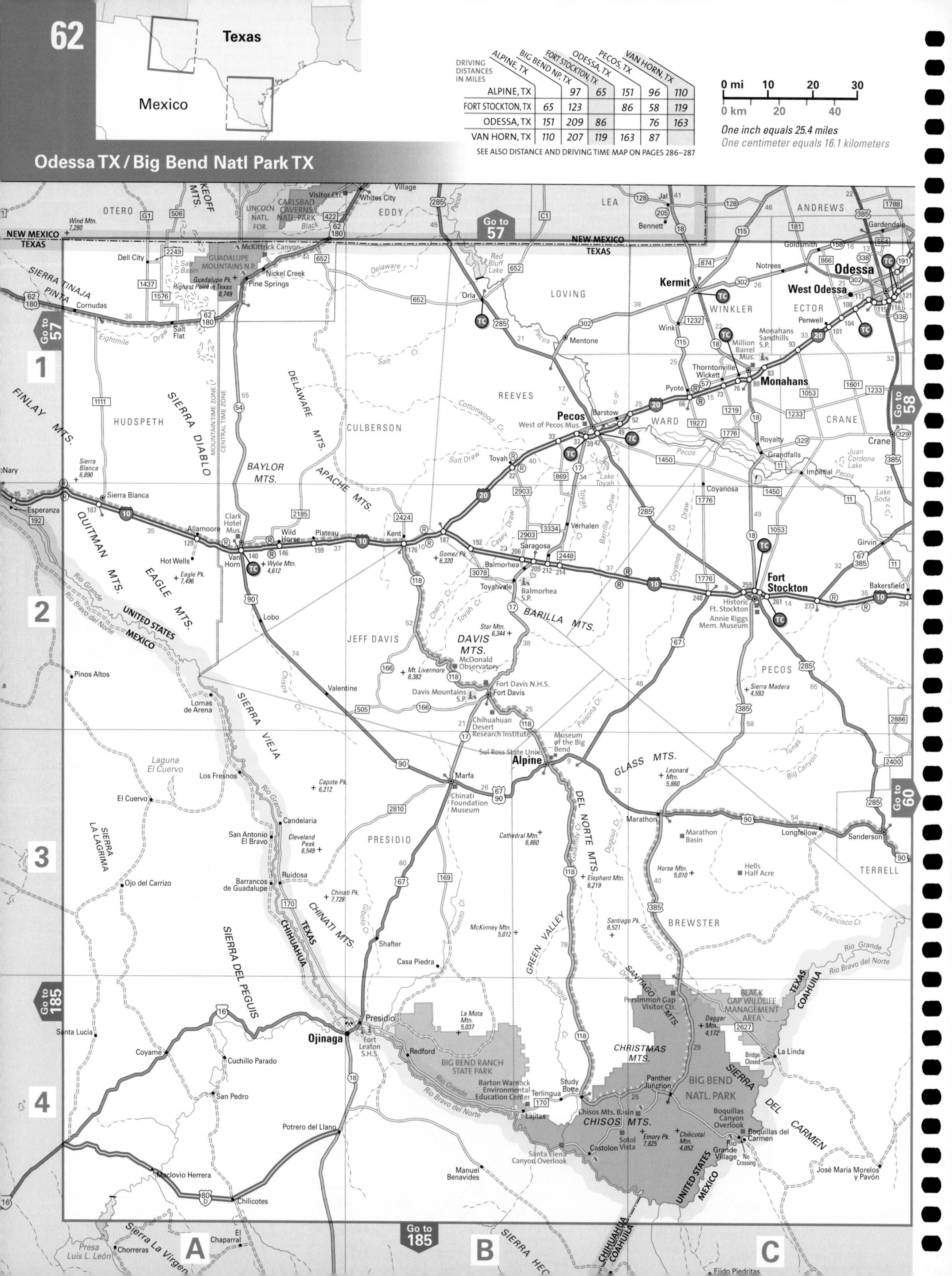

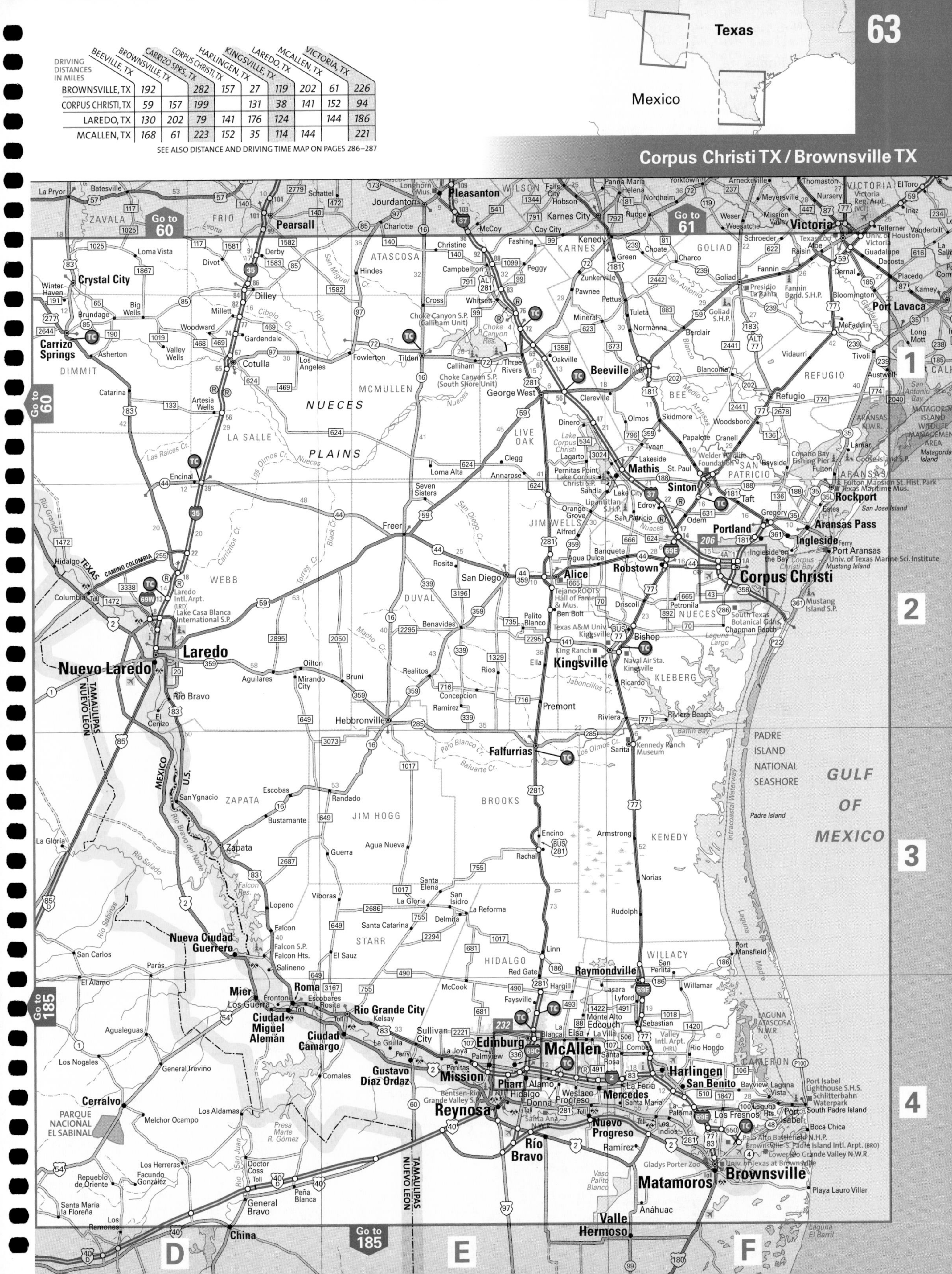

DRIVING DISTANCES IN MILES

	BEEVILLE, TX	BROWNSVILLE, TX	CARRIZO SPRS., TX	CORPUS CHRISTI, TX	HARLINGEN, TX	KINGSVILLE, TX	LAREDO, TX	MCALLEN, TX	VICTORIA, TX
BROWNSVILLE, TX	192		282	157	27	119	202	61	226
CORPUS CHRISTI, TX	59	157	199		131	38	141	152	94
LAREDO, TX	130	202	79	141	176	124		144	186
MCALLEN, TX	168	61	223	152	35	114	144		221

SEE ALSO DISTANCE AND DRIVING TIME MAP ON PAGES 286–287

Duluth MN / International Falls MN

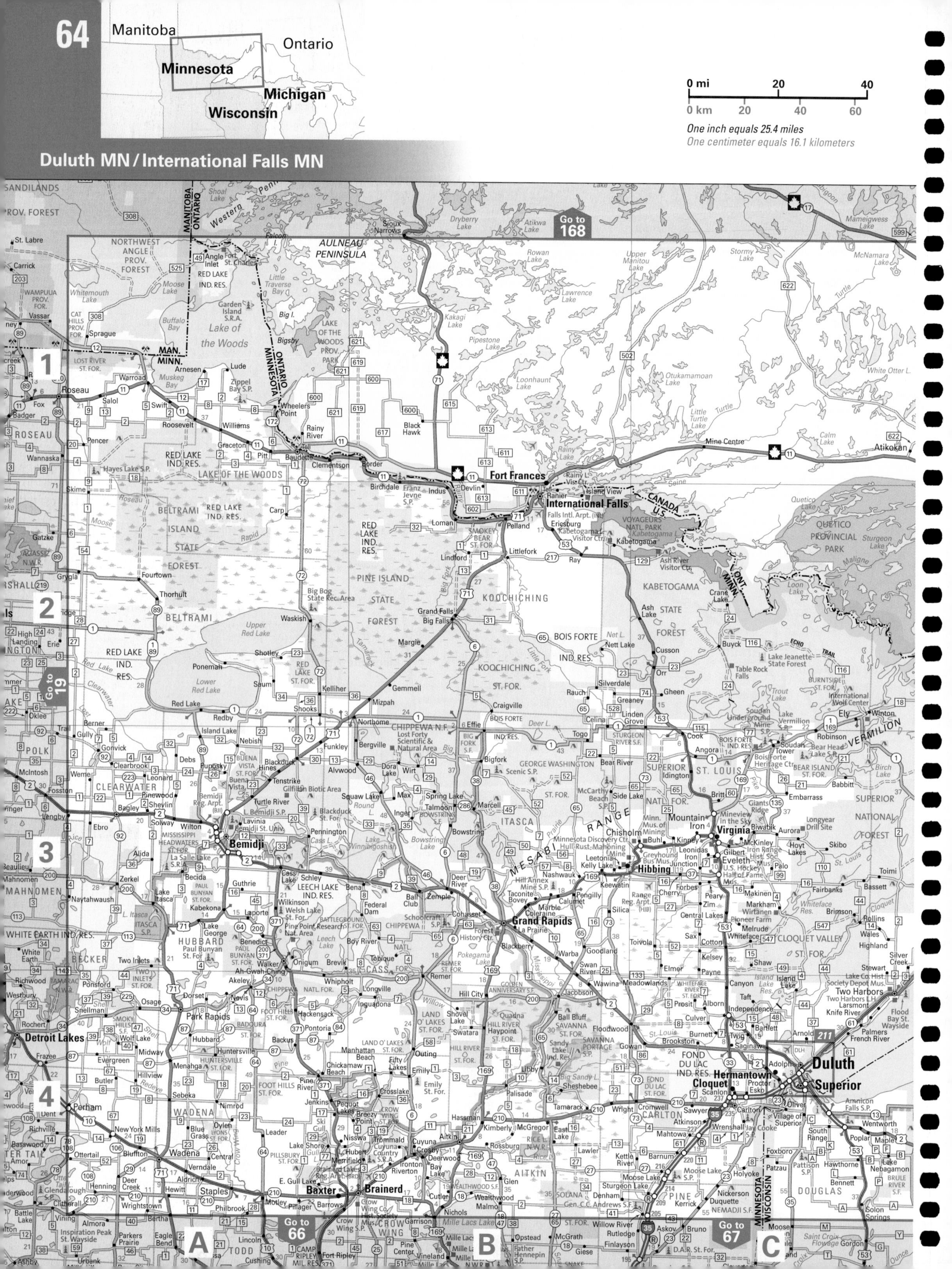

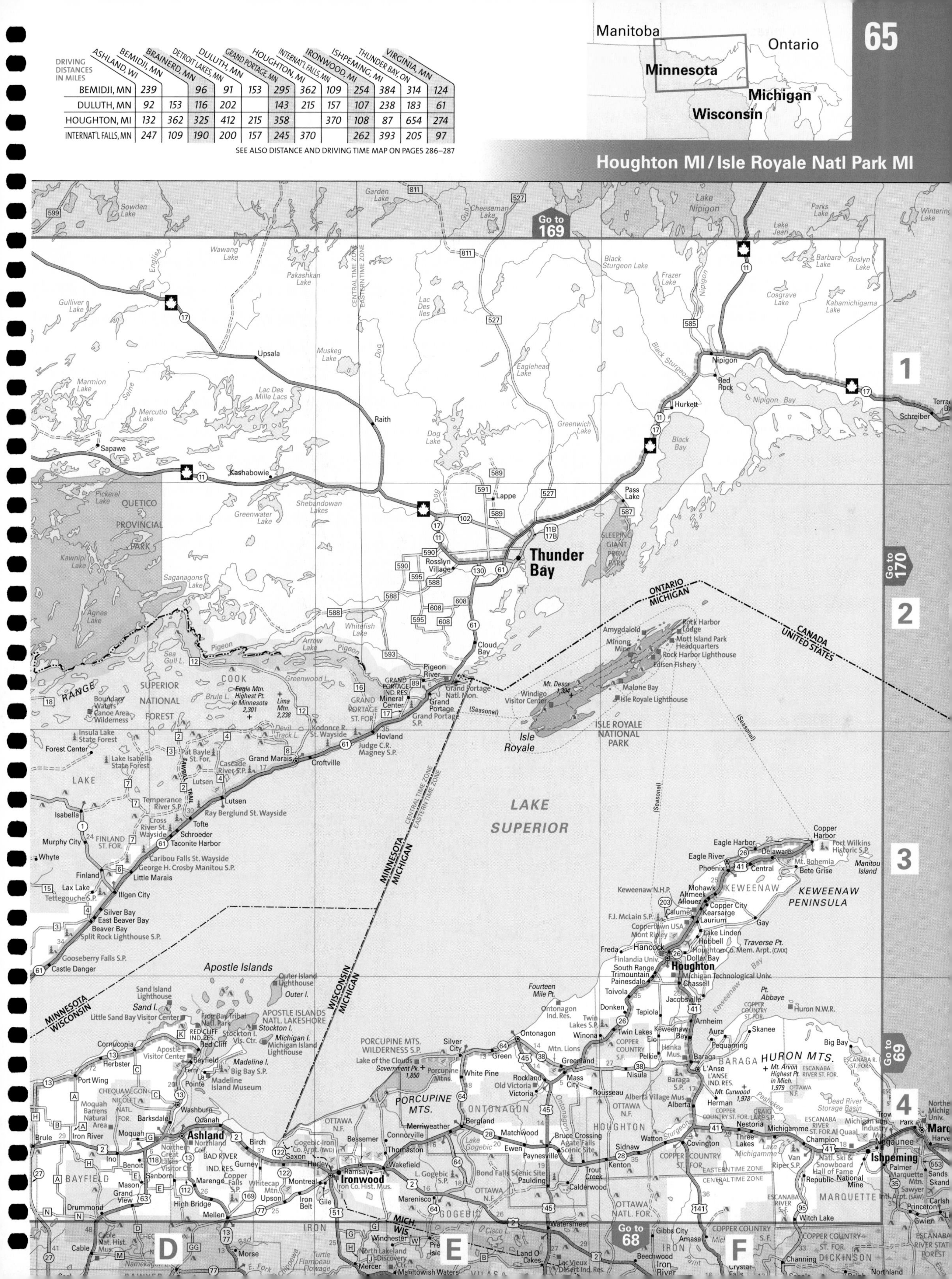

DRIVING DISTANCES IN MILES	ASHLAND, WI	BEMIDJI, MN	BRAINERD, MN	DETROIT LAKES, MN	DULUTH, MN	GRAND PORTAGE, MN	HOUGHTON, MI	INTERNAT'L FALLS, MN	IRONWOOD, MI	ISHPEMING, MI	THUNDER BAY, ON	VIRGINIA, MN
BEMIDJI, MN	239		96	91	153	295	362	109	254	384	314	124
DULUTH, MN	92	153	116	202		143	215	157	107	238	183	61
HOUGHTON, MI	132	362	325	412	215	358		370	108	87	654	274
INTERNAT'L FALLS, MN	247	109	190	200	157	245	370		262	393	205	97

SEE ALSO DISTANCE AND DRIVING TIME MAP ON PAGES 286–287

St Cloud MN / Willmar MN

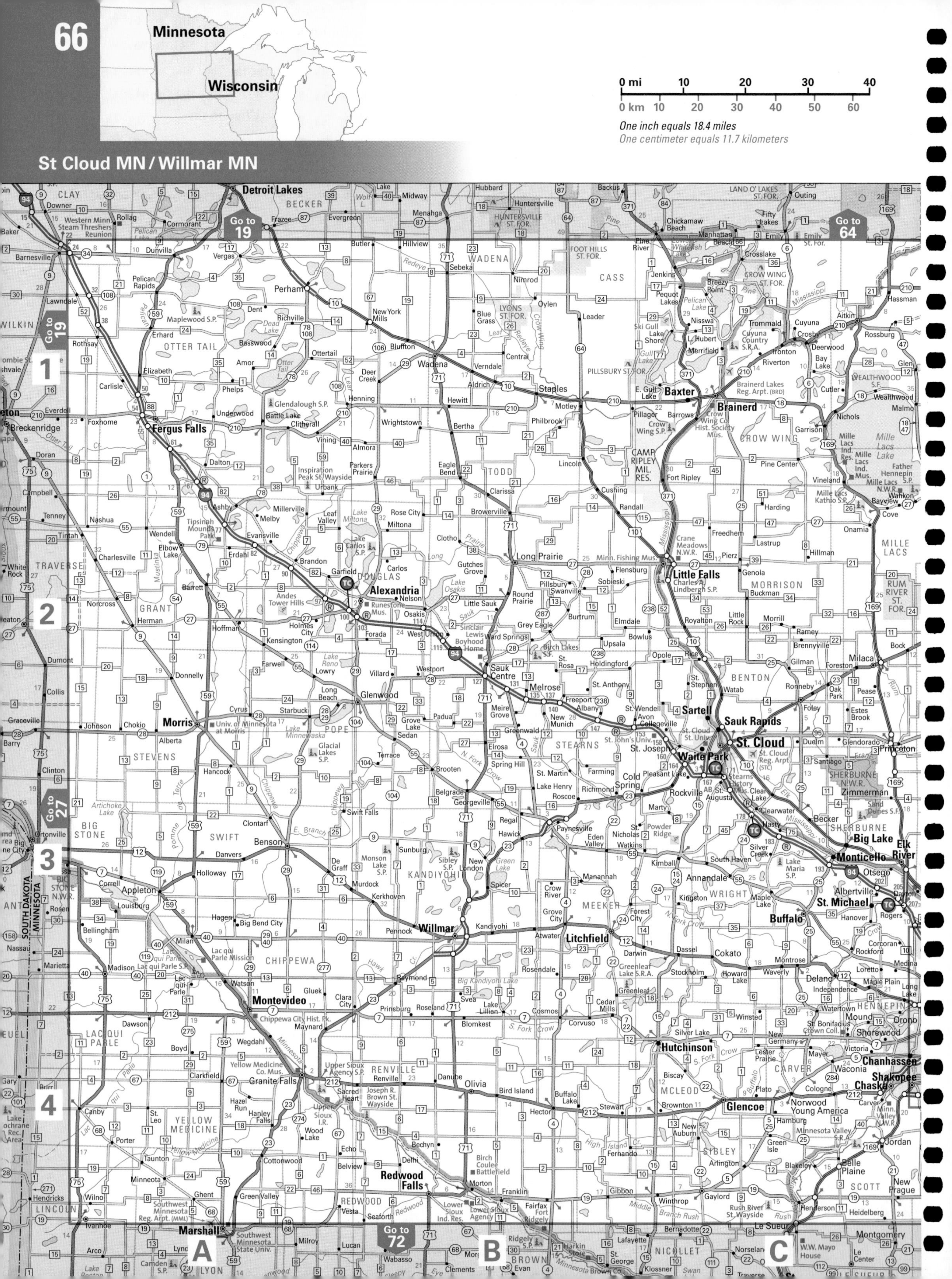

DRIVING DISTANCES IN MILES

	ASHLAND, WI	BRAINERD, MN	DULUTH, MN	EAU CLAIRE, WI	FERGUS FALLS, MN	MARSHALL, MN	MINNEAPOLIS, MN	MORRIS, MN	RICE LAKE, WI	ST. CLOUD, MN	ST. PAUL, MN	WILLMAR, MN
EAU CLAIRE, WI	167	220	155		267	236	93	247	57	156	83	193
MINNEAPOLIS, MN	196	129	158	93	176	148		156	103	64	10	92
ST. CLOUD, MN	205	62	149	156	117	131	64	98	155		73	63
WILLMAR, MN	263	112	206	193	113	68	92	57	196	63	102	

SEE ALSO DISTANCE AND DRIVING TIME MAP ON PAGES 286–287

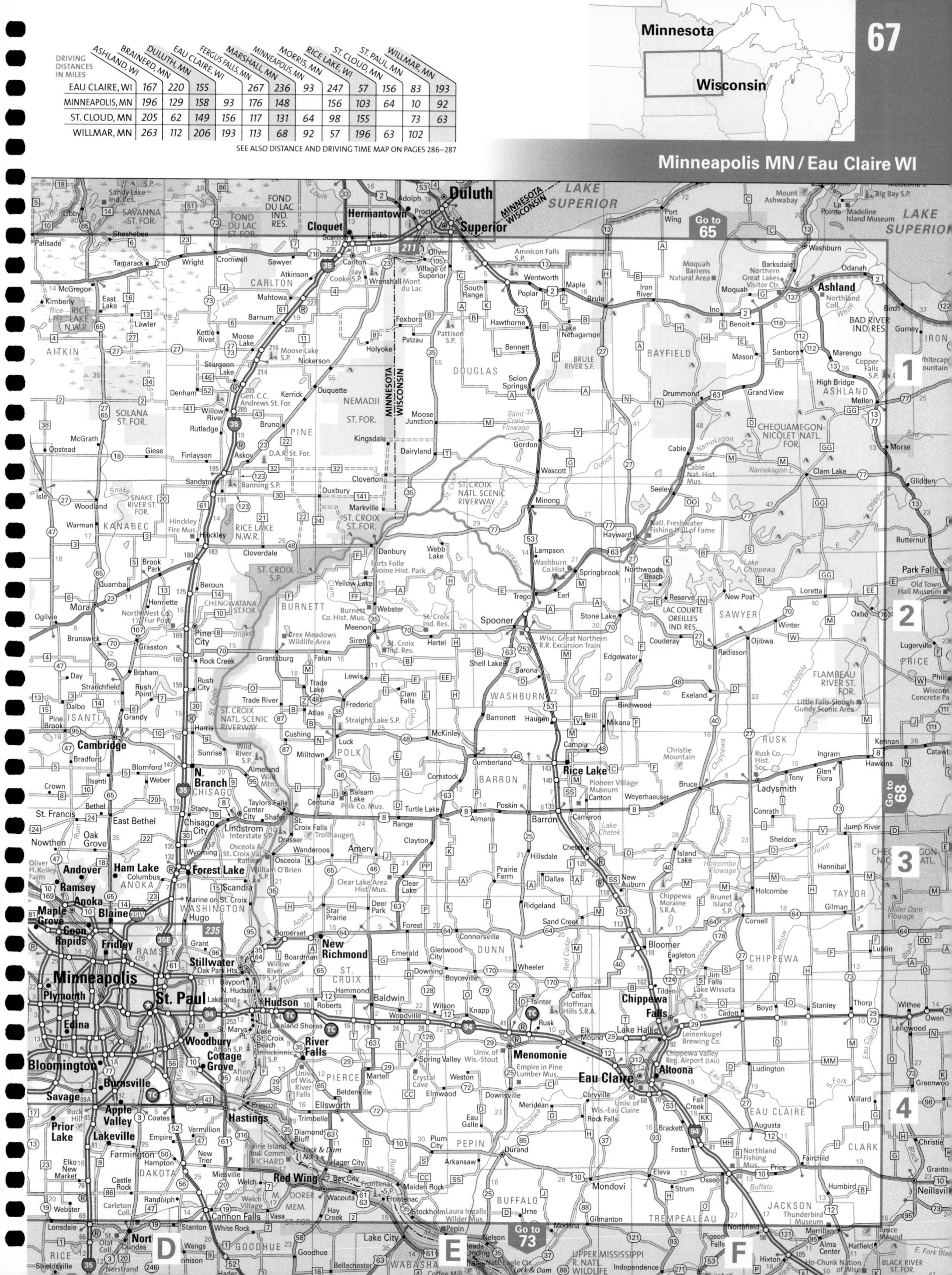

Wisconsin
Michigan

0 mi 10 20 30 40
0 km 10 20 30 40 50 60

One inch equals 18.4 miles
One centimeter equals 11.7 kilometers

Green Bay WI / Wausau WI

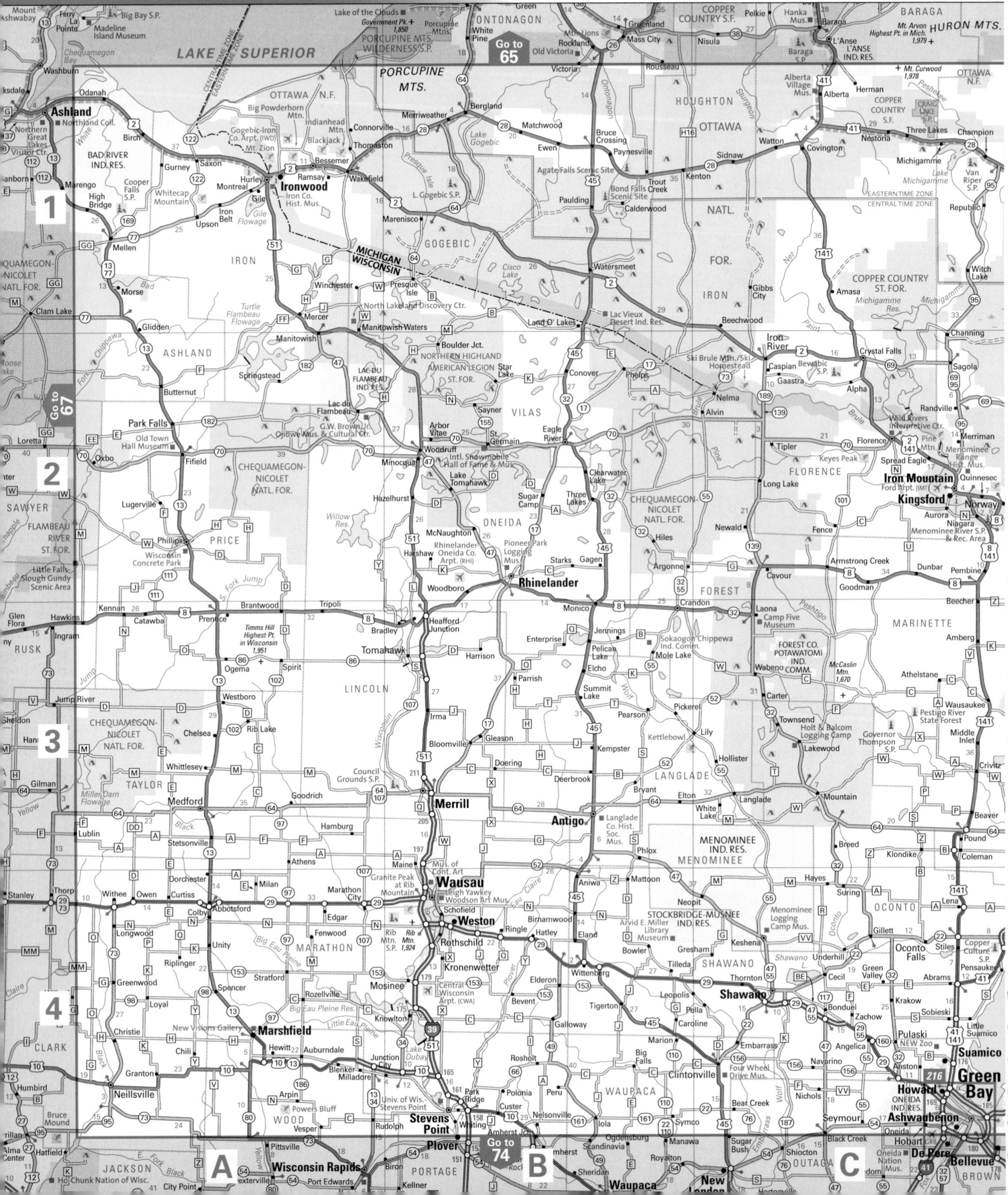

Go to 65
Go to 67
Go to 74

LAKE SUPERIOR
CENTRAL TIME ZONE
EASTERN TIME ZONE
MICHIGAN
WISCONSIN
PORCUPINE MTS.
PORCUPINE MTS. WILDERNESS S.P.
ONTONAGON
HOUGHTON
BARAGA
HURON MTS.
COPPER COUNTRY S.F.
OTTAWA N.F.
GOGEBIC
IRON
VILAS
ONEIDA
FOREST
FLORENCE
MARINETTE
ASHLAND
PRICE
SAWYER
RUSK
TAYLOR
LINCOLN
LANGLADE
MARATHON
MENOMINEE
MENOMINEE IND. RES.
SHAWANO
OCONTO
CLARK
WOOD
PORTAGE
WAUPACA
OUTAGAMIE
BROWN
JACKSON
CHEQUAMEGON-NICOLET NATL. FOR.
NORTHERN HIGHLAND AMERICAN LEGION ST. FOR.
COPPER COUNTRY ST. FOR.
BAD RIVER IND. RES.
LAC DU FLAMBEAU IND. RES.
STOCKBRIDGE-MUNSEE IND. RES.
FOREST CO. POTAWATOMI IND. COMM.
ONEIDA IND. RES.

Ashland
Ironwood
Hurley
Bessemer
Wakefield
Watersmeet
Iron River
Iron Mountain
Kingsford
Norway
Park Falls
Phillips
Medford
Rhinelander
Eagle River
Minocqua
Woodruff
Tomahawk
Merrill
Antigo
Wausau
Weston
Schofield
Rothschild
Mosinee
Marshfield
Stevens Point
Plover
Wisconsin Rapids
Shawano
Oconto Falls
Green Bay
Howard
Ashwaubenon
De Pere
Bellevue
Suamico
Waupaca
New London
Clintonville
Crandon
Laona
Abbotsford
Colby
Neillsville
Greenwood
Spencer
Athens
Prentice
Crivitz
Marinette

Timms Hill Highest Pt. in Wisconsin 1,951
Rib Mtn. 1,924
Mt. Arvon Highest Pt. in Mich. 1,979
Mt. Curwood 1,978
Government Pk. 1,850
McCaslin Mtn. 1,670

EASTERN TIME ZONE
CENTRAL TIME ZONE

A
B
C
1
2
3
4

DRIVING DISTANCES IN MILES

	ESCANABA, MI	GREEN BAY, WI	IRON MOUNTAIN, MI	IRONWOOD, MI	L'ANSE, MI	MANISTIQUE, MI	MARINETTE, WI	MARQUETTE, MI	RHINELANDER, WI	STEVENS POINT, WI	TRAVERSE CITY, MI	WAUSAU, WI
ESCANABA, MI		111	52	178	134	54	57	65	132	185	252	171
GREEN BAY, WI	111		96	202	178	165	54	175	124	87	363	93
MARQUETTE, MI	65	175	79	145	70	86	122		147	238	269	204
WAUSAU, WI	171	93	133	121	176	225	112	204	58	35	423	

SEE ALSO DISTANCE AND DRIVING TIME MAP ON PAGES 286–287

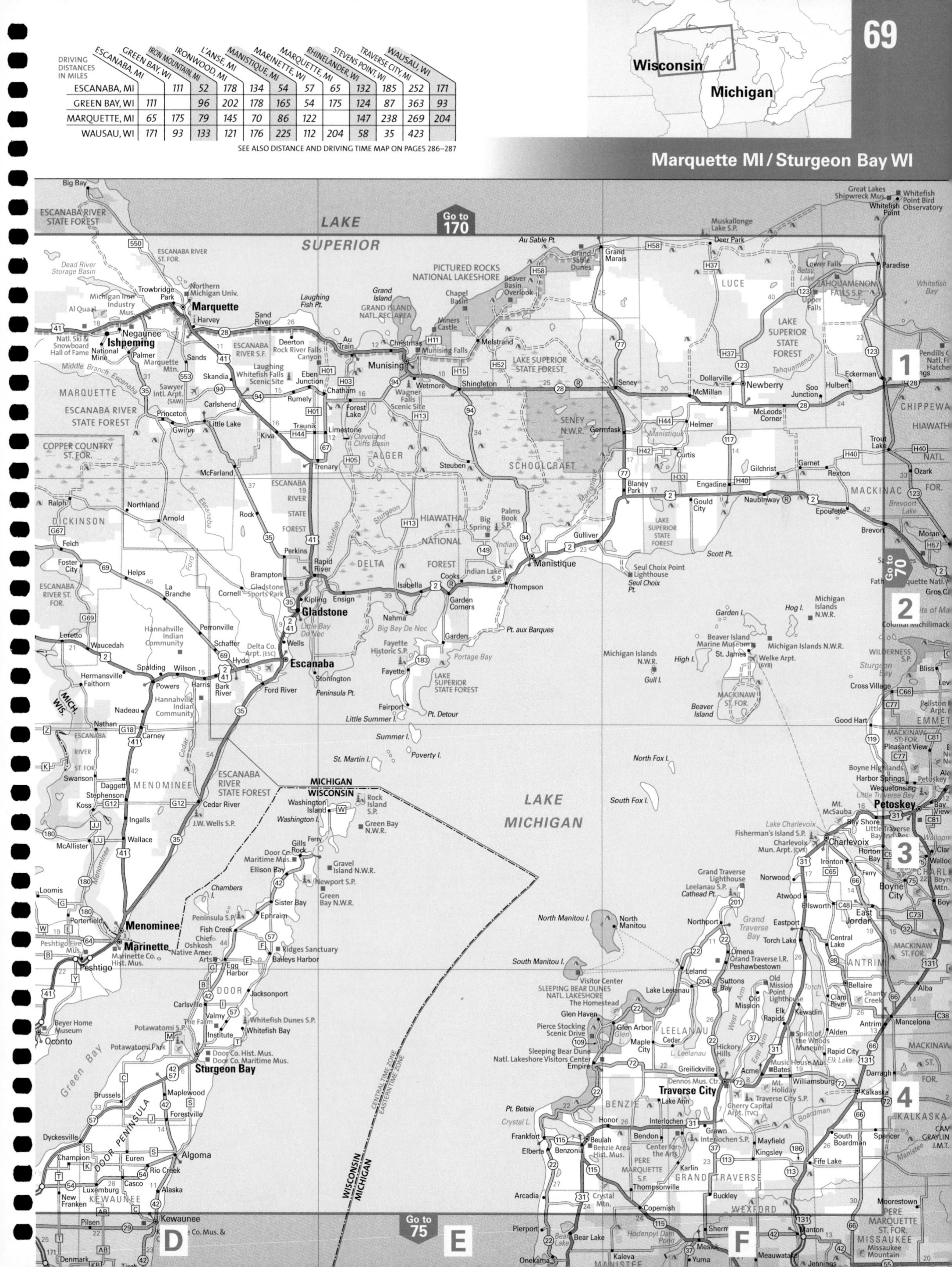

Ontario
Michigan

Sault Ste Marie MI / Traverse City MI

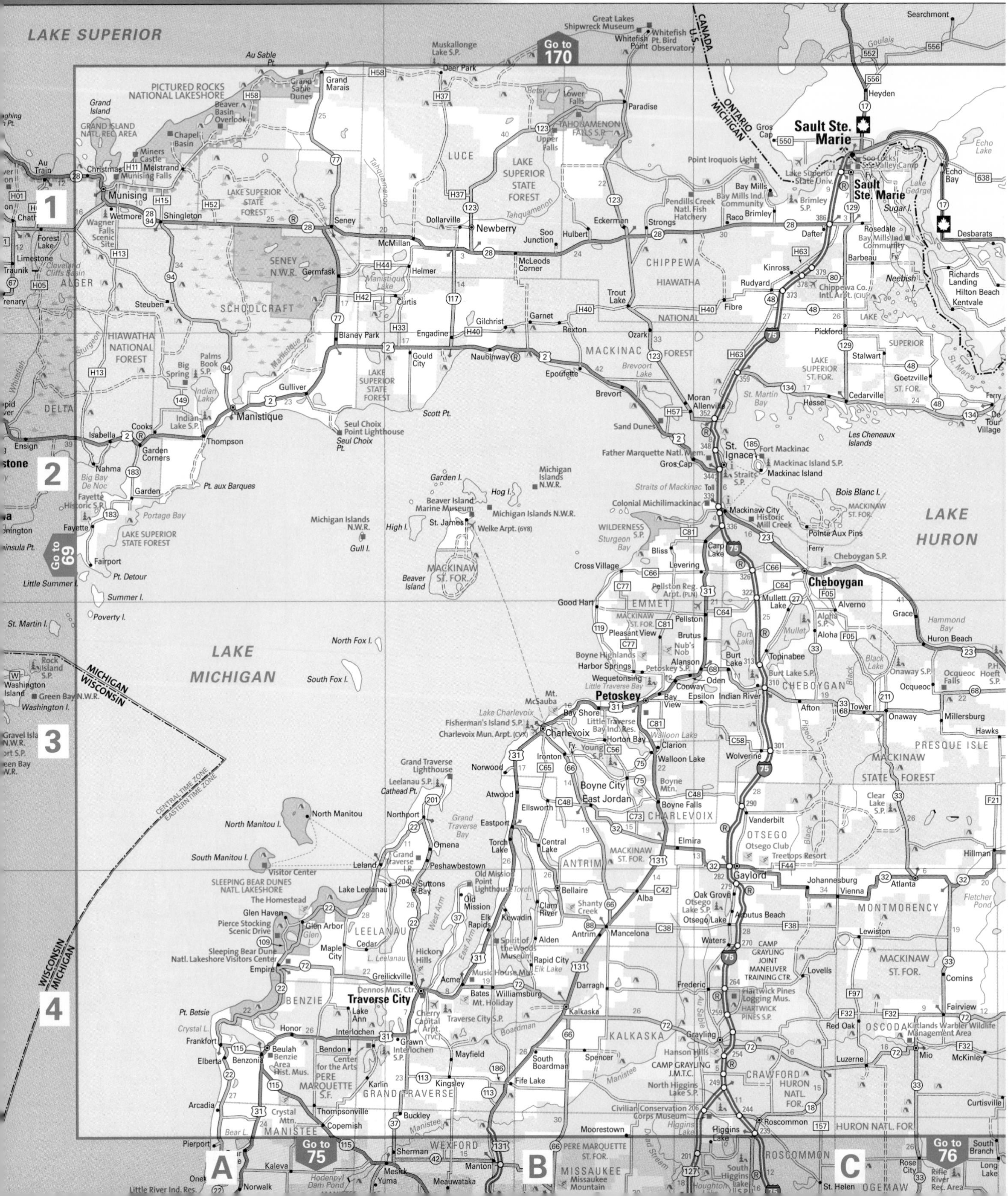

0 mi 10 20 30 40
0 km 10 20 30 40 50 60
One inch equals 18.4 miles
One centimeter equals 11.7 kilometers

Go to 170
Go to 69
Go to 75
Go to 76

LAKE SUPERIOR
LAKE MICHIGAN
LAKE HURON
CANADA U.S.
ONTARIO MICHIGAN
MICHIGAN WISCONSIN
CENTRAL TIME ZONE EASTERN TIME ZONE

1 2 3 4
A B C

Great Lakes Shipwreck Museum
Whitefish Point
Whitefish Pt. Bird Observatory
Muskallonge Lake S.P.
Au Sable Pt.
Deer Park
Grand Marais
PICTURED ROCKS NATIONAL LAKESHORE
Grand Sable Dunes
Beaver Basin Overlook
Grand Island
GRAND ISLAND NATL. REC. AREA
Chapel Basin
Miners Castle
Munising Falls
Christmas
Melstrand
Au Train
Munising
Wetmore
Shingleton
Wagner Falls Scenic Site
Forest Lake
Limestone
Traunik
Chatham
ALGER
Cleveland Cliffs Basin
LAKE SUPERIOR STATE FOREST
SENEY N.W.R.
Germfask
Seney
SCHOOLCRAFT
Steuben
HIAWATHA NATIONAL FOREST
Big Spring
Palms Book S.P.
Indian Lake
Indian Lake S.P.
Manistique
Gulliver
Thompson
Cooks
Isabella
Garden Corners
Ensign
DELTA
Nahma
Big Bay De Noc
Garden
Pt. aux Barques
Fayette Historic S.P.
Fayette
Portage Bay
Fairport
Pt. Detour
Little Summer I.
Summer I.
Poverty I.
St. Martin I.
Rock Island S.P.
Washington Island
Green Bay N.W.R.
Washington I.
Gravel Island N.W.R.
LUCE
LAKE SUPERIOR STATE FOREST
Tahquamenon
Lower Falls
Upper Falls
TAHQUAMENON FALLS S.P.
Paradise
Betsy Lake
Dollarville
Newberry
McMillan
Helmer
Manistique Lake
Curtis
Blaney Park
Engadine
Gould City
Gilchrist
Garnet
Naubinway
Rexton
Soo Junction
Hulbert
Eckerman
Strongs
McLeods Corner
CHIPPEWA
HIAWATHA
NATIONAL
Trout Lake
MACKINAC
FOREST
Ozark
Epoufette
Brevort Lake
Brevort
Moran
Allenville
Sand Dunes
Seul Choix Point Lighthouse
Seul Choix Pt.
Scott Pt.
Pendills Creek Natl. Fish Hatchery
Point Iroquois Light
Bay Mills
Bay Mills Ind. Community
Brimley
Brimley S.P.
Raco
Gros Cap
Sault Ste. Marie
Lake Superior State Univ.
Soo Locks
Sault Ste. Marie
Sugar I.
Lake George
Echo Lake
Echo Bay
Searchmont
Goulais
Heyden
Desbarats
Dafter
Rosedale
Bay Mills Ind. Community
Barbeau
Kinross
Rudyard
Chippewa Co. Intl. Arpt.
Neebish I.
Richards Landing
Hilton Beach
Kentvale
Fibre
Pickford
Stalwart
SUPERIOR
LAKE SUPERIOR ST. FOR.
Goetzville
Cedarville
Hessel
St. Martin Bay
Les Cheneaux Islands
De Tour Village
St. Ignace
Fort Mackinac
Mackinac Island S.P.
Mackinac Island
Straits S.P.
Straits of Mackinac
Father Marquette Natl. Mem.
Gros Cap
Bois Blanc I.
MACKINAW ST. FOR.
Colonial Michilimackinac
Mackinaw City
Historic Mill Creek
Pointe Aux Pins
Cheboygan S.P.
Cheboygan
Michigan Islands N.W.R.
Garden I.
Hog I.
Beaver Island Marine Museum
St. James
Welke Arpt.
High I.
Gull I.
Beaver Island
MACKINAW ST. FOR.
North Fox I.
South Fox I.
WILDERNESS S.P.
Sturgeon Bay
Bliss
Cross Village
Levering
Carp Lake
Good Hart
EMMET
Pellston
Pellston Reg. Arpt.
Mullett Lake
Alverno
Grace
Hammond Bay
Huron Beach
Brutus
Alanson
Harbor Springs
Boyne Highlands
Nub's Nob
Petoskey S.P.
Wequetonsing
Little Traverse Bay
Petoskey
Bay View
Conway
Oden
Burt Lake
Burt Lake S.P.
Topinabee
Aloha
Black Lake
Onaway S.P.
Ocqueoc
Ocqueoc Falls
P.H. Hoeft S.P.
CHEBOYGAN
Indian River
Epsilon
Afton
Tower
Onaway
Millersburg
Hawks
PRESQUE ISLE
MACKINAW STATE FOREST
Mt. McSauba
Bay Shore
Fisherman's Island S.P.
Charlevoix
Charlevoix Mun. Arpt.
Lake Charlevoix
Little Traverse Bay Ind. Res.
Walloon Lake
Horton Bay
Clarion
Young S.P.
Ironton
Norwood
Walloon Lake
Wolverine
Boyne City
Boyne Mtn.
East Jordan
Boyne Falls
Atwood
Ellsworth
CHARLEVOIX
Vanderbilt
Clear Lake S.P.
Grand Traverse Lighthouse
Leelanau S.P.
Cathead Pt.
Northport
Grand Traverse Bay
Eastport
North Manitou I.
North Manitou
South Manitou I.
Visitor Center
Leland
Omena
Peshawbestown
Torch Lake
Central Lake
ANTRIM
MACKINAW ST. FOR.
Elmira
OTSEGO
Otsego Club
Treetops Resort
Gaylord
Johannesburg
Vienna
Atlanta
Hillman
Fletcher Pond
SLEEPING BEAR DUNES NATL. LAKESHORE
The Homestead
Lake Leelanau
Suttons Bay
Old Mission Point Lighthouse
Old Mission
Bellaire
Alba
Oak Grove
Otsego Lake S.P.
Otsego Lake
Arbutus Beach
MONTMORENCY
Lewiston
Glen Haven
Pierce Stocking Scenic Drive
Glen Arbor
Glen Lake
LEELANAU
Sleeping Bear Dune Natl. Lakeshore Visitors Center
Maple City
Cedar
L. Leelanau
Hickory Hills
Elk Rapids
Kewadin
Clam River
Shanty Creek
Spirit of the Woods Museum
Alden
Rapid City
Elk Lake
Antrim
Mancelona
Waters
CAMP GRAYLING JOINT MANEUVER TRAINING CTR.
Lovells
MACKINAW ST. FOR.
Comins
Empire
Greilickville
Acme
Music House Mus.
Williamsburg
Darragh
Frederic
Hartwick Pines Logging Mus.
HARTWICK PINES S.P.
BENZIE
Traverse City
Dennos Mus. Ctr.
Bates
Mt. Holiday
Lake Ann
Cherry Capital Arpt.
Traverse City S.P.
Boardman
Kalkaska
KALKASKA
Grayling
Red Oak
OSCODA
Kirtlands Warbler Wildlife Management Area
Fairview
Pt. Betsie
Crystal L.
Frankfort
Elberta
Honor
Interlochen
Beulah
Benzonia
Benzie Area Hist. Mus.
Bendon
Interlochen Center for the Arts
Grawn
Interlochen S.P.
PERE MARQUETTE S.F.
Karlin
GRAND TRAVERSE
Mayfield
Kingsley
Fife Lake
South Boardman
Spencer
Manistee
Hanson Hills
CAMP GRAYLING J.M.T.C.
North Higgins Lake S.P.
CRAWFORD
HURON NATL. FOR.
Luzerne
Mio
McKinley
Curtisville
Arcadia
Thompsonville
Copemish
Crystal Mtn.
Bear L.
MANISTEE
Buckley
Civilian Conservation Corps Museum
Higgins Lake
Moorestown
Roscommon
HURON NATL. FOR.
Pierport
Onekama
Kaleva
Norwalk
Little River Ind. Res.
Hodenpyl Dam Pond
Sherman
WEXFORD
Mesick
Yuma
Manton
Meauwataka
PERE MARQUETTE ST. FOR.
MISSAUKEE
Missaukee Mountain
South Higgins Lake S.P.
Houghton
ROSCOMMON
St. Helen
OGEMAW
Rose City
Rifle River Rec. Area
South Branch
Long Lake

DRIVING DISTANCES IN MILES	ALPENA, MI	CHEBOYGAN, MI	GAYLORD, MI	GRAYLING, MI	MACKINAW CITY, MI	MANISTIQUE, MI	MUNISING, MI	PETOSKEY, MI	ROGERS CITY, MI	SAULT STE. MARIE, MI	SUDBURY, ON	TRAVERSE CITY, MI
ALPENA, MI		78	76	95	94	187	215	101	38	148	334	141
MACKINAW CITY, MI	94	16	60	87		95	123	38	58	57	242	106
SAULT STE. MARIE, MI	148	71	114	142	57	120	120	93	112		186	160
TRAVERSE CITY, MI	141	115	65	52	106	198	226	67	135	160	346	

SEE ALSO DISTANCE AND DRIVING TIME MAP ON PAGES 286–287

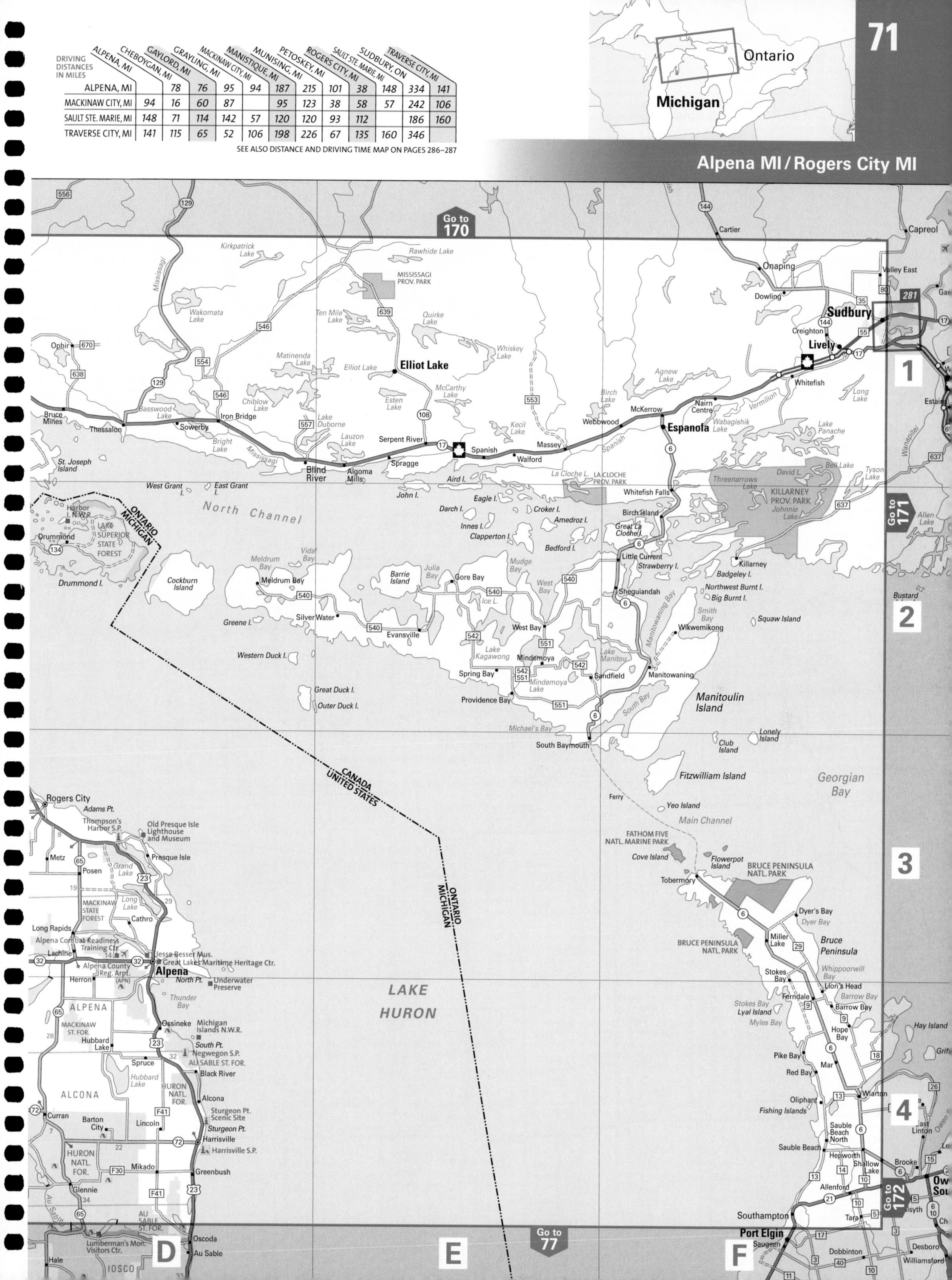

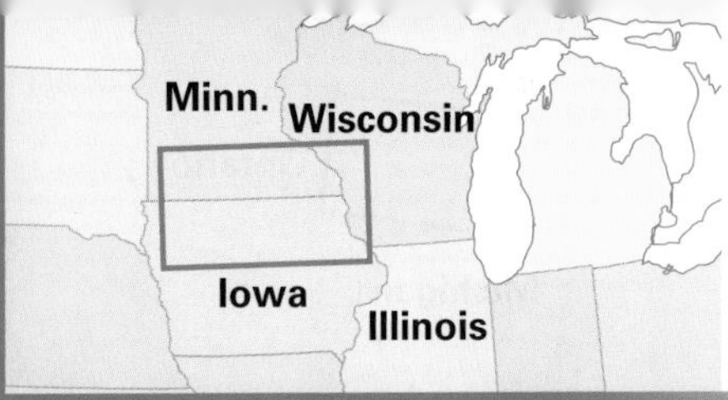

Minn. Wisconsin Iowa Illinois

0 mi 10 20 30 40
0 km 10 20 30 40 50 60

One inch equals 18.4 miles
One centimeter equals 11.7 kilometers

Mankato MN / Fort Dodge IA

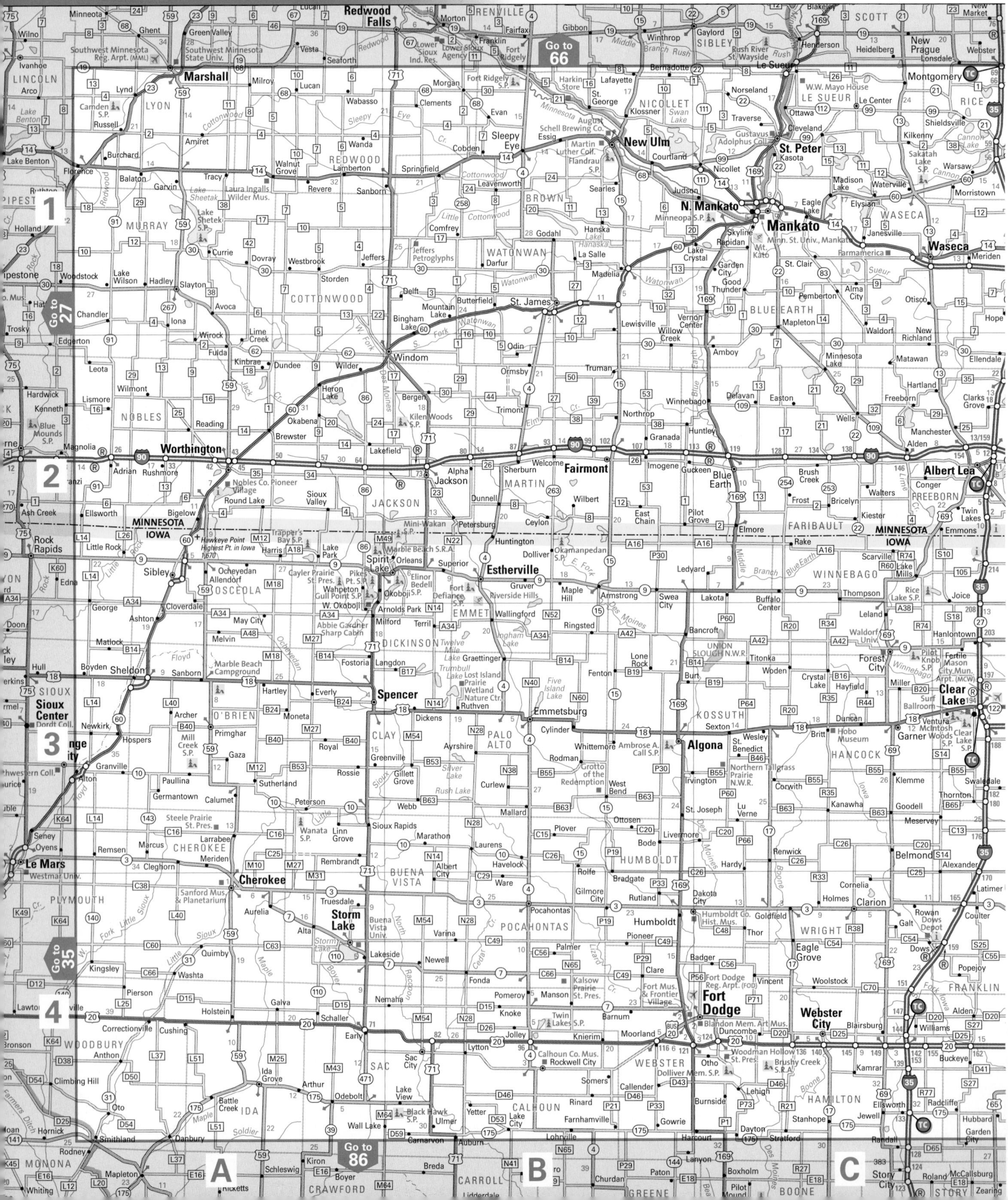

Go to 66
Go to 27
Go to 35
Go to 86

1 2 3 4 A B C

Redwood Falls, Marshall, New Ulm, St. Peter, N. Mankato, Mankato, Waseca, Worthington, Windom, St. James, Fairmont, Blue Earth, Albert Lea, Jackson, Spirit Lake, Estherville, Spencer, Emmetsburg, Algona, Clear Lake, Sheldon, Sioux Center, Le Mars, Cherokee, Storm Lake, Humboldt, Fort Dodge, Webster City, Eagle Grove, Clarion

MINNESOTA
IOWA

DRIVING DISTANCES IN MILES	ALBERT LEA, MN	DECORAH, IA	DUBUQUE, IA	FORT DODGE, IA	LA CROSSE, WI	MANKATO, MN	MASON CITY, IA	ROCHESTER, MN	SPENCER, IA	WATERLOO, IA	WINONA, MN	WORTHINGTON, MN
FORT DODGE, IA	124	186	200		245	138	97	183	95	108	225	148
MANKATO, MN	56	151	253	138	149		100	80	123	186	128	108
ROCHESTER, MN	62	68	170	183	71	80	103		189	116	51	174
WATERLOO, IA	130	79	93	108	138	186	79	116	189		144	244

SEE ALSO DISTANCE AND DRIVING TIME MAP ON PAGES 286–287

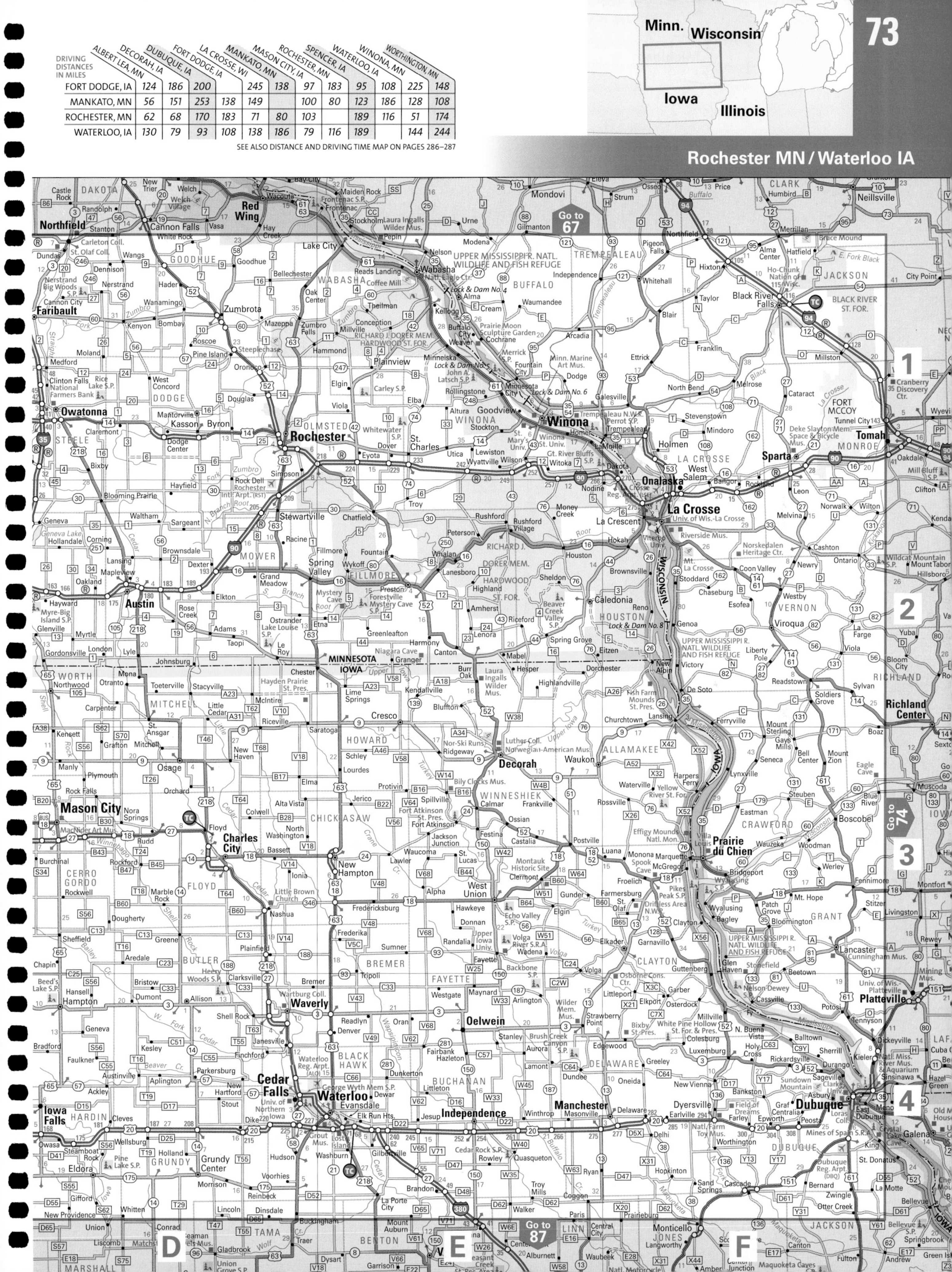

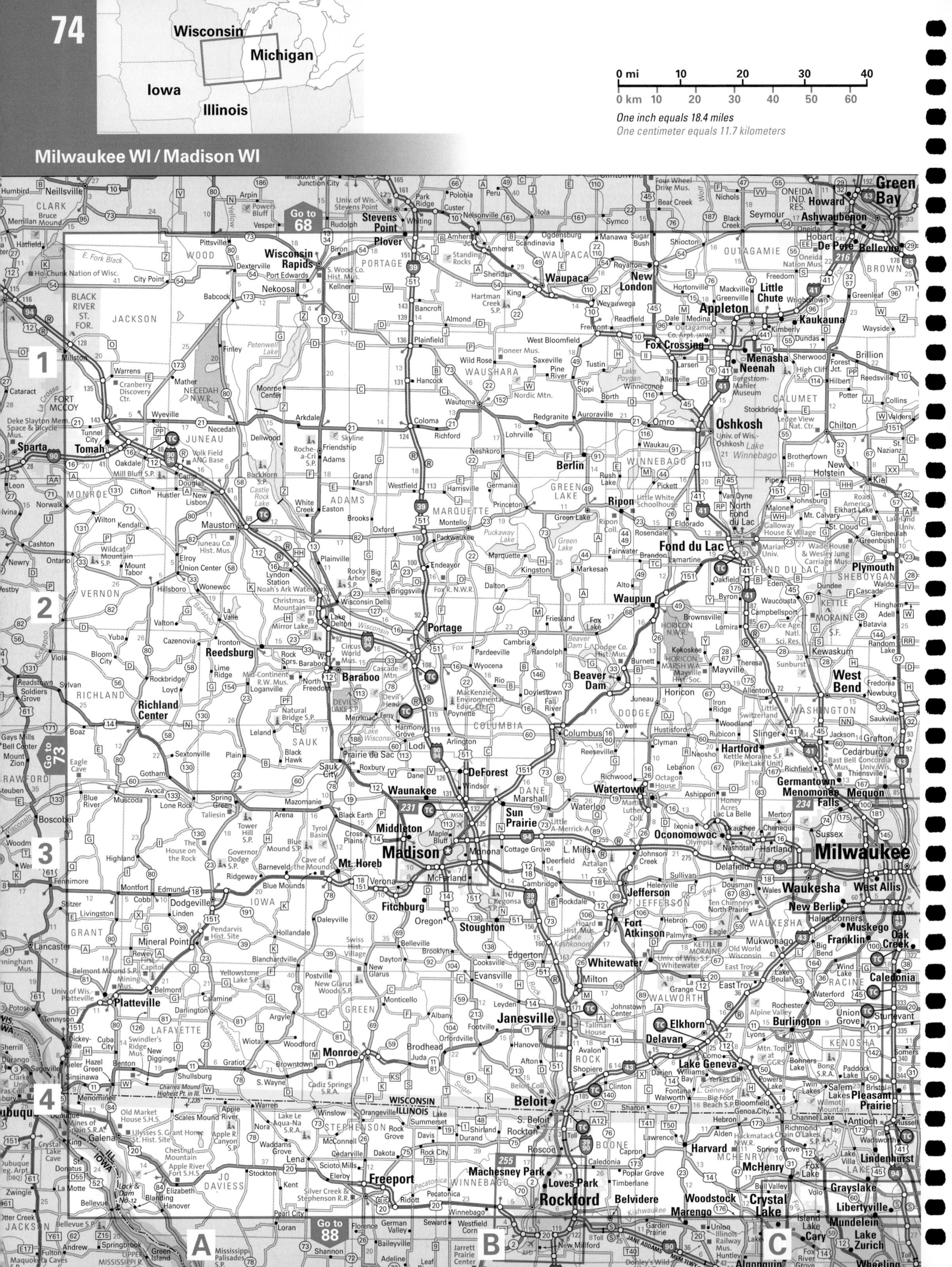
Wisconsin
Michigan
Iowa
Illinois
0 mi 10 20 30 40
0 km 10 20 30 40 50 60
One inch equals 18.4 miles
One centimeter equals 11.7 kilometers
Go to 68
Go to 73
Go to 88
Green Bay
Appleton
Oshkosh
Fond du Lac
Milwaukee
Madison
Waukesha
Janesville
Beloit
Rockford
Portage
Baraboo
Wisconsin Rapids
Stevens Point
Tomah
Sparta
Platteville
Monroe
Freeport
Galena
Dubuque
Waupaca
Neenah
Menasha
Ripon
Waupun
Beaver Dam
Watertown
West Bend
Sheboygan
Plymouth
Kenosha
Racine
Elkhorn
Lake Geneva
Burlington
Fort Atkinson
Whitewater
Jefferson
Stoughton
Fitchburg
Middleton
Sun Prairie
Reedsburg
Richland Center
Mauston
WISCONSIN
ILLINOIS

DRIVING DISTANCES IN MILES

	CADILLAC, MI	DUBUQUE, IA	GRAND RAPIDS, MI	GREEN BAY, WI	KALAMAZOO, MI	MADISON, WI	MILWAUKEE, WI	MUSKEGON, MI	OSHKOSH, WI	ROCKFORD, IL	SHEBOYGAN, WI	TOMAH, WI
GRAND RAPIDS, MI	99	364		393	53	335	277	40	363	271	332	424
GREEN BAY, WI	492	229	393		362	135	115	400	50	211	61	162
MADISON, WI	434	93	335	135	304		78	341	86	78	132	98
MILWAUKEE, WI	377	167	277	115	247	78		285	87	95	54	168

SEE ALSO DISTANCE AND DRIVING TIME MAP ON PAGES 286–287

Ontario
Michigan

0 mi 10 20 30 40
0 km 10 20 30 40 50 60

One inch equals 18.4 miles
One centimeter equals 11.7 kilometers

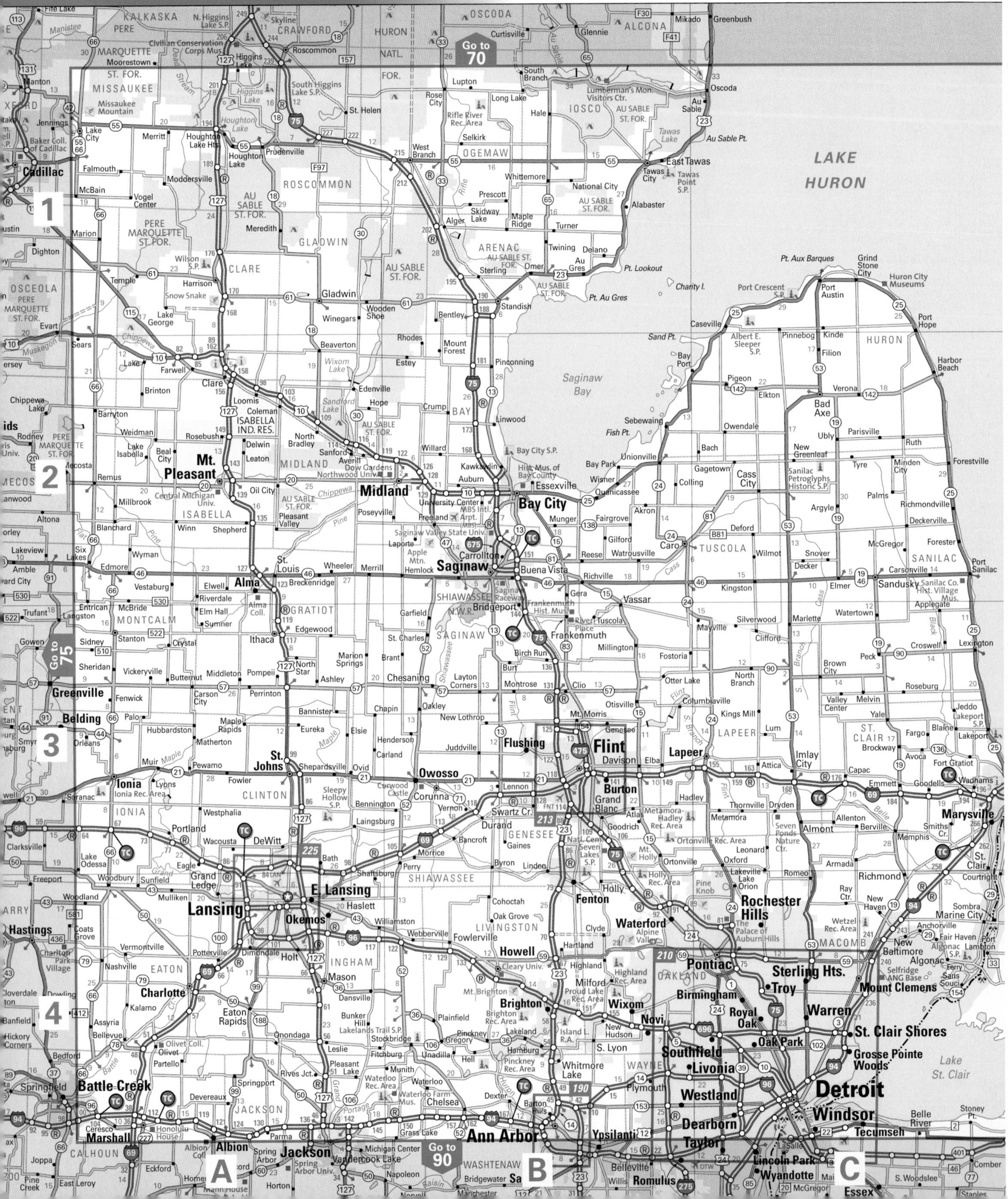

Detroit MI / Lansing MI

Go to 70

Go to 75

Go to 90

1
2
3
4

A B C

LAKE HURON

Saginaw Bay

Lake St. Clair

Lansing
E. Lansing
Flint
Saginaw
Bay City
Midland
Detroit
Windsor
Ann Arbor
Pontiac
Jackson
Battle Creek
Mt. Pleasant

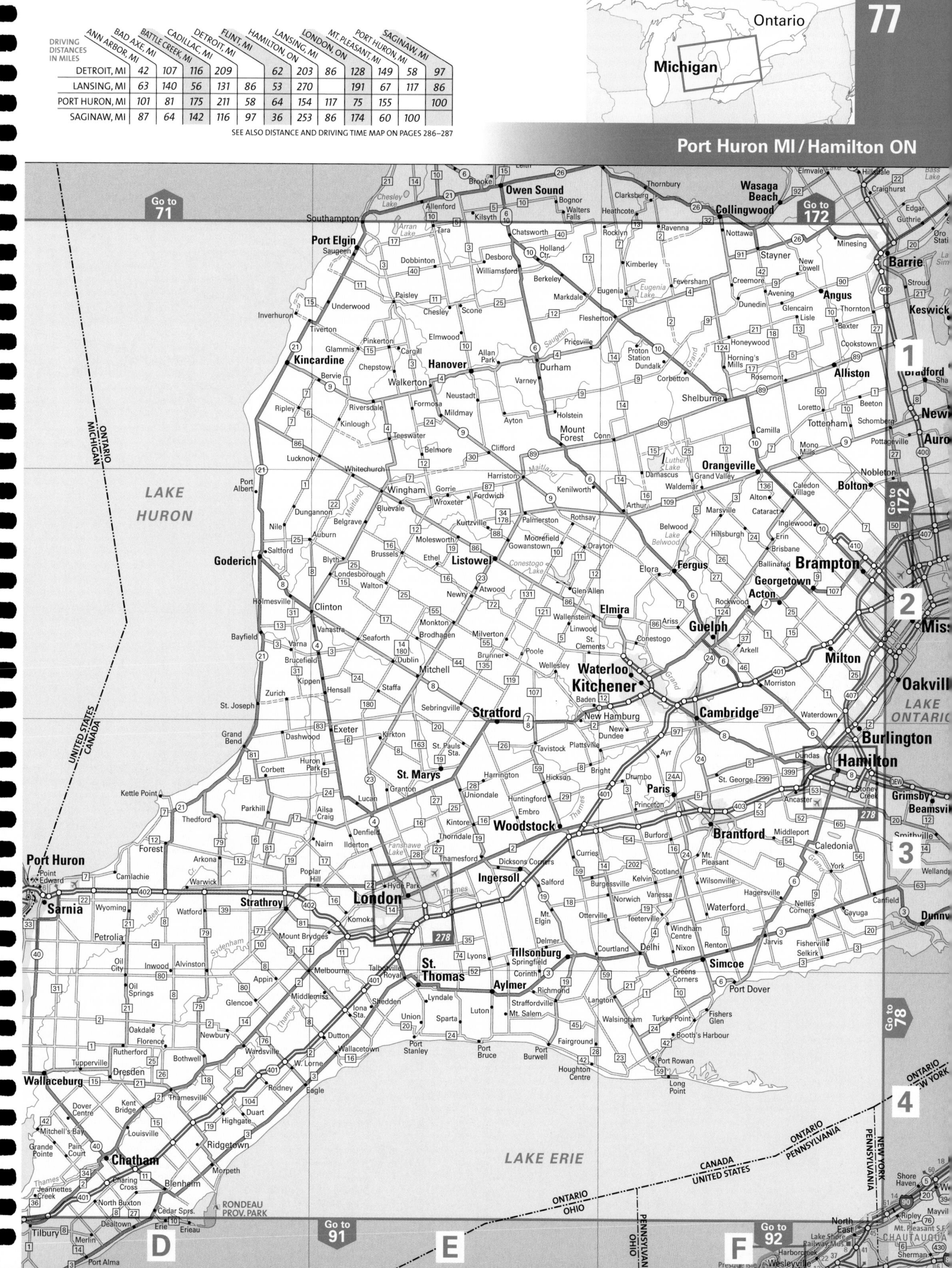

DRIVING DISTANCES IN MILES	ANN ARBOR, MI	BAD AXE, MI	BATTLE CREEK, MI	CADILLAC, MI	DETROIT, MI	FLINT, MI	HAMILTON, ON	LANSING, MI	LONDON, ON	MT. PLEASANT, MI	PORT HURON, MI	SAGINAW, MI
DETROIT, MI	42	107	116	209		62	203	86	128	149	58	97
LANSING, MI	63	140	56	131	86	53	270		191	67	117	86
PORT HURON, MI	101	81	175	211	58	64	154	117	75	155		100
SAGINAW, MI	87	64	142	116	97	36	253	86	174	60	100	

SEE ALSO DISTANCE AND DRIVING TIME MAP ON PAGES 286–287

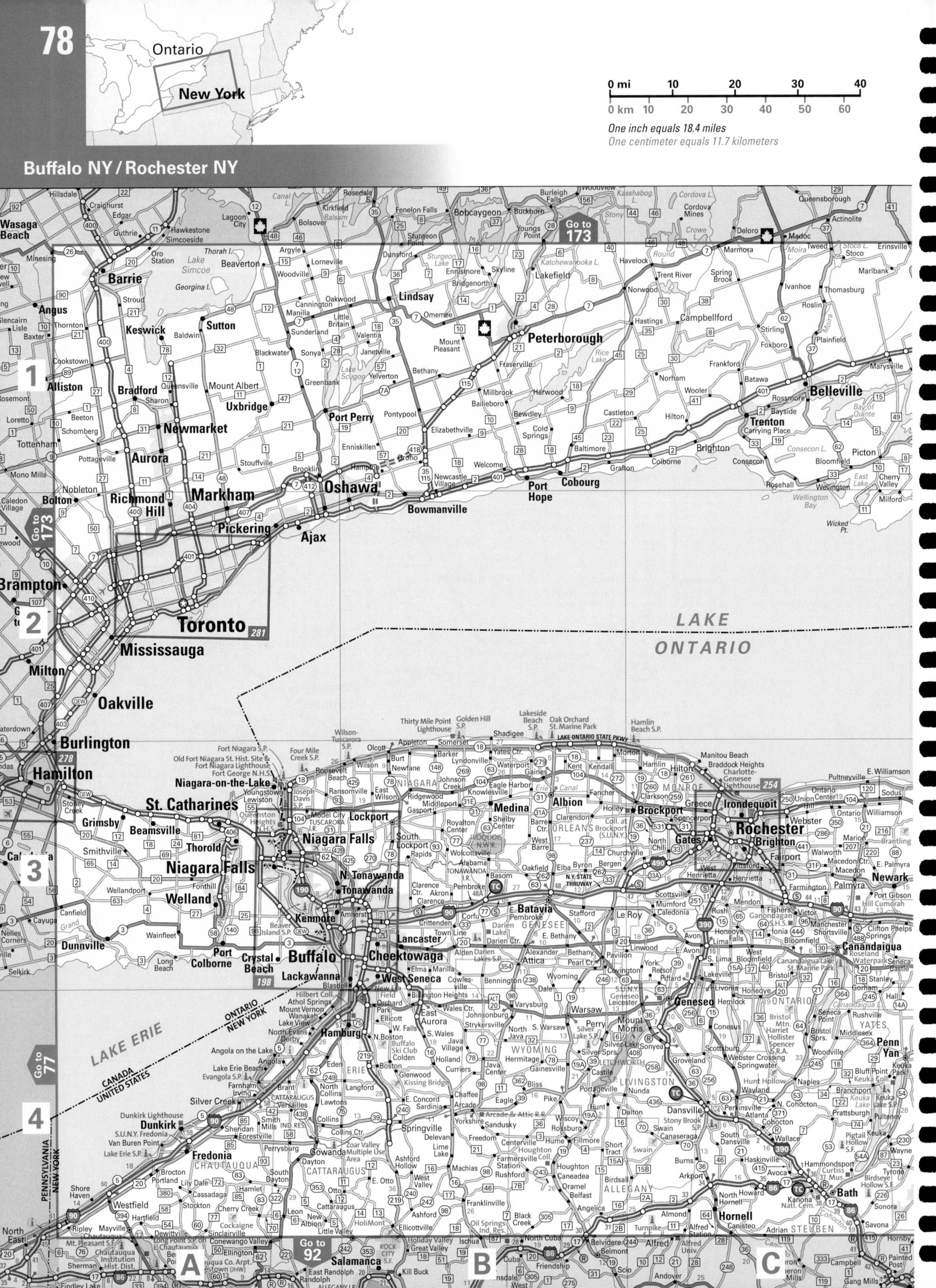
Ontario
New York
0 mi 10 20 30 40
0 km 10 20 30 40 50 60
One inch equals 18.4 miles
One centimeter equals 11.7 kilometers
Go to 173
Go to 77
Go to 92
1
2
3
4
A
B
C
LAKE ONTARIO
LAKE ERIE
ONTARIO
NEW YORK
CANADA
UNITED STATES
PENNSYLVANIA
NEW YORK
Wasaga Beach
Barrie
Angus
Alliston
Bradford
Keswick
Sutton
Newmarket
Aurora
Uxbridge
Lindsay
Peterborough
Port Perry
Oshawa
Markham
Richmond Hill
Pickering
Ajax
Bowmanville
Port Hope
Cobourg
Belleville
Trenton
Picton
Bolton
Brampton
Toronto
Mississauga
Milton
Oakville
Burlington
Hamilton
St. Catharines
Niagara-on-the-Lake
Niagara Falls
Welland
Thorold
Grimsby
Beamsville
Port Colborne
Dunnville
Crystal Beach
Buffalo
Lackawanna
Cheektowaga
West Seneca
Lancaster
Kenmore
Tonawanda
N. Tonawanda
Lockport
Medina
Albion
Brockport
Batavia
Le Roy
Rochester
Irondequoit
Greece
Gates
Brighton
Fairport
Webster
Newark
Canandaigua
Geneseo
Dansville
Hornell
Bath
Penn Yan
Hamburg
Dunkirk
Fredonia
Salamanca
Westfield
Lake Ontario State Pkwy
N.Y. State Thruway

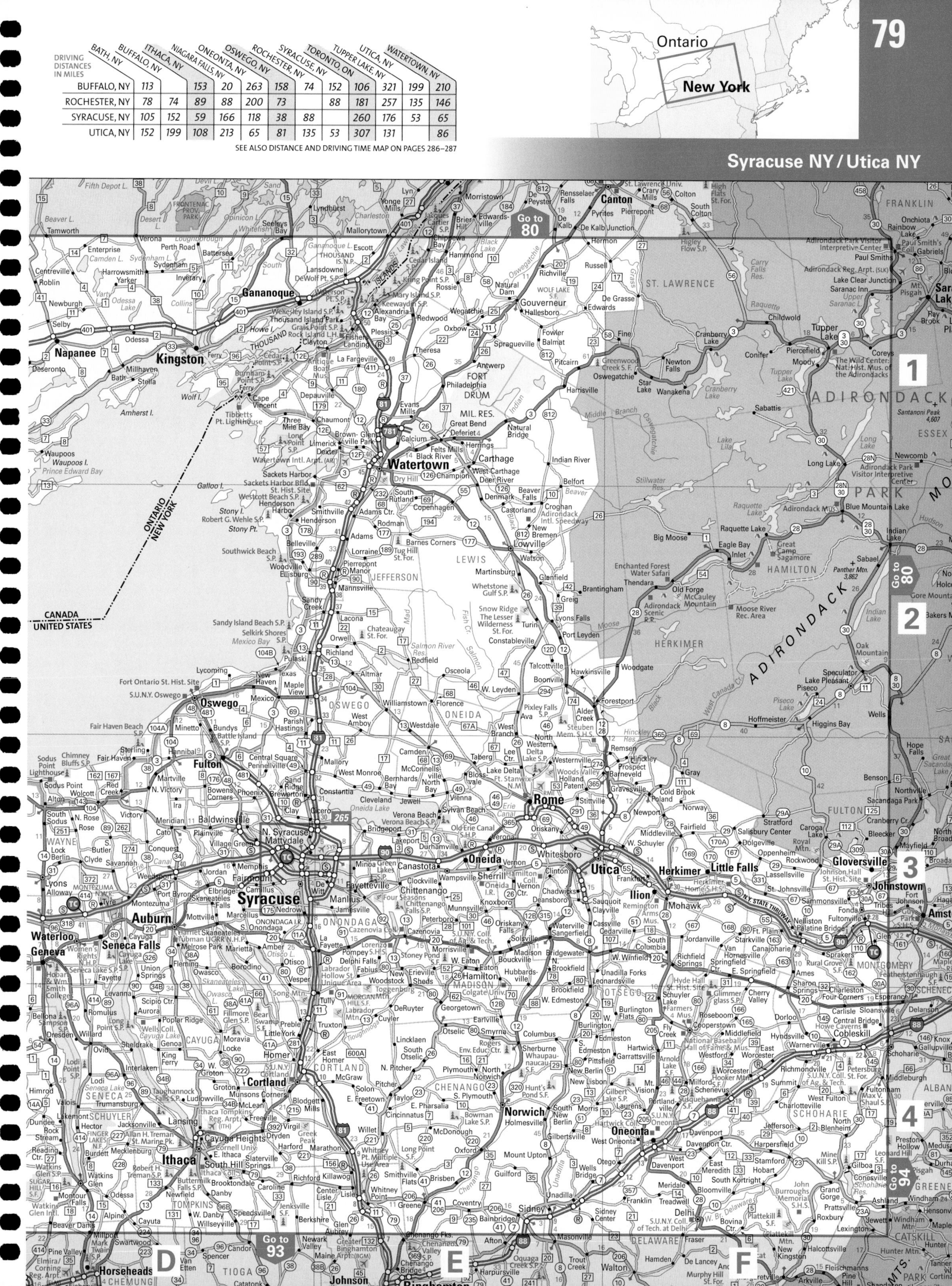

DRIVING DISTANCES IN MILES

	BATH, NY	BUFFALO, NY	ITHACA, NY	NIAGARA FALLS, NY	ONEONTA, NY	OSWEGO, NY	ROCHESTER, NY	SYRACUSE, NY	TORONTO, ON	TUPPER LAKE, NY	UTICA, NY	WATERTOWN, NY
BUFFALO, NY	113		153	20	263	158	74	152	106	321	199	210
ROCHESTER, NY	78	74	89	88	200	73		88	181	257	135	146
SYRACUSE, NY	105	152	59	166	118	38	88		260	176	53	65
UTICA, NY	152	199	108	213	65	81	135	53	307	131		86

SEE ALSO DISTANCE AND DRIVING TIME MAP ON PAGES 286–287

Watertown NY / Lake Placid NY

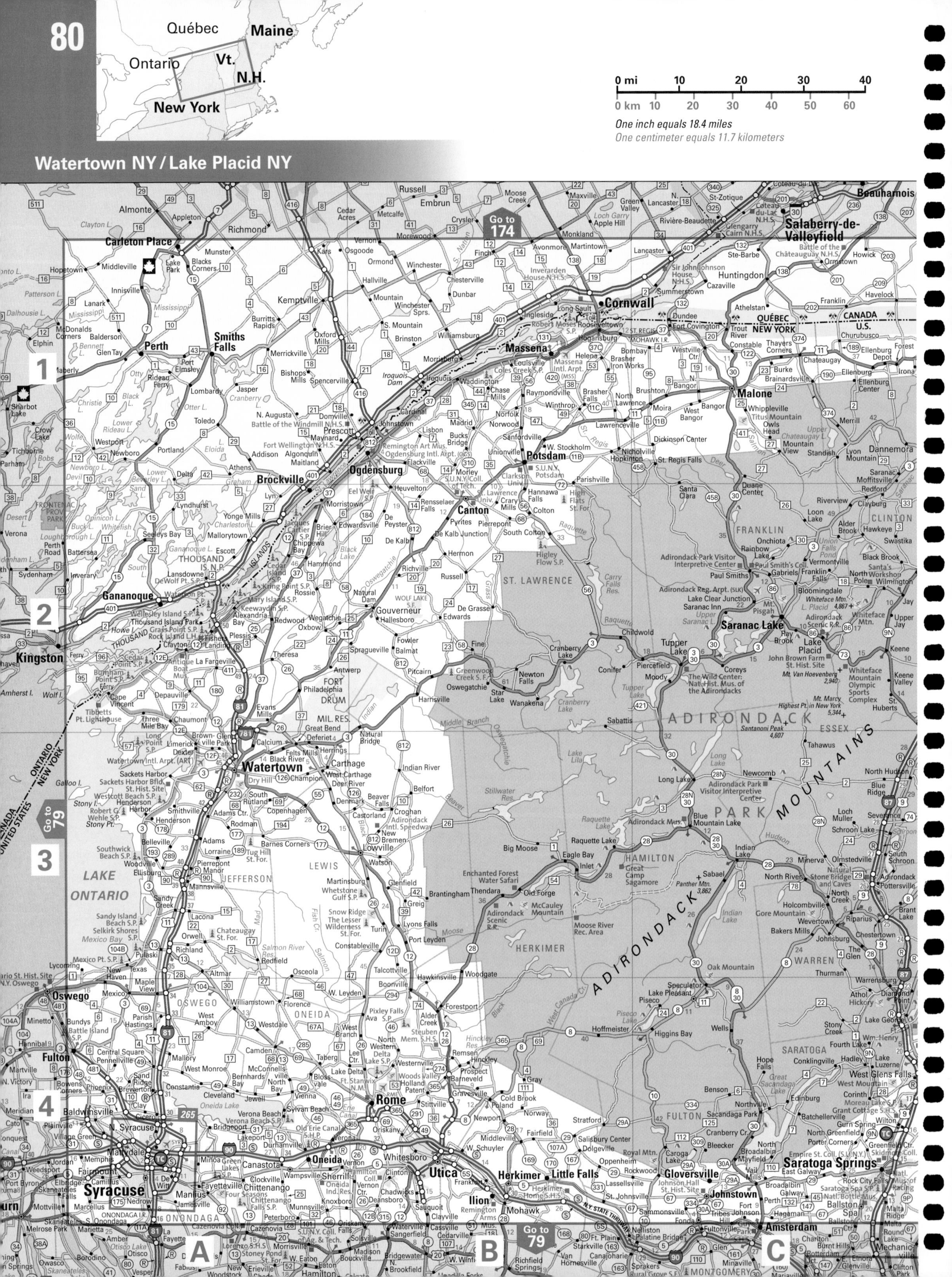

DRIVING DISTANCES IN MILES

	BURLINGTON, VT	CONCORD, NH	LAKE PLACID, NY	OGDENSBURG, NY	PLATTSBURGH, NY	RUTLAND, VT	ST. JOHNSBURY, VT	SARATOGA SPRS., NY	SYRACUSE, NY	UTICA, NY	WATERTOWN, NY	WHITE RIVER JCT., VT
BURLINGTON, VT		150	68	208	51	69	76	115	230	183	195	91
CONCORD, NH	150		215	357	198	104	104	173	280	228	312	59
LAKE PLACID, NY	68	215		96	49	133	141	106	192	148	126	156
WATERTOWN, NY	195	312	126	68	167	244	319	179	65	86		289

SEE ALSO DISTANCE AND DRIVING TIME MAP ON PAGES 286–287

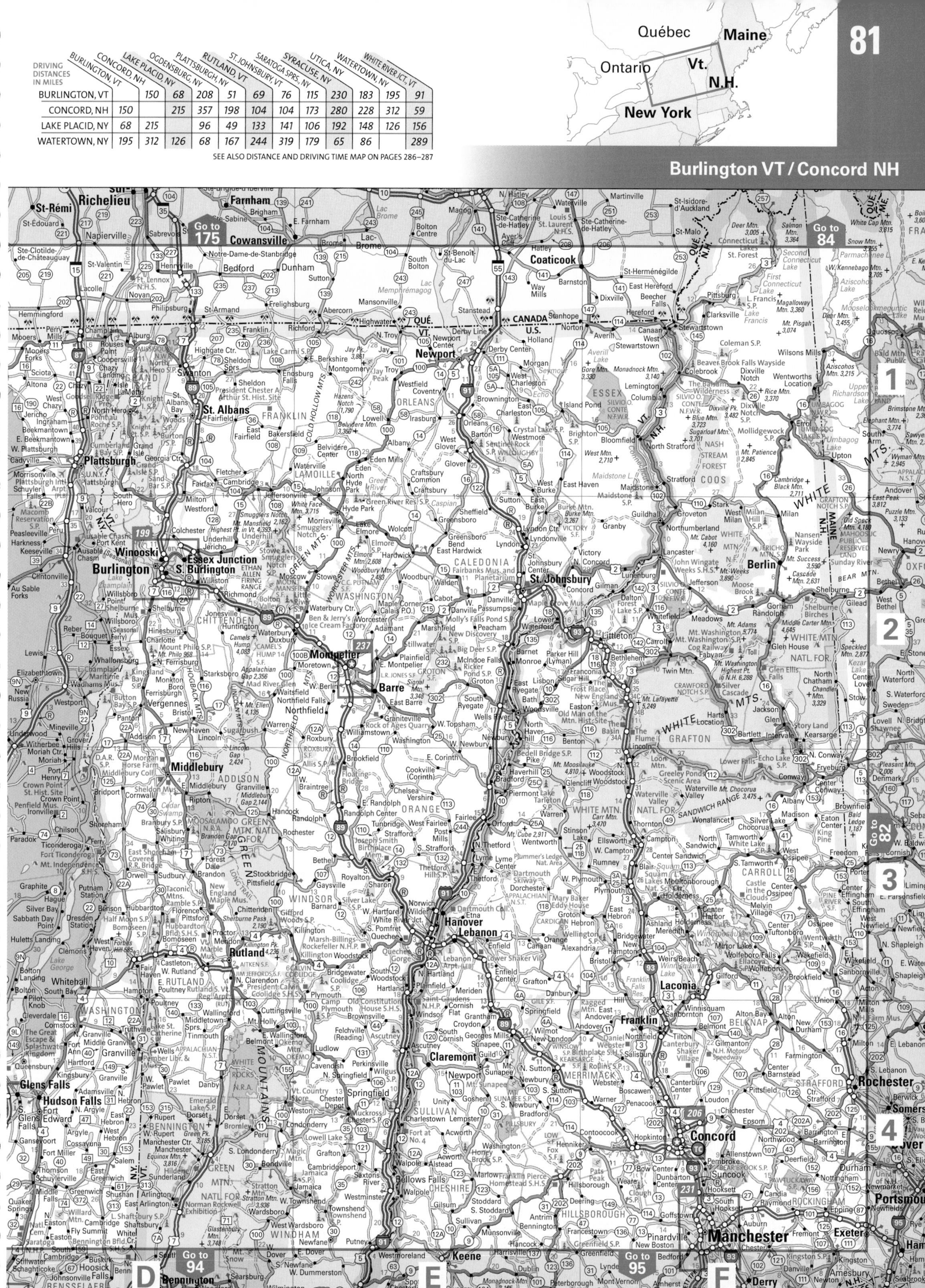

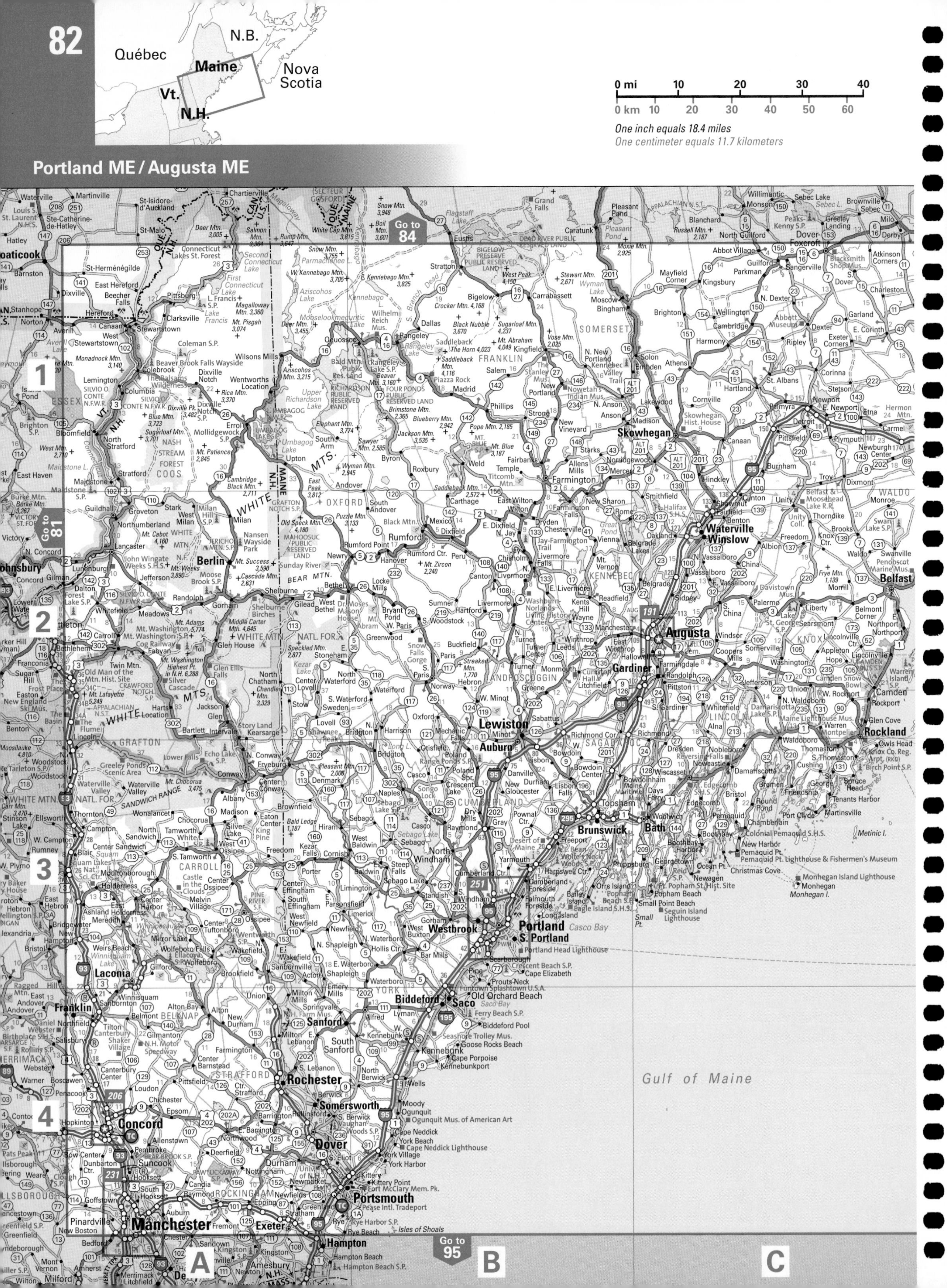

Québec
N.B.
Maine
Nova Scotia
Vt.
N.H.
0 mi 10 20 30 40
0 km 10 20 30 40 50 60
One inch equals 18.4 miles
One centimeter equals 11.7 kilometers
Go to 84
Go to 81
Go to 95
1
2
3
4
A
B
C
Augusta
Portland
S. Portland
Lewiston
Auburn
Waterville
Winslow
Skowhegan
Farmington
Rumford
Berlin
Gardiner
Brunswick
Bath
Rockland
Belfast
Camden
Biddeford
Saco
Sanford
Rochester
Somersworth
Dover
Portsmouth
Exeter
Hampton
Concord
Manchester
Laconia
Franklin
Westbrook
Topsham
Old Orchard Beach
Kennebunk
Kennebunkport
Wells
Ogunquit
York Harbor
Kittery
Freeport
Yarmouth
Norway
Bethel
Rangeley
Conway
Lancaster
Colebrook
Stewartstown
Pittsburg
Gorham
Casco Bay
Gulf of Maine
Saco Bay
Isles of Shoals
Monhegan I.
Metinic I.
WHITE MTS.
WHITE MTN. NATL. FOR.
FRANKLIN
OXFORD
SOMERSET
KENNEBEC
ANDROSCOGGIN
CUMBERLAND
SAGADAHOC
LINCOLN
KNOX
WALDO
YORK
CARROLL
STRAFFORD
ROCKINGHAM
BELKNAP
GRAFTON
COOS
ESSEX

DRIVING DISTANCES IN MILES

	AUGUSTA, ME	BANGOR, ME	BAR HARBOR, ME	BERLIN, NH	CALAIS, ME	CONCORD, NH	CONWAY, NH	LEWISTON, ME	MACHIAS, ME	PORTLAND, ME	PORTSMOUTH, NH	WATERVILLE, ME
AUGUSTA, ME		77	120	110	173	141	97	35	158	58	110	20
BANGOR, ME	77		45	160	97	214	170	108	83	131	184	56
BAR HARBOR, ME	120	45		204	112	257	214	151	71	175	227	100
PORTLAND, ME	58	131	175	93	228	83	62	36	213		53	84

SEE ALSO DISTANCE AND DRIVING TIME MAP ON PAGES 286–287

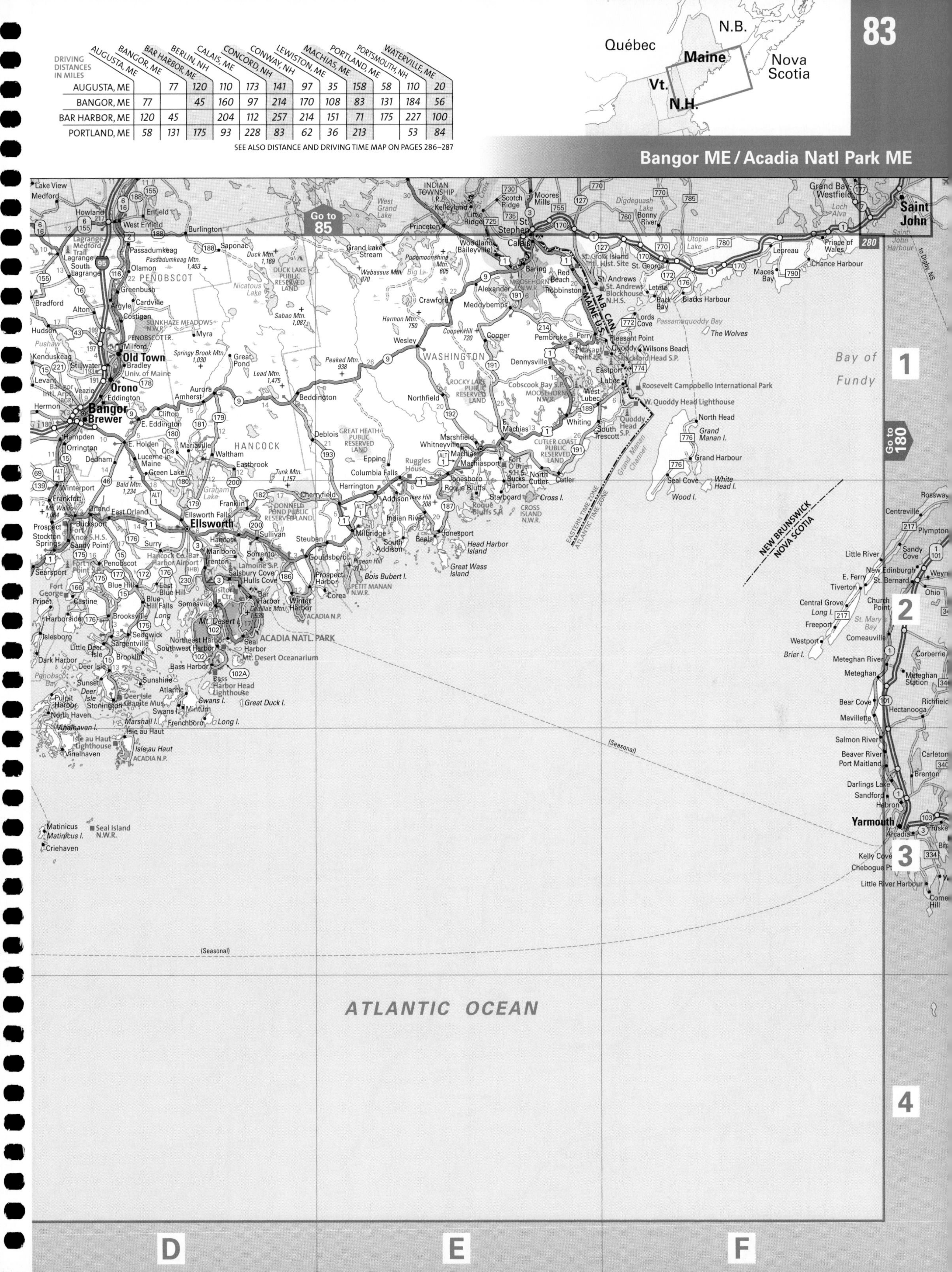

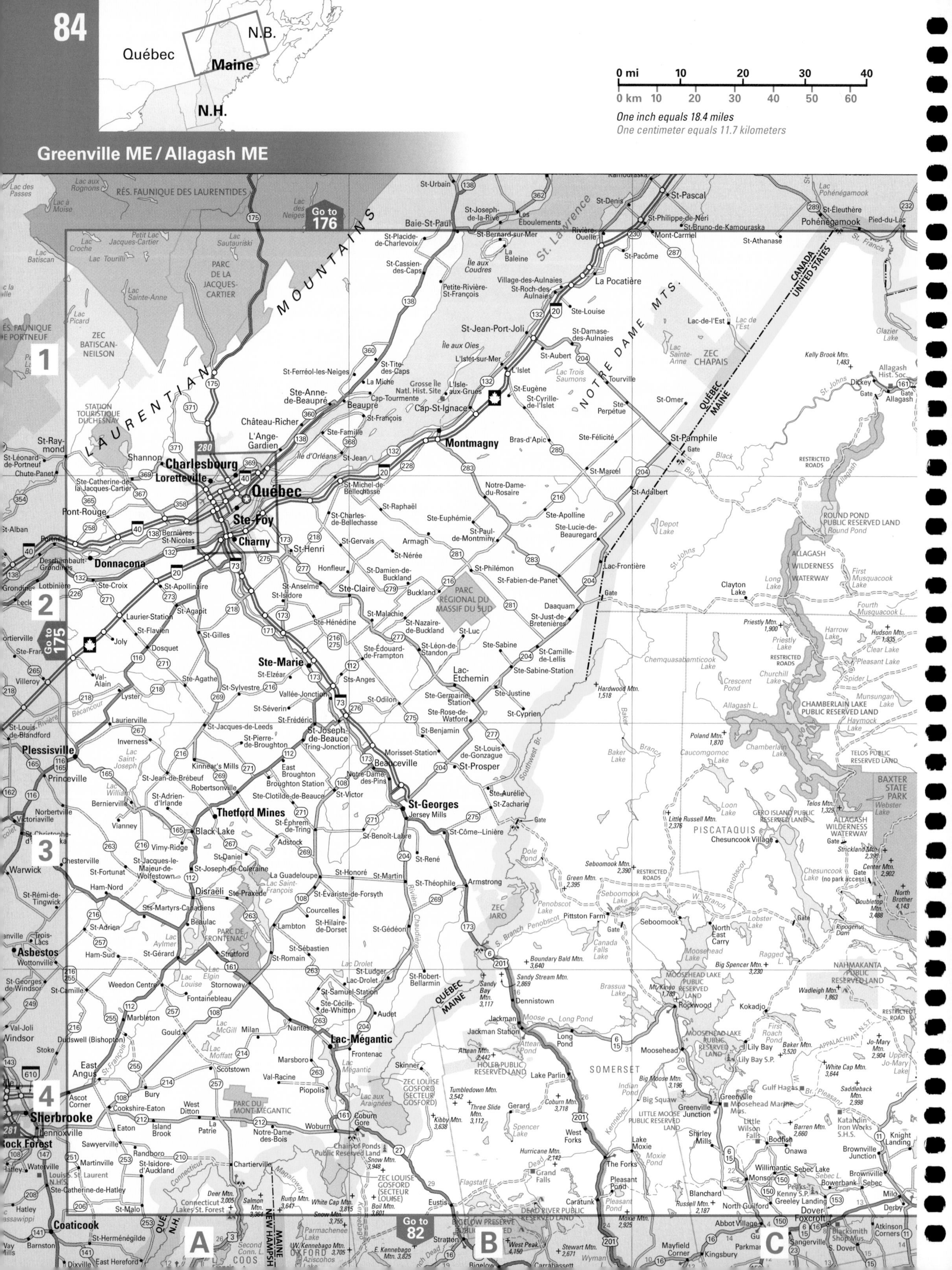
84
Québec
N.B.
Maine
N.H.
Greenville ME / Allagash ME
0 mi 10 20 30 40
0 km 10 20 30 40 50 60
One inch equals 18.4 miles
One centimeter equals 11.7 kilometers
Go to 176
Go to 175
Go to 82
RÉS. FAUNIQUE DES LAURENTIDES
PARC DE LA JACQUES-CARTIER
ZEC BATISCAN-NEILSON
LAURENTIAN MOUNTAINS
NOTRE DAME MTS.
St. Lawrence
CANADA UNITED STATES
QUÉBEC MAINE
ZEC CHAPAIS
PARC RÉGIONAL DU MASSIF DU SUD
ROUND POND PUBLIC RESERVED LAND
ALLAGASH WILDERNESS WATERWAY
CHAMBERLAIN LAKE PUBLIC RESERVED LAND
TELOS PUBLIC RESERVED LAND
BAXTER STATE PARK
GERO ISLAND PUBLIC RESERVED LAND
PISCATAQUIS
SOMERSET
ZEC JARO
MOOSEHEAD LAKE PUBLIC RESERVED LAND
NAHMAKANTA PUBLIC RESERVED LAND
HOLEB PUBLIC RESERVED LAND
LITTLE MOOSE PUBLIC RESERVED LAND
ZEC LOUISE GOSFORD (SECTEUR GOSFORD)
PARC DU MONT-MÉGANTIC
PARC DE FRONTENAC
DEAD RIVER PUBLIC RESERVED LAND
BIGELOW PRESERVE
Québec
Ste-Foy
Charny
Charlesbourg
Loretteville
Montmagny
La Pocatière
St-Jean-Port-Joli
Baie-St-Paul
Ste-Anne-de-Beaupré
Donnacona
Plessisville
Thetford Mines
Ste-Marie
St-Georges
Beauceville
Lac-Mégantic
Sherbrooke
Coaticook
Asbestos
Lac-Etchemin
St-Pamphile
Pohénégamook
Allagash
Chesuncook Village
Rockwood
Greenville
Jackman
The Forks
Dover-Foxcroft
Monson
Kokadjo
A
B
C
1
2
3
4

DRIVING DISTANCES IN MILES	BANGOR, ME	CALAIS, ME	CARIBOU, ME	FREDERICTON, NB	GREENVILLE, ME	HOULTON, ME	JACKMAN, ME	LINCOLN, ME	MADAWASKA, ME	MILLINOCKET, ME	PRESQUE ISLE, ME	QUÉBEC, QC
HOULTON, ME	122	91	55	73	155		204	83	102	73	42	286
LINCOLN, ME	51	77	135	114	83	83	132		174	35	122	231
MADAWASKA, ME	214	207	50	167	212	102	269	174		164	62	182
PRESQUE ISLE, ME	162	133	13	113	166	42	215	122	62	113		246

SEE ALSO DISTANCE AND DRIVING TIME MAP ON PAGES 286–287

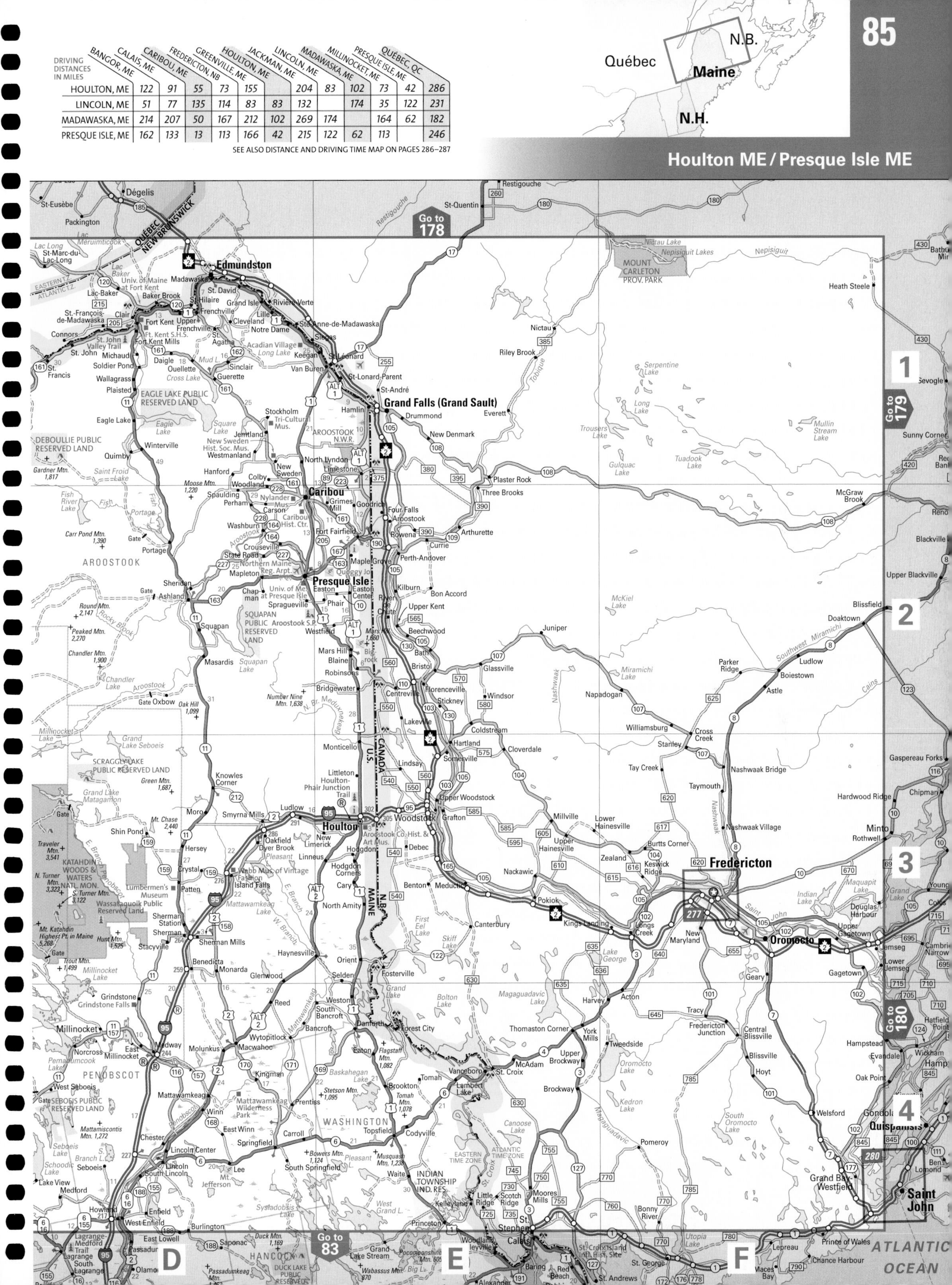

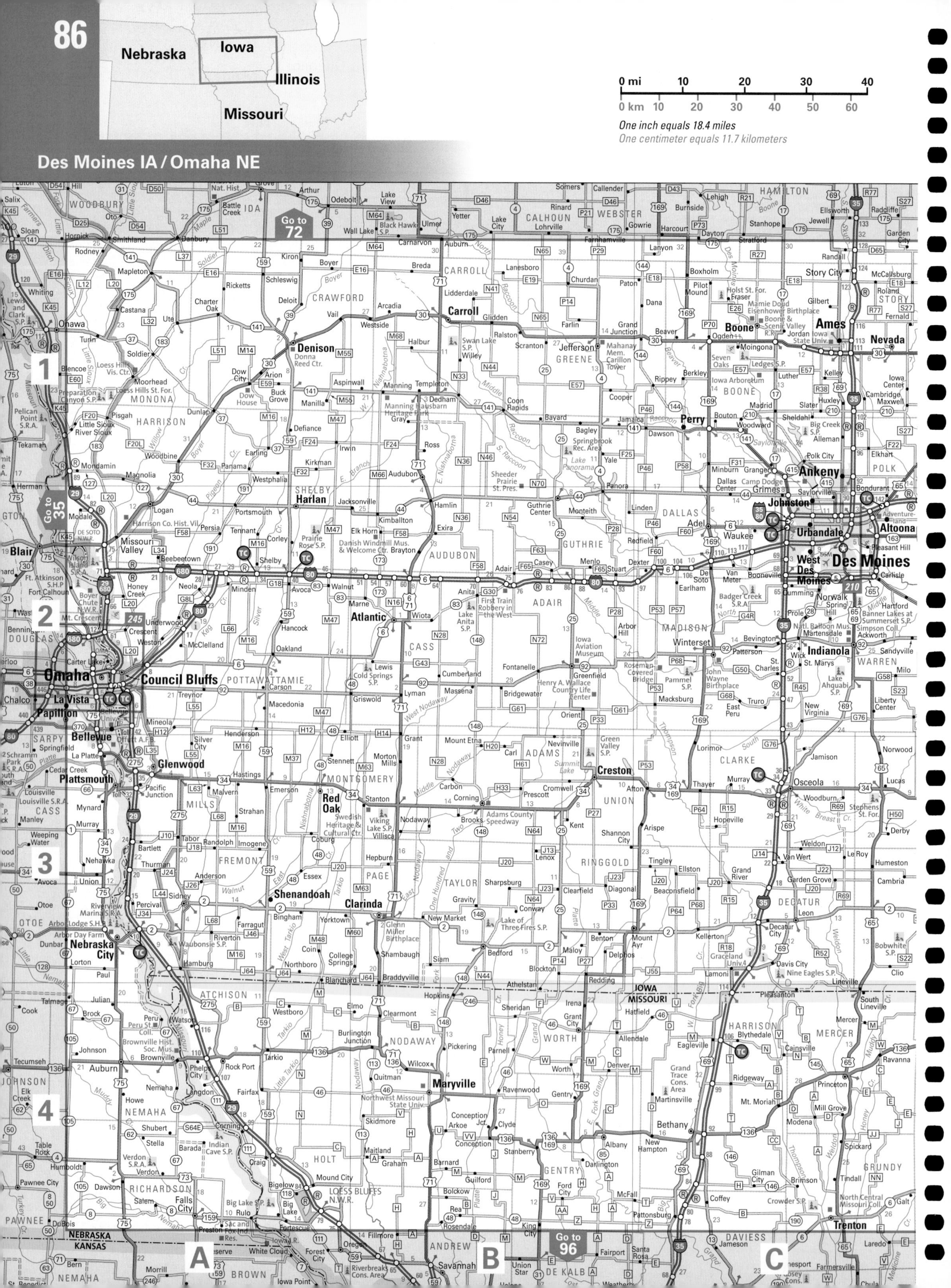
Nebraska
Iowa
Illinois
Missouri
0 mi 10 20 30 40
0 km 10 20 30 40 50 60
One inch equals 18.4 miles
One centimeter equals 11.7 kilometers
Go to 72
Go to 35
Go to 96
WOODBURY
CRAWFORD
CARROLL
CALHOUN
WEBSTER
HAMILTON
GREENE
BOONE
STORY
MONONA
HARRISON
SHELBY
AUDUBON
GUTHRIE
DALLAS
POLK
POTTAWATTAMIE
CASS
ADAIR
MADISON
WARREN
MILLS
MONTGOMERY
ADAMS
UNION
CLARKE
FREMONT
PAGE
TAYLOR
RINGGOLD
DECATUR
ATCHISON
NODAWAY
WORTH
HARRISON
MERCER
HOLT
GENTRY
GRUNDY
ANDREW
DE KALB
DAVIESS
DOUGLAS
SARPY
CASS
OTOE
JOHNSON
NEMAHA
RICHARDSON
PAWNEE
BROWN
NEBRASKA
KANSAS
IOWA
MISSOURI
Omaha
Council Bluffs
Des Moines
West Des Moines
Ames
Ankeny
Urbandale
Johnston
Altoona
Boone
Carroll
Denison
Harlan
Atlantic
Red Oak
Shenandoah
Clarinda
Creston
Osceola
Indianola
Winterset
Perry
Glenwood
Plattsmouth
Bellevue
Papillion
La Vista
Nebraska City
Maryville
Blair
Missouri Valley
Bethany
Trenton
Auburn
Falls City
Savannah
A
B
C
1
2
3
4

DRIVING DISTANCES IN MILES	AMES, IA	BURLINGTON, IA	CARROLL, IA	CEDAR RAPIDS, IA	CRESTON, IA	DAVENPORT, IA	DES MOINES, IA	IOWA CITY, IA	KIRKSVILLE, MO	MARYVILLE, MO	OMAHA, NE	OTTUMWA, IA
CEDAR RAPIDS, IA	108	106	173		211	87	129	28	170	276	266	111
DES MOINES, IA	34	157	90	129	81	171		113	145	146	136	86
IOWA CITY, IA	136	82	195	28	195	59	113		143	260	250	83
OMAHA, NE	171	328	97	266	98	308	136	250	275	112		221

SEE ALSO DISTANCE AND DRIVING TIME MAP ON PAGES 286–287

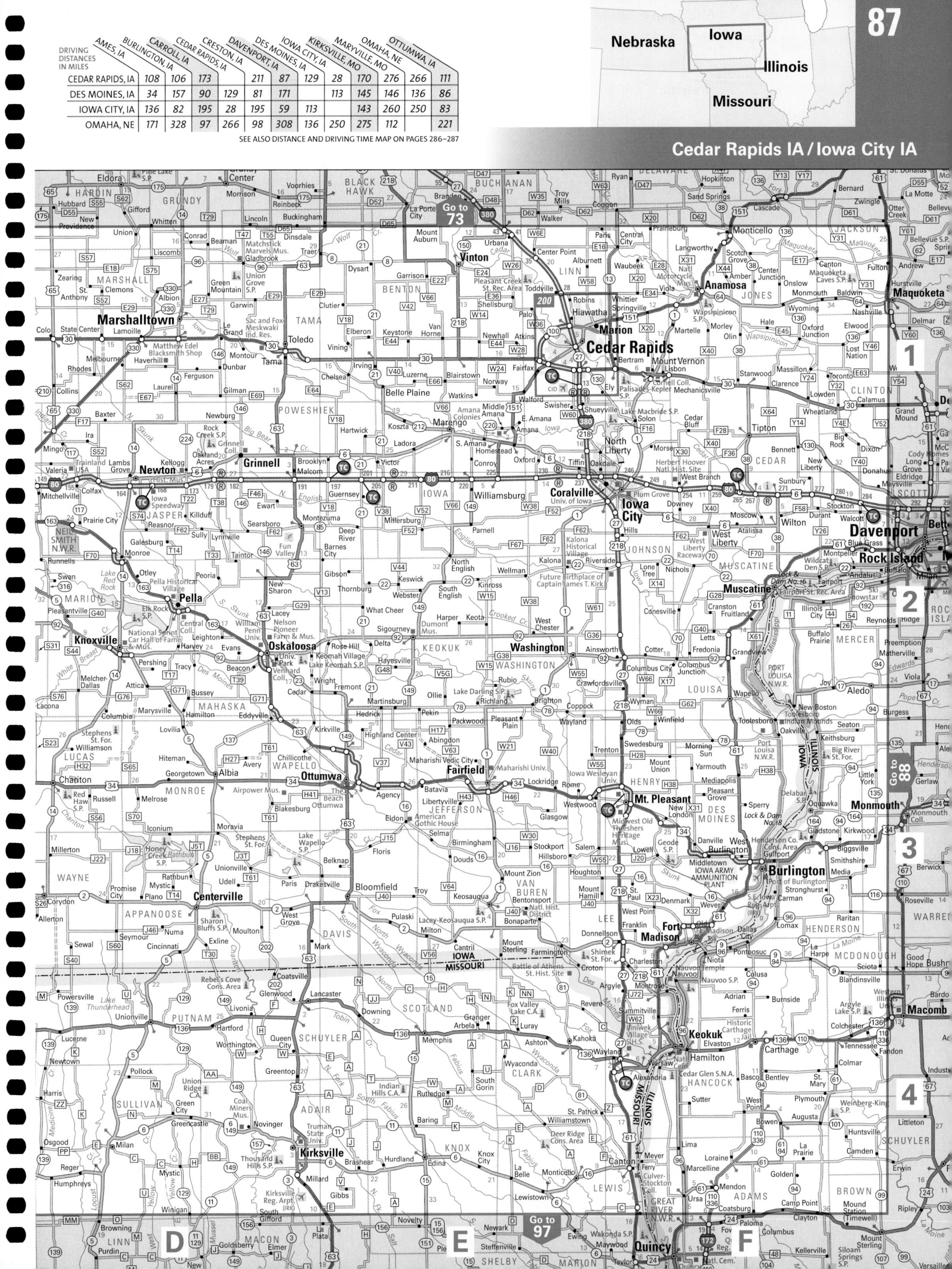

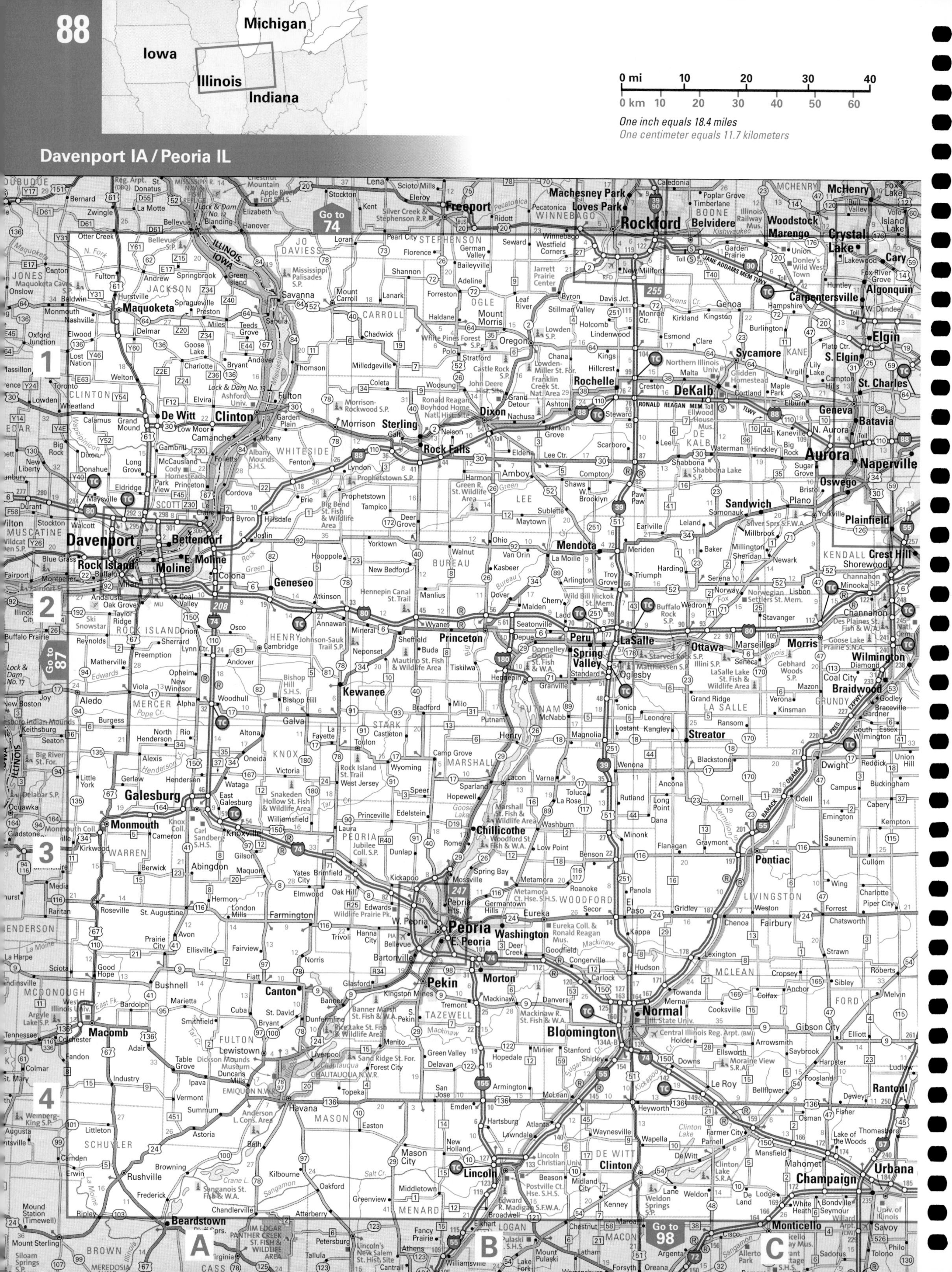
Michigan
Iowa
Illinois
Indiana
0 mi 10 20 30 40
0 km 10 20 30 40 50 60
One inch equals 18.4 miles
One centimeter equals 11.7 kilometers
Go to 74
Go to 87
Go to 98
Davenport
Rock Island
Moline
Bettendorf
E. Moline
Clinton
De Witt
Maquoketa
Savanna
Freeport
Rockford
Machesney Park
Loves Park
Belvidere
Woodstock
Marengo
McHenry
Crystal Lake
Algonquin
Carpentersville
Elgin
S. Elgin
St. Charles
Geneva
Batavia
Aurora
Naperville
Oswego
Plainfield
Sycamore
DeKalb
Rochelle
Dixon
Sterling
Rock Falls
Mendota
Princeton
Peru
LaSalle
Ottawa
Morris
Spring Valley
Streator
Pontiac
Kewanee
Geneseo
Galesburg
Monmouth
Macomb
Peoria
E. Peoria
Pekin
Washington
Chillicothe
Canton
Bloomington
Normal
Lincoln
Clinton
Champaign
Urbana
Rantoul
Monticello
Beardstown
Havana
Wilmington
Braidwood
Dwight
Crest Hill
Shorewood
Minooka
Channahon
A
B
C
1
2
3
4

DRIVING DISTANCES IN MILES

	BLOOMINGTON, IL	CHAMPAIGN, IL	CHICAGO, IL	DAVENPORT, IA	JOLIET, IL	KALAMAZOO, MI	KOKOMO, IN	LAFAYETTE, IN	LA SALLE, IL	PEORIA, IL	ROCKFORD, IL	SOUTH BEND, IN
CHAMPAIGN, IL	54		141	192	115	255	145	94	117	94	189	198
CHICAGO, IL	135	141		170	40	150	158	121	98	168	86	93
PEORIA, IL	41	94	168	99	132	291	235	184	63		135	234
SOUTH BEND, IN	201	198	93	248	105	76	86	104	164	234	183	

SEE ALSO DISTANCE AND DRIVING TIME MAP ON PAGES 286–287

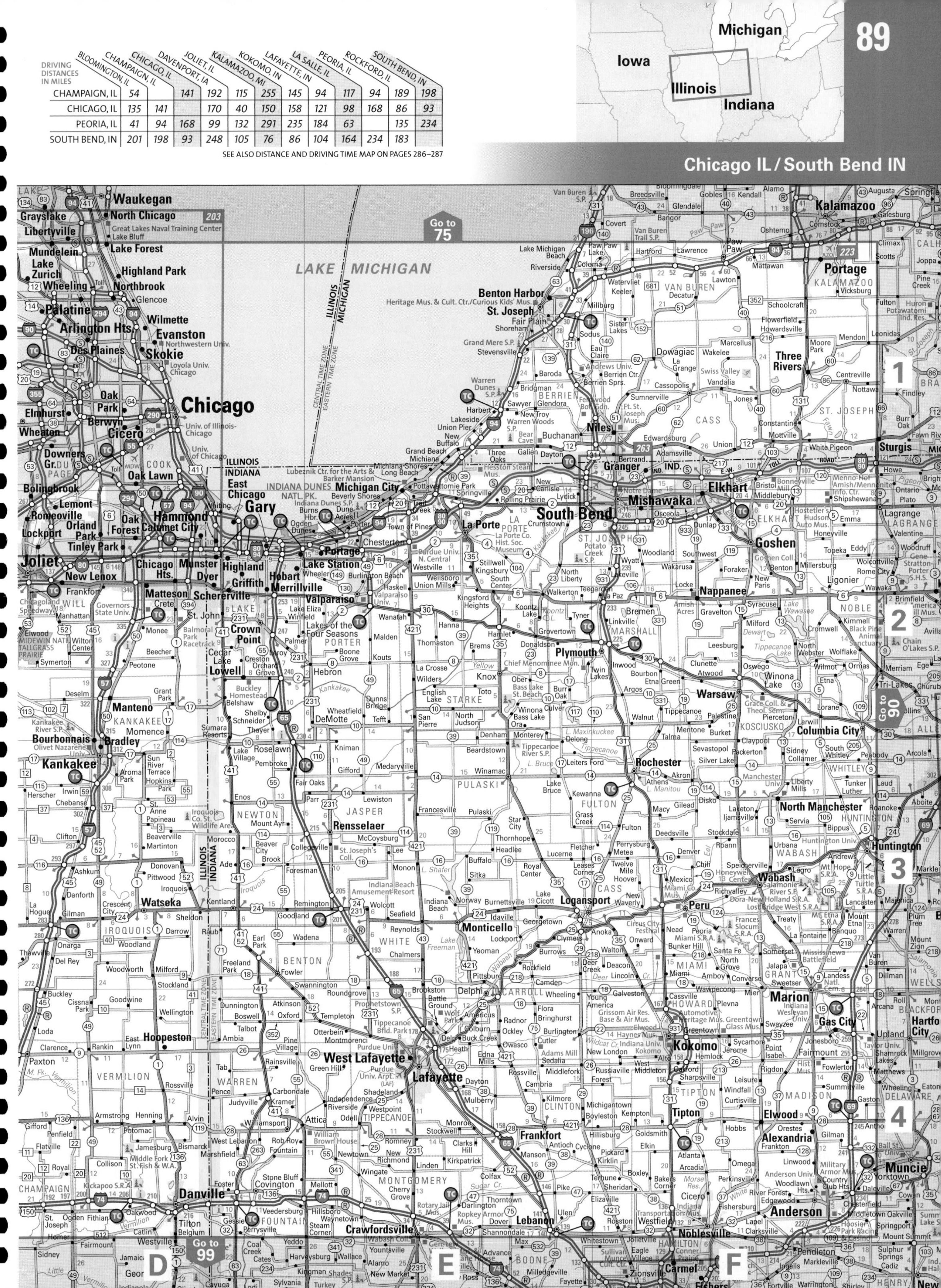

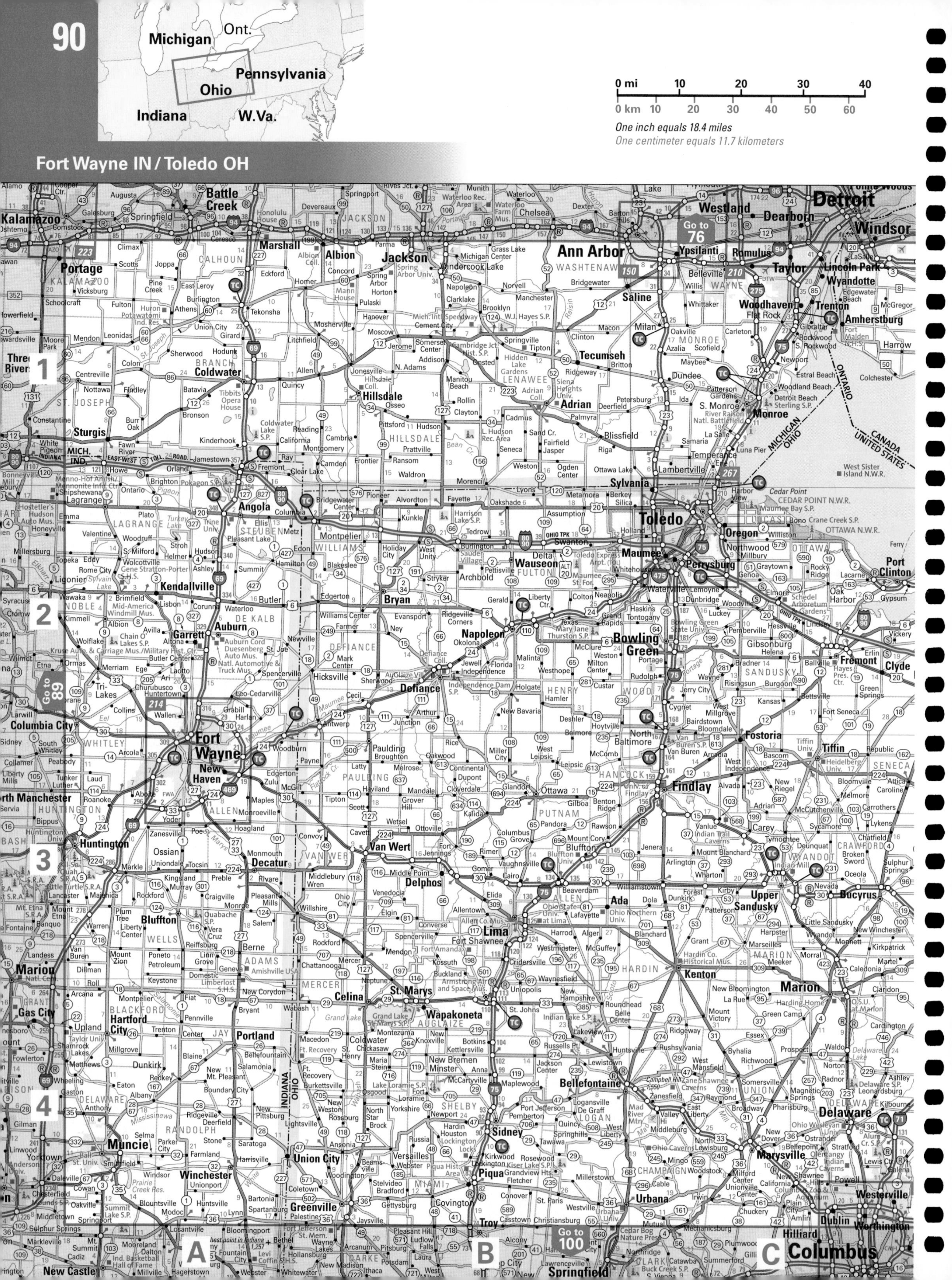
90
Michigan
Ont.
Pennsylvania
Ohio
Indiana
W.Va.
Fort Wayne IN / Toledo OH
0 mi 10 20 30 40
0 km 10 20 30 40 50 60
One inch equals 18.4 miles
One centimeter equals 11.7 kilometers
Go to 76
Go to 89
Go to 100
Kalamazoo
Battle Creek
Jackson
Ann Arbor
Detroit
Windsor
Dearborn
Westland
Ypsilanti
Romulus
Taylor
Lincoln Park
Wyandotte
Monroe
Toledo
Sylvania
Maumee
Perrysburg
Oregon
Bowling Green
Fremont
Fostoria
Tiffin
Findlay
Lima
Defiance
Bryan
Napoleon
Wauseon
Adrian
Tecumseh
Hillsdale
Coldwater
Sturgis
Angola
Kendallville
Auburn
Garrett
Fort Wayne
New Haven
Huntington
Decatur
Bluffton
Van Wert
Delphos
Celina
St. Marys
Wapakoneta
Sidney
Piqua
Troy
Urbana
Bellefontaine
Kenton
Marion
Bucyrus
Upper Sandusky
Delaware
Marysville
Dublin
Columbus
Springfield
Muncie
Portland
Hartford City
Union City
Greenville
Winchester
Marion
Gas City
Portage
Marshall
Albion
Port Clinton
Clyde
Ottawa
A
B
C
1
2
3
4
INDIANA
OHIO
MICHIGAN
OHIO
ONTARIO
MICHIGAN
CANADA
UNITED STATES

DRIVING DISTANCES IN MILES	AKRON, OH	CLEVELAND, OH	COLUMBUS, OH	DETROIT, MI	ERIE, PA	FORT WAYNE, IN	LIMA, OH	MANSFIELD, OH	MUNCIE, IN	TOLEDO, OH	WHEELING, WV	YOUNGSTOWN, OH
CLEVELAND, OH	38		144	171	106	214	163	81	287	119	16	275
FORT WAYNE, IN	237	214	186	170	322		66	151	75	109	290	274
MANSFIELD, OH	66	81	67	156	179	151	93		209	105	141	112
TOLEDO, OH	142	119	148	60	227	109	83	105	180		261	179

SEE ALSO DISTANCE AND DRIVING TIME MAP ON PAGES 286–287

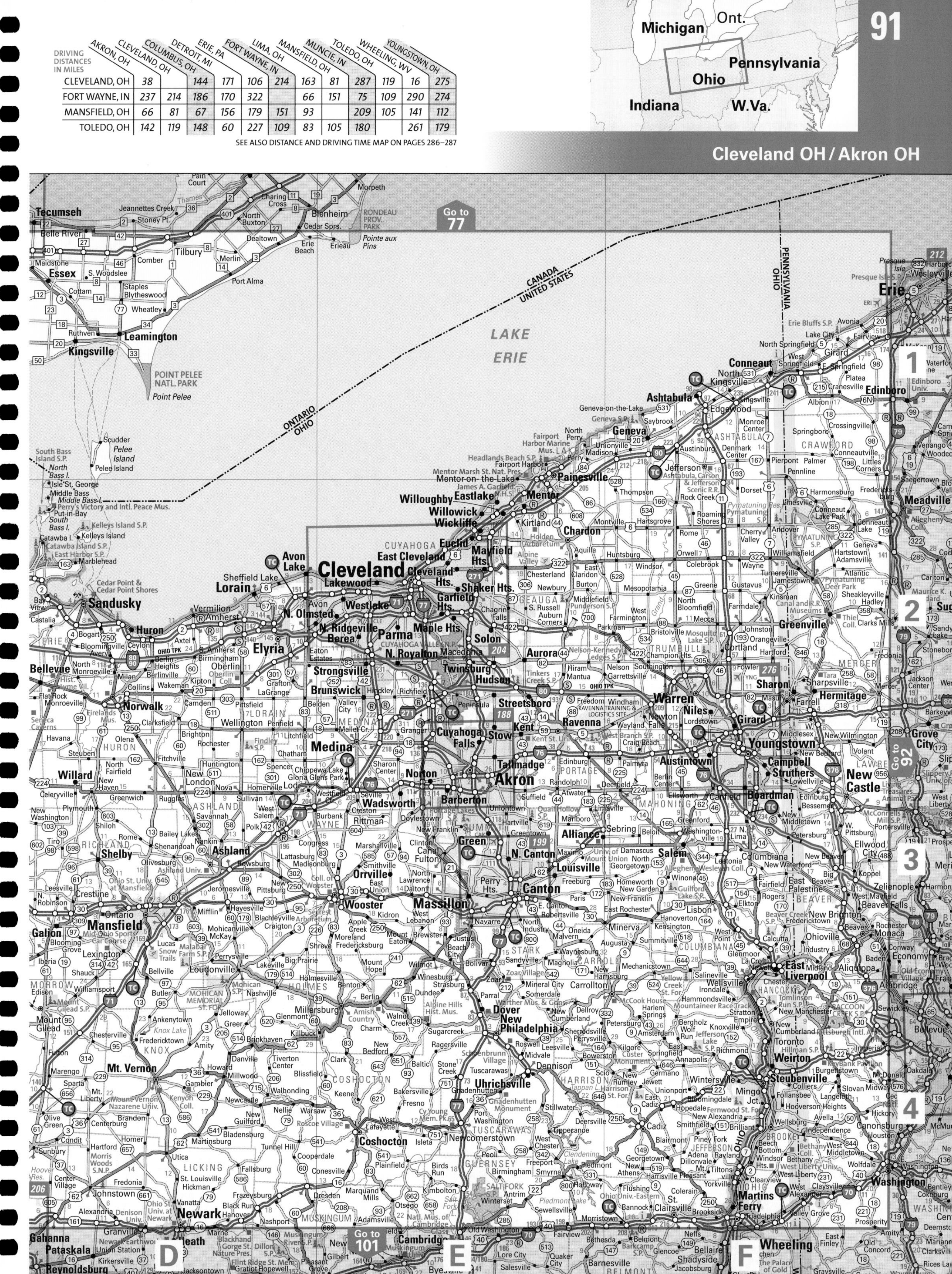

Pittsburgh PA / Erie PA

0 mi 10 20 30 40
0 km 10 20 30 40 50 60
One inch equals 18.4 miles
One centimeter equals 11.7 kilometers

DRIVING DISTANCES IN MILES	ALLENTOWN, PA	ALTOONA, PA	BINGHAMTON, NY	ELMIRA, NY	ERIE, PA	HARRISBURG, PA	JOHNSTOWN, PA	PITTSBURGH, PA	READING, PA	SCRANTON, PA	STATE COLLEGE, PA	WILLIAMSPORT, PA
ALLENTOWN, PA		218	132	188	361	82	217	284	37	76	165	116
HARRISBURG, PA	82	140	181	157	298		138	205	65	119	88	83
PITTSBURGH, PA	284	99	363	284	126	205	73		262	301	139	215
SCRANTON, PA	76	185	61	117	317	119	233	301	103		149	83

SEE ALSO DISTANCE AND DRIVING TIME MAP ON PAGES 286–287

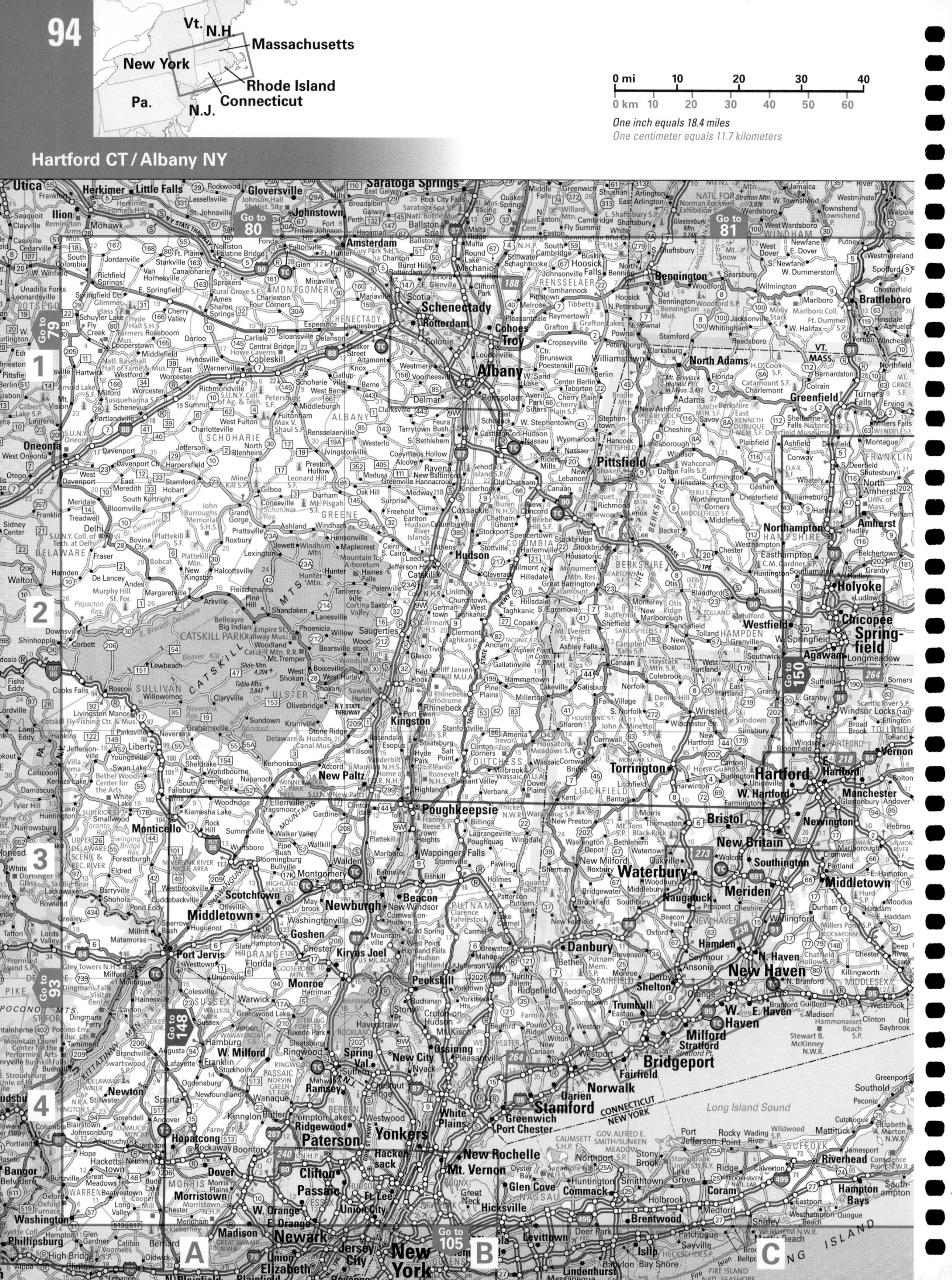

94
Vt.
N.H.
Massachusetts
New York
Rhode Island
Pa.
Connecticut
N.J.
Hartford CT / Albany NY
0 mi 10 20 30 40
0 km 10 20 30 40 50 60
One inch equals 18.4 miles
One centimeter equals 11.7 kilometers
Go to 80
Go to 81
Go to 79
Go to 150
Go to 93
Go to 148
Go to 105
1
2
3
4
A
B
C
Utica
Saratoga Springs
Gloversville
Johnstown
Amsterdam
Schenectady
Troy
Cohoes
Albany
Rensselaer
Bennington
North Adams
Brattleboro
Greenfield
Pittsfield
Northampton
Amherst
Holyoke
Chicopee
Springfield
Westfield
Oneonta
Hudson
Catskill
Kingston
New Paltz
Poughkeepsie
Torrington
Hartford
Bristol
New Britain
Waterbury
Meriden
Middletown
Danbury
New Haven
Bridgeport
Norwalk
Stamford
Newburgh
Middletown
Port Jervis
Peekskill
Yonkers
New Rochelle
Paterson
Newark
New York
Long Island Sound

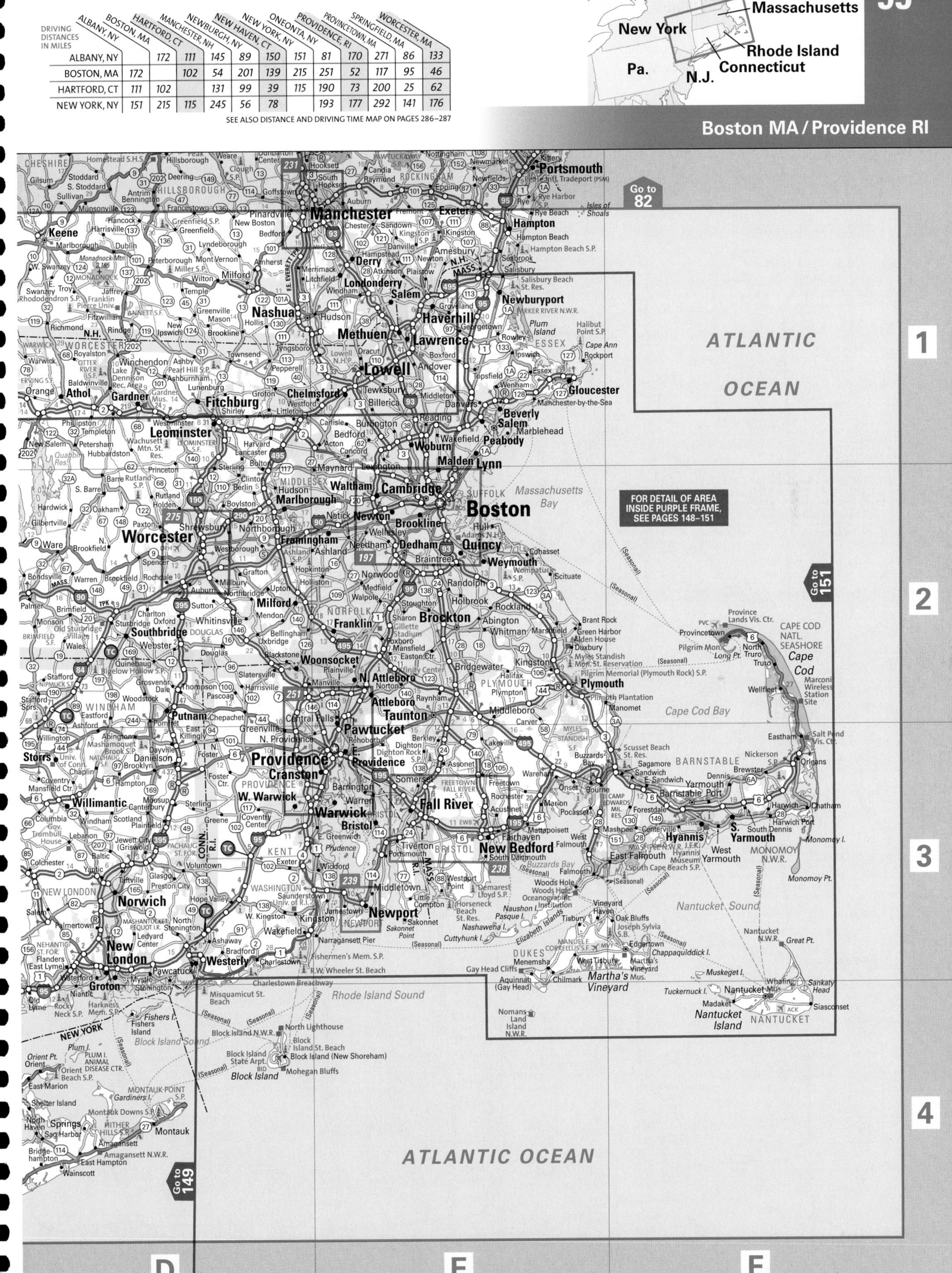

DRIVING DISTANCES IN MILES

	ALBANY, NY	BOSTON, MA	HARTFORD, CT	MANCHESTER, NH	NEWBURGH, NY	NEW HAVEN, CT	NEW YORK, NY	ONEONTA, NY	PROVIDENCE, RI	PROVINCETOWN, MA	SPRINGFIELD, MA	WORCESTER, MA
ALBANY, NY		172	111	145	89	150	151	81	170	271	86	133
BOSTON, MA	172		102	54	201	139	215	251	52	117	95	46
HARTFORD, CT	111	102		131	99	39	115	190	73	200	25	62
NEW YORK, NY	151	215	115	245	56	78		193	177	292	141	176

SEE ALSO DISTANCE AND DRIVING TIME MAP ON PAGES 286–287

Kansas City MO / Topeka KS

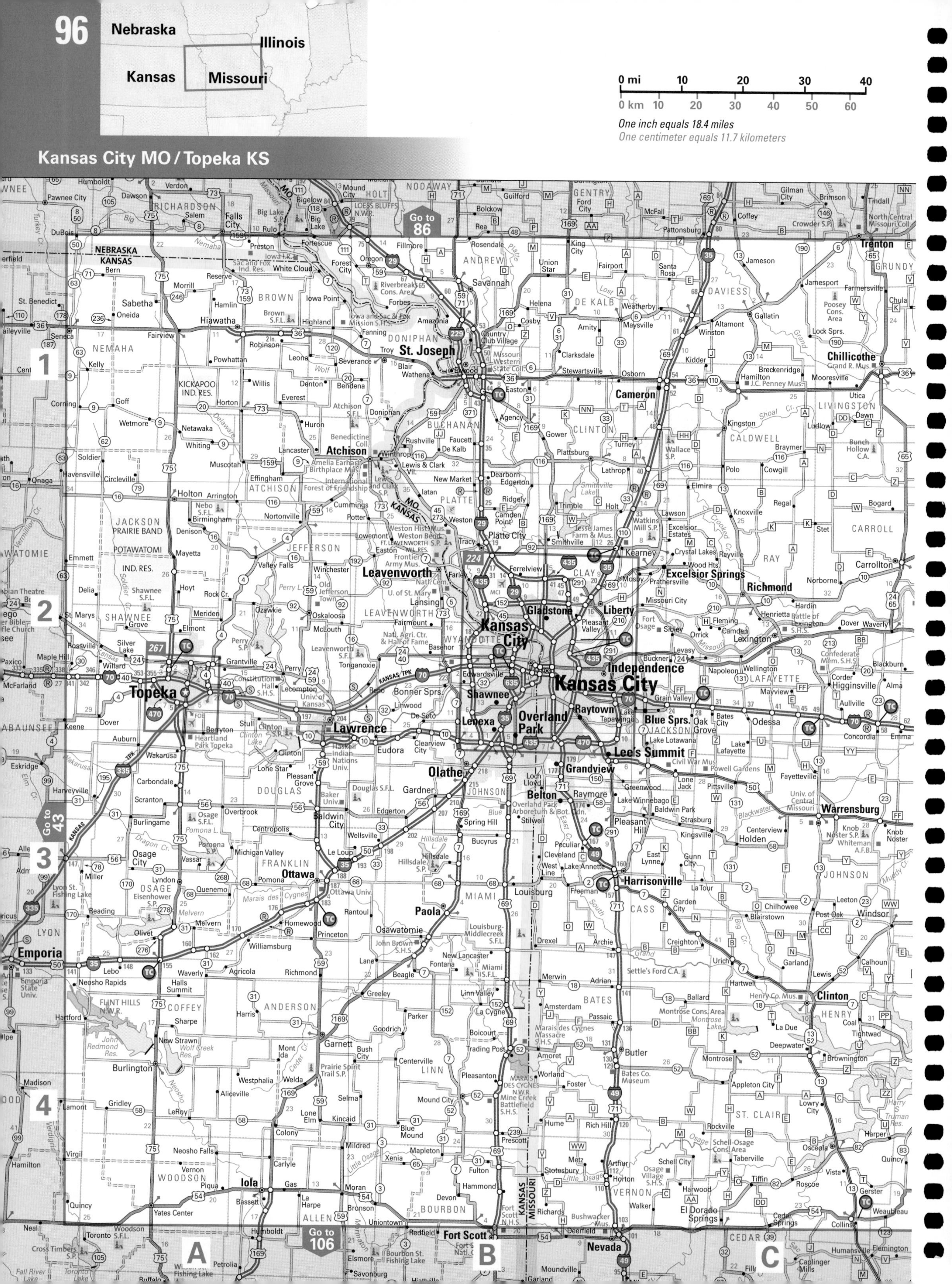

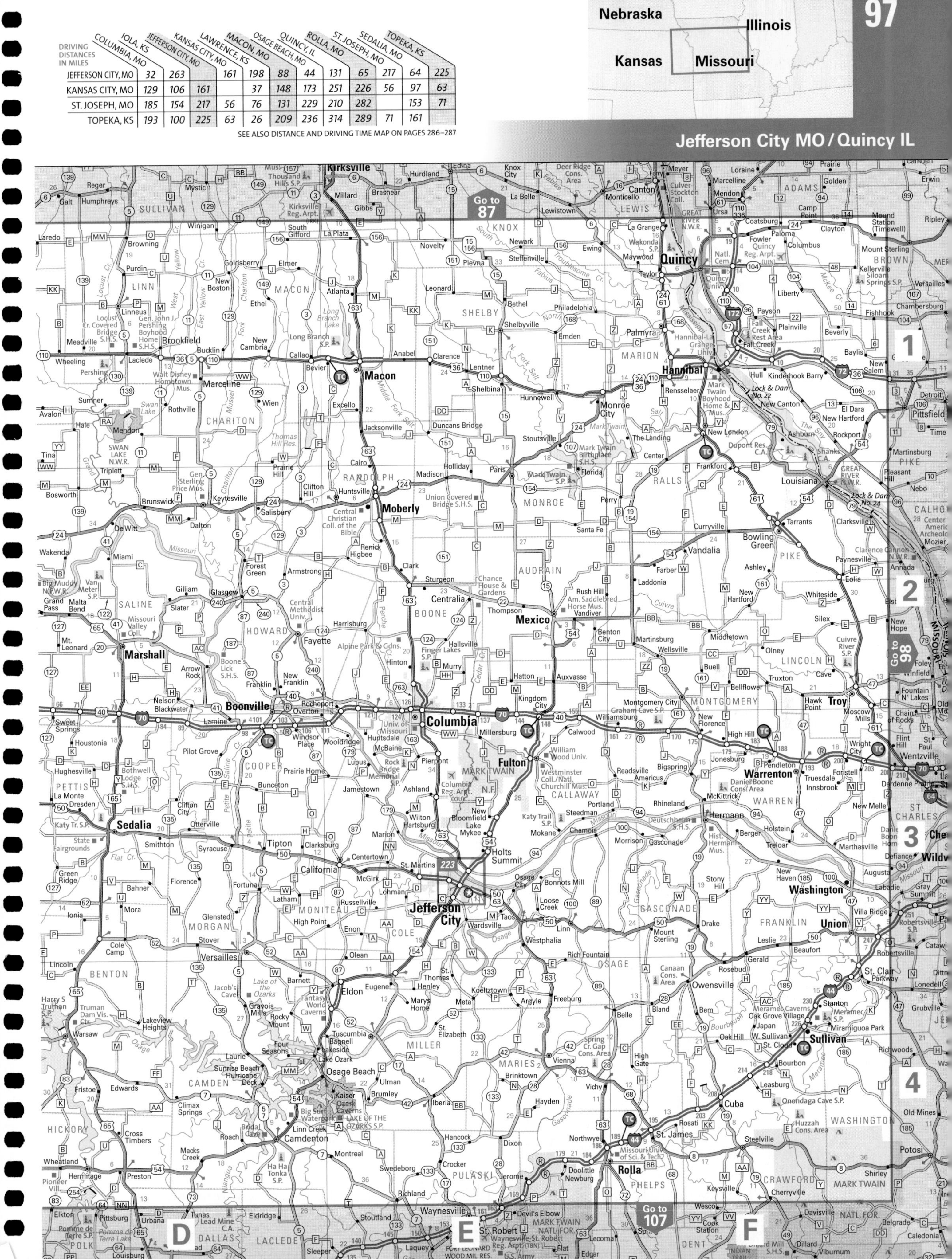

DRIVING DISTANCES IN MILES

	COLUMBIA, MO	IOLA, KS	JEFFERSON CITY, MO	KANSAS CITY, MO	LAWRENCE, KS	MACON, MO	OSAGE BEACH, MO	QUINCY, IL	ROLLA, MO	ST. JOSEPH, MO	SEDALIA, MO	TOPEKA, KS
JEFFERSON CITY, MO	32	263		161	198	88	44	131	65	217	64	225
KANSAS CITY, MO	129	106	161		37	148	173	251	226	56	97	63
ST. JOSEPH, MO	185	154	217	56	76	131	229	210	282		153	71
TOPEKA, KS	193	100	225	63	26	209	236	314	289	71	161	

SEE ALSO DISTANCE AND DRIVING TIME MAP ON PAGES 286–287

St Louis MO / Springfield IL

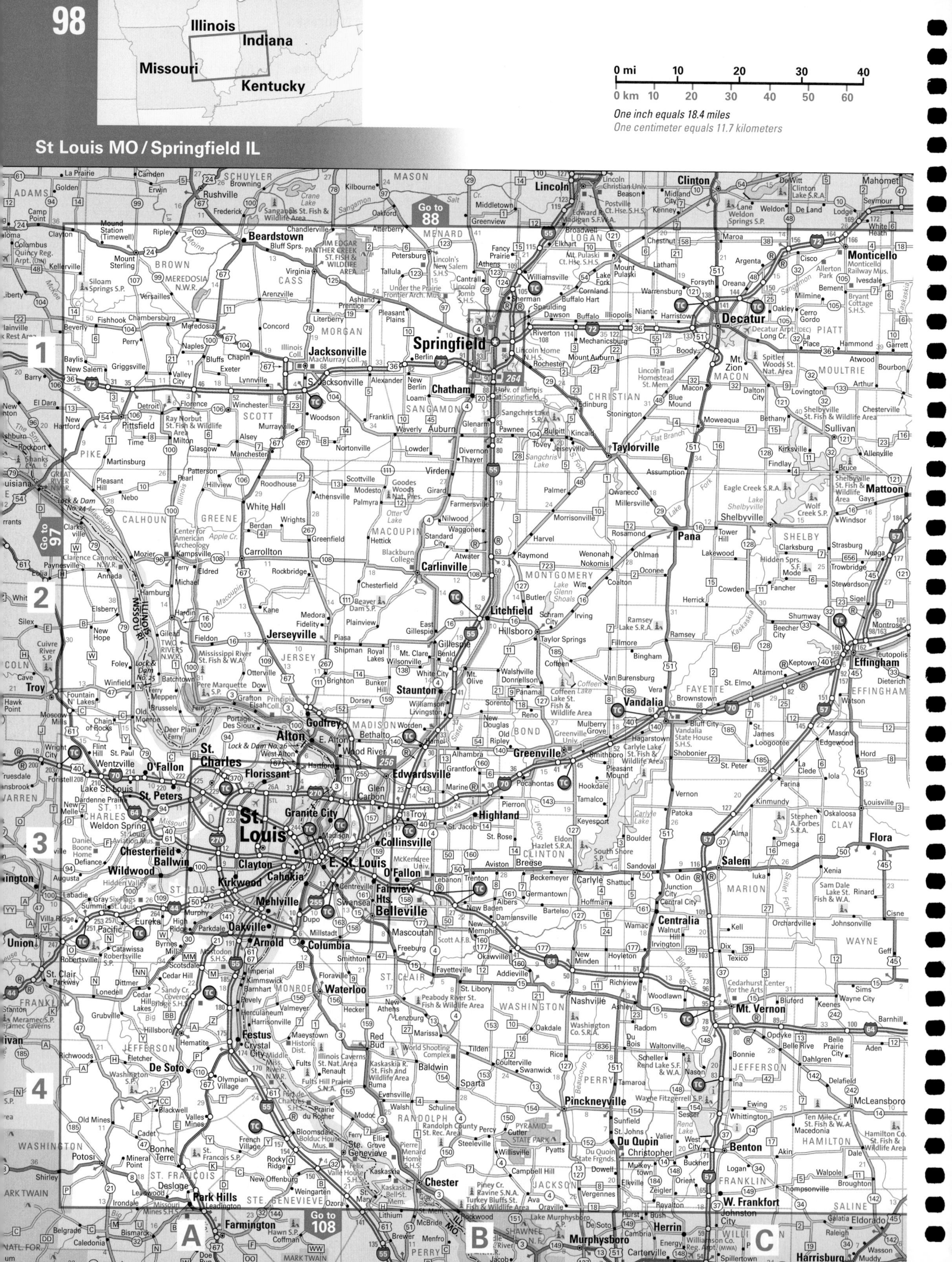

DRIVING DISTANCES IN MILES

	BLOOMINGTON, IN	CHAMPAIGN, IL	DECATUR, IL	EFFINGHAM, IL	EVANSVILLE, IN	INDIANAPOLIS, IN	LOUISVILLE, KY	MT. VERNON, IL	ST. LOUIS, MO	SPRINGFIELD, IL	TERRE HAUTE, IN	VINCENNES, IN
EVANSVILLE, IN	117	192	184	117		166	114	90	170	247	107	51
INDIANAPOLIS, IN	47	123	177	137	166		112	205	239	212	77	123
ST. LOUIS, MO	223	179	116	103	170	239	264	81		97	169	185
SPRINGFIELD, IL	209	87	40	89	247	212	326	158	97		155	169

SEE ALSO DISTANCE AND DRIVING TIME MAP ON PAGES 286–287

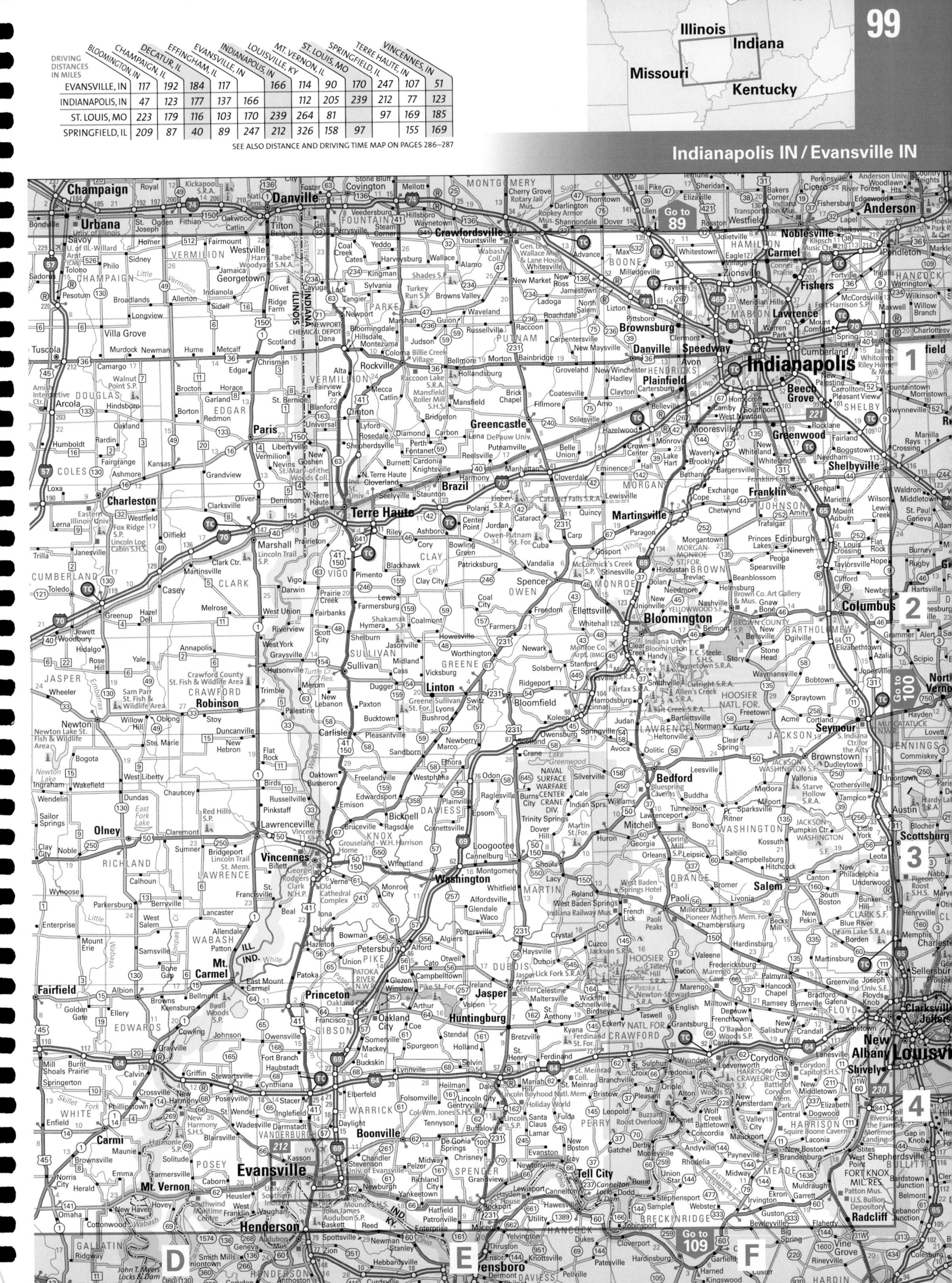

Ohio
Indiana
W.Va.
Kentucky

0 mi 10 20 30 40
0 km 10 20 30 40 50 60

One inch equals 18.4 miles
One centimeter equals 11.7 kilometers

Cincinnati OH / Louisville KY

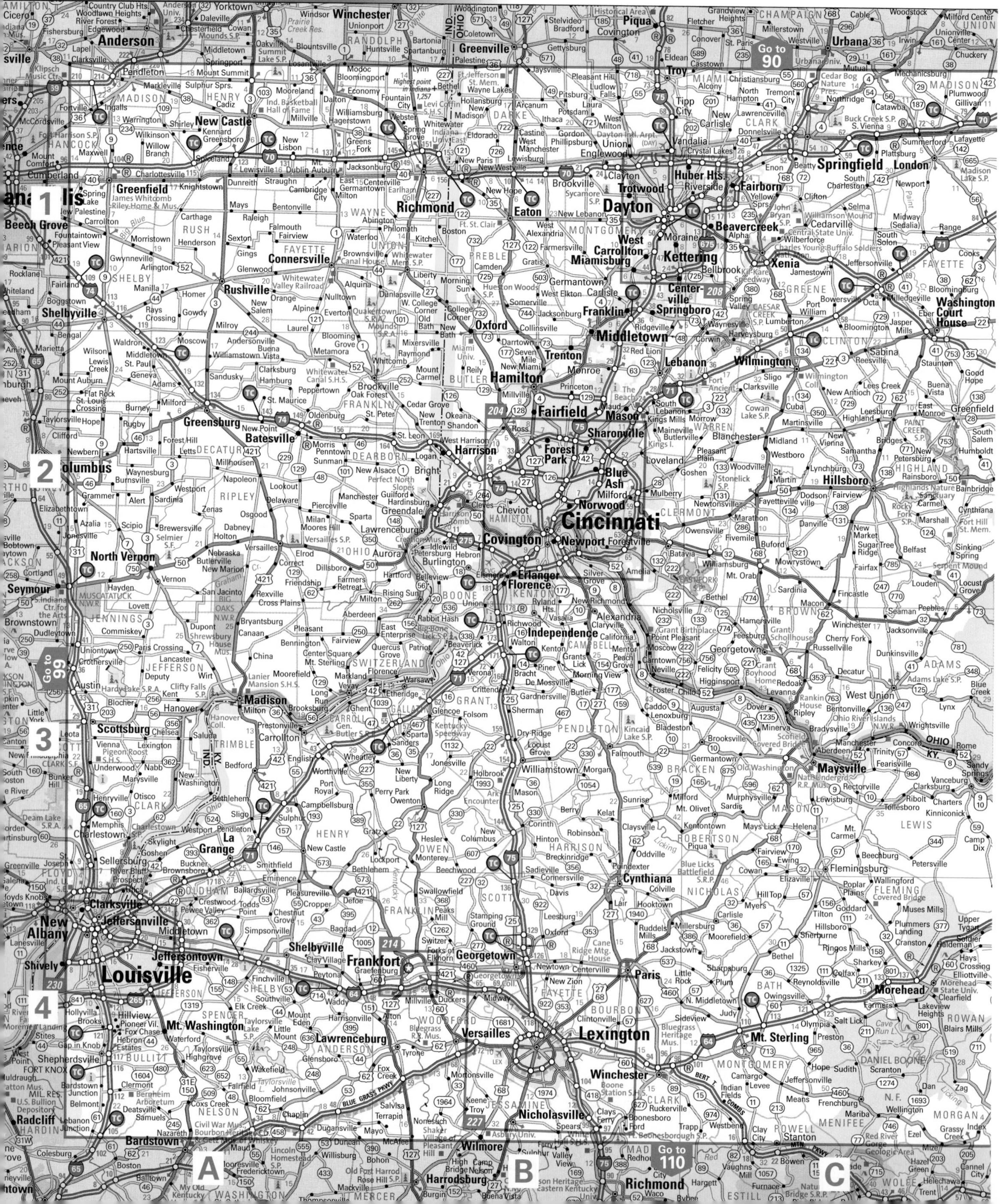

Go to 90

Go to 99

Go to 110

Anderson
Muncie
Winchester
Greenville
Piqua
Troy
Urbana
New Castle
Richmond
Eaton
Dayton
Springfield
Beavercreek
Kettering
Xenia
Greenfield
Connersville
Rushville
Shelbyville
Greensburg
Batesville
Oxford
Hamilton
Middletown
Lebanon
Wilmington
Washington Court House
Fairfield
Mason
Harrison
Columbus
North Vernon
Seymour
Cincinnati
Covington
Newport
Florence
Independence
Hillsboro
Madison
Scottsburg
Maysville
La Grange
Cynthiana
Flemingsburg
Clarksville
New Albany
Jeffersonville
Louisville
Shelbyville
Frankfort
Georgetown
Paris
Lexington
Versailles
Lawrenceburg
Mt. Washington
Mt. Sterling
Morehead
Winchester
Nicholasville
Bardstown
Wilmore
Harrodsburg
Richmond

1 2 3 4
A B C

Ohio
Indiana
W.Va.
Kentucky

DRIVING DISTANCES IN MILES	CHARLESTON, WV	CHILLICOTHE, OH	CINCINNATI, OH	COLUMBUS, OH	DAYTON, OH	HUNTINGTON, WV	LEXINGTON, KY	LOUISVILLE, KY	MAYSVILLE, KY	PARKERSBURG, WV	WHEELING, WV	ZANESVILLE, OH
CHARLESTON, WV		121	202	168	198	52	176	251	155	73	176	155
CINCINNATI, OH	202	108		109	52	150	85	100	63	191	235	164
COLUMBUS, OH	168	47	109		70	135	193	207	114	108	130	58
LEXINGTON, KY	176	191	85	193	135	126		80	67	249	319	247

SEE ALSO DISTANCE AND DRIVING TIME MAP ON PAGES 286–287

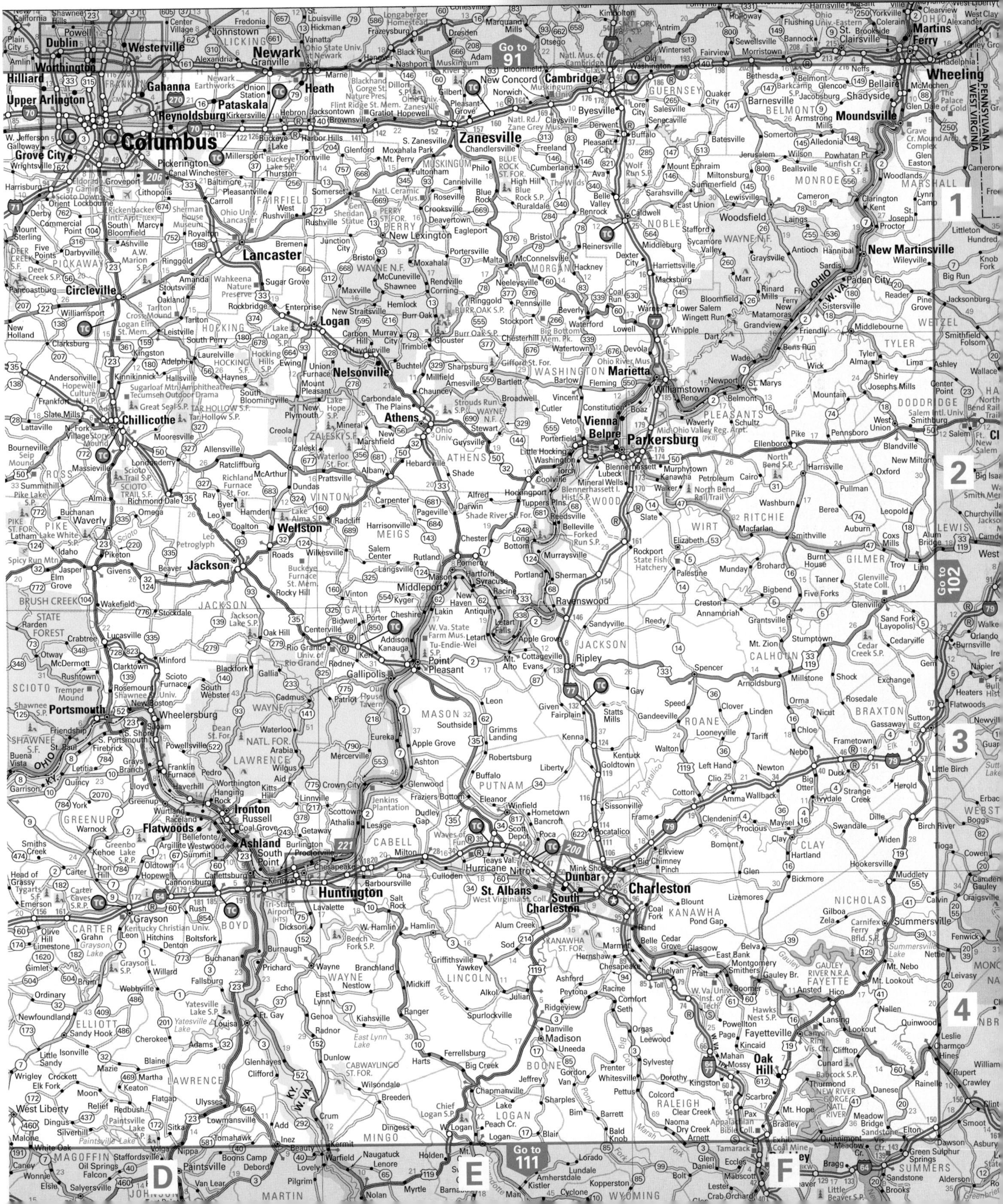

Go to 91

Go to 102

Go to 111

Pennsylvania
Ohio
Md.
Delaware
W.Va.
Virginia

0 mi 10 20 30 40
0 km 10 20 30 40 50 60
One inch equals 18.4 miles
One centimeter equals 11.7 kilometers

Charlottesville VA / Morgantown WV

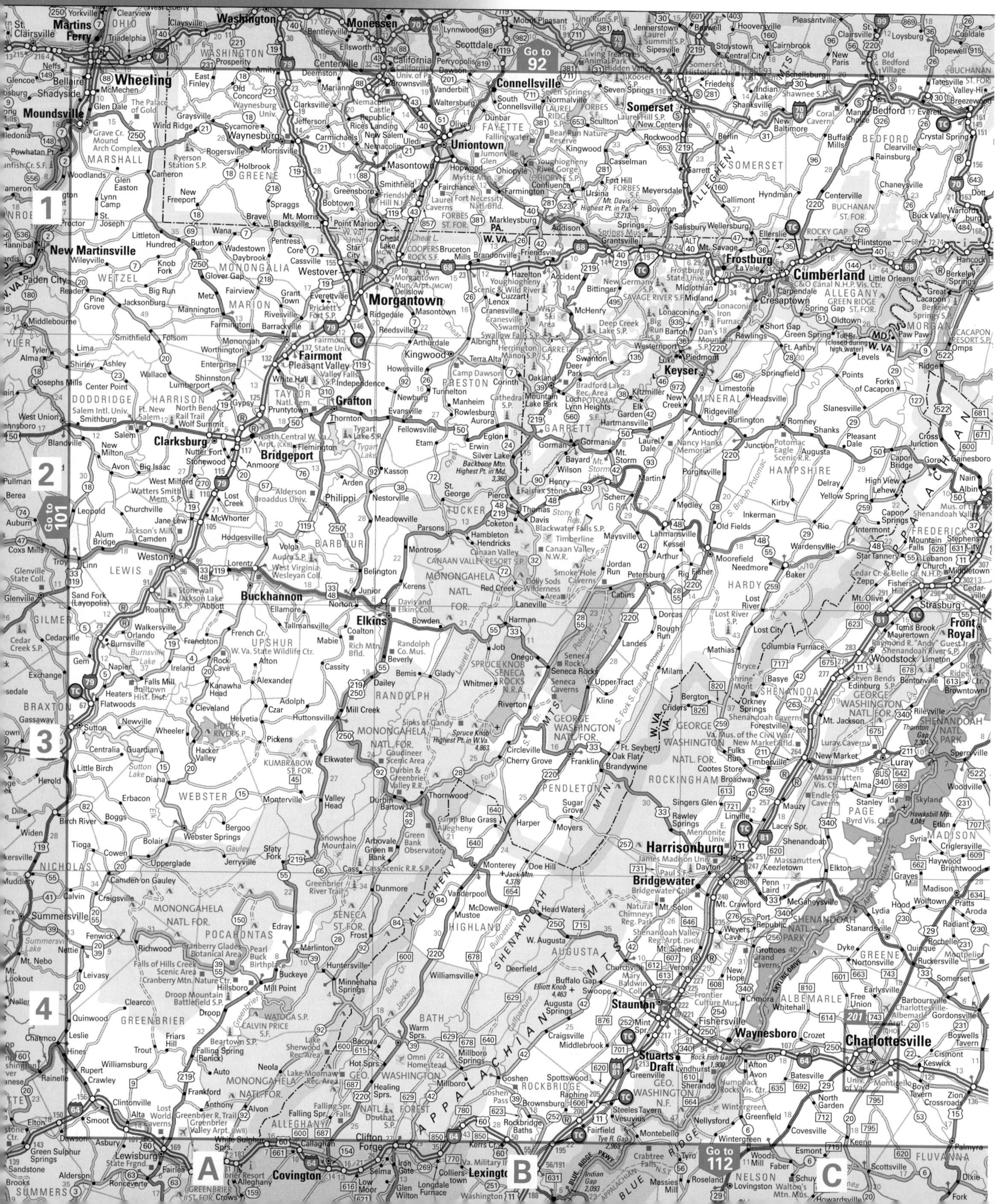

Go to 92
Go to 101
Go to 112

Wheeling
Moundsville
Washington
Monessen
Connellsville
Uniontown
Somerset
Bedford
Waynesburg
New Martinsville
Morgantown
Fairmont
Grafton
Clarksburg
Bridgeport
Frostburg
Cumberland
Keyser
Weston
Buckhannon
Elkins
Philippi
Harrisonburg
Bridgewater
Staunton
Waynesboro
Charlottesville
Stuarts Draft
Winchester
Front Royal
Strasburg
Woodstock
Luray
Lewisburg
Covington
Lexington
Summersville
Sutton
Flatwoods

PA.
W. VA.
MD.
W. VA.
W. VA.
VA.

MARSHALL
WETZEL
MONONGALIA
MARION
TAYLOR
HARRISON
DODDRIDGE
LEWIS
UPSHUR
BARBOUR
PRESTON
TUCKER
RANDOLPH
GRANT
MINERAL
HAMPSHIRE
HARDY
PENDLETON
WEBSTER
BRAXTON
NICHOLAS
GREENBRIER
POCAHONTAS
HIGHLAND
BATH
AUGUSTA
ROCKINGHAM
ROCKBRIDGE
ALLEGHANY
SHENANDOAH
PAGE
GREENE
ALBEMARLE
MADISON
NELSON
FLUVANNA
FREDERICK
GARRETT
ALLEGANY
SOMERSET
BEDFORD
FAYETTE
GREENE
WASHINGTON
MORGAN
GILMER
SUMMERS

MONONGAHELA NATL. FOR.
GEORGE WASHINGTON NATL. FOR.
SHENANDOAH NATL. PARK
ALLEGHENY
APPALACHIAN MTS.
SHENANDOAH MTN.
BLUE RIDGE

1
2
3
4
A
B
C

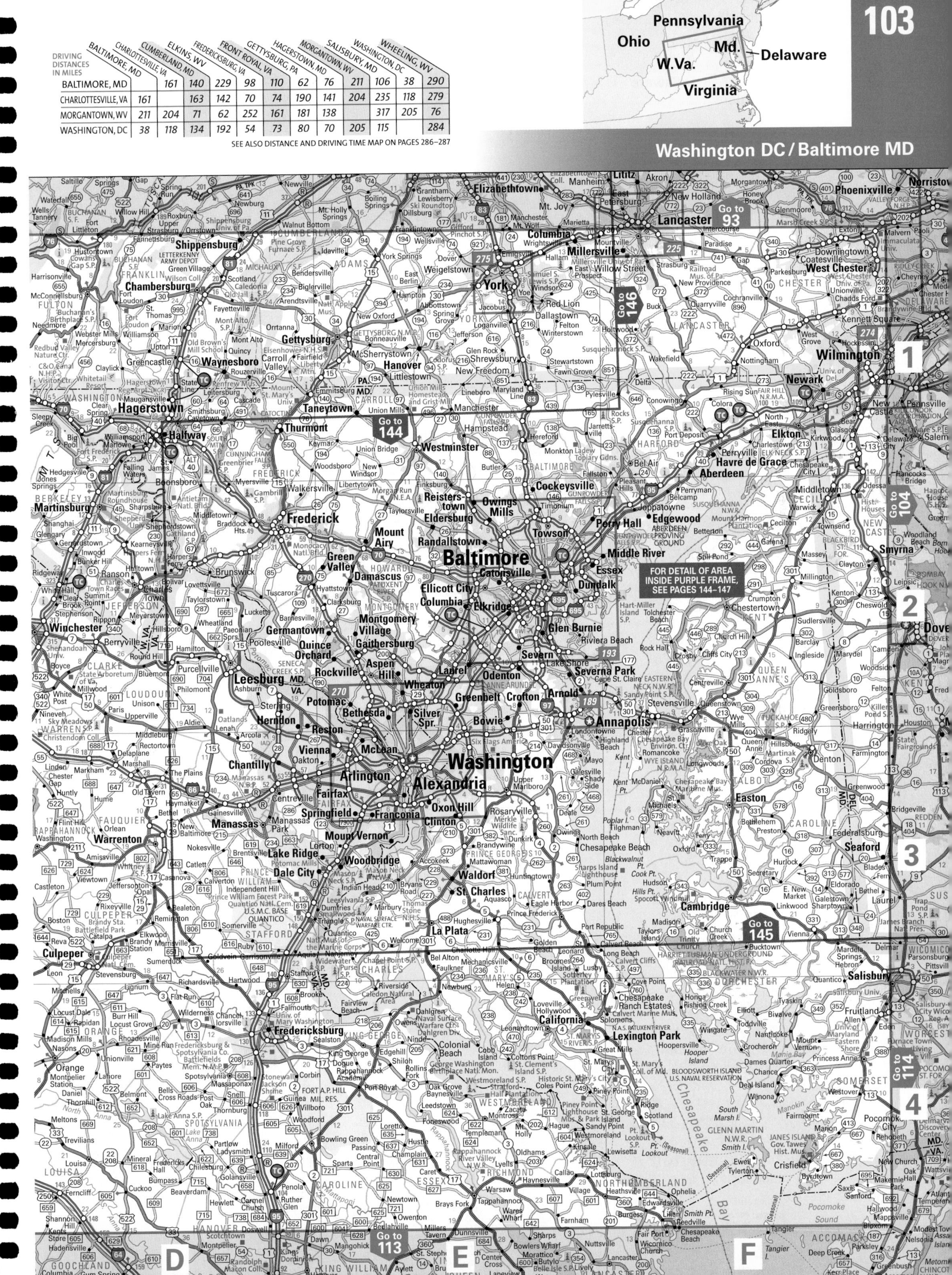

DRIVING DISTANCES IN MILES

	BALTIMORE, MD	CHARLOTTESVILLE, VA	CUMBERLAND, MD	ELKINS, WV	FREDERICKSBURG, VA	FRONT ROYAL, VA	GETTYSBURG, PA	HAGERSTOWN, MD	MORGANTOWN, WV	SALISBURY, MD	WASHINGTON, DC	WHEELING, WV
BALTIMORE, MD		161	140	229	98	110	62	76	211	106	38	290
CHARLOTTESVILLE, VA	161		163	142	70	74	190	141	204	235	118	279
MORGANTOWN, WV	211	204	71	62	252	161	181	138		317	205	76
WASHINGTON, DC	38	118	134	192	54	73	80	70	205	115		284

SEE ALSO DISTANCE AND DRIVING TIME MAP ON PAGES 286–287

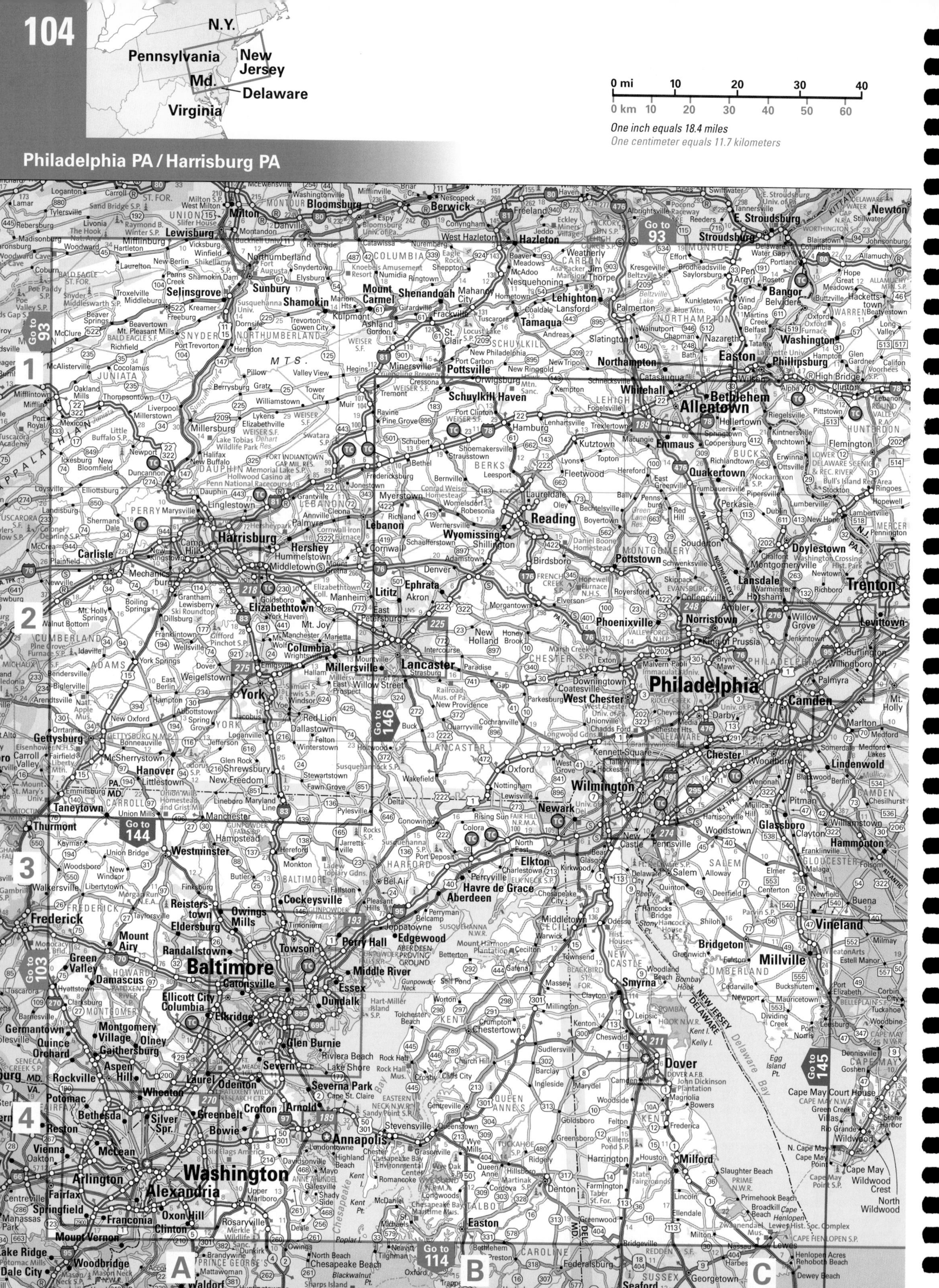

104
N.Y.
Pennsylvania
New Jersey
Md.
Delaware
Virginia
Philadelphia PA / Harrisburg PA
0 mi 10 20 30 40
0 km 10 20 30 40 50 60
One inch equals 18.4 miles
One centimeter equals 11.7 kilometers
Go to 93
Go to 144
Go to 146
Go to 103
Go to 114
Go to 145
Bloomsburg
Berwick
Hazleton
Milton
Lewisburg
Sunbury
Selinsgrove
Shamokin
Mount Carmel
Shenandoah
Pottsville
Tamaqua
Lehighton
Schuylkill Haven
Stroudsburg
E. Stroudsburg
Bangor
Washington
Easton
Phillipsburg
Northampton
Whitehall
Bethlehem
Allentown
Emmaus
Quakertown
Reading
Wyomissing
Pottstown
Doylestown
Lansdale
Trenton
Harrisburg
Carlisle
Hershey
Lebanon
Elizabethtown
Lititz
Ephrata
Lancaster
Millersville
Columbia
York
Gettysburg
Hanover
Phoenixville
Norristown
Philadelphia
Camden
West Chester
Chester
Wilmington
Newark
Levittown
Taneytown
Westminster
Frederick
Baltimore
Towson
Cockeysville
Aberdeen
Havre de Grace
Elkton
Annapolis
Washington
Alexandria
Arlington
Bethesda
Rockville
Dover
Smyrna
Milford
Vineland
Millville
Bridgeton
Glassboro
Salem
Easton
Denton
Seaford
Georgetown
Cape May
Wildwood
Lewes
A
B
C
1
2
3
4

DRIVING DISTANCES IN MILES

	ALLENTOWN, PA	ATLANTIC CITY, NJ	BALTIMORE, MD	DOVER, DE	HARRISBURG, PA	LANCASTER, PA	NEWARK, NJ	NEW YORK, NY	PHILADELPHIA, PA	TRENTON, NJ	WASHINGTON, DC	WILMINGTON, DE
HARRISBURG, PA	82	171	83	126		44	154	165	109	135	123	102
NEW YORK, NY	84	125	192	160	165	165	11		91	55	228	120
PHILADELPHIA, PA	63	62	104	74	109	79	80	91		34	140	30
WASHINGTON, DC	188	186	38	94	123	123	218	228	140	179		110

SEE ALSO DISTANCE AND DRIVING TIME MAP ON PAGES 286–287

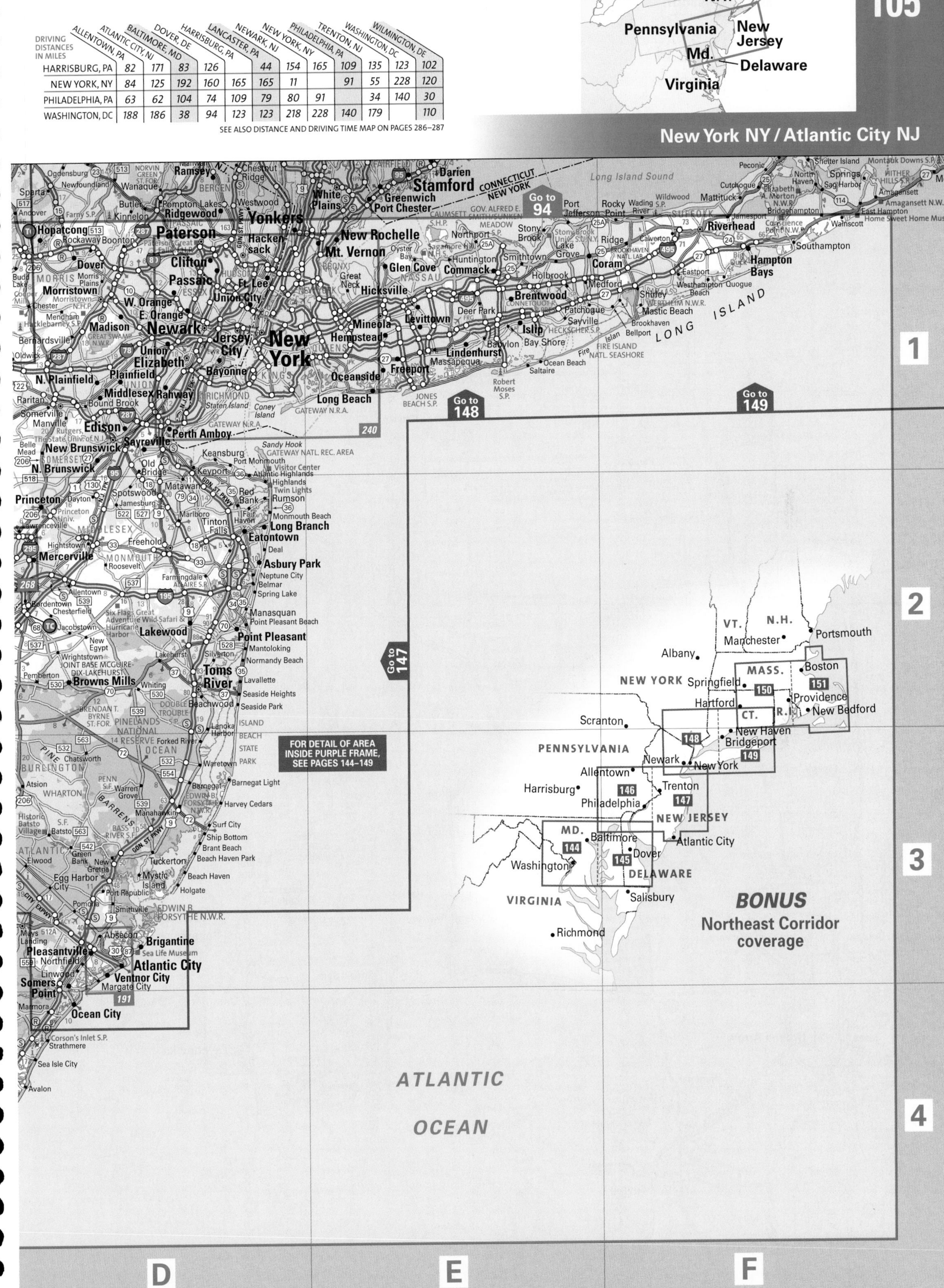

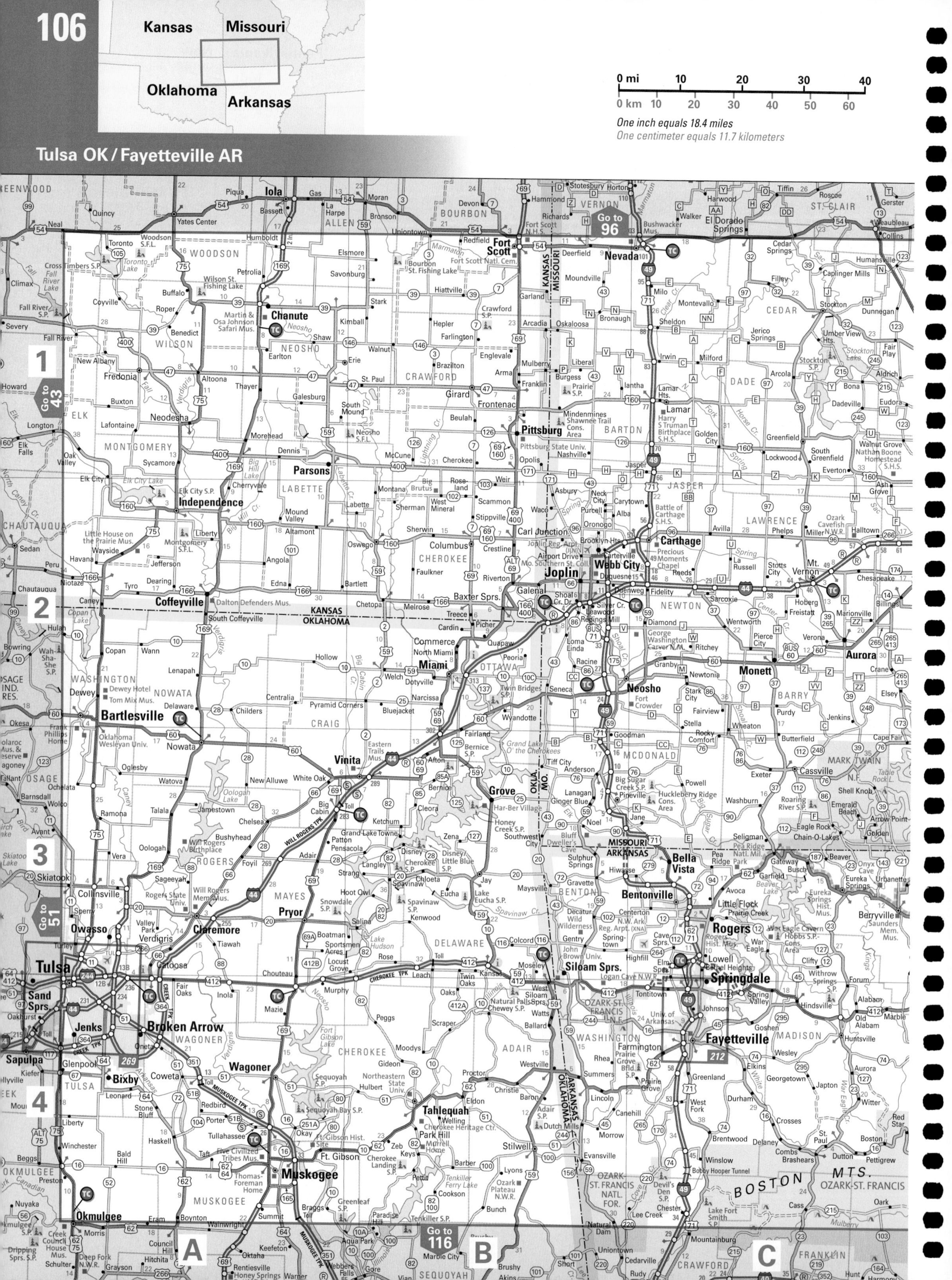
106
Kansas
Missouri
Oklahoma
Arkansas
0 mi 10 20 30 40
0 km 10 20 30 40 50 60
One inch equals 18.4 miles
One centimeter equals 11.7 kilometers
Tulsa OK / Fayetteville AR
Go to 96
Go to 43
Go to 51
Go to 116
1
2
3
4
A
B
C
Iola
Chanute
Fort Scott
Nevada
Pittsburg
Parsons
Independence
Coffeyville
Joplin
Webb City
Carthage
Miami
Bartlesville
Vinita
Neosho
Monett
Aurora
Grove
Bella Vista
Bentonville
Rogers
Springdale
Fayetteville
Siloam Sprs.
Pryor
Claremore
Owasso
Tulsa
Sand Sprs.
Broken Arrow
Jenks
Sapulpa
Bixby
Wagoner
Muskogee
Tahlequah
Okmulgee
KANSAS
OKLAHOMA
MISSOURI
ARKANSAS
BOSTON MTS.
OZARK-ST. FRANCIS
WOODSON
WILSON
NEOSHO
ALLEN
BOURBON
VERNON
ST. CLAIR
CRAWFORD
CEDAR
DADE
BARTON
JASPER
LAWRENCE
NEWTON
MCDONALD
BARRY
BENTON
WASHINGTON
MADISON
ADAIR
CHEROKEE
DELAWARE
MAYES
ROGERS
TULSA
WAGONER
MUSKOGEE
OKMULGEE
OSAGE
WASHINGTON
NOWATA
CRAIG
OTTAWA
LABETTE
MONTGOMERY
ELK
CHAUTAUQUA
FRANKLIN
SEQUOYAH
MARK TWAIN

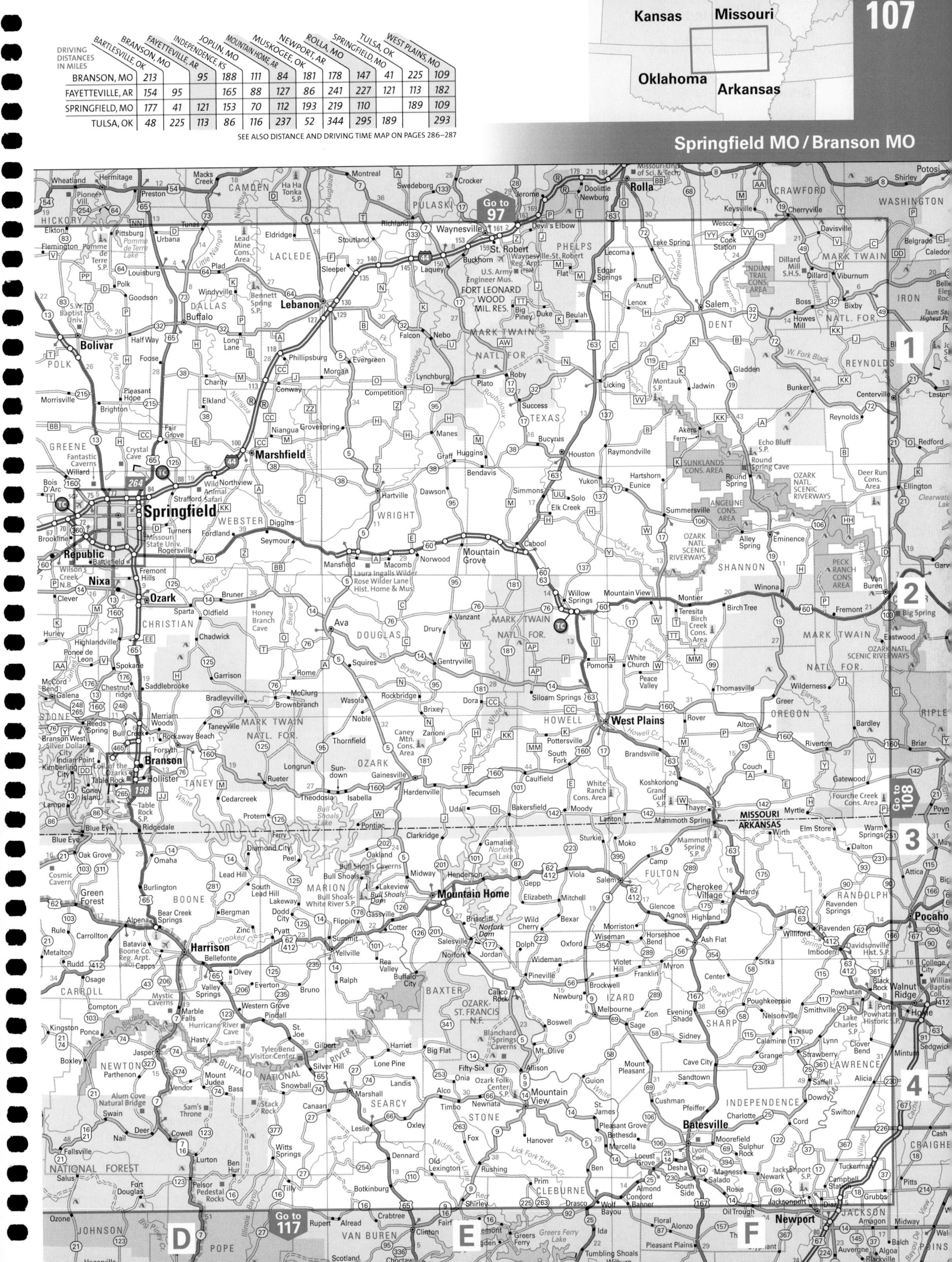

DRIVING DISTANCES IN MILES

	BARTLESVILLE, OK	BRANSON, MO	FAYETTEVILLE, AR	INDEPENDENCE, KS	JOPLIN, MO	MOUNTAIN HOME, AR	MUSKOGEE, OK	NEWPORT, AR	ROLLA, MO	SPRINGFIELD, MO	TULSA, OK	WEST PLAINS, MO
BRANSON, MO	213		95	188	111	84	181	178	147	41	225	109
FAYETTEVILLE, AR	154	95		165	88	127	86	241	227	121	113	182
SPRINGFIELD, MO	177	41	121	153	70	112	193	219	110		189	109
TULSA, OK	48	225	113	86	116	237	52	344	295	189		293

SEE ALSO DISTANCE AND DRIVING TIME MAP ON PAGES 286–287

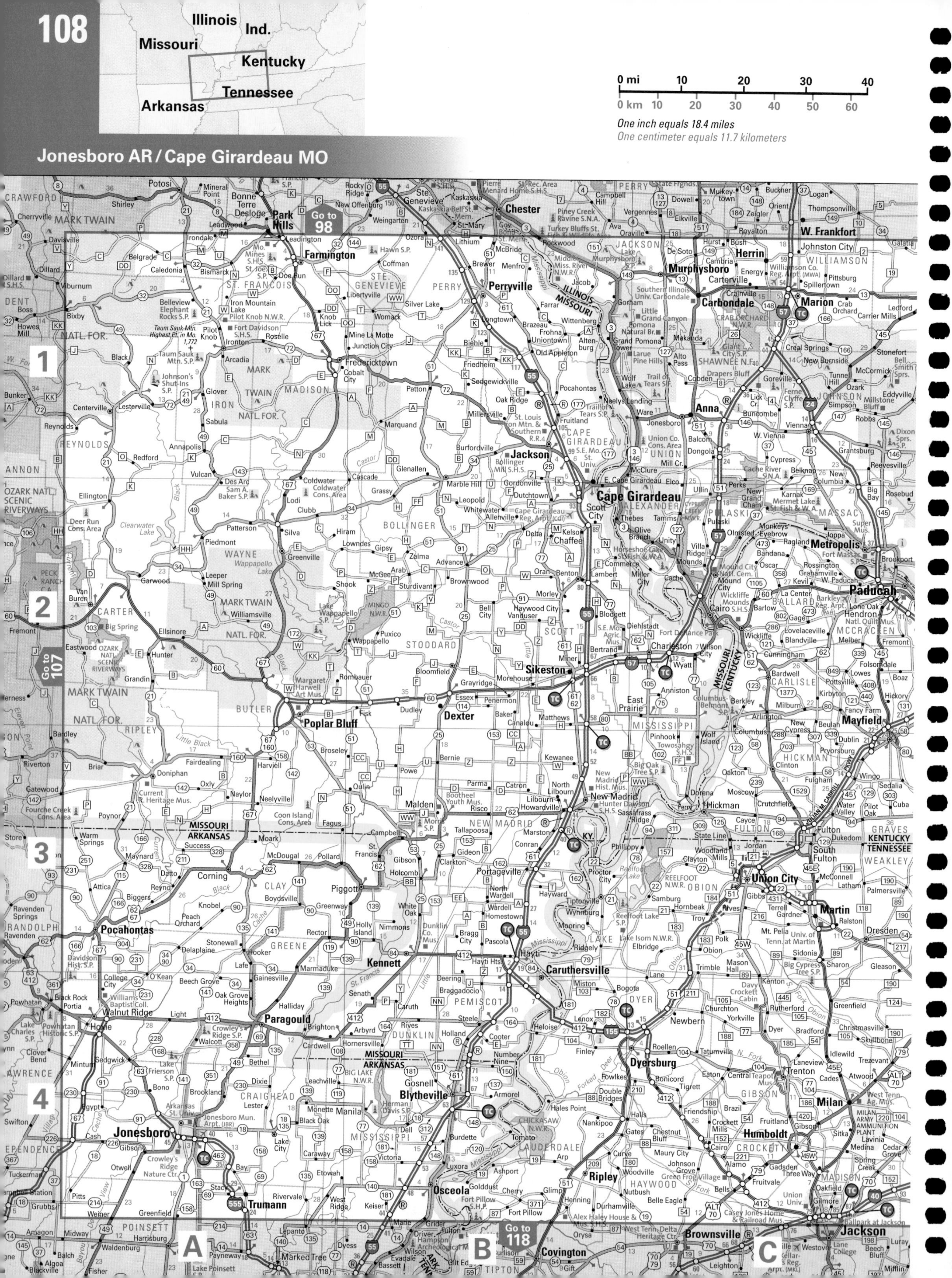
Illinois
Ind.
Missouri
Kentucky
Tennessee
Arkansas
0 mi 10 20 30 40
0 km 10 20 30 40 50 60
One inch equals 18.4 miles
One centimeter equals 11.7 kilometers
Go to 98
Go to 107
Go to 118
1
2
3
4
A
B
C
Park Hills
Farmington
Chester
Perryville
Murphysboro
Herrin
Carbondale
Marion
W. Frankfort
Anna
Jackson
Cape Girardeau
Scott City
Chaffee
Metropolis
Paducah
Mayfield
Sikeston
Charleston
Poplar Bluff
Dexter
Malden
New Madrid
Hickman
Union City
Martin
Kennett
Caruthersville
Dyersburg
Pocahontas
Walnut Ridge
Paragould
Blytheville
Jonesboro
Trumann
Osceola
Ripley
Humboldt
Milan
Covington
Brownsville
Jackson
MISSOURI
ARKANSAS
KENTUCKY
TENNESSEE
ILLINOIS
MISSOURI
MISSOURI
KENTUCKY
MARK TWAIN NATL. FOR.
SHAWNEE N.F.
OZARK NATL. SCENIC RIVERWAYS

DRIVING DISTANCES IN MILES	BOWLING GREEN, KY	CAPE GIRARDEAU, MO	CARBONDALE, IL	CLARKSVILLE, TN	DYERSBURG, TN	HOPKINSVILLE, KY	JACKSON, TN	JONESBORO, AR	NASHVILLE, TN	OWENSBORO, KY	PADUCAH, KY	POPLAR BLUFF, MO
BOWLING GREEN, KY		199	206	63	217	63	196	349	68	76	135	239
CAPE GIRARDEAU, MO	199		46	155	112	136	161	155	197	168	67	75
JONESBORO, AR	349	155	199	268	101	249	160		285	304	178	81
NASHVILLE, TN	68	197	204	46	178	68	132	285		141	133	237

SEE ALSO DISTANCE AND DRIVING TIME MAP ON PAGES 286–287

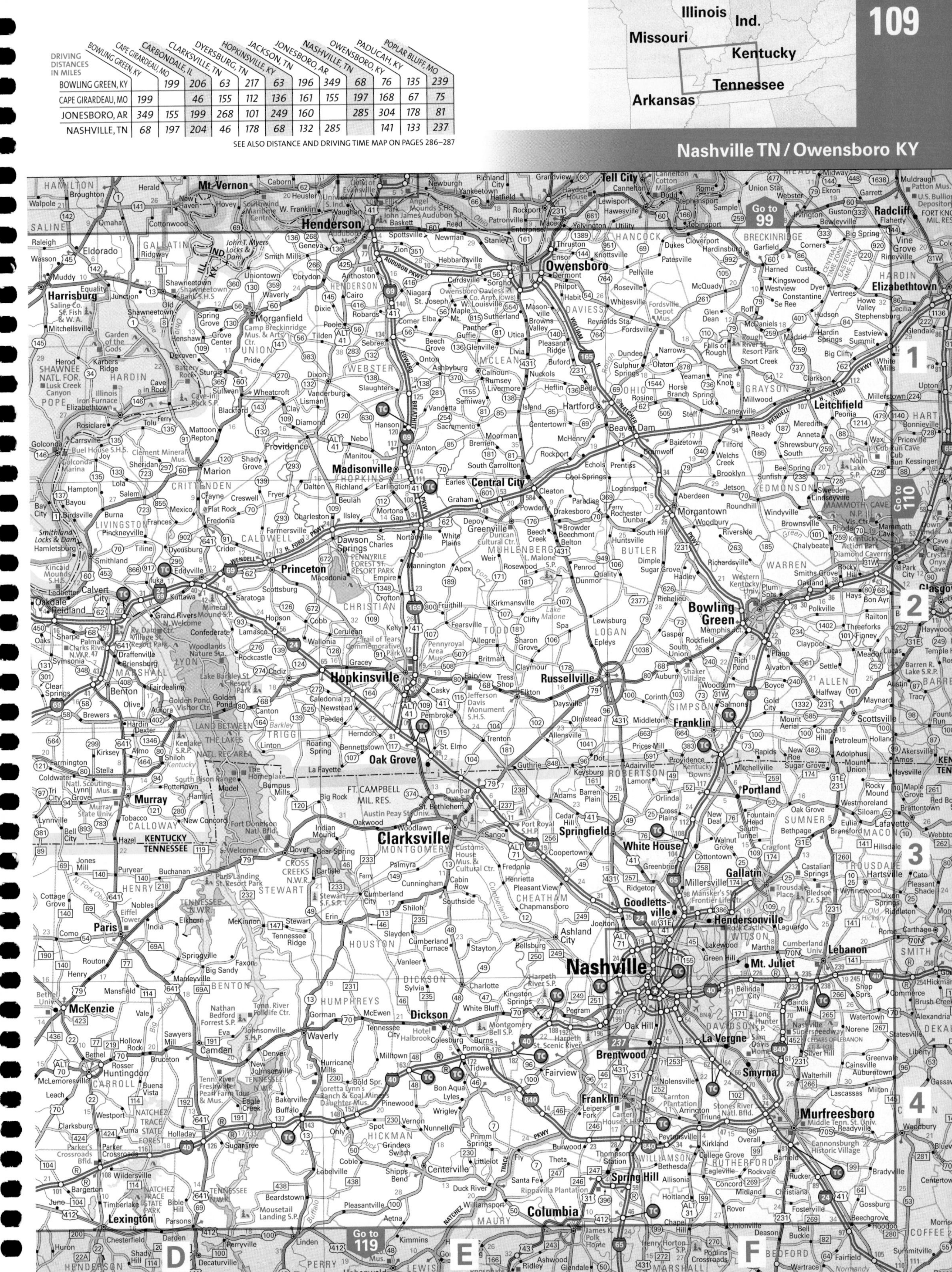

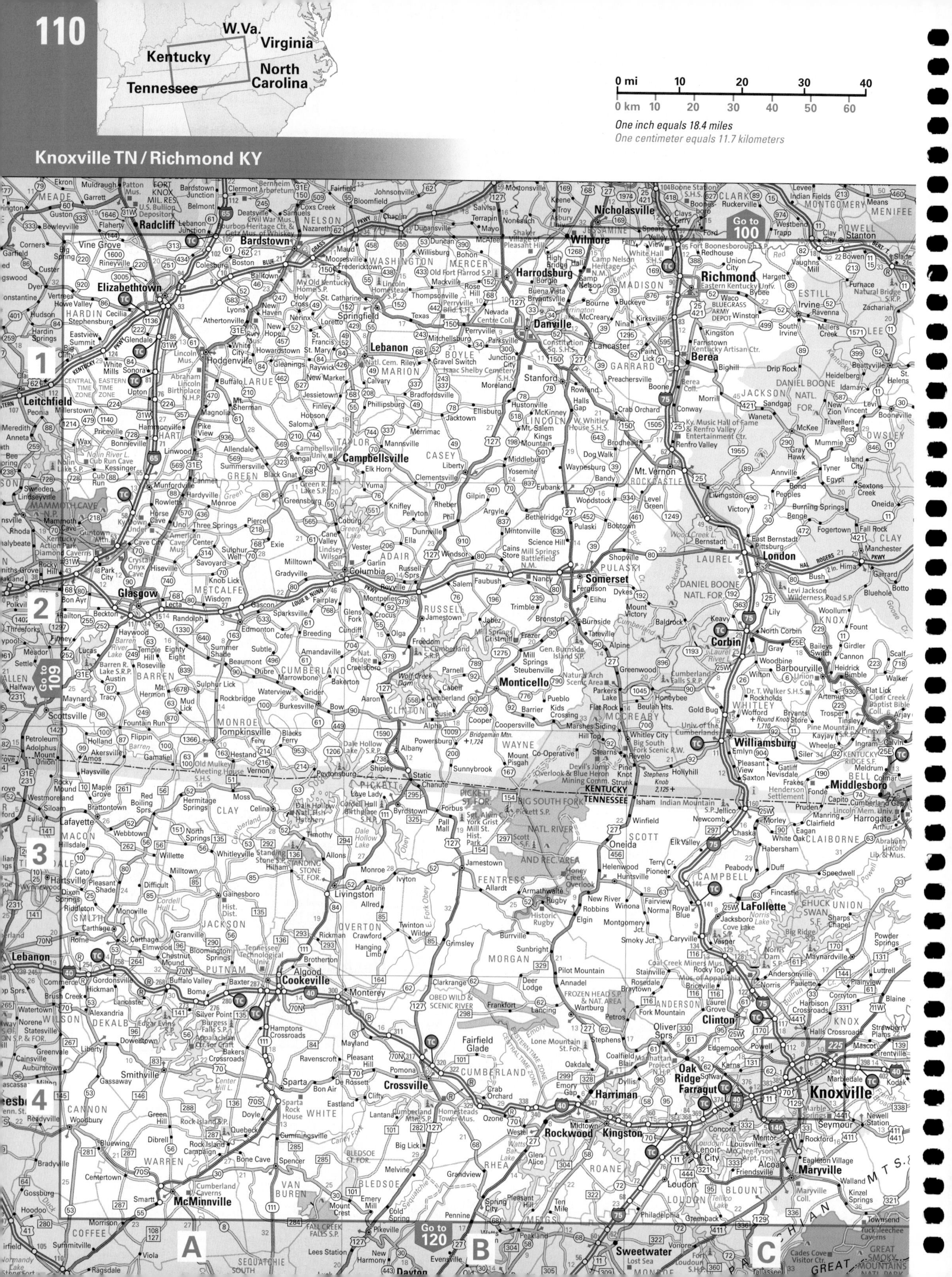
W.Va.
Virginia
Kentucky
North Carolina
Tennessee
0 mi 10 20 30 40
0 km 10 20 30 40 50 60
One inch equals 18.4 miles
One centimeter equals 11.7 kilometers
Go to 100
Go to 109
Go to 120
1
2
3
4
A
B
C
Radcliff
Bardstown
Elizabethtown
Nicholasville
Wilmore
Harrodsburg
Richmond
Danville
Lebanon
Berea
Leitchfield
Campbellsville
Mt. Vernon
London
Somerset
Glasgow
Columbia
Corbin
Monticello
Williamsburg
Middlesboro
LaFollette
Lebanon
Cookeville
Crossville
Harriman
Oak Ridge
Farragut
Clinton
Knoxville
Rockwood
Kingston
Maryville
McMinnville
Sweetwater
DANIEL BOONE NATL. FOR.
MAMMOTH CAVE N.P.
BIG SOUTH FORK NATL. RIVER AND REC. AREA
KENTUCKY
TENNESSEE
CENTRAL TIME ZONE
EASTERN TIME ZONE

DRIVING DISTANCES IN MILES	ASHEVILLE, NC	BECKLEY, WV	BRISTOL, TN/VA	COOKEVILLE, TN	GATLINBURG, TN	HICKORY, NC	JOHNSON CITY, TN	KNOXVILLE, TN	LONDON, KY	MAMMOTH CAVE NP, KY	PIKEVILLE, KY	RICHMOND, KY
BRISTOL, TN/VA	83	140		224	118	98	24	117	213	348	116	265
HICKORY, NC	78	196	98	291	147		98	185	280	415	214	332
KNOXVILLE, TN	109	256	117	107	40	185	107		100	234	202	151
LONDON, KY	205	287	213	129	136	280	203	100		136	121	53

SEE ALSO DISTANCE AND DRIVING TIME MAP ON PAGES 286–287

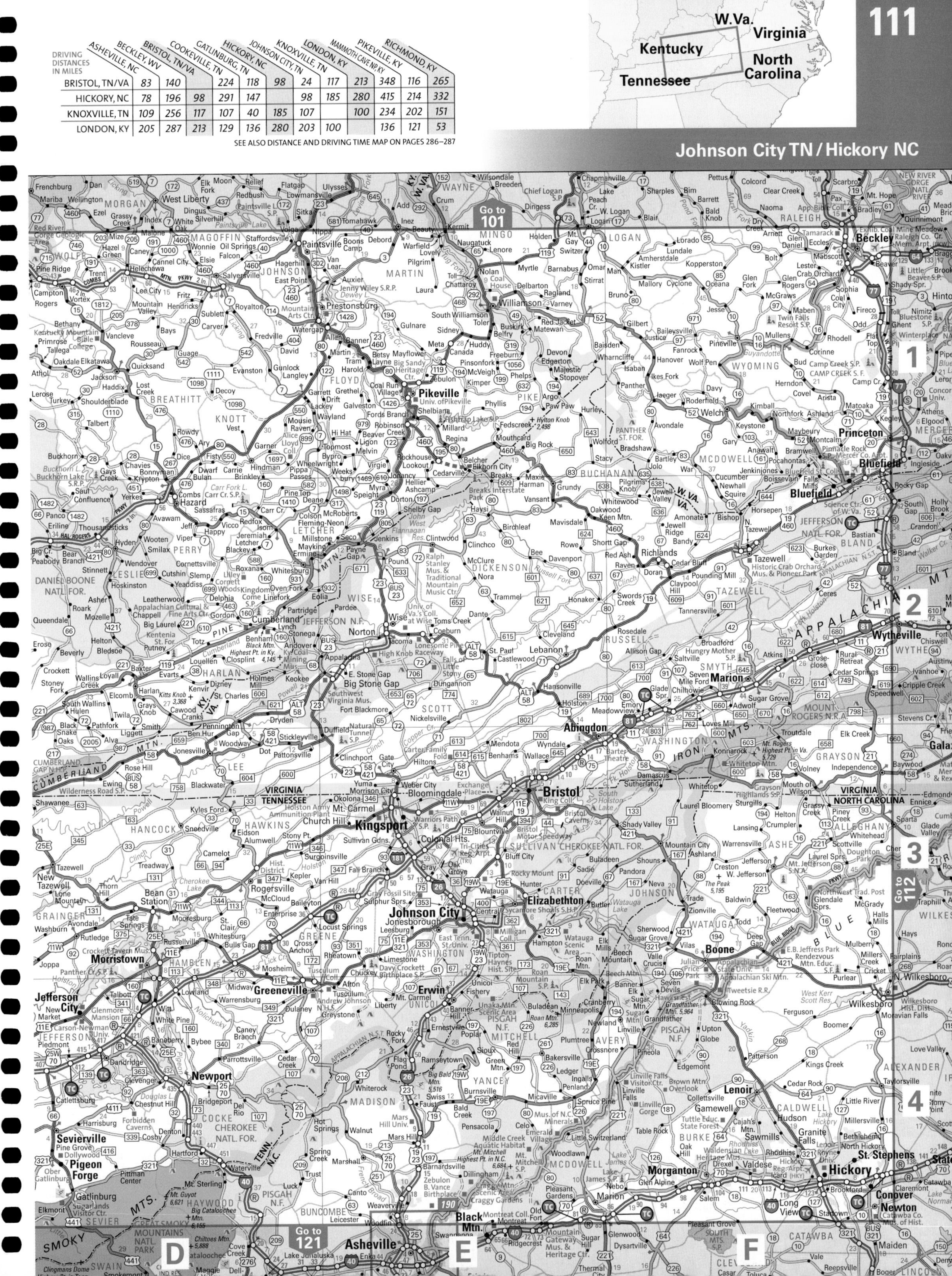

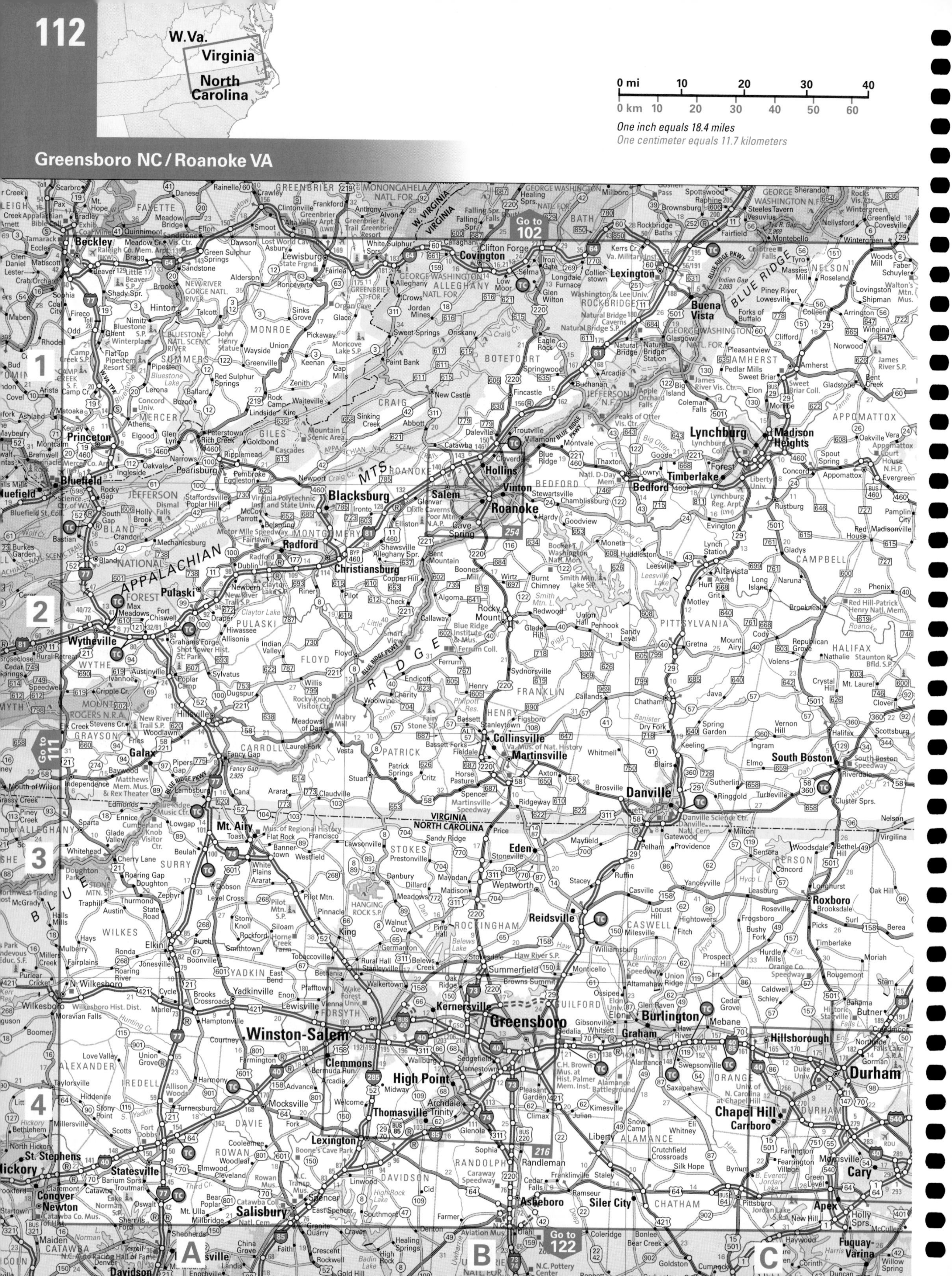

W.Va.
Virginia
North Carolina
0 mi 10 20 30 40
0 km 10 20 30 40 50 60
One inch equals 18.4 miles
One centimeter equals 11.7 kilometers
Go to 102
Go to 111
Go to 122
1
2
3
4
A
B
C
Beckley
Bluefield
Princeton
Blacksburg
Christiansburg
Radford
Pulaski
Wytheville
Galax
Salem
Roanoke
Vinton
Hollins
Lexington
Buena Vista
Covington
Clifton Forge
Lynchburg
Madison Heights
Timberlake
Bedford
Rocky Mount
Collinsville
Martinsville
Danville
South Boston
Mt. Airy
Eden
Reidsville
Roxboro
Winston-Salem
Greensboro
Burlington
Graham
Hillsborough
Durham
Chapel Hill
Carrboro
High Point
Thomasville
Lexington
Clemmons
Kernersville
Statesville
Salisbury
Asheboro
Siler City
Hickory
Conover
Newton
St. Stephens
Cary
Apex
Fuquay-Varina
APPALACHIAN
BLUE RIDGE
VIRGINIA
NORTH CAROLINA

DRIVING DISTANCES IN MILES	DANVILLE, VA	GREENSBORO, NC	LYNCHBURG, VA	NORFOLK, VA	RALEIGH, NC	RICHMOND, VA	ROANOKE, VA	ROANOKE RAPIDS, NC	ROCKY MOUNT, NC	WILLIAMSBURG, VA	WINSTON-SALEM, NC	WYTHEVILLE, VA
GREENSBORO, NC	46		106	230	69	200	101	132	124	237	30	120
RALEIGH, NC	89	69	140	179		157	156	84	54	204	96	186
RICHMOND, VA	160	200	114	91	157		192	91	127	49	228	256
ROANOKE, VA	83	101	55	285	156	192		190	211	243	107	78

SEE ALSO DISTANCE AND DRIVING TIME MAP ON PAGES 286–287

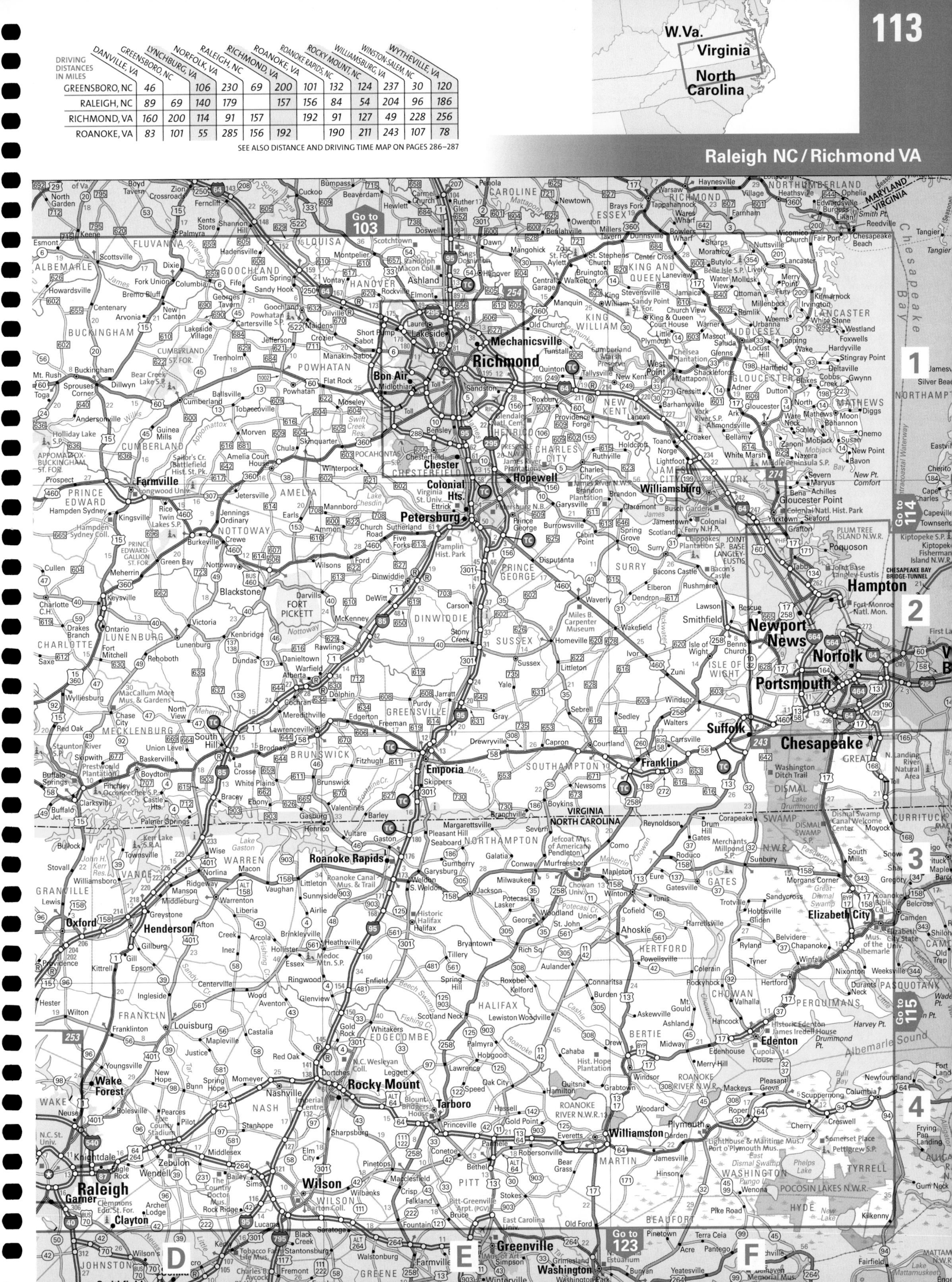

Md.
Delaware
Virginia
North Carolina
0 mi 10 20 30 40
0 km 10 20 30 40 50 60
One inch equals 18.4 miles
One centimeter equals 11.7 kilometers
Go to 104
Go to 103
Go to 144
Go to 145
Go to 113
Go to 115
FOR DETAIL OF AREA INSIDE PURPLE FRAME, SEE PAGES 144–145
Washington
Alexandria
Arlington
Annapolis
Fredericksburg
Richmond
Petersburg
Williamsburg
Hampton
Newport News
Norfolk
Portsmouth
Virginia Beach
Chesapeake
Suffolk
Salisbury
Ocean City
Cambridge
Easton
Seaford
Lewes
Dover
Chesapeake Bay
ATLANTIC
OCEAN
MARYLAND
VIRGINIA
1
2
3
4
A
B
C

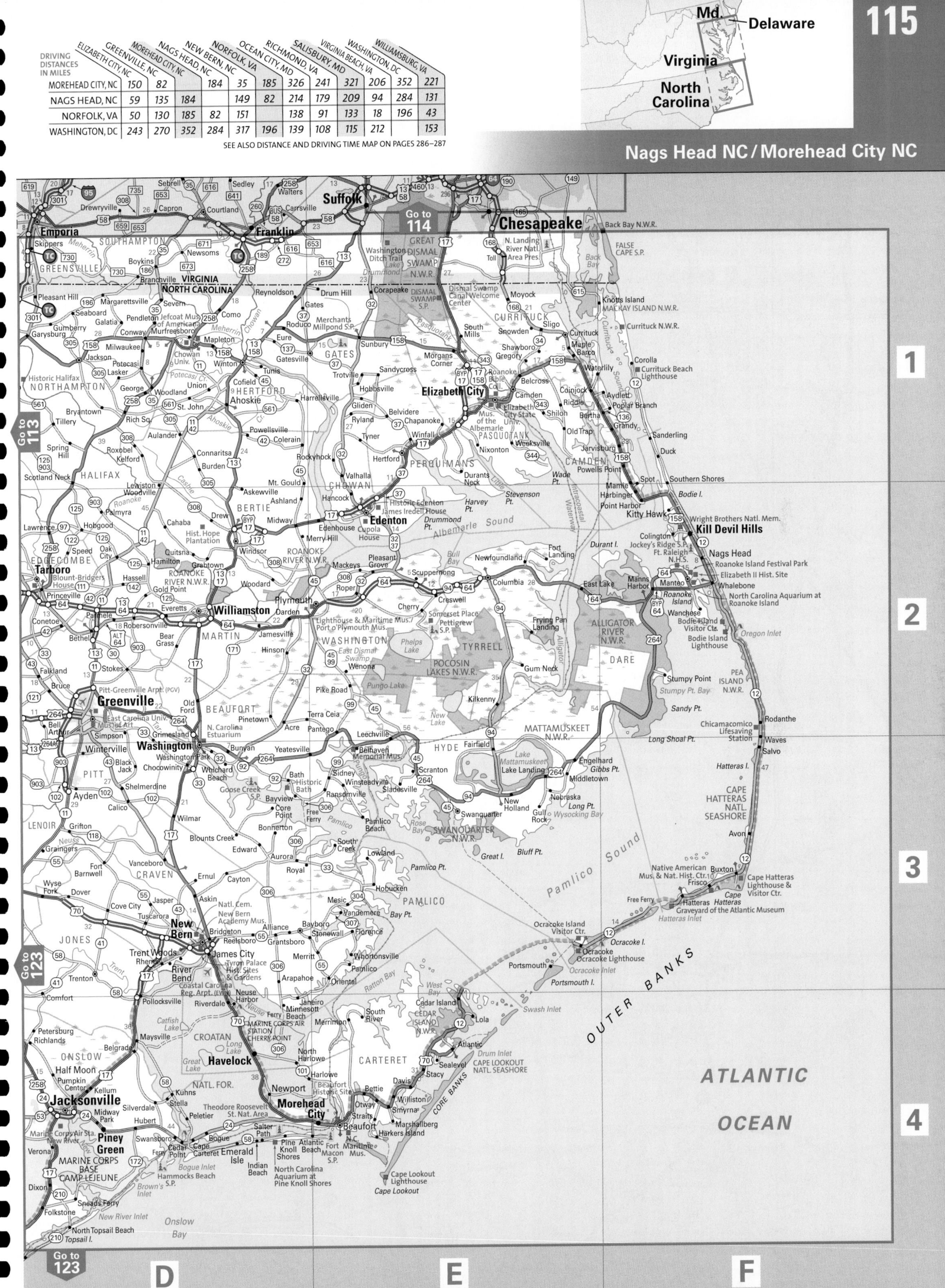

DRIVING DISTANCES IN MILES

	ELIZABETH CITY, NC	GREENVILLE, NC	MOREHEAD CITY, NC	NAGS HEAD, NC	NEW BERN, NC	NORFOLK, VA	OCEAN CITY, MD	RICHMOND, VA	SALISBURY, MD	VIRGINIA BEACH, VA	WASHINGTON, DC	WILLIAMSBURG, VA
MOREHEAD CITY, NC	150	82		184	35	185	326	241	321	206	352	221
NAGS HEAD, NC	59	135	184		149	82	214	179	209	94	284	131
NORFOLK, VA	50	130	185	82	151		138	91	133	18	196	43
WASHINGTON, DC	243	270	352	284	317	196	139	108	115	212		153

SEE ALSO DISTANCE AND DRIVING TIME MAP ON PAGES 286–287

Fort Smith AR / Texarkana AR–TX

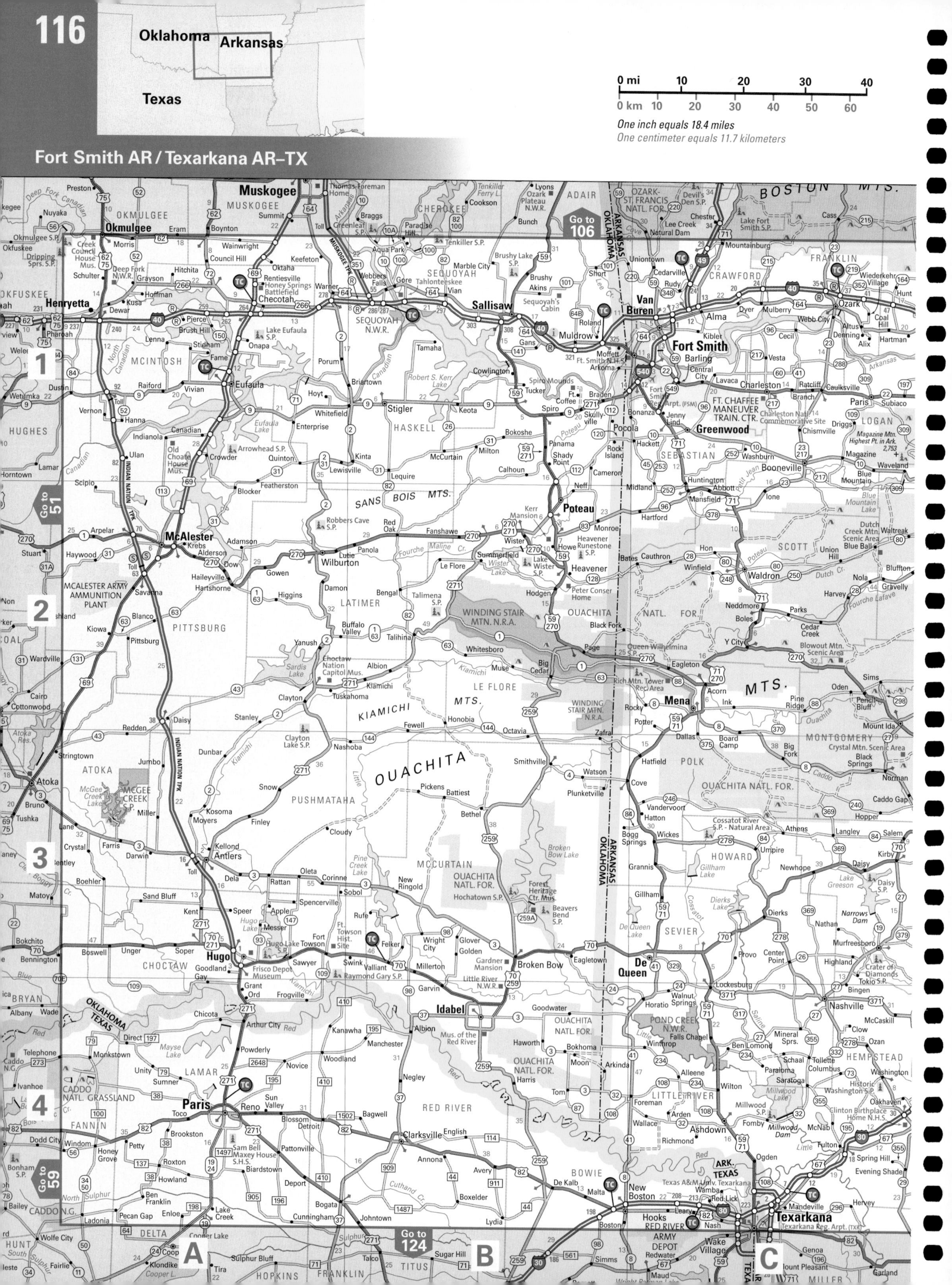

DRIVING DISTANCES IN MILES	ARKADELPHIA, AR	FORT SMITH, AR	HENRYETTA, OK	HOT SPRINGS, AR	LITTLE ROCK, AR	MCALESTER, OK	MENA, AR	NEWPORT, AR	PARIS, TX	PINE BLUFF, AR	RUSSELLVILLE, AR	TEXARKANA, AR/TX
FORT SMITH, AR	152		100	126	165	114	81	220	214	210	87	180
HOT SPRINGS, AR	37	126	224		65	193	75	154	207	76	67	117
LITTLE ROCK, AR	72	165	263	65		278	141	89	242	45	81	153
TEXARKANA, AR/TX	83	180	227	117	153	188	99	241	92	163	180	

SEE ALSO DISTANCE AND DRIVING TIME MAP ON PAGES 286–287

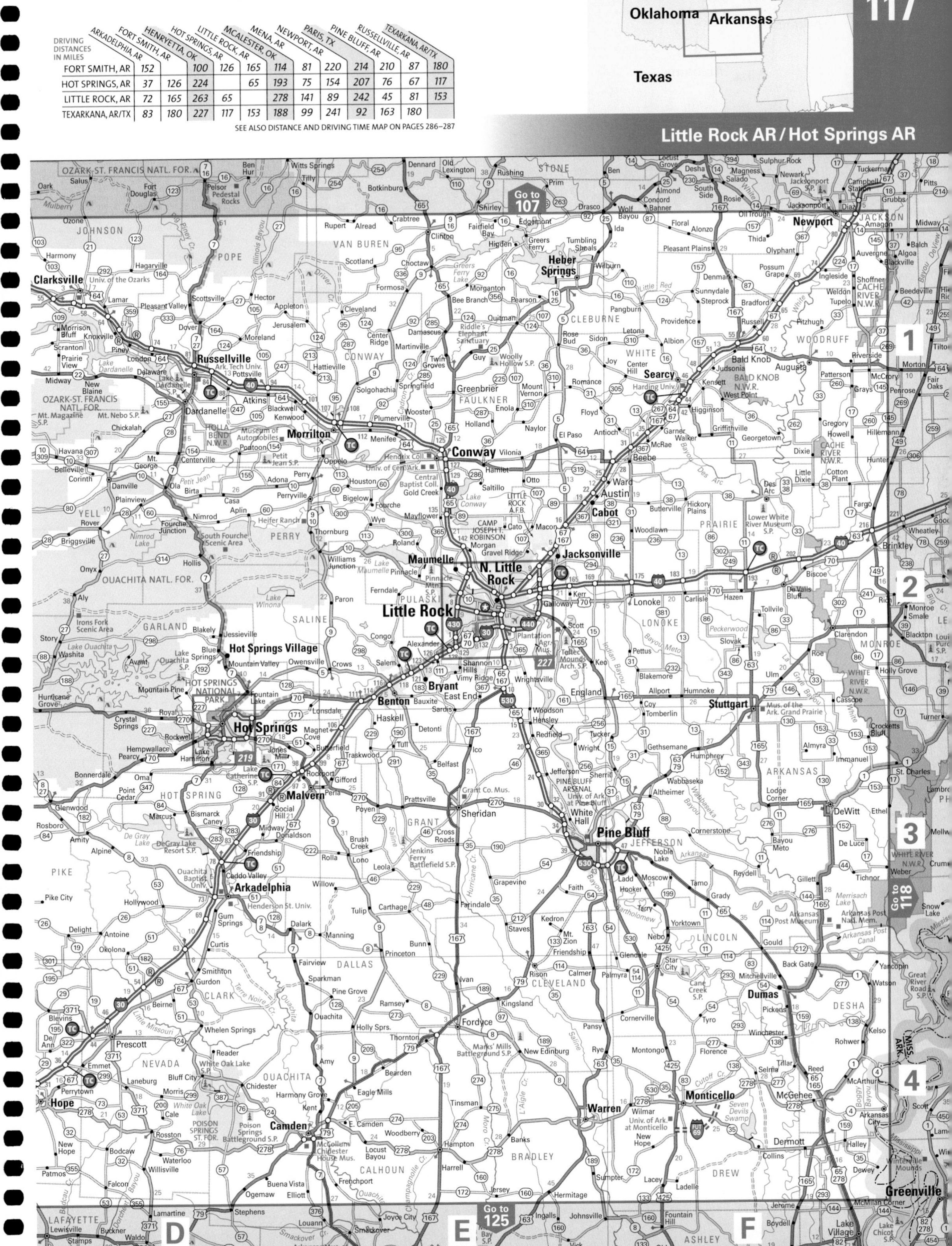

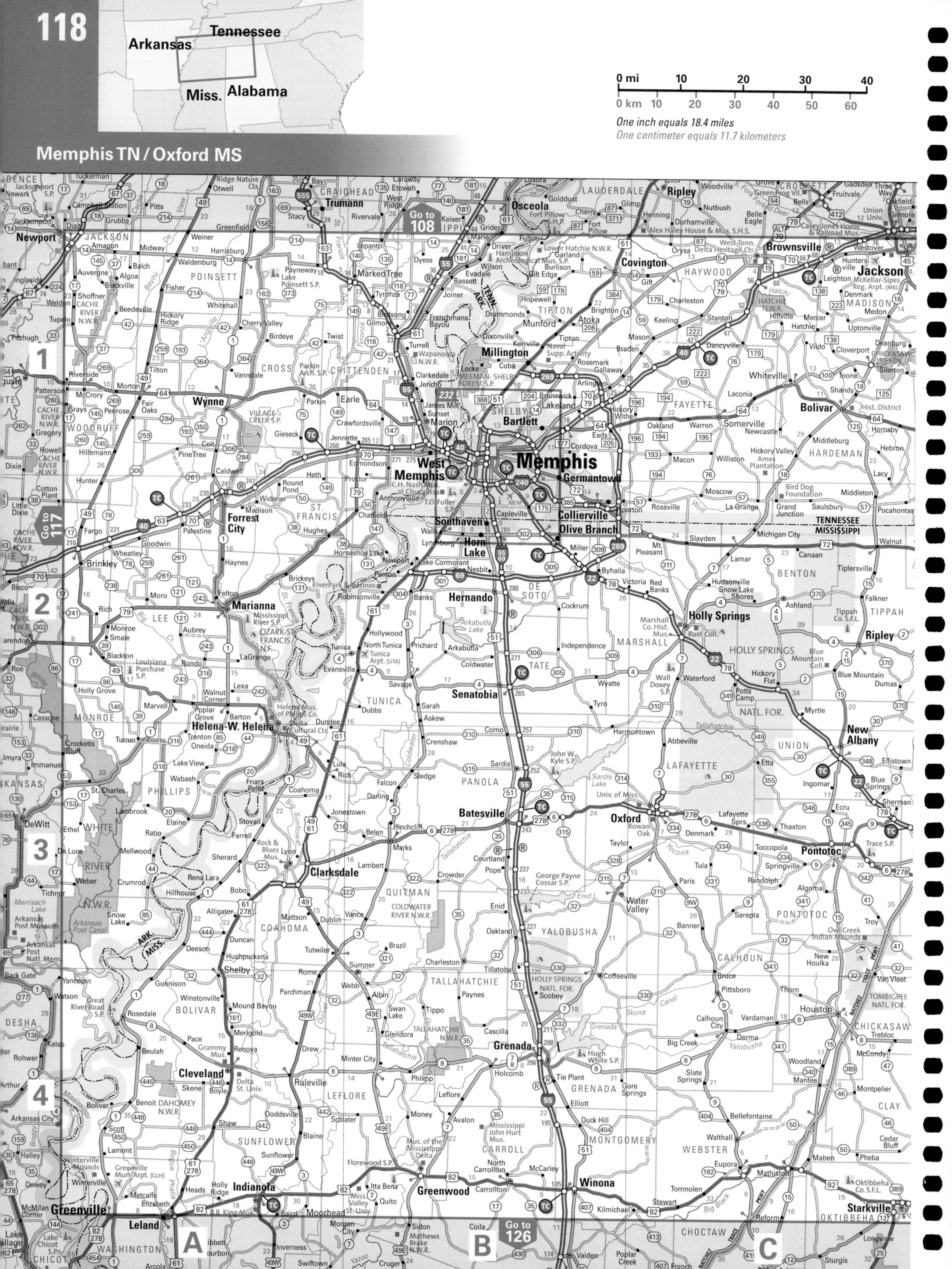

Arkansas
Tennessee
Miss.
Alabama
Memphis TN / Oxford MS
0 mi 10 20 30 40
0 km 10 20 30 40 50 60
One inch equals 18.4 miles
One centimeter equals 11.7 kilometers
Go to 108
Go to 117
Go to 126
Memphis
West Memphis
Germantown
Collierville
Olive Branch
Southaven
Horn Lake
Bartlett
Millington
Covington
Brownsville
Jackson
Bolivar
Somerville
Holly Springs
Hernando
Senatobia
Batesville
Oxford
Clarksdale
Helena-W. Helena
Marianna
Forrest City
Wynne
Osceola
Trumann
Newport
Brinkley
Cleveland
Greenville
Leland
Indianola
Greenwood
Grenada
Winona
Starkville
Pontotoc
New Albany
Ripley
TENNESSEE
MISSISSIPPI

DRIVING DISTANCES IN MILES	BIRMINGHAM, AL	CLARKSDALE, MS	COLUMBIA, TN	COLUMBUS, MS	DECATUR, AL	FLORENCE, AL	GREENVILLE, MS	HUNTSVILLE, AL	JACKSON, TN	MEMPHIS, TN	OXFORD, MS	TUPELO, MS
BIRMINGHAM, AL		248	161	122	83	121	286	101	223	241	185	136
HUNTSVILLE, AL	101	260	79	163	25	65	318		205	216	196	148
MEMPHIS, TN	241	76	210	175	191	156	148	216	91		85	109
TUPELO, MS	136	113	159	66	123	92	172	148	107	109	50	

SEE ALSO DISTANCE AND DRIVING TIME MAP ON PAGES 286–287

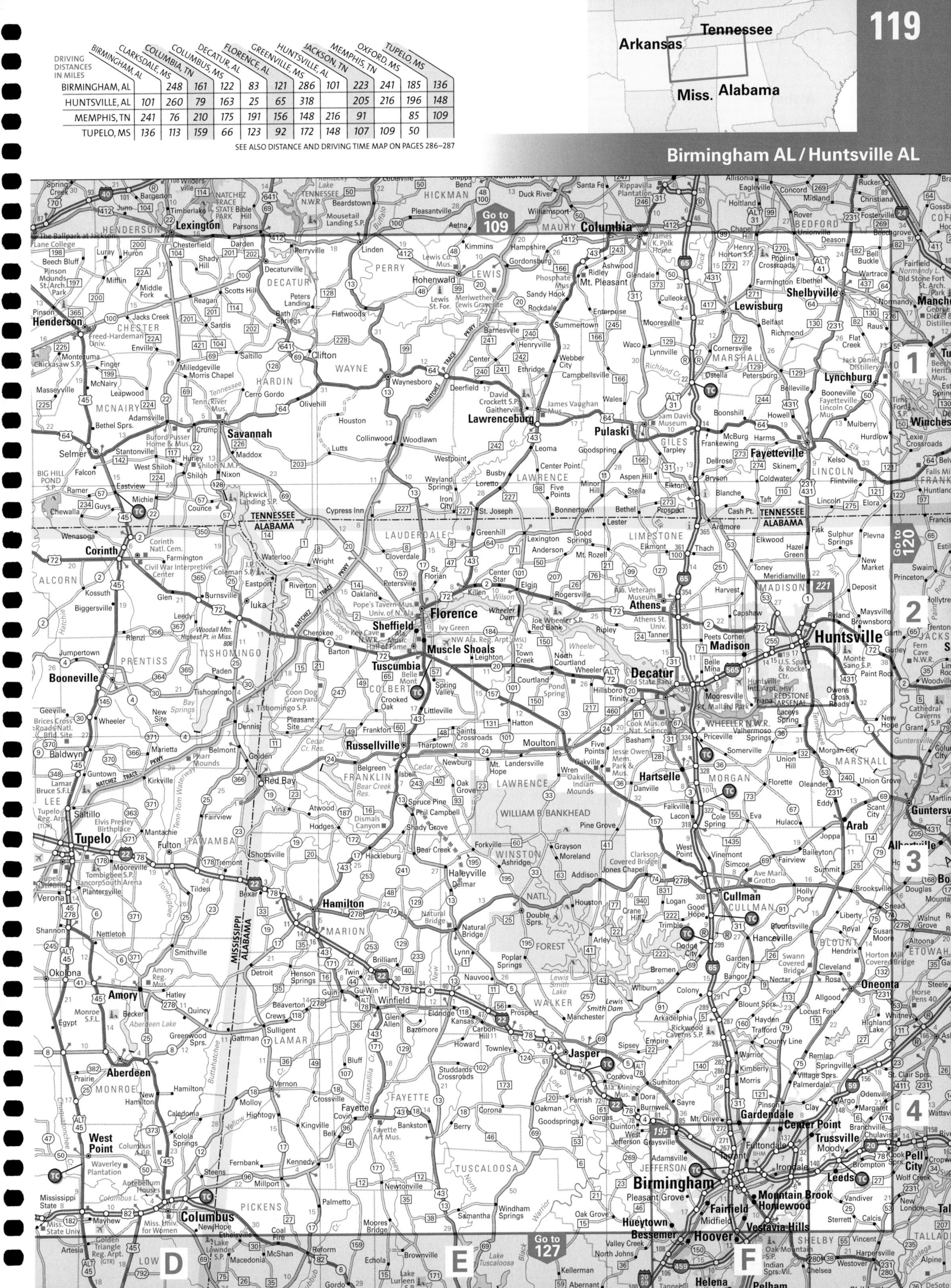

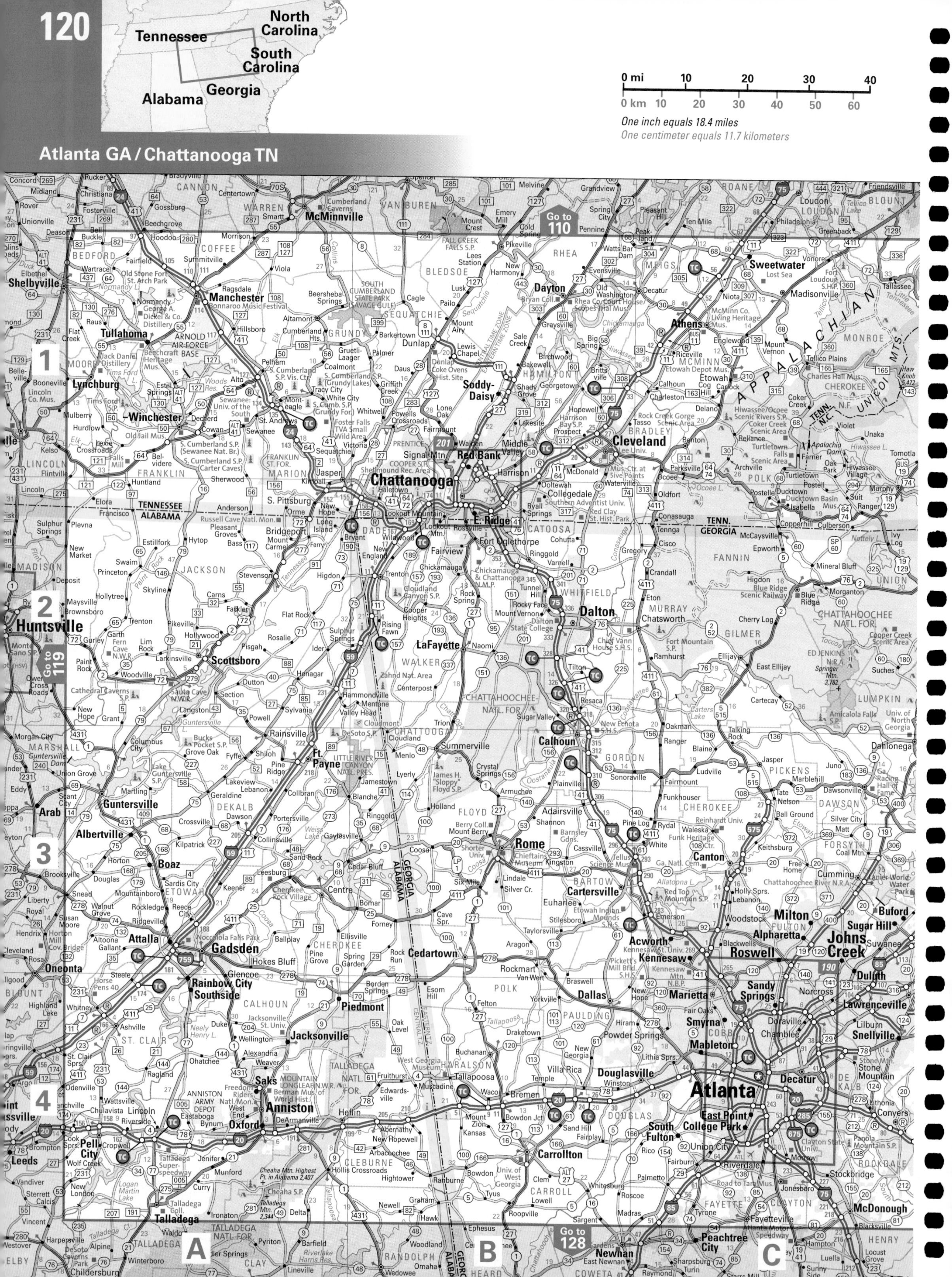

Tennessee
North Carolina
South Carolina
Alabama
Georgia
0 mi 10 20 30 40
0 km 10 20 30 40 50 60
One inch equals 18.4 miles
One centimeter equals 11.7 kilometers
Atlanta GA / Chattanooga TN
Go to 110
Go to 119
Go to 128
1
2
3
4
A
B
C
Chattanooga
Atlanta
Huntsville
Gadsden
Anniston
Rome
Dalton
Cleveland
Manchester
Tullahoma
McMinnville
Athens
Marietta
Roswell
Johns Creek
Kennesaw
Cartersville
Calhoun
Carrollton
Douglasville
Scottsboro
Guntersville
Albertville
Fort Payne
Talladega
Oxford
Decatur
Sandy Springs
Smyrna
East Point
Newnan
Peachtree City
McDonough

DRIVING DISTANCES IN MILES	ANNISTON, AL	ASHEVILLE, NC	ATHENS, GA	ATLANTA, GA	AUGUSTA, GA	CHATTANOOGA, TN	GADSDEN, AL	GATLINBURG, TN	GREENVILLE, SC	HUNTSVILLE, AL	MANCHESTER, TN	SPARTANBURG, SC
ATLANTA, GA	91	207	70		149	113	117	187	146	191	180	173
AUGUSTA, GA	240	179	97	149		266	266	240	110	334	333	118
CHATTANOOGA, TN	120	225	170	113	266		94	156	245	109	69	272
GREENVILLE, SC	238	64	104	146	110	245	264	125		313	311	30

SEE ALSO DISTANCE AND DRIVING TIME MAP ON PAGES 286–287

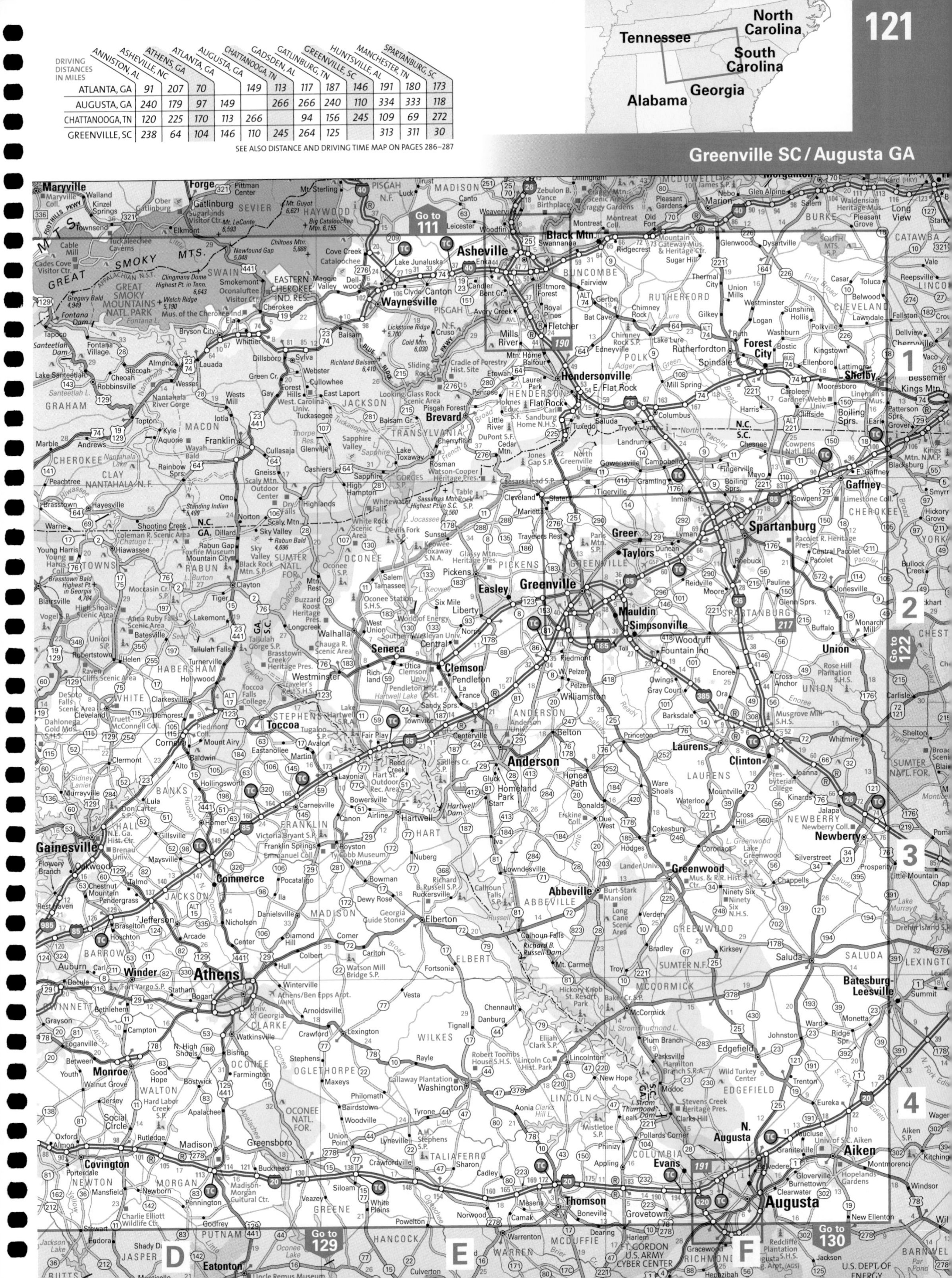

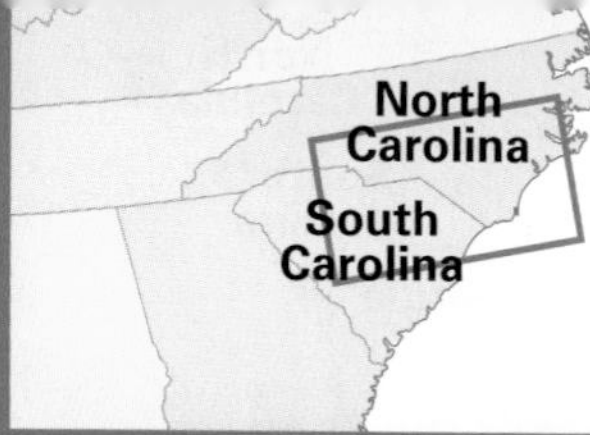

North Carolina
South Carolina

Charlotte NC / Columbia SC

0 mi 10 20 30 40
0 km 10 20 30 40 50 60

One inch equals 18.4 miles
One centimeter equals 11.7 kilometers

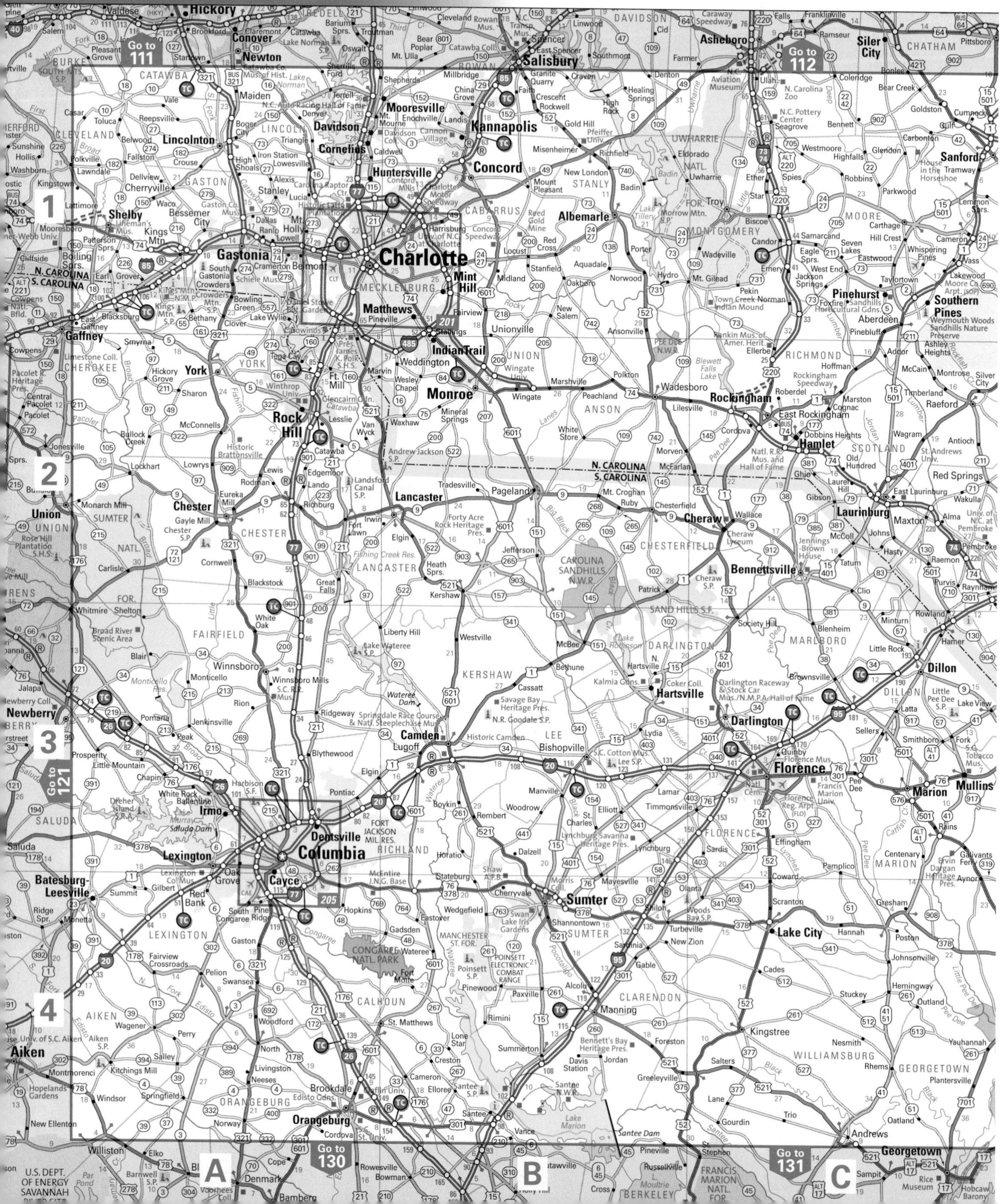

Go to 111
Go to 112
Go to 121
Go to 130
Go to 131

1
2
3
4
A B C

North Carolina
South Carolina

DRIVING DISTANCES IN MILES

	CHARLOTTE, NC	COLUMBIA, SC	FAYETTEVILLE, NC	FLORENCE, SC	GOLDSBORO, NC	HICKORY, NC	LUMBERTON, NC	MOREHEAD CITY, NC	MYRTLE BEACH, SC	ROCK HILL, SC	SUMTER, SC	WILMINGTON, NC
CHARLOTTE, NC		91	139	107	208	47	128	298	173	26	115	205
COLUMBIA, SC	91		170	80	240	139	139	289	146	70	45	199
MYRTLE BEACH, SC	173	146	116	66	170	220	83	165		181	93	71
WILMINGTON, NC	205	199	92	120	100	292	77	95	71	220	158	

SEE ALSO DISTANCE AND DRIVING TIME MAP ON PAGES 286–287

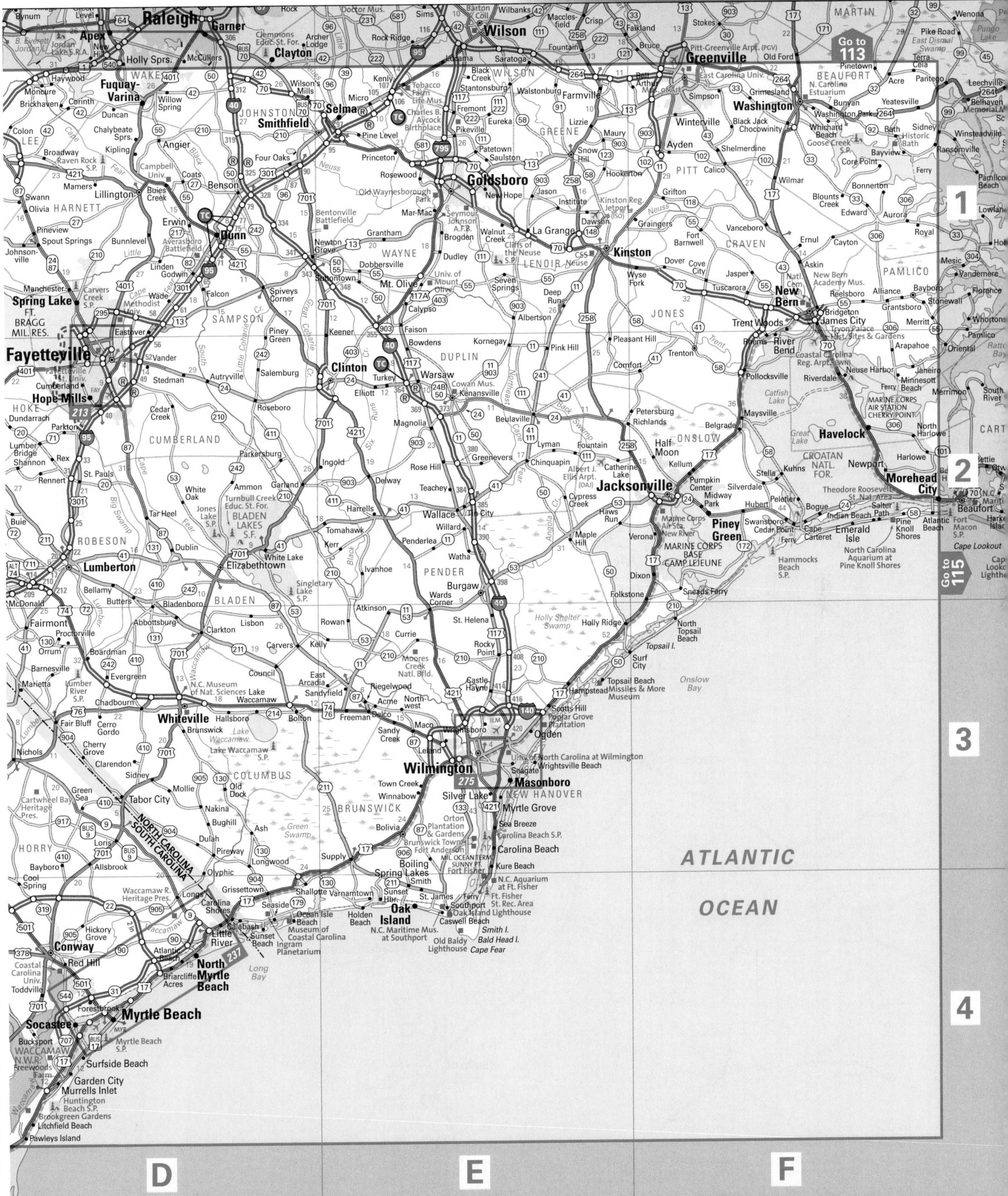

Go to 113

Go to 115

ATLANTIC OCEAN

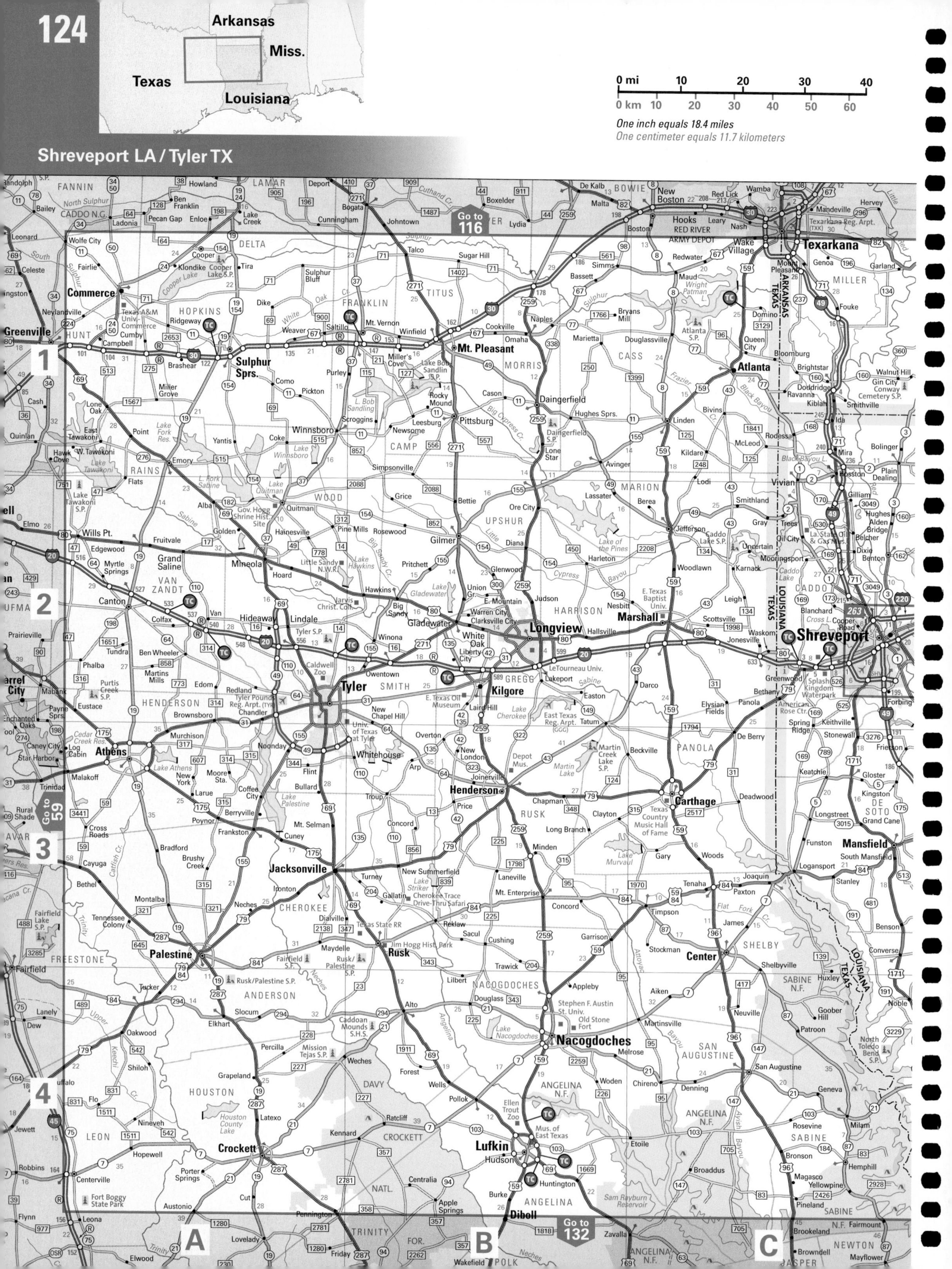
124
Shreveport LA / Tyler TX
Arkansas
Miss.
Texas
Louisiana
0 mi 10 20 30 40
0 km 10 20 30 40 50 60
One inch equals 18.4 miles
One centimeter equals 11.7 kilometers
Go to 116
Go to 59
Go to 132
Texarkana
Shreveport
Tyler
Longview
Marshall
Mt. Pleasant
Sulphur Sprs.
Commerce
Greenville
Atlanta
Kilgore
Henderson
Carthage
Mansfield
Center
Jacksonville
Palestine
Rusk
Nacogdoches
Lufkin
Crockett
Athens
Diboll
Daingerfield
Pittsburg
Gilmer
Mineola
Canton
Winnsboro
Jefferson
Sulphur Bluff
Grand Saline
Lindale
Gladewater
Whitehouse
FANNIN
LAMAR
DELTA
HOPKINS
HUNT
FRANKLIN
TITUS
RED RIVER
BOWIE
MORRIS
CASS
MILLER
CAMP
WOOD
RAINS
UPSHUR
MARION
VAN ZANDT
SMITH
GREGG
HARRISON
CADDO
HENDERSON
RUSK
PANOLA
DE SOTO
CHEROKEE
ANDERSON
FREESTONE
NACOGDOCHES
SHELBY
SABINE
SAN AUGUSTINE
HOUSTON
LEON
ANGELINA
TRINITY
POLK
JASPER
NEWTON
DAVY CROCKETT NATL. FOR.
ANGELINA N.F.
SABINE N.F.
Lake of the Pines
Caddo Lake
Lake Palestine
Sam Rayburn Reservoir
Toledo Bend
Tyler Pounds Reg. Arpt.
Texarkana Reg. Arpt.
Stephen F. Austin St. Univ.
Univ. of Texas at Tyler
LeTourneau Univ.
1
2
3
4
A
B
C

DRIVING DISTANCES IN MILES

	ALEXANDRIA, LA	EL DORADO, AR	GREENVILLE, TX	LONGVIEW, TX	LUFKIN, TX	MONROE, LA	NACOGDOCHES, TX	NATCHEZ, MS	NATCHITOCHES, LA	SHREVEPORT, LA	TEXARKANA, AR/TX	TYLER, TX
ALEXANDRIA, LA		147	276	179	160	96	167	76	55	121	190	213
MONROE, LA	96	86	267	170	223		203	95	100	103	172	204
SHREVEPORT, LA	121	96	165	68	121	103	101	198	73		69	102
TYLER, TX	213	196	77	42	82	204	76	288	164	102	118	

SEE ALSO DISTANCE AND DRIVING TIME MAP ON PAGES 286–287

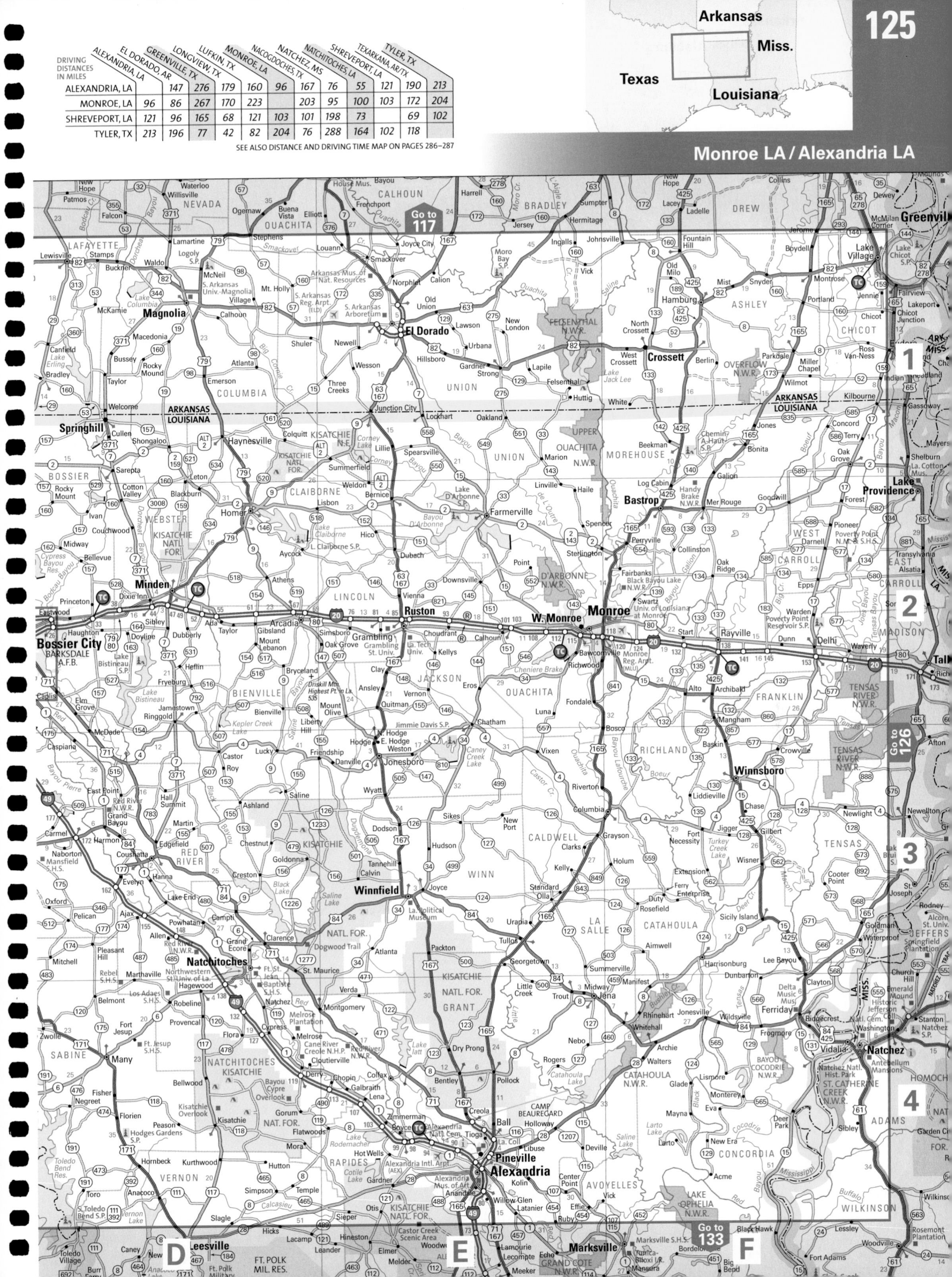

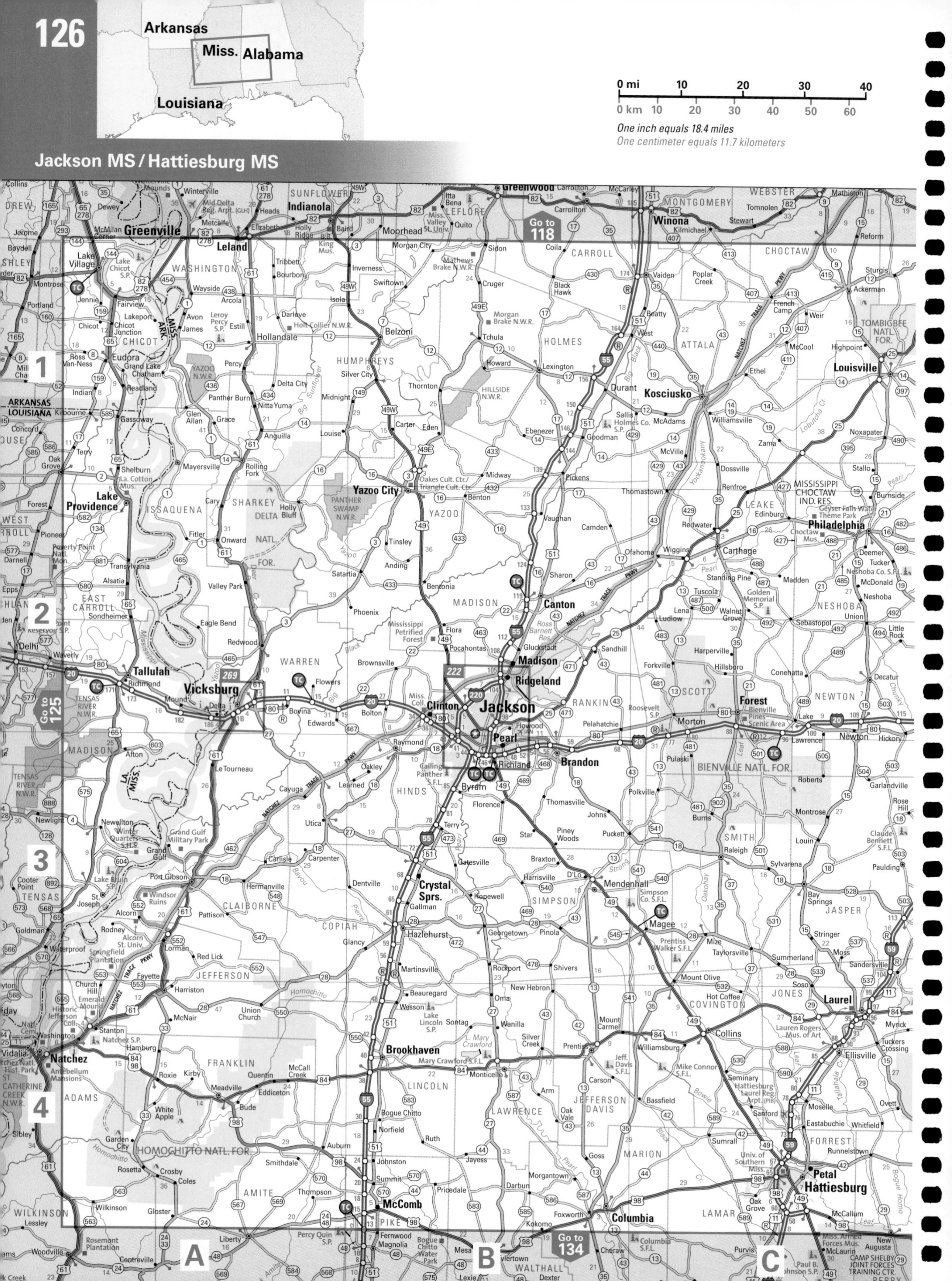
126
Arkansas
Miss.
Alabama
Louisiana
0 mi 10 20 30 40
0 km 10 20 30 40 50 60
One inch equals 18.4 miles
One centimeter equals 11.7 kilometers
Jackson MS / Hattiesburg MS
Greenwood
Indianola
Greenville
Leland
Winona
Go to 118
WASHINGTON
CARROLL
CHOCTAW
MONTGOMERY
WEBSTER
SUNFLOWER
LEFLORE
HOLMES
ATTALA
HUMPHREYS
CHICOT
Lake Village
Eudora
Belzoni
Kosciusko
Louisville
Lexington
Durant
Yazoo City
YAZOO
ISSAQUENA
SHARKEY
Lake Providence
MADISON
Canton
LEAKE
Carthage
Philadelphia
NESHOBA
MISSISSIPPI CHOCTAW IND. RES.
EAST CARROLL
Madison
Ridgeland
WARREN
Vicksburg
Tallulah
Delhi
Go to 125
Jackson
Clinton
Pearl
Brandon
Flowood
Richland
RANKIN
SCOTT
Forest
NEWTON
Newton
Morton
BIENVILLE NATL. FOR.
HINDS
Raymond
Byram
Port Gibson
CLAIBORNE
Crystal Sprs.
COPIAH
Hazlehurst
SIMPSON
Mendenhall
Magee
SMITH
JASPER
Bay Springs
JEFFERSON
Fayette
COVINGTON
Collins
JONES
Laurel
Natchez
Vidalia
ADAMS
FRANKLIN
Meadville
Brookhaven
LINCOLN
LAWRENCE
Monticello
JEFFERSON DAVIS
MARION
Columbia
FORREST
Hattiesburg
Petal
LAMAR
Ellisville
HOMOCHITTO NATL. FOR.
WILKINSON
AMITE
PIKE
McComb
Liberty
Woodville
WALTHALL
Tylertown
Go to 134
1
2
3
4
A
B
C

DRIVING DISTANCES IN MILES

	BIRMINGHAM, AL	EVERGREEN, AL	GREENVILLE, MS	HATTIESBURG, MS	JACKSON, MS	McCOMB, MS	MERIDIAN, MS	NATCHEZ, MS	SELMA, AL	TUSCALOOSA, AL	VICKSBURG, MS	WINONA, MS
HATTIESBURG, MS	239	184	215		90	75	89	142	193	183	132	180
JACKSON, MS	241	243	125	90		76	91	102	195	185	42	94
MERIDIAN, MS	149	152	216	89	91	167		194	104	94	133	113
TUSCALOOSA, AL	61	211	225	183	185	261	94	287	82		227	144

SEE ALSO DISTANCE AND DRIVING TIME MAP ON PAGES 286–287

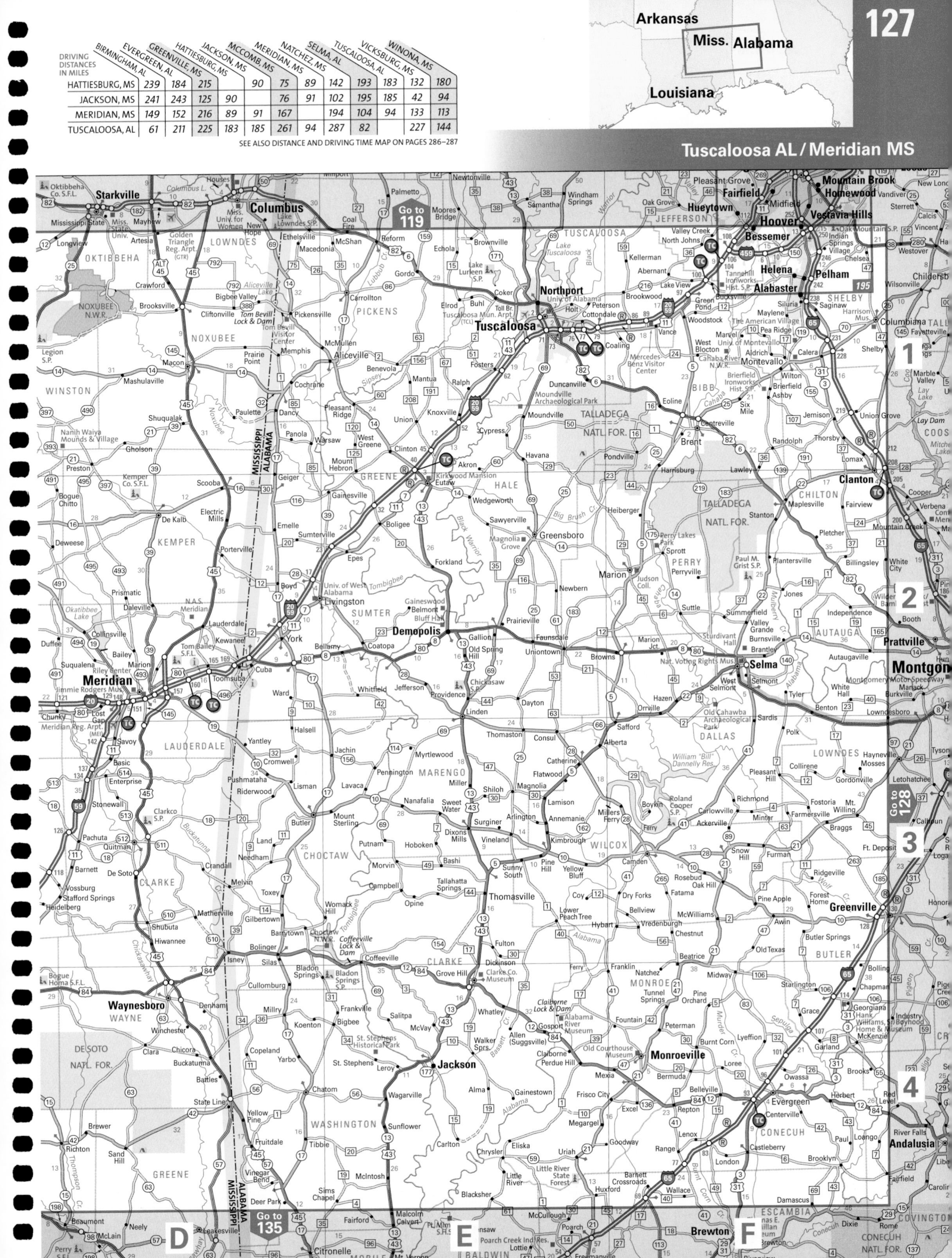

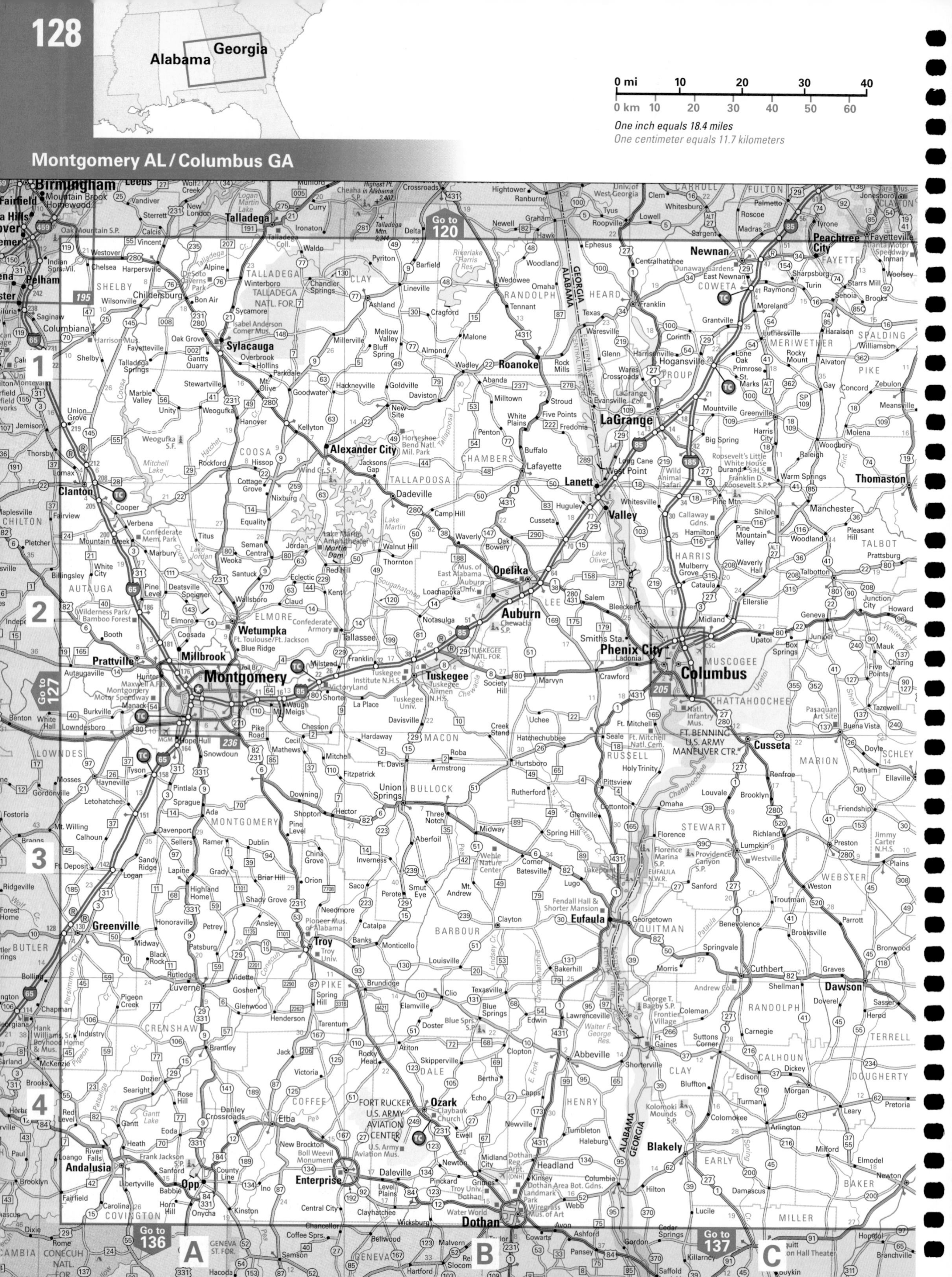
Alabama
Georgia
0 mi 10 20 30 40
0 km 10 20 30 40 50 60
One inch equals 18.4 miles
One centimeter equals 11.7 kilometers
Go to 120
Go to 127
Go to 136
Go to 137
1
2
3
4
A
B
C
Birmingham
Talladega
Sylacauga
Roanoke
LaGrange
Newnan
Peachtree City
Alexander City
Dadeville
Lafayette
Lanett
Valley
Thomaston
Clanton
Opelika
Auburn
Wetumpka
Millbrook
Prattville
Montgomery
Tuskegee
Phenix City
Columbus
Cusseta
Union Springs
Greenville
Troy
Eufaula
Luverne
Dawson
Cuthbert
Abbeville
Ozark
Blakely
Andalusia
Opp
Enterprise
Dothan
TALLADEGA
CLAY
RANDOLPH
HEARD
COWETA
FAYETTE
SHELBY
COOSA
TALLAPOOSA
CHAMBERS
TROUP
MERIWETHER
SPALDING
PIKE
CHILTON
AUTAUGA
ELMORE
LEE
HARRIS
TALBOT
MUSCOGEE
CHATTAHOOCHEE
MARION
SCHLEY
MACON
RUSSELL
BULLOCK
MONTGOMERY
LOWNDES
BUTLER
CRENSHAW
BARBOUR
STEWART
WEBSTER
QUITMAN
RANDOLPH
TERRELL
CALHOUN
DOUGHERTY
CLAY
HENRY
DALE
COFFEE
EARLY
BAKER
MILLER
COVINGTON
GENEVA
GEORGIA
ALABAMA
FT. BENNING U.S. ARMY MANEUVER CTR.
FORT RUCKER U.S. ARMY AVIATION CENTER
TALLADEGA NATL. FOR.
TUSKEGEE NATL. FOR.
CONECUH NATL. FOR.

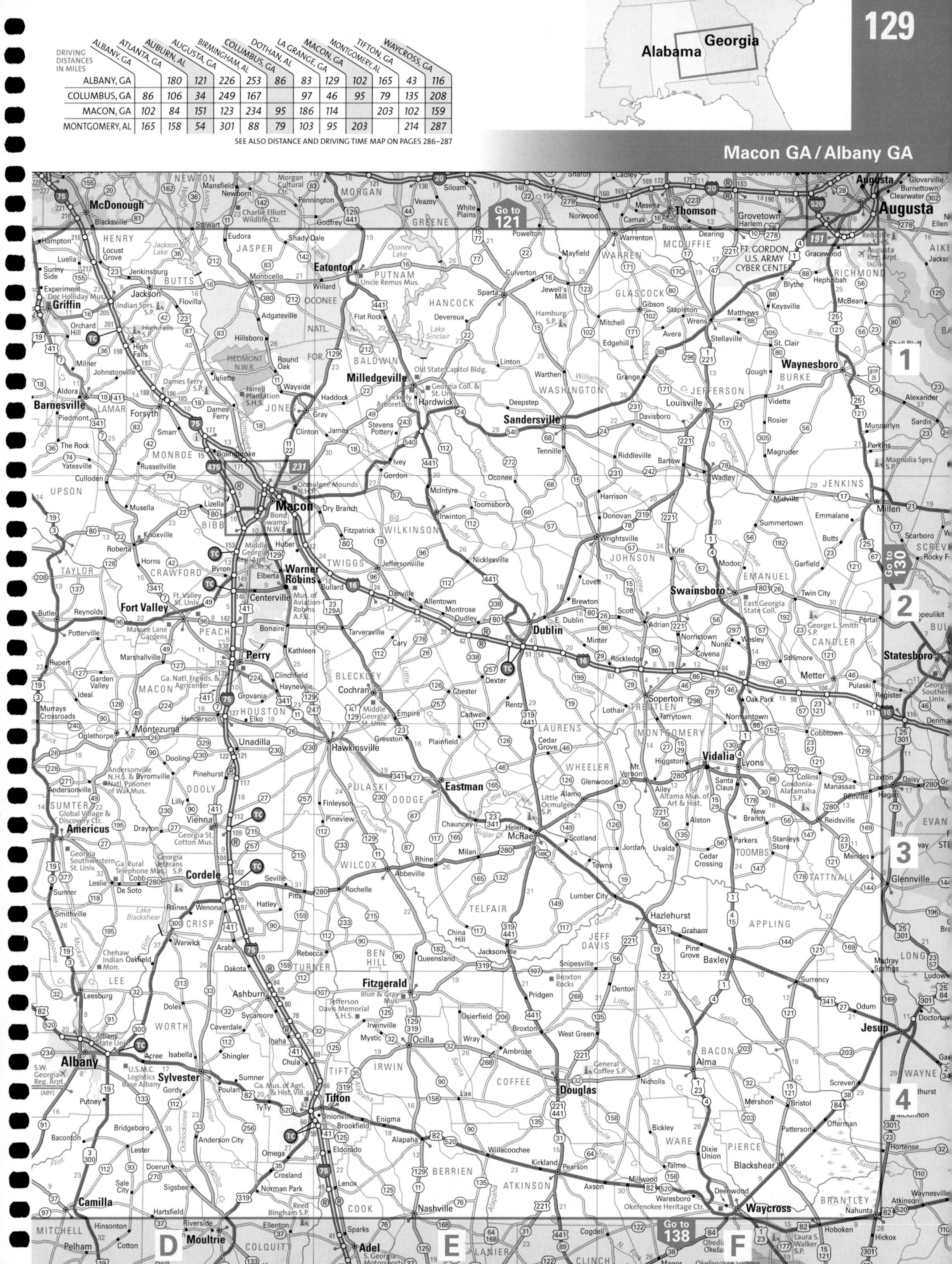

DRIVING DISTANCES IN MILES

	ALBANY, GA	ATLANTA, GA	AUBURN, AL	AUGUSTA, GA	BIRMINGHAM, AL	COLUMBUS, GA	DOTHAN, AL	LA GRANGE, GA	MACON, GA	MONTGOMERY, AL	TIFTON, GA	WAYCROSS, GA
ALBANY, GA		180	121	226	253	86	83	129	102	165	43	116
COLUMBUS, GA	86	106	34	249	167		97	46	95	79	135	208
MACON, GA	102	84	151	123	234	95	186	114		203	102	159
MONTGOMERY, AL	165	158	54	301	88	79	103	95	203		214	287

SEE ALSO DISTANCE AND DRIVING TIME MAP ON PAGES 286–287

South Carolina
Georgia

0 mi 10 20 30 40
0 km 10 20 30 40 50 60
One inch equals 18.4 miles
One centimeter equals 11.7 kilometers

Savannah GA / Hilton Head Island SC

Go to 121
Go to 129
Go to 138
Go to 139

1
2
3
4
A
B
C

Augusta
N. Augusta
Evans
Thomson
Orangeburg
Barnwell
Blackville
Williston
Denmark
Bamberg
Allendale
Hampton
Walterboro
Waynesboro
Louisville
Sandersville
Millen
Sylvania
Swainsboro
Statesboro
Metter
Vidalia
Lyons
Reidsville
Claxton
Glennville
Hinesville
Hazlehurst
Baxley
Jesup
Alma
Blackshear
Waycross
Brunswick
St. Simons Island
Savannah
Garden City
Pooler
Rincon
Richmond Hill
Wilmington Island
Tybee Island
Ridgeland
Hardeeville
Bluffton
Beaufort
Hilton Head Island
Daufuskie Island
Skidaway Island
Wassaw Island
Ossabaw Island
St. Catherines Island
Sapelo Island
Little St. Simons Island
Sea Island
Jekyll Island

MCDUFFIE
RICHMOND
GLASCOCK
JEFFERSON
BURKE
JENKINS
SCREVEN
EMANUEL
CANDLER
BULLOCH
EFFINGHAM
TREUTLEN
MONTGOMERY
TOOMBS
TATTNALL
EVANS
BRYAN
CHATHAM
LIBERTY
LONG
JEFF DAVIS
APPLING
WAYNE
MCINTOSH
BACON
PIERCE
WARE
BRANTLEY
GLYNN
COFFEE
AIKEN
BARNWELL
BAMBERG
ALLENDALE
HAMPTON
JASPER
BEAUFORT
COLLETON
DORCHESTER

S. CAROLINA
GEORGIA

U.S. DEPT. OF ENERGY SAVANNAH RIVER SITE
FORT STEWART MIL. RES.
Savannah N.W.R.
Tybee N.W.R.
Wassaw N.W.R.
Ossabaw Island Heritage Pres.
Blackbeard Island N.W.R.
Sapelo Island Natl. Estuarine Research Reserve
Hilton Head Island Arpt. (HHH)
Ft. Pulaski Natl. Mon.
Georgia Southern Univ.
Marine Corps Air Sta. Beaufort
M.C. Recruit Depot Parris Island

DRIVING DISTANCES IN MILES	AUGUSTA, GA	BEAUFORT, SC	BRUNSWICK, GA	CHARLESTON, SC	GEORGETOWN, SC	HILTON HEAD I., SC	HINESVILLE, GA	ORANGEBURG, SC	SAVANNAH, GA	STATESBORO, GA	WALTERBORO, SC	WAYCROSS, GA
AUGUSTA, GA		126	194	142	181	127	157	74	135	81	111	184
CHARLESTON, SC	142	66	175		58	95	138	73	107	150	51	203
HILTON HEAD I., SC	127	32	113	95	157		75	116	35	88	64	141
SAVANNAH, GA	135	42	78	107	163	35	41	123		53	71	106

SEE ALSO DISTANCE AND DRIVING TIME MAP ON PAGES 286–287

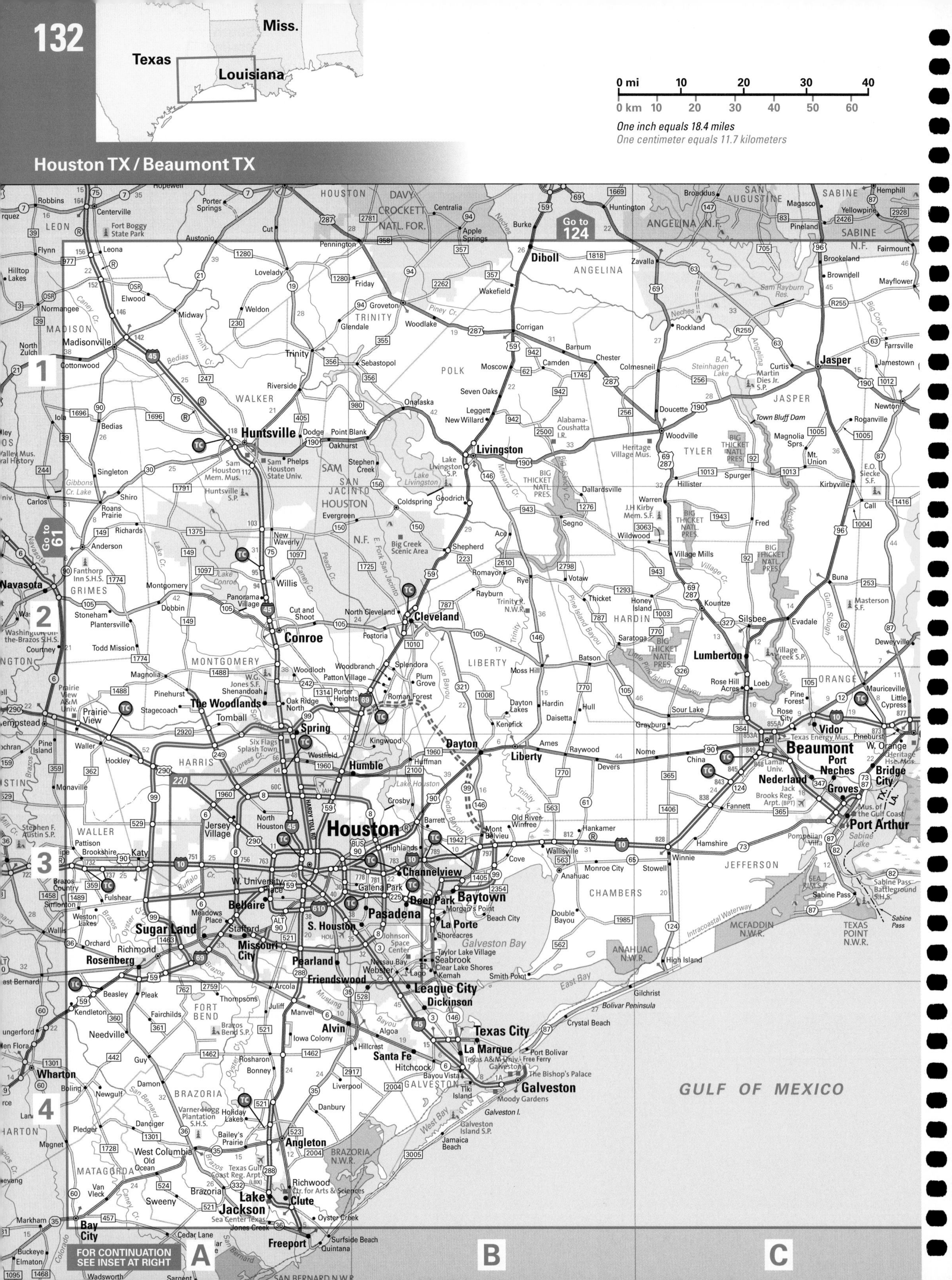

132
Houston TX / Beaumont TX
Texas
Louisiana
Miss.
0 mi 10 20 30 40
0 km 10 20 30 40 50 60
One inch equals 18.4 miles
One centimeter equals 11.7 kilometers
Go to 124
Go to 61
Houston
Beaumont
Port Arthur
Galveston
Huntsville
Conroe
The Woodlands
Spring
Humble
Baytown
Pasadena
Sugar Land
Missouri City
Pearland
Friendswood
League City
Dickinson
Texas City
La Marque
Alvin
Angleton
Lake Jackson
Clute
Freeport
Rosenberg
Bay City
Wharton
Navasota
Cleveland
Dayton
Liberty
Livingston
Diboll
Jasper
Lumberton
Vidor
Nederland
Port Neches
Bridge City
Groves
Silsbee
Katy
Bellaire
S. Houston
Deer Park
La Porte
Channelview
GULF OF MEXICO
Galveston Bay
East Bay
West Bay
Sabine Lake
Lake Livingston
Lake Houston
Lake Conroe
Intracoastal Waterway
ANGELINA N.F.
SAM HOUSTON N.F.
DAVY CROCKETT NATL. FOR.
SABINE N.F.
BIG THICKET NATL. PRES.
ANAHUAC N.W.R.
MCFADDIN N.W.R.
BRAZORIA N.W.R.
TEXAS POINT N.W.R.
SAN BERNARD N.W.R.
HARRIS
MONTGOMERY
WALKER
GRIMES
WALLER
FORT BEND
BRAZORIA
GALVESTON
CHAMBERS
JEFFERSON
ORANGE
HARDIN
LIBERTY
SAN JACINTO
POLK
TYLER
JASPER
ANGELINA
TRINITY
HOUSTON
MADISON
LEON
MATAGORDA
WHARTON
Sam Rayburn Res.
B.A. Steinhagen Lake
FOR CONTINUATION SEE INSET AT RIGHT
A
B
C
1
2
3
4

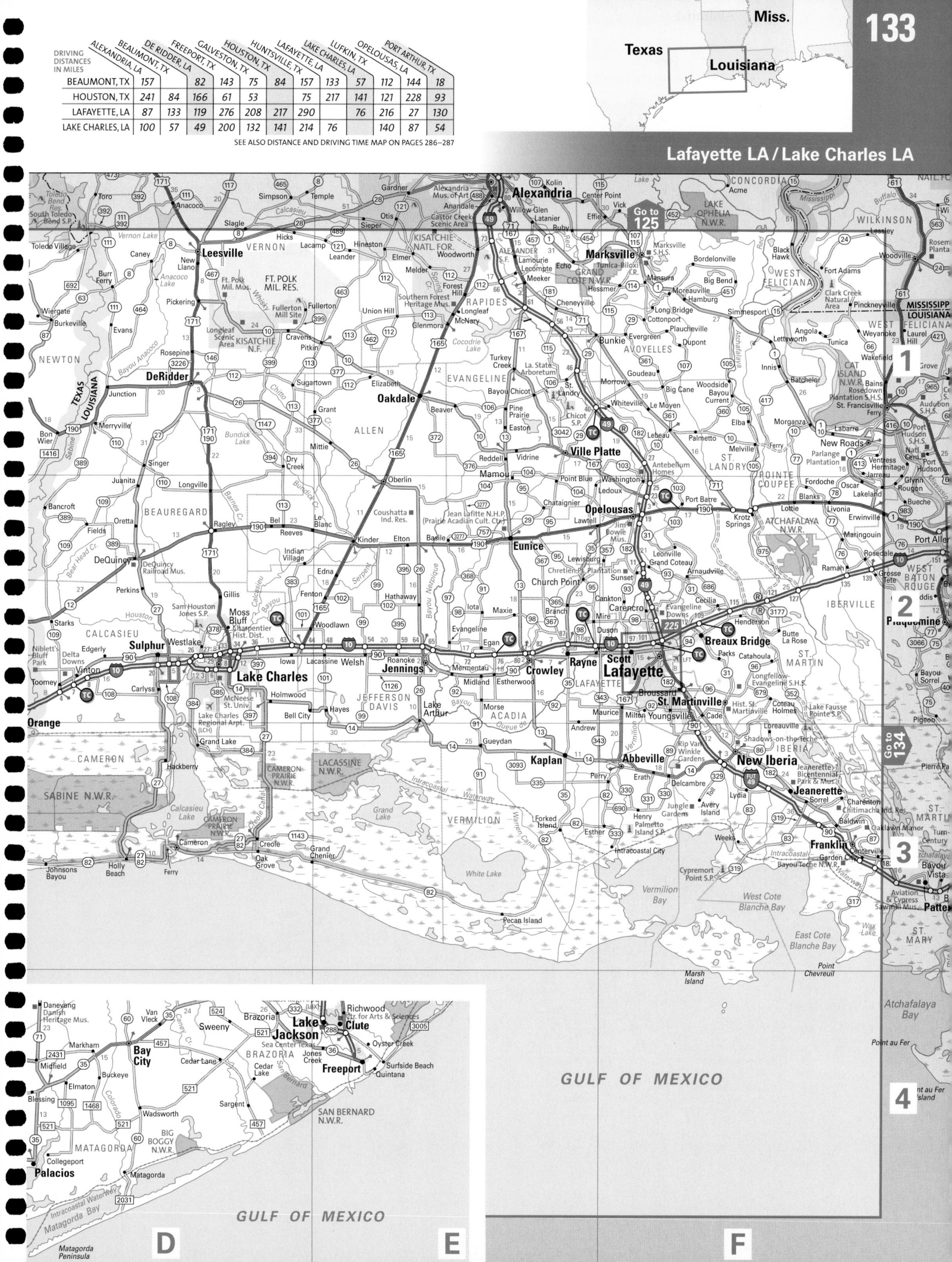

DRIVING DISTANCES IN MILES	ALEXANDRIA, LA	BEAUMONT, TX	DE RIDDER, LA	FREEPORT, TX	GALVESTON, TX	HOUSTON, TX	HUNTSVILLE, TX	LAFAYETTE, LA	LAKE CHARLES, LA	LUFKIN, TX	OPELOUSAS, LA	PORT ARTHUR, TX
BEAUMONT, TX	157		82	143	75	84	157	133	57	112	144	18
HOUSTON, TX	241	84	166	61	53		75	217	141	121	228	93
LAFAYETTE, LA	87	133	119	276	208	217	290		76	216	27	130
LAKE CHARLES, LA	100	57	49	200	132	141	214	76		140	87	54

SEE ALSO DISTANCE AND DRIVING TIME MAP ON PAGES 286–287

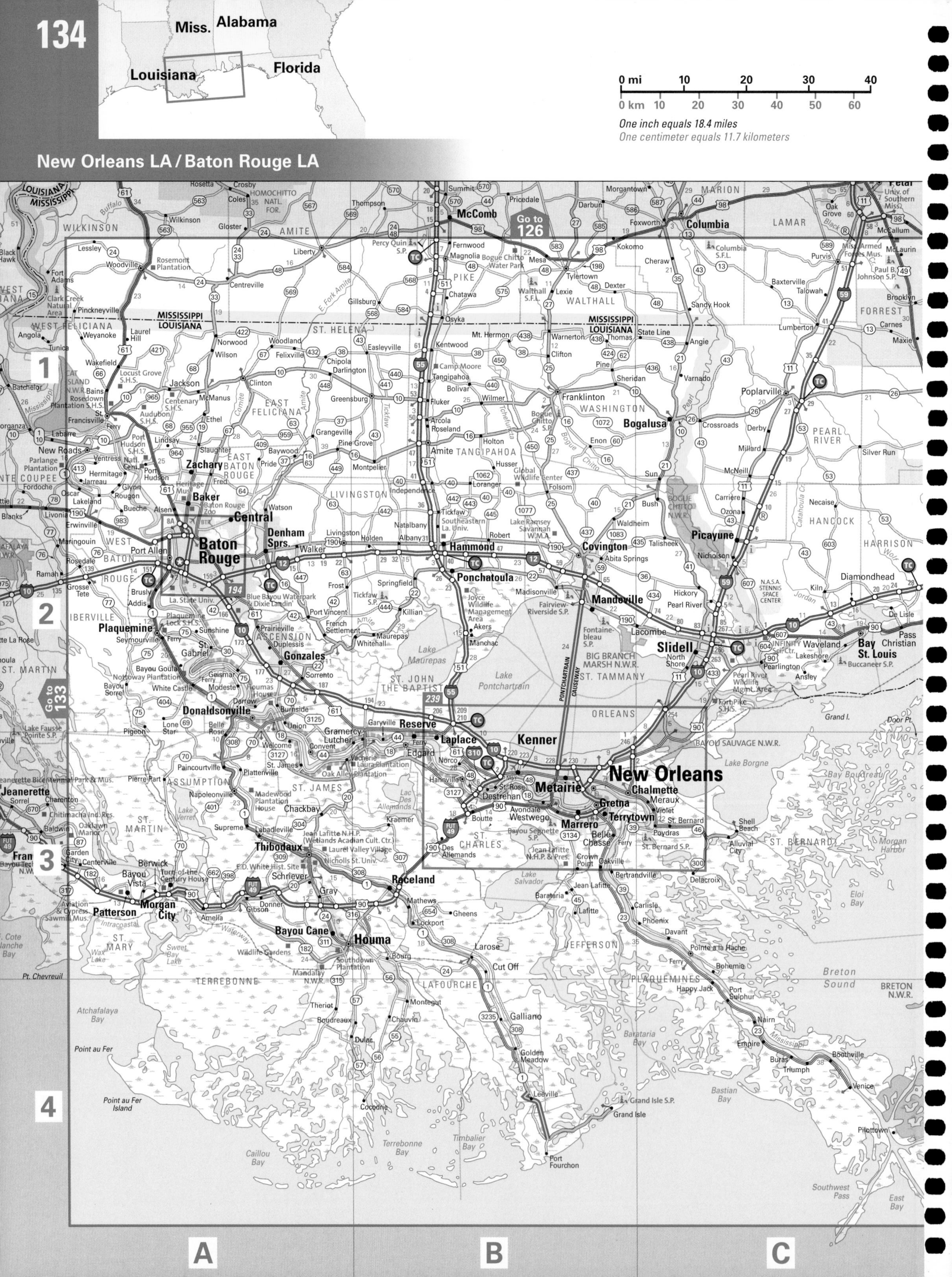
Miss.
Alabama
Louisiana
Florida
0 mi 10 20 30 40
0 km 10 20 30 40 50 60
One inch equals 18.4 miles
One centimeter equals 11.7 kilometers
Go to 126
Go to 133
McComb
Columbia
Magnolia
Liberty
Woodville
Centreville
Gloster
Tylertown
MISSISSIPPI
LOUISIANA
WILKINSON
AMITE
PIKE
WALTHALL
MARION
LAMAR
FORREST
WEST FELICIANA
EAST FELICIANA
ST. HELENA
WASHINGTON
TANGIPAHOA
LIVINGSTON
EAST BATON ROUGE
WEST BATON ROUGE
POINTE COUPEE
IBERVILLE
ASCENSION
ST. JAMES
ST. JOHN THE BAPTIST
ST. CHARLES
ORLEANS
ST. TAMMANY
PEARL RIVER
HANCOCK
HARRISON
ASSUMPTION
ST. MARTIN
ST. MARY
TERREBONNE
LAFOURCHE
JEFFERSON
PLAQUEMINES
ST. BERNARD
Baton Rouge
Central
Baker
Zachary
Denham Sprs.
Walker
Port Allen
Plaquemine
Gonzales
Donaldsonville
Hammond
Ponchatoula
Amite
Franklinton
Bogalusa
Picayune
Poplarville
Covington
Mandeville
Slidell
Bay St. Louis
Waveland
Reserve
Laplace
Kenner
Metairie
New Orleans
Chalmette
Gretna
Marrero
Terrytown
Thibodaux
Raceland
Houma
Bayou Cane
Morgan City
Patterson
Lake Maurepas
Lake Pontchartrain
Lake Borgne
Breton Sound
Atchafalaya Bay
Terrebonne Bay
Timbalier Bay
Caillou Bay
Barataria Bay
Grand Isle
Port Fourchon
Golden Meadow
Galliano
Cut Off
Venice
Boothville
Empire
Port Sulphur
Pointe a la Hache
1
2
3
4
A
B
C

DRIVING DISTANCES IN MILES	BATON ROUGE, LA	BILOXI, MS	GULFPORT, MS	GULF SHORES, AL	HAMMOND, LA	HATTIESBURG, MS	HOUMA, LA	MCCOMB, MS	MOBILE, AL	NEW ORLEANS, LA	PASCAGOULA, MS	PENSACOLA, FL
BATON ROUGE, LA		151	140	254	51	174	101	102	205	91	170	264
BILOXI, MS	151		12	110	106	82	148	161	61	93	20	120
MOBILE, AL	205	61	75	48	159	97	201	215		146	41	58
NEW ORLEANS, LA	91	93	81	195	57	115	57	111	146		112	205

SEE ALSO DISTANCE AND DRIVING TIME MAP ON PAGES 286–287

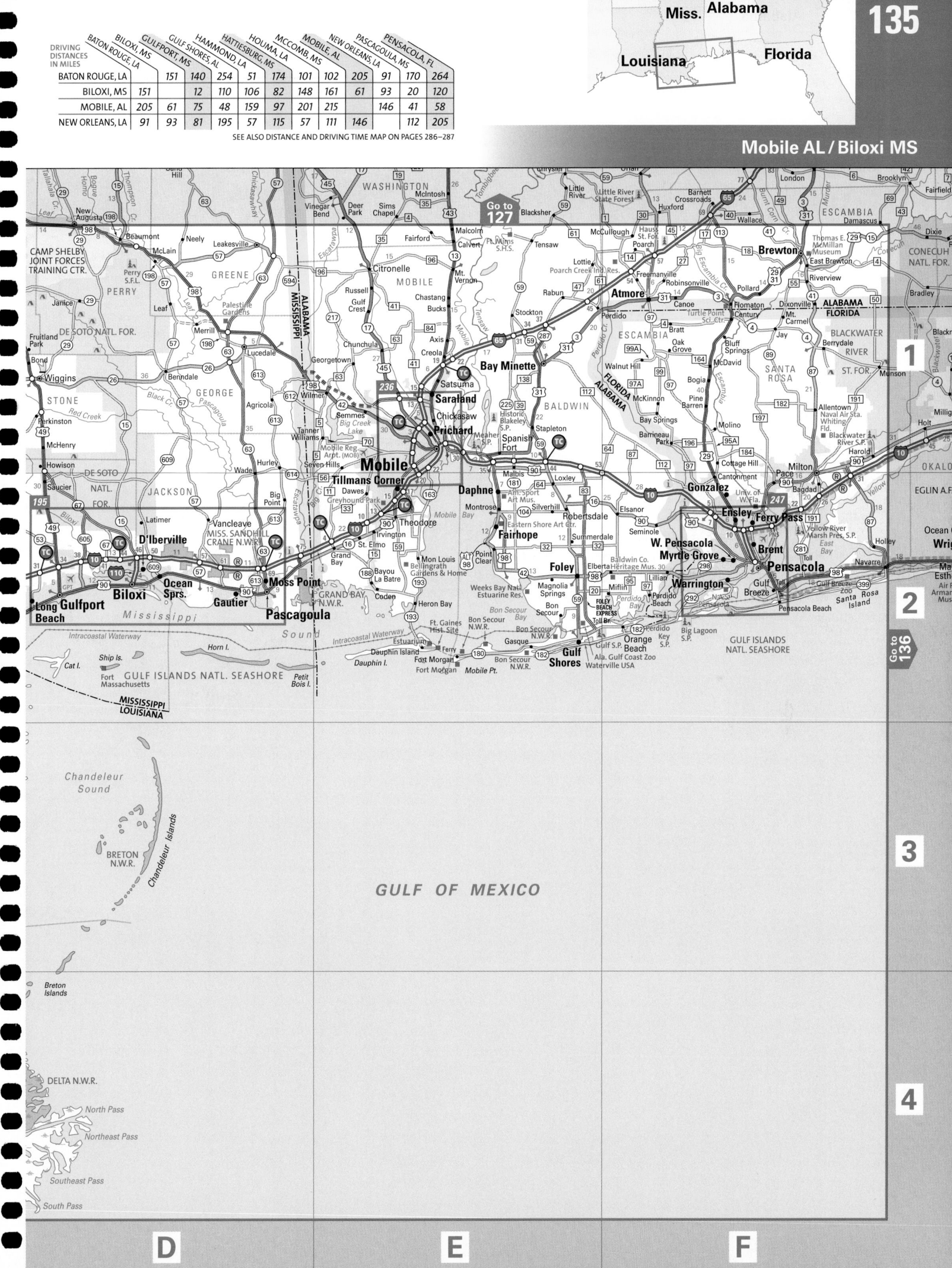

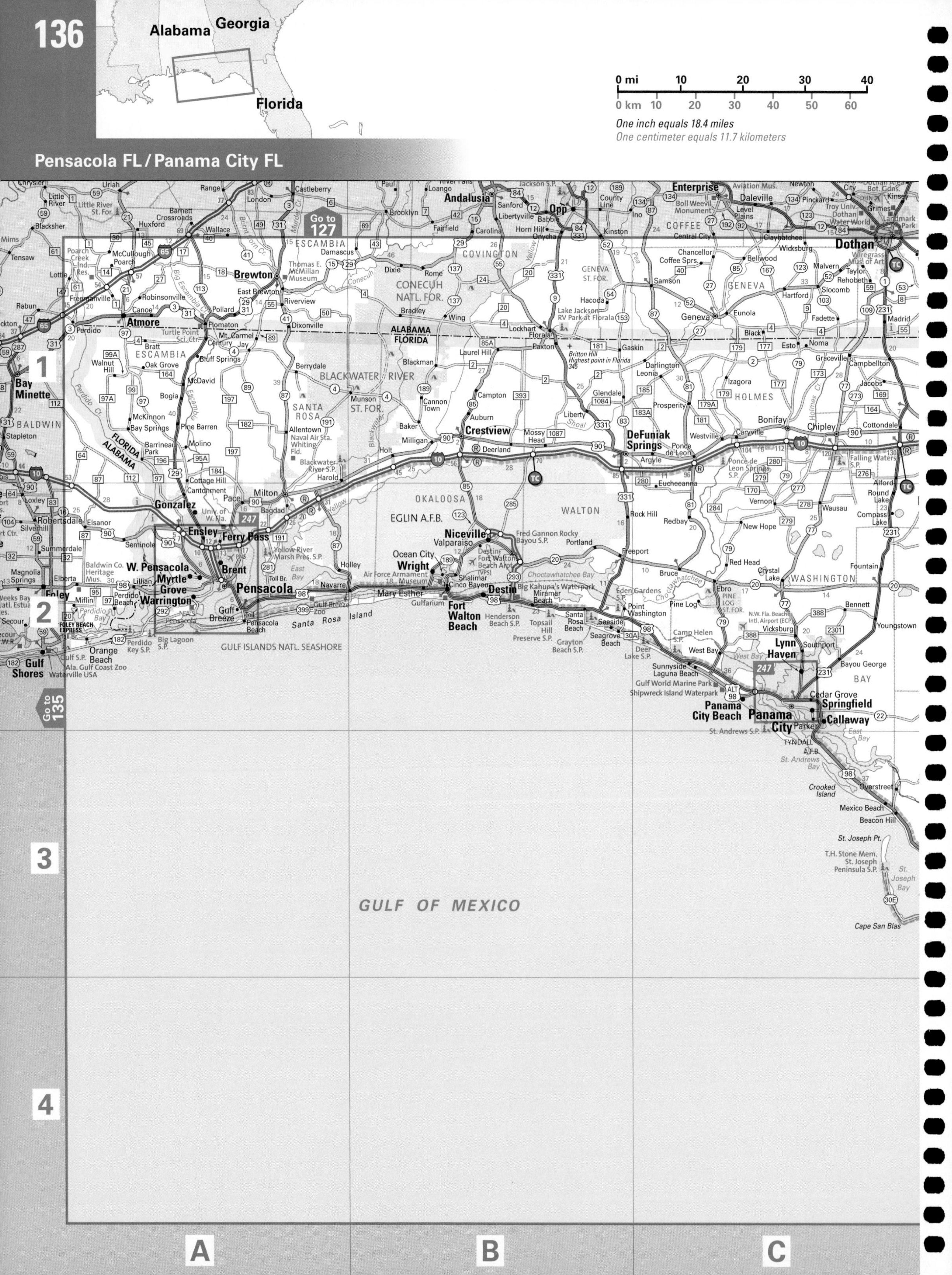
Alabama
Georgia
Florida
0 mi 10 20 30 40
0 km 10 20 30 40 50 60
One inch equals 18.4 miles
One centimeter equals 11.7 kilometers
Go to 127
Go to 135
1
2
3
4
A
B
C
GULF OF MEXICO
GULF ISLANDS NATL. SEASHORE
Santa Rosa Island
ESCAMBIA
COVINGTON
COFFEE
GENEVA
HOLMES
WASHINGTON
WALTON
OKALOOSA
SANTA ROSA
BALDWIN
BAY
ALABAMA
FLORIDA
CONECUH NATL. FOR.
BLACKWATER RIVER ST. FOR.
EGLIN A.F.B.
TYNDALL A.F.B.
Andalusia
Opp
Enterprise
Dothan
Brewton
Atmore
Bay Minette
Crestview
DeFuniak Springs
Niceville
Valparaiso
Destin
Fort Walton Beach
Wright
Mary Esther
Navarre
Milton
Pace
Gonzalez
Ensley
Ferry Pass
Brent
W. Pensacola
Myrtle Grove
Warrington
Pensacola
Gulf Breeze
Foley
Gulf Shores
Orange Beach
Robertsdale
Elberta
Freeport
Bonifay
Chipley
Panama City
Panama City Beach
Lynn Haven
Springfield
Callaway
Cedar Grove
Parker
Mexico Beach
Beacon Hill
Port St. Joe
Cape San Blas
St. Joseph Pt.
Crooked Island
Choctawhatchee Bay
East Bay
West Bay
St. Andrews Bay
St. Joseph Bay
Britton Hill
Highest point in Florida 345

DRIVING DISTANCES IN MILES

	BREWTON, AL	DE FUNIAK SPRS., FL	DOTHAN, AL	FT. WALTON BEACH, FL	MARIANNA, FL	MOBILE, AL	PANAMA CITY, FL	PENSACOLA, FL	PERRY, FL	TALLAHASSEE, FL	THOMASVILLE, GA	VALDOSTA, GA
PANAMA CITY, FL	143	65	82	64	61	160		102	160	104	134	186
PENSACOLA, FL	57	82	152	39	138	58	102		256	200	230	282
TALLAHASSEE, FL	201	123	110	166	68	247	104	200	52		35	85
VALDOSTA, GA	283	204	133	247	149	329	186	282	66	85	42	

SEE ALSO DISTANCE AND DRIVING TIME MAP ON PAGES 286–287

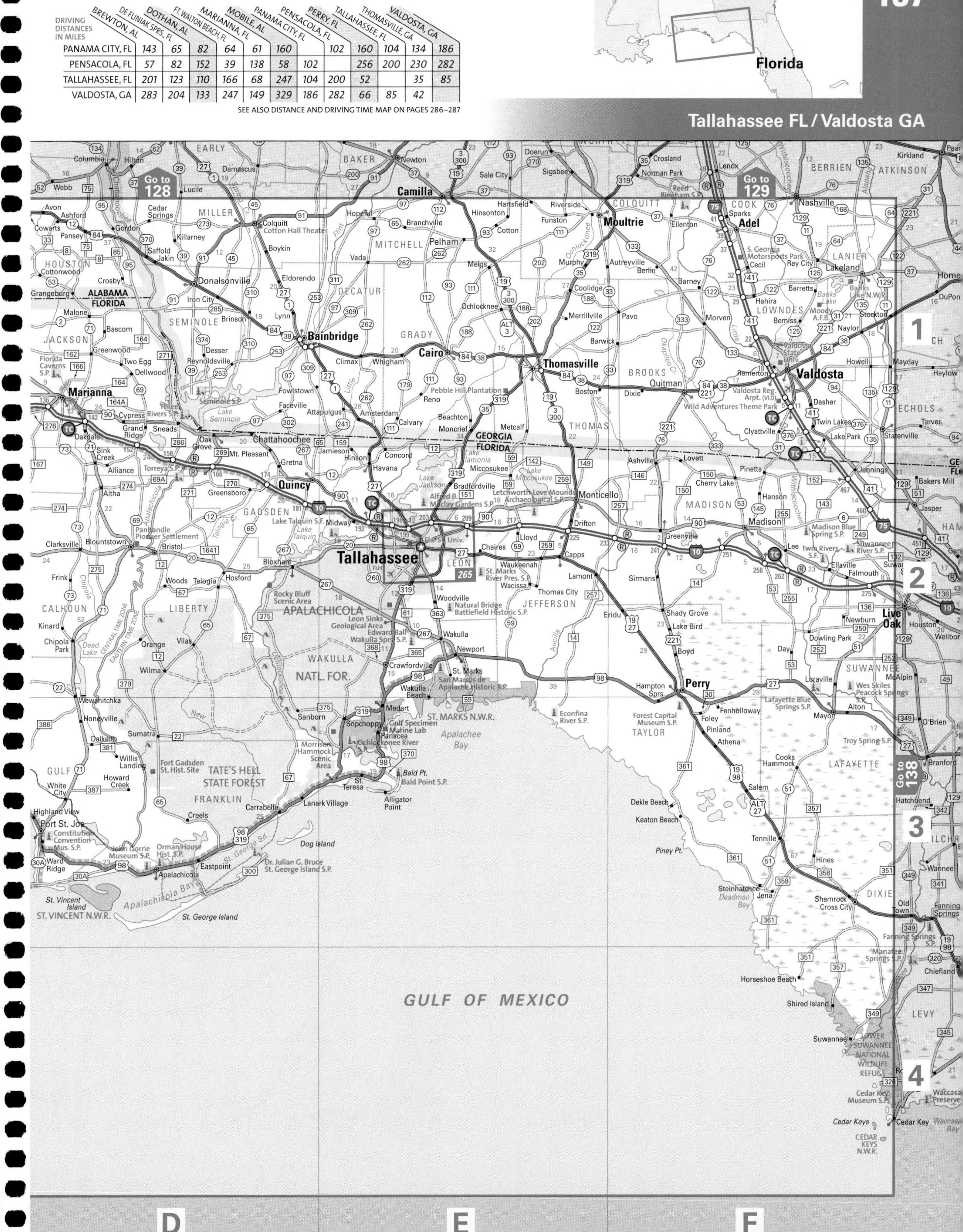

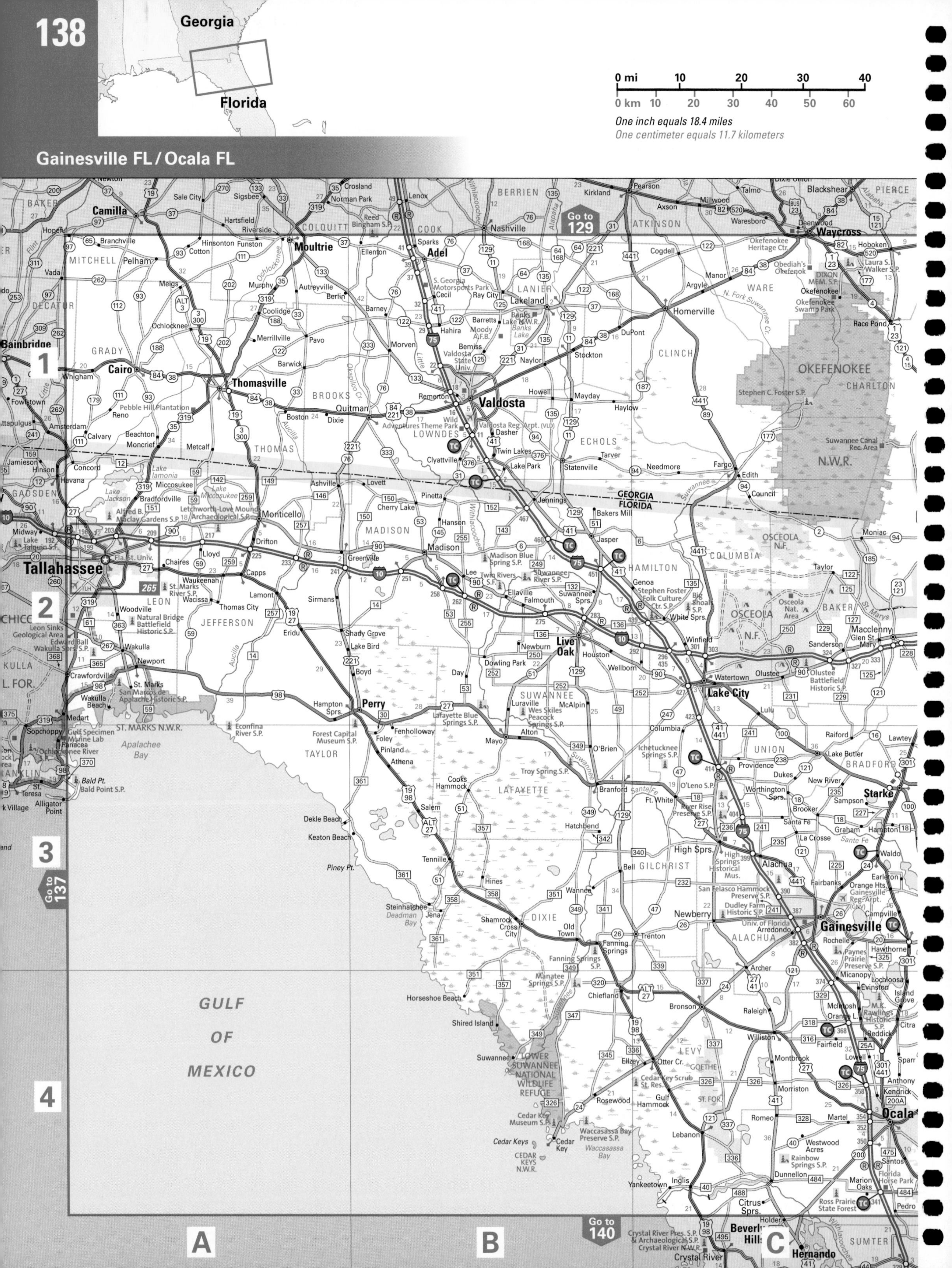
Georgia
Florida
0 mi 10 20 30 40
0 km 10 20 30 40 50 60
One inch equals 18.4 miles
One centimeter equals 11.7 kilometers
Go to 129
Go to 137
Go to 140
1
2
3
4
A
B
C
GEORGIA
FLORIDA
GULF
OF
MEXICO
Apalachee Bay
Deadman Bay
Waccasassa Bay
Cedar Keys
Piney Pt.
OKEFENOKEE
N.W.R.
OSCEOLA N.F.
OSCEOLA
N.F.
ST. MARKS N.W.R.
LOWER SUWANNEE NATIONAL WILDLIFE REFUGE
CEDAR KEYS N.W.R.
BAKER
MITCHELL
DECATUR
GRADY
THOMAS
BROOKS
COLQUITT
COOK
BERRIEN
LANIER
LOWNDES
ECHOLS
CLINCH
WARE
ATKINSON
PIERCE
CHARLTON
GADSDEN
LEON
JEFFERSON
MADISON
TAYLOR
HAMILTON
SUWANNEE
LAFAYETTE
COLUMBIA
BAKER
UNION
BRADFORD
GILCHRIST
ALACHUA
DIXIE
LEVY
SUMTER
Camilla
Moultrie
Adel
Nashville
Valdosta
Thomasville
Cairo
Bainbridge
Quitman
Waycross
Homerville
Blackshear
Tallahassee
Monticello
Madison
Perry
Live Oak
Jasper
Lake City
Starke
Gainesville
Ocala
Alachua
Chiefland
Cedar Key
Crystal River
Hernando
Beverly Hills
Williston
High Sprs.
Mayo
Cross City
Trenton
Bronson
Newberry
Macclenny
Fargo
Lakeland
Hahira
Pelham
Havana
Quincy
Woodville
Crawfordville
Wakulla
Medart
Sopchoppy
Steinhatchee
Horseshoe Beach
Suwannee
Yankeetown
Inglis
Dunnellon
Keaton Beach
Dekle Beach
Branford
Fort White
Micanopy
Waldo
Hawthorne
Reddick
Citra
Lowell
Belleview
Santos
Okefenokee Swamp Park
Stephen C. Foster S.P.
Suwannee Canal Rec. Area
Olustee Battlefield Historic S.P.
Ichetucknee Springs S.P.
O'Leno S.P.
Manatee Springs S.P.
Fanning Springs S.P.
Cedar Key Museum S.P.
Waccasassa Bay Preserve S.P.
Rainbow Springs S.P.
Paynes Prairie Preserve S.P.
Forest Capital Museum S.P.
Econfina River S.P.
Lafayette Blue Springs S.P.
Madison Blue Spring S.P.
Suwannee River S.P.
Stephen Foster Folk Culture Ctr. S.P.
Big Shoals S.P.
Natural Bridge Battlefield Historic S.P.
Wakulla Springs S.P.
Leon Sinks Geological Area
San Marcos de Apalache Historic S.P.
Alfred B. Maclay Gardens S.P.
Letchworth-Love Mounds Archaeological S.P.
Lake Talquin S.F.
Lake Jackson
Lake Iamonia
Lake Miccosukee
Valdosta Reg. Arpt. (VLD)
Gainesville Reg. Arpt. (GNV)
Moody A.F.B.
Ross Prairie State Forest
Crystal River Pres. S.P.
Crystal River N.W.R.

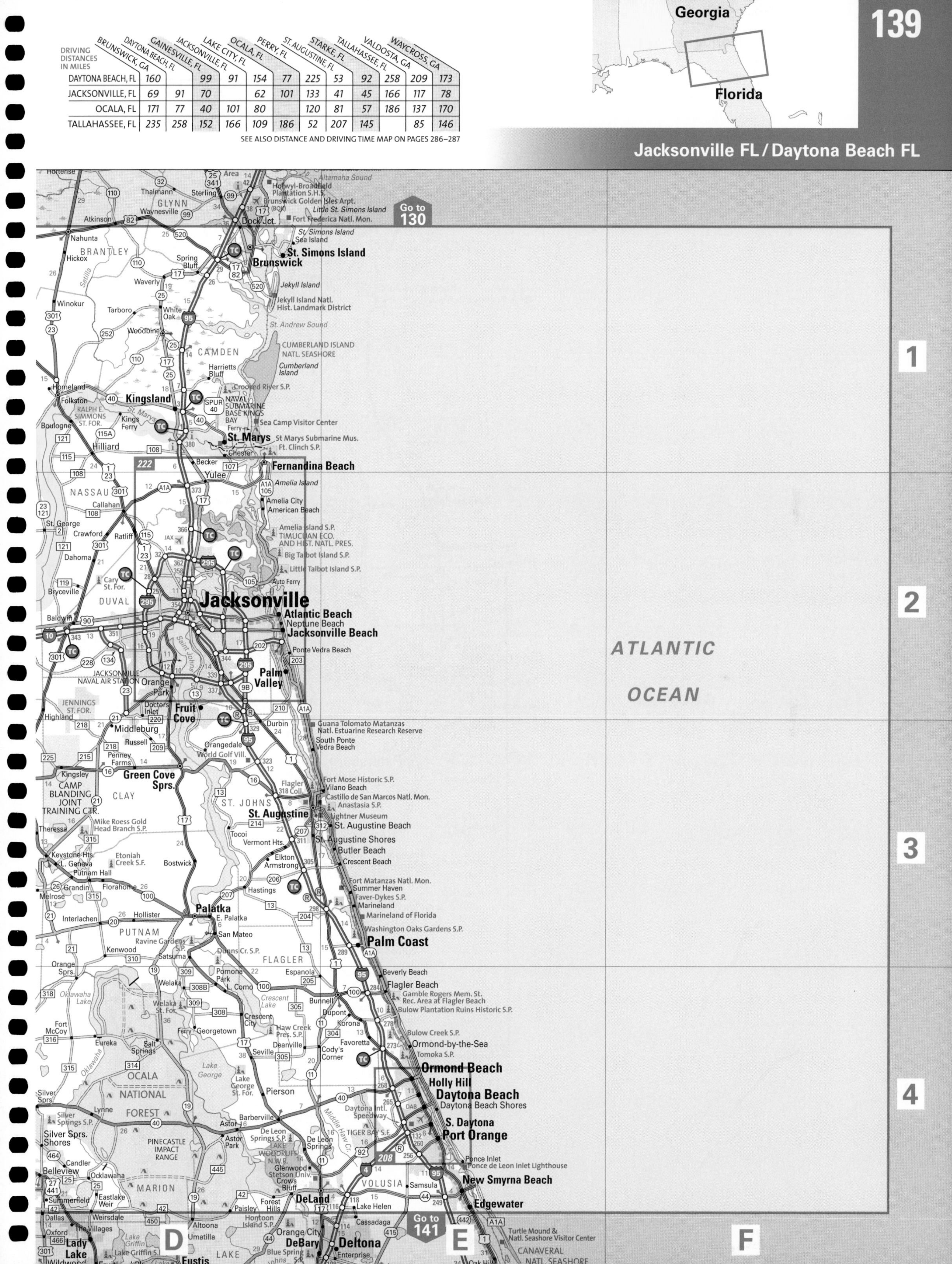

DRIVING DISTANCES IN MILES

	BRUNSWICK, GA	DAYTONA BEACH, FL	GAINESVILLE, FL	JACKSONVILLE, FL	LAKE CITY, FL	OCALA, FL	PERRY, FL	ST. AUGUSTINE, FL	STARKE, FL	TALLAHASSEE, FL	VALDOSTA, GA	WAYCROSS, GA
DAYTONA BEACH, FL	160		99	91	154	77	225	53	92	258	209	173
JACKSONVILLE, FL	69	91	70		62	101	133	41	45	166	117	78
OCALA, FL	171	77	40	101	80		120	81	57	186	137	170
TALLAHASSEE, FL	235	258	152	166	109	186	52	207	145		85	146

SEE ALSO DISTANCE AND DRIVING TIME MAP ON PAGES 286–287

Florida

0 mi 10 20 30 40
0 km 10 20 30 40 50 60

One inch equals 18.4 miles
One centimeter equals 11.7 kilometers

Tampa FL / Sarasota FL

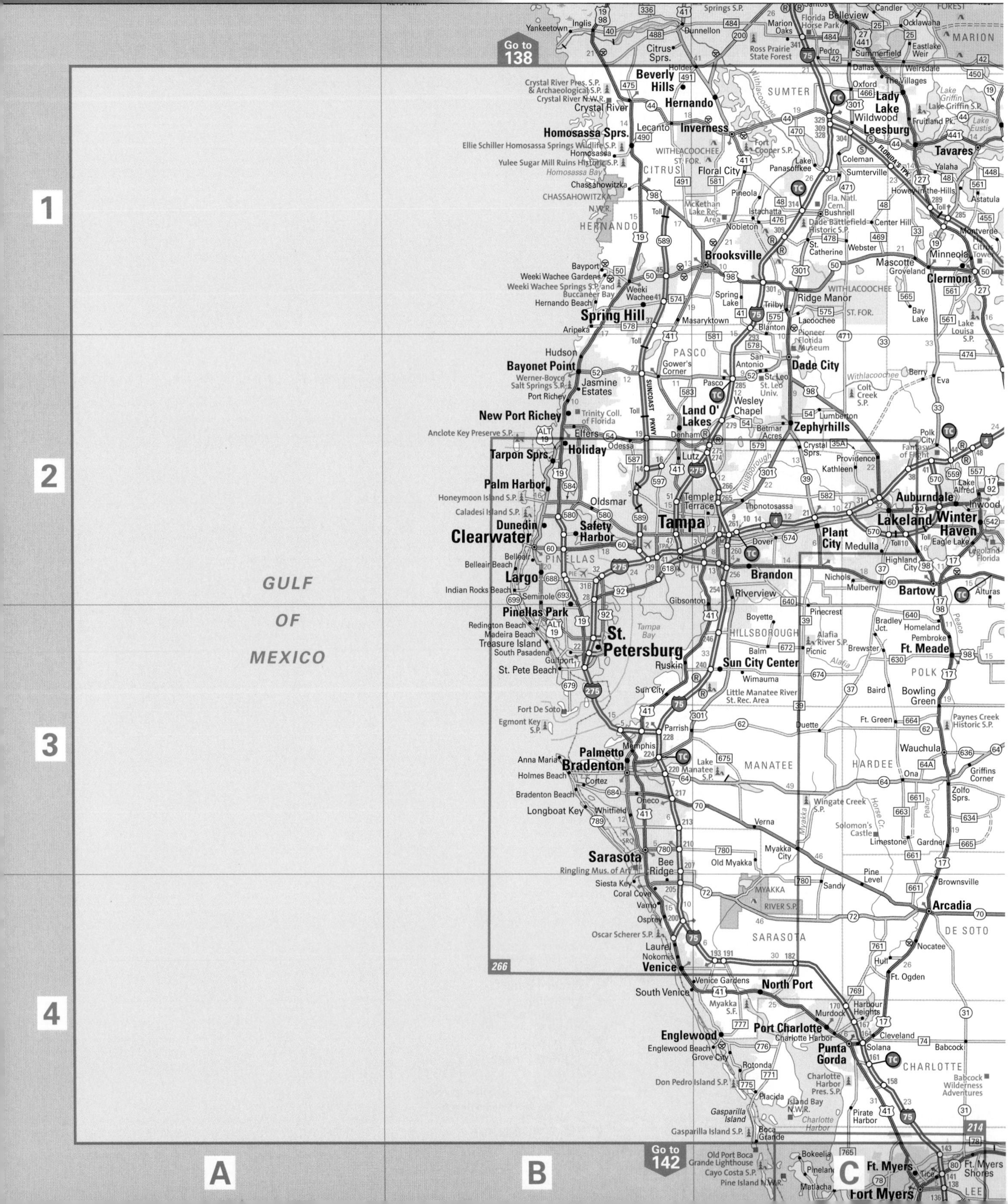

Go to 138

GULF OF MEXICO

Crystal River, Beverly Hills, Hernando, Inverness, Homosassa Sprs., Lady Lake, Wildwood, Leesburg, Tavares, Floral City, Brooksville, Clermont, Spring Hill, Bayonet Point, Dade City, New Port Richey, Land O' Lakes, Zephyrhills, Tarpon Sprs., Holiday, Palm Harbor, Clearwater, Dunedin, Safety Harbor, Tampa, Plant City, Lakeland, Auburndale, Winter Haven, Largo, Brandon, Bartow, Pinellas Park, St. Petersburg, Sun City Center, Ft. Meade, Bradenton, Palmetto, Sarasota, Bee Ridge, Arcadia, Venice, North Port, Englewood, Port Charlotte, Punta Gorda, Ft. Myers, Fort Myers

SUMTER, CITRUS, HERNANDO, PASCO, PINELLAS, HILLSBOROUGH, POLK, MANATEE, HARDEE, SARASOTA, DE SOTO, CHARLOTTE, LEE, MARION

1 2 3 4
A B C

Go to 142
266
214

DRIVING DISTANCES IN MILES	FORT MYERS, FL	FORT PIERCE, FL	LAKELAND, FL	MELBOURNE, FL	OKEECHOBEE, FL	ORLANDO, FL	PUNTA GORDA, FL	ST. PETERSBURG, FL	SARASOTA, FL	TAMPA, FL	TITUSVILLE, FL	W. PALM BEACH, FL
FORT PIERCE, FL	126		122	57	36	120	127	197	150	172	95	57
ORLANDO, FL	155	120	56	72	108		131	107	130	82	40	169
SARASOTA, FL	74	150	85	190	114	130	50	35		60	170	184
TAMPA, FL	123	172	37	142	162	82	99	25	60		121	223

SEE ALSO DISTANCE AND DRIVING TIME MAP ON PAGES 286–287

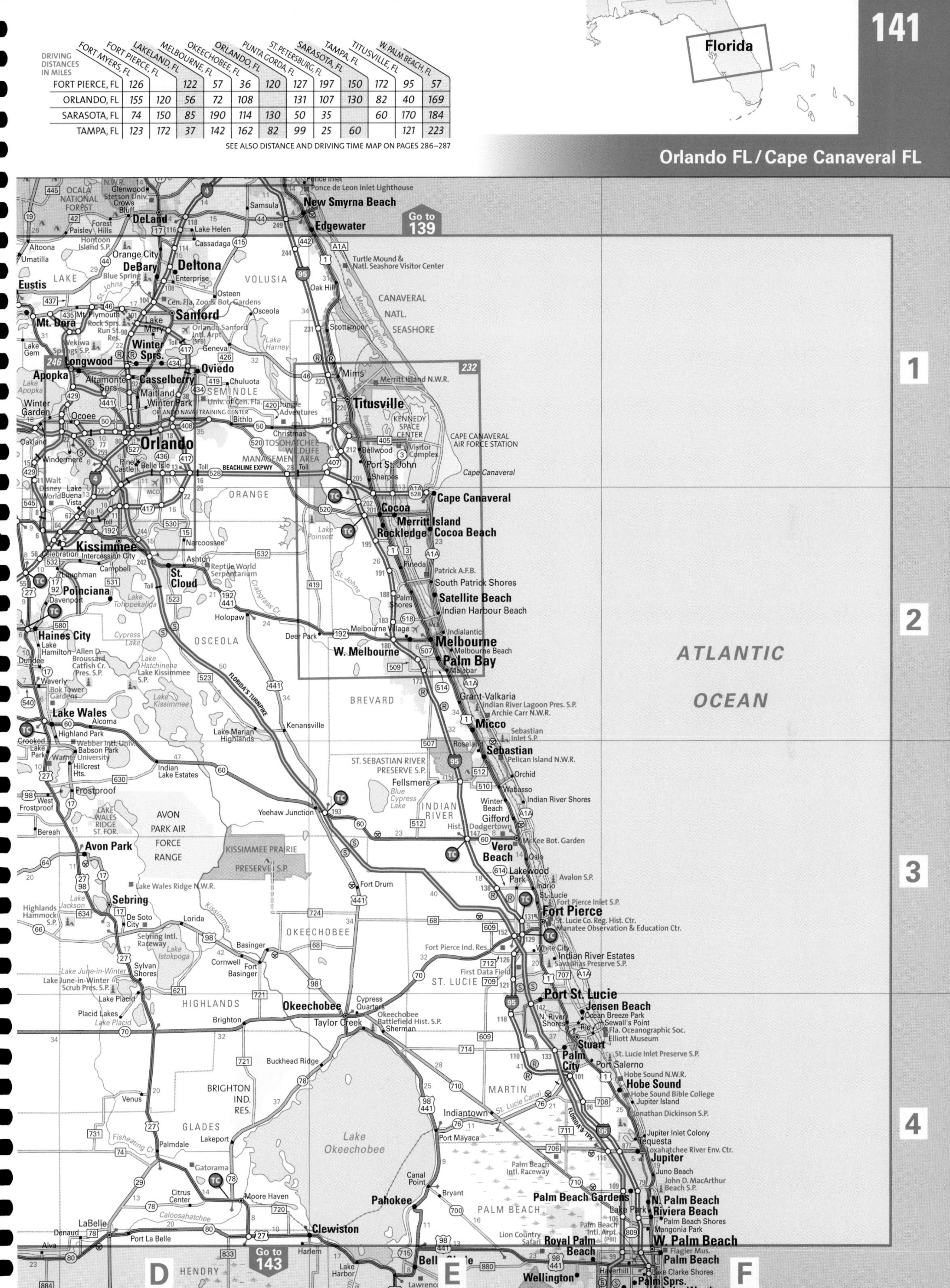

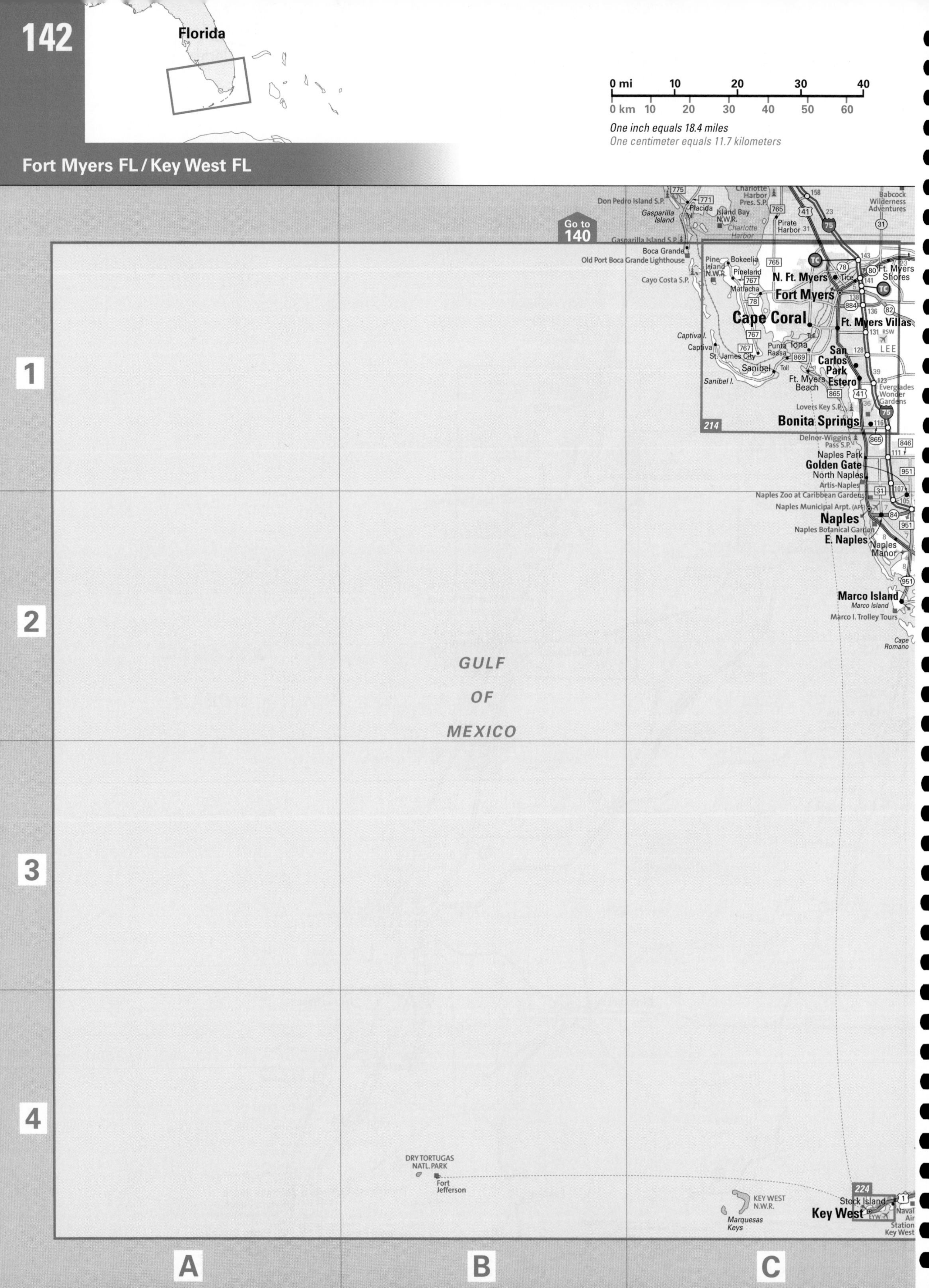
Florida
0 mi 10 20 30 40
0 km 10 20 30 40 50 60
One inch equals 18.4 miles
One centimeter equals 11.7 kilometers
Go to 140
Don Pedro Island S.P.
Gasparilla Island
Placida
Island Bay N.W.R.
Charlotte Harbor Pres. S.P.
Charlotte Harbor
Pirate Harbor
Babcock Wilderness Adventures
Gasparilla Island S.P.
Boca Grande
Old Port Boca Grande Lighthouse
Cayo Costa S.P.
Pine Island N.W.R.
Bokeelia
Pineland
Matlacha
N. Ft. Myers
Tice
Ft. Myers Shores
Fort Myers
Cape Coral
Ft. Myers Villas
RSW
LEE
Captiva I.
Captiva
St. James City
Punta Rassa
Iona
Sanibel
Sanibel I.
San Carlos Park
Ft. Myers Beach
Estero
Everglades Wonder Gardens
Lovers Key S.P.
Bonita Springs
214
Delnor-Wiggins Pass S.P.
Naples Park
Golden Gate
North Naples
Artis-Naples
Naples Zoo at Caribbean Gardens
Naples Municipal Arpt. (APF)
Naples
Naples Botanical Garden
E. Naples
Naples Manor
Marco Island
Marco Island
Marco I. Trolley Tours
Cape Romano
GULF
OF
MEXICO
DRY TORTUGAS NATL. PARK
Fort Jefferson
KEY WEST N.W.R.
Marquesas Keys
224
Stock Island
Key West
Naval Air Station Key West
1
2
3
4
A
B
C

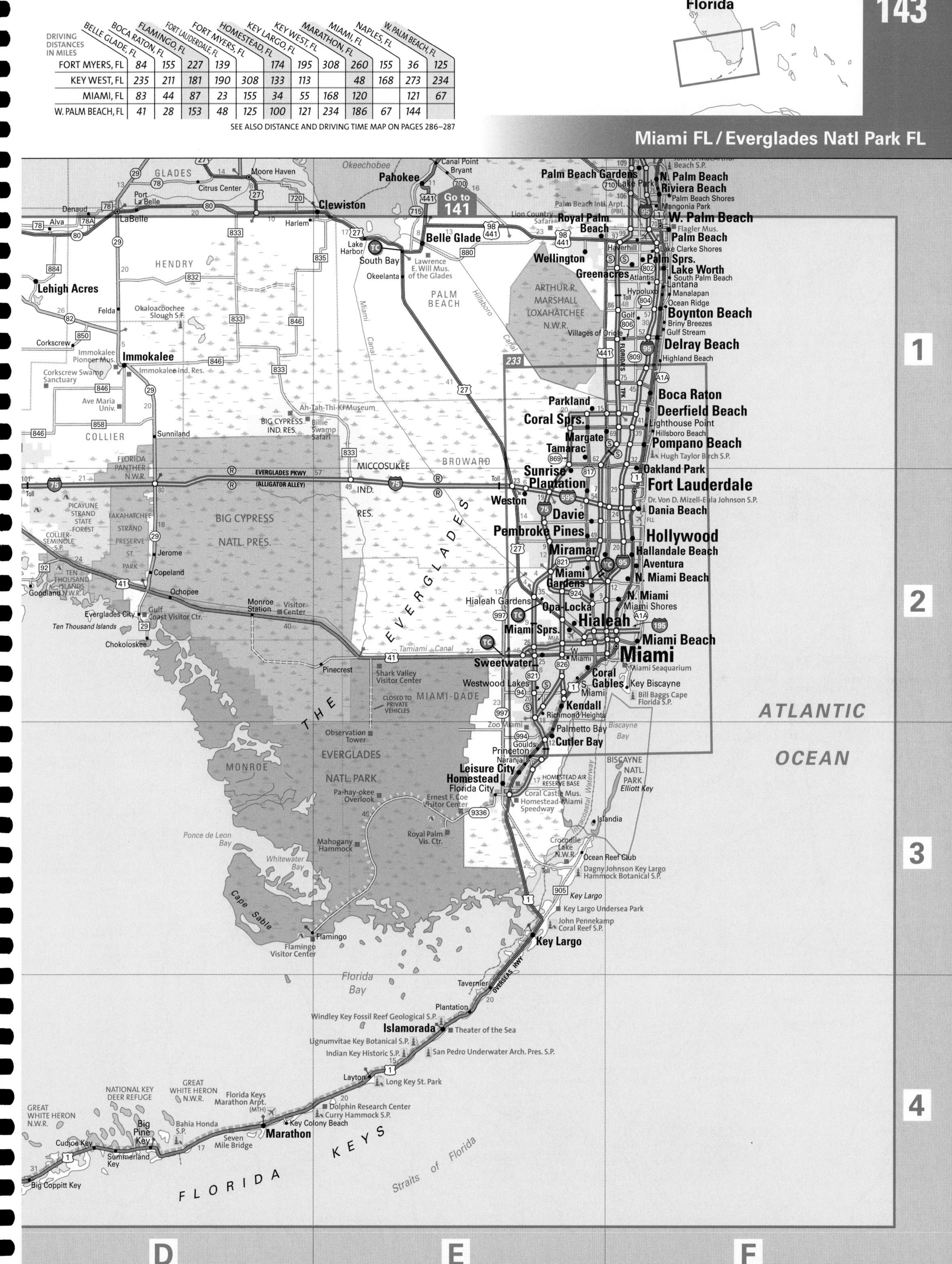

DRIVING DISTANCES IN MILES

	BELLE GLADE, FL	BOCA RATON, FL	FLAMINGO, FL	FORT LAUDERDALE, FL	FORT MYERS, FL	HOMESTEAD, FL	KEY LARGO, FL	KEY WEST, FL	MARATHON, FL	MIAMI, FL	NAPLES, FL	W. PALM BEACH, FL
FORT MYERS, FL	84	155	227	139		174	195	308	260	155	36	125
KEY WEST, FL	235	211	181	190	308	133	113		48	168	273	234
MIAMI, FL	83	44	87	23	155	34	55	168	120		121	67
W. PALM BEACH, FL	41	28	153	48	125	100	121	234	186	67	144	

SEE ALSO DISTANCE AND DRIVING TIME MAP ON PAGES 286–287

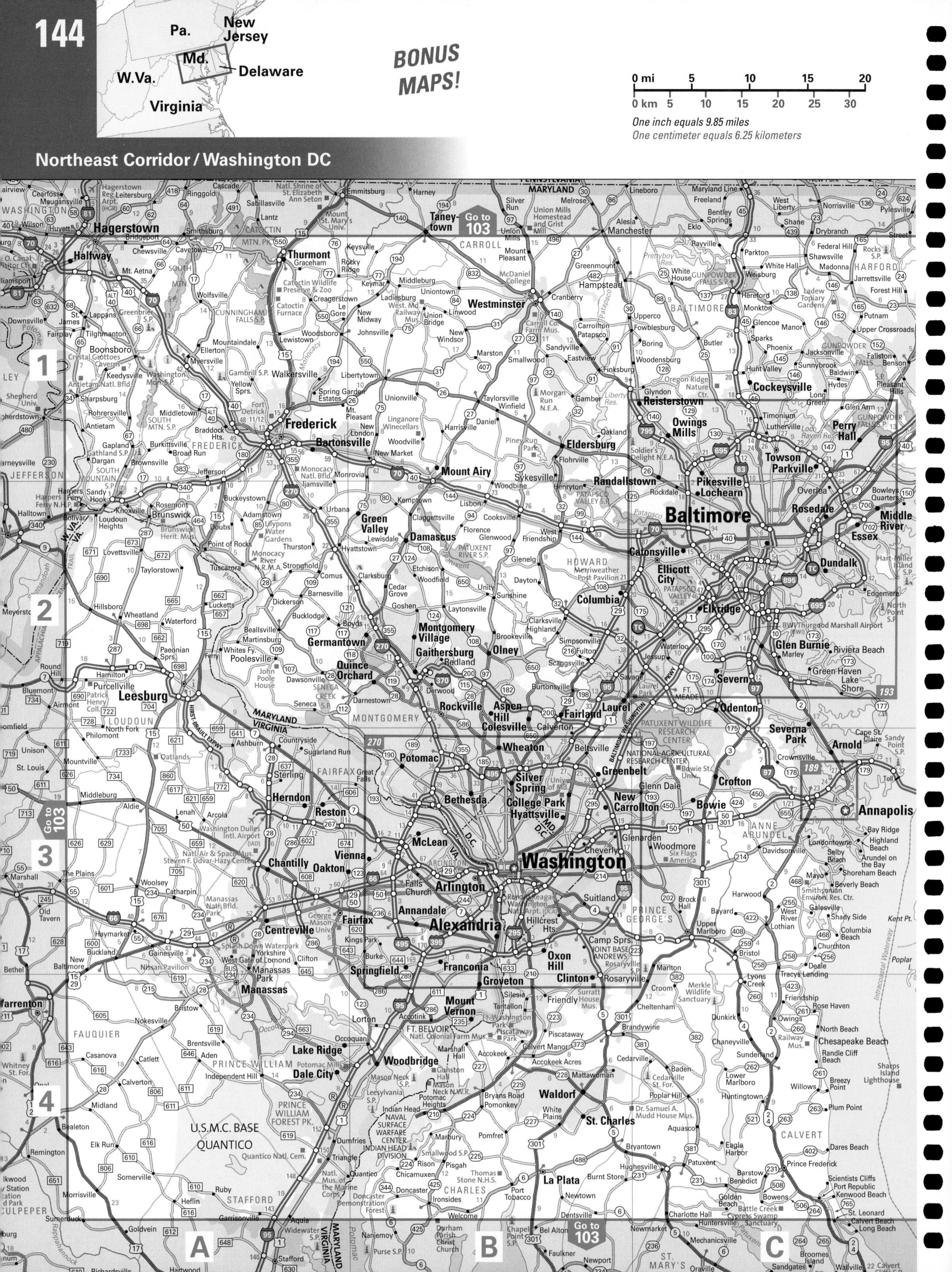
Pa.
New Jersey
Md.
Delaware
W.Va.
Virginia
BONUS MAPS!
0 mi 5 10 15 20
0 km 5 10 15 20 25 30
One inch equals 9.85 miles
One centimeter equals 6.25 kilometers
Northeast Corridor / Washington DC
Go to 103
Hagerstown
Frederick
Westminster
Baltimore
Columbia
Annapolis
Washington
Alexandria
Arlington
Leesburg
Manassas
Waldorf
La Plata
Woodbridge
Gaithersburg
Rockville
Bethesda
Silver Spring
Towson
Glen Burnie
Bowie
Fairfax
Herndon
Reston
Chantilly
Germantown
Damascus
Mount Airy
Eldersburg
Ellicott City
Laurel
193
189
270
Go to 103
A
B
C
1
2
3
4

BONUS MAPS!

DRIVING DISTANCES IN MILES	ANNAPOLIS, MD	BALTIMORE, MD	CAMBRIDGE, MD	DOVER, DE	ELKTON, MD	FREDERICK, MD	HAGERSTOWN, MD	LEESBURG, VA	MANASSAS, VA	REHOBOTH BEACH, DE	VINELAND, NJ	WASHINGTON, DC
BALTIMORE, MD	25		78	98	58	51	76	71	67	111	109	38
DOVER, DE	62	98	64		40	135	160	135	131	43	77	94
FREDERICK, MD	73	51	128	135	106		28	25	61	161	158	44
WASHINGTON, DC	31	38	87	94	94	44	70	38	31	120	145	

SEE ALSO DISTANCE AND DRIVING TIME MAP ON PAGES 286–287

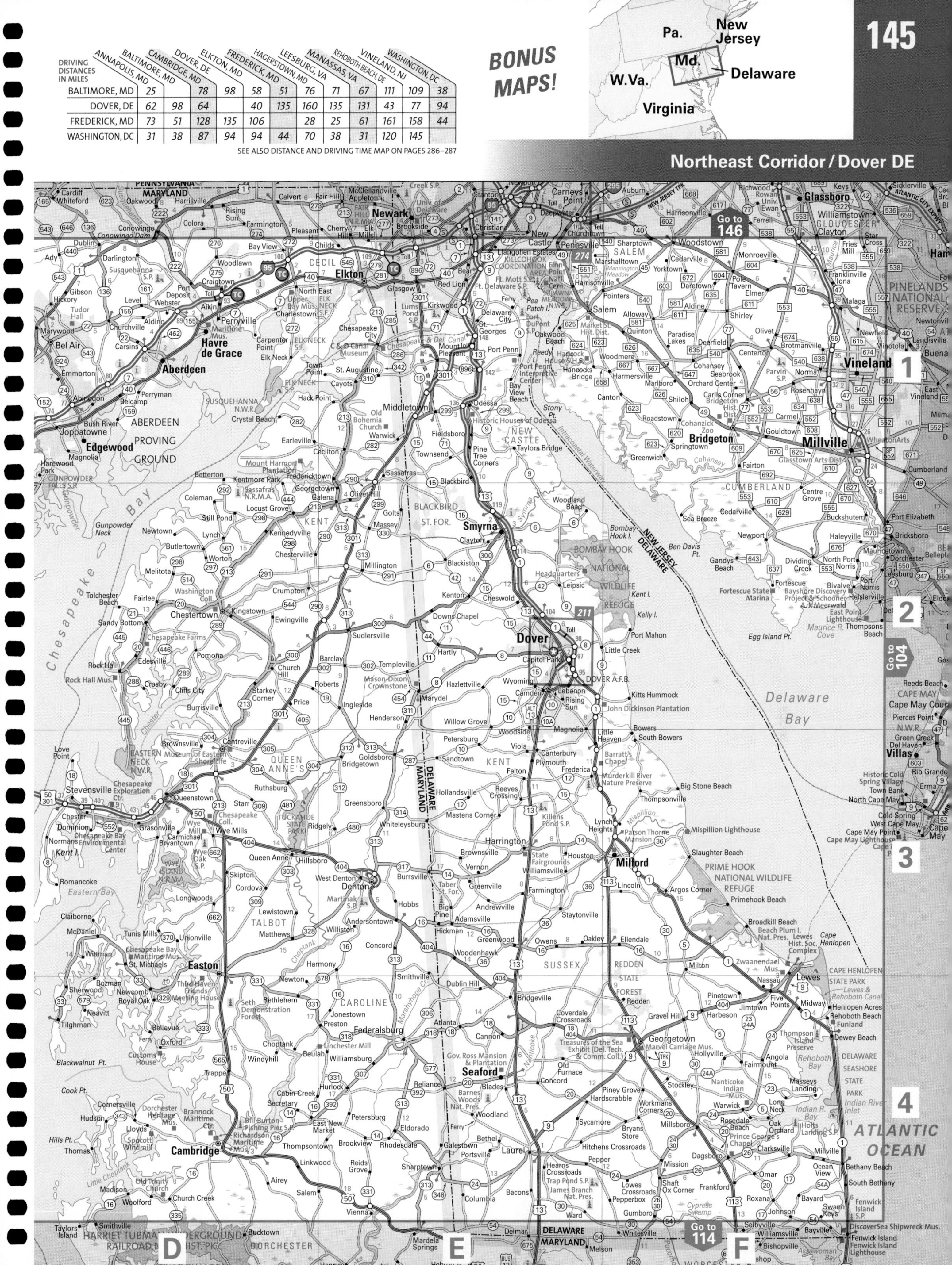

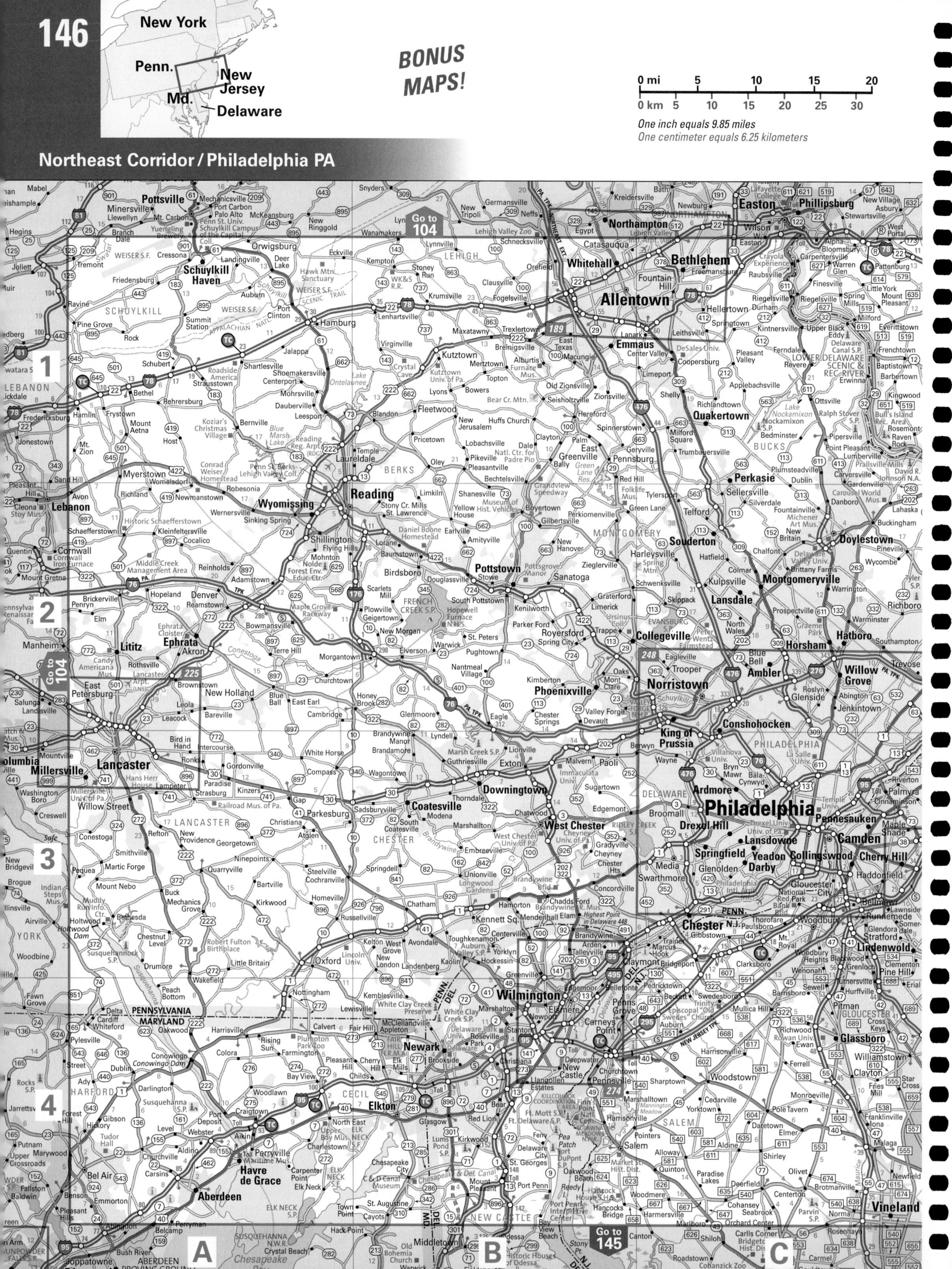
New York
Penn.
New Jersey
Md.
Delaware
BONUS MAPS!
0 mi 5 10 15 20
0 km 5 10 15 20 25 30
One inch equals 9.85 miles
One centimeter equals 6.25 kilometers
Northeast Corridor / Philadelphia PA
Go to 104
Go to 145
Pottsville
Allentown
Bethlehem
Easton
Phillipsburg
Reading
Lancaster
Pottstown
Norristown
Philadelphia
Camden
Wilmington
West Chester
Newark
Elkton
Chester
Vineland
Havre de Grace
Aberdeen
Lebanon
Quakertown
Doylestown
Hatboro
Horsham
Lansdale
Collegeville
Phoenixville
Downingtown
Coatesville
Ephrata
Lititz
Hamburg
Kutztown
Emmaus
Northampton
Whitehall
A
B
C
1
2
3
4

BONUS MAPS!

New York
Penn.
New Jersey
Md.
Delaware

Northeast Corridor / Trenton NJ

DRIVING DISTANCES IN MILES	ALLENTOWN, PA	ATLANTIC CITY, NJ	ELKTON, MD	LANCASTER, PA	LONG BRANCH, NJ	NEW BRUNSWICK, NJ	NEW YORK, NY	PHILADELPHIA, PA	READING, PA	TOMS RIVER, NJ	TRENTON, NJ	WILMINGTON, DE
NEW YORK, NY	84	125	137	165	55	34		91	118	75	55	120
PHILADELPHIA, PA	63	62	50	79	77	55	91		63	58	34	30
TRENTON, NJ	66	77	88	105	53	22	55	34	89	48		68
WILMINGTON, DE	77	86	20	53	106	90	120	30	56	85	68	

SEE ALSO DISTANCE AND DRIVING TIME MAP ON PAGES 286–287

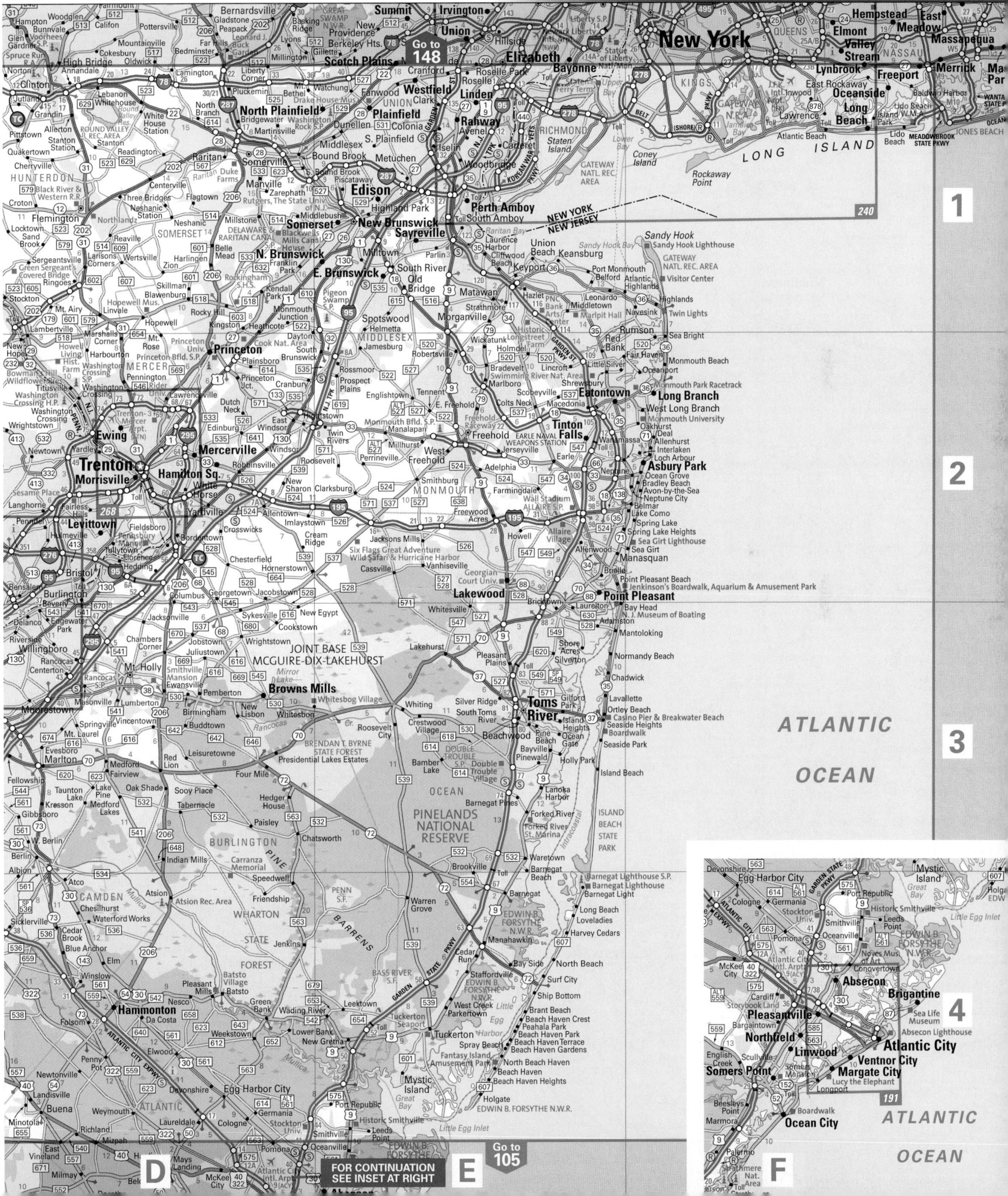

Go to 148

FOR CONTINUATION SEE INSET AT RIGHT

Go to 105

ATLANTIC OCEAN

1
2
3
4

D E F

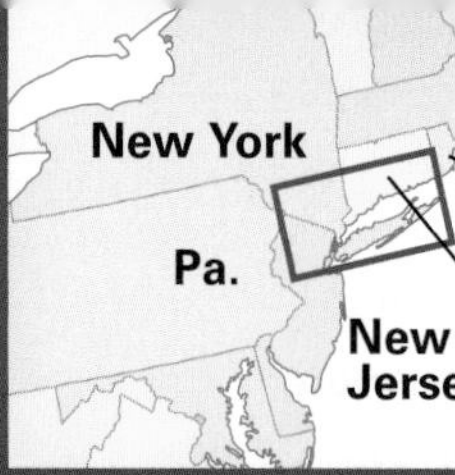

New York
Rhode Island
Pa.
Conn.
New Jersey

BONUS MAPS!

0 mi 5 10 15 20
0 km 5 10 15 20 25 30

One inch equals 9.85 miles
One centimeter equals 6.25 kilometers

Northeast Corridor / New York NY

Go to 94
Go to 94
Go to 147
240
264
238

1
2
3
4
A
B
C

BONUS MAPS!

DRIVING DISTANCES IN MILES

	BRIDGEPORT, CT	DANBURY, CT	HARTFORD, CT	NEWARK, NJ	NEWBURGH, NY	NEW HAVEN, CT	NEW LONDON, CT	NEW YORK, NY	PATERSON, NJ	RIVERHEAD, NY	STAMFORD, CT	WATERBURY, CT
BRIDGEPORT, CT		31	56	69	73	19	64	60	71	115	21	33
NEWARK, NJ	69	79	125		66	88	134	11	18	88	48	108
NEW HAVEN, CT	19	35	39	88	78		46	78	89	133	40	30
NEW YORK, NY	60	69	115	11	56	78	124		16	78	38	99

SEE ALSO DISTANCE AND DRIVING TIME MAP ON PAGES 286–287

Massachusetts
Rhode Island
Connecticut

BONUS MAPS!

0 mi 5 10 15 20
0 km 5 10 15 20 25 30

One inch equals 9.85 miles
One centimeter equals 6.25 kilometers

Northeast Corridor / Hartford CT

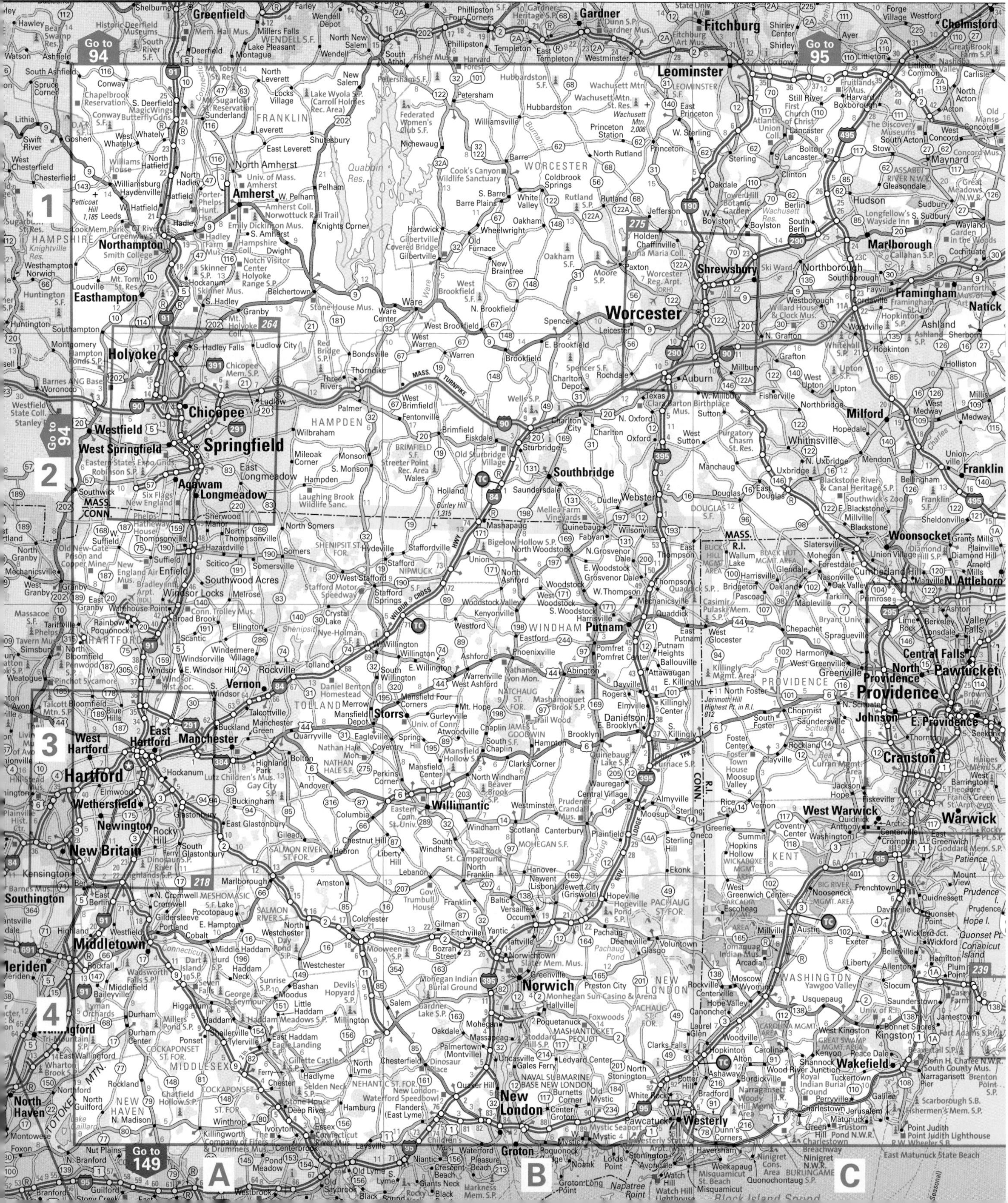

Go to 94
Go to 95
Go to 149

DRIVING DISTANCES IN MILES	BOSTON, MA	GLOUCESTER, MA	HARTFORD, CT	HYANNIS, MA	NEW BEDFORD, MA	NEW LONDON, CT	NEWPORT, RI	PLYMOUTH, MA	PROVIDENCE, RI	PROVINCETOWN, MA	SPRINGFIELD, MA	WORCESTER, MA
BOSTON, MA		35	102	72	60	109	73	41	52	117	95	46
HARTFORD, CT	102	136		155	104	46	85	127	73	200	25	62
PROVIDENCE, RI	52	92	73	71	33	58	33	41		117	75	43
SPRINGFIELD, MA	95	129	25	148	127	71	111	120	75	193		55

SEE ALSO DISTANCE AND DRIVING TIME MAP ON PAGES 286–287

BONUS MAPS!

Massachusetts
Rhode Island
Connecticut

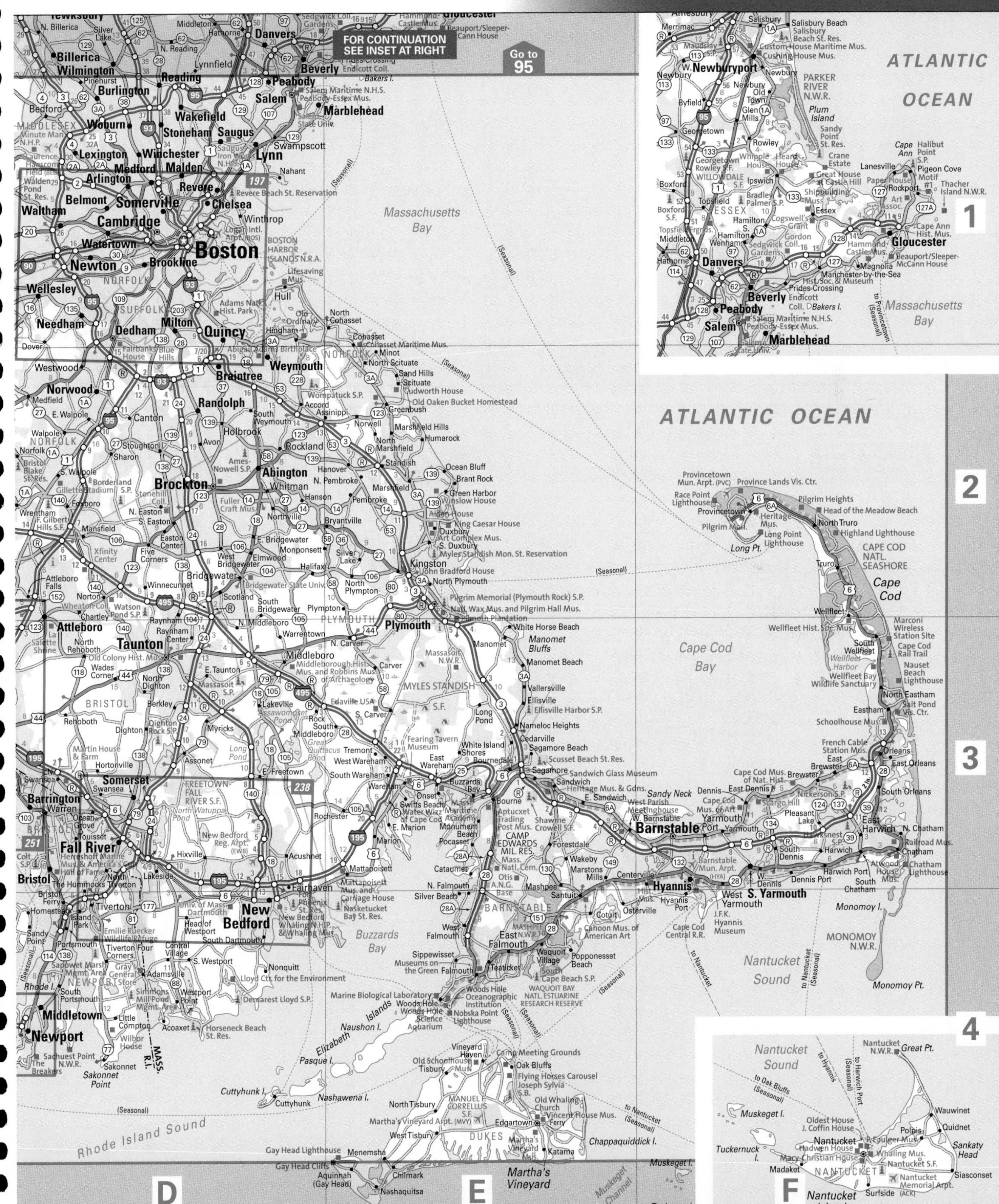

Honolulu HI / Lihue HI

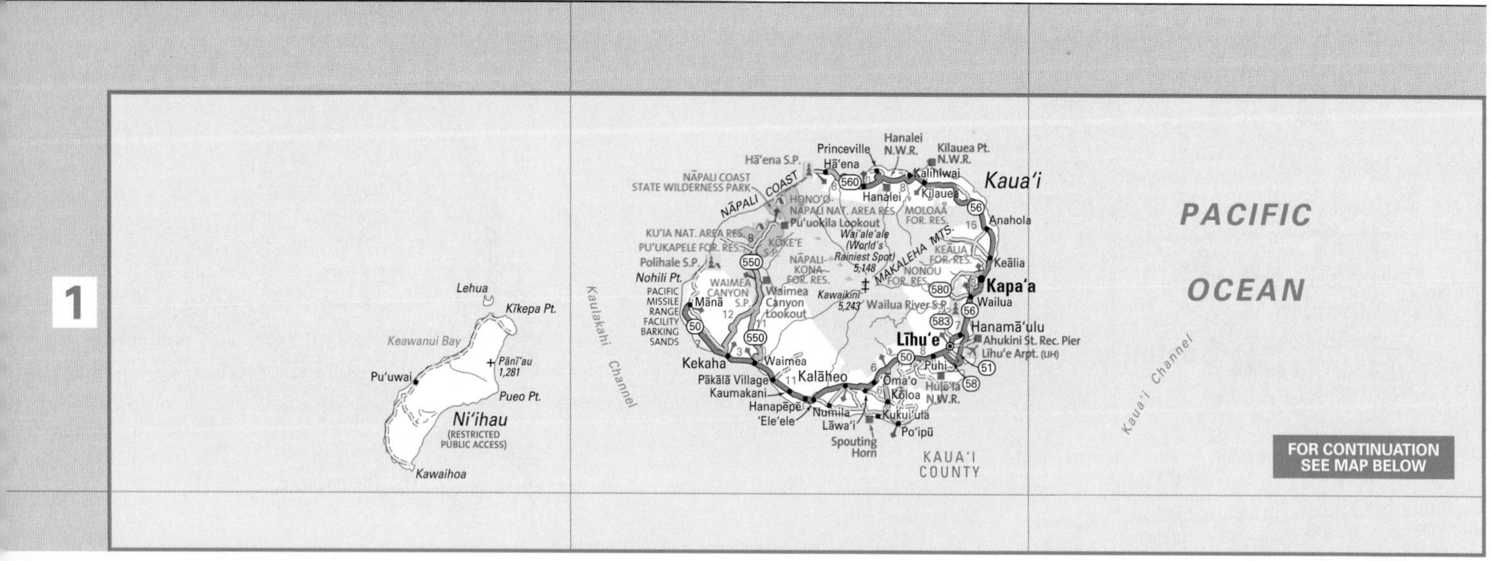

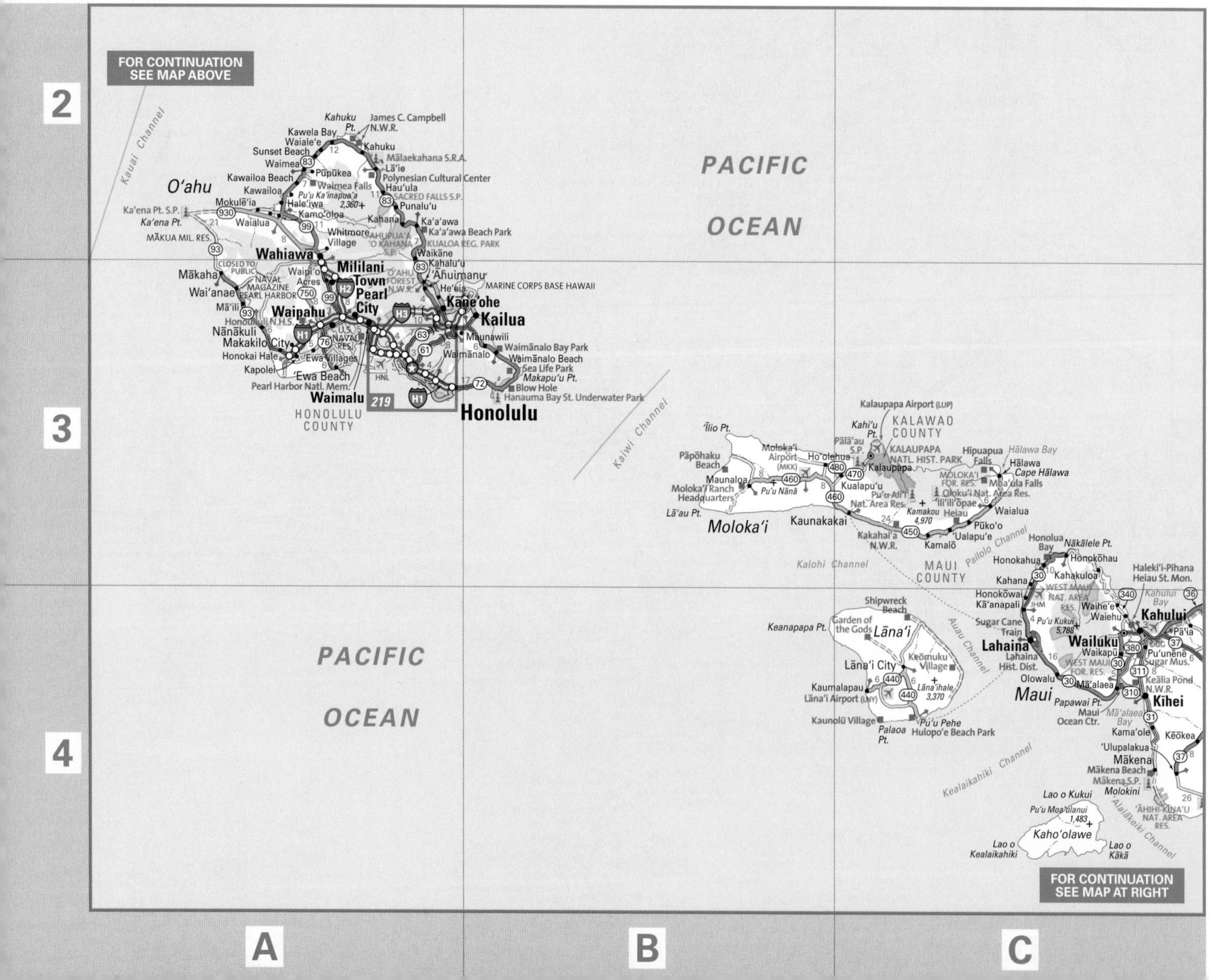

DRIVING DISTANCES IN MILES

	HĀNA	HILO	HONOLULU	HO'OLEHUA	KAHULUI	KAILUA	KAILUA-KONA	LAHAINA	LANAI CITY	LIHUE	WAHIAWĀ	WAIMEA
HILO	149*		217*	169*	121*	235*	88	142*	155*	319*	234*	54
HONOLULU	129*	217*		54*	101*	14	185*	92*	74*	102*	23	172*
KAHULUI	42	121*	101*	76*		119*	109*	23	57*	202*	118*	79*
LIHUE	230*	319*	102*	156*	202*	120*	285*	225*	176*		119*	174*

*DISTANCE INCLUDES AIR TRAVEL

SEE ALSO DISTANCE AND DRIVING TIME MAP ON PAGES 286–287

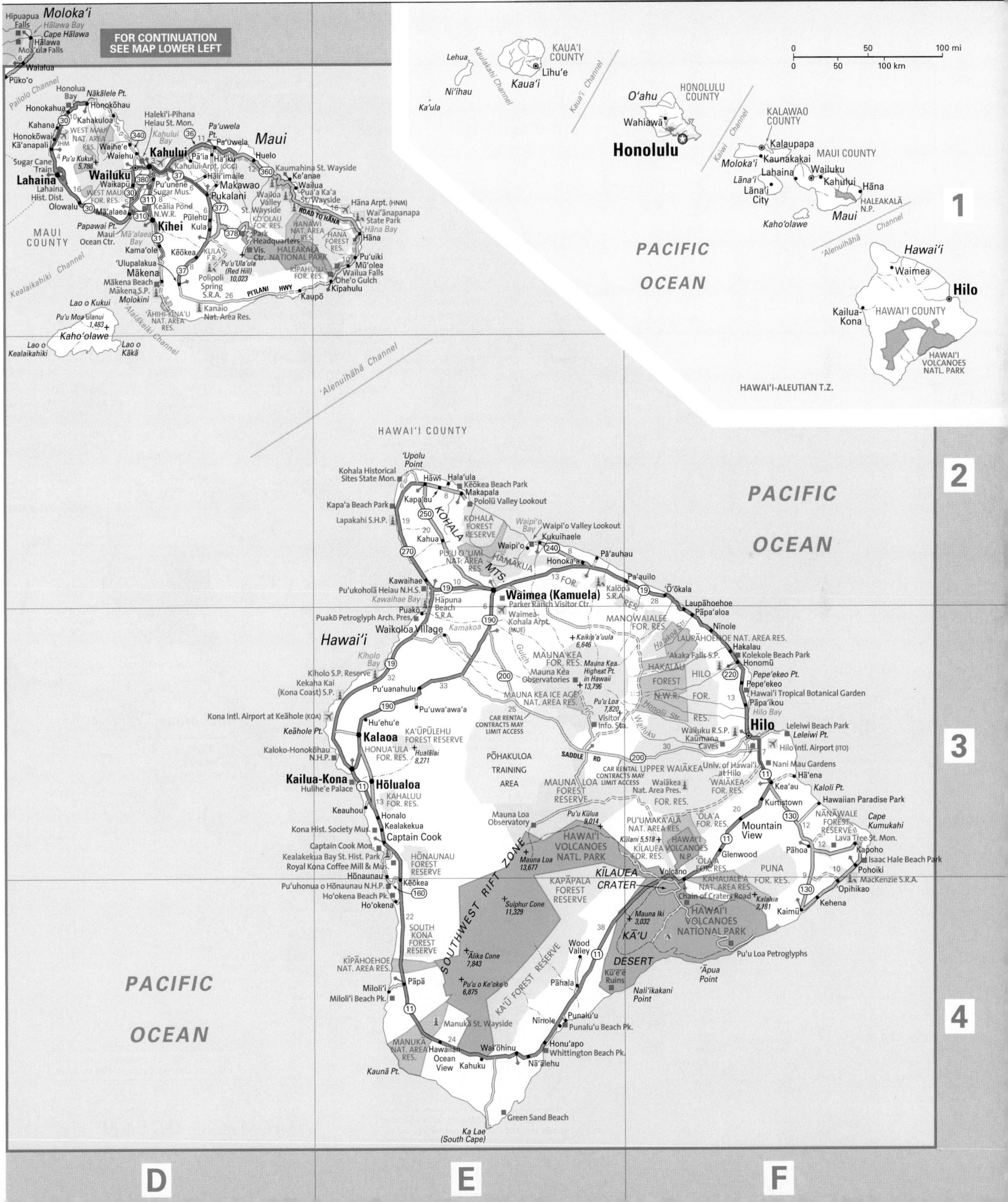

CANADA
UNITED STATES
MEXICO
HAWAII

FOR CONTINUATION SEE MAP LOWER LEFT

Moloka'i
Maui
Lahaina
Wailuku
Kahului
Kīhei
Makawao
Pukalani
Kula
Hāna
Kīpahulu
Kaupō
MAUI COUNTY
HALEAKALĀ NATIONAL PARK
ROAD TO HĀNA
PI'ILANI HWY
Kaho'olawe
Molokini
Kealaikahiki Channel
Alalākeiki Channel
'Alenuihāhā Channel

KAUA'I COUNTY
Kaua'i
Līhu'e
Ni'ihau
Lehua
Ka'ula
HONOLULU COUNTY
O'ahu
Wahiawā
Honolulu
KALAWAO COUNTY
Kalaupapa
Kaunakakai
Moloka'i
Lāna'i
Lāna'i City
Lahaina
Wailuku
Kahului
Hāna
Maui
HALEAKALĀ N.P.
Kaho'olawe
Hawai'i
Waimea
Hilo
Kailua-Kona
HAWAI'I COUNTY
HAWAI'I VOLCANOES NATL. PARK
PACIFIC OCEAN
HAWAI'I-ALEUTIAN T.Z.
0 50 100 mi
0 50 100 km

HAWAI'I COUNTY
Hawai'i
'Upolu Point
Hāwī
Kapa'au
KOHALA MTS.
Waipi'o Valley Lookout
Honoka'a
Waimea (Kamuela)
Waikoloa Village
Kona Intl. Airport at Keāhole (KOA)
Kalaoa
Kailua-Kona
Hōlualoa
Captain Cook
Hōnaunau
Ho'okena
Mauna Kea
Mauna Kea Observatories
Mauna Loa
Mauna Loa Observatory
SADDLE RD
PŌHAKULOA TRAINING AREA
Hilo
Hilo Intl. Airport (ITO)
Kea'au
Kurtistown
Mountain View
Glenwood
Volcano
KĪLAUEA CRATER
HAWAI'I VOLCANOES NATIONAL PARK
KA'Ū DESERT
SOUTHWEST RIFT ZONE
Pāhala
Punalu'u
Nā'ālehu
Wai'ōhinu
Hawaiian Ocean View
Pāhoa
Kapoho
Ka Lae (South Cape)
Green Sand Beach
PACIFIC OCEAN

1
2
3
4

D
E
F

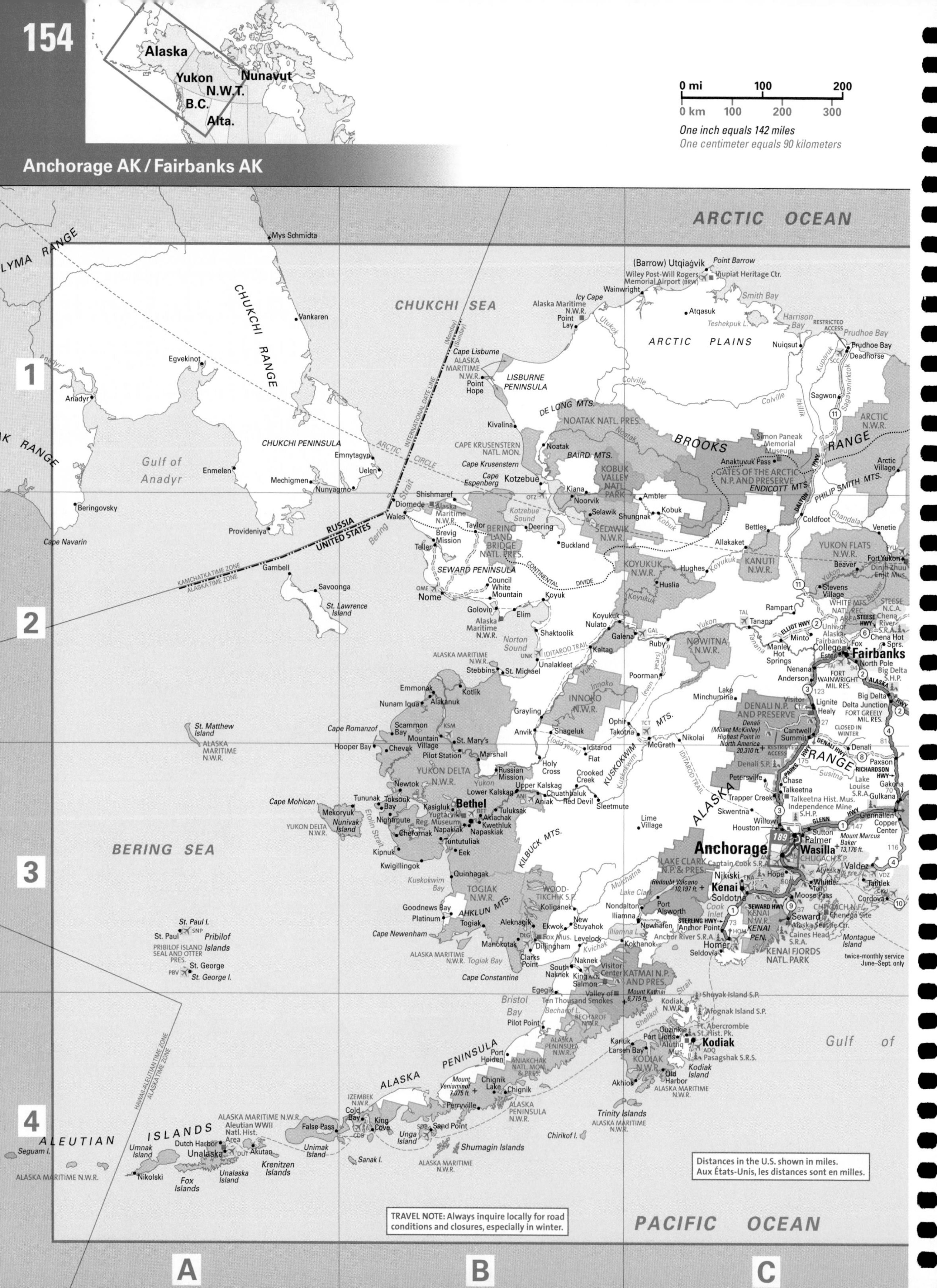
Alaska
Yukon
Nunavut
N.W.T.
B.C.
Alta.
0 mi 100 200
0 km 100 200 300
One inch equals 142 miles
One centimeter equals 90 kilometers
ARCTIC OCEAN
CHUKCHI SEA
BERING SEA
PACIFIC OCEAN
Gulf of
Gulf of Anadyr
KOLYMA RANGE
CHUKCHI RANGE
CHUKCHI PENINSULA
Mys Schmidta
Vankaren
Egvekinot
Anadyr
Enmelen
Mechigmen
Nunyamo
Emnytagyn
Uelen
Beringovsky
Provideniya
Cape Navarin
RUSSIA
UNITED STATES
KAMCHATKA TIME ZONE
ALASKA TIME ZONE
INTERNATIONAL DATE LINE
ARCTIC CIRCLE
Bering Strait
Gambell
Savoonga
St. Lawrence Island
(Barrow) Utqiaġvik
Point Barrow
Iñupiat Heritage Ctr.
Wiley Post-Will Rogers Memorial Airport (BRW)
Wainwright
Icy Cape
Alaska Maritime N.W.R.
Point Lay
Atqasuk
Smith Bay
Harrison Bay
Teshekpuk L.
ARCTIC PLAINS
Nuiqsut
Prudhoe Bay
Deadhorse
Cape Lisburne
ALASKA MARITIME N.W.R.
Point Hope
LISBURNE PENINSULA
DE LONG MTS.
NOATAK NATL. PRES.
Kivalina
CAPE KRUSENSTERN NATL. MON.
Noatak
BAIRD MTS.
Cape Krusenstern
KOBUK VALLEY NATL. PARK
Cape Espenberg
Kotzebue
Kiana
Noorvik
Ambler
Kobuk
Shungnak
Selawik
SELAWIK N.W.R.
BROOKS RANGE
Simon Paneak Memorial Museum
Anaktuvuk Pass
GATES OF THE ARCTIC N.P. AND PRESERVE
ENDICOTT MTS.
PHILIP SMITH MTS.
ARCTIC N.W.R.
Arctic Village
Sagwon
Coldfoot
Bettles
Venetie
Shishmaref
Diomede
Wales
Alaska Maritime N.W.R.
Taylor
BERING LAND BRIDGE NATL. PRES.
Kotzebue Sound
Deering
Buckland
Brevig Mission
Teller
SEWARD PENINSULA
CONTINENTAL DIVIDE
Council
White Mountain
Nome
Golovin
Elim
Koyuk
Alaska Maritime N.W.R.
Allakaket
KANUTI N.W.R.
KOYUKUK N.W.R.
Hughes
Huslia
YUKON FLATS N.W.R.
Beaver
Fort Yukon
Dinjii Zhuu Enjit Mus.
Stevens Village
WHITE MTS. NATL. REC. AREA
STEESE N.C.A.
Chena River S.R.A.
Chena Hot Sprs.
Rampart
Tanana
ELLIOT HWY
STEESE HWY
Univ. of Alaska Fairbanks
Fox
Minto
College
Fairbanks
Ester
North Pole
Manley Hot Springs
Nenana
Anderson
FORT WAINWRIGHT MIL. RES.
Big Delta S.H.P.
Big Delta
Delta Junction
FORT GREELY MIL. RES.
Koyukuk
Nulato
Galena
Ruby
NOWITNA N.W.R.
Kaltag
Norton Sound
IDITAROD TRAIL
Shaktoolik
Unalakleet
ALASKA MARITIME N.W.R.
Stebbins
St. Michael
Poorman
INNOKO N.W.R.
Lake Minchumina
DENALI N.P. AND PRESERVE
Denali (Mount McKinley) Highest Point in North America 20,310 ft.
Healy
Lignite
Cantwell
Summit
CLOSED IN WINTER
Denali
DENALI HWY
RANGE
Paxson
RICHARDSON HWY
Denali S.P.
Emmonak
Kotlik
Alakanuk
Nunam Iqua
Scammon Bay
Cape Romanzof
Mountain Village
St. Mary's
Hooper Bay
Chevak
Pilot Station
Marshall
Grayling
Anvik
Shageluk
Ophir
Takotna
McGrath
Nikolai
Iditarod
Flat
KUSKOKWIM MTS.
Holy Cross
Russian Mission
YUKON DELTA N.W.R.
Newtok
Tununak
Toksook Bay
Nightmute
Mekoryuk
Nunivak Island
Cape Mohican
Etolin Strait
YUKON DELTA N.W.R.
Crooked Creek
Upper Kalskag
Lower Kalskag
Chuathbaluk
Aniak
Red Devil
Sleetmute
Kasigluk
Yugtarvik Reg. Museum
Bethel
Tuluksak
Akiachak
Kwethluk
Napakiak
Napaskiak
Chefornak
Tuntutuliak
Kipnuk
Eek
Kwigillingok
Kuskokwim Bay
Quinhagak
KILBUCK MTS.
Lime Village
Petersville
Chase
Talkeetna
Talkeetna Hist. Mus.
Trapper Creek
Independence Mine S.H.P.
Skwentna
Willow
Houston
ALASKA RANGE
Lake Louise S.R.A.
Gakona
Gulkana
Glennallen
Copper Center
GLENN HWY
Sutton
Palmer
Wasilla
Mount Marcus Baker 13,176 ft.
Anchorage
CHUGACH S.P.
Valdez
Tatitlek
Cordova
LAKE CLARK N.P. & PRES.
Captain Cook S.R.A.
Redoubt Volcano 10,197 ft.
Nikiski
Kenai
Soldotna
Hope
Whittier
Moose Pass
Port Alsworth
Lake Clark
Nondalton
Iliamna
Newhalen
Cook Inlet
STERLING HWY
SEWARD HWY
Anchor Point
Anchor River S.R.A.
KENAI N.W.R.
KENAI PEN.
Seward
Alaska SeaLife Ctr.
Caines Head S.R.A.
CHUGACH N.F.
Chenega Site
Montague Island
Homer
Seldovia
KENAI FJORDS NATL. PARK
twice-monthly service June–Sept. only
TOGIAK N.W.R.
AHKLUN MTS.
WOOD-TIKCHIK S.P.
Koliganek
Goodnews Bay
Platinum
Togiak
Aleknagik
Ekwok
New Stuyahok
Fox Mus.
Dillingham
Levelock
Manokotak
Cape Newenham
ALASKA MARITIME N.W.R.
Togiak Bay
Clarks Point
Iliamna L.
Kokhanok
Naknek
South Naknek
King Salmon
KATMAI N.P. AND PRES.
Visitor Center
Cape Constantine
Egegik
Valley of Ten Thousand Smokes
Mount Katmai 6,715 ft.
Becharof L.
BECHAROF N.W.R.
Bristol Bay
Pilot Point
Shuyak Island S.P.
Afognak Island S.P.
Shelikof Strait
Kodiak N.W.R.
Ouzinkie
Ft. Abercrombie St. Hist. Pk.
Port Lions
Alutiiq Mus.
Kodiak
Pasagshak S.R.S.
Karluk
Larsen Bay
KODIAK N.W.R.
Kodiak Island
Old Harbor
Akhiok
ALASKA MARITIME N.W.R.
ALASKA PENINSULA N.W.R.
ALASKA PENINSULA
Port Heiden
ANIAKCHAK NATL. MON. & PRES.
Mount Veniaminof 7,075 ft.
Chignik Lake
Chignik
Perryville
ALASKA PENINSULA N.W.R.
Trinity Islands
Chirikof I.
IZEMBEK N.W.R.
Cold Bay
King Cove
False Pass
Unimak Island
Sand Point
Unga Island
Shumagin Islands
Sanak I.
ALASKA MARITIME N.W.R.
ALASKA MARITIME N.W.R.
Aleutian WWII Natl. Hist. Area
ALEUTIAN ISLANDS
Dutch Harbor
Unalaska
Akutan
Krenitzen Islands
Umnak Island
Unalaska Island
Fox Islands
Nikolski
Seguam I.
ALASKA MARITIME N.W.R.
HAWAII-ALEUTIAN TIME ZONE
ALASKA TIME ZONE
St. Matthew Island
ALASKA MARITIME N.W.R.
St. Paul I.
St. Paul
Pribilof Islands
PRIBILOF ISLAND SEAL AND OTTER PRES.
St. George
St. George I.
Distances in the U.S. shown in miles.
Aux États-Unis, les distances sont en milles.
TRAVEL NOTE: Always inquire locally for road conditions and closures, especially in winter.
1
2
3
4
A
B
C

DRIVING DISTANCES IN MILES	ANCHORAGE, AK	DAWSON CREEK, BC	DENALI NP, AK	FAIRBANKS, AK	HOMER, AK	JUNEAU, AK	PRINCE GEORGE, BC	PRINCE RUPERT, BC	SKAGWAY, AK	TOK, AK	WHITEHORSE, YT	YELLOWKNIFE, NT
ANCHORAGE, AK		1516	275	378	225	841*	1679	1514	807	323	697	1844
DAWSON CREEK, BC	1516		1503	1400	1740	963*	224	625	862	1193	819	741
FAIRBANKS, AK	378	1400	103		603	726*	1564	1398	691	207	581	1729
WHITEHORSE, YT	697	819	684	581	921	211*	982	817	110	374		1147

*DISTANCE INCLUDES FERRY TRAVEL

SEE ALSO DISTANCE AND DRIVING TIME MAP ON PAGES 286–287

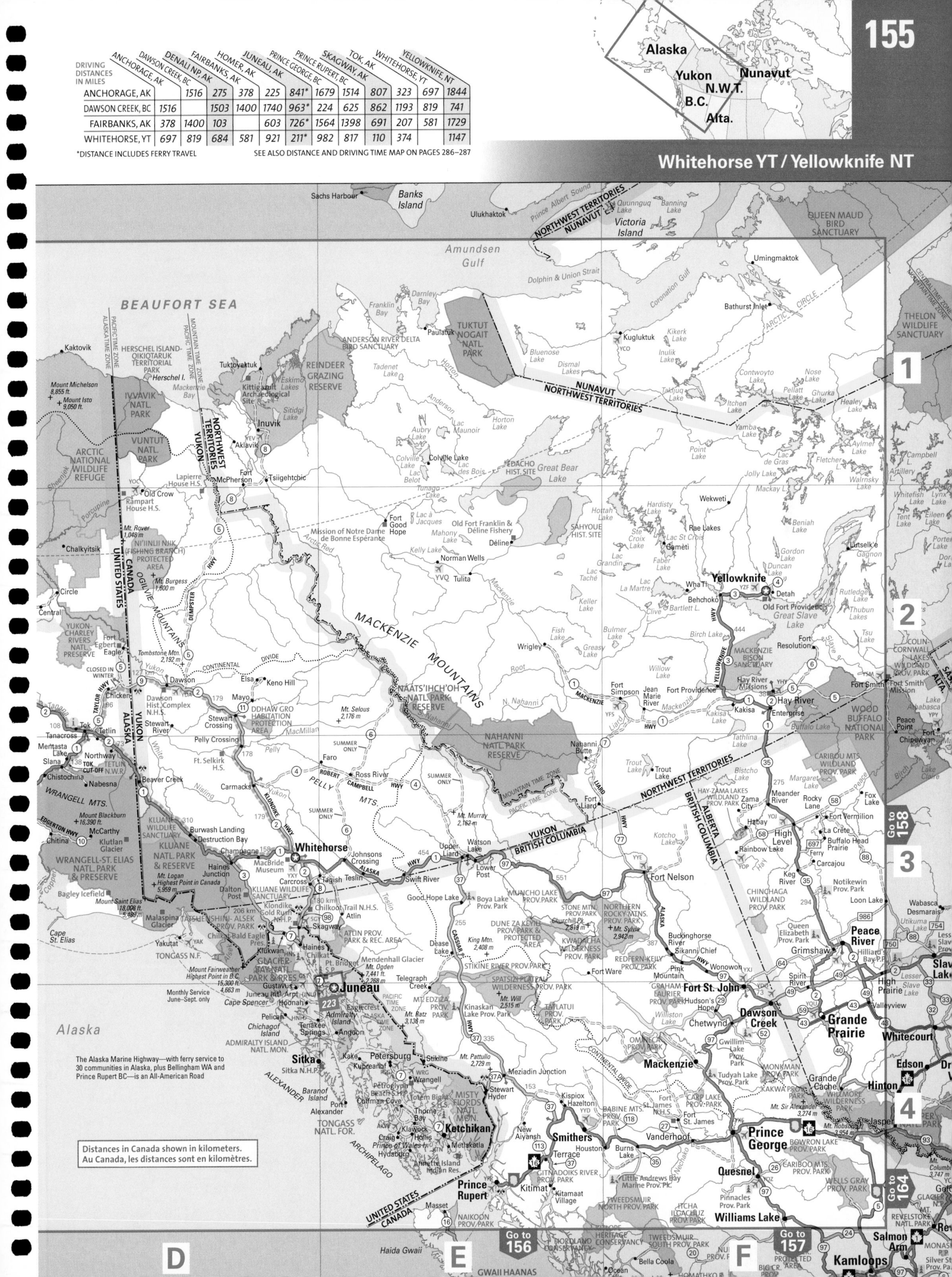

Alaska
British Columbia
Alberta

0 mi 20 40 60
0 km 20 40 60 80

One inch equals 40.3 miles/Un pouce équivaut à 40.3 milles
One centimeter equals 25.4 km/Un cm équivaut à 25.4 km

Prince Rupert BC / Terrace BC

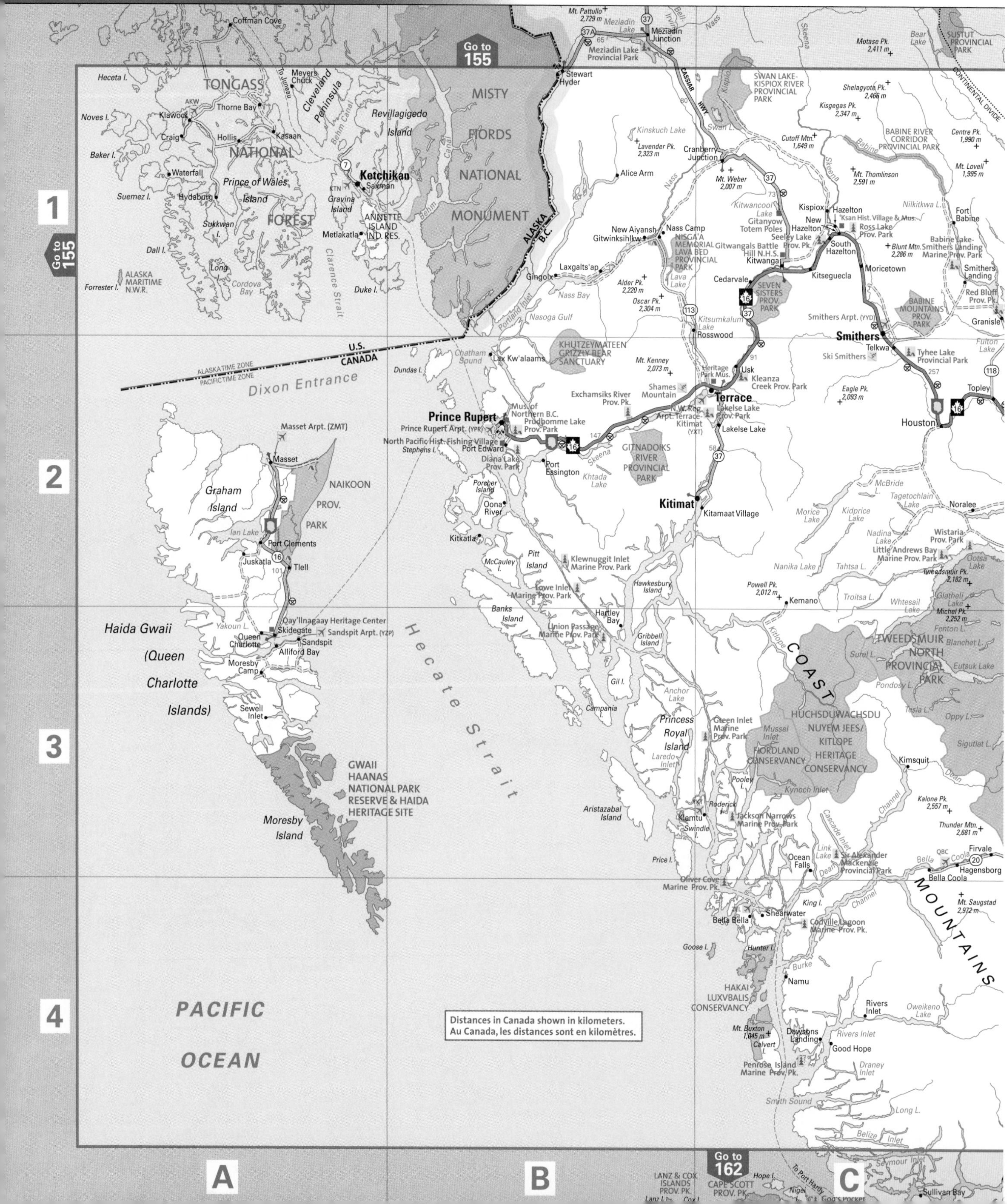

Go to 155

Go to 162

Distances in Canada shown in kilometers.
Au Canada, les distances sont en kilomètres.

TONGASS NATIONAL FOREST
MISTY FIORDS NATIONAL MONUMENT
Prince of Wales Island
Revillagigedo Island
Cleveland Peninsula
Ketchikan
Saxman
Metlakatla
ANNETTE ISLAND IND. RES.
Gravina Island
Coffman Cove
Meyers Chuck
Thorne Bay
Klawock
Craig
Hollis
Kasaan
Waterfall
Hydaburg
Heceta I.
Noyes I.
Baker I.
Suemez I.
Dall I.
Long I.
Sukkwan I.
Forrester I.
ALASKA MARITIME N.W.R.
Cordova Bay
Clarence Strait
Duke I.
Stewart
Hyder
Mt. Pattullo 2,729 m
Meziadin Lake
Meziadin Junction
Meziadin Lake Provincial Park
CASSIAR HWY.
ALASKA B.C.
U.S.
CANADA
ALASKA TIME ZONE
PACIFIC TIME ZONE
Dixon Entrance
Dundas I.
Chatham Sound
Lax Kw'alaams
KHUTZEYMATEEN GRIZZLY BEAR SANCTUARY
Portland Inlet
Nasoga Gulf
Nass Bay
Gingolx
Laxgalts'ap
New Aiyansh
Gitwinksihlkw
Nass Camp
NISGA'A MEMORIAL LAVA BED PROVINCIAL PARK
Lava Lake
Alice Arm
Kinskuch Lake
Lavender Pk. 2,323 m
Cranberry Junction
Mt. Weber 2,007 m
Kitwancool Lake
Gitanyow Totem Poles
Gitwangak Battle Hill N.H.S.
Kitwanga
Seeley Lake Prov. Pk.
Cedarvale
SEVEN SISTERS PROV. PARK
Alder Pk. 2,220 m
Oscar Pk. 2,304 m
Kitsumkalum Lake
Rosswood
Mt. Kenney 2,073 m
Heritage Park Mus.
Usk
Kleanza Creek Prov. Park
Shames Mountain
Exchamsiks River Prov. Pk.
Terrace
N.W. Reg. Arpt. Terrace-Kitimat (YXT)
Lakelse Lake Prov. Park
Lakelse Lake
GITNADOIKS RIVER PROVINCIAL PARK
Prince Rupert
Mus. of Northern B.C.
Prince Rupert Arpt. (YPR)
Prudhomme Lake Prov. Park
North Pacific Hist. Fishing Village
Port Edward
Stephens I.
Diana Lake Prov. Park
Port Essington
Khtada Lake
Porcher Island
Oona River
Kitkatla
McCauley I.
Pitt Island
Klewnuggit Inlet Marine Prov. Park
Lowe Inlet Marine Prov. Park
Banks Island
Hartley Bay
Union Passage Marine Prov. Park
Gribbell Island
Hawkesbury Island
Kitimat
Kitamaat Village
Gil I.
Campania
Anchor Lake
Princess Royal Island
Laredo Inlet
Green Inlet Marine Prov. Park
Aristazabal Island
Roderick
Klemtu
Swindle I.
Jackson Narrows Marine Prov. Park
Pooley I.
Price I.
Oliver Cove Marine Prov. Pk.
Ocean Falls
Link Lake
Sir Alexander Mackenzie Provincial Park
Shearwater
Bella Bella
King I.
Codville Lagoon Marine Prov. Pk.
Goose I.
Hunter I.
Namu
HAKAI LUXVBALIS CONSERVANCY
Mt. Buxton 1,045 m
Calvert I.
Penrose Island Marine Prov. Pk.
Dawsons Landing
Rivers Inlet
Good Hope
Oweikeno Lake
Draney Inlet
Smith Sound
Long L.
Belize Inlet
Seymour Inlet
Sullivan Bay
Hope I.
Nigei
God's Pocket
To Port Hardy
LANZ & COX ISLANDS PROV. PK.
CAPE SCOTT PROV. PK.
Masset Arpt. (ZMT)
Masset
Graham Island
NAIKOON PROV. PARK
Ian Lake
Port Clements
Juskatla
Tlell
Haida Gwaii (Queen Charlotte Islands)
Yakoun L.
Qay'llnagaay Heritage Center
Skidegate
Queen Charlotte
Sandspit Arpt. (YZP)
Sandspit
Alliford Bay
Moresby Camp
Sewell Inlet
GWAII HAANAS NATIONAL PARK RESERVE & HAIDA HERITAGE SITE
Moresby Island
Hecate Strait
PACIFIC OCEAN
SWAN LAKE-KISPIOX RIVER PROVINCIAL PARK
Swan L.
Kispiox
Hazelton
'Ksan Hist. Village & Mus.
New Hazelton
Ross Lake Prov. Park
South Hazelton
Kitseguecla
Moricetown
Cutoff Mtn. 1,649 m
Kisgegas Pk. 2,347 m
Shelagyote Pk. 2,466 m
Mt. Thomlinson 2,591 m
BABINE RIVER CORRIDOR PROVINCIAL PARK
Motase Pk. 2,411 m
Bear Lake
SUSTUT PROVINCIAL PARK
CONTINENTAL DIVIDE
Centre Pk. 1,990 m
Mt. Lovell 1,995 m
Nilkitkwa L.
Fort Babine
Blunt Mtn. 2,286 m
Babine Lake-Smithers Landing Marine Prov. Park
Smithers Landing
Red Bluff Prov. Pk.
BABINE MOUNTAINS PROV. PARK
Granisle
Smithers Arpt. (YYD)
Smithers
Telkwa
Ski Smithers
Tyhee Lake Provincial Park
Fulton Lake
Topley
Houston
Eagle Pk. 2,093 m
McBride
Tagetochlain Lake
Noralee
Morice Lake
Kidprice Lake
Nadina Lake
Wistaria Prov. Park
Little Andrews Bay Marine Prov. Park
Nanika Lake
Tahtsa L.
Ootsa Lake
Tweedsmuir Pk. 2,182 m
Powell Pk. 2,012 m
Kemano
Troitsa L.
Whitesail Lake
Glatheli Lake
Michel Pk. 2,252 m
Fenton L.
TWEEDSMUIR NORTH PROVINCIAL PARK
Blanchet L.
Surel L.
Eutsuk Lake
Pondosy L.
Tesla L.
Oppy L.
Kitlope
COAST MOUNTAINS
HUCHSDUWACHSDU NUYEM JEES/KITLOPE HERITAGE CONSERVANCY
Mussel Inlet
FIORDLAND CONSERVANCY
Kynoch Inlet
Sigutlat L.
Kimsquit
Dean Channel
Kalone Pk. 2,557 m
Thunder Mtn. 2,681 m
Cascade Inlet
Bella Coola
QBC
Firvale
Hagensborg
Mt. Saugstad 2,972 m
Burke Channel
Rivers Inlet

A B C
1 2 3 4

DRIVING DISTANCES IN KM / DISTANCES ROUTIÈRES EN KM

	DAWSON CREEK, BC	GRANDE PRAIRIE, AB	KAMLOOPS, BC	KITIMAT, BC	100 MILE HOUSE, BC	PRINCE GEORGE, BC	PRINCE RUPERT, BC	SMITHERS, BC	STEWART, BC	TERRACE, BC	VALEMOUNT, BC	WILLIAMS LAKE, BC
DAWSON CREEK, BC		124	931	1041	734	406	1130	777	1109	983	642	644
PRINCE GEORGE, BC	406	530	525	635	328		724	371	703	577	295	238
PRINCE RUPERT, BC	1130	1254	1249	205	1052	724		353	463	147	1019	962
WILLIAMS LAKE, BC	644	768	287	873	90	238	962	609	941	815	332	

SEE ALSO DISTANCE AND DRIVING TIME MAP ON PAGES 286–287 / VOIR AUSSI CARTE DES DISTANCES ET DES TEMPS DE PARCOURS PAGES 286–287

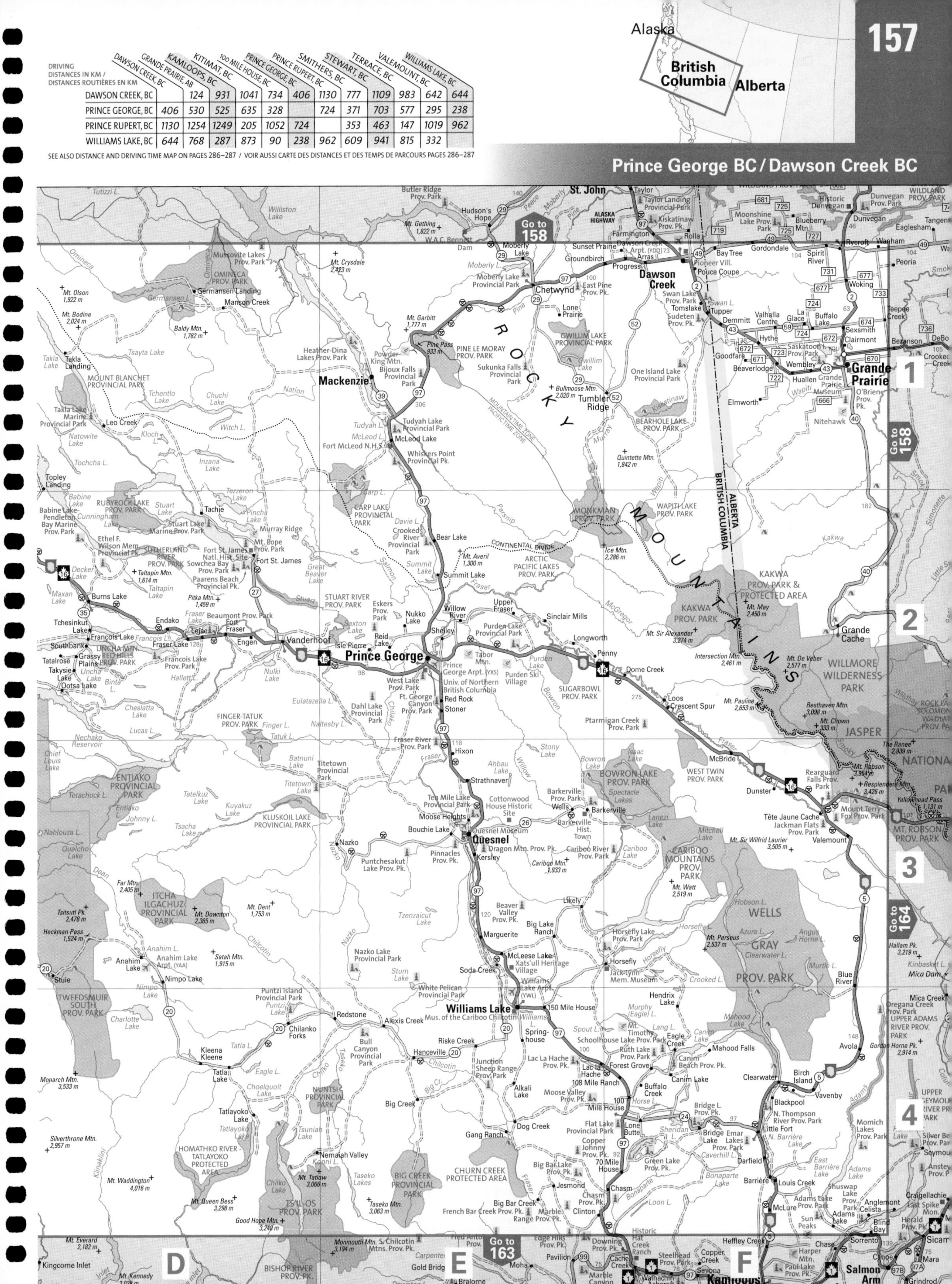

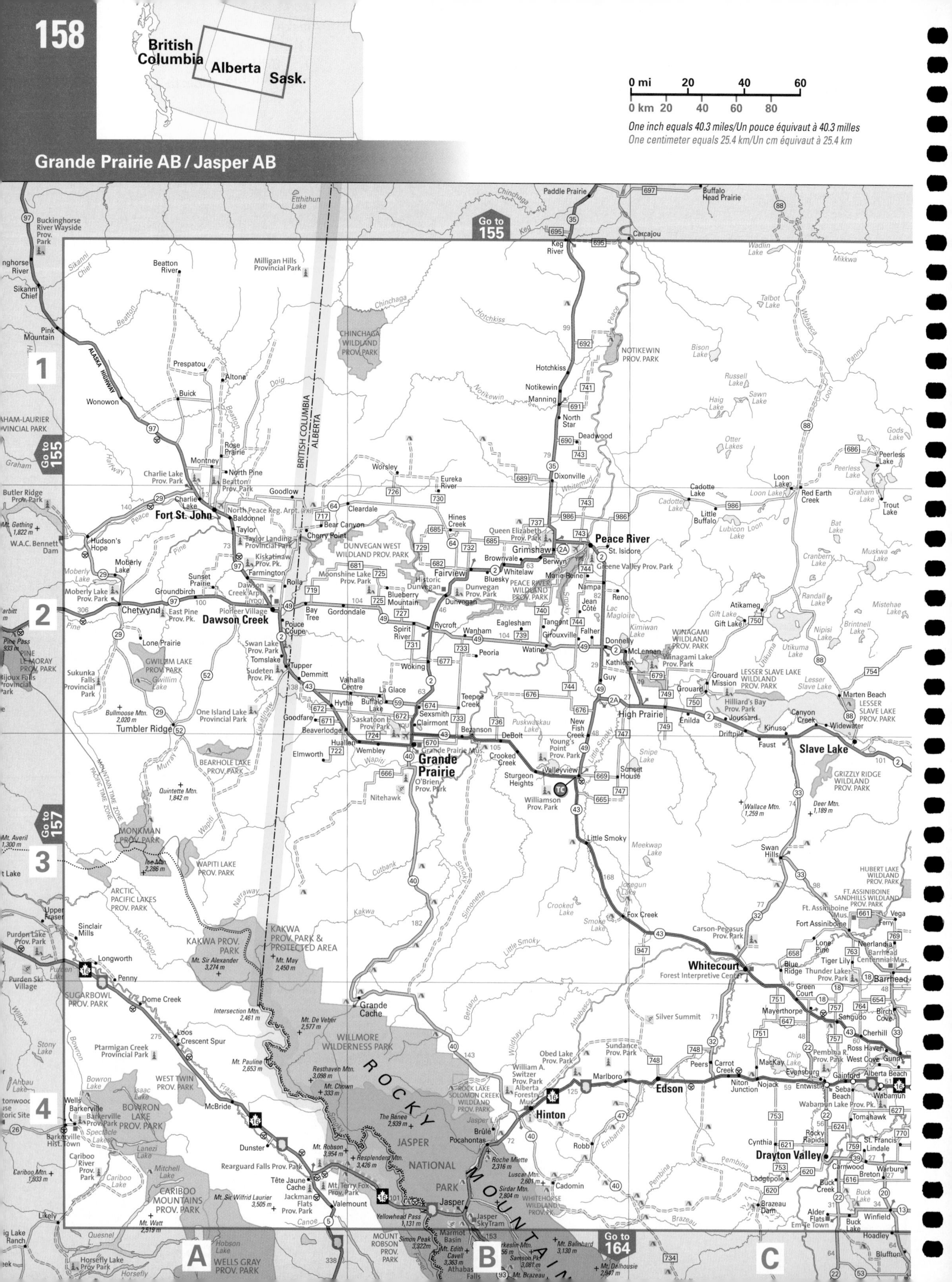

Grande Prairie AB / Jasper AB

DRIVING DISTANCES IN KM / DISTANCES ROUTIÈRES EN KM

	DAWSON CREEK, BC	EDMONTON, AB	FORT MCMURRAY, AB	GRANDE PRAIRIE, AB	JASPER, AB	LLOYDMINSTER, AB/SK	MEADOW LAKE, SK	N. BATTLEFORD, SK	PEACE RIVER, AB	SLAVE LAKE, AB	VALEMOUNT, BC	WHITECOURT, AB
EDMONTON, AB	597		439	462	367	238	415	375	484	251	488	177
GRANDE PRAIRIE, AB	124	462	756		397	700	824	837	197	318	518	279
JASPER, AB	521	367	796	397		605	782	742	578	464	121	271
N. BATTLEFORD, SK	972	375	814	837	742	137	158		866	633	863	559

SEE ALSO DISTANCE AND DRIVING TIME MAP ON PAGES 286–287 / VOIR AUSSI CARTE DES DISTANCES ET DES TEMPS DE PARCOURS PAGES 286–287

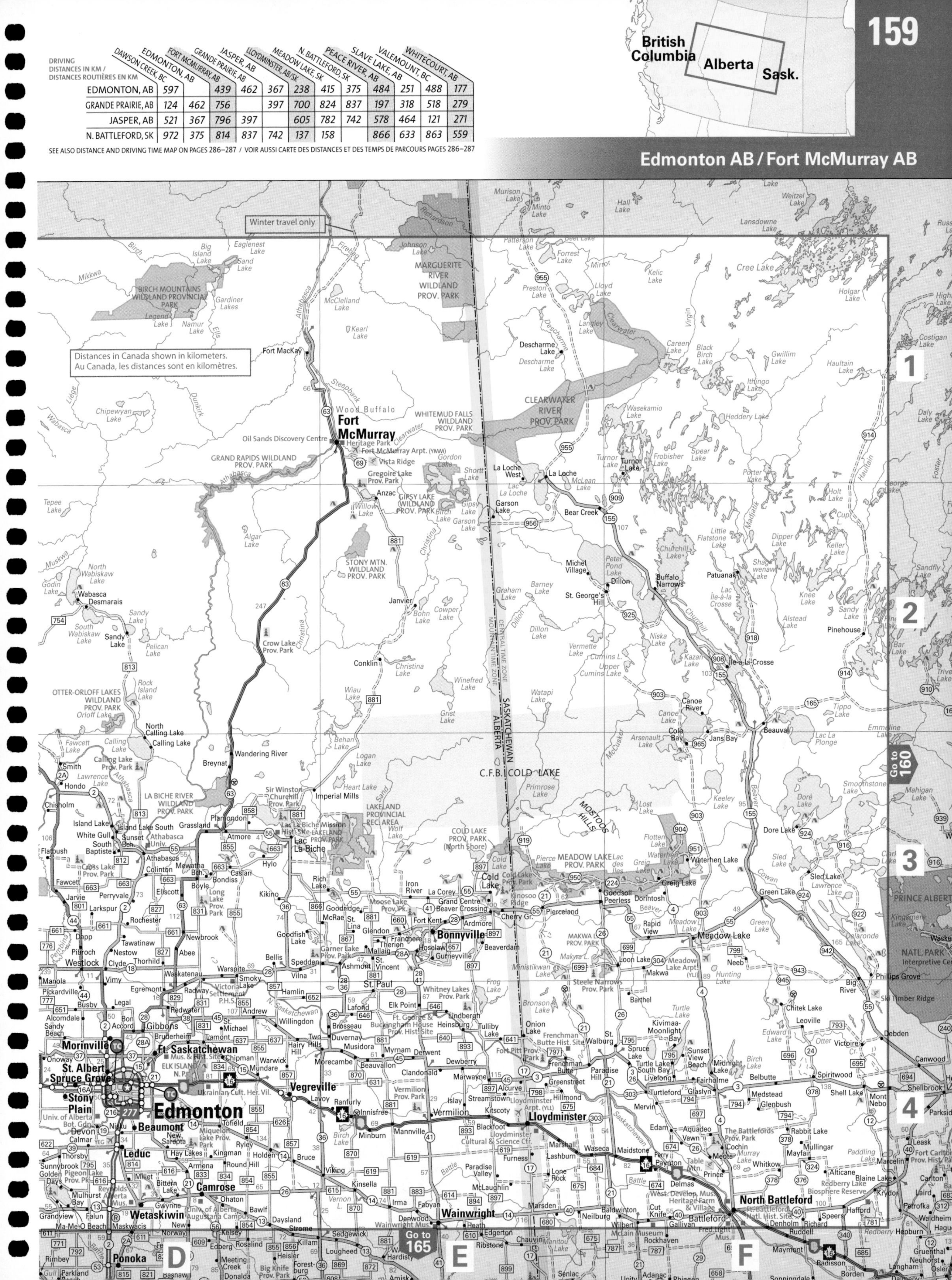

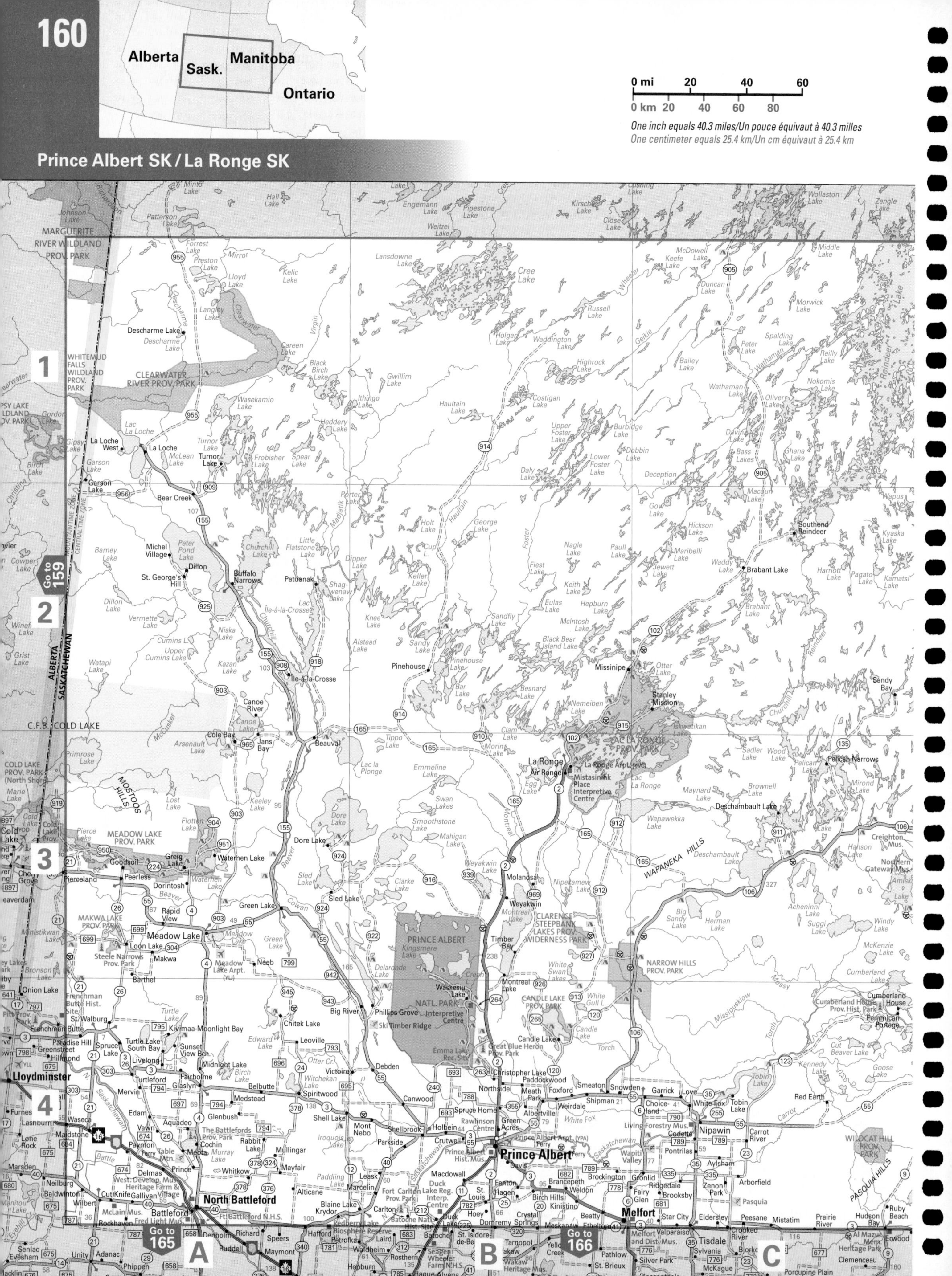
Alberta
Sask.
Manitoba
Ontario
0 mi 20 40 60
0 km 20 40 60 80
One inch equals 40.3 miles/Un pouce équivaut à 40.3 milles
One centimeter equals 25.4 km/Un cm équivaut à 25.4 km
1
2
3
4
A
B
C
Go to 159
Go to 165
Go to 166
ALBERTA
SASKATCHEWAN
MOUNTAIN TIME ZONE
CENTRAL TIME ZONE
MARGUERITE RIVER WILDLAND PROV. PARK
WHITEMUD FALLS WILDLAND PROV. PARK
CLEARWATER RIVER PROV. PARK
Descharme Lake
La Loche
La Loche West
Turnor Lake
Garson Lake
Bear Creek
Michel Village
Dillon
St. George's Hill
Buffalo Narrows
Patuanak
Île-à-la-Crosse
Pinehouse
Canoe River
Cole Bay
Jans Bay
Beauval
C.F.B. COLD LAKE
COLD LAKE PROV. PARK
MOSTOOS HILLS
MEADOW LAKE PROV. PARK
Goodsoil
Pierceland
Peerless
Dorintosh
Greig Lake
Waterhen Lake
Dore Lake
Sled Lake
Green Lake
Rapid View
Meadow Lake
Loon Lake
Makwa
Steele Narrows Prov. Park
Barthel
Neeb
MAKWA LAKE PROV. PARK
Lloydminster
Onion Lake
Frenchman Butte
St. Walburg
Paradise Hill
Kivimaa-Moonlight Bay
Turtle Lake South Bay
Livelong
Spruce Lake
Sunset View Bch.
Midnight Lake
Turtleford
Fairholme
Glaslyn
Mervin
Medstead
Belbutte
Spiritwood
Leoville
Chitek Lake
Big River
Phillips Grove
Ski Timber Ridge
Debden
Victoire
Canwood
Shell Lake
Mont Nebo
Shellbrook
Parkside
Leask
Marcelin
Blaine Lake
Krydor
Hafford
Edam
Vawn
Aquadeo
Glenbush
Paynton
Cochin
Meota
Rabbit Lake
Mullingar
Mayfair
Whitkow
Delmas
Battleford
North Battleford
Cut Knife
Gallivan
Baldwinton
Wilbert
Marsden
Neilburg
Waseca
Maidstone
Lashburn
Lone Rock
Rockhaven
Denholm
Richard
Speers
Ruddell
Maymont
PRINCE ALBERT NATL. PARK
Waskesiu Lake
Emma Lake
Christopher Lake
Northside
Meath Park
Paddockwood
Foxford
Holbein
Spruce Home
Crutwell
Prince Albert
Albertville
Weirdale
Smeaton
Snowden
Choiceland
Garrick
White Fox
Love
Tobin Lake
Nipawin
Codette
Carrot River
Aylsham
Arborfield
Pontrilas
Brockington
Gronlid
Ridgedale
Brooksby
Zenon Park
Fairy Glen
Melfort
Star City
Tisdale
Eldersley
Peesane
Mistatim
Prairie River
Hudson Bay
Ruby Beach
Birch Hills
Kinistino
Brancepeth
Weldon
Hagen
St. Louis
Duck Lake
Batoche
Rosthern
Waldheim
Laird
Hepburn
Carlton
Macdowall
Fenton
Hoey
Domremy
Crystal Springs
Wakaw
Molanosa
Weyakwin
Timber Bay
Montreal Lake
CLARENCE-STEEPBANK LAKES PROV. WILDERNESS PARK
CANDLE LAKE PROV. PARK
Candle Lake
NARROW HILLS PROV. PARK
WILDCAT HILL PROV. PARK
PASQUIA HILLS
WAPANEKA HILLS
La Ronge
Air Ronge
LAC LA RONGE PROV. PARK
Missinipe
Stanley Mission
Sandy Bay
Pelican Narrows
Deschambault Lake
Creighton
Cumberland House
Southend Reindeer
Brabant Lake
Cree Lake

DRIVING DISTANCES IN KM / DISTANCES ROUTIÈRES EN KM

	FLIN FLON, MB	GILLAM, MB	GRAND RAPIDS, MB	LA LOCHE, SK	LA RONGE, SK	LYNN LAKE, MB	MEADOW LAKE, SK	NIPAWIN, SK	N. BATTLEFORD, SK	PRINCE ALBERT, SK	THE PAS, MB	THOMPSON, MB
FLIN FLON, MB		676	402	889	613	703	633	388	571	375	141	380
MEADOW LAKE, SK	633	1309	867	305	496	1336		399	158	258	569	1013
PRINCE ALBERT, SK	375	1051	609	514	238	1078	258	141	196		311	781
THOMPSON, MB	380	296	328	1269	697	323	1013	640	977	781	470	

SEE ALSO DISTANCE AND DRIVING TIME MAP ON PAGES 286–287 / VOIR AUSSI CARTE DES DISTANCES ET DES TEMPS DE PARCOURS PAGES 286–287

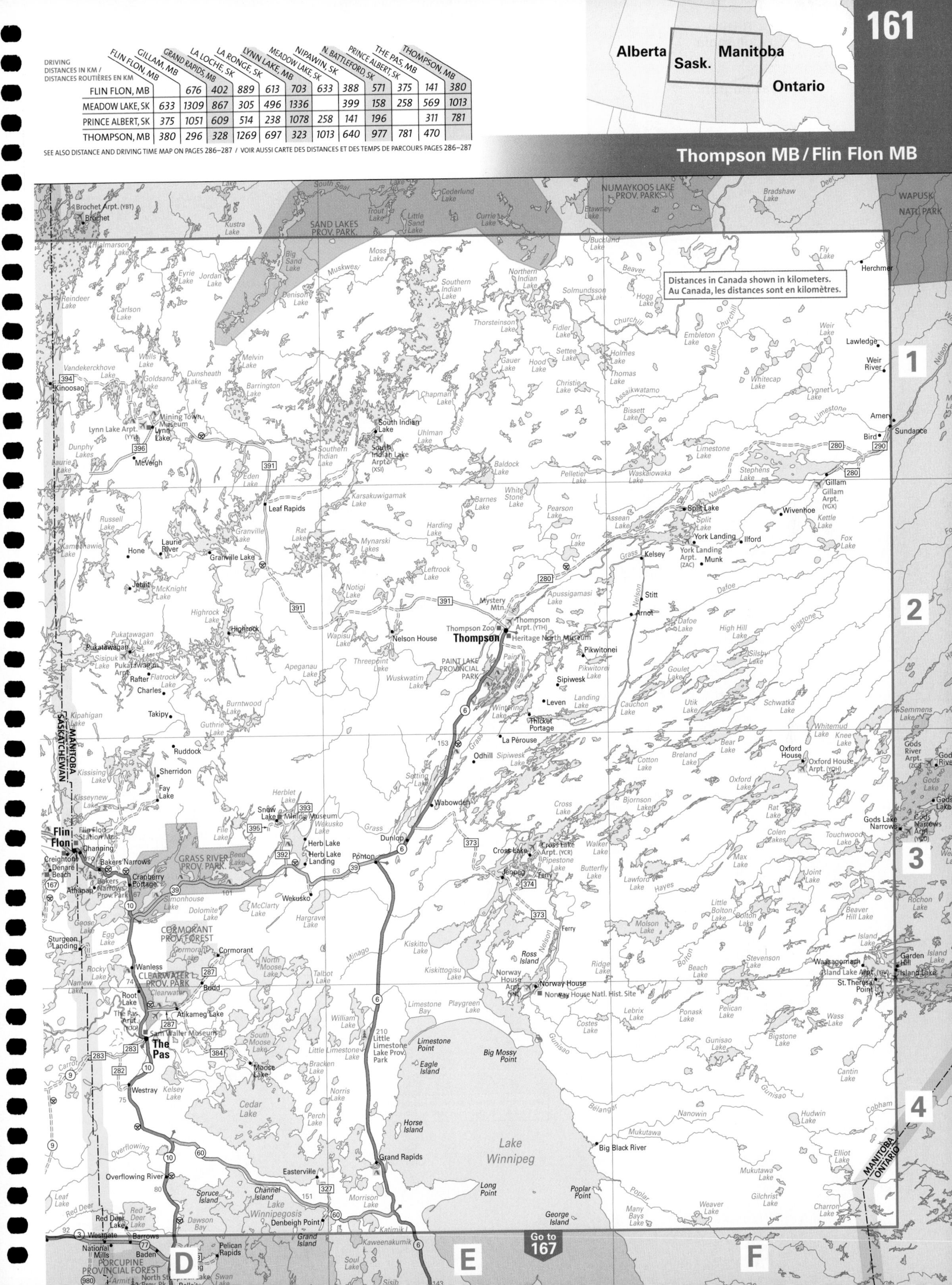

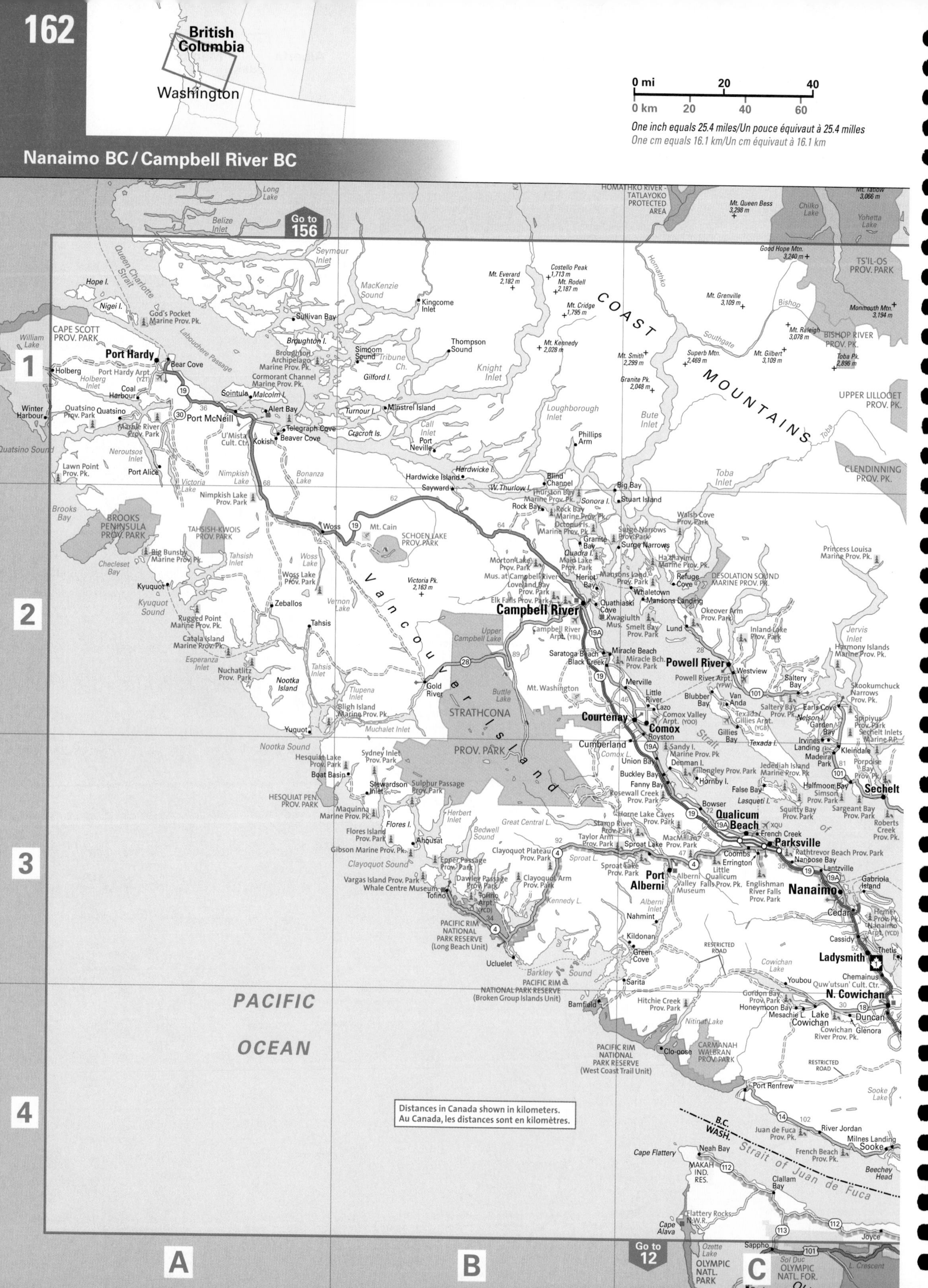
British Columbia
Washington
0 mi 20 40
0 km 20 40 60
One inch equals 25.4 miles/Un pouce équivaut à 25.4 milles
One cm equals 16.1 km/Un cm équivaut à 16.1 km
Go to 156
Go to 12
COAST MOUNTAINS
Vancouver Island
PACIFIC OCEAN
Distances in Canada shown in kilometers.
Au Canada, les distances sont en kilomètres.
CAPE SCOTT PROV. PARK
Port Hardy
Bear Cove
Holberg
Port Hardy Arpt.
Coal Harbour
Winter Harbour
Quatsino
Quatsino Sound
Port McNeill
Sointula
Malcolm I.
Alert Bay
Telegraph Cove
Beaver Cove
Kokish
U'Mista Cult. Ctr.
Port Alice
Lawn Point Prov. Pk.
Nimpkish Lake
Nimpkish Lake Prov. Park
Woss
Mt. Cain
SCHOEN LAKE PROV. PARK
BROOKS PENINSULA PROV. PARK
TAHSISH-KWOIS PROV. PARK
Big Bunsby Marine Prov. Pk.
Kyuquot
Kyuquot Sound
Zeballos
Tahsis
Rugged Point Marine Prov. Pk.
Catala Island Marine Prov. Pk.
Esperanza Inlet
Nuchatlitz Prov. Park
Nootka Island
Gold River
Bligh Island Marine Prov. Pk.
Yuquot
Nootka Sound
Hesquiat Lake Prov. Park
Boat Basin
HESQUIAT PEN. PROV. PARK
Sydney Inlet Prov. Park
Stewardson Inlet
Sulphur Passage Prov. Park
Maquinna Marine Prov. Pk.
Flores I.
Flores Island Prov. Park
Ahousat
Gibson Marine Prov. Pk.
Clayoquot Sound
Vargas Island Prov. Park
Whale Centre Museum
Tofino
Tofino Arpt.
PACIFIC RIM NATIONAL PARK RESERVE (Long Beach Unit)
Ucluelet
Barkley Sound
PACIFIC RIM NATIONAL PARK RESERVE (Broken Group Islands Unit)
Bamfield
Clo-oose
CARMANAH WALBRAN PROV. PARK
PACIFIC RIM NATIONAL PARK RESERVE (West Coast Trail Unit)
Port Renfrew
Juan de Fuca Prov. Pk.
River Jordan
French Beach Prov. Pk.
Sooke
Milnes Landing
Strait of Juan de Fuca
B.C. WASH.
Cape Flattery
Neah Bay
MAKAH IND. RES.
Clallam Bay
Cape Alava
Sappho
Forks
OLYMPIC NATL. PARK
OLYMPIC NATL. FOR.
STRATHCONA PROV. PARK
Upper Campbell Lake
Buttle Lake
Mt. Washington
Victoria Pk. 2,163 m
Campbell River
Campbell River Arpt.
Quathiaski Cove
Heriot Bay
Quadra I.
Saratoga Beach
Black Creek
Miracle Beach
Merville
Courtenay
Comox
Comox Valley Arpt.
Cumberland
Royston
Union Bay
Denman I.
Hornby I.
Buckley Bay
Fanny Bay
Bowser
Qualicum Beach
Parksville
French Creek
Coombs
Errington
Port Alberni
Sproat Lake
Great Central L.
Taylor Arm Prov. Park
Nahmint
Kildonan
Green Cove
Sarita
Nanaimo
Lantzville
Nanoose Bay
Gabriola Island
Cedar
Cassidy
Ladysmith
Chemainus
N. Cowichan
Duncan
Lake Cowichan
Youbou
Cowichan Lake
Powell River
Powell River Arpt.
Westview
Lund
Texada I.
Lasqueti I.
Saltery Bay
Earls Cove
Sechelt
Halfmoon Bay
Madeira Park
Irvines Landing
Kleindale
Refuge Cove
Whaletown
Mansons Landing
DESOLATION SOUND MARINE PROV. PK.
Stuart Island
Big Bay
Sayward
Hardwicke Island
Blind Channel
Rock Bay
Port Neville
Kingcome Inlet
Sullivan Bay
Simoom Sound
Minstrel Island
Thompson Sound
Knight Inlet
Loughborough Inlet
Bute Inlet
Phillips Arm
Toba Inlet
Jervis Inlet
Mt. Queen Bess 3,298 m
Good Hope Mtn. 3,240 m
TS'IL-OS PROV. PARK
BISHOP RIVER PROV. PARK
UPPER LILLOOET PROV. PK.
CLENDINNING PROV. PK.
HOMATHKO RIVER - TATLAYOKO PROTECTED AREA
Mt. Waddington
A
B
C
1
2
3
4

DRIVING DISTANCES IN KM / DISTANCES ROUTIÈRES EN KM

	CAMPBELL RIVER, BC	KAMLOOPS, BC	KELOWNA, BC	MERRITT, BC	NANAIMO, BC	OSOYOOS, BC	PORT ALBERNI, BC	PORT HARDY, BC	SALMON ARM, BC	VANCOUVER, BC	VICTORIA, BC	WHISTLER, BC
KAMLOOPS, BC	512		163	87	363	231	441	750	108	355	393	475
NANAIMO, BC	153	363	403	279		404	82	391	471	23	113	104
VANCOUVER, BC	172	355	395	271	23	396	101	410	463		69	123
VICTORIA, BC	266	393	433	309	113	434	195	504	501	69		192

SEE ALSO DISTANCE AND DRIVING TIME MAP ON PAGES 286–287 / VOIR AUSSI CARTE DES DISTANCES ET DES TEMPS DE PARCOURS PAGES 286–287

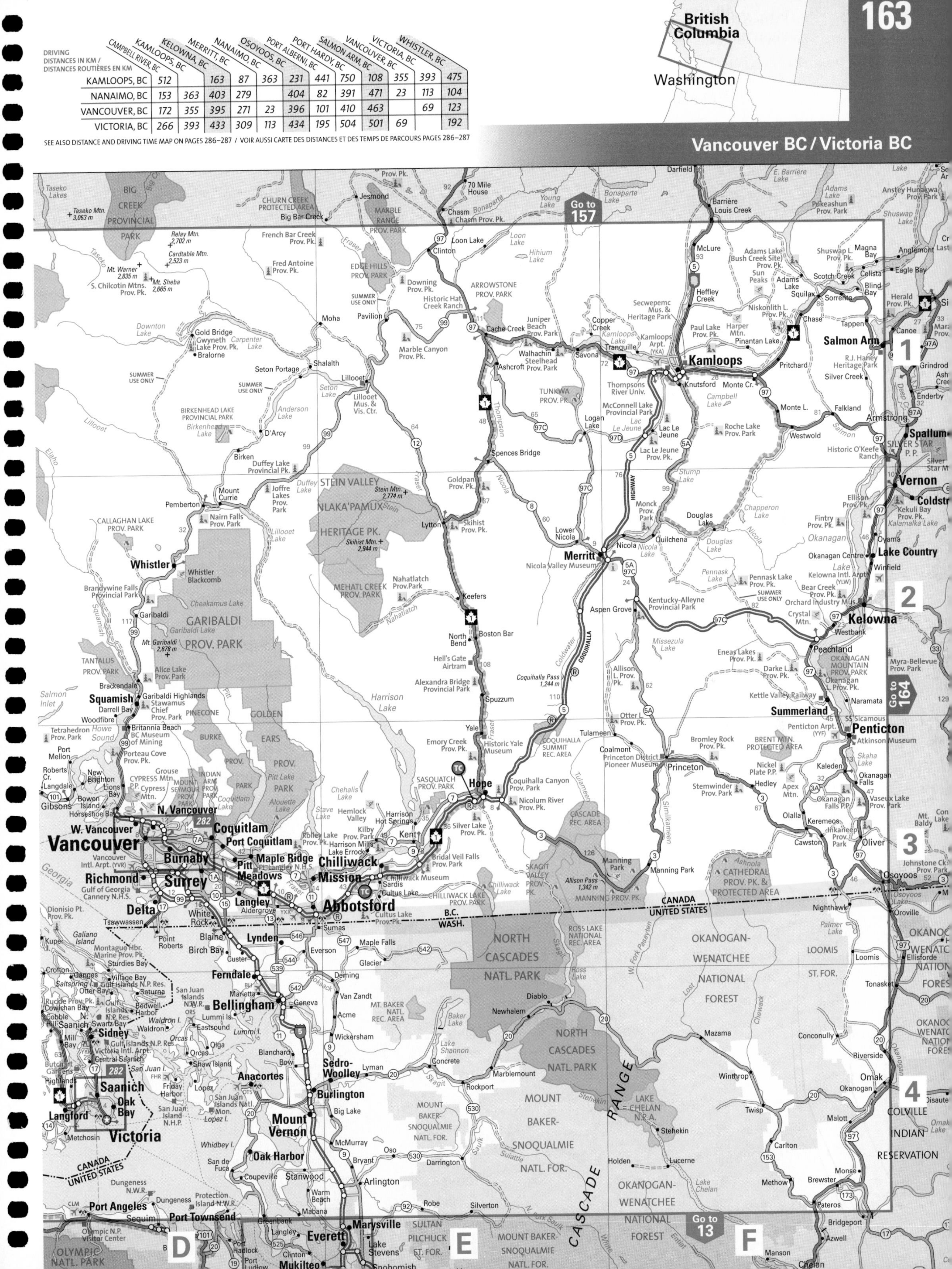

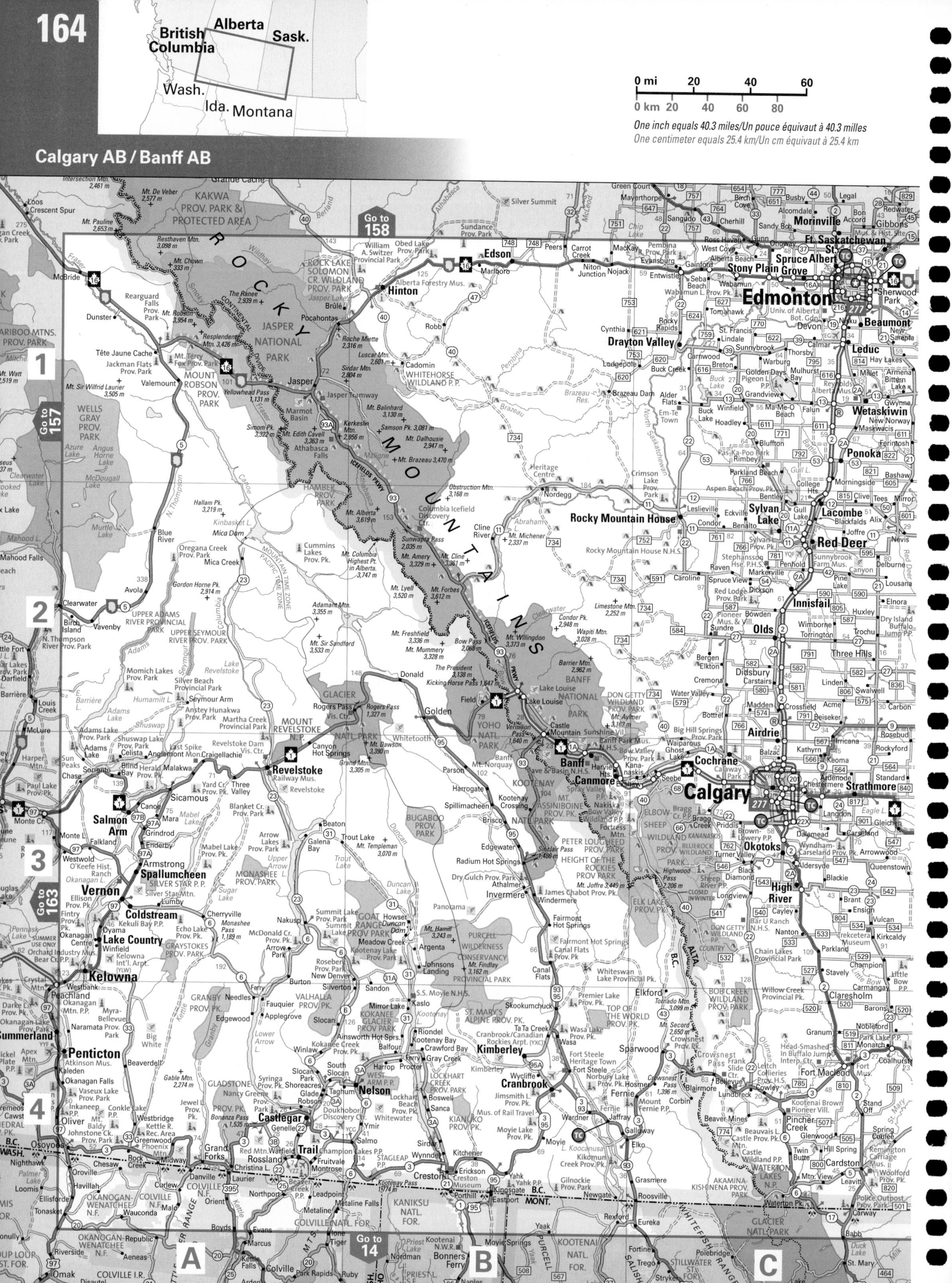
British Columbia
Alberta
Sask.
Wash.
Ida.
Montana
0 mi 20 40 60
0 km 20 40 60 80
One inch equals 40.3 miles/Un pouce équivaut à 40.3 milles
One centimeter equals 25.4 km/Un cm équivaut à 25.4 km
Go to 158
Go to 157
Go to 163
Go to 14
ROCKY MOUNTAINS
JASPER NATIONAL PARK
BANFF NATIONAL PARK
YOHO NATL. PARK
KOOTENAY NATL. PARK
GLACIER NATL. PARK
MOUNT REVELSTOKE N.P.
MOUNT ROBSON PROV. PARK
WELLS GRAY PROV. PARK
KAKWA PROV. PARK & PROTECTED AREA
Edmonton
Calgary
Red Deer
Banff
Canmore
Jasper
Hinton
Edson
Lake Louise
Golden
Revelstoke
Salmon Arm
Vernon
Kelowna
Penticton
Nelson
Castlegar
Trail
Cranbrook
Kimberley
Fernie
Invermere
Radium Hot Springs
Cochrane
Airdrie
Okotoks
High River
Olds
Innisfail
Lacombe
Wetaskiwin
Ponoka
Leduc
Spruce Grove
St. Albert
Drayton Valley
Rocky Mountain House
Sylvan Lake
Strathmore
Claresholm
Fort Macleod
Pincher Creek
Cardston
Waterton Pk.
Valemount
Blue River
Clearwater
McBride
Osoyoos
Oliver
Grand Forks
Creston
Sparwood
Elkford
B.C.
ALTA.
WASH.
MONT.
A
B
C
1
2
3
4

DRIVING DISTANCES IN KM / DISTANCES ROUTIÈRES EN KM

	BANFF, AB	CALGARY, AB	CRANBROOK, BC	EDMONTON, AB	JASPER, AB	KELOWNA, BC	LETHBRIDGE, AB	LLOYDMINSTER, AB/SK	MEDICINE HAT, AB	RED DEER, AB	SASKATOON, SK	SWIFT CURRENT, SK
CALGARY, AB	128		383	296	396	638	216	534	285	145	620	503
EDMONTON, AB	412	296	679		367	934	512	238	579	150	513	676
LETHBRIDGE, AB	344	216	306	512	612	809		605	164	360	650	382
SASKATOON, SK	748	620	969	513	880	1255	650	275	486	639		267

SEE ALSO DISTANCE AND DRIVING TIME MAP ON PAGES 286–287 / VOIR AUSSI CARTE DES DISTANCES ET DES TEMPS DE PARCOURS PAGES 286–287

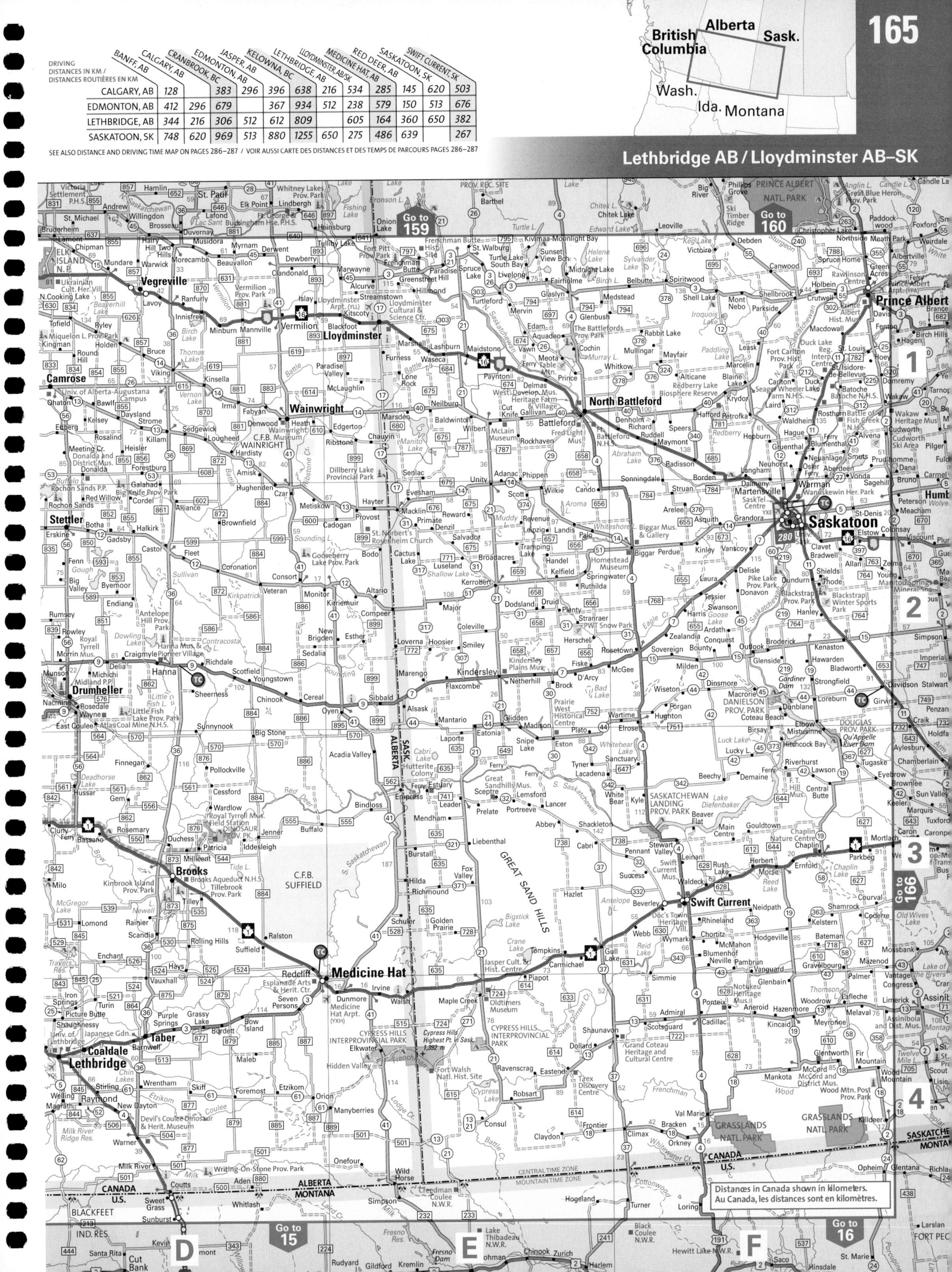

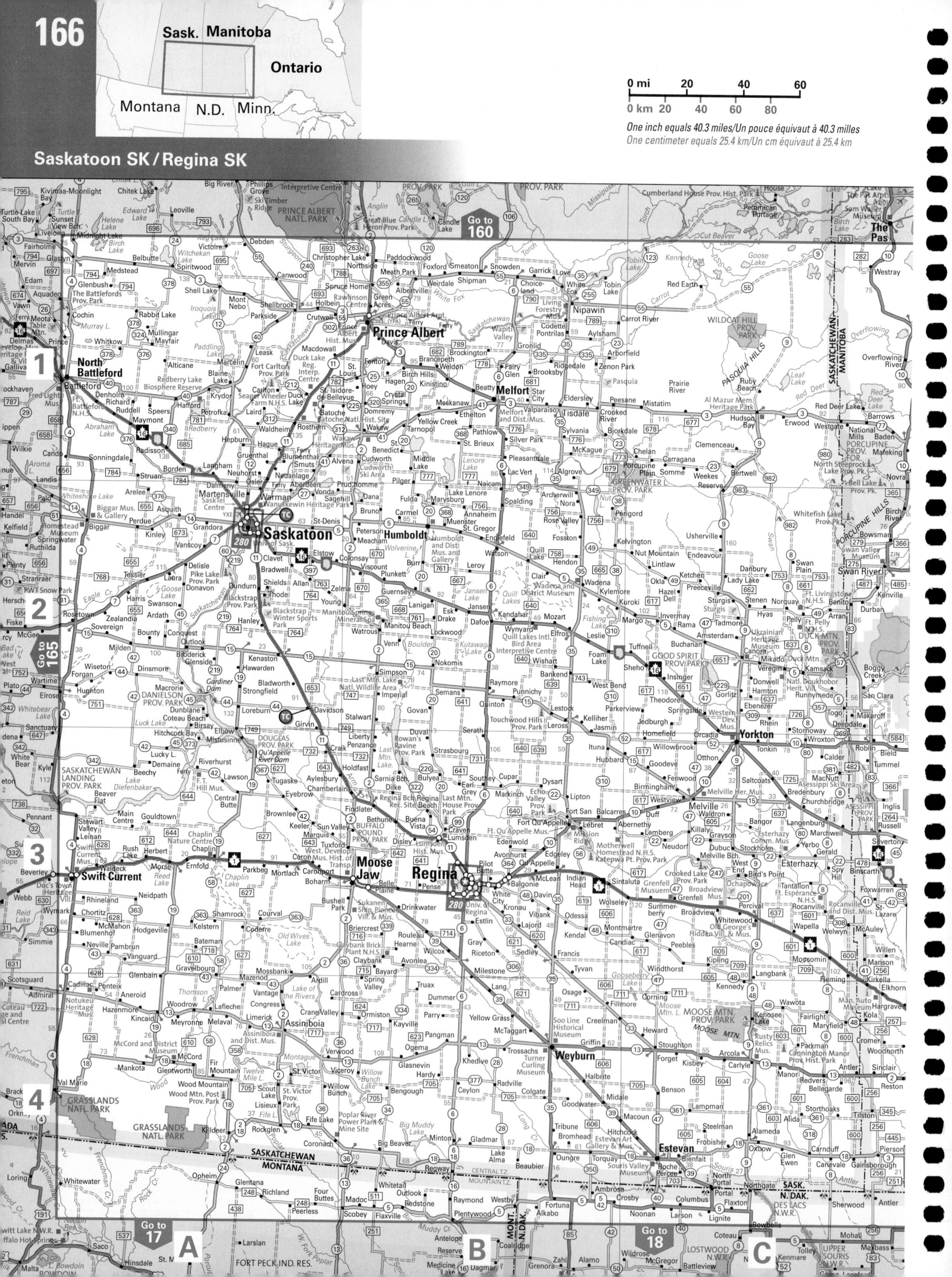
Sask.
Manitoba
Ontario
Montana
N.D.
Minn.
0 mi 20 40 60
0 km 20 40 60 80
One inch equals 40.3 miles/Un pouce équivaut à 40.3 milles
One centimeter equals 25.4 km/Un cm équivaut à 25.4 km
Saskatoon SK / Regina SK
Go to 160
Go to 165
Go to 17
Go to 18
Prince Albert
North Battleford
Saskatoon
Humboldt
Melfort
Nipawin
Tisdale
Yorkton
Melville
Swift Current
Moose Jaw
Regina
Weyburn
Estevan
The Pas
Swan River
SASKATCHEWAN
MANITOBA
MONTANA
N. DAK.
PRINCE ALBERT NATL. PARK
GRASSLANDS NATL. PARK
A
B
C
1
2
3
4

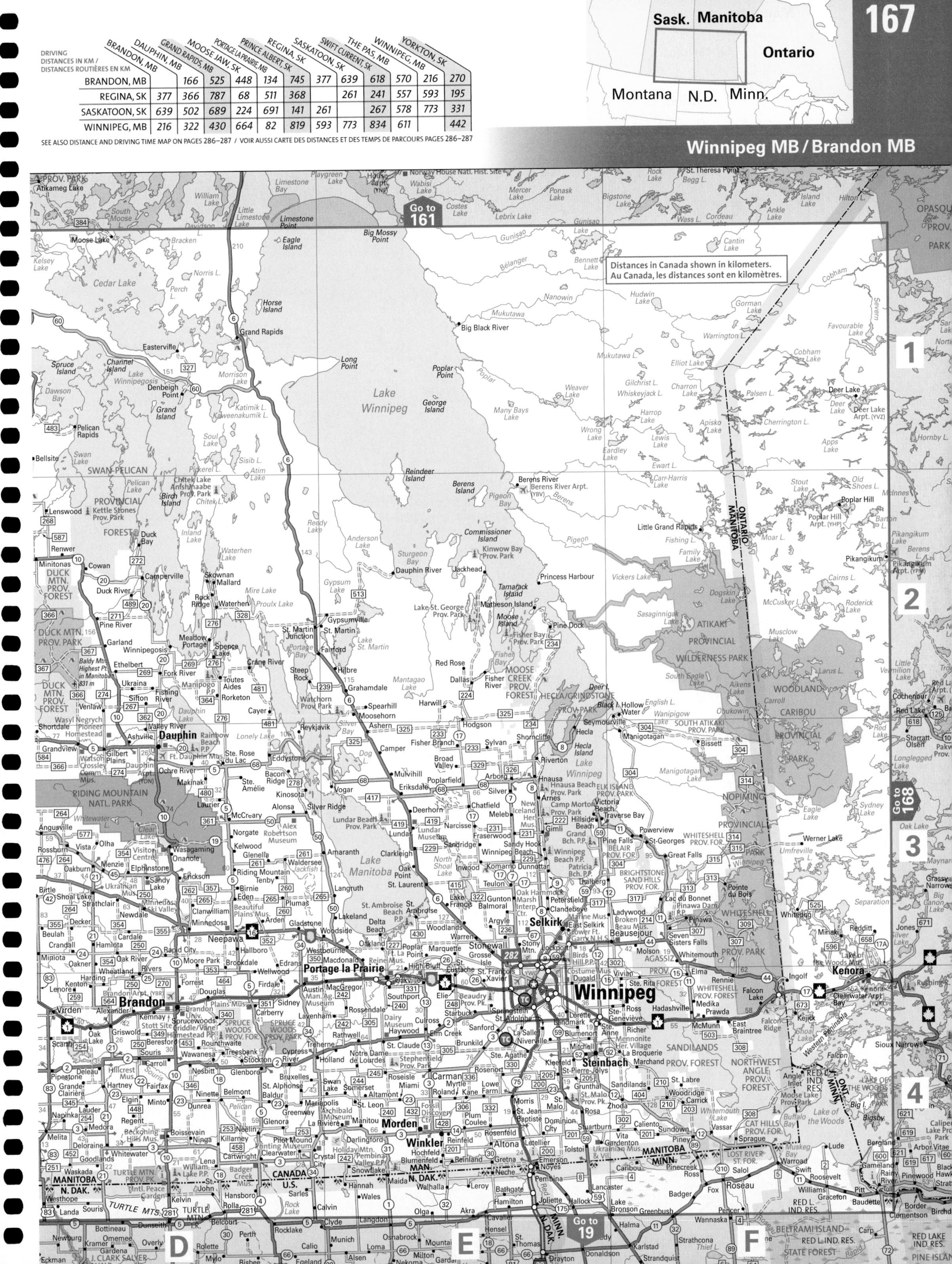

DRIVING DISTANCES IN KM / DISTANCES ROUTIÈRES EN KM

	BRANDON, MB	DAUPHIN, MB	GRAND RAPIDS, MB	MOOSE JAW, SK	PORTAGE LA PRAIRIE, MB	PRINCE ALBERT, SK	REGINA, SK	SASKATOON, SK	SWIFT CURRENT, SK	THE PAS, MB	WINNIPEG, MB	YORKTON, SK
BRANDON, MB		166	525	448	134	745	377	639	618	570	216	270
REGINA, SK	377	366	787	68	511	368		261	241	557	593	195
SASKATOON, SK	639	502	689	224	691	141	261		267	578	773	331
WINNIPEG, MB	216	322	430	664	82	819	593	773	834	611		442

SEE ALSO DISTANCE AND DRIVING TIME MAP ON PAGES 286–287 / VOIR AUSSI CARTE DES DISTANCES ET DES TEMPS DE PARCOURS PAGES 286–287

Kenora ON / Fort Frances ON

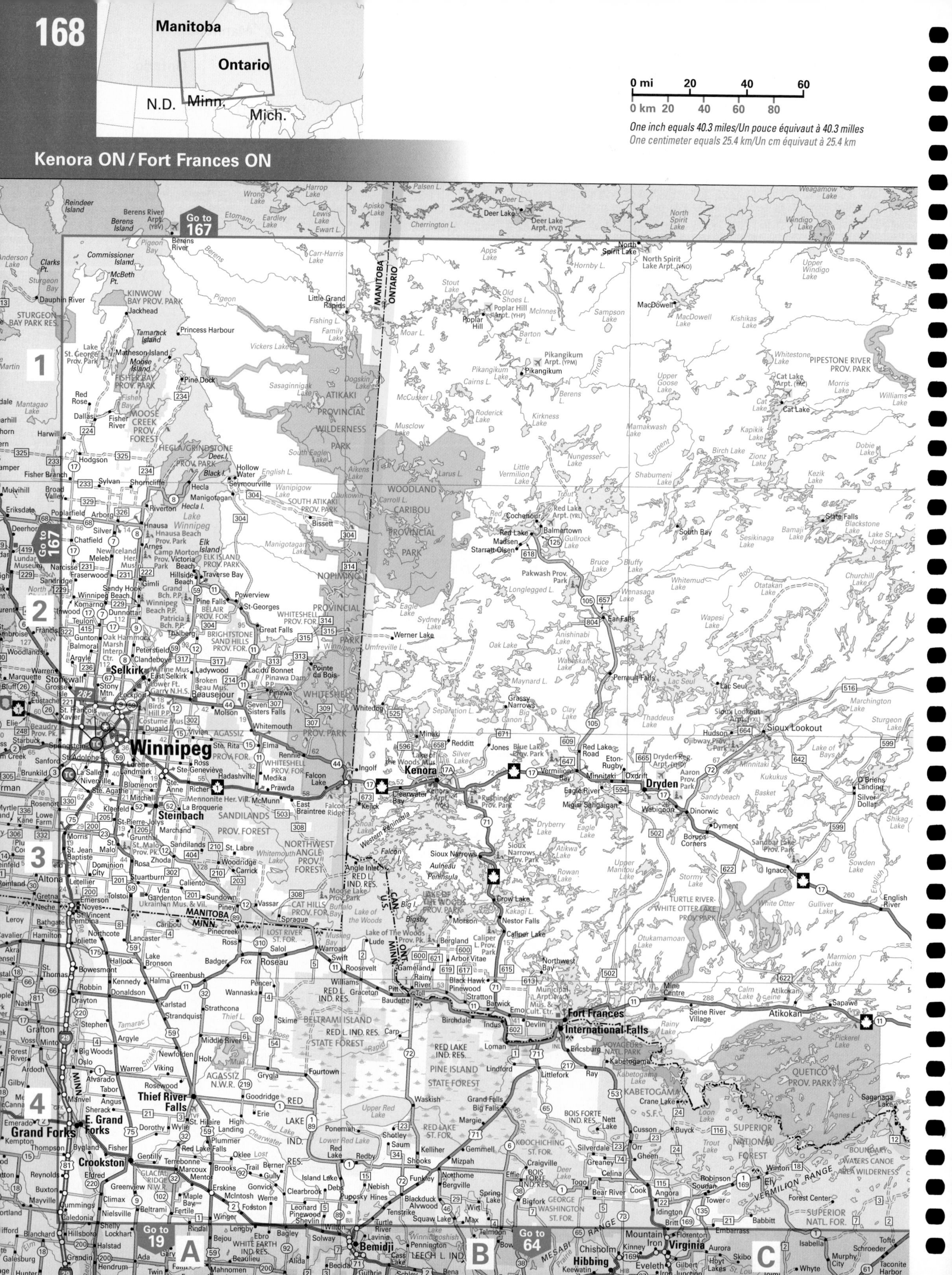

DRIVING DISTANCES IN KM / DISTANCES ROUTIÈRES EN KM

	DRYDEN, ON	FORT FRANCES, ON	GERALDTON, ON	GRAND FORKS, ND	HEARST, ON	KENORA, ON	MARATHON, ON	NIPIGON, ON	STEINBACH, MB	THUNDER BAY, ON	WAWA, ON	WINNIPEG, MB
FORT FRANCES, ON	190		627	315	845	215	641	445	310	335	805	420
KENORA, ON	140	215	772	429	990		786	585	184	480	950	205
THUNDER BAY, ON	340	335	292	650	510	480	306	110	664		470	685
WINNIPEG, MB	345	420	977	228	1195	205	991	790	55	685	1155	

SEE ALSO DISTANCE AND DRIVING TIME MAP ON PAGES 286–287 / VOIR AUSSI CARTE DES DISTANCES ET DES TEMPS DE PARCOURS PAGES 286–287

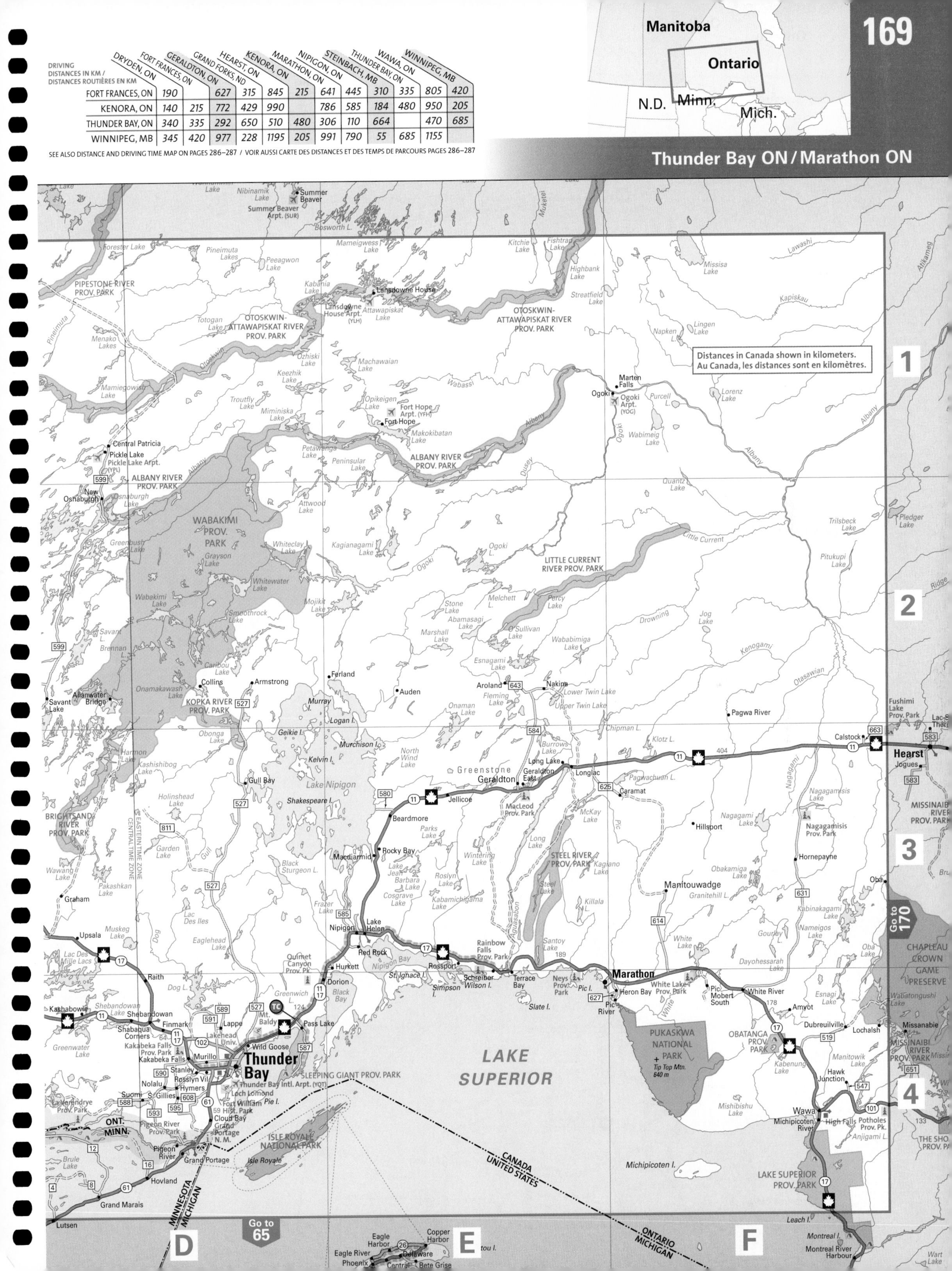

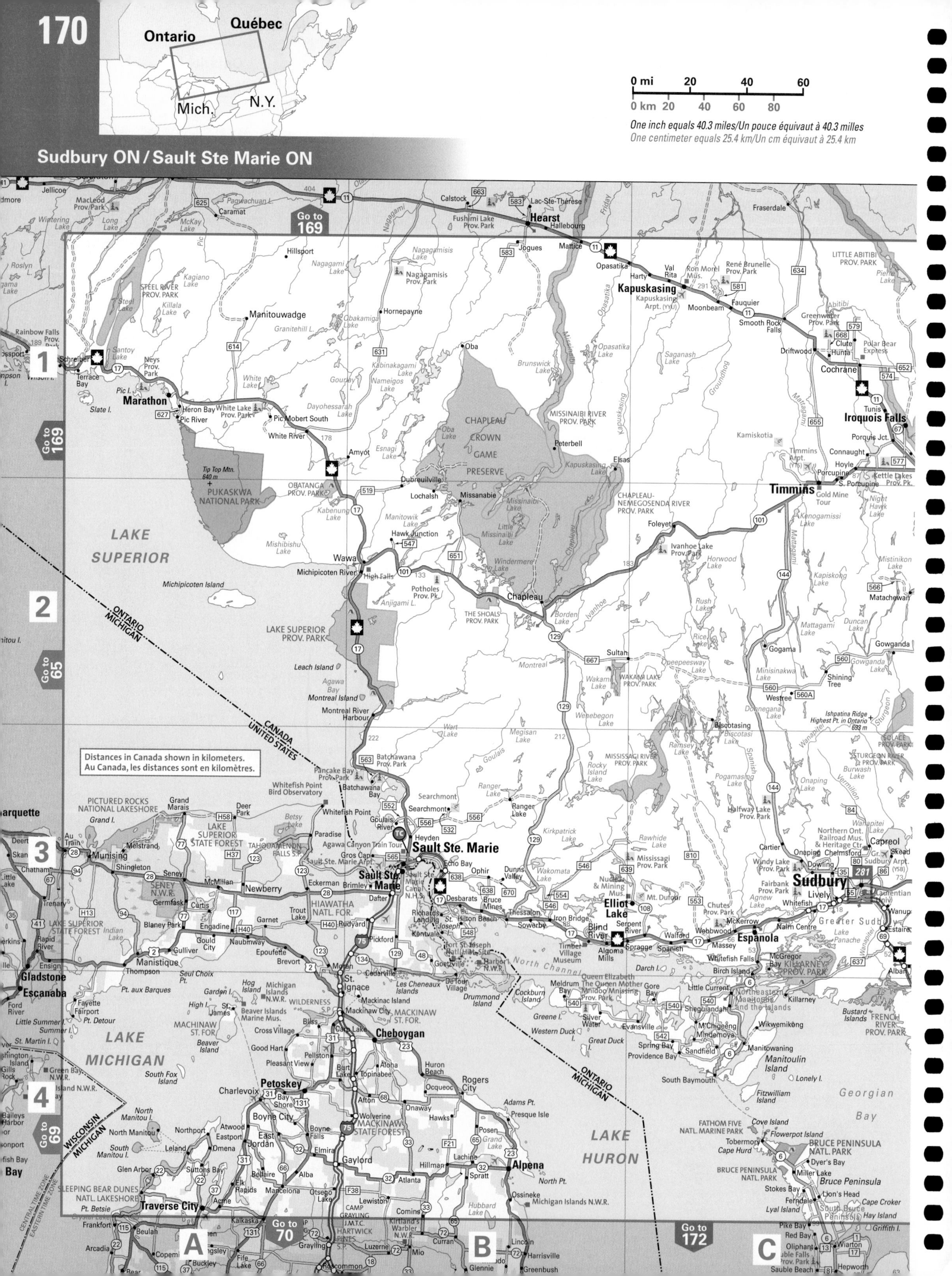
Ontario
Québec
Mich.
N.Y.
0 mi 20 40 60
0 km 20 40 60 80
One inch equals 40.3 miles/Un pouce équivaut à 40.3 milles
One centimeter equals 25.4 km/Un cm équivaut à 25.4 km
Distances in Canada shown in kilometers.
Au Canada, les distances sont en kilomètres.
Go to 169
Go to 65
Go to 69
Go to 70
Go to 172
LAKE SUPERIOR
LAKE MICHIGAN
LAKE HURON
Georgian Bay
CANADA
UNITED STATES
ONTARIO
MICHIGAN
WISCONSIN
CENTRAL TIME ZONE
EASTERN TIME ZONE
Hearst
Kapuskasing
Cochrane
Iroquois Falls
Timmins
Marathon
White River
Wawa
Chapleau
CHAPLEAU CROWN GAME PRESERVE
PUKASKWA NATIONAL PARK
LAKE SUPERIOR PROV. PARK
Michipicoten Island
Sault Ste. Marie
Elliot Lake
Espanola
Sudbury
Greater Sudbury
Manitoulin Island
BRUCE PENINSULA NATL. PARK
FATHOM FIVE NATL. MARINE PARK
Cheboygan
Petoskey
Alpena
Traverse City
Gaylord
Escanaba
Gladstone
Manistique
Newberry
St. Ignace
Mackinaw City
PICTURED ROCKS NATIONAL LAKESHORE
SLEEPING BEAR DUNES NATL. LAKESHORE
HIAWATHA NATL. FOR.
1
2
3
4
A
B
C

DRIVING DISTANCES IN KM / DISTANCES ROUTIÈRES EN KM

	HEARST, ON	HUNTSVILLE, ON	KIRKLAND LAKE, ON	MONT-LAURIER, QC	NORTH BAY, ON	ORILLIA, ON	OTTAWA, ON	ROUYN-NORANDA, QC	SAULT STE. MARIE, ON	SUDBURY, ON	TIMMINS, ON	WAWA, ON
KIRKLAND LAKE, ON	370	370		505	250	578	610	154	580	315	140	475
OTTAWA, ON	955	350	610	209	364	415		456	787	488	730	1015
SAULT STE. MARIE, ON	545	560	580	1004	430	562	787	734		305	440	225
SUDBURY, ON	550	250	315	699	124	263	488	469	305		290	530

SEE ALSO DISTANCE AND DRIVING TIME MAP ON PAGES 286–287 / VOIR AUSSI CARTE DES DISTANCES ET DES TEMPS DE PARCOURS PAGES 286–287

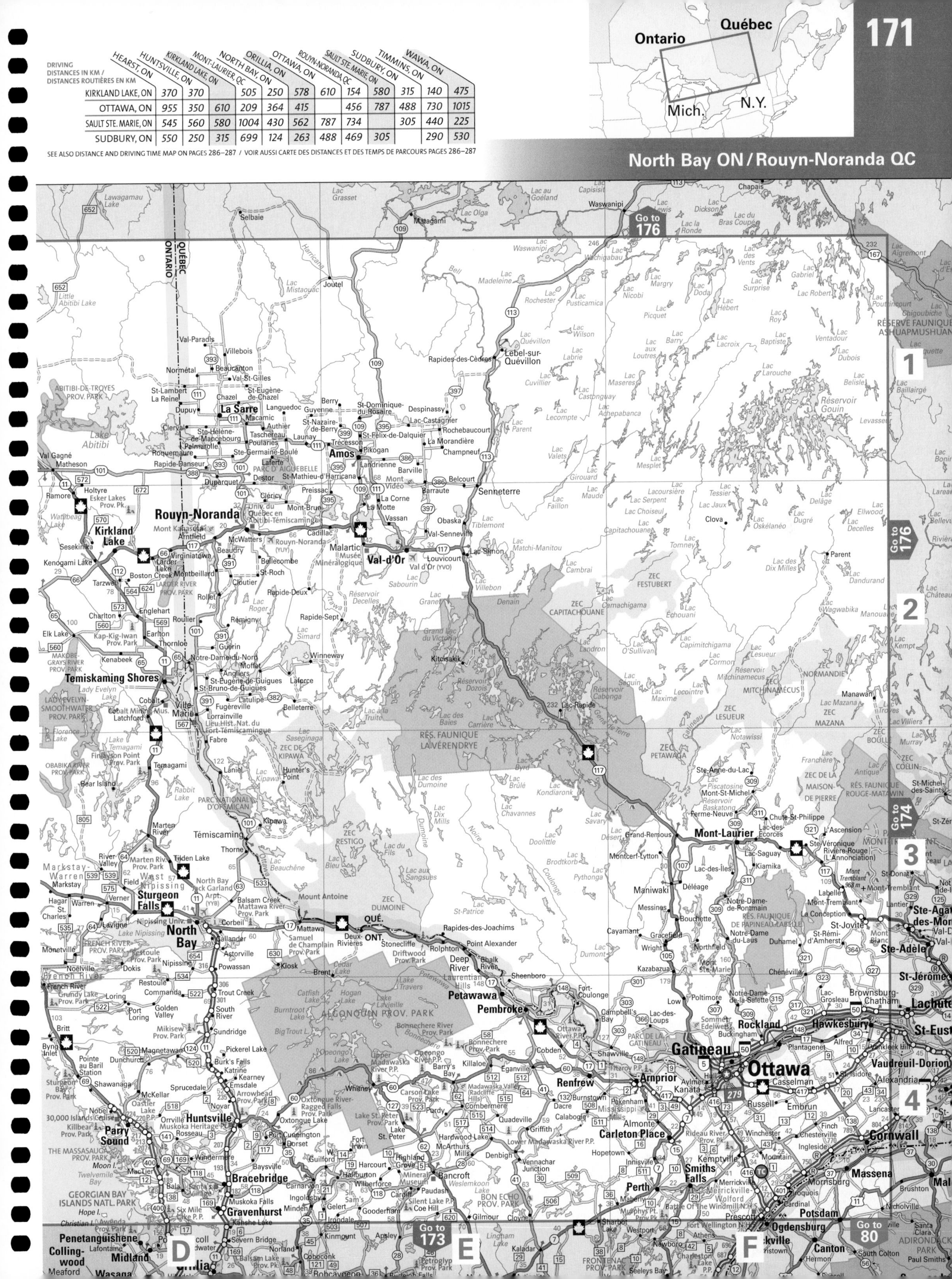

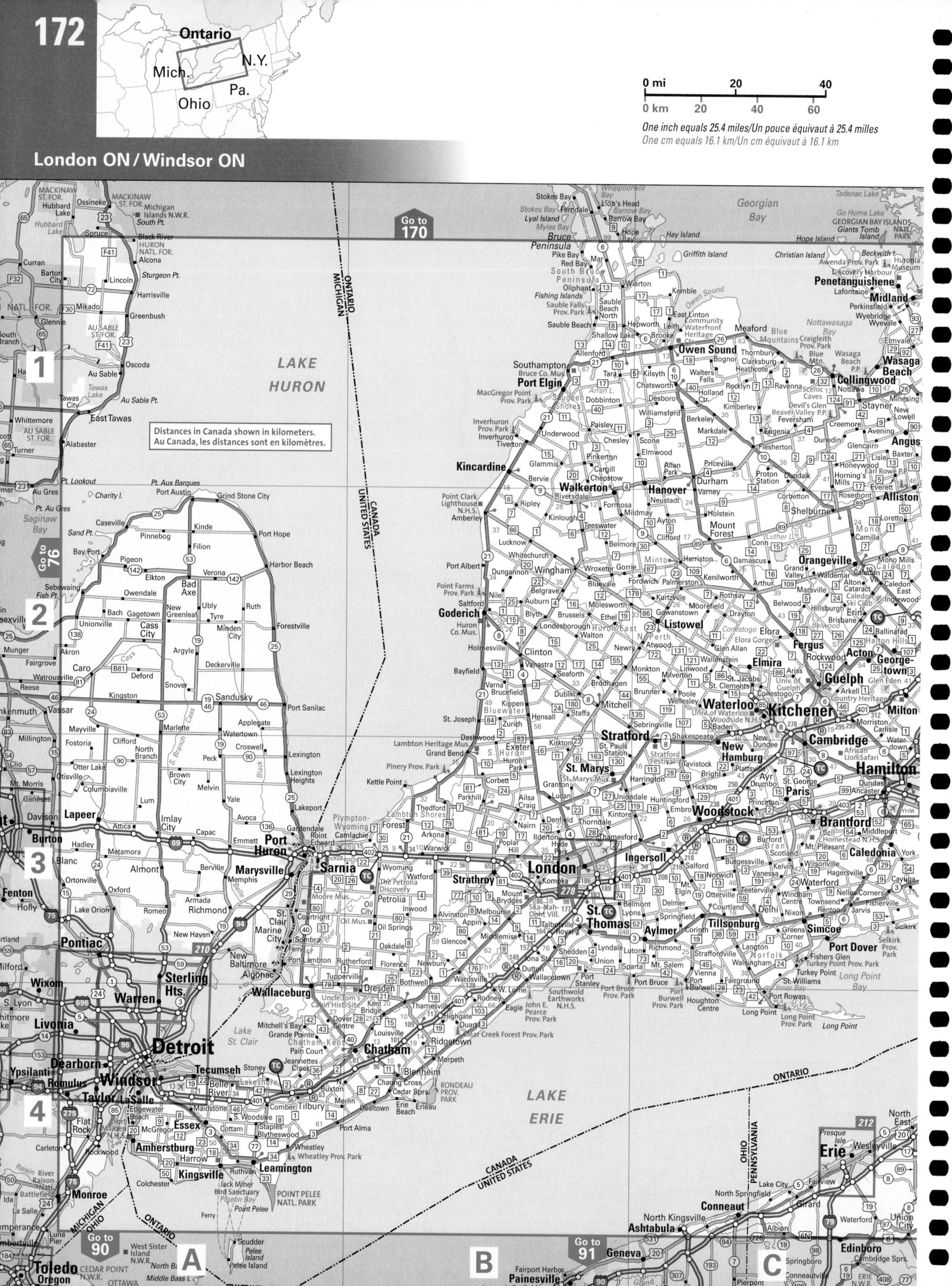
Ontario
Mich.
N.Y.
Pa.
Ohio
0 mi
20
40
0 km
20
40
60
One inch equals 25.4 miles/Un pouce équivaut à 25.4 milles
One cm equals 16.1 km/Un cm équivaut à 16.1 km
Go to 170
Go to 76
Go to 90
Go to 91
Go to 212
LAKE HURON
Georgian Bay
LAKE ERIE
Lake St. Clair
Saginaw Bay
Distances in Canada shown in kilometers.
Au Canada, les distances sont en kilomètres.
ONTARIO
MICHIGAN
CANADA
UNITED STATES
OHIO
PENNSYLVANIA
Bruce Peninsula
Owen Sound
Collingwood
Wasaga Beach
Midland
Penetanguishene
Orangeville
Kincardine
Port Elgin
Southampton
Walkerton
Hanover
Goderich
Listowel
Wingham
Clinton
Stratford
St. Marys
Waterloo
Kitchener
Guelph
Cambridge
Hamilton
Brantford
Paris
Woodstock
Ingersoll
London
St. Thomas
Aylmer
Tillsonburg
Simcoe
Port Dover
Strathroy
Sarnia
Port Huron
Marysville
Chatham
Wallaceburg
Windsor
Detroit
Tecumseh
Leamington
Kingsville
Essex
Amherstburg
Tilbury
Blenheim
Ridgetown
Erie
Ashtabula
Conneaut
Geneva
Painesville
Toledo
Oregon
Monroe
Taylor
Dearborn
Livonia
Warren
Sterling Hts.
Pontiac
Flint
Lapeer
Burton
Fenton
Oscoda
Au Sable
East Tawas
Alcona
Harrisville
Caseville
Bad Axe
Port Austin
Harbor Beach
Sandusky
Caro
Vassar
Lexington
Imlay City
Capac
Almont
Richmond
Fergus
Elmira
Elora
Acton
Georgetown
Milton
Caledonia
Alliston
Shelburne
Mount Forest
Durham
Exeter
Point Pelee Natl. Park
Pinery Prov. Park
Long Point
A
B
C
1
2
3
4

DRIVING DISTANCES IN KM / DISTANCES ROUTIÈRES EN KM

	BARRIE, ON	HAMILTON, ON	KINGSTON, ON	KITCHENER, ON	LONDON, ON	NIAGARA FALLS, ON	ORILLIA, ON	OWEN SOUND, ON	PETERBOROUGH, ON	SARNIA, ON	TORONTO, ON	WINDSOR, ON
KINGSTON, ON	350	330		430	430	390	317	430	180	530	260	620
NIAGARA FALLS, ON	200	68	390	130	190		237	260	260	290	130	380
TORONTO, ON	90	70	260	105	185	130	127	190	135	280		370
WINDSOR, ON	430	310	620	285	190	380	467	390	490	160	370	

SEE ALSO DISTANCE AND DRIVING TIME MAP ON PAGES 286–287 / VOIR AUSSI CARTE DES DISTANCES ET DES TEMPS DE PARCOURS PAGES 286–287

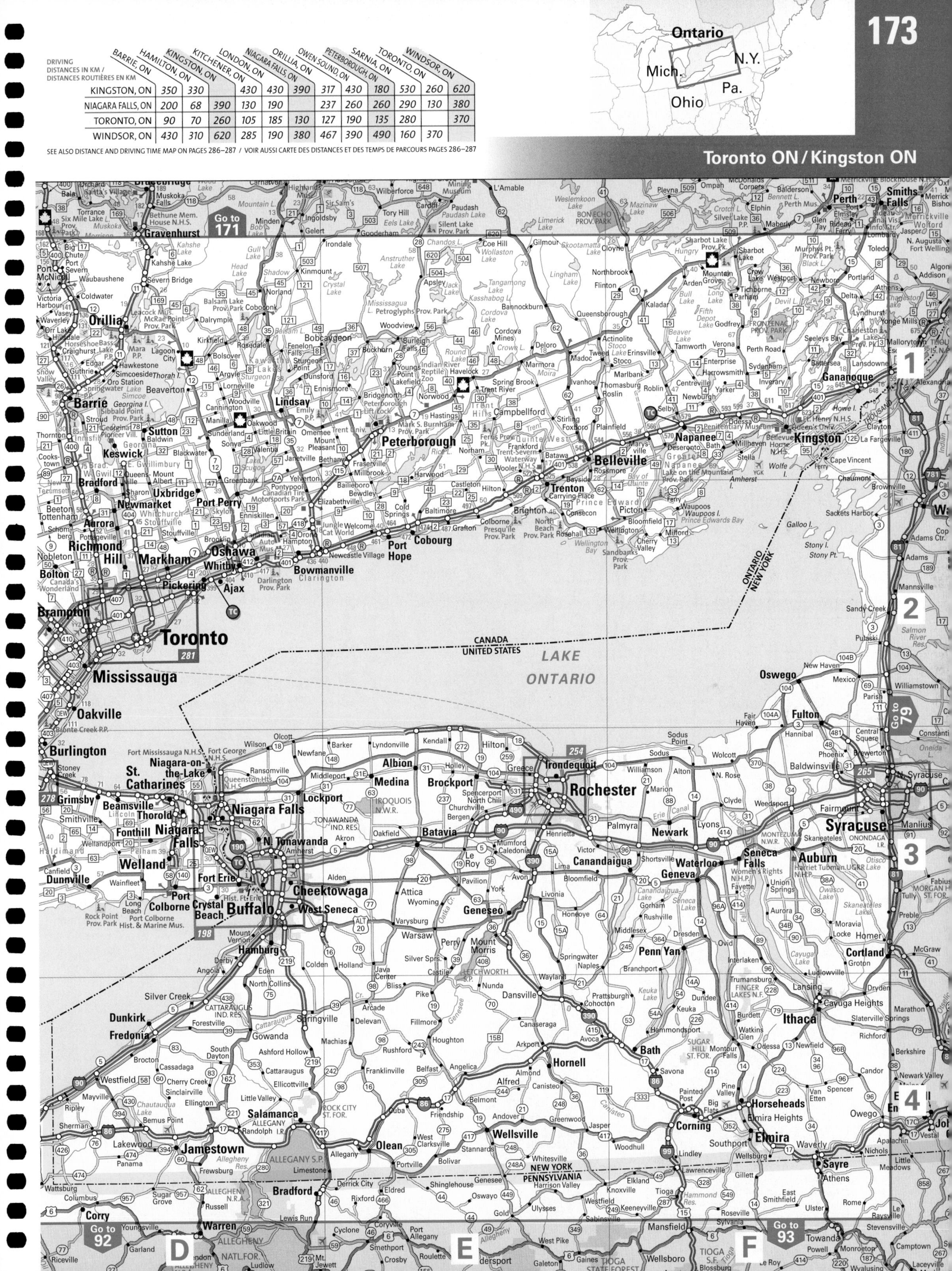

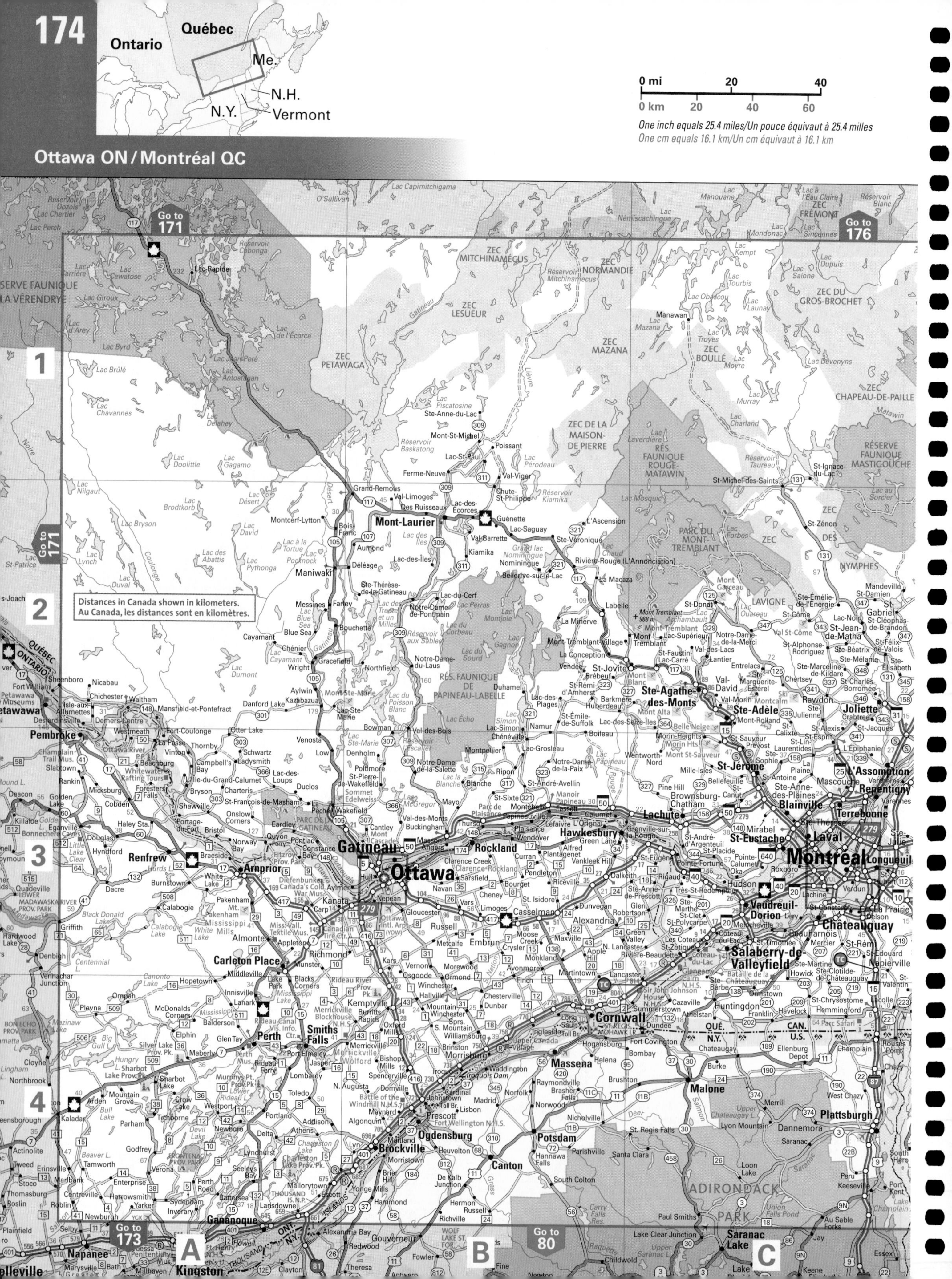
Ontario
Québec
Me.
N.H.
N.Y.
Vermont
0 mi
20
40
0 km
20
40
60
One inch equals 25.4 miles/Un pouce équivaut à 25.4 milles
One cm equals 16.1 km/Un cm équivaut à 16.1 km
Go to 171
Go to 176
Go to 173
Go to 80
Distances in Canada shown in kilometers.
Au Canada, les distances sont en kilomètres.
1
2
3
4
A
B
C
ZEC MITCHINAMÉCUS
ZEC NORMANDIE
ZEC LESUEUR
ZEC PETAWAGA
ZEC MAZANA
ZEC BOULLÉ
ZEC DU GROS-BROCHET
ZEC CHAPEAU-DE-PAILLE
ZEC FRÉMONT
ZEC DE LA MAISON-DE PIERRE
RÉS. FAUNIQUE ROUGE-MATAWIN
RÉSERVE FAUNIQUE MASTIGOUCHE
RÉS. FAUNIQUE DE PAPINEAU-LABELLE
PARC DU MONT-TREMBLANT
ZEC DES NYMPHES
ADIRONDACK PARK
Mont-Laurier
Maniwaki
Gatineau
Ottawa
Montréal
Laval
Longueuil
Terrebonne
Repentigny
Joliette
St-Jérôme
Ste-Adèle
Ste-Agathe-des-Monts
Lachute
Hawkesbury
Rockland
Casselman
Alexandria
Cornwall
Massena
Salaberry-de-Valleyfield
Vaudreuil-Dorion
Châteauguay
Pembroke
Petawawa
Renfrew
Arnprior
Kanata
Nepean
Carleton Place
Smiths Falls
Perth
Kemptville
Brockville
Ogdensburg
Prescott
Gananoque
Kingston
Napanee
Potsdam
Canton
Malone
Plattsburgh
Saranac Lake
Lake Placid
Hudson
Mirabel
St-Eustache
Blainville
Mascouche
L'Assomption
Chambly
Huntingdon
Valleyfield

DRIVING DISTANCES IN KM / DISTANCES ROUTIÈRES EN KM	BURLINGTON, VT	CORNWALL, ON	DRUMMONDVILLE, QC	KINGSTON, ON	MONT-LAURIER, QC	MONTRÉAL, QC	MONT-TREMBLANT, QC	OTTAWA, ON	QUÉBEC, QC	ST-GEORGES, QC	SHERBROOKE, QC	TROIS-RIVIÈRES, QC
MONTRÉAL, QC	153	103	116	283	230		126	194	250	325	143	146
OTTAWA, ON	360	97	310	175	209	194	208		444	485	337	340
QUÉBEC, QC	394	353	151	533	445	250	298	444		102	233	135
SHERBROOKE, QC	174	246	82	426	402	143	269	337	233	148		158

SEE ALSO DISTANCE AND DRIVING TIME MAP ON PAGES 286–287 / VOIR AUSSI CARTE DES DISTANCES ET DES TEMPS DE PARCOURS PAGES 286–287

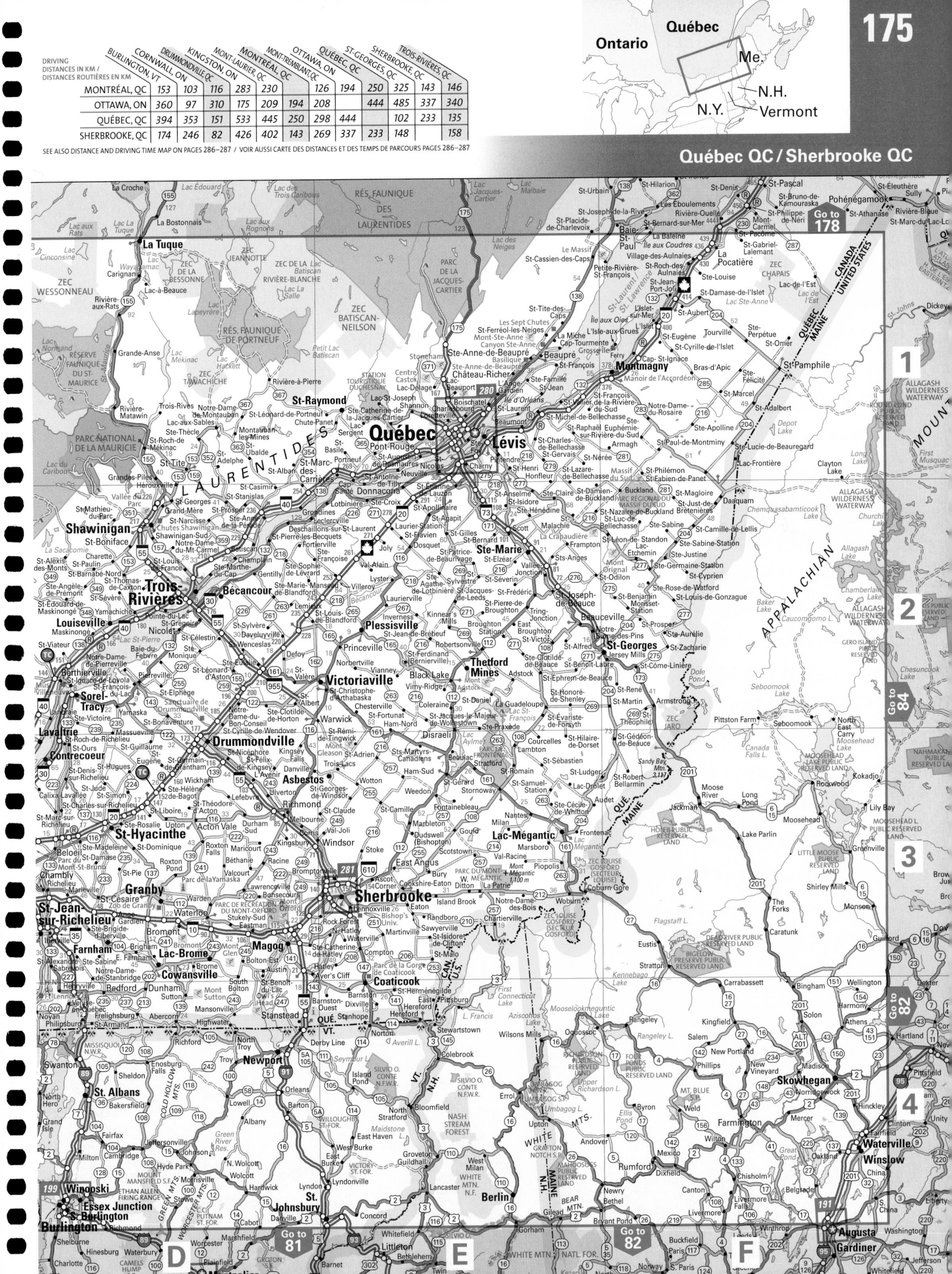

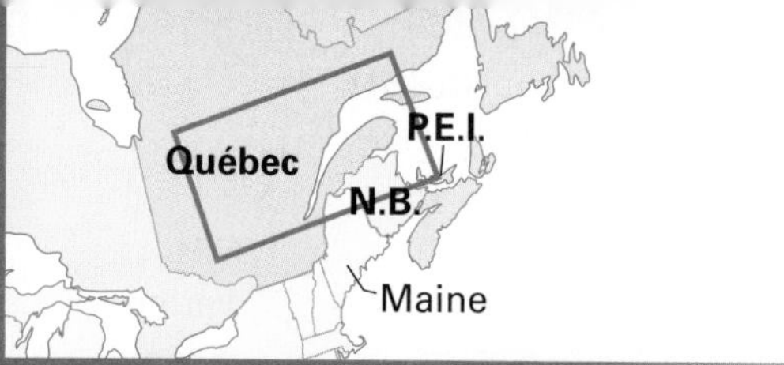

Québec P.E.I. N.B. Maine

Chicoutimi QC / Chibougamau QC

0 mi 20 40 60
0 km 20 40 60 80

One inch equals 40.3 miles/Un pouce équivaut à 40.3 milles
One centimeter equals 25.4 km/Un cm équivaut à 25.4 km

Distances in Canada shown in kilometers.
Au Canada, les distances sont en kilomètres.

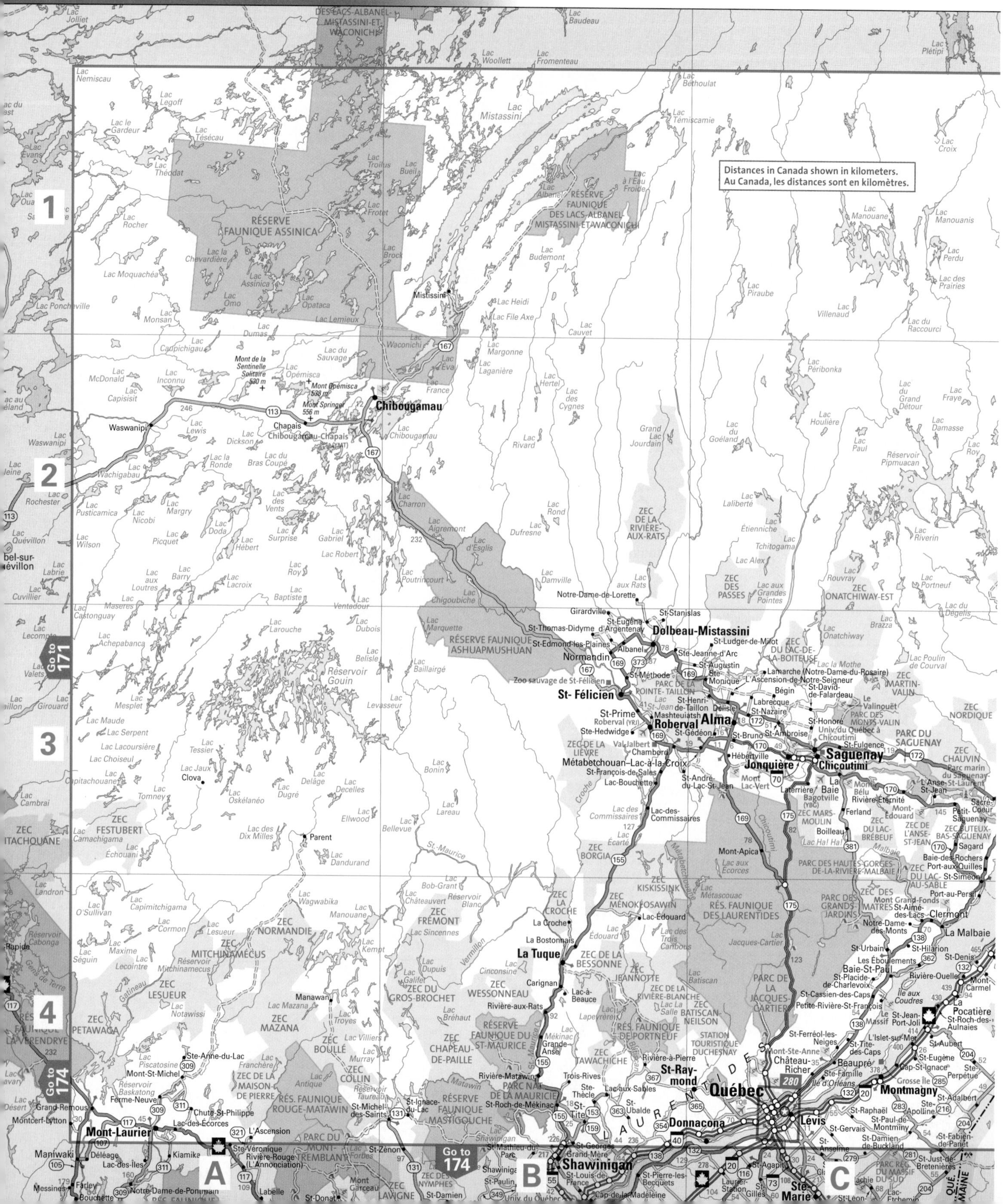

Go to 171

Go to 174

Go to 174

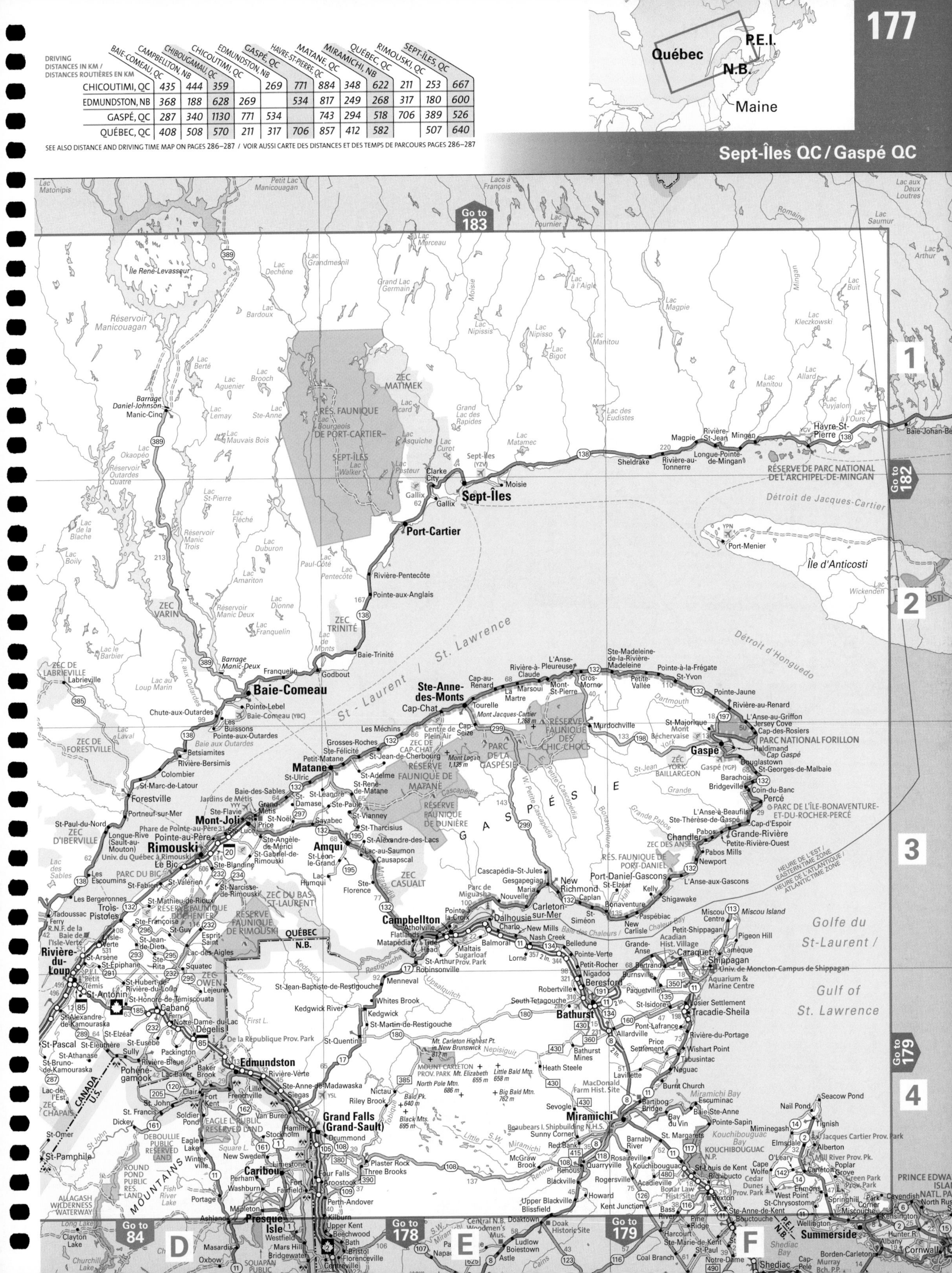

DRIVING DISTANCES IN KM / DISTANCES ROUTIÈRES EN KM

	BAIE-COMEAU, QC	CAMPBELLTON, NB	CHIBOUGAMAU, QC	CHICOUTIMI, QC	EDMUNDSTON, NB	GASPÉ, QC	HAVRE-ST-PIERRE, QC	MATANE, QC	MIRAMICHI, NB	QUÉBEC, QC	RIMOUSKI, QC	SEPT-ÎLES, QC
CHICOUTIMI, QC	435	444	359		269	771	884	348	622	211	253	667
EDMUNDSTON, NB	368	188	628	269		534	817	249	268	317	180	600
GASPÉ, QC	287	340	1130	771	534		743	294	518	706	389	526
QUÉBEC, QC	408	508	570	211	317	706	857	412	582		507	640

SEE ALSO DISTANCE AND DRIVING TIME MAP ON PAGES 286–287 / VOIR AUSSI CARTE DES DISTANCES ET DES TEMPS DE PARCOURS PAGES 286–287

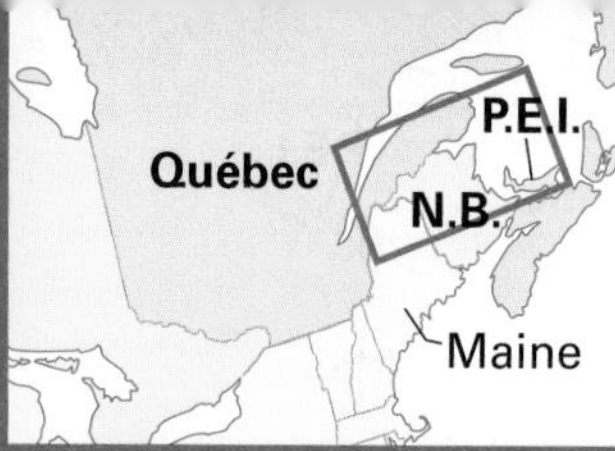

Québec
P.E.I.
N.B.
Maine

0 mi 20 40
0 km 20 40 60

One inch equals 25.4 miles/Un pouce équivaut à 25.4 milles
One cm equals 16.1 km/Un cm équivaut à 16.1 km

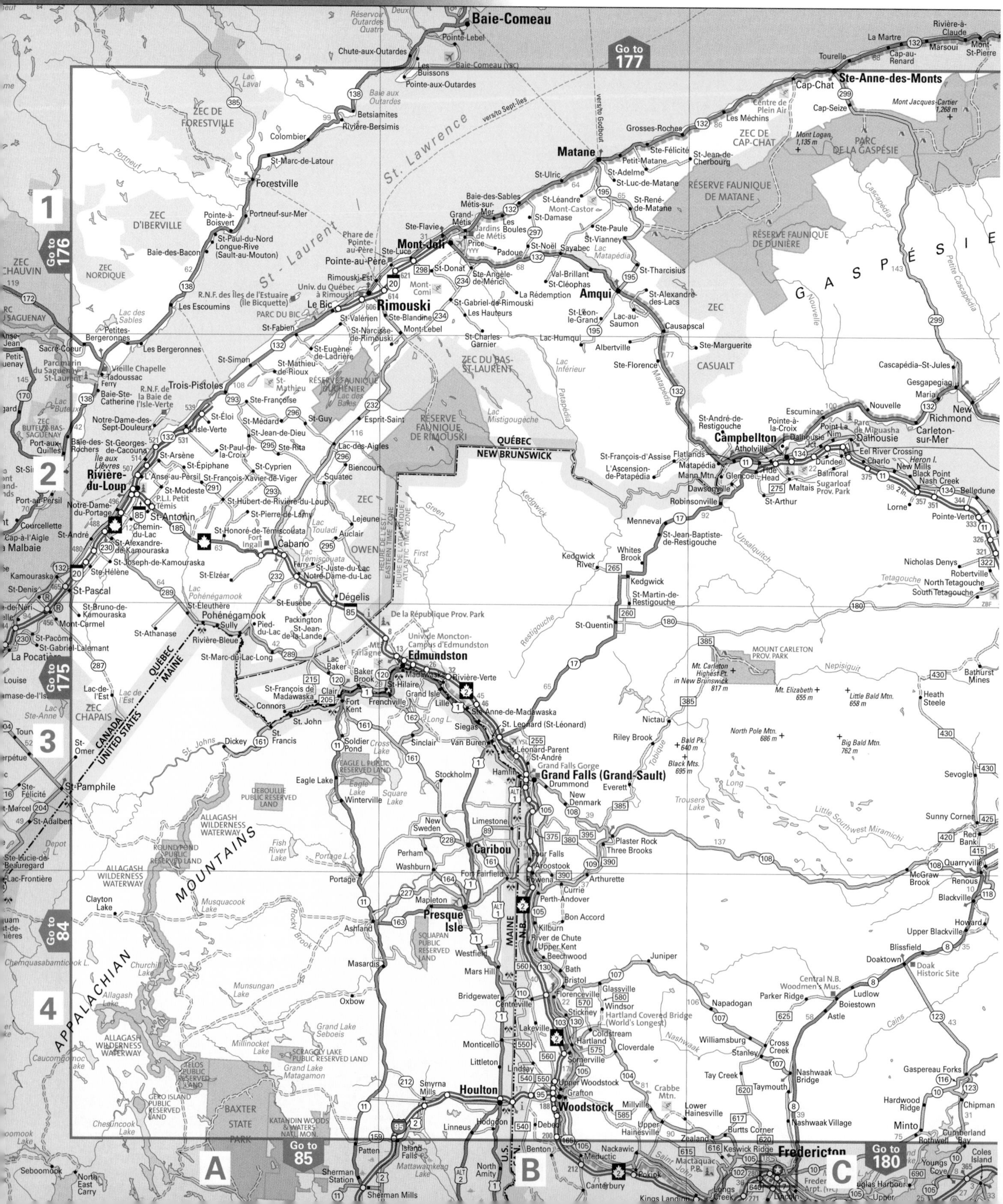

Rimouski QC / Edmundston NB

Baie-Comeau
Pointe-Lebel
Chute-aux-Outardes
Les Buissons
Pointe-aux-Outardes
Réservoir Outardes Quatre
Go to 177
Lac Laval
ZEC DE FORESTVILLE
Betsiamites
Rivière-Bersimis
Colombier
St-Marc-de-Latour
Forestville
St. Lawrence
St-Laurent
vers/to Sept-Îles
vers/to Godbout
Matane
La Martre
Rivière-à-Claude
Marsoui
Mont-St-Pierre
Tourelle
Cap-au-Renard
Ste-Anne-des-Monts
Cap-Chat
Cap-Seize
Centre de Plein Air
Les Méchins
Mont Jacques-Cartier 1,268 m
Mont Logan 1,135 m
PARC DE LA GASPÉSIE
ZEC DE CAP-CHAT
Grosses-Roches
Ste-Félicité
St-Jean-de-Cherbourg
Petit-Matane
St-Adelme
St-Luc-de-Matane
St-Ulric
RÉSERVE FAUNIQUE DE MATANE
RÉSERVE FAUNIQUE DE DUNIÈRE
St-Léandre
Mont-Castor
St-Damase
St-René-de-Matane
Ste-Paule
St-Vianney
Baie-des-Sables
Métis-sur-Mer
Grand-Métis
Jardins de Métis
Les Boules
Price
Padoue
St-Noël
Sayabec
Lac Matapédia
Ste-Flavie
Mont-Joli
Ste-Luce
Pointe-au-Père
Phare de Pointe-au-Père
St-Donat
Ste-Angèle-de-Mérici
Val-Brillant
St-Cléophas
La Rédemption
Amqui
St-Tharcisius
St-Alexandre-des-Lacs
GASPÉSIE
ZEC
ZEC D'IBERVILLE
Pointe-à-Boisvert
Portneuf-sur-Mer
St-Paul-du-Nord
Longue-Rive (Sault-au-Mouton)
Baie-des-Bacon
ZEC NORDIQUE
ZEC CHAUVIN
Go to 176
R.N.F. des Îles de l'Estuaire (Île Bicquette)
Les Escoumins
Rimouski-Est
Univ. du Québec à Rimouski
Le Bic
PARC DU BIC
Rimouski
Mont-Comi
St-Gabriel-de-Rimouski
Les Hauteurs
Ste-Blandine
Mont-Lebel
St-Valérien
St-Fabien
St-Narcisse-de-Rimouski
St-Léon-le-Grand
Lac-au-Saumon
Lac-Humqui
Causapscal
Ste-Marguerite
Albertville
St-Charles-Garnier
ZEC DU BAS-ST-LAURENT
Lac Inférieur
Ste-Florence
CASUALT
Cascapédia–St-Jules
Gesgapegiag
Maria
New Richmond
Carleton-sur-Mer
Nouvelle
Escuminac
Pointe-à-la-Croix
Point La Nim
Parc de Miguasha
Dalhousie
Dalhousie Jct.
Eel River Crossing
Charlo
Heron I.
New Mills
Black Point
Nash Creek
Belledune
Campbellton
Atholville
Tide Head
Dundee
Balmoral
Maltais
Sugarloaf Prov. Park
St-Arthur
Lorne
Pointe-Verte
St-André-de-Restigouche
Flatlands
Matapédia
Mann Mtn.
Glencoe
Dawsonville
St-François-d'Assise
L'Ascension-de-Patapédia
Robinsonville
Menneval
St-Jean-Baptiste-de-Restigouche
Whites Brook
Kedgwick River
Kedgwick
St-Martin-de-Restigouche
St-Quentin
Nicholas Denys
Robertville
North Tetagouche
South Tetagouche
Tetagouche
Sacré-Cœur
Les Bergeronnes
Petites-Bergeronnes
Parc marin du Saguenay–St-Laurent
Vieille Chapelle
Tadoussac
Ferry
R.N.F. de la Baie de l'Isle-Verte
Baie-Ste-Catherine
ZEC BUTEUX-BAS-SAGUENAY
Port-aux-Quilles
Trois-Pistoles
St-Simon
St-Mathieu-de-Rioux
St-Eugène-de-Ladrière
St-Mathieu
RÉSERVE FAUNIQUE DUCHÉNIER
Lac des Baies
Ste-Françoise
St-Éloi
Isle-Verte
St-Médard
St-Guy
Esprit-Saint
Lac Mistigougèche
RÉSERVE FAUNIQUE DE RIMOUSKI
QUÉBEC
NEW BRUNSWICK
Notre-Dame-des-Sept-Douleurs
Baie-des-Rochers
St-Georges-de-Cacouna
Île aux Lièvres
St-Arsène
St-Épiphane
St-Paul-de-la-Croix
St-Jean-de-Dieu
Ste-Rita
Lac-des-Aigles
Biencourt
Squatec
Rivière-du-Loup
L'Anse-au-Persil
St-Cyprien
St-François-Xavier-de-Viger
St-Modeste
P.L.I. Petit Témis
St-Hubert-de-Rivière-du-Loup
St-Pierre-de-Lamy
Lejeune
Notre-Dame-du-Portage
St-Antonin
Chemin-du-Lac
St-Honoré-de-Témiscouata
Lac Touladi
Auclair
St-André
St-Alexandre-de-Kamouraska
Fort Ingall
Cabano
Lac Témiscouata
OWEN
St-Joseph-de-Kamouraska
Ferry
St-Juste-du-Lac
Notre-Dame-du-Lac
Ste-Hélène
St-Elzéar
Kamouraska
St-Denis
St-Pascal
Dégelis
Lac Pohénégamook
St-Eusèbe
HEURE DE L'EST/EASTERN TIME ZONE
HEURE DE L'ATLANTIQUE/ATLANTIC TIME ZONE
St-Bruno-de-Kamouraska
Mont-Carmel
St-Éleuthère
Pohénégamook
Sully
Packington
Pied-du-Lac
St-Jean-de-la-Lande
De la République Prov. Park
St-Athanase
St-Pacôme
St-Gabriel-Lalemant
La Pocatière
Go to 175
Rivière-Bleue
St-Marc-du-Lac-Long
Univ. de Moncton-Campus d'Edmundston
Edmundston
Lac Baker
Baker Brook
Madawaska
Rivière-Verte
St-Hilaire
Grand Isle
Lille
Ste-Anne-de-Madawaska
St-François-de-Madawaska
Clair
Fort Kent
Frenchville
Connors
St. John
St. Francis
Dickey
QUÉBEC
MAINE
CANADA
UNITED STATES
Lac de l'Est
Lac-de-l'Est
ZEC CHAPAIS
St-Omer
St-Pamphile
Ste-Félicité
St-Adalbert
Ste-Lucie-de-Beauregard
Lac-Frontière
Go to 84
Long L.
Siegas
St. Leonard (St-Léonard)
Van Buren
Sinclair
Soldier Pond
Cross Lake
EAGLE L. PUBLIC RESERVED LAND
Eagle Lake
Square Lake
Winterville
Stockholm
St-Léonard-Parent
St-André
Grand Falls Gorge
Hamlin
Grand Falls (Grand-Sault)
Drummond
New Denmark
Everett
Riley Brook
Nictau
Mt. Carleton Highest Pt. in New Brunswick 817 m
MOUNT CARLETON PROV. PARK
Mt. Elizabeth 655 m
Little Bald Mtn. 658 m
North Pole Mtn. 686 m
Bald Pk. 640 m
Black Mts. 695 m
Big Bald Mtn. 762 m
Nepisiguit
Bathurst Mines
Heath Steele
Sevogle
Little Southwest Miramichi
Trousers Lake
DEBOULLIE PUBLIC RESERVED LAND
ALLAGASH WILDERNESS WATERWAY
ROUND POND PUBLIC RESERVED LAND
Fish River Lake
Portage L.
Portage
New Sweden
Limestone
Caribou
Perham
Washburn
Fort Fairfield
Four Falls
Aroostook
Plaster Rock
Three Brooks
Arthurette
Perth-Andover
Currie
Bon Accord
Sunny Corner
Red Bank
Quarryville
McGraw Brook
Renous
Blackville
Howard
Upper Blackville
Blissfield
Doaktown
Doak Historic Site
APPALACHIAN MOUNTAINS
Musquacook Lake
Rocky Brook
Clayton Lake
Mapleton
Presque Isle
SQUAPAN PUBLIC RESERVED LAND
Ashland
Masardis
Westfield
Mars Hill
Kilburn
River de Chute
Upper Kent
Beechwood
Bath
Bristol
Juniper
Chemquasabamticook L.
Churchill Lake
Allagash Lake
Munsungan Lake
Oxbow
Bridgewater
Centreville
Florenceville
Glassville
Windsor
Stickney
Hartland Covered Bridge (World's Longest)
Napadogan
Central N.B. Woodmen's Mus.
Parker Ridge
Ludlow
Boiestown
Astle
Cains
Nashwaak
Williamsburg
Stanley
Cross Creek
Grand Lake Seboeis
ALLAGASH WILDERNESS WATERWAY
Millinocket Lake
SCRAGGLY LAKE PUBLIC RESERVED LAND
Grand Lake Matagamon
TELOS PUBLIC RESERVED LAND
Caucomgomoc Lake
Monticello
Littleton
Lakeville
Hartland
Coldstream
Cloverdale
Somerville
Tay Creek
Taymouth
Nashwaak Bridge
Gaspereau Forks
Lindsay
Smyrna Mills
Houlton
Upper Woodstock
Grafton
Woodstock
Millville
Crabbe Mtn.
Lower Hainesville
Upper Hainesville
Hardwood Ridge
Chipman
Cumberland Bay
Rothwell
Minto
Nashwaak Village
Burtts Corner
GERO ISLAND PUBLIC RESERVED LAND
BAXTER STATE PARK
KATAHDIN WOODS & WATERS NATL. MON.
Chesuncook Lake
Linneus
Hodgdon
Debec
Benton
Zealand
Keswick Ridge
Nackawic
Meductic
Saint John
Mactaquac P.P.
Fredericton
Go to 180
Go to 85
Patten
Island Falls
Mattawamkeag Lake
North Amity
Canterbury
Pokiok
Kings Landing
Long Creek
Sherman Station
Sherman Mills
Seboomook
North East Carry
Youngs Cove
Coles Island
Douglas Harbour
Fredericton Arpt. (YFC)
Upper
MAINE
N.B.
U.S.
CAN.
1 2 3 4
A B C

DRIVING DISTANCES IN KM / DISTANCES ROUTIÈRES EN KM

	BATHURST, NB	BORDEN-CARLETON, PE	CAMPBELLTON, NB	CHARLOTTETOWN, PE	EDMUNDSTON, NB	FREDERICTON, NB	GASPÉ, QC	GRAND FALLS, NB	MATANE, QC	MIRAMICHI, NB	MONCTON, NB	RIMOUSKI, QC
CHARLOTTETOWN, PE	338	56	438		629	362	791	581	562	273	164	596
EDMUNDSTON, NB	189	428	188	638		279	534	57	249	268	447	180
MATANE, QC	262	506	168	562	249	553	294	331		346	487	95
MONCTON, NB	206	108	306	164	447	170	659	390	487	141		502

SEE ALSO DISTANCE AND DRIVING TIME MAP ON PAGES 286–287 / VOIR AUSSI CARTE DES DISTANCES ET DES TEMPS DE PARCOURS PAGES 286–287

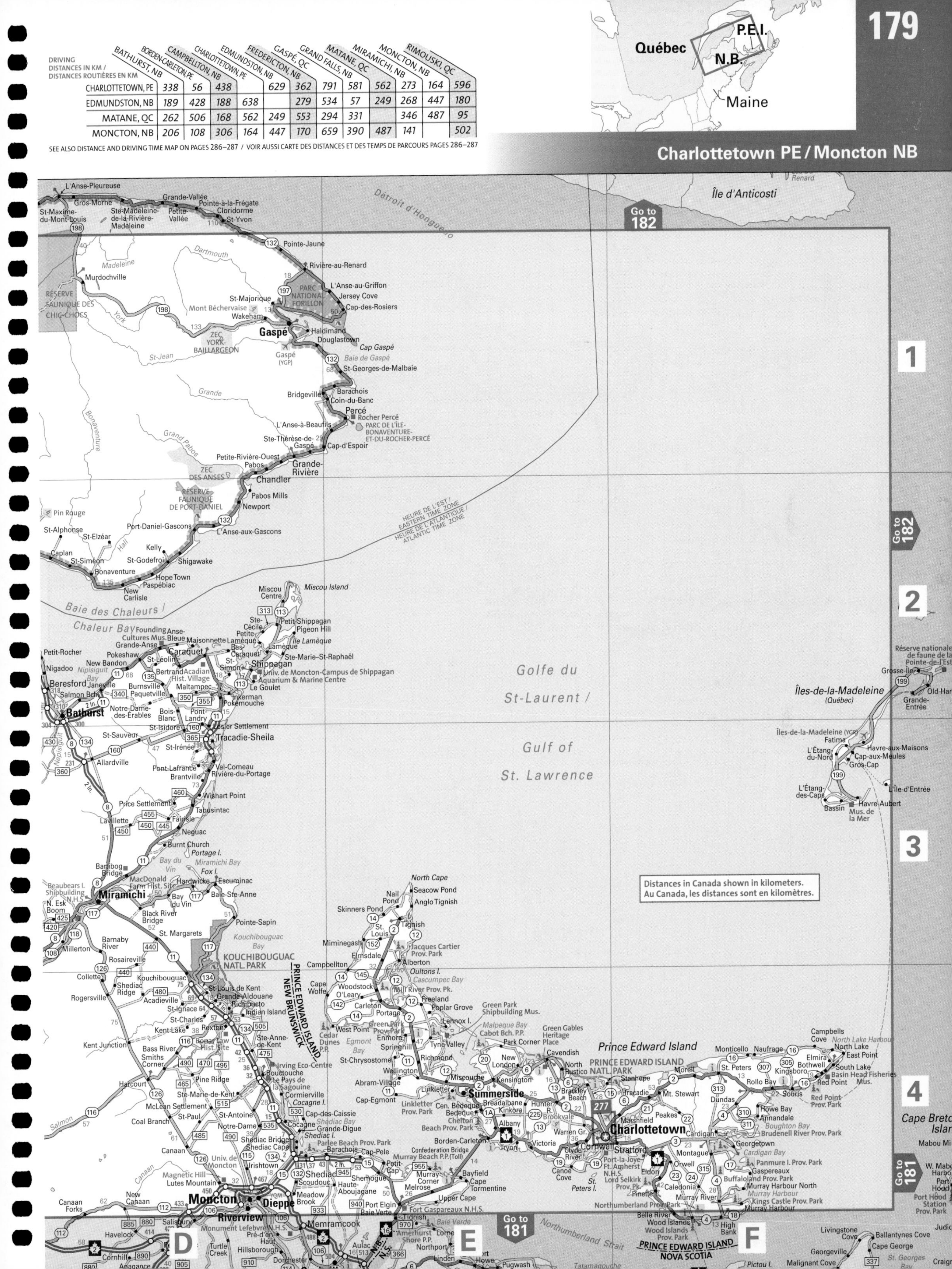

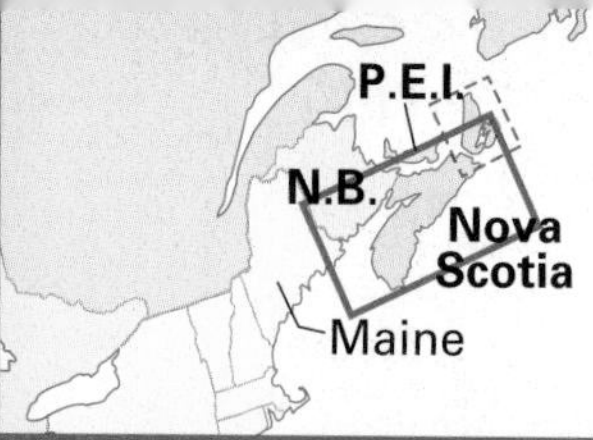

P.E.I.
N.B.
Nova Scotia
Maine

0 mi 20 40
0 km 20 40 60
One inch equals 25.4 miles/Un pouce équivaut à 25.4 milles
One cm equals 16.1 km/Un cm équivaut à 16.1 km

Saint John NB / Yarmouth NS

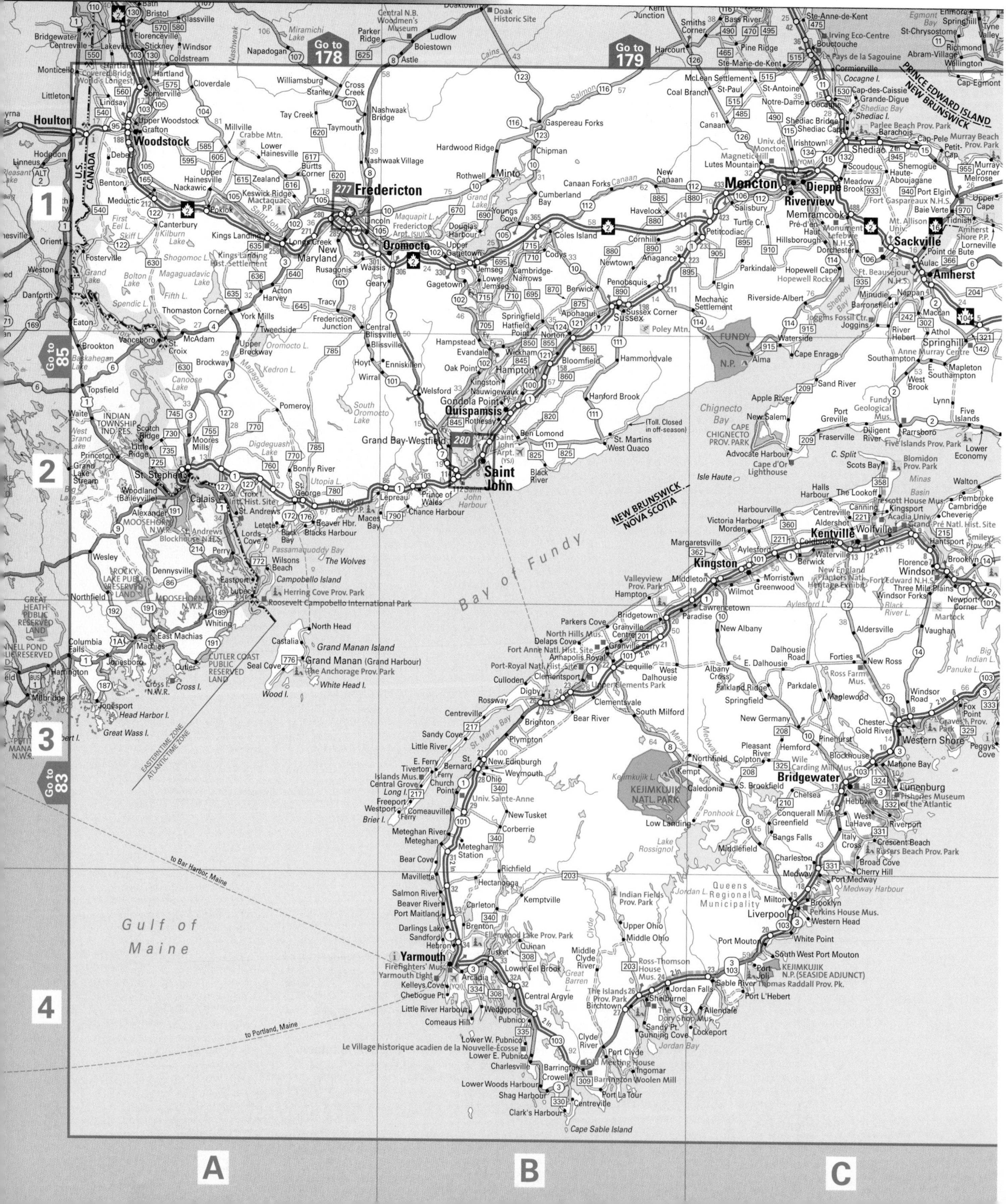

Go to 178
Go to 179
Go to 85
Go to 83

Bath
Bristol
Glassville
Bridgewater
Centreville
Florenceville
Stickney
Windsor
Coldstream
Lakeville
Monticello
Hartland
Covered Bridge (World's Longest)
Somerville
Cloverdale
Littleton
Lindsay
Houlton
Upper Woodstock
Grafton
Woodstock
Millville
Crabbe Mtn.
Lower Hainesville
Upper Hainesville
Nackawic
Zealand
Keswick Ridge
Mactaquac P.P.
Debec
Hodgdon
Linneus
Benton
Meductic
Canterbury
Kilburn Lake
First Eel L.
Skiff L.
Kings Landing
Kings Landing Hist. Settlement
Long Creek
New Maryland
Fredericton
Oromocto
Fosterville
Orient
Weston
Danforth
Shogomoc L.
Magaguadavic Lake
Bolton Lake
Grand Lake
Spendic L.
Fifth L.
Thomaston Corner
York Mills
Acton
Harvey
Tweedside
Eaton
McAdam
Vanceboro
St. Croix
Brookton
Baskahegan Lake
Upper Brockway
Oromocto L.
Brockway
Kedron L.
Canoose Lake
Topsfield
Pomeroy
Waite
Indian Township Ind. Res.
Scotch Ridge
Moores Mills
Digdeguash Lake
Bonny River
West Grand Lake
Princeton
Grand Lake Stream
Little Ridge
St. Stephen
Calais
Woodland (Baileyville)
Alexander
Moosehorn N.W.R.
St. Croix Intl. Hist. Site
St. Andrews
St. Andrews Blockhouse N.H.S.
Perry
Lords Cove
Letete
Back Bay
Beaver Hbr.
Blacks Harbour
Passamaquoddy Bay
The Wolves
Wesley
Rocky Lake Public Reserved Land
Dennysville
Wilsons Beach
Campobello Island
Herring Cove Prov. Park
Roosevelt Campobello International Park
Eastport
Lubec
Great Heath Public Reserved Land
Northfield
Whiting
East Machias
Machias
Columbia Falls
Jonesboro
Cutler
Cutler Coast Public Reserved Land
Harrington
Milbridge
Jonesport
Head Harbor I.
Great Wass I.
Cross I. N.W.R.
Cross I.
Eastern Time Zone / Atlantic Time Zone
St. George
Utopia L.
New River Beach P.P.
Lepreau
Prince of Wales
Chance Harbour
Maces Bay
Grand Bay-Westfield
Saint John
Saint John Harbour
Black River
Ben Lomond
St. Martins
West Quaco
Quispamsis
Rothesay
Gondola Point
Nauwigewauk
Hampton
Wickham
Norton
Evandale
Hampstead
Oak Point
Welsford
Enniskillen
Hoyt
Wirral
Blissville
Central Blissville
Fredericton Junction
Tracy
Rusagonis
Waasis
Geary
Gagetown
Upper Gagetown
Jemseg
Lower Jemseg
Cambridge-Narrows
Douglas Harbour
Maquapit L.
Lincoln
Youngs Cove
Grand Lake
Minto
Rothwell
Chipman
Cumberland Bay
Coles Island
Cody's
Springfield
Hatfield Point
Kingston
Bloomfield
Hammondvale
Hanford Brook
Poley Mtn.
Sussex
Sussex Corner
Apohaqui
Penobsquis
Berwick
Newtown
Anagance
Cornhill
Havelock
Canaan Forks
New Canaan
Petitcodiac
Salisbury
Turtle Cr.
Elgin
Mechanic Settlement
Fundy N.P.
Alma
Waterside
Cape Enrage
Riverside-Albert
Hopewell Cape
Hopewell Rocks
Shepody Bay
Hillsborough
Memramcook
Pré-d'en-Haut
Dorchester
Moncton
Riverview
Dieppe
Lutes Mountain
Magnetic Hill
Univ. de Moncton
Irishtown
Shediac
Shediac Bridge
Shediac Cape
Shediac Bay
Parlee Beach Prov. Park
Barachois
Cap-Pelé
Murray Beach Prov. Park
Scoudouc
Shemogue
Haute-Aboujagane
Meadow Brook
Port Elgin
Fort Gaspareaux N.H.S.
Baie Verte
Upper Cape
Murray Corner
Melrose
Petit-Cap
Cocagne I.
Cap-des-Caissie
Grande-Digue
Cocagne
Notre-Dame
St-Antoine
St-Paul
McLean Settlement
Coal Branch
Canaan
Harcourt
Smiths Corner
Bass River
Pine Ridge
Ste-Marie-de-Kent
Ste-Anne-de-Kent
Irving Eco-Centre
Bouctouche
Le Pays de la Sagouine
Cormierville
Kent Junction
Doak Historic Site
Central N.B. Woodmen's Museum
Parker Ridge
Ludlow
Boiestown
Astle
Miramichi Lake
Napadogan
Williamsburg
Stanley
Cross Creek
Tay Creek
Taymouth
Nashwaak Bridge
Nashwaak Village
Hardwood Ridge
Gaspereau Forks
Egmont Bay
Springhill
Tyne Valley
Enmore
St-Chrysostome
Richmond
Abram-Village
Wellington
Cap-Egmont
Prince Edward Island / New Brunswick
Sackville
Mt. Allison Univ.
Tidnish
Amherst Shore P.P.
Lorneville
Point de Bute
Aulac
Ft. Beauséjour N.H.S.
Amherst
Minudie
Nappan
Barronsfield
Maccan
Joggins Fossil Ctr.
Joggins
River Hebert
Athol
Springhill
Anne Murray Centre
Southampton
Mapleton
E. Southampton
West Brook
Sand River
Apple River
Fundy Geological Mus.
Parrsboro
Lynn
Five Islands
Port Greville
New Salem
Fraserville
Diligent River
Five Islands Prov. Park
Lower Economy
Chignecto Bay
Cape Chignecto Prov. Park
Advocate Harbour
Cape d'Or Lighthouse
C. Split
Scots Bay
Blomidon Prov. Park
Minas Basin
Isle Haute
New Brunswick / Nova Scotia
Halls Harbour
The Lookoff
Walton
Pembroke
Cambridge
Prescott House Mus.
Kingsport
Canning
Acadia Univ.
Cheverie
Grand-Pré Natl. Hist. Site
Hantsport
Smileys Prov. Pk.
Harbourville
Centreville
Victoria Harbour
Aldershot
Morden
Kentville
Wolfville
Coldbrook
Margaretsville
Aylesford
Waterville
Berwick
Kingston
Florence
Windsor
Brooklyn
Fort Edward N.H.S.
Three Mile Plains
Windsor Forks
Newport Corner
Black River L.
Martock
Vaughan
Aldersville
Morristown
New England Planters Natl. Heritage Exhibit
Greenwood
Wilmot
Middleton
Valleyview Prov. Park
Hampton
Lawrencetown
Paradise
Bridgetown
Parkers Cove
Granville Centre
Granville Ferry
North Hills Mus.
Delaps Cove
Fort Anne Natl. Hist. Site
Annapolis Royal
Port-Royal Natl. Hist. Site
Clementsport
Upper Clements Park
Lequille
West Dalhousie
Culloden
Digby
Clementsvale
Bear River
Rossway
Brighton
South Milford
Albany Cross
Falkland Ridge
Springfield
New Albany
Dalhousie Road
E. Dalhousie
Forties
New Ross
Ross Farm Mus.
Parkdale
Maplewood
Windsor Road
Fox Point
Graves I. Prov. Park
Chester
Chester Gold River
Western Shore
Peggys Cove
New Germany
Pinehurst
Pleasant River
Hemford
Wile Carding Mill Mus.
Colpton
Blockhouse
Mahone Bay
Northfield
Bridgewater
Lunenburg
Fisheries Museum of the Atlantic
Kempt
Caledonia
S. Brookfield
Chelsea
Hebbville
West LaHave
Conquerall Mills
Greenfield
Riverport
Bangs Falls
Italy Cross
Crescent Beach
Rissers Beach Prov. Park
Charleston
Broad Cove
Cherry Hill
Medway
Port Medway
Medway Harbour
Milton
Brooklyn
Perkins House Mus.
Western Head
Liverpool
White Point
South West Port Mouton
Port Mouton
Kejimkujik N.P. (Seaside Adjunct)
Port Joli
Thomas Raddall Prov. Pk.
Sable River
Port L'Hebert
Jordan Falls
Allendale
Shelburne
The Dory Shop Mus.
Sandy Pt.
Gunning Cove
Lockeport
Jordan Bay
The Islands Prov. Park
Birchtown
Ross-Thomson House Mus.
Kejimkujik Natl. Park
Kejimkujik L.
Low Landing
Ponhook L.
Middlefield
Lake Rossignol
Queens Regional Municipality
Indian Fields Prov. Park
Upper Ohio
Middle Ohio
Middle Clyde River
Clyde River
Great Barren L.
Port Clyde
Old Meeting House
Ingomar
Barrington Woolen Mill
Barrington
Crowell
Port La Tour
Shag Harbour
Centreville
Clark's Harbour
Cape Sable Island
Lower Woods Harbour
Charlesville
Lower E. Pubnico
Lower W. Pubnico
Le Village historique acadien de la Nouvelle-Écosse
Pubnico
Comeaus Hill
Little River Harbour
Wedgeport
Chebogue Pt.
Kelleys Cove
Yarmouth Light
Firefighters' Mus.
Yarmouth
Arcadia
Tusket
Lower Eel Brook
Central Argyle
Quinan
Ellenwood Lake Prov. Park
Hebron
Sandford
Darlings Lake
Brenton
Port Maitland
Beaver River
Salmon River
Carleton
Kemptville
Hectanooga
Richfield
Mavillette
Bear Cove
Meteghan Station
Meteghan
Meteghan River
Corberrie
New Tusket
Brier I.
Westport
Freeport
Comeauville
Long I.
Central Grove
Islands Mus.
Church Point
Univ. Sainte-Anne
E. Ferry
Tiverton
St. Bernard
Ohio
Weymouth
New Edinburgh
Little River
Sandy Cove
Plympton
Centreville
St. Mary's Bay
Bay of Fundy
North Head
Castalia
Grand Manan Island
Grand Manan (Grand Harbour)
Seal Cove
The Anchorage Prov. Park
White Head I.
Wood I.
Gulf of Maine
to Bar Harbor, Maine
to Portland, Maine
(Toll. Closed in off-season)

1 2 3 4
A B C

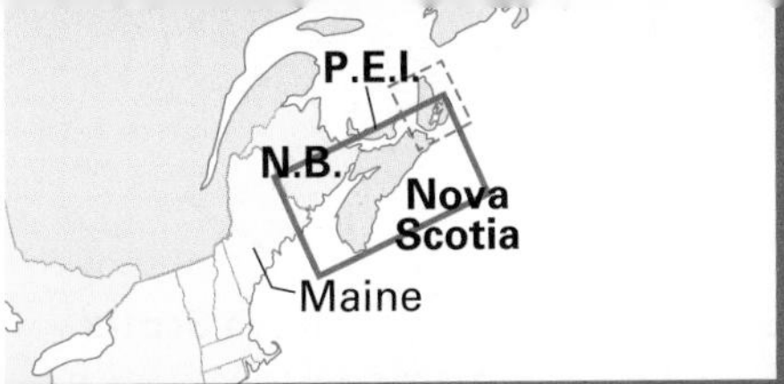

P.E.I.
N.B.
Nova Scotia
Maine

DRIVING DISTANCES IN KM / DISTANCES ROUTIÈRES EN KM

	CHARLOTTETOWN, PE	CHETICAMP, NS	DIGBY, NS	FREDERICTON, NB	HALIFAX, NS	MONCTON, NB	PORT HAWKESBURY, NS	SAINT JOHN, NB	ST. STEPHEN, NB	SYDNEY, NS	TRURO, NS	YARMOUTH, NS
HALIFAX, NS	322	425	235	462		260	265	410	515	415	89	339
MONCTON, NB	164	481	231	170	260		374	150	278	497	182	599
SAINT JOHN, NB	350	640	72	114	410	150	497		119	647	321	176
SYDNEY, NS	374	173	623	689	415	497	123	647	766		326	727

SEE ALSO DISTANCE AND DRIVING TIME MAP ON PAGES 286–287 / VOIR AUSSI CARTE DES DISTANCES ET DES TEMPS DE PARCOURS PAGES 286–287

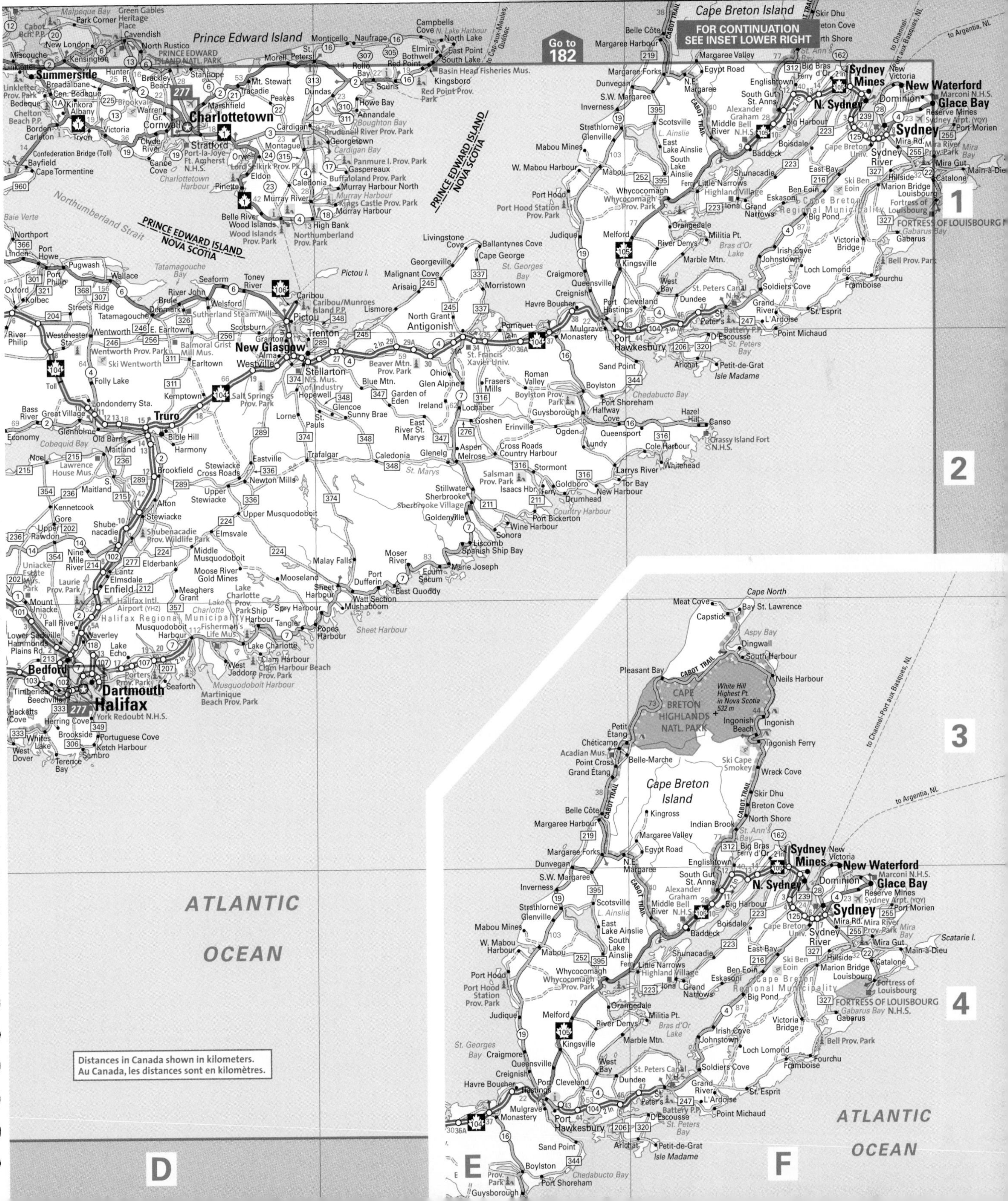

Prince Edward Island
Charlottetown
Summerside
Cape Breton Island
FOR CONTINUATION SEE INSET LOWER RIGHT
Go to 182
Northumberland Strait
PRINCE EDWARD ISLAND / NOVA SCOTIA
New Glasgow
Truro
Antigonish
Port Hawkesbury
Sydney
Glace Bay
Dartmouth
Halifax
Bedford
ATLANTIC OCEAN
Cape Breton Highlands Natl. Park
Distances in Canada shown in kilometers.
Au Canada, les distances sont en kilomètres.
1
2
3
4
D
E
F

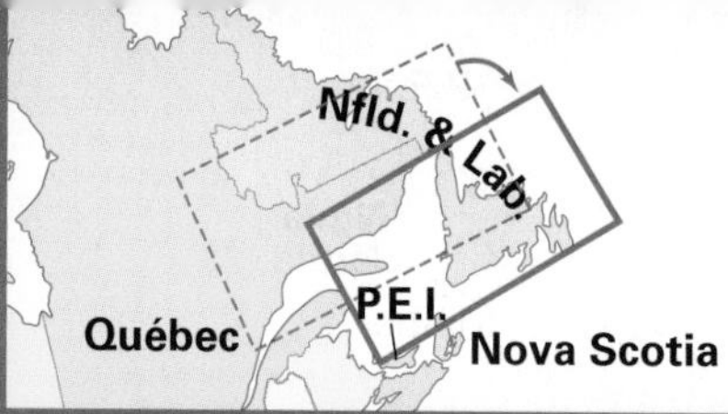

Nfld. & Lab.
Québec
P.E.I.
Nova Scotia

0 mi 20 40 60
0 km 20 40 60 80

One inch equals 40.3 miles/Un pouce équivaut à 40.3 milles
One centimeter equals 25.4 km/Un cm équivaut à 25.4 km

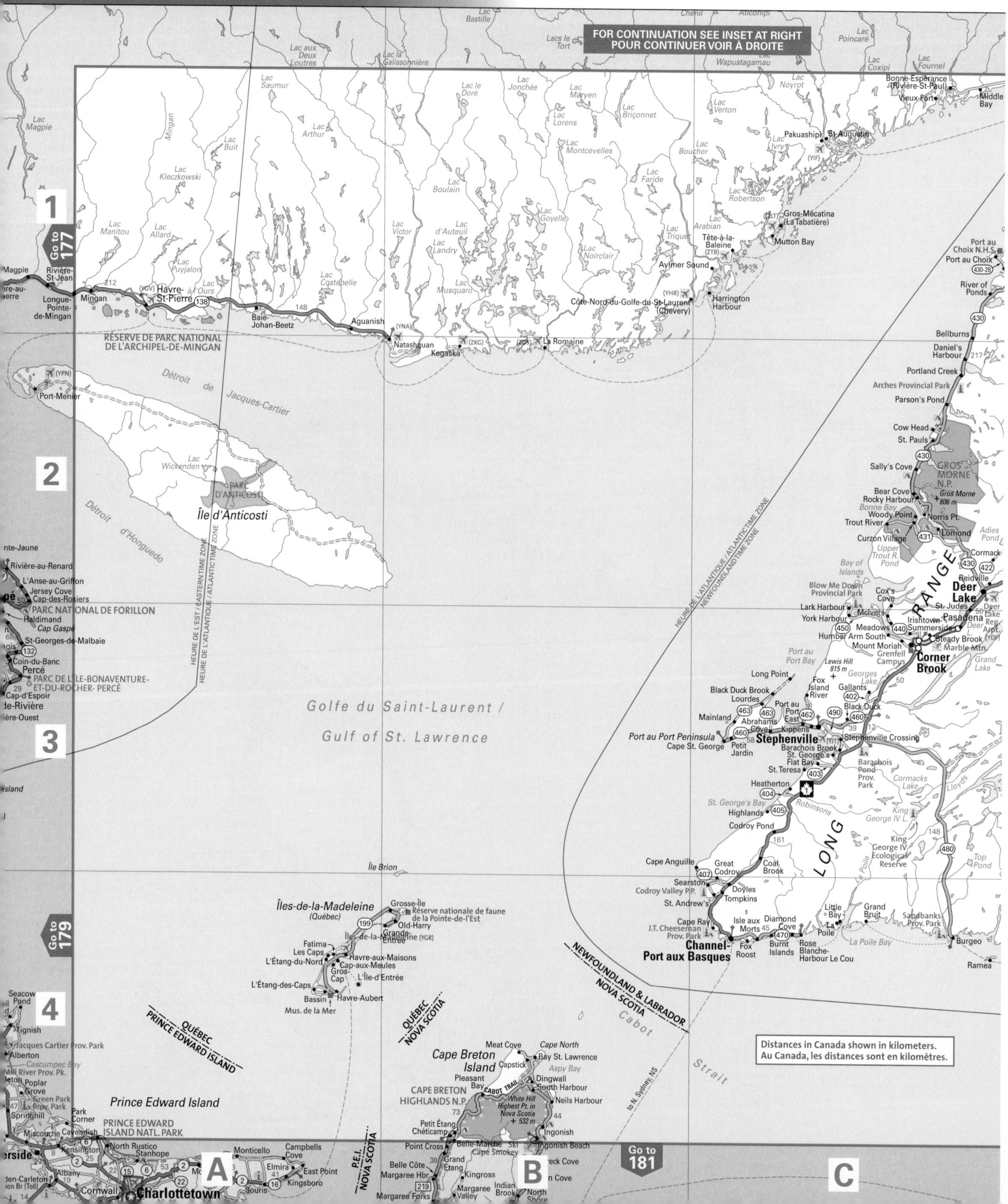

FOR CONTINUATION SEE INSET AT RIGHT
POUR CONTINUER VOIR À DROITE
1
2
3
4
Go to 177
Go to 179
Go to 181
A
B
C
Distances in Canada shown in kilometers.
Au Canada, les distances sont en kilomètres.
Golfe du Saint-Laurent /
Gulf of St. Lawrence
Détroit de Jacques-Cartier
Détroit d'Honguedo
Île d'Anticosti
PARC D'ANTICOSTI
Port-Menier
Lac Wickenden
Havre-St-Pierre
Mingan
Magpie
Rivière-St-Jean
Longue-Pointe-de-Mingan
Baie-Johan-Beetz
Aguanish
Natashquan
Kegaska
La Romaine
Côte-Nord-du-Golfe-du-St-Laurent (Chevery)
Harrington Harbour
Aylmer Sound
Tête-à-la-Baleine
Mutton Bay
Gros-Mécatina (La Tabatière)
Pakuashipi
St-Augustin
Bonne-Espérance (Rivière-St-Paul)
Vieux-Fort
Middle Bay
RÉSERVE DE PARC NATIONAL DE L'ARCHIPEL-DE-MINGAN
HEURE DE L'EST / EASTERN TIME ZONE
HEURE DE L'ATLANTIQUE / ATLANTIC TIME ZONE
HEURE DE L'ATLANTIQUE / ATLANTIC TIME ZONE
NEWFOUNDLAND TIME ZONE
Port au Choix N.H.S.
Port au Choix
River of Ponds
Bellburns
Daniel's Harbour
Portland Creek
Arches Provincial Park
Parson's Pond
Cow Head
St. Pauls
Sally's Cove
GROS MORNE N.P.
Gros Morne 806 m
Bear Cove
Rocky Harbour
Bonne Bay
Woody Point
Norris Pt.
Trout River
Lomond
Curzon Village
Cormack
Reidville
Deer Lake
St. Judes
Pasadena
Irishtown-Summerside
Steady Brook
Marble Mtn.
Corner Brook
Grenfell Campus
Mount Moriah
Humber Arm South
Meadows
York Harbour
Lark Harbour
Cox's Cove
McIvers
Blow Me Down Provincial Park
Bay of Islands
LONG RANGE
Port au Port Bay
Lewis Hill 815 m
Long Point
Fox Island River
Gallants
Black Duck Brook
Lourdes
Mainland
Abrahams Cove
Port au Port East
Black Duck
Kippens
Stephenville
Stephenville Crossing
Port au Port Peninsula
Cape St. George
Petit Jardin
Barachois Brook
St. George's
Flat Bay
St. Teresa
Barachois Pond Prov. Park
Heatherton
St. George's Bay
Highlands
Codroy Pond
Robinsons
King George IV Ecological Reserve
Cape Anguille
Great Codroy
Coal Brook
Searston
Codroy Valley P.P.
Doyles
Tompkins
St. Andrew's
Cape Ray
J.T. Cheeseman Prov. Park
Isle aux Morts
Diamond Cove
Channel-Port aux Basques
Fox Roost
Burnt Islands
Rose Blanche-Harbour Le Cou
Little Bay
La Poile
Grand Bruit
Sandbanks Prov. Park
Burgeo
Ramea
La Poile Bay
Cabot Strait
NEWFOUNDLAND & LABRADOR
NOVA SCOTIA
to N. Sydney, NS
Île Brion
Îles-de-la-Madeleine (Québec)
Grosse-Île
Réserve nationale de faune de la Pointe-de-l'Est
Old-Harry
Grande-Entrée
Fatima
Les Caps
L'Étang-du-Nord
Havre-aux-Maisons
Cap-aux-Meules
Gros-Cap
L'Île-d'Entrée
L'Étang-des-Caps
Bassin
Havre-Aubert
Mus. de la Mer
QUÉBEC
PRINCE EDWARD ISLAND
QUÉBEC
NOVA SCOTIA
P.E.I.
NOVA SCOTIA
Cape Breton Island
Meat Cove
Cape North
Bay St. Lawrence
Capstick
Aspy Bay
Dingwall
South Harbour
Pleasant Bay
CABOT TRAIL
CAPE BRETON HIGHLANDS N.P.
White Hill Highest Pt. in Nova Scotia 532 m
Neils Harbour
Petit Étang
Chéticamp
Ingonish
Ingonish Beach
Point Cross
Belle-Marche
Cape Smokey
Belle Côte
Grand Étang
Margaree Hbr.
Kingross
Margaree Forks
Margaree Valley
Indian Brook
North Shore
Prince Edward Island
PRINCE EDWARD ISLAND NATL. PARK
Cavendish
North Rustico
Stanhope
Kensington
Charlottetown
Cornwall
Albany
Monticello
Campbells Cove
Elmira
East Point
Kingsboro
Souris
Tignish
Alberton
Jacques Cartier Prov. Park
Cascumpec Bay
Mill River Prov. Pk.
Poplar Grove
Green Park Prov. Park
Springhill
Miscouche
Park Corner
Seacow Pond
Rivière-au-Renard
L'Anse-au-Griffon
Jersey Cove
Cap-des-Rosiers
PARC NATIONAL DE FORILLON
Haldimand
Cap Gaspé
St-Georges-de-Malbaie
Coin-du-Banc
Percé
PARC DE L'ÎLE-BONAVENTURE-ET-DU-ROCHER-PERCÉ
Cap-d'Espoir

DRIVING DISTANCES IN KM / DISTANCES ROUTIÈRES EN KM

	ARGENTIA, NL	BISHOP'S FALLS, NL	BONAVISTA, NL	CHAN.-PT. AUX BASQUES, NL	CORNER BROOK, NL	DEER LAKE, NL	GANDER, NL	GRAND FALLS-WINDSOR, NL	MARYSTOWN, NL	ST. ANTHONY, NL	ST. JOHN'S, NL	STEPHENVILLE, NL
BISHOP'S FALLS, NL	363		307	482	280	225	72	18	384	628	393	339
CHAN.-PT. AUX BASQUES, NL	845	482	789		202	257	554	464	866	660	875	151
CORNER BROOK, NL	643	280	587	202		55	352	262	664	458	673	59
ST. JOHN'S, NL	134	393	296	875	673	618	321	411	293	1021		732

SEE ALSO DISTANCE AND DRIVING TIME MAP ON PAGES 286–287 / VOIR AUSSI CARTE DES DISTANCES ET DES TEMPS DE PARCOURS PAGES 286–287

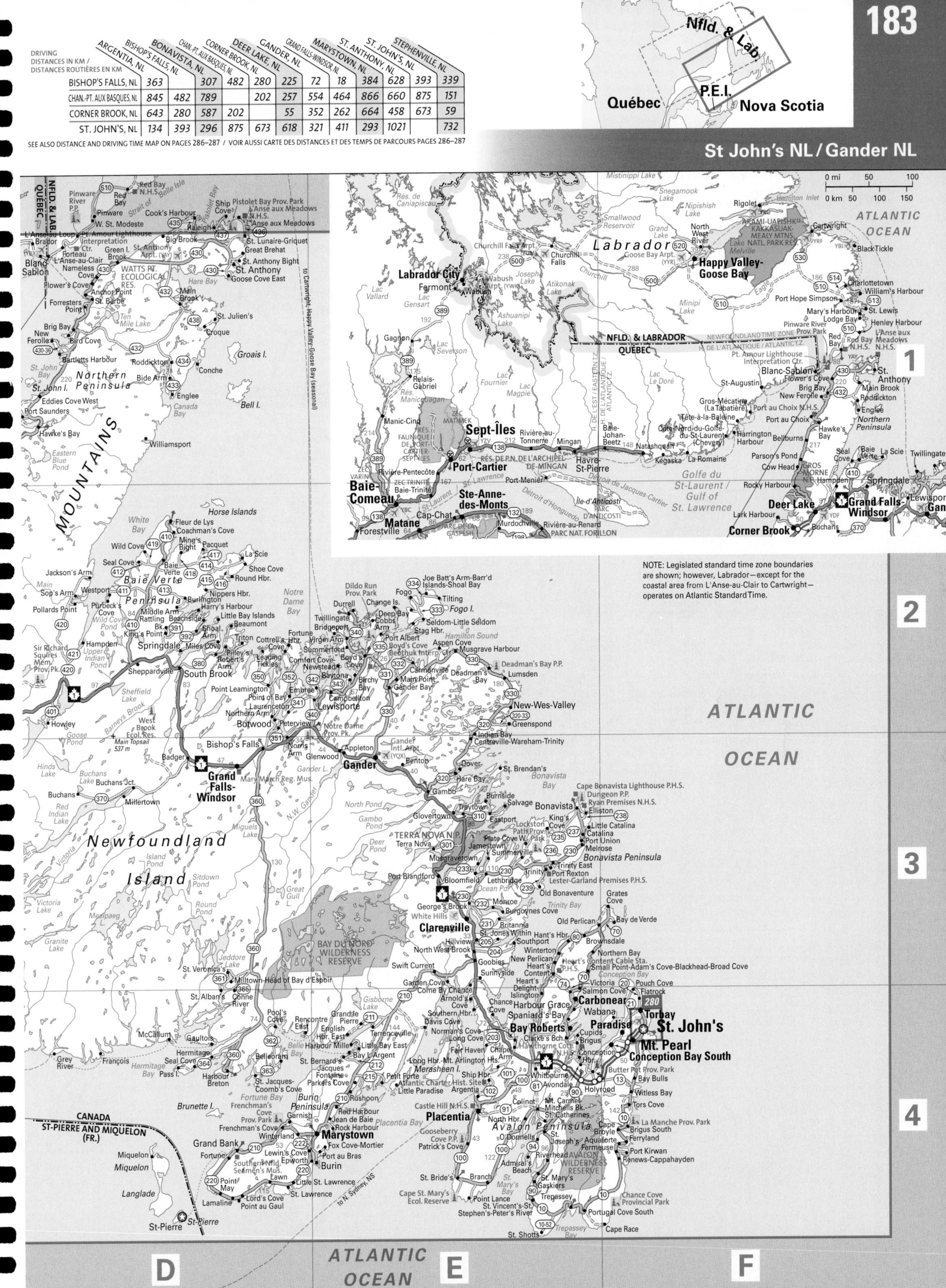

NOTE: Legislated standard time zone boundaries are shown; however, Labrador—except for the coastal area from L'Anse-au-Clair to Cartwright—operates on Atlantic Standard Time.

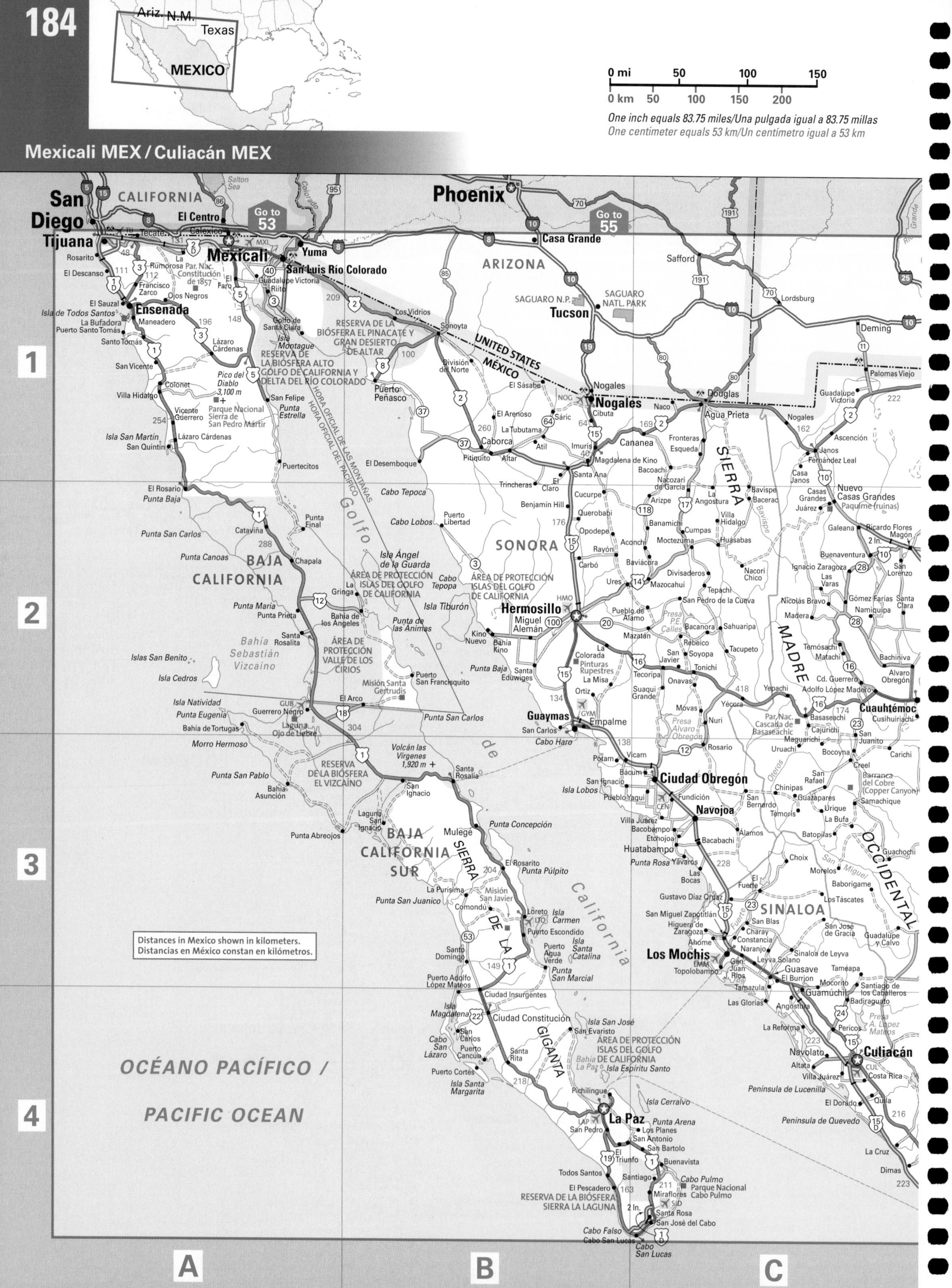
Ariz.
N.M.
Texas
MEXICO
0 mi 50 100 150
0 km 50 100 150 200
One inch equals 83.75 miles/Una pulgada igual a 83.75 millas
One centimeter equals 53 km/Un centímetro igual a 53 km
San Diego
Tijuana
CALIFORNIA
El Centro
Calexico
Go to 53
Phoenix
Go to 55
Mexicali
Yuma
San Luis Río Colorado
Casa Grande
ARIZONA
Safford
Tucson
SAGUARO N.P.
SAGUARO NATL. PARK
Lordsburg
Deming
Ensenada
Rosarito
El Descanso
Tecate
Rumorosa
Parque Nacional Constitución de 1857
Ojos Negros
Maneadero
El Sauzal
Isla de Todos Santos
La Bufadora
Puerto Santo Tomás
Santo Tomás
San Vicente
Lázaro Cárdenas
Colonet
Villa Hidalgo
Vicente Guerrero
Pico del Diablo 3,100 m
Parque Nacional Sierra de San Pedro Mártir
Isla San Martín
San Quintín
Golfo de Santa Clara
Isla Montague
RESERVA DE LA BIÓSFERA EL PINACATE Y GRAN DESIERTO DE ALTAR
RESERVA DE LA BIÓSFERA ALTO GOLFO DE CALIFORNIA Y DELTA DEL RÍO COLORADO
San Felipe
Punta Estrella
Los Vidrios
Sonoyta
Puerto Peñasco
UNITED STATES
MÉXICO
Nogales
Douglas
Agua Prieta
Naco
Cananea
Palomas Viejo
HORA OFICIAL DE LAS MONTAÑAS
HORA OFICIAL DEL PACÍFICO
Puertecitos
El Rosario
Punta Baja
Punta San Carlos
Cataviña
Punta Final
Punta Canoas
BAJA CALIFORNIA
Chapala
El Desemboque
Caborca
Altar
Magdalena de Kino
Santa Ana
Imuris
Cabo Tepoca
Cabo Lobos
Puerto Libertad
SONORA
Golfo
Isla Ángel de la Guarda
ÁREA DE PROTECCIÓN ISLAS DEL GOLFO DE CALIFORNIA
Isla Tiburón
Hermosillo
Miguel Alemán
Kino Nuevo
Bahía Kino
Punta María
Punta Prieta
Bahía de los Ángeles
Santa Rosalita
Bahía Sebastián Vizcaíno
ÁREA DE PROTECCIÓN VALLE DE LOS CIRIOS
Islas San Benito
Isla Cedros
Isla Natividad
Punta Eugenia
Bahía de Tortugas
Guerrero Negro
Laguna Ojo de Liebre
Morro Hermoso
El Arco
Misión Santa Gertrudis
Puerto San Francisquito
Punta San Carlos
Guaymas
San Carlos
Empalme
Cabo Haro
Volcán las Vírgenes 1,920 m
RESERVA DE LA BIÓSFERA EL VIZCAÍNO
Punta San Pablo
Bahía Asunción
Santa Rosalía
San Ignacio
Laguna San Ignacio
Punta Abreojos
BAJA CALIFORNIA SUR
Mulegé
SIERRA DE LA GIGANTA
Punta Concepción
El Rosarito
Punta Púlpito
California
Loreto
Isla Carmen
Puerto Escondido
Isla Santa Catalina
Punta San Marcial
Distances in Mexico shown in kilometers.
Distancias en México constan en kilómetros.
Santo Domingo
Puerto Adolfo López Mateos
Ciudad Insurgentes
Ciudad Constitución
Isla Magdalena
Isla San José
San Evaristo
Puerto Cortés
Isla Santa Margarita
OCÉANO PACÍFICO / PACIFIC OCEAN
La Paz
Pichilingue
Isla Espíritu Santo
Isla Cerralvo
Punta Arena
Los Planes
San Antonio
San Bartolo
El Triunfo
Buenavista
Todos Santos
Santiago
El Pescadero
Cabo Pulmo
Parque Nacional Cabo Pulmo
Miraflores
RESERVA DE LA BIÓSFERA SIERRA LA LAGUNA
Santa Rosa
San José del Cabo
Cabo Falso
Cabo San Lucas
Ciudad Obregón
Navojoa
Huatabampo
Los Mochis
Topolobampo
Guasave
Guamúchil
Culiacán
Costa Rica
Península de Lucenilla
Península de Quevedo
La Cruz
Dimas
SINALOA
SIERRA MADRE OCCIDENTAL
Cuauhtémoc
Nuevo Casas Grandes
Casas Grandes
Paquimé (ruinas)
Janos
Ascensión
Basaseachi
Par. Nac. Cascada de Basaseachic
Creel
Barranca del Cobre (Copper Canyon)
Batopilas
Guachochi
Yécora
Álamos
El Fuerte
Choix
Badiraguato
1
2
3
4
A
B
C

DRIVING DISTANCES IN KM / DISTANCIAS DE MANEJO EN KM	CHIHUAHUA	CIUDAD JUÁREZ	CIUDAD VICTORIA	CULIACÁN	DURANGO	HERMOSILLO	MAZATLÁN	MÉXICO	MONTERREY	SAN LUIS POTOSÍ	TIJUANA	TORREÓN
CHIHUAHUA		385	1086	919	686	579	1209	1538	808	1155	1456	449
HERMOSILLO	579	795	1666	706	941		729	1810	1387	1416	884	1028
MONTERREY	808	1236	288	924	689	1387	901	892		509	2362	359
TORREÓN	449	834	637	914	266	1028	892	1089	359	706	1905	

SEE ALSO DISTANCE AND DRIVING TIME MAP ON PAGES 286–287 / CONSULTE, PARA DISTANCIAS Y TIEMPO DE MANEJO, EN LAS PÁGINAS 286-287

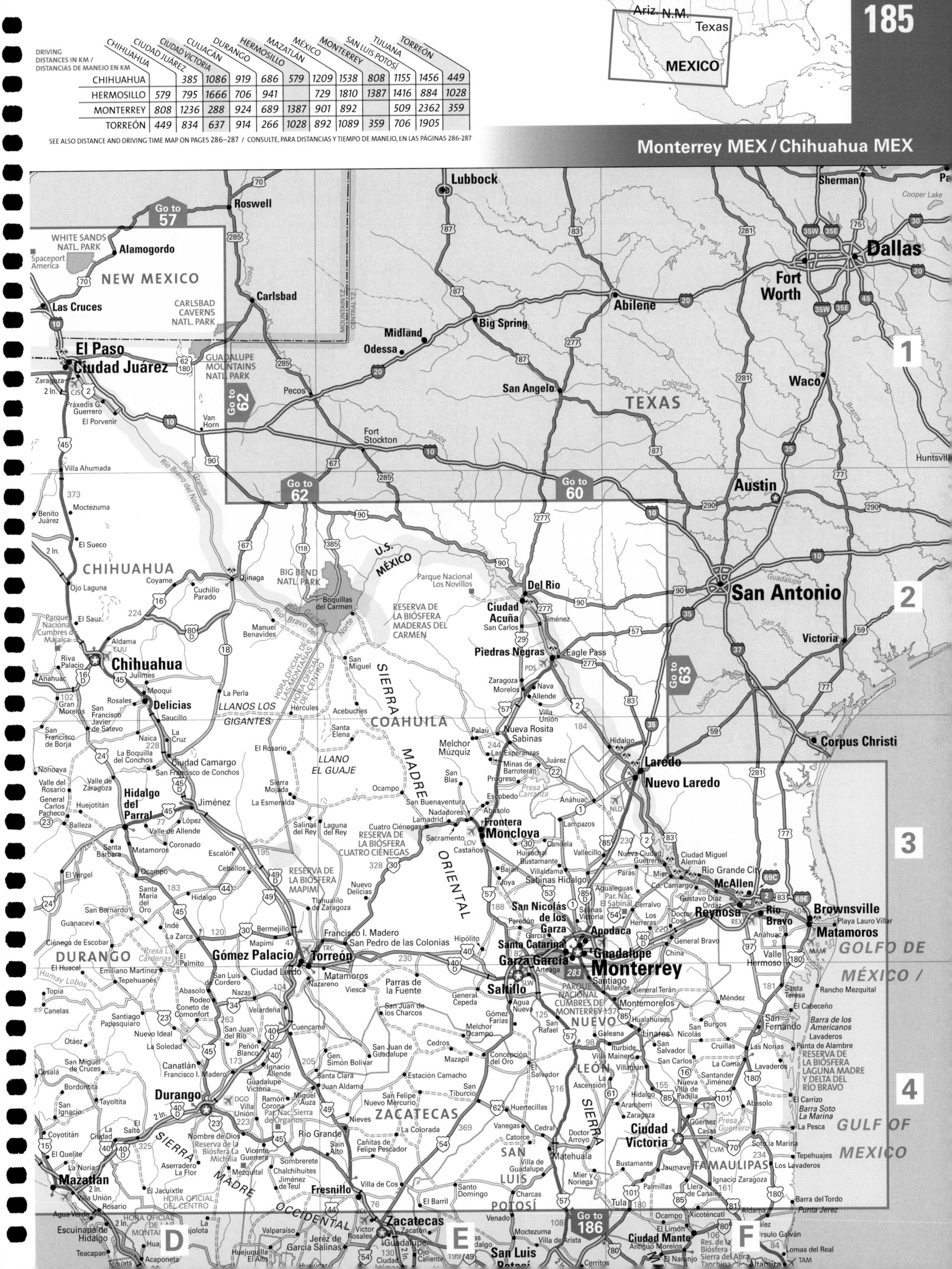

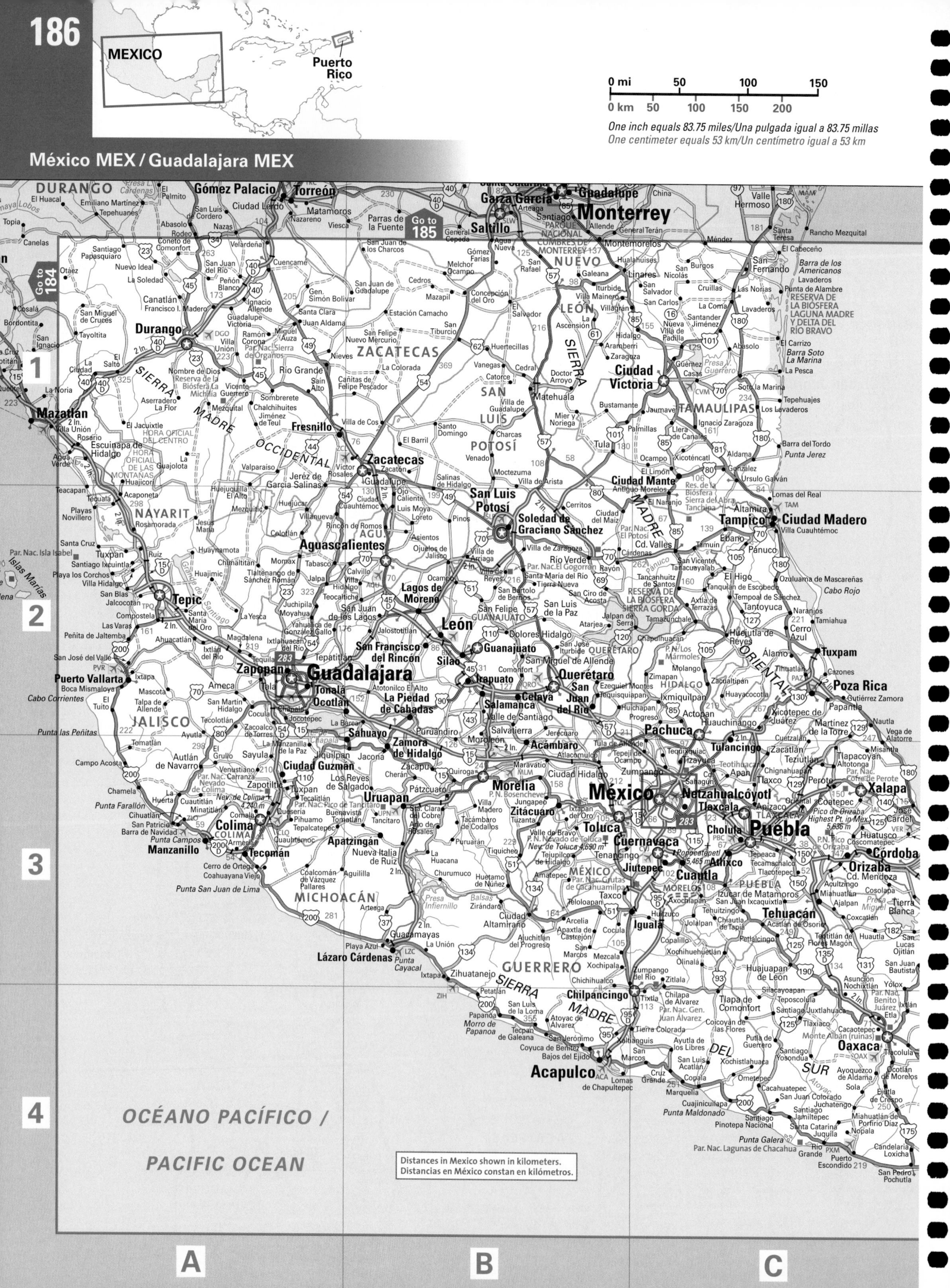
MEXICO
Puerto Rico
0 mi 50 100 150
0 km 50 100 150 200
One inch equals 83.75 miles/Una pulgada igual a 83.75 millas
One centimeter equals 53 km/Un centímetro igual a 53 km
Go to 185
Go to 184
DURANGO
ZACATECAS
SAN LUIS POTOSÍ
NUEVO LEÓN
TAMAULIPAS
NAYARIT
JALISCO
COLIMA
MICHOACÁN
GUERRERO
MÉXICO
MORELOS
PUEBLA
TLAXCALA
HIDALGO
QUERÉTARO
GUANAJUATO
AGUASCALIENTES
SIERRA MADRE OCCIDENTAL
SIERRA MADRE ORIENTAL
SIERRA MADRE DEL SUR
Monterrey
Saltillo
Torreón
Gómez Palacio
Durango
Mazatlán
Zacatecas
Fresnillo
Ciudad Victoria
Tampico
Ciudad Madero
San Luis Potosí
Soledad de Graciano Sánchez
Aguascalientes
Lagos de Moreno
León
Guanajuato
Querétaro
Celaya
Irapuato
Tepic
Puerto Vallarta
Guadalajara
Zapopan
Tonalá
Ciudad Guzmán
Colima
Manzanillo
Tecomán
Morelia
Uruapan
Apatzingán
Lázaro Cárdenas
Pachuca
Tulancingo
Poza Rica
Tuxpam
Xalapa
México
Netzahualcóyotl
Toluca
Cuernavaca
Tlaxcala
Puebla
Cholula
Orizaba
Córdoba
Tehuacán
Cuautla
Iguala
Chilpancingo
Acapulco
Oaxaca
Zihuatanejo
OCÉANO PACÍFICO / PACIFIC OCEAN
Distances in Mexico shown in kilometers.
Distancias en México constan en kilómetros.
1
2
3
4
A
B
C

MEXICO

Puerto Rico

DRIVING DISTANCES IN KM / DISTANCIAS DE MANEJO EN KM

	ACAPULCO	CANCÚN	CIUDAD VICTORIA	DURANGO	GUADALAJARA	MAZATLÁN	MÉRIDA	MÉXICO	PUEBLA	SAN LUIS POTOSÍ	TUXTLA GUTIÉRREZ	VERACRUZ
GUADALAJARA	897	2275	774	599		523	1904	578	691	336	1510	943
MÉRIDA	1777	321	1725	2182	1904	2408		1326	1282	1707	786	995
MÉXICO	422	1736	682	856	578	1081	1326		133	381	932	365
SAN LUIS POTOSÍ	834	2161	438	475	336	687	1707	381	496		1313	747

SEE ALSO DISTANCE AND DRIVING TIME MAP ON PAGES 286–287 / CONSULTE, PARA DISTANCIAS Y TIEMPO DE MANEJO, EN LAS PÁGINAS 286-287

PUERTO RICO

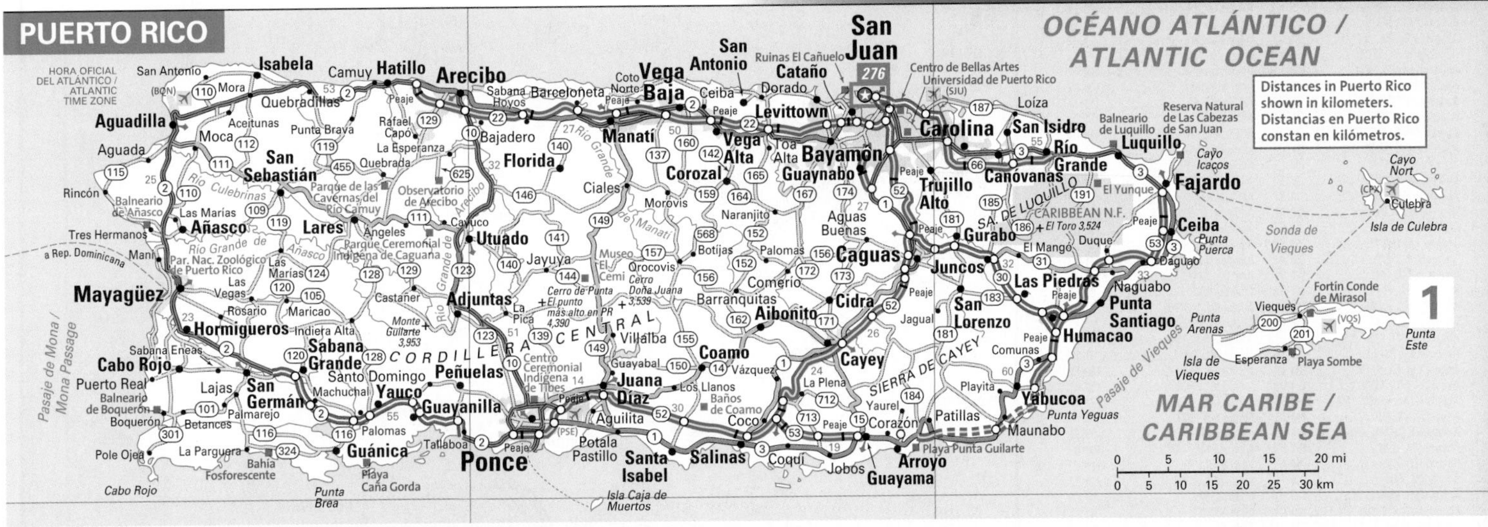

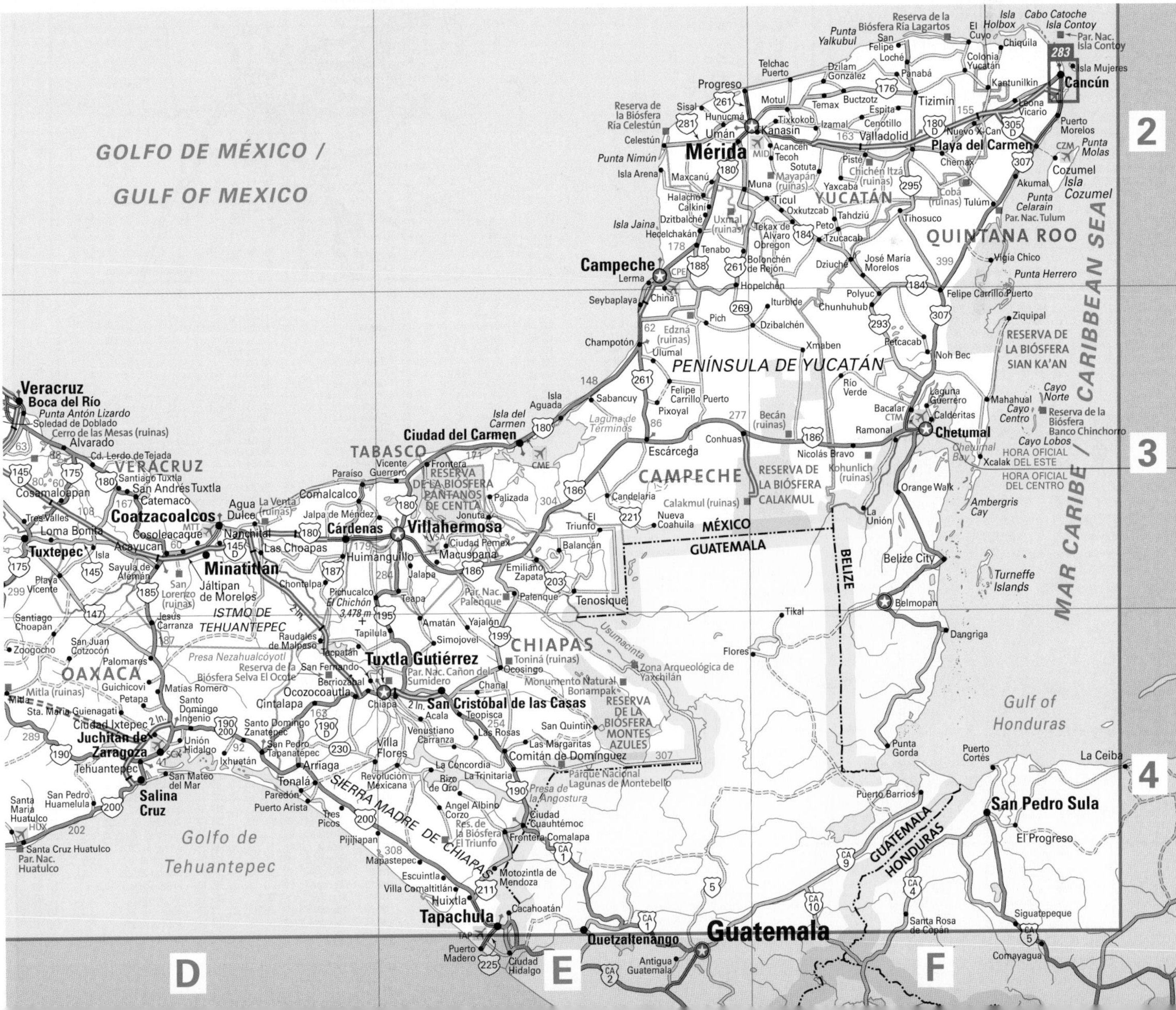

HORA OFICIAL DEL ATLÁNTICO / ATLANTIC TIME ZONE

OCÉANO ATLÁNTICO / ATLANTIC OCEAN

Distances in Puerto Rico shown in kilometers. Distancias en Puerto Rico constan en kilómetros.

MAR CARIBE / CARIBBEAN SEA

CORDILLERA CENTRAL

0 5 10 15 20 mi
0 5 10 15 20 25 30 km

GOLFO DE MÉXICO / GULF OF MEXICO

PENÍNSULA DE YUCATÁN

MAR CARIBE / CARIBBEAN SEA

Gulf of Honduras

Golfo de Tehuantepec

D E F

1 2 3 4

Figures after entries indicate population, page number, and grid reference.

UNITED STATES

A

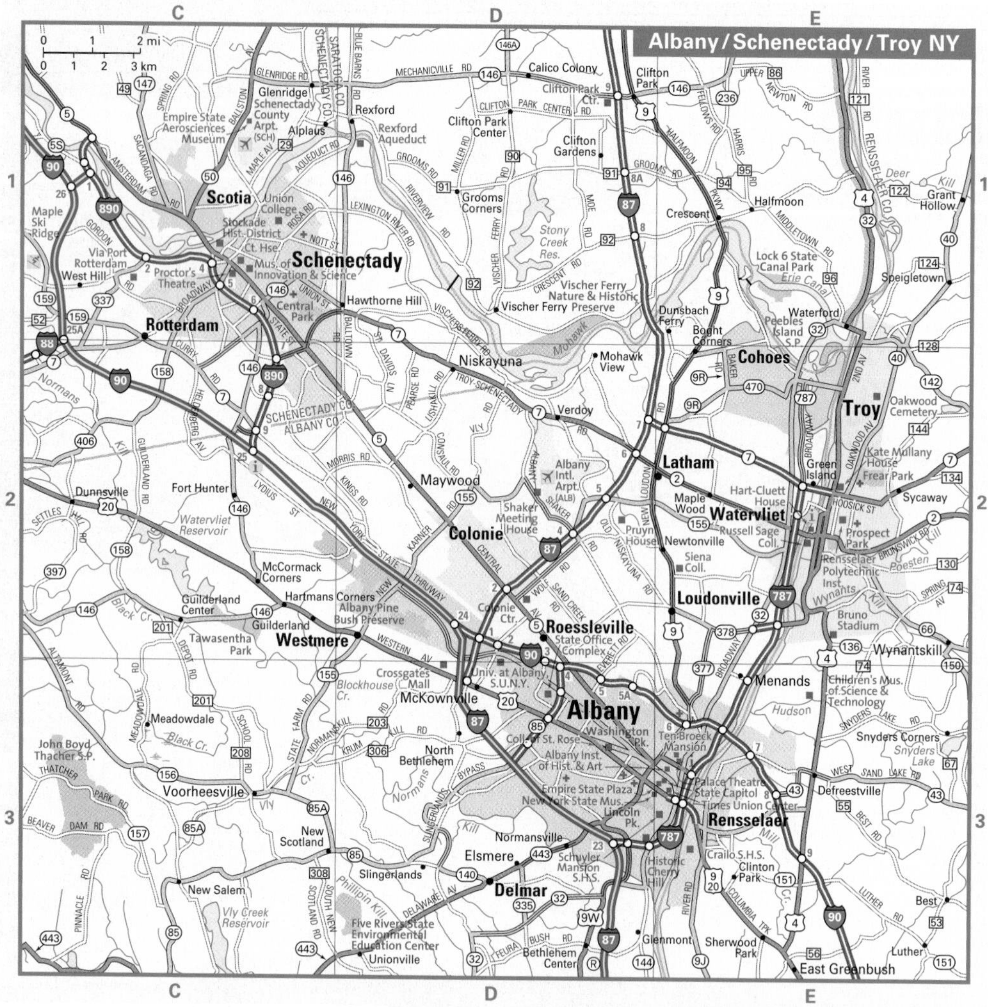

Akron OH

Entries in **bold black** indicate counties or parishes.
Entries in **bold color** indicate cities with detailed inset maps.

Albuquerque NM

Amarillo TX

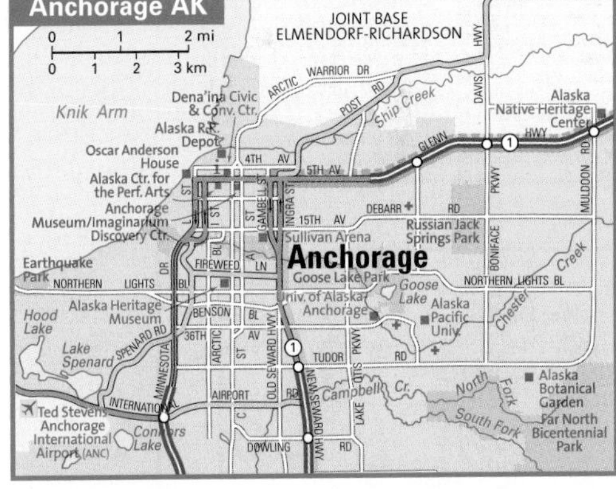

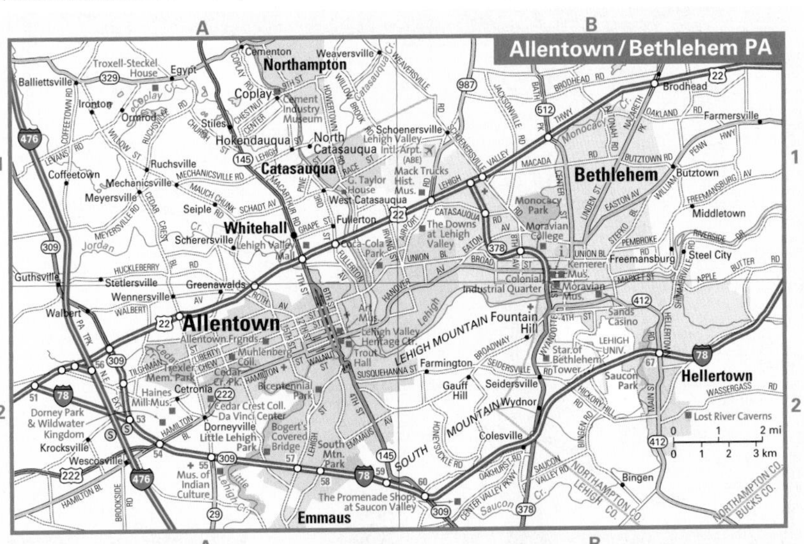

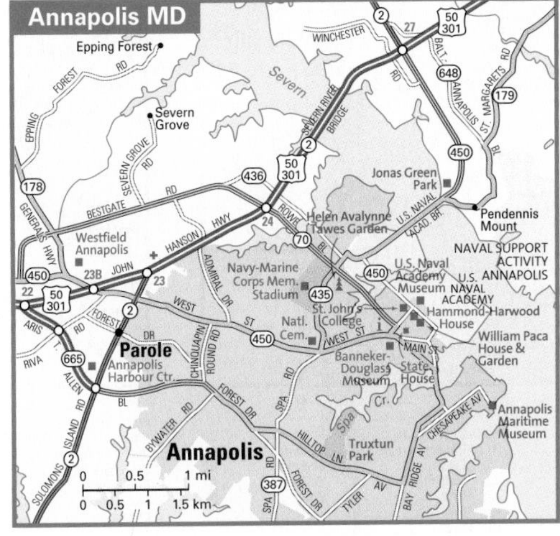

Figures after entries indicate population, page number, and grid reference.

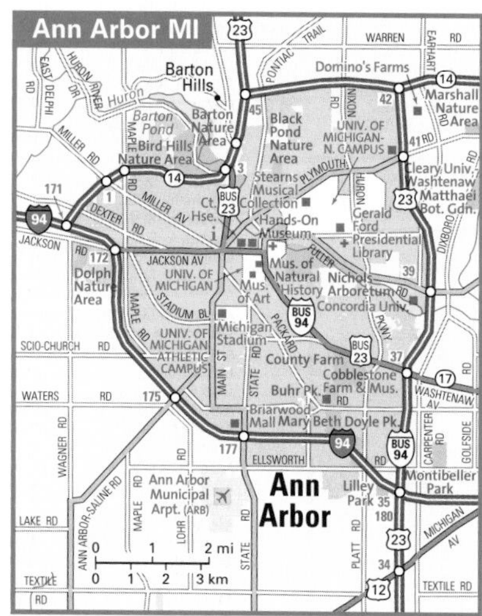

Anoka Co. MN, *330844* **67** D3
Ansley NE, *441* **35** D3
Anson ME, *752* **82** B1
Anson TX, *2430* **58** C2
Anson Co. NC, *26948* **122** B2
Ansonia CT, *19249* **149** D2
Ansonia OH, *1174* **90** A4
Ansonville NC, *631* **122** B1
Ansted WV, *1404* **101** F4
Antelope SD, *826* **26** C4
Antelope Acres CA, *1000* **52** C1
Antelope Co. NE, *6685* **35** E2
Anthon IA, *565* **72** A4
Anthony FL, *1600* **138** C4
Anthony KS, *2269* **43** E4
Anthony NM, *9360* **56** C3
Anthony TX, *5011* **56** C3
Antigo WI, *8234* **68** B3
Antioch CA, *102372* **36** B3
Antioch IL, *14430* **74** C4
Antlers OK, *2453* **116** A3
Anton TX, *1126* **58** A1
Antonito CO, *781* **49** D1
Antrim NH, *1397* **81** E4
Antrim Co. MI, *23580* **70** B3
Antwerp NY, *686* **79** E1
Antwerp OH, *1736* **90** A2
Apache OK, *1444* **51** D3
Apache Co. AZ, *71518* **47** F3
Apache Jct. AZ, *35840* **54** C1
Apalachicola FL, *2231* **137** D3
Apalachin NY, *1131* **93** E1
Apex NC, *37476* **112** C4
Aplington IA, *1128* **73** D4
Apollo PA, *1647* **92** A4
Apollo Beach FL, *14055* **266** C3
Apopka FL, *41542* **141** D1
Appalachia VA, *1754* **111** E2
Appanoose Co. IA, *12887* **87** D3
Apple Creek OH, *1173* **91** E3
Applegate CA, *800* **36** C2
Appleton MN, *1412* **27** F2
Appleton WI, *72623* **74** C1
Appleton City MO, *1127* **96** C4
Apple Valley CA, *69135* **53** D2
Apple Valley MN, *49084* **67** D4
Applewood CO, *7160* **209** B3
Appling GA, *225* **121** F4
Appling Co. GA, *18236* **129** F3
Appomattox VA, *1733* **112** C1
Appomattox Co. VA, *14973* **112** C1
Aptos CA, *6220* **44** B2
Aquebogue NY, *2438* **149** E3
Arab AL, *8050* **119** F3
Arabi LA, *3635* **239** C1
Aragon GA, *1249* **120** B3
Aransas Co. TX, *23158* **61** F4
Aransas Pass TX, *8204* **63** F2
Arapaho OK, *796* **51** D3
Arapahoe NE, *1026* **34** C4
Arapahoe WY, *1656* **32** B1
Arapahoe Co. CO, *572003* **41** E1
Arbuckle CA, *3028* **36** B2
Arbutus MD, *20483* **193** B3
Arbyrd MO, *509* **108** B4
Arcade CA, *96025* **255** B2

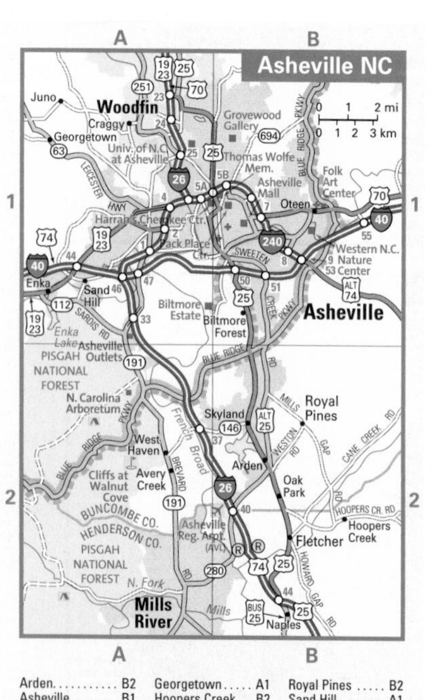

A		B	

Arden B2
Asheville B1
Avery Creek A2
Biltmore Forest B1
Craggy A1
Enka A1
Fletcher B2
Georgetown A1
Hoopers Creek B2
Juno A1
Mills River A2
Naples B2
Oak Park B2
Oteen B1
Royal Pines B2
Sand Hill A1
Skyland B2
W. Haven A2
Woodfin A1

Atlanta GA

Alpharetta E1
Atlanta C4
Avondale Estates E3
Belvedere Park E4
Brookhaven D3
Cedar Grove E5
Chamblee E2
Chattahoochee Plantation D2
Clarkston E3
College Park C5
Constitution D4
Decatur E4
Doraville E2
Druid Hills D3
Dunwoody E2
E. Point C4
Ellenwood E5
Fair Oaks C2
Fairview E5
Forest Park D5
Gresham Park E4
Hapeville D5
Johns Creek E1
Lake City D5
Marietta C1
Mechanicsville E2
Mount Bethel D1
N. Atlanta E2
N. Decatur E3
N. Druid Hills E3
Oakdale C3
Panthersville E4
Peachtree Corners E1
Red Oak C5
Rehoboth E3
Roswell D1
Sandy Plains C1
Sandy Sprs. D2
Scottdale E3
Smyrna C2
S. Fulton C5
Tucker E2
Union City C5
Vinings C2

Entries in **bold black** indicate counties or parishes.
Entries in **bold color** indicate cities with detailed inset maps.

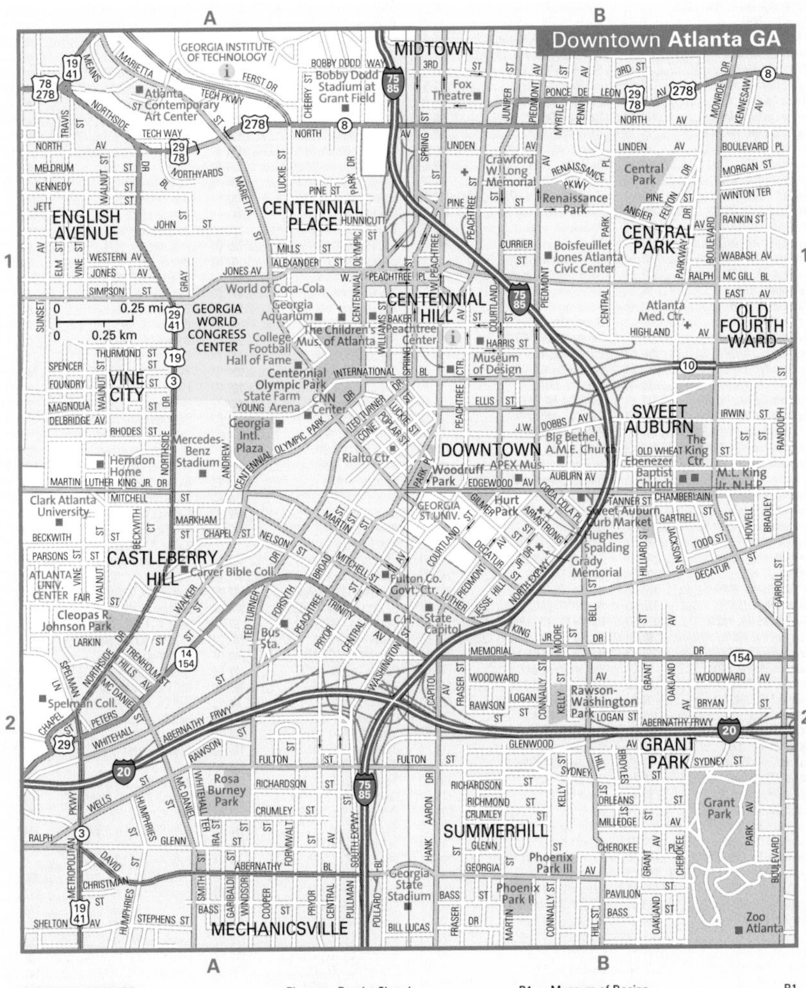

POINTS OF INTEREST

APEX Museum B1
Atlanta Contemporary Art Center A1
Atlanta University Center A2
Big Bethel African Meth. Episcopal Church . B1
Bobby Dodd Stadium at Grant Field A1
Boisfeuillet Jones Atlanta Civic Center B1
Bus Station A2
Carver Bible College A2
City Hall A2
Clark Atlanta University A2
CNN Center A1
Ebenezer Baptist Church B1
Fox Theatre B1
Fulton County Government Center A2
Georgia Aquarium A1
Georgia Institute of Technology A1
Georgia State Stadium A2
Georgia State University B2
Georgia World Congress Center A1
Herndon Home A1
The King Center B1
Martin Luther King, Jr. Natl. Hist. Park B1
Mercedes-Benz Stadium A1
Museum of Design B1
Peachtree Center B1
Rialto Center A1
Spelman College A2
State Capitol B2
State Farm Arena A1
Sweet Auburn Curb Market B2
The Children's Mus. of Atlanta A1
World of Coca-Cola A1
Zoo Atlanta B2

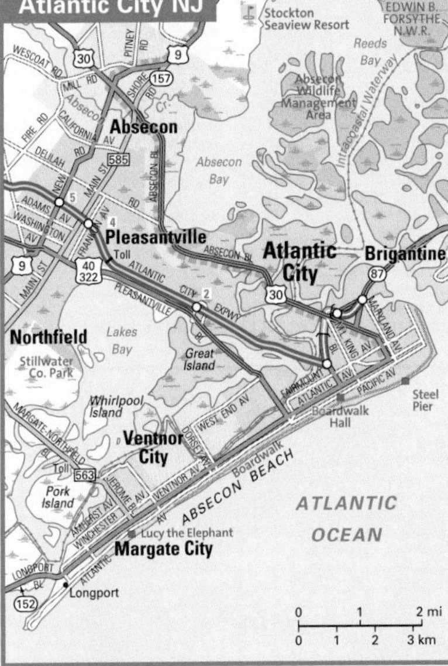

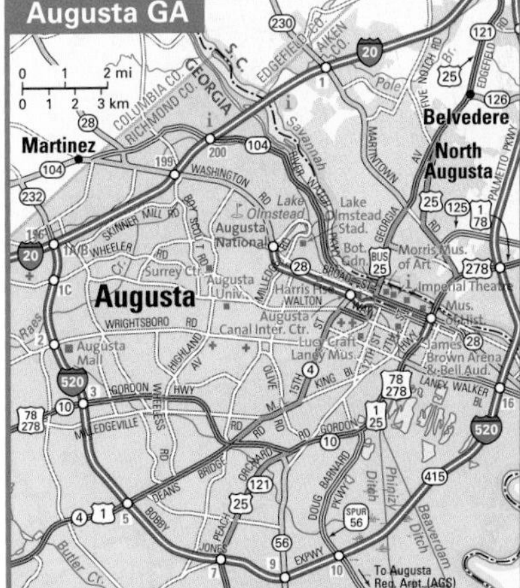

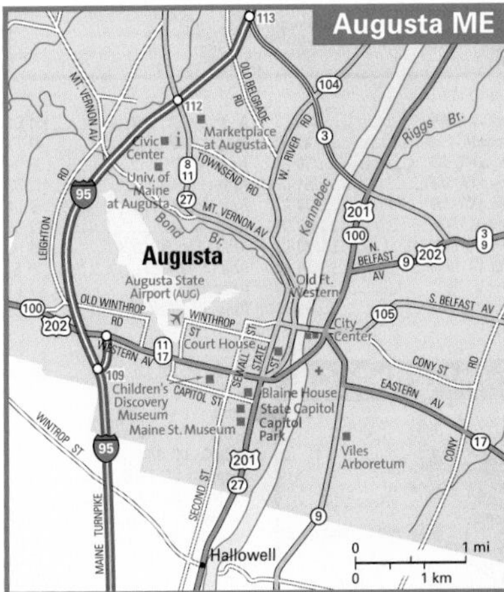

Figures after entries indicate population, page number, and grid reference.

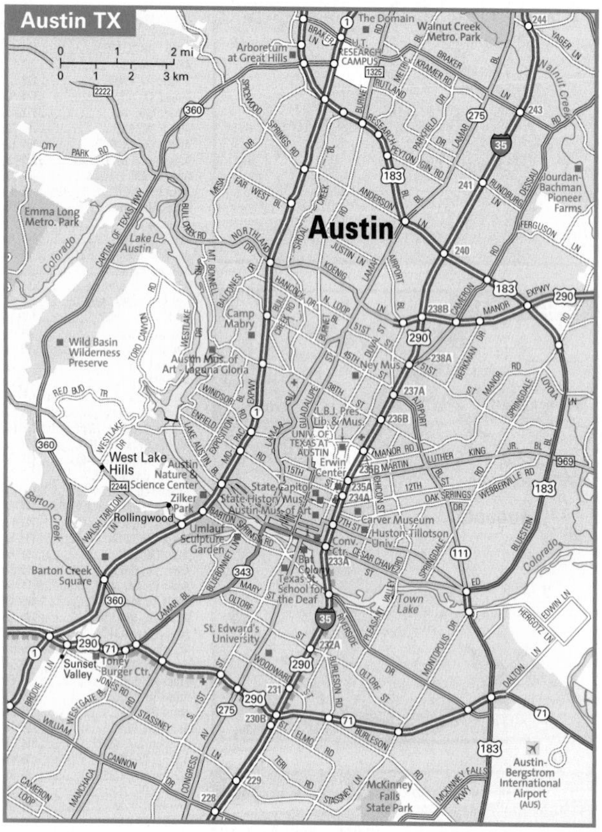

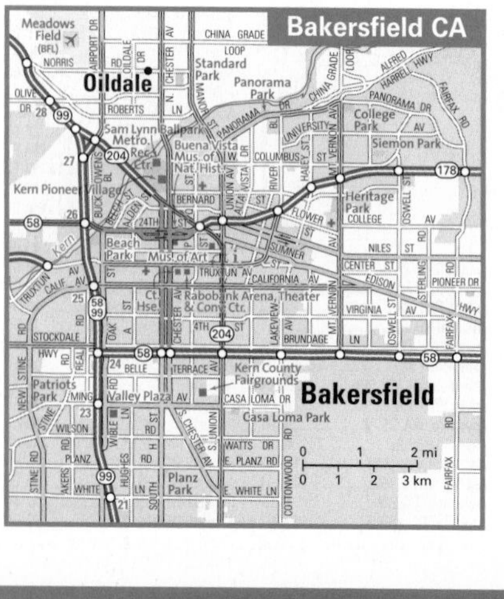

Entries in **bold black** indicate counties or parishes.
Entries in **bold color** indicate cities with detailed inset maps.

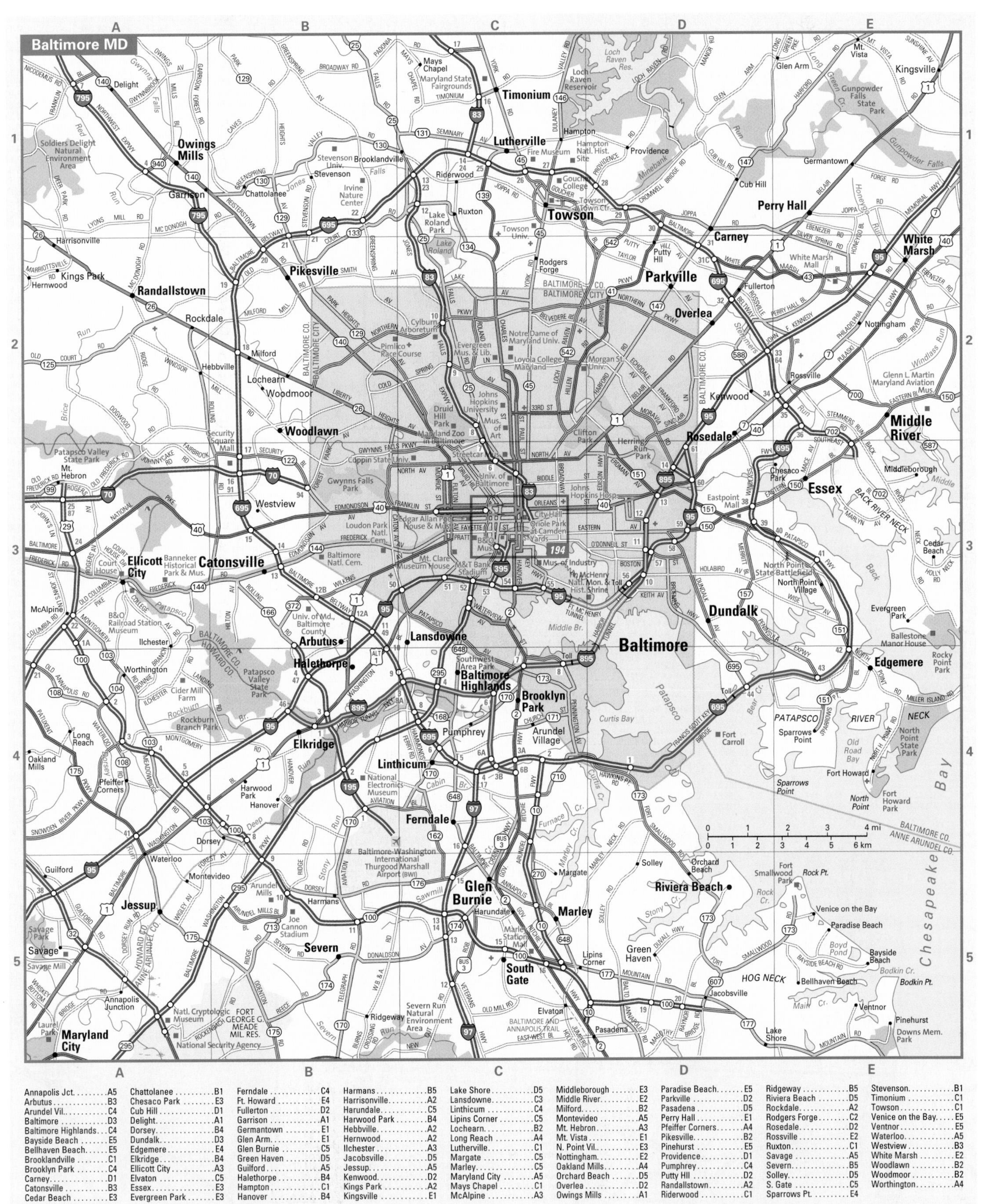

Annapolis Jct. A5
Arbutus B3
Arundel Vil. C4
Baltimore D3
Baltimore Highlands. . .C4
Bayside Beach E5
Bellhaven Beach. E5
Brooklandville C1
Brooklyn Park C4
Carney. D1
Catonsville B3
Cedar Beach E3
Chattolanee B1
Chesaco Park E3
Cub Hill D1
Delight. A1
Dorsey. B4
Dundalk. D3
Edgemere E4
Elkridge. B4
Ellicott City A3
Elvaton C5
Essex. E3
Evergreen Park E3
Ferndale C4
Ft. Howard E4
Fullerton D2
Garrison A1
Germantown E1
Glen Arm. E1
Glen Burnie C5
Green Haven D5
Guilford A5
Halethorpe B4
Hampton C1
Hanover B4
Harmans B5
Harrisonville. A2
Harundale. C5
Harwood Park B4
Hebbville. A2
Hernwood. A2
Ilchester A3
Jacobsville. D5
Jessup. A5
Kenwood. D2
Kings Park A2
Kingsville E1
Lake Shore D5
Lansdowne. C3
Linthicum C4
Lipins Corner C5
Lochearn. B2
Long Reach A4
Lutherville. C1
Margate C5
Marley. C5
Maryland City A5
Mays Chapel C1
McAlpine A3
Middleborough E3
Middle River. E2
Milford. B2
Montevideo A5
Mt. Hebron. A3
Mt. Vista E1
N. Point Vil.. . . . . E3
Nottingham. E2
Oakland Mills. A4
Orchard Beach D5
Overlea D2
Owings Mills A1
Paradise Beach. E5
Parkville D2
Pasadena D5
Perry Hall E1
Pfeiffer Corners. A4
Pikesville. B2
Pinehurst E5
Providence. D1
Pumphrey C4
Putty Hll D2
Randallstown. A2
Riderwood C1
Ridgeway B5
Riviera Beach D5
Rockdale. A2
Rodgers Forge. C2
Rosedale. D2
Rossville E2
Ruxton. C1
Savage A5
Severn. B5
Solley. D5
S. Gate C5
Sparrows Pt. E4
Stevenson. B1
Timonium C1
Towson C1
Venice on the Bay. E5
Ventnor E5
Waterloo. A5
Westview B3
White Marsh E2
Woodlawn B2
Woodmoor B2
Worthington. A4

Figures after entries indicate population, page number, and grid reference.

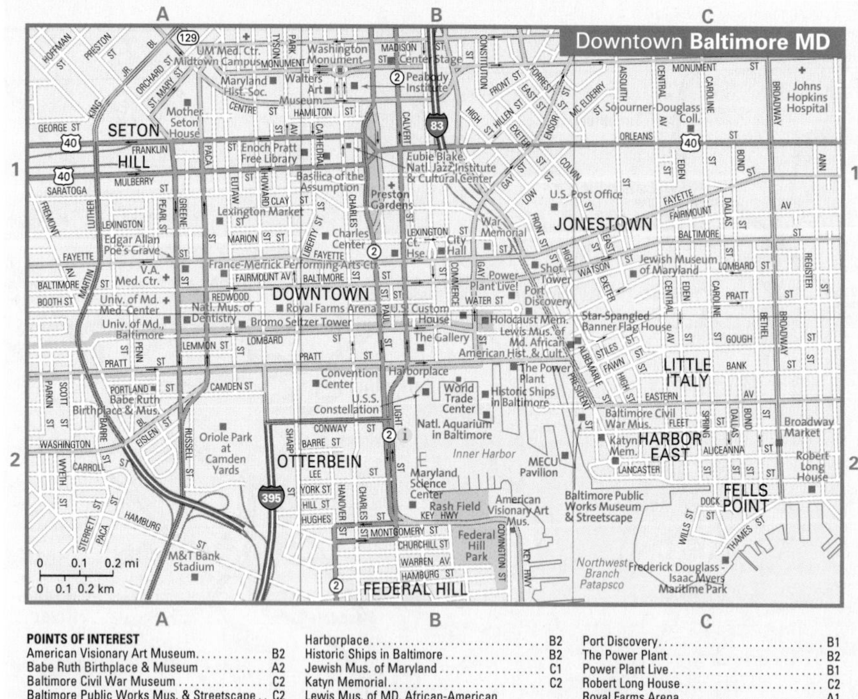

POINTS OF INTEREST

American Visionary Art Museum ... B2
Babe Ruth Birthplace & Museum ... A2
Baltimore Civil War Museum ... C2
Baltimore Public Works Mus. & Streetscape ... C2
Basilica of the Assumption ... B1
Broadway Market ... C2
Bromo Seltzer Tower ... A2
Charles Center ... B1
Convention Center ... B2
Edgar Allan Poe's Grave ... A1
Enoch Pratt Free Library ... A1
Eubie Blake Natl. Jazz Institute & Cult. Ctr. ... B1
France-Merrick Performing Arts Center ... A1
Frederick Douglass-Isaac Myers Maritime Pk. ... C2
The Gallery ... B2
Harborplace ... B2
Historic Ships in Baltimore ... B2
Jewish Mus. of Maryland ... C1
Katyn Memorial ... C2
Lewis Mus. of MD. African-American History & Culture ... B2
Lexington Market ... A1
M&T Bank Stadium ... A2
Maryland Historical Society ... A1
Maryland Science Center ... B2
MECU Pavilion ... B2
Mother Seton House ... A1
National Aquarium in Baltimore ... B2
National Museum of Dentistry ... A2
Oriole Park at Camden Yards ... A2
Peabody Institute ... B1
Port Discovery ... B1
The Power Plant ... B2
Power Plant Live ... B1
Robert Long House ... C2
Royal Farms Arena ... A1
Shot Tower ... B1
Sojourner-Douglas College ... C1
Star-Spangled Banner Flag House ... C2
U.S. Custom House ... B2
Univ. of Maryland, Baltimore ... A2
U.S.S. Constellation ... B2
Walters Art Museum ... B1
War Memorial ... B1
Washington Monument ... B1
World Trade Center ... B2

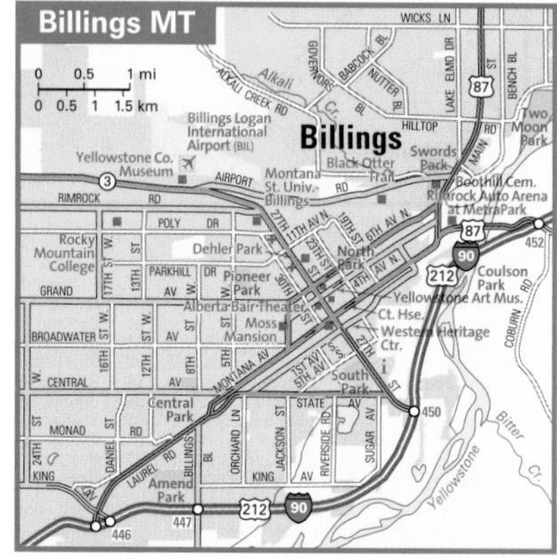

Entries in **bold black** indicate counties or parishes.
Entries in **bold color** indicate cities with detailed inset maps.

Biloxi/Gulfport MS

Birmingham AL

Figures after entries indicate population, page number, and grid reference.

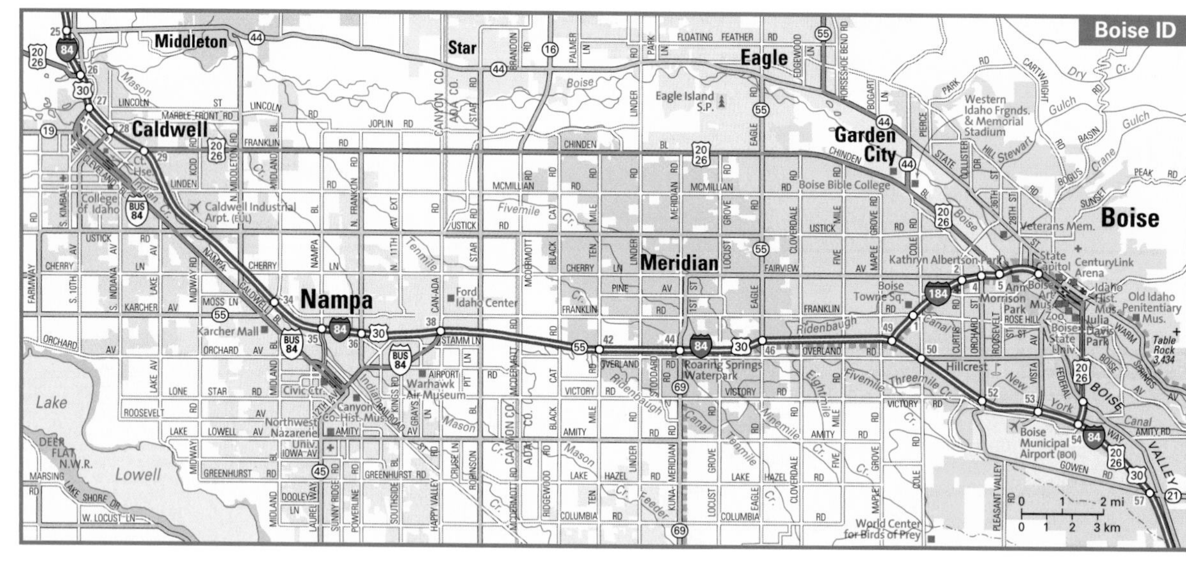

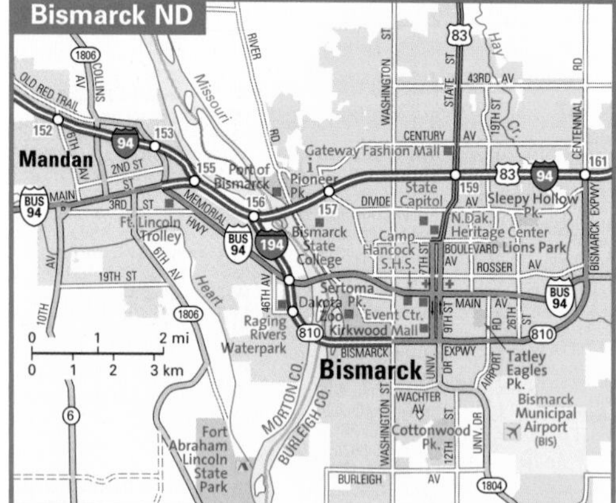

Entries in **bold black** indicate counties or parishes.
Entries in **bold color** indicate cities with detailed inset maps.

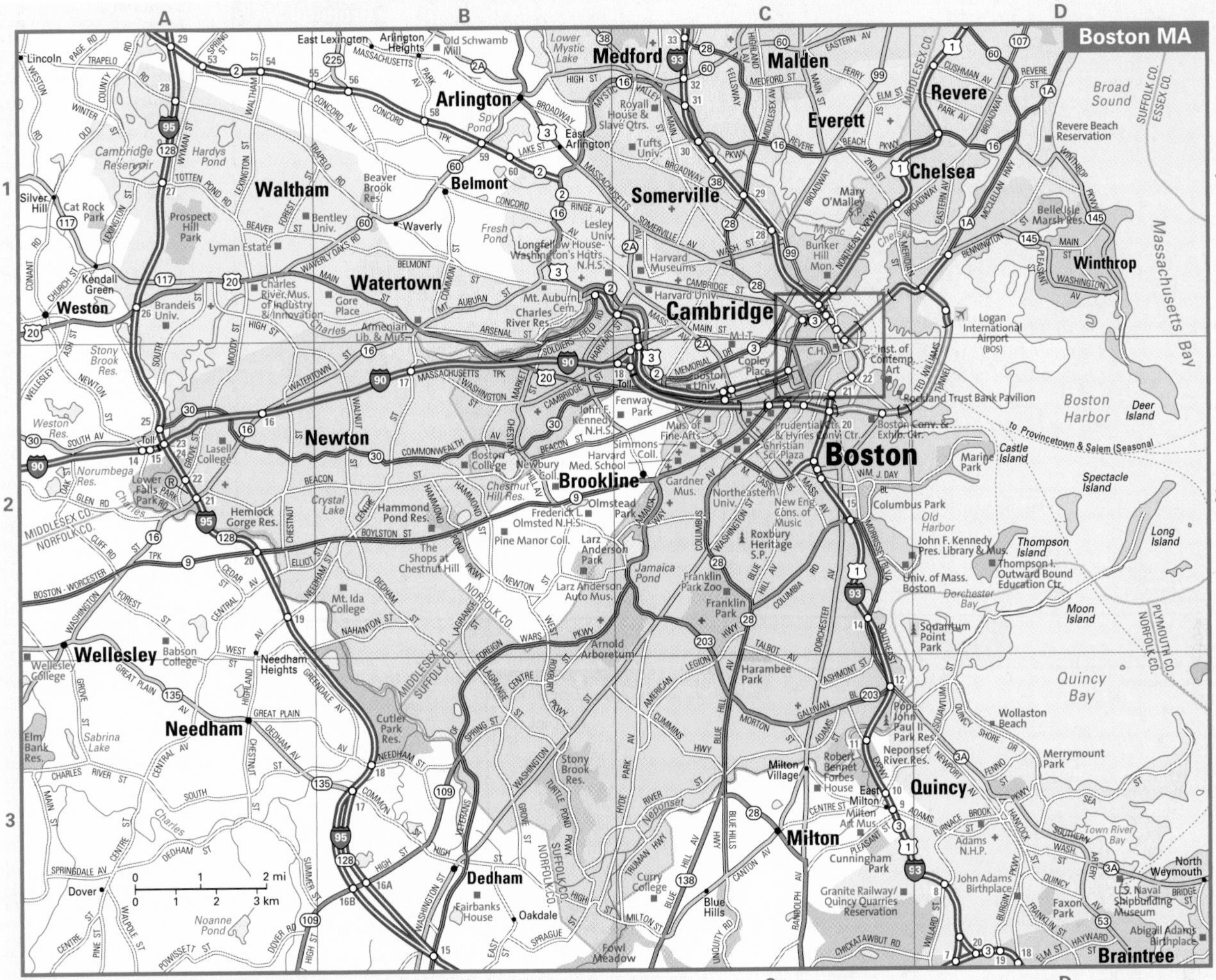

Boston MA

Arlington B1
Arlington Hts. B1
Belmont B1
Blue Hills C3
Boston C2
Brookline C2
Cambridge C1
Chelsea D1
Dedham B3
Dover A3
E. Arlington B1
E. Lexington B1
E. Milton C3
Everett C1
Kendall Green A1
Lincoln A1
Malden C1
Medford C1
Milton C3
Milton Vil. C3
Needham A3
Needham Hts. A2
Newton B2
N. Weymouth D3
Oakdale B3
Quincy D3
Revere D1
Silver Hill A1
Somerville C1
Waltham A1
Watertown B1
Waverly B1
Wellesley A2
Weston A1
Winthrop D1

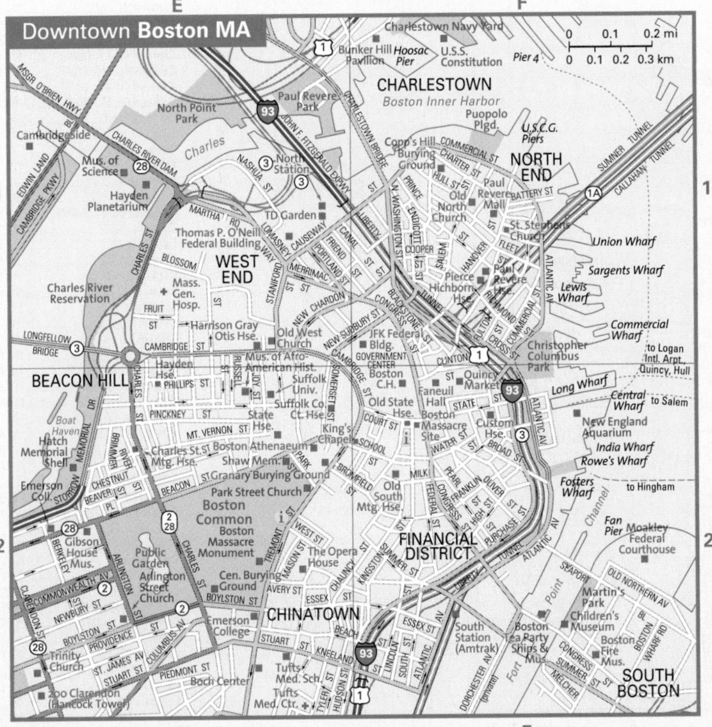

POINTS OF INTEREST

200 Clarendon (Hancock Tower) E2
Arlington Street Church E2
Boch Center E2
Boston Athenaeum E2
Boston City Hall F2
Boston Fire Museum F2
Boston Massacre Monument E2
Boston Massacre Site F2
Boston Tea Party Ships & Museum F2
Bunker Hill Pavilion F1
Central Burying Ground E2
Charles Street Meeting House E2
Children's Museum F2
Copp's Hill Burying Ground F1
Custom House F2
Emerson College E2
Faneuil Hall F2
Gibson House Museum E2
Granary Burying Ground E2
Harrison Gray Otis House E1
Hatch Memorial Shell E2
Hayden House E2
Hayden Planetarium E1
JFK Federal Building F1
King's Chapel E2
Moakley Federal Courthouse F2
Museum of Afro-American Hist. E2
Museum of Science E1
New England Aquarium F2
North Station E1
Old North Church F1
Old South Meeting House F2
Old State House F2
Old West Church E1
The Opera House E2
Park Street Church E2
Paul Revere House F1
Paul Revere Mall F1
Pierce Hichborn House F1
Quincy Market F2
St. Stephens Church F1
Shaw Memorial E2
South Station (Amtrak) F2
State House E2
Suffolk County Court House E2
Suffolk Univ. E1
TD Garden E1
Thomas P. O'Neill Federal Building E1
Trinity Church E2
Suffolk County Court House E2
Tufts Medical School E2
U.S.S. Constitution F1

Figures after entries indicate population, page number, and grid reference.

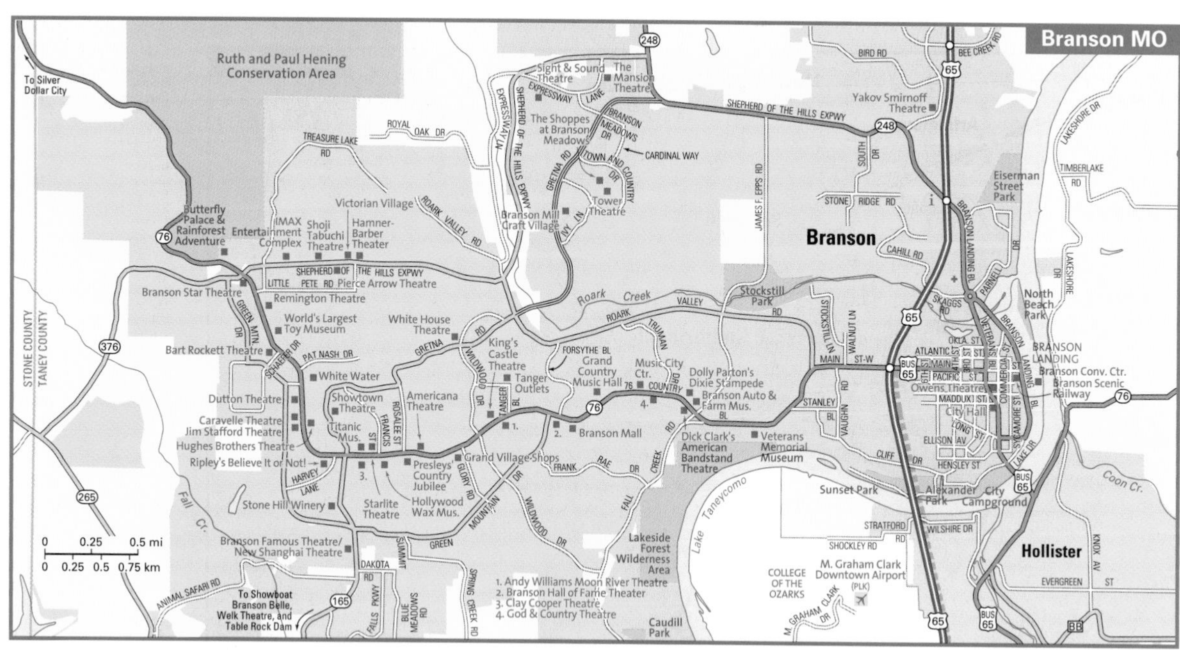

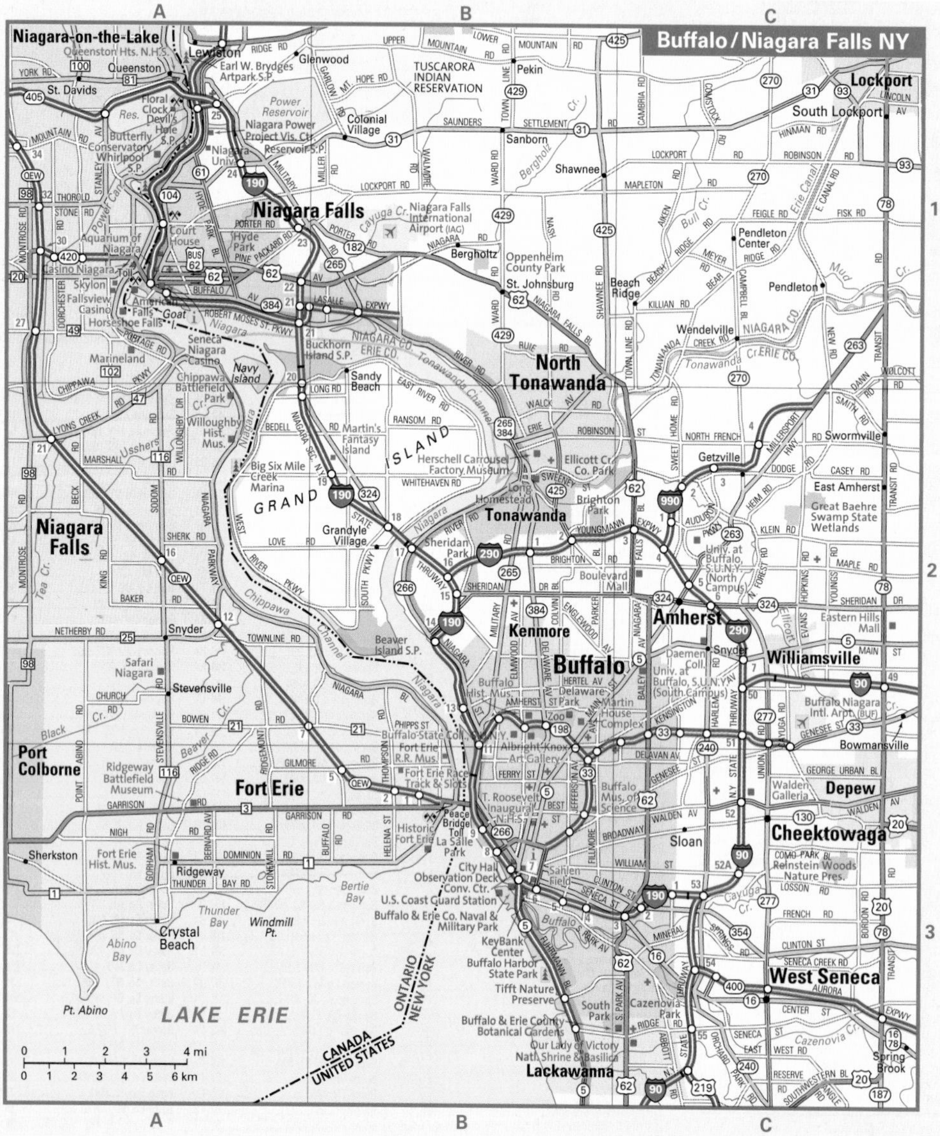

Buffalo / Niagara Falls NY

Entries in **bold black** indicate counties or parishes.
Entries in **bold color** indicate cities with detailed inset maps.

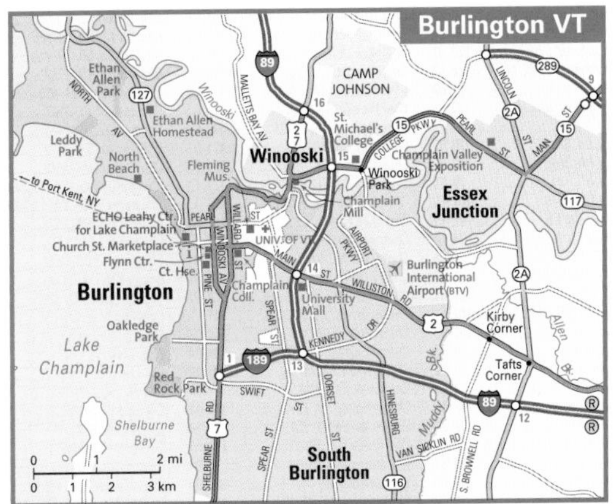

Canton OH

Cairo ... B1	Green ... A1	McDonaldsville ... A1	Perry Hts. ... A2
Canton ... B1	Hills and Dales ... A1	Meyers Lake ... B2	Reedurban ... A2
Crystal Sprs. ... A1	Louisville ... B1	Middlebranch ... B1	Richville ... A2
Fairhope ... B1	Massillon ... A2	N. Canton ... B1	Waco ... B2

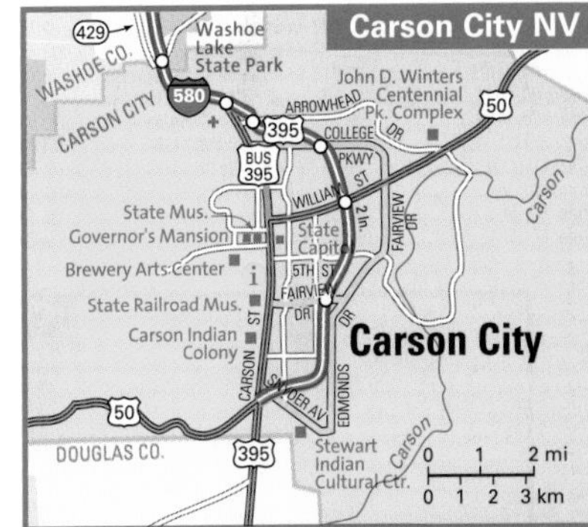

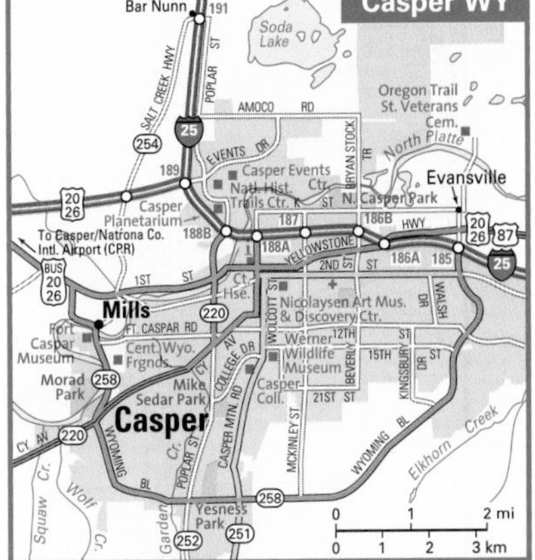

Figures after entries indicate population, page number, and grid reference.

Cedar Rapids IA

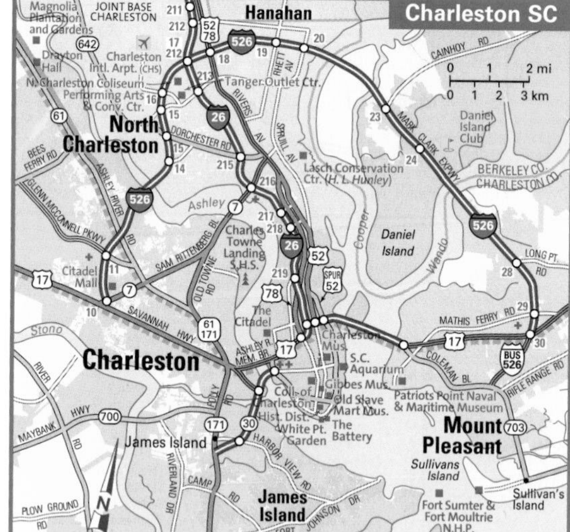

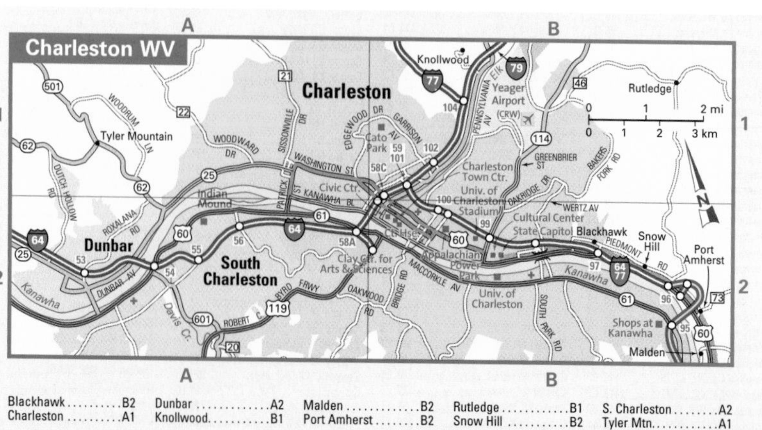

Entries in **bold black** indicate counties or parishes.
Entries in **bold color** indicate cities with detailed inset maps.

Chisholm ME, *1380* ... **82** B2
Chisholm MN, *4976* ... **64** C3
Chittenango NY, *5081* ... **79** E3
Chittenden VT, *1182* ... **81** D3
Chittenden Co. VT, *156545* ... **81** D2
Chocowinity NC, *820* ... **115** D3
Choctaw OK, *11146* ... **51** E3
Choctaw Co. AL, *13859* ... **127** E3
Choctaw Co. MS, *8547* ... **126** C1
Choctaw Co. OK, *15205* ... **116** A3
Choteau MT, *1684* ... **15** E3
Choudrant LA, *845* ... **125** E2
Chouteau OK, *2097* ... **106** A3
Chouteau Co. MT, *5813* ... **15** F2
Chowan Co. NC, *14793* ... **113** F4
Chowchilla CA, *18720* ... **44** C2
Chrisman IL, *1343* ... **99** D1
Chrisney IN, *481* ... **99** E4
Christiana PA, *1168* ... **146** A3
Christian Co. IL, *34800* ... **98** B1
Christian Co. KY, *73955* ... **109** E2
Christian Co. MO, *77422* ... **107** D2
Christiansburg OH, *526* ... **90** B4
Christiansburg VA, *21041* ... **112** A2
Christmas FL, *1146* ... **141** D1
Christopher IL, *2382* ... **98** C4
Chualar CA, *1190* ... **44** B3
Chubbuck ID, *13922* ... **31** E1
Chugwater WY, *212* ... **33** E2
Chuichu AZ, *269* ... **54** C2
Chula Vista CA, *243916* ... **53** D4
Chuluota FL, *2483* ... **141** D1
Church Hill MD, *745* ... **145** D2
Church Hill TN, *6737* ... **111** E3
Churchill OH, *2149* ... **276** C2
Churchill PA, *3011* ... **250** D2
Churchill Co. NV, *24877* ... **37** F1
Church Pt. LA, *4560* ... **133** E2
Church Rock NM, *1128* ... **48** A3
Churchton MD, *1800* ... **144** C3
Churchtown NJ, *3300* ... **146** B4
Churchville MD, *1200* ... **145** D1
Churchville NY, *1961* ... **78** C3
Churubusco IN, *1796* ... **90** A2
Cibecue AZ, *1713* ... **55** D1
Cibola Co. NM, *27213* ... **48** B4
Cibolo TX, *15349* ... **257** F1
Cicero IL, *83891* ... **89** D1
Cicero IN, *4812* ... **89** F4
Cimarron KS, *2184* ... **42** C4
Cimarron NM, *1021* ... **49** E1
Cimarron Co. OK, *2475* ... **50** A1
Cincinnati OH, *296943* ... **100** B2
Cinnaminson NJ, *15569* ... **146** C3
Circle MT, *615* ... **17** E3
Circle Pines MN, *4918* ... **235** C1
Circleville NY, *900* ... **148** A1
Circleville OH, *13314* ... **101** D1
Circleville UT, *547* ... **39** E3
Cisco TX, *3899* ... **59** D3
Cisne IL, *672* ... **98** C3
Cissna Park IL, *846* ... **89** D4
Citra FL, *800* ... **138** C4
Citronelle AL, *3905* ... **135** E1
Citrus Co. FL, *141236* ... **140** B1
Citrus Hts. CA, *83301* ... **36** C3
Citrus Park FL, *24252* ... **266** B1
Citrus Sprs. FL, *8622* ... **138** C4
City View SC, *1345* ... **217** A2
Clackamas OR, *5177* ... **251** D3
Clackamas Co. OR, *375992* ... **20** C2
Claflin KS, *645* ... **43** D3
Claiborne Co. MS, *9604* ... **126** A3
Claiborne Co. TN, *32213* ... **110** C3
Claiborne Par. LA, *17195* ... **125** D2
Clairton PA, *6796* ... **92** A4
Clallam Bay WA, *363* ... **12** B2
Clallam Co. WA, *71404* ... **12** B2
Clancy MT, *1661* ... **15** E4
Clanton AL, *8619* ... **127** F2
Clara City MN, *1360* ... **66** B4
Clare MI, *3118* ... **76** A2
Clare Co. MI, *30926* ... **76** A1
Claremont CA, *34926* ... **229** G2
Claremont MN, *548* ... **73** D1
Claremont NH, *13355* ... **81** E4
Claremont NC, *1352* ... **112** A4
Claremont VA, *378* ... **113** F2
Claremore OK, *18581* ... **106** A3
Clarence IA, *974* ... **87** F1
Clarence LA, *499* ... **125** D3
Clarence MO, *813* ... **97** E1
Clarence PA, *626* ... **92** C3
Clarence Ctr. NY, *2257* ... **78** B3
Clarendon AR, *1664* ... **117** F2
Clarendon TX, *2026* ... **50** B3
Clarendon Co. SC, *34971* ... **122** B4
Clarendon Hills IL, *8427* ... **203** C5
Clarinda IA, *5572* ... **86** B3
Clarion IA, *2850* ... **72** C4
Clarion PA, *5276* ... **92** B2
Clarion Co. PA, *39988* ... **92** A3
Clarissa MN, *681* ... **66** B2
Clark NJ, *14756* ... **147** E1
Clark SD, *1139* ... **27** E2
Clark Co. AR, *22995* ... **117** D4
Clark Co. ID, *982* ... **23** E3
Clark Co. IL, *16335* ... **99** D2
Clark Co. IN, *110232* ... **100** A3
Clark Co. KS, *2215* ... **42** C4
Clark Co. KY, *35613* ... **100** B4
Clark Co. MO, *7139* ... **87** E4
Clark Co. NV, *1951269* ... **46** A1
Clark Co. OH, *138333* ... **100** C1
Clark Co. SD, *3691* ... **27** E2
Clark Co. WA, *425363* ... **20** C1
Clark Co. WI, *34690* ... **67** F4
Clarkdale AZ, *4097* ... **47** D4
Clarke Co. AL, *25833* ... **127** E4
Clarke Co. GA, *116714* ... **121** D4
Clarke Co. IA, *9286* ... **86** C3
Clarke Co. MS, *16732* ... **127** D3
Clarke Co. VA, *14034* ... **103** D2
Clarkesville GA, *1733* ... **121** D2
Clarkfield MN, *863* ... **66** A4
Clark Fork ID, *536* ... **14** B2
Clarks LA, *1017* ... **125** E3
Clarksboro NJ, *2600* ... **146** C3
Clarksburg MD, *13766* ... **144** B2
Clarksburg WV, *16578* ... **102** A2
Clarksdale MS, *17962* ... **118** A3
Clarks Green PA, *1476* ... **261** E1
Clarks Grove MN, *706* ... **72** C2
Clarks Hill IN, *611* ... **89** E4
Clarkson KY, *875* ... **109** F1
Clarkson NE, *658* ... **35** F2
Clarks Summit PA, *5116* ... **93** F2
Clarkston GA, *7554* ... **190** E3

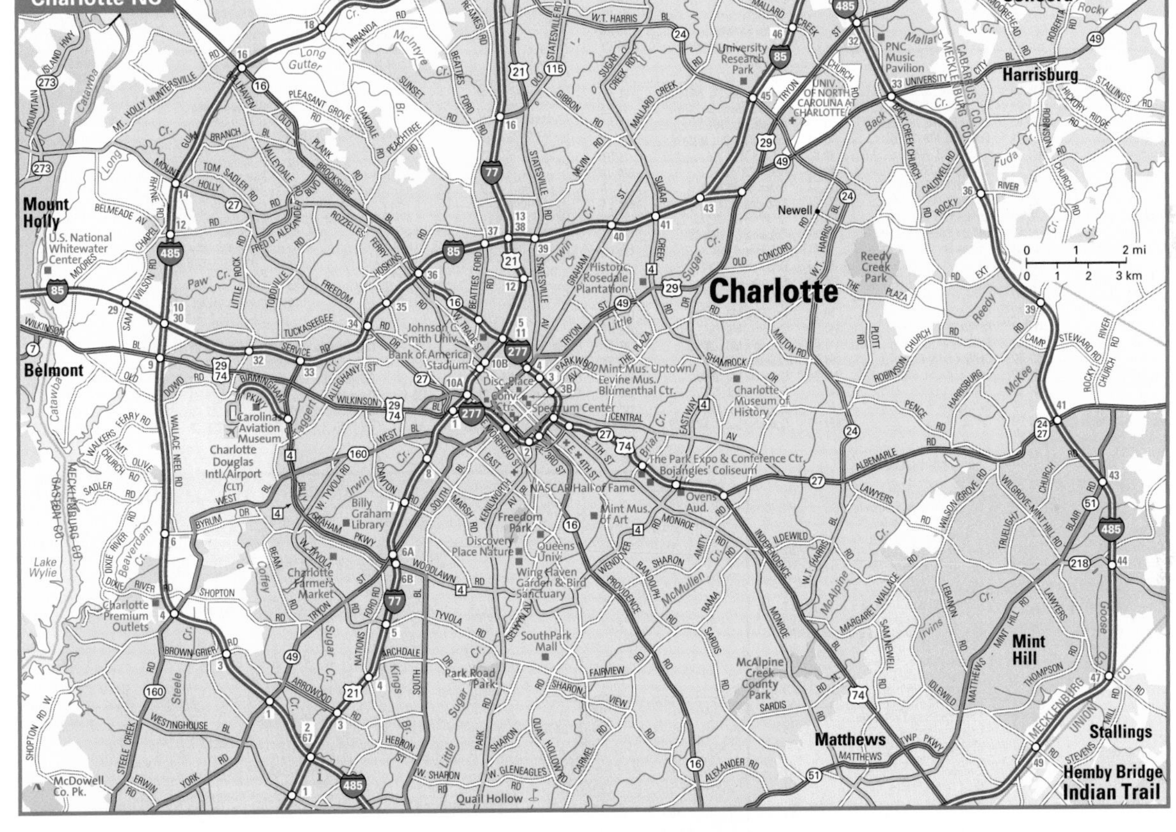

Clarkston UT, *666* ... **31** E2
Clarkston WA, *7229* ... **14** B4
Clarksville AR, *9178* ... **117** D1
Clarksville DE, *900* ... **145** F4
Clarksville IN, *21724* ... **100** A4
Clarksville IA, *1439* ... **73** D4
Clarksville MD, *900* ... **144** B2
Clarksville MO, *442* ... **97** F2
Clarksville TN, *132929* ... **109** E3
Clarksville TX, *3285* ... **116** B4
Clarksville VA, *1139* ... **113** D3
Clarksville City TX, *865* ... **124** B2
Clarkton MO, *1288* ... **108** B3
Clarkton NC, *837* ... **123** D3
Claryville KY, *2355* ... **100** B3
Clatskanie OR, *1737* ... **20** B1
Clatsop Co. OR, *37039* ... **20** B1
Claude TX, *1196* ... **50** B3
Claverack NY, *913* ... **94** B2
Clawson MI, *11825* ... **210** C2
Claxton GA, *2746* ... **130** A3
Clay AL, *9708* ... **119** F4
Clay KY, *1181* ... **109** D1
Clay WV, *491* ... **101** F3
Clay Ctr. KS, *4334* ... **43** E2
Clay Ctr. NE, *760* ... **35** E4
Clay City IL, *959* ... **99** D3
Clay City IN, *861* ... **99** E2
Clay City KY, *1077* ... **110** C1
Claycomo MO, *1430* ... **224** C2
Clay Co. AL, *13932* ... **128** B1
Clay Co. AR, *16083* ... **108** A3
Clay Co. FL, *190865* ... **139** D3
Clay Co. GA, *3183* ... **128** C4
Clay Co. IL, *13815* ... **98** C3
Clay Co. IN, *26890* ... **99** E2
Clay Co. IA, *16667* ... **72** B3
Clay Co. KS, *8535* ... **43** E2
Clay Co. KY, *21730* ... **110** C2
Clay Co. MN, *58999* ... **19** F4
Clay Co. MS, *20634* ... **118** C4
Clay Co. MO, *221939* ... **96** B2
Clay Co. NE, *6542* ... **35** E4
Clay Co. NC, *10587* ... **121** D1
Clay Co. SD, *13864* ... **35** F1
Clay Co. TN, *7861* ... **110** A3
Clay Co. TX, *10752* ... **59** D1
Clay Co. WV, *9386* ... **101** F3
Clayhatchee AL, *589* ... **128** B4
Claymont DE, *8253* ... **146** B3
Claypool AZ, *1538* ... **55** D1
Claypool Hill VA, *1776* ... **111** F2
Claysburg PA, *1625* ... **92** C4
Claysville PA, *829* ... **91** F4
Clayton AL, *3008* ... **128** B3
Clayton CA, *10897* ... **259** E2
Clayton DE, *2918* ... **145** E2
Clayton GA, *2047* ... **121** D2
Clayton IL, *709* ... **87** F4
Clayton IN, *972* ... **99** F1
Clayton LA, *711* ... **125** F4
Clayton MO, *15939* ... **98** A3
Clayton NJ, *8179* ... **146** C4
Clayton NM, *2980* ... **49** F1
Clayton NY, *1978* ... **79** E1
Clayton NC, *16116* ... **113** D4
Clayton OH, *13209* ... **100** B1
Clayton OK, *821* ... **116** A2
Clayton Co. GA, *259424* ... **120** C4
Clayton Co. IA, *18129* ... **73** F3
Clearbrook MN, *518* ... **64** A3
Clear Creek IN, *1800* ... **99** F2
Clear Creek Co. CO, *9088* ... **41** D1
Clearfield PA, *6215* ... **92** C3
Clearfield UT, *30112* ... **31** E3
Clearfield Co. PA, *81642* ... **92** C3
Clearlake CA, *15250* ... **36** B2
Clear Lake IA, *7777* ... **72** C3
Clear Lake SD, *1273* ... **27** F3
Clear Lake WA, *1002* ... **12** C2
Clear Lake WI, *1070* ... **67** E3
Clearlake Oaks CA, *2359* ... **36** B2
Clear Lake Shores TX, *1063* ... **132** B3
Clear Spr. MD, *358* ... **103** D1
Clearview WV, *565* ... **91** F4
Clearwater FL, *107685* ... **140** B2
Clearwater KS, *2481* ... **43** E4
Clearwater MN, *1735* ... **66** C3
Clearwater SC, *4370* ... **121** F4
Clearwater Co. ID, *8761* ... **14** C4
Clearwater Co. MN, *8695* ... **64** A3
Cleaton KY, *500* ... **109** E2
Cleburne TX, *29337* ... **59** E3
Cleburne Co. AL, *14972* ... **120** B4
Cleburne Co. AR, *25970* ... **107** E4
Cle Elum WA, *1872* ... **13** D3
Clementon NJ, *5000* ... **146** C3
Clemmons NC, *18627* ... **112** A4
Clemson SC, *13905* ... **121** E2
Clendenin WV, *1227* ... **101** F3
Cleona PA, *2080* ... **93** E4
Cleora OK, *1463* ... **106** B3
Clermont FL, *28742* ... **140** C1
Clermont IN, *1356* ... **99** F1
Clermont IA, *632* ... **73** E3
Clermont Co. OH, *197363* ... **100** C2
Cleveland AL, *1303* ... **119** F3
Cleveland FL, *2990* ... **140** C4
Cleveland GA, *3410* ... **121** D2
Cleveland MN, *719* ... **72** C1
Cleveland MS, *12334* ... **118** A4
Cleveland MO, *661* ... **96** B3
Cleveland NY, *750* ... **79** E3
Cleveland NC, *871* ... **112** A4
Cleveland OH, *396815* ... **91** E2
Cleveland OK, *3251* ... **51** F2
Cleveland TN, *41285* ... **120** B1
Cleveland TX, *7675* ... **132** B2
Cleveland UT, *464* ... **39** F2
Cleveland WI, *1485* ... **75** D2
Cleveland Co. AR, *8689* ... **117** E4
Cleveland Co. NC, *98078* ... **121** F1
Cleveland Co. OK, *255755* ... **51** E3
Cleveland Hts. OH, *46121* ... **91** E2
Clever MO, *2139* ... **107** D2
Cleves OH, *3234* ... **100** B2
Clewiston FL, *7155* ... **141** E4
Cliffside NC, *611* ... **121** F1
Cliffside Park NJ, *23594* ... **148** B3
Cliffwood Beach NJ, *3194* ... **147** E1
Clifton AZ, *3311* ... **55** E2
Clifton CO, *19889* ... **40** B2
Clifton ID, *259* ... **31** E2
Clifton IL, *1468* ... **89** D3
Clifton KS, *554* ... **43** E1
Clifton NJ, *84136* ... **148** B3
Clifton TN, *2694* ... **119** D1
Clifton TX, *3442* ... **59** E4
Clifton Forge VA, *3884* ... **112** B1
Clifton Hts. PA, *6652* ... **248** B3
Clifton Park NY, *4600* ... **94** B1
Clifton Sprs. NY, *2127* ... **78** C3
Climax MI, *767* ... **75** F4
Clinchco VA, *337* ... **111** E2
Clinch Co. GA, *6798* ... **138** C1
Clint TX, *926* ... **56** C4

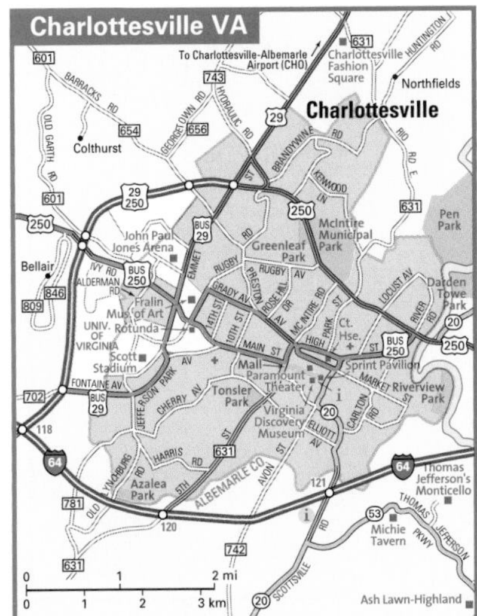

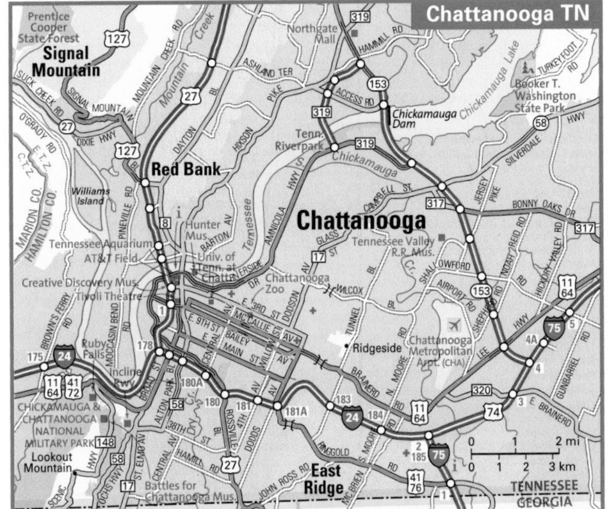

Figures after entries indicate population, page number, and grid reference.

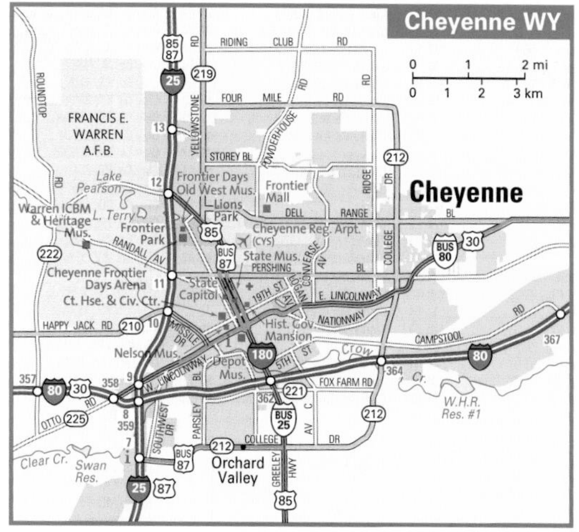

CHICAGO MAP INDEX

Addison ... C4
Algonquin ... A2
Alsip ... D6
Arlington Hts. ... C2
Aurora ... A5
Bannockburn ... C2
Barrington ... B2
Barrington Hills ... A2
Bartlett ... A3
Batavia ... A4
Bedford Park ... D5
Bellwood ... C4
Bensenville ... C4
Berkeley ... C4
Berwyn ... D4
Bloomingdale ... B3
Blue Island ... D6
Bolingbrook ... B6
Bridgeview ... D5
Broadview ... C4
Brookfield ... C5
Buffalo Grove ... C2
Burbank ... D5
Burnham ... E6
Burr Ridge ... C5
Burtons Bridge ... A1
Calumet City ... E6
Calumet Park ... E6
Carol Stream ... B4
Carpentersville ... A2
Cary ... A2
Chicago ... E4
Chicago Ridge ... D5
Cicero ... D4
Clarendon Hills ... C5
Countryside ... C5
Crest Hill ... B6
Crestwood ... D6
Crystal Lake ... A1
Darien ... C5
Deerfield ... C2
Deer Park ... B2
Des Plaines ... C3
Diamond Lake ... B1
Dixmoor ... E6
Dolton ... E6
Downers Grove ... B5
E. Dundee ... A2
Elgin ... A3
Elk Grove Vil. ... C3
Elmhurst ... C4
Elmwood Park ... D4
Evanston ... D3
Evergreen Park ... D5
Forest Lake ... B1
Forest Park ... D4
Forest View ... D5
Fox River Grove ... A2
Franklin Park ... C4
Geneva ... A4
Glencoe ... D2
Glendale Hts. ... B4
Glen Ellyn ... B4
Glenview ... D2
Golf ... D3
Grayslake ... B1
Green Oaks ... C1
Hanover Park ... B3
Harvey ... E6
Harwood Hts. ... D3
Hawthorn Woods ... B1
Hazel Crest ... E6
Hickory Hills ... D5
Highland Park ... D2
Highwood ... D1
Hillside ... C4
Hinsdale ... C5
Hodgkins ... C5
Hoffman Estates ... B3
Holiday Hills ... A1
Homer Glen ... C6
Hometown ... D5
Indian Creek ... C1
Indian Head Park ... C5
Inverness ... B2
Island Lake ... A1
Itasca ... B3
Ivanhoe ... B1
Justice ... D5
Kenilworth ... D2
Kildeer ... B2
Knollwood ... C1
La Grange ... C5
La Grange Park ... C4
Lake Barrington ... B1
Lake Bluff ... C1
Lake Forest ... C1
Lake in the Hills ... A2
Lakemoor ... A1
Lake Zurich ... B2
Lemont ... B6
Libertyville ... C1
Lincolnshire ... C2
Lincolnwood ... D3
Lisle ... B5
Lockport ... B6
Lombard ... B4
Long Grove ... C2
Lyons ... D5
Markham ... D6
Maywood ... C4
McCook ... D5
McHenry ... A1
Medinah ... B3
Melrose Park ... C4
Merrionette Park ... D6
Mettawa ... C1
Midlothian ... D6
Montgomery ... A5
Morton Grove ... D3
Mount Prospect ... C3
Mundelein ... B1
Naperville ... B5
Niles ... D3
Norridge ... D3
N. Aurora ... A5
N. Barrington ... B2
Northbrook ... D2
N. Chicago ... C1
Northfield ... D2
Northlake ... C4
N. Riverside ... D4
Oak Brook ... C4
Oakbrook Terrace ... C4
Oak Forest ... D6
Oak Lawn ... D5
Oak Park ... D4
Oakwood Hills ... A1
Orland Hills ... C6
Orland Park ... C6
Oswego ... A5
Palatine ... B2
Palos Hts. ... D6
Palos Hills ... D5
Palos Park ... D6
Park Ridge ... C3
Phoenix ... E6
Plainfield ... A6
Port Barrington ... A1
Posen ... D6
Prairie Grove ... A1
Prospect Hts. ... C2
Riverdale ... E6
River Forest ... D4
River Grove ... D4
Riverside ... D4
Riverwoods ... C2
Robbins ... D6
Rolling Meadows ... B3
Romeoville ... B6
Rondout ... C1
Roselle ... B3
Rosemont ... C3
St. Charles ... A4
Schaumburg ... B3
Schiller Park ... C3
Skokie ... D3
Sleepy Hollow ... A2
S. Barrington ... B2
S. Elgin ... A3
S. Holland ... E6
Stickney ... D5
Stone Park ... C4
Streamwood ... B3
Summit ... D5
Tinley Park ... D6
Tower Lakes ... B1
Trout Valley ... A1
Valley View ... A3
Vernon Hills ... C1
Villa Park ... C4
Volo ... B1
Warrenville ... A4
Wauconda ... B1
Wayne ... A4
Westchester ... C4
W. Chicago ... A4
W. Dundee ... A2
Western Sprs. ... C5
Westmont ... C5
Wheaton ... B4
Wheeling ... C2
Willowbrook ... C5
Willow Sprs. ... C5
Wilmette ... D3
Winfield ... B4
Winnetka ... D2
Wood Dale ... C3
Woodridge ... B5
Worth ... D6

POINTS OF INTEREST

875 N. Michigan Av. (John Hancock Ctr.) ... B1
900 North Michigan Shops ... B1
Adler Planetarium & Astronomy Museum ... C3
American Writers Museum ... B2
Art Institute of Chicago ... B2
Auditorium Building ... B2
Buckingham Fountain ... B2
Cadillac Palace Theatre ... B2
Centennial Fountain & Arc ... B2
Chicago Architecture Foundation ... B2
Chicago Board of Trade ... B2
Chicago Children's Museum ... C1
Chicago Cultural Center ... B2
Chicago Fire Marker ... A3
Chicago Mercantile Exchange ... A2
Chicago Stock Exchange ... B2
Chicago Theatre ... B2
Chicago Yacht Club ... C2
CIBC Theatre ... B2
City Hall ... B2
Civic Opera House ... A2
Cloud Gate ... B2
Credit Union 1 Arena ... A3
Crown Fountain ... B2
Daley Plaza ... B2
Dearborn Station ... B3
East-West University ... B3
The Field Museum ... C3
Ford Center for the Performing Arts ... B2
Goodman Theatre ... B2
Harris Theater ... B2
Harold Washington Library Center ... B2
Huntington Bank Pavilion at Northerly Island ... C3
James R. Thompson Center ... B2
Jane Addams' Hull House Mus. ... A3
John G. Shedd Aquarium ... C3
Merchandise Mart ... A2
Monadnock Building ... B2
Moody Bible Institute ... B1
Mus. of Broadcast Communications ... B2
Mus. of Contemporary Art ... B1
Mus. of Contemporary Photography ... B3
Navy Pier ... C1
Newberry Library ... B1
New Maxwell Street Market ... A3
Northwestern Univ. (Chi. Campus) ... C1
Petrillo Band Shell ... B2
Pritzker Pavillion ... B2
The Shops at North Bridge ... B1
Soldier Field ... C3
Spertus Institute ... B3
Symphony Center ... B2
Tribune Tower ... B1
Trump Intl. Hotel & Tower ... B2
Union Station ... A2
Univ. of Illinois at Chicago ... A3
Water Tower ... B1
Water Tower Place ... B1
Willis Tower ... A2
Wrigley Building ... B1

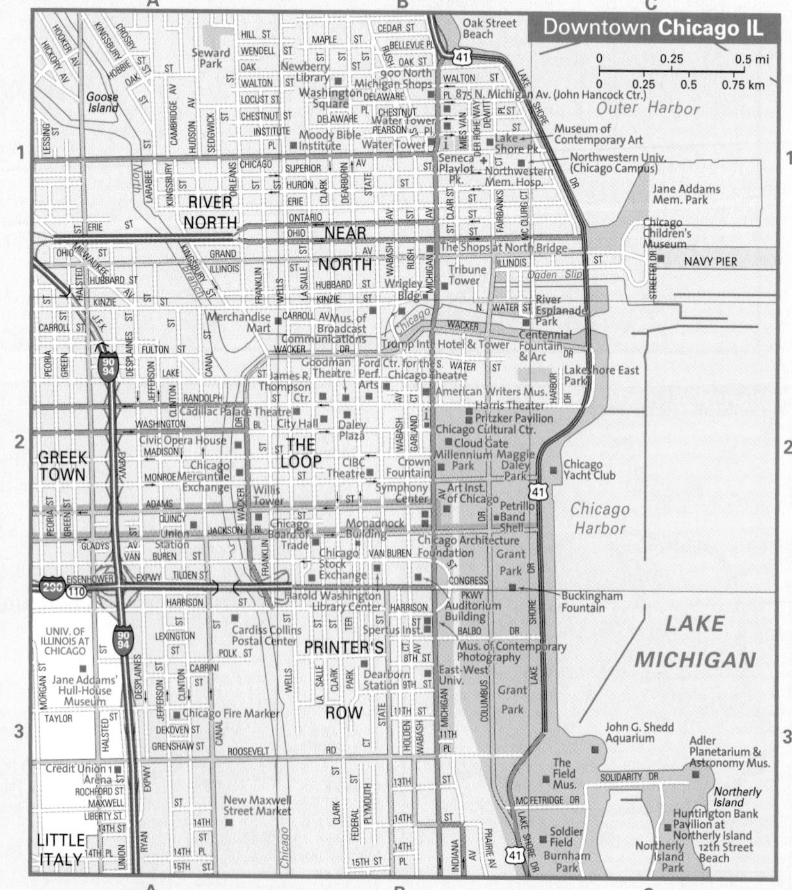

Entries in **bold black** indicate counties or parishes.
Entries in **bold color** indicate cities with detailed inset maps.

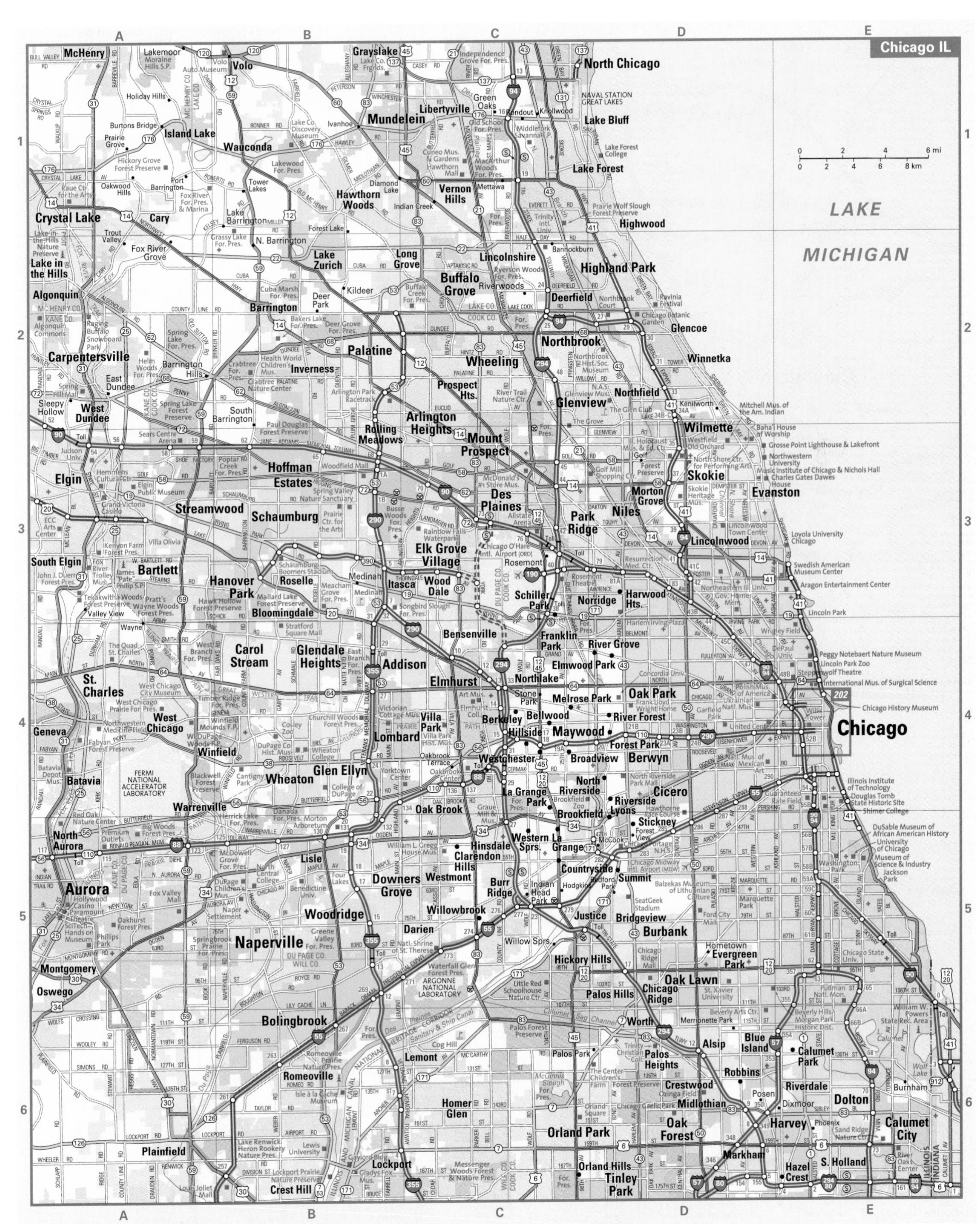

Figures after entries indicate population, page number, and grid reference.

Cincinnati OH

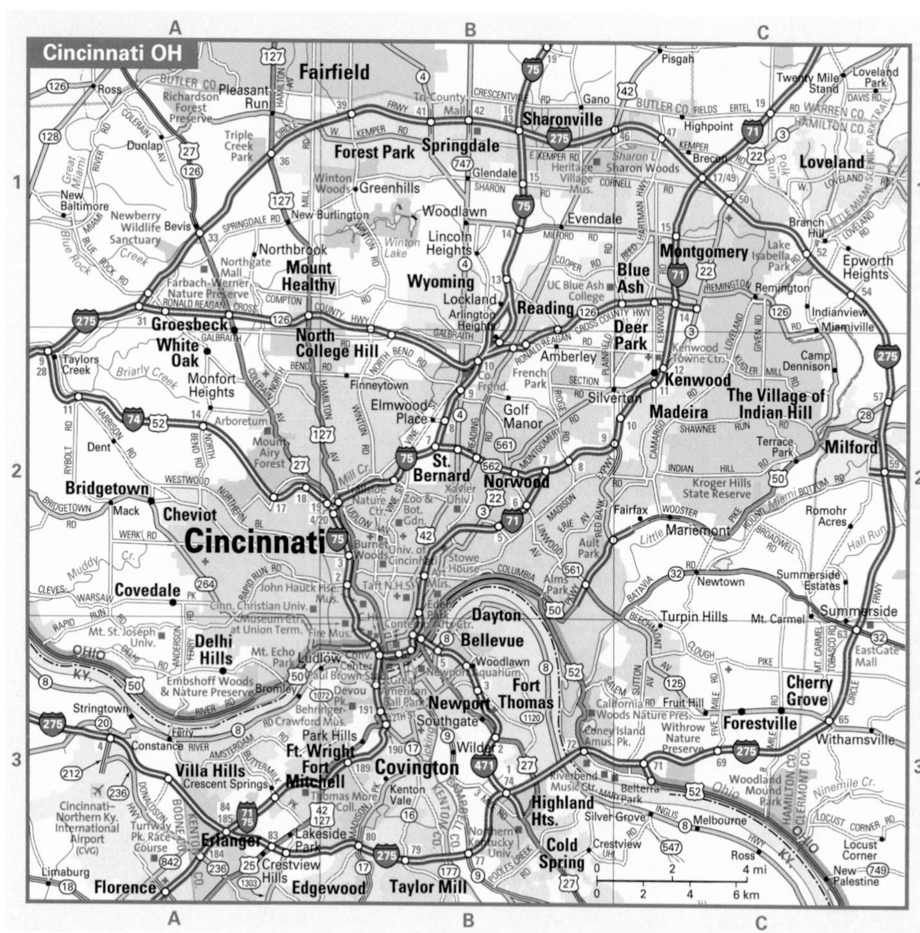

Cleveland OH

Entries in **bold black** indicate counties or parishes.
Entries in **bold color** indicate cities with detailed inset maps.

Black Forest........ D1
Cascade............ C1
Chipita Park C1
Colorado Sprs....... D1
Crystola............ C1
Fountain D2
Green Mtn. Falls C1
Manitou Sprs. C2
Security-Widefield .. D2
Stratmoor Hills...... D2

Arcadia Lakes F1
Arthurtown..............F2
Cayce E2
Columbia...............F2
Denny Terrace..........E1
Dentsville F1
Dixiana E2
Forest Acres F1
Olympia................E2
Pineridge E2
St. Andrews............E1
Springdale E2
W. Columbia............E2

POINTS OF INTEREST
Burke-Lakefront Airport........................B1
Cleveland Arcade...............................A2
Cleveland Police Museum........................A1
Cleveland State University.....................B2
Convention Center..............................A1
FirstEnergy Stadium............................A1
Galleria at Erieview...........................B1
Great Lakes Science Center.....................A1
International Women's Air & Space Museum.......B1
Jacobs Pavilion at Nautica.....................A1
Playhouse Square...............................B2
Progressive Field..............................A2
Quicken Loans Arena............................A2
Rock and Roll Hall of Fame & Museum............A1
Tower City Center..............................A2
U.S.S. Cod.....................................B1
West Side Market...............................A2
William G. Mather Museum.......................A1

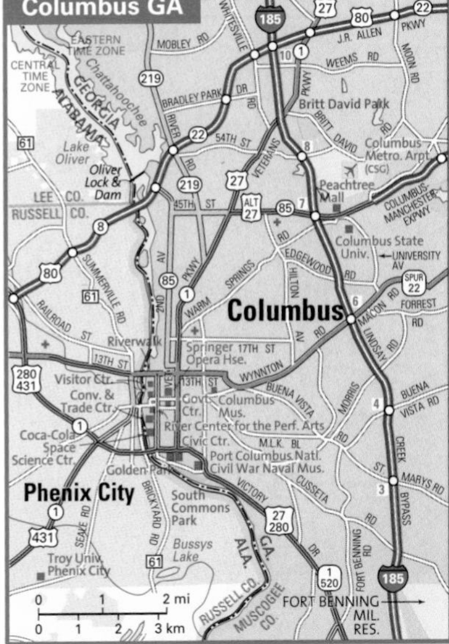

Figures after entries indicate population, page number, and grid reference.

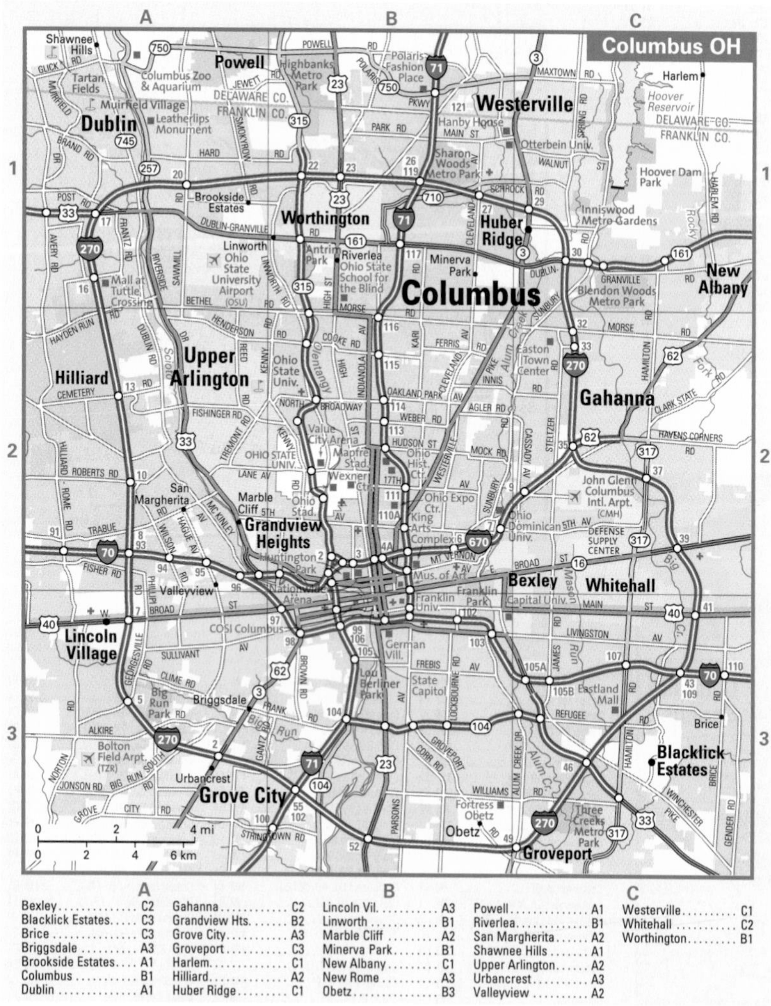

Concord NH

Corpus Christi TX

Entries in **bold black** indicate counties or parishes.
Entries in **bold color** indicate cities with detailed inset maps.

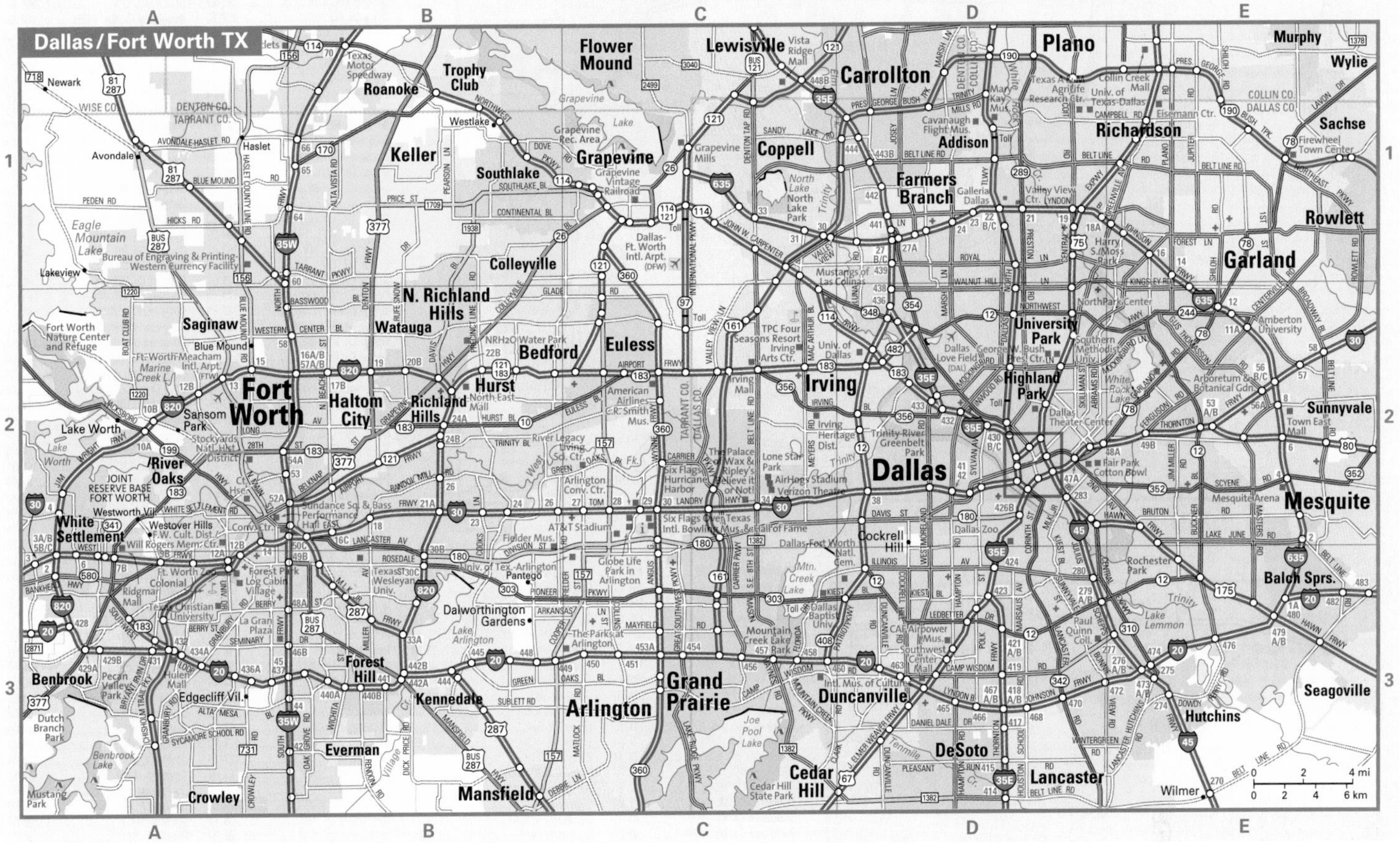

Dallas/Fort Worth TX

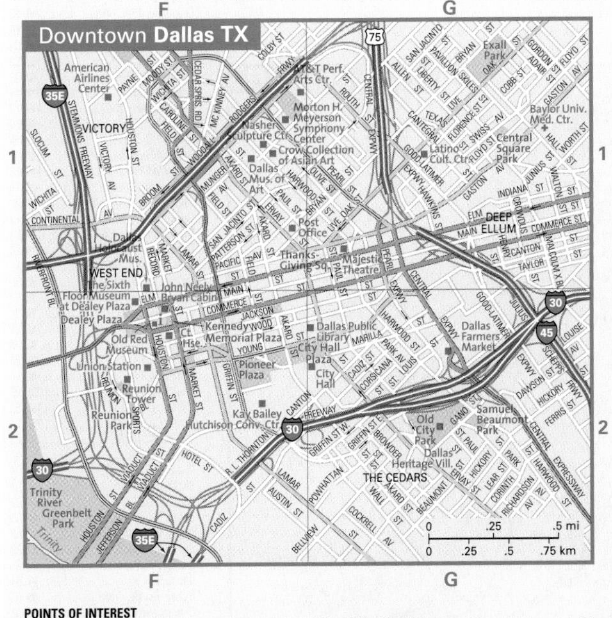

POINTS OF INTEREST

Figures after entries indicate population, page number, and grid reference.

Barstow C2
Bettendorf B1
Buffalo A2
Carbon Cliff C2
Cleveland C2
Coal Valley B2
Colona C2
Davenport A1
E. Moline B1
Hampton C1
Le Claire C1
Milan B2
Moline B2
Panorama Park B1
Port Byron C1
Rapids City C1
Riverdale B1
Rock Island A2
Silvis C2

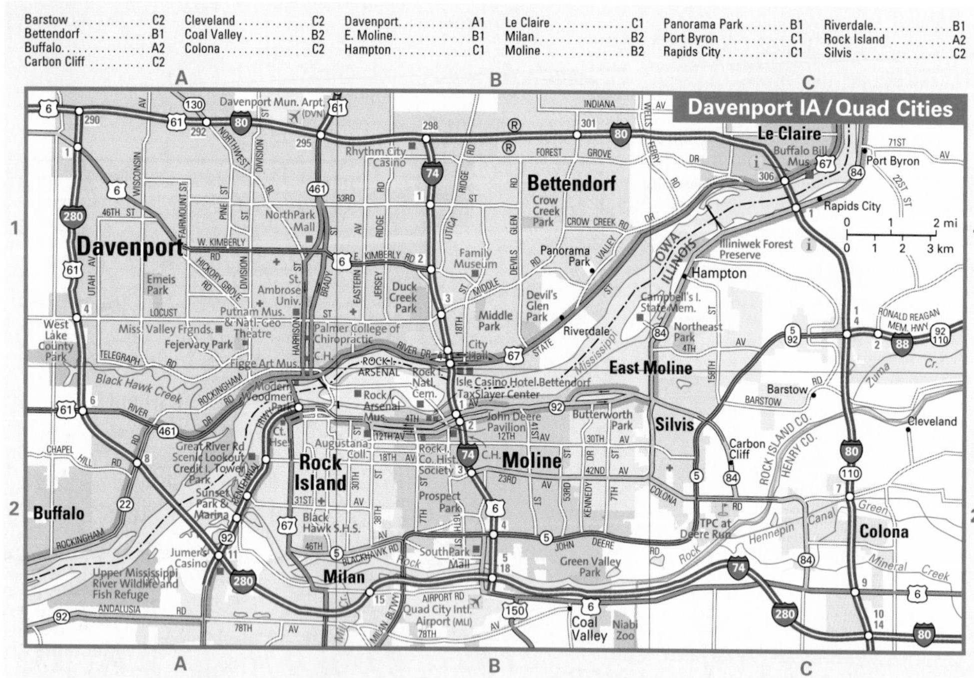

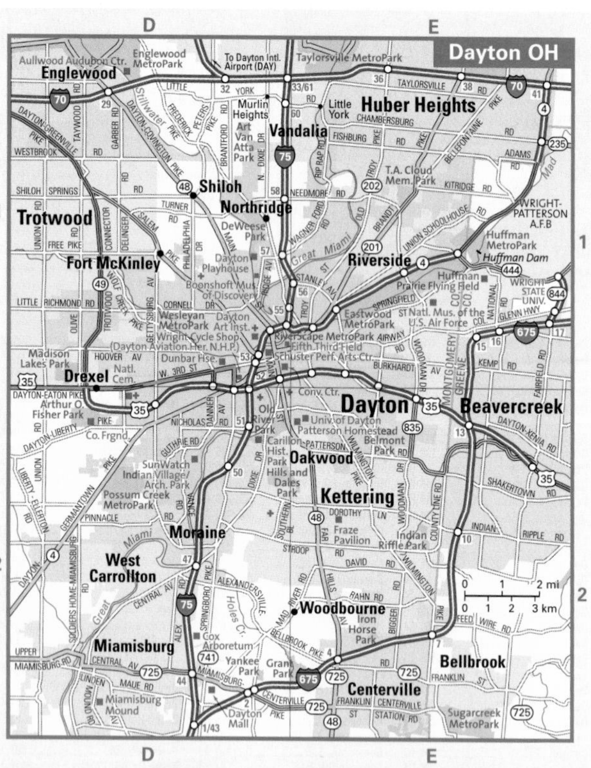

Beavercreek E2
Bellbrook E2
Centerville E2
Dayton E2
Drexel D1
Englewood D1
Ft. McKinley D1
Huber Hts. E1
Kettering E2
Little York E1
Miamisburg D2
Moraine D2
Murlin Hts. D1
Northridge D1
Oakwood E2
Riverside E1
Shiloh D1
Trotwood D1
Vandalia E1
W. Carrollton D2
Woodbourne E2

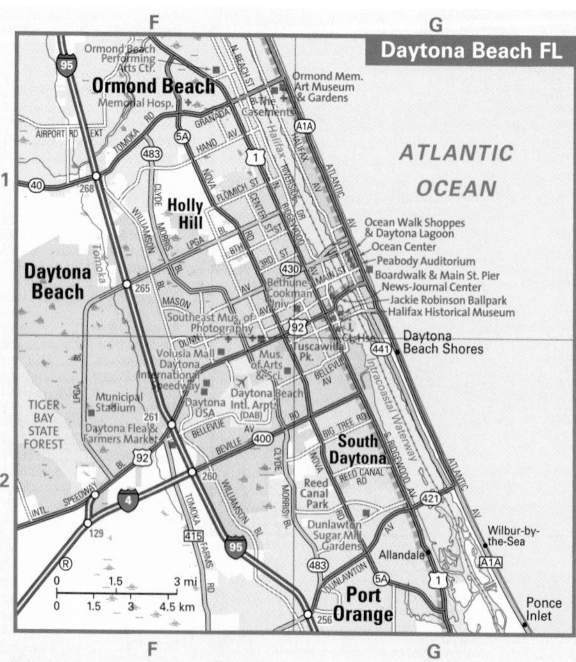

Allandale G2
Daytona Beach F1
Daytona Beach Shores G2
Holly Hill F1
Ormond Beach F1
Ponce Inlet G2
Port Orange G2
S. Daytona G2
Wilbur-by-the-Sea G2

Denver CO

Applewood........... B3
Arvada............... B2
Aspen Park........... A4
Aurora............... D3
Bergen Park.......... A3
Boulder.............. A1
Bow Mar.............. B4
Brighton............. D1
Broomfield........... B1
Centennial........... C4
Cherry Hills Vil..... C4
Columbine Valley..... B4
Commerce City........ C2
Denver............... C3
Dupont............... C2
Edgewater............ B3
Eldorado Sprs........ A1
El Rancho............ A3
Englewood............ C3
Erie................. B1
Evergreen............ A4
Federal Hts.......... B2
Foxfield............. D4
Glendale............. C3
Golden............... A3
Greenwood Vil........ C4
Henderson............ C2
Highlands Ranch...... C4
Idledale............. A3
Indian Hills......... A4
Kittredge............ A4
Lafayette............ B1
Lakeside............. B3
Lakewood............. B3
Littleton............ B4
Lochbuie............. D1
Lone Tree............ C4
Louisville........... B1
Morrison............. A4
Mtn. View............ B3
Northglenn........... C2
Parker............... D4
Pleasant View........ B3
Sheridan............. B4
Superior............. B1
Thornton............. C1
Watkins.............. D3
Wattenberg........... C1
Welby................ C2
Westminster.......... B2
Wheat Ridge.......... B3

Downtown Denver CO

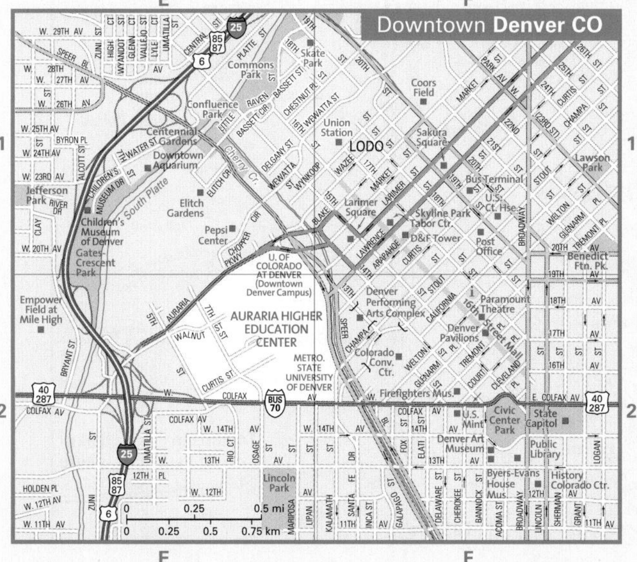

POINTS OF INTEREST

16th Street Mall................ F2
Auraria Higher Education Center........ E2
Bus Terminal................ F1
Byers-Evans House................ F2
Children's Museum of Denver................ E1
Colorado Convention Center................ F2
Coors Field................ F1
D&F Tower................ F1
Denver Art Museum................ F2
Denver Pavilions................ F2
Denver Performing Arts Complex................ F2
Downtown Aquarium................ E1
Elitch Gardens................ E1
Empower Field at Mile High................ E2
Firefighters Museum................ F2
History Colorado Center................ F2
Larimer Square................ F1
LoDo................ F1
Metropolitan State Coll. of Denver................ E2
Paramount Theatre................ F2
Pepsi Center................ E1
Post Office................ F1
Public Library................ F2
Sakura Square................ F1
Skate Park................ E1
State Capitol................ F2
Tabor Center................ F1
Union Station................ F1
U.S. Court House................ F1
U.S. Mint................ F2
Univ. of Colorado at Denver (Downtown Denver Campus)................ E2

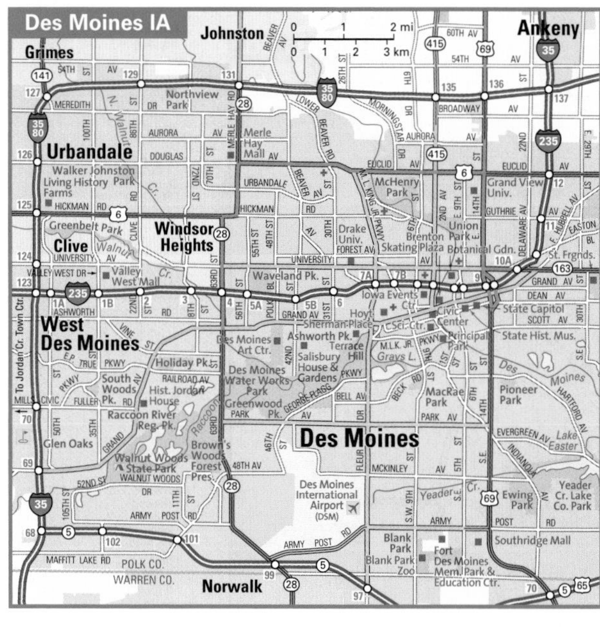

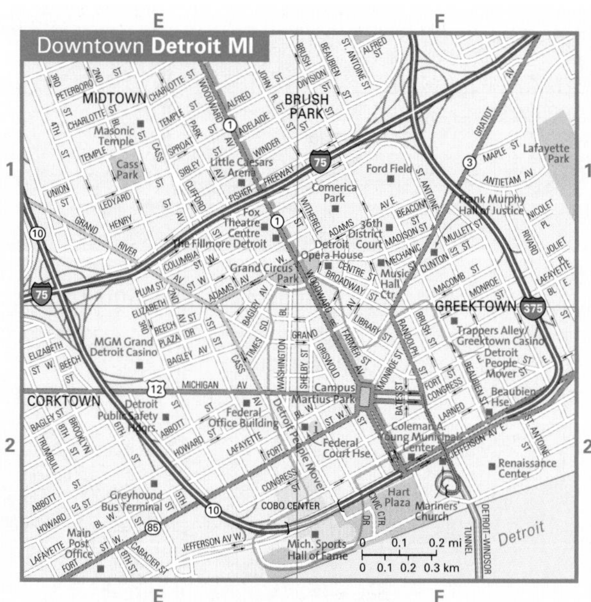

POINTS OF INTEREST

- 36th District Court . . . F1
- Beaubien House . . . F2
- Cobo Center . . . F2
- Coleman A. Young Municipal Center . . . F2
- Comerica Park . . . F1
- Detroit Opera House . . . F1
- Detroit People Mover . . . F2
- Detroit Public Safety Headquarters . . . F1
- Federal Court House . . . F2
- Federal Office Building . . . E2
- The Fillmore Detroit . . . E1
- Ford Field . . . F1
- Fox Theatre Centre . . . E1
- Frank Murphy Hall of Justice . . . F1
- Greyhound Bus Terminal . . . E2
- Little Caesars Arena . . . E1
- Main Post Office . . . E2
- Mariners Church . . . F2
- Masonic Temple . . . E1
- MGM Grand Detroit Casino . . . E2
- Michigan Sports Hall of Fame . . . F2
- Music Hall Center . . . F1
- Renaissance Center . . . F2
- Trappers Alley/Greektown Casino . . F2

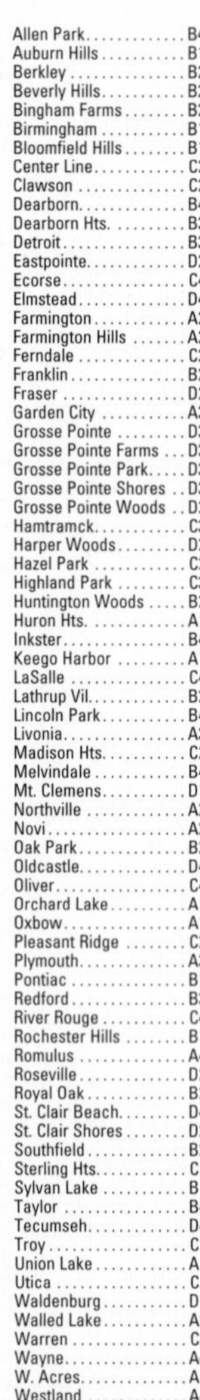

- Allen Park . . . B4
- Auburn Hills . . . B1
- Berkley . . . B2
- Beverly Hills . . . B2
- Bingham Farms . . . B2
- Birmingham . . . B1
- Bloomfield Hills . . . B1
- Center Line . . . C2
- Clawson . . . C2
- Dearborn . . . B4
- Dearborn Hts. . . . B3
- Detroit . . . B3
- Eastpointe . . . D2
- Ecorse . . . C4
- Elmstead . . . D4
- Farmington . . . A2
- Farmington Hills . . . A2
- Ferndale . . . C2
- Franklin . . . B2
- Fraser . . . D2
- Garden City . . . A3
- Grosse Pointe . . . D3
- Grosse Pointe Farms . . . D3
- Grosse Pointe Park . . . D3
- Grosse Pointe Shores . . . D3
- Grosse Pointe Woods . . D2
- Hamtramck . . . C3
- Harper Woods . . . D2
- Hazel Park . . . C2
- Highland Park . . . C3
- Huntington Woods . . . B2
- Huron Hts. . . . A1
- Inkster . . . B4
- Keego Harbor . . . A1
- LaSalle . . . C4
- Lathrup Vil. . . . B2
- Lincoln Park . . . B4
- Livonia . . . A3
- Madison Hts. . . . C2
- Melvindale . . . B4
- Mt. Clemens . . . D1
- Northville . . . A2
- Novi . . . A2
- Oak Park . . . B2
- Oldcastle . . . D4
- Oliver . . . C4
- Orchard Lake . . . A1
- Oxbow . . . A1
- Pleasant Ridge . . . C2
- Plymouth . . . A3
- Pontiac . . . B1
- Redford . . . B3
- River Rouge . . . C4
- Rochester Hills . . . B1
- Romulus . . . A4
- Roseville . . . D2
- Royal Oak . . . B2
- St. Clair Beach . . . D4
- St. Clair Shores . . . D2
- Southfield . . . B2
- Sterling Hts. . . . C1
- Sylvan Lake . . . B1
- Taylor . . . B4
- Tecumseh . . . D4
- Troy . . . C1
- Union Lake . . . A1
- Utica . . . C1
- Waldenburg . . . D1
- Walled Lake . . . A2
- Warren . . . C2
- Wayne . . . A4
- W. Acres . . . A1
- Westland . . . A4
- Windsor . . . C4
- Wolverine Lake . . . A1

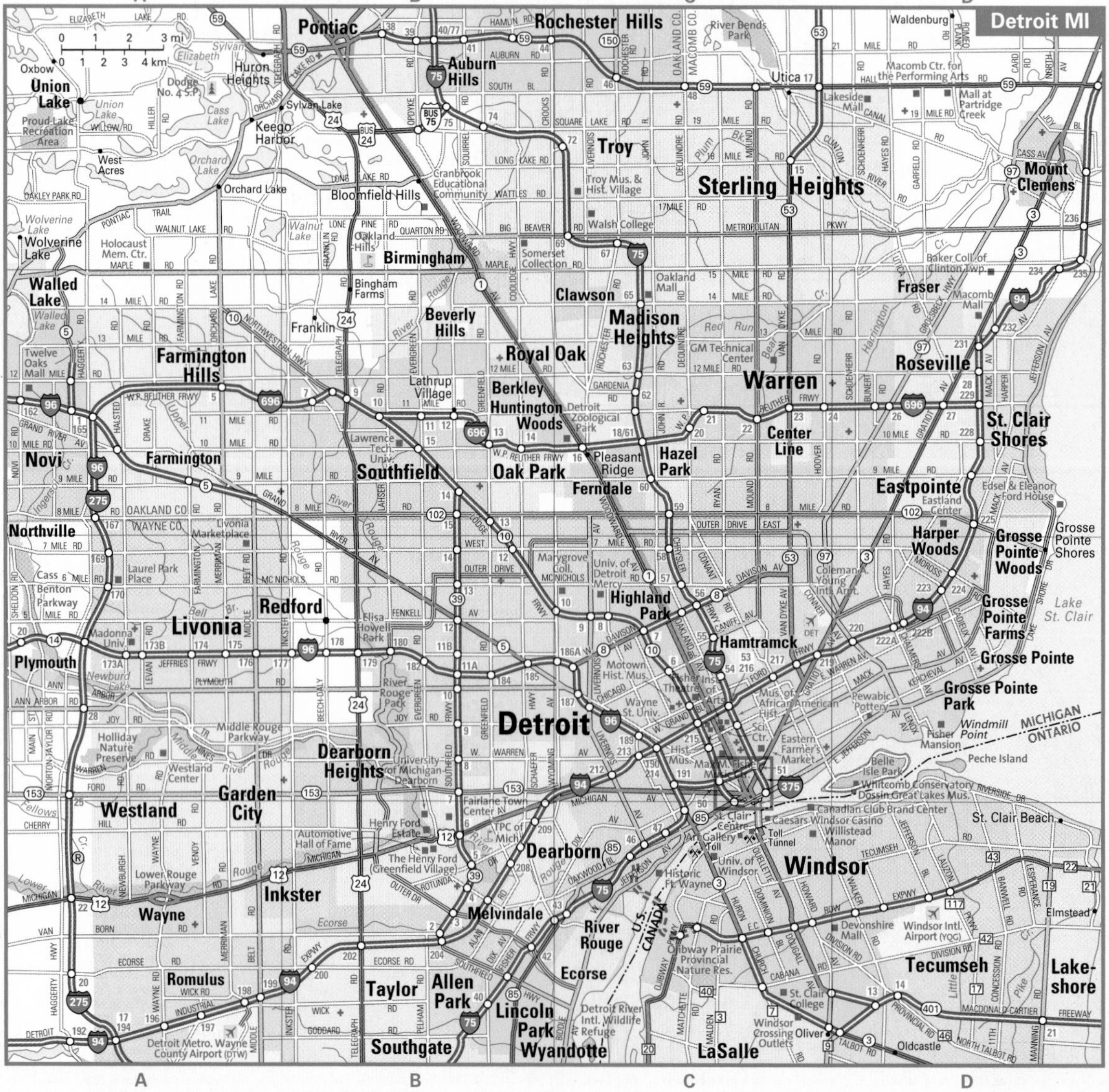

Detroit MI

Entries in **bold black** indicate counties or parishes.
Entries in **bold color** indicate cities with detailed inset maps.

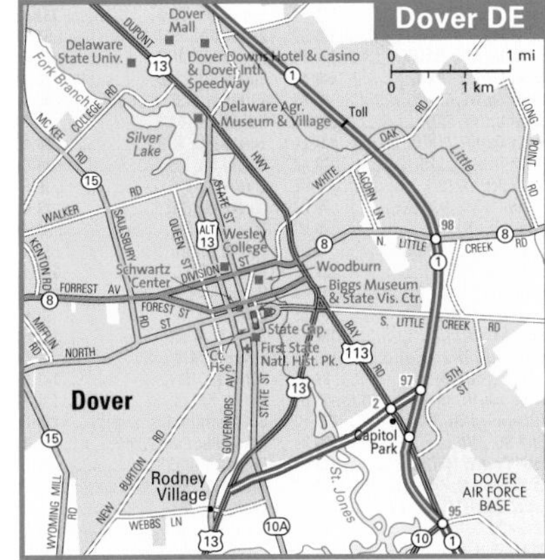

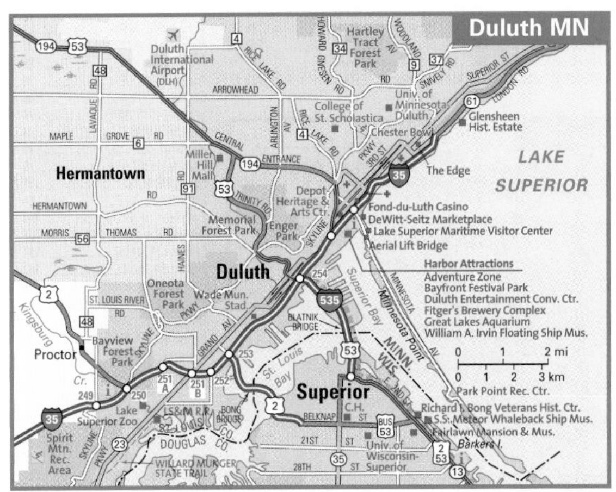

E

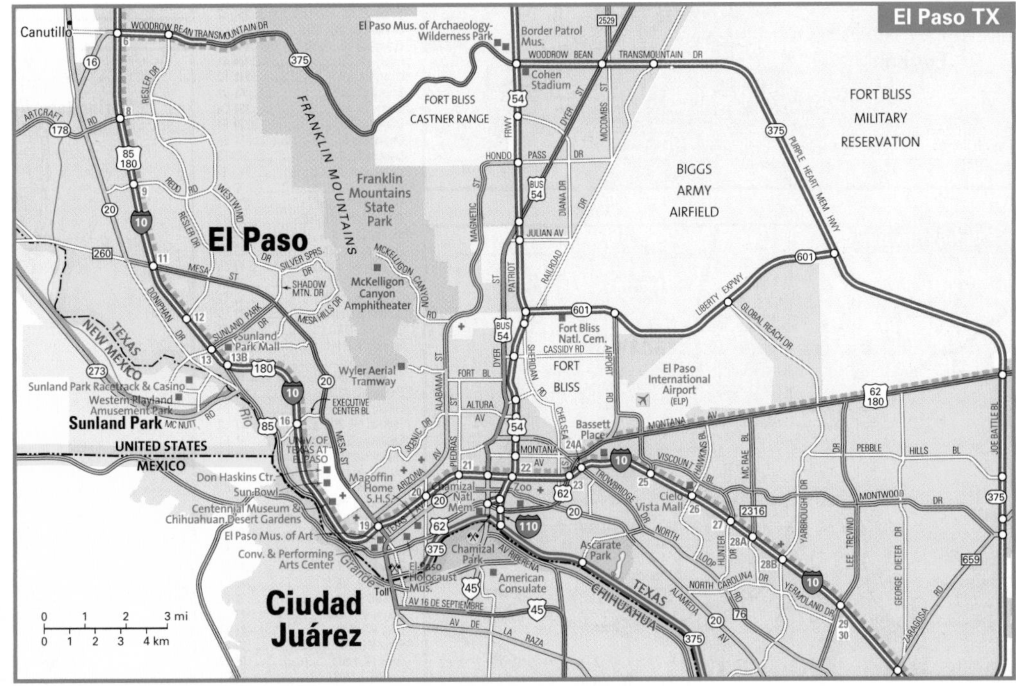

Figures after entries indicate population, page number, and grid reference.

Erie PA

Lake Erie
Presque Isle Lighthouse
Presque Isle State Park
Lawrence Park
Wesleyville
Erie
Kearsarge
Five Points

Fargo ND

Hector International Airport (FAR)
Fargodome
North Dakota State University
Moorhead
Fargo
Red River Zoo

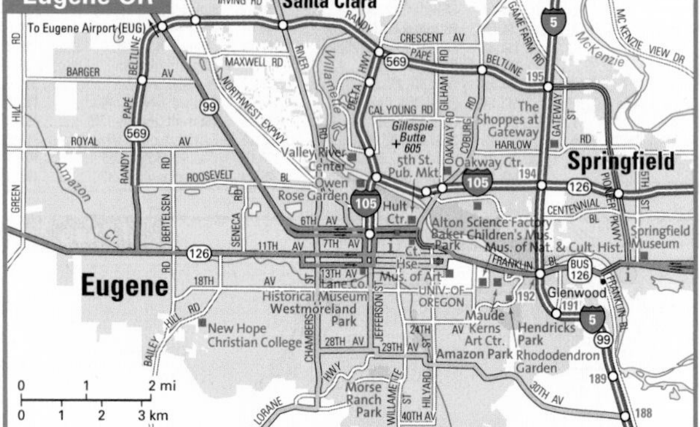

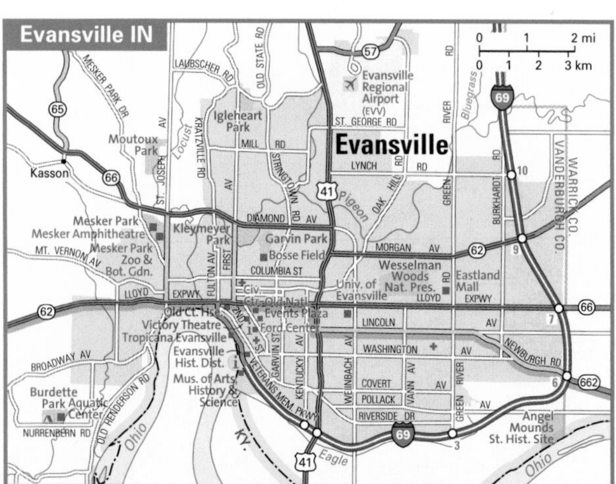

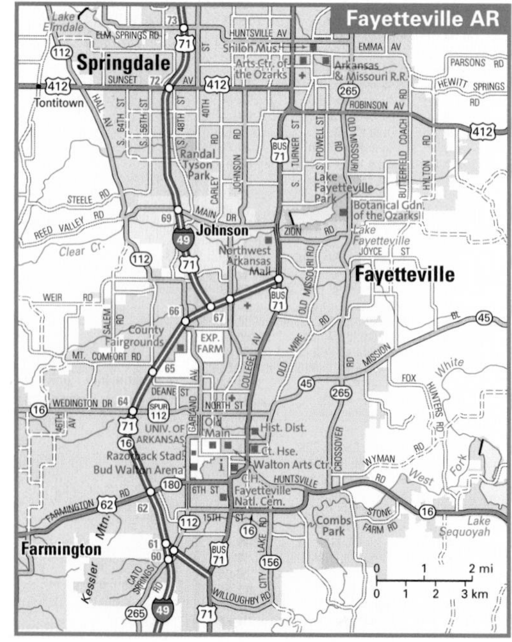

Entries in **bold black** indicate counties or parishes.
Entries in **bold color** indicate cities with detailed inset maps.

Fayetteville NC

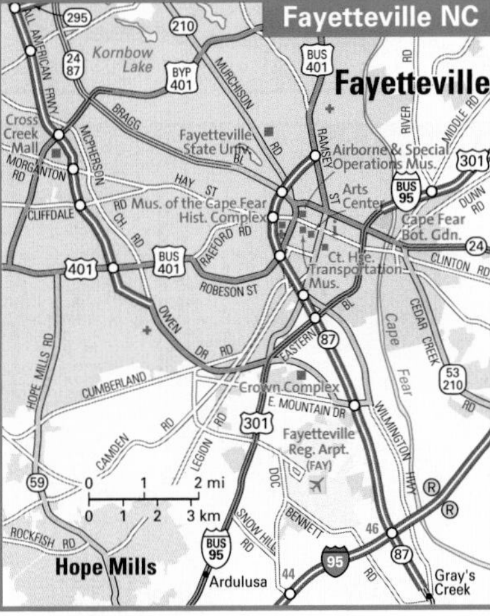

Flagstaff AZ

Flint MI

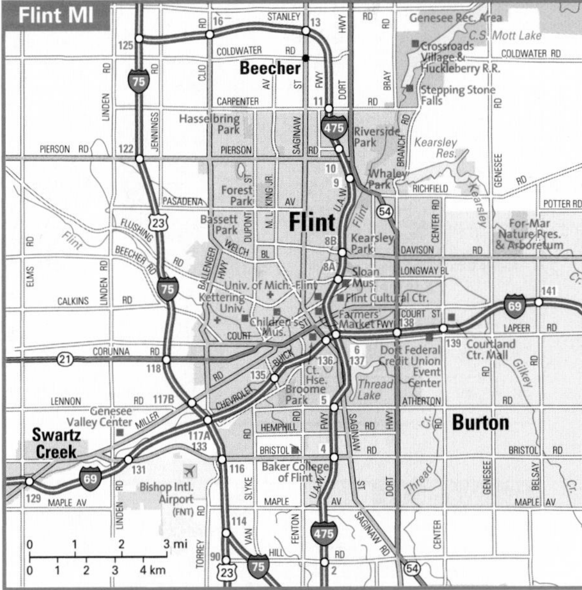

Fort Collins CO

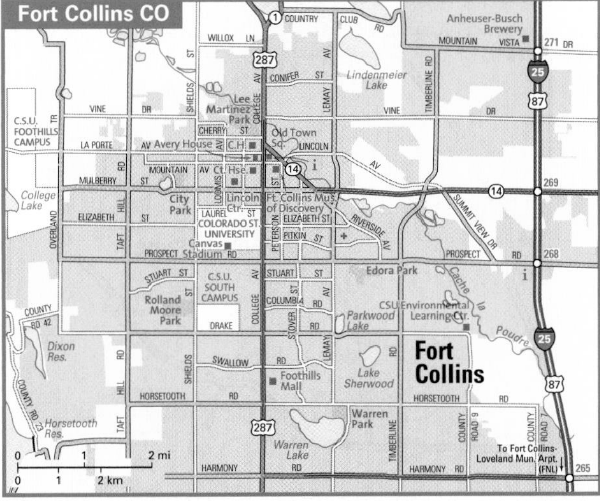

Figures after entries indicate population, page number, and grid reference.

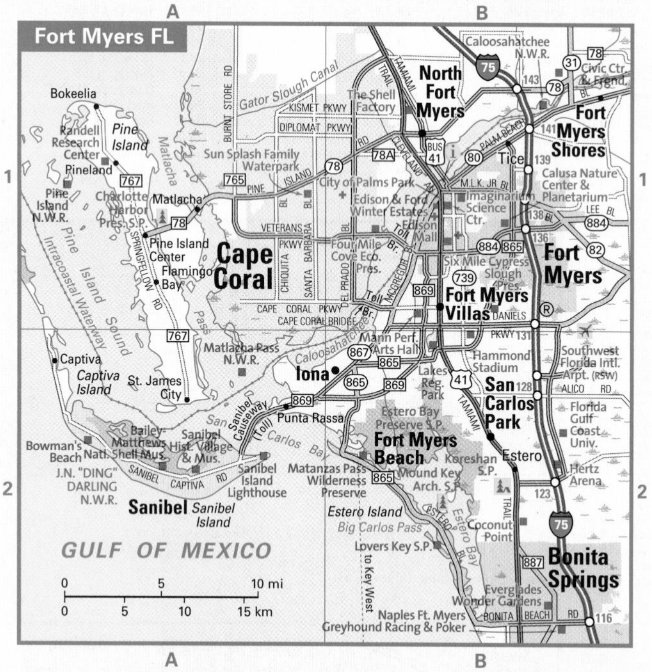

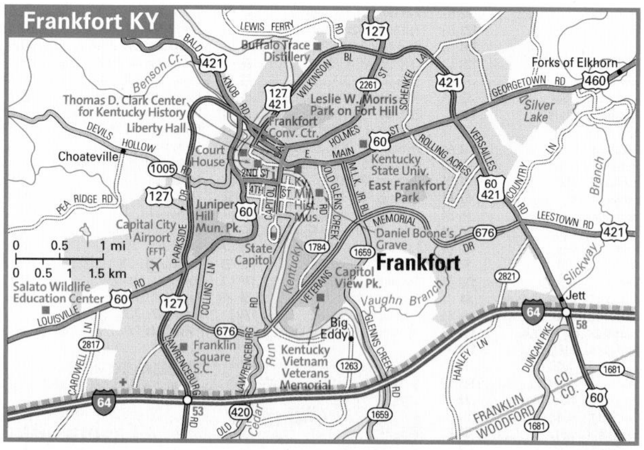

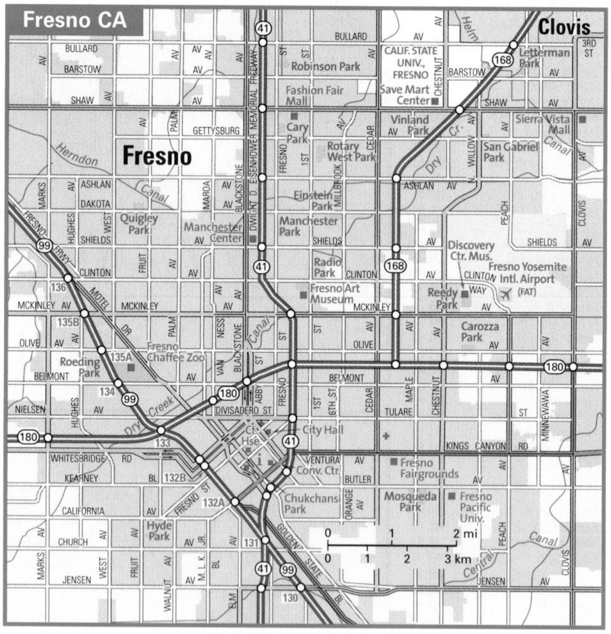

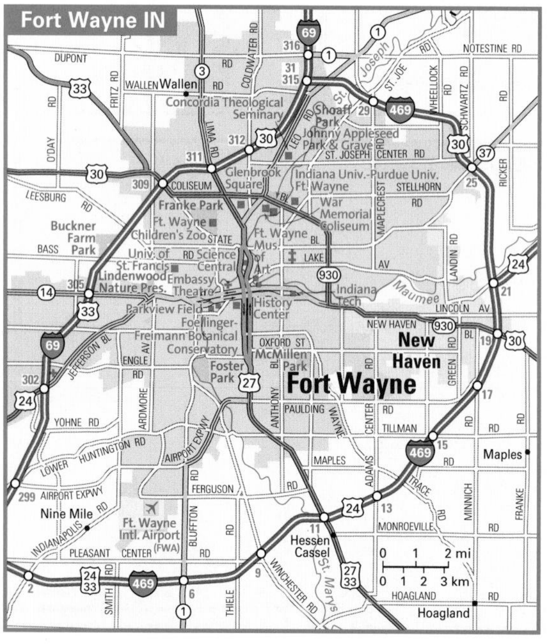

Fort Myers FL

Frankfort KY

Fresno CA

Fort Wayne IN

Entries in **bold black** indicate counties or parishes.
Entries in **bold color** indicate cities with detailed inset maps.

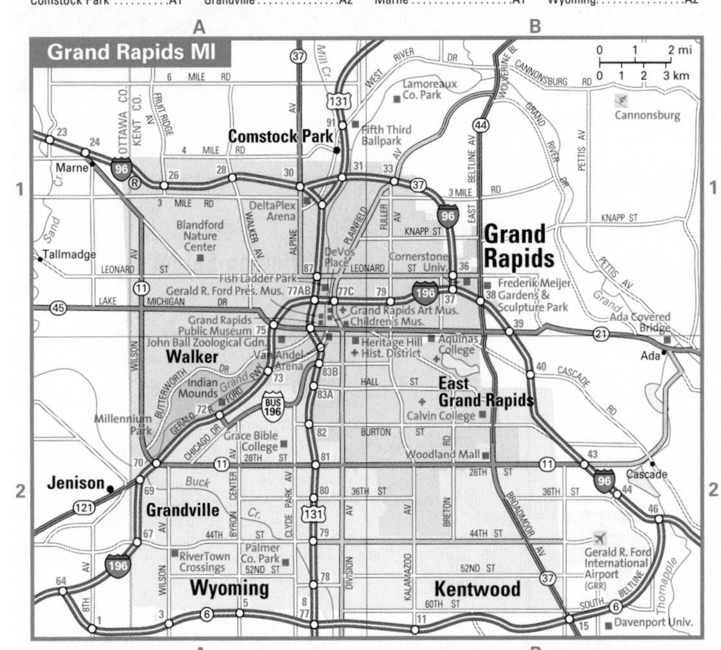

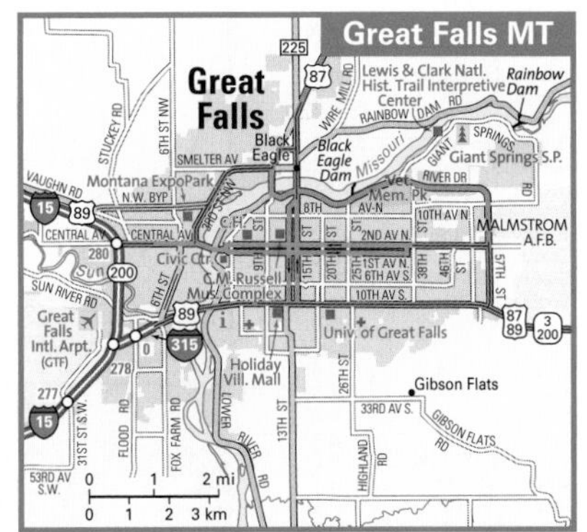

Figures after entries indicate population, page number, and grid reference.

Green Bay WI

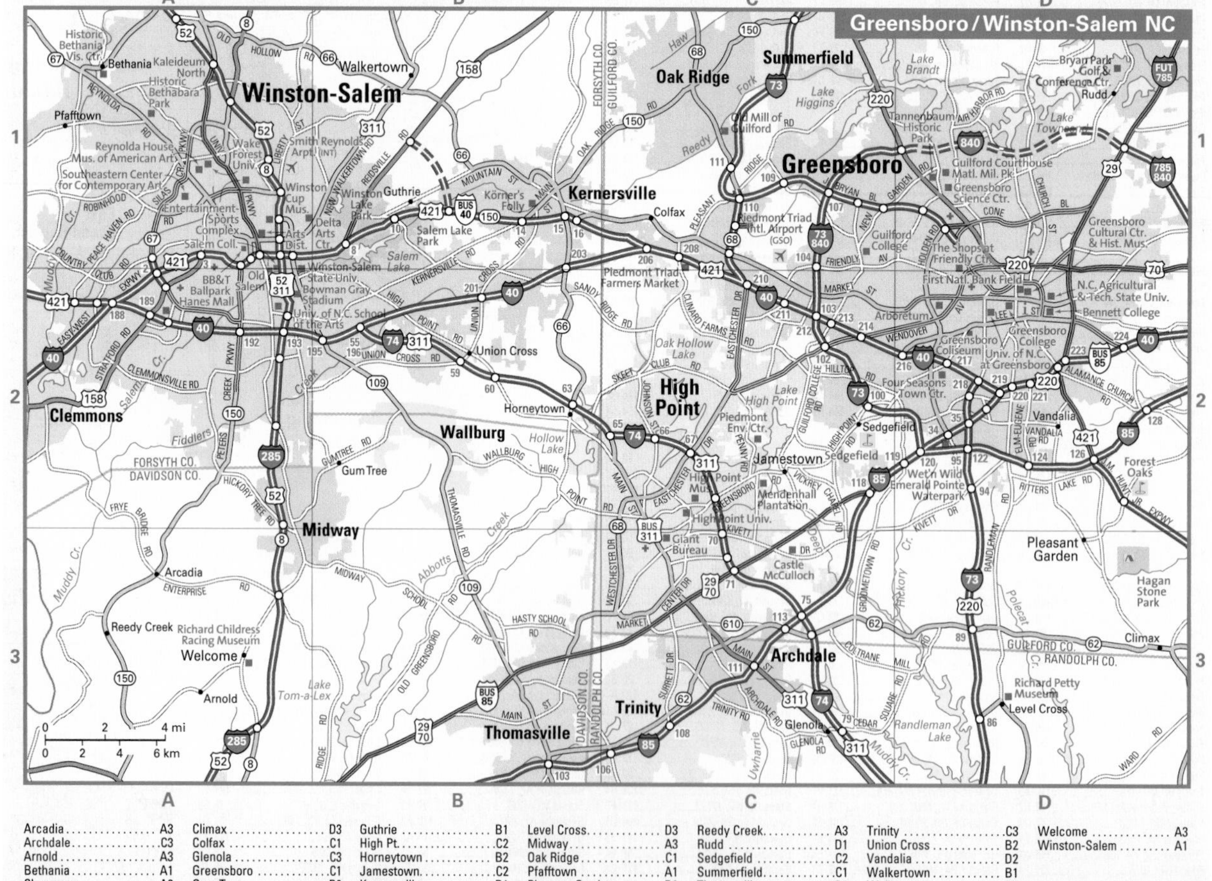

Arcadia A3	Climax D3	Guthrie B1	Level Cross D3	Reedy Creek A3	Trinity C3	Welcome A3
Archdale C3	Colfax C1	High Pt. C2	Midway A3	Rudd D1	Union Cross B2	Winston-Salem A1
Arnold A3	Glenola C3	Horneytown B2	Oak Ridge C1	Sedgefield C2	Vandalia D2	
Bethania A1	Greensboro C1	Jamestown C2	Pfafftown A1	Summerfield C1	Walkertown B1	
Clemmons A2	Gum Tree B2	Kernersville B1	Pleasant Garden D3	Thomasville B3	Wallburg B2	

Entries in **bold black** indicate counties or parishes.
Entries in **bold color** indicate cities with detailed inset maps.

Greenville / Spartanburg SC

Figures after entries indicate population, page number, and grid reference.

Harrisburg PA

Hartford CT

Entries in **bold black** indicate counties or parishes.
Entries in **bold color** indicate cities with detailed inset maps.

Honolulu HI

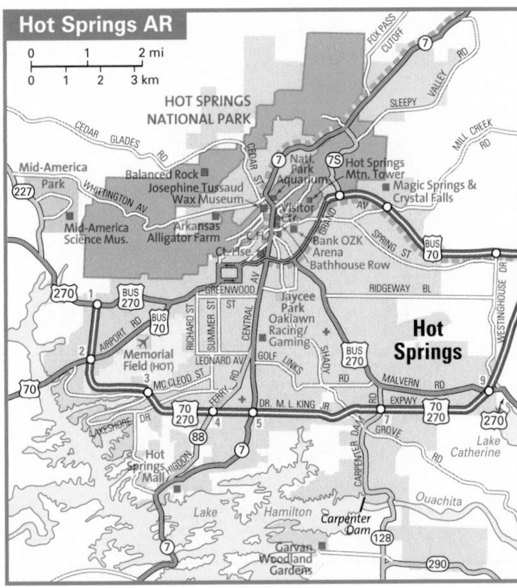

Figures after entries indicate population, page number, and grid reference.

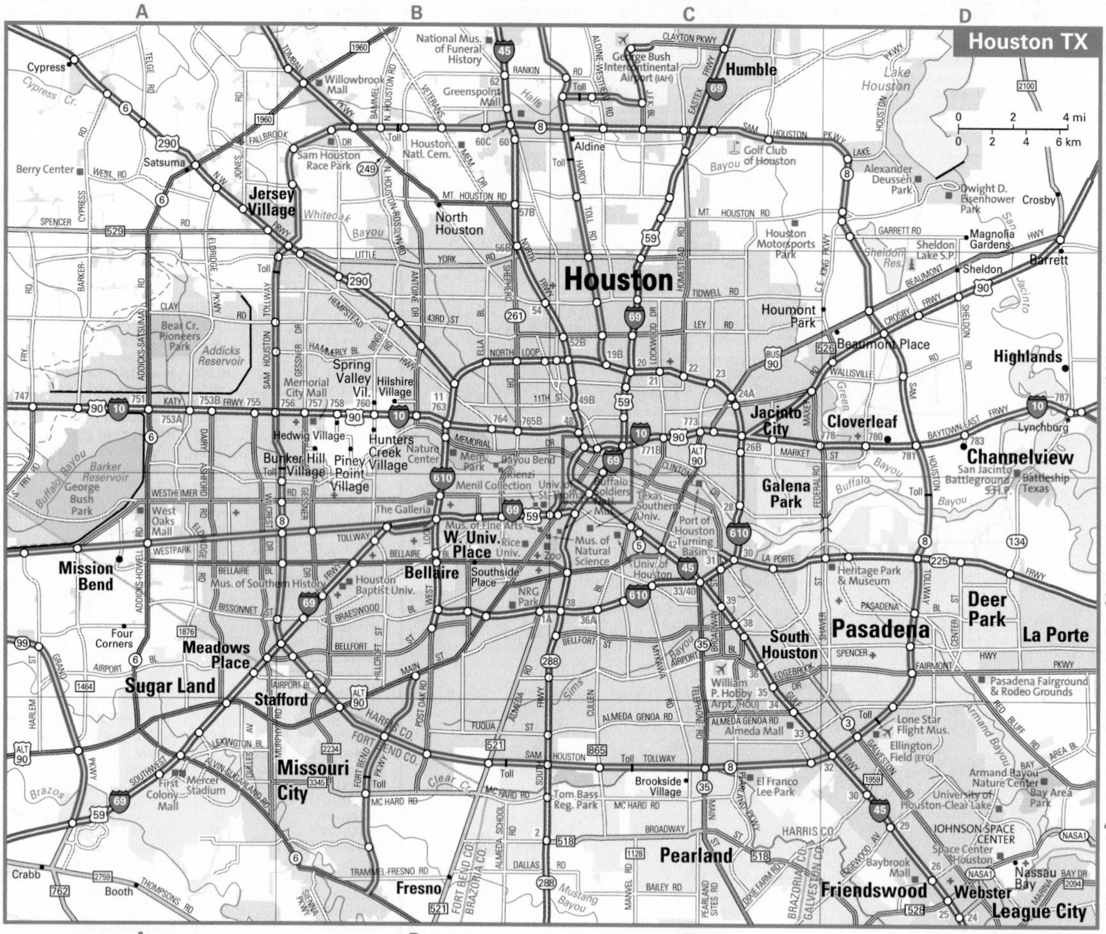

Houston TX

Downtown Houston TX

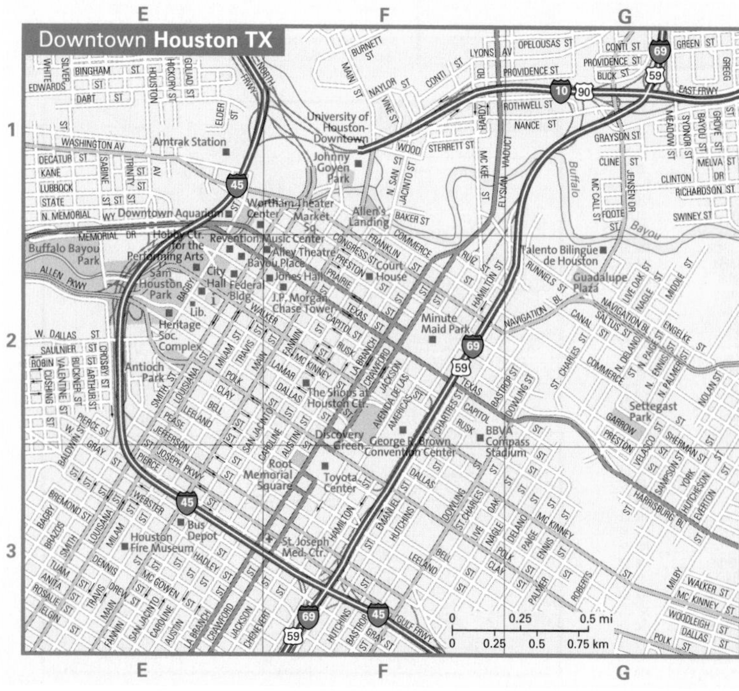

POINTS OF INTEREST

Entries in **bold black** indicate counties or parishes.
Entries in **bold color** indicate cities with detailed inset maps.

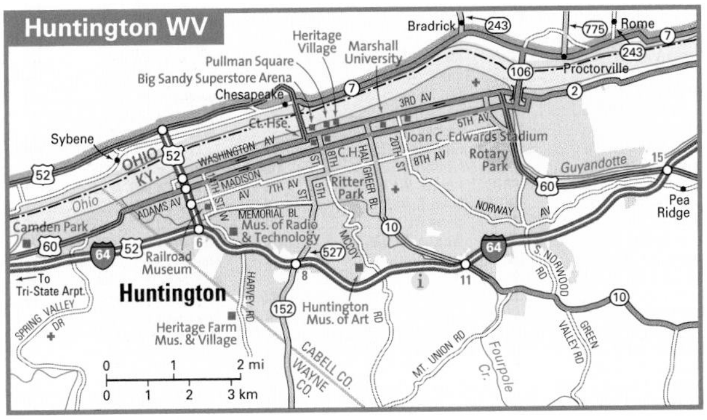

Huntington WV

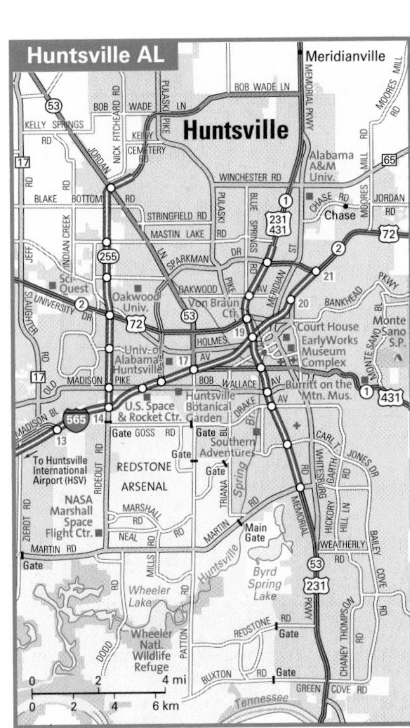

Indianapolis IN

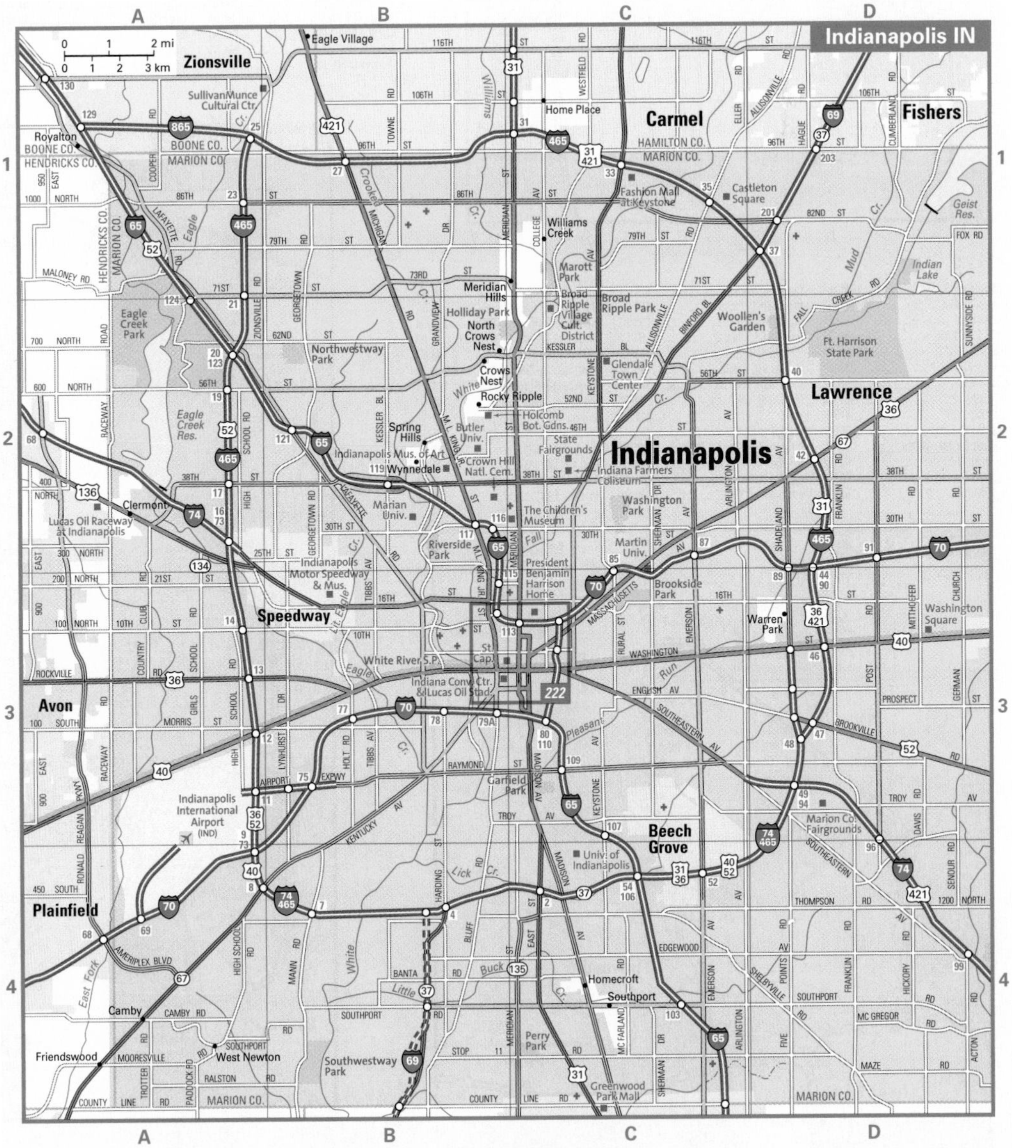

Figures after entries indicate population, page number, and grid reference.

POINTS OF INTEREST

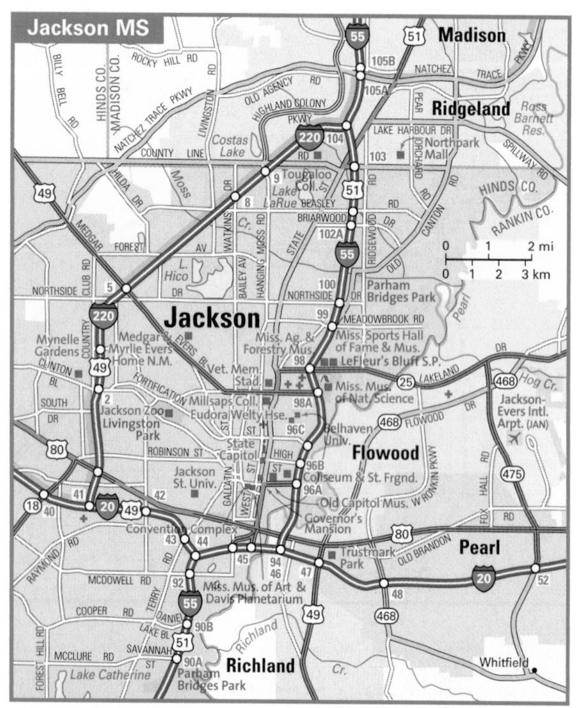

J

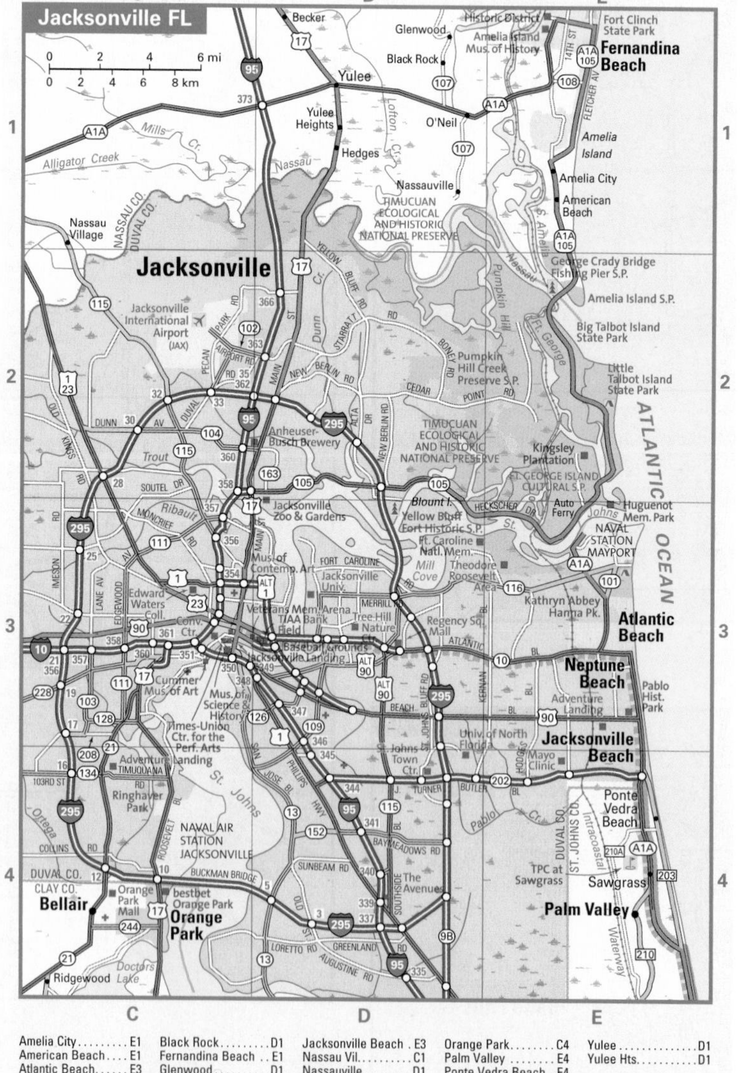

Entries in **bold black** indicate counties or parishes.
Entries in **bold color** indicate cities with detailed inset maps.

Jefferson City MO

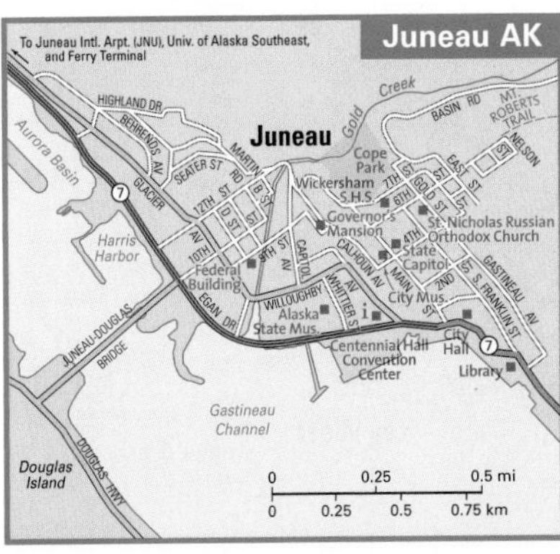

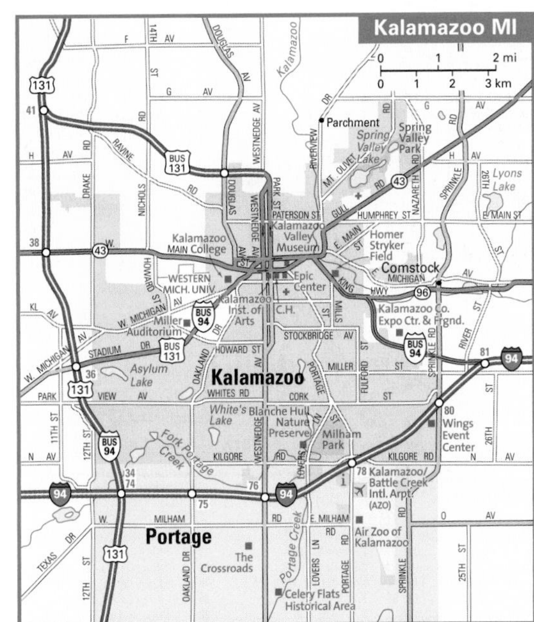

Figures after entries indicate population, page number, and grid reference.

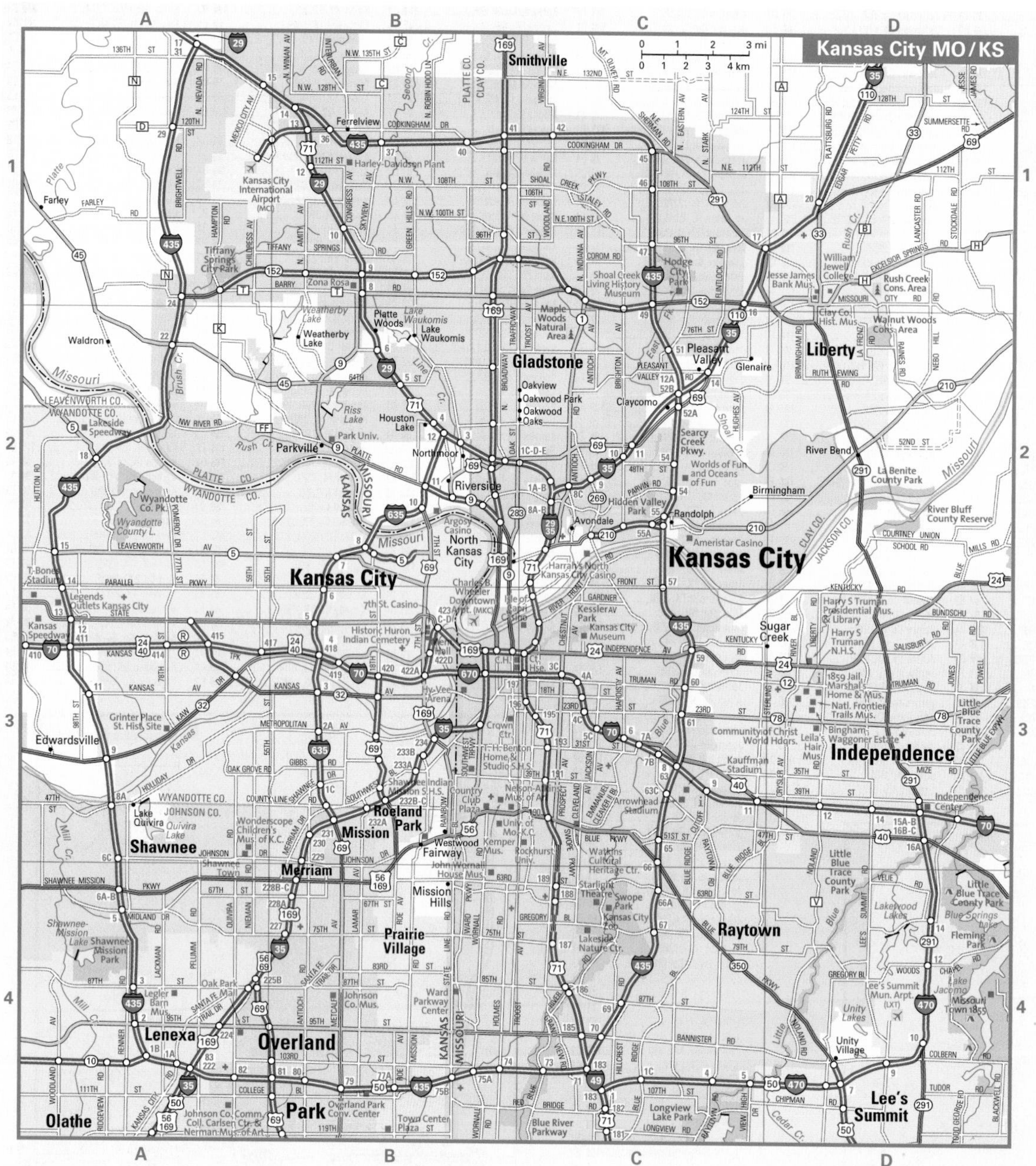

Keytesville MO, *471* **97** D2
Key West FL, *24649* **142** C4
Kezar Falls ME, *750* **82** A3
Kiamesha Lake NY, *700* **148** A1
Kiawah Island SC, *1626* **131** D2
Kibler AR, *961* **116** C1
Kidder Co. ND, *2435* **18** C4
Kiefer OK, *1685* **51** F2
Kiel WI, *3738* **74** C2
Kiester MN, *501* **72** C2
Kihei HI, *20881* **153** D1
Kilauea HI, *2803* **152** B1
Kilbourne LA, *416* **125** F1
Kildeer IL, *3968* **203** B2
Kilgore TX, *12975* **124** B2
Killbuck OH, *817* **91** E4
Killdeer ND, *751* **18** A3
Kill Devil Hills NC, *6683* **115** F2
Killeen TX, *127921* **59** E4
Killen AL, *1108* **119** E2
Killian LA, *1206* **134** B2
Killona LA, *793* **239** A1
Kilmarnock VA, *1487* **113** F1
Kilmichael MS, *699* **118** C4
Kiln MS, *2238* **134** C2
Kimball MN, *762* **66** C3
Kimball NE, *2496* **33** F3
Kimball SD, *703* **27** D4
Kimball TN, *1395* **120** A2
Kimball WV, *194* **111** F1
Kimball Co. NE, *3821* **33** F3
Kimberling City MO, *2400* **107** D3
Kimberly AL, *2711* **119** F4
Kimberly ID, *3264* **30** C1
Kimberly WI, *6468* **74** C1
Kimberton PA, *2500* **146** B2
Kimble Co. TX, *4607* **60** C1
Kincaid IL, *1505* **98** B1
Kinde MI, *448* **76** C1
Kinder LA, *2477* **133** E2
Kinderhook NY, *1211* **94** B2
Kindred ND, *692* **19** E4
King NC, *6904* **112** A3
King WI, *1750* **74** B1
King and Queen Co. VA, *6945* **113** F1
King and Queen C.H. VA, *85* **113** F1
King City CA, *12874* **44** B3
King City MO, *1013* **86** B4
King City OR, *3111* **251** C3
King Co. TX, *286* **58** C1
King Co. WA, *1931249* **12** C3
King Cove AK, *938* **154** B4
Kingfield ME, *997* **82** B1
Kingfisher OK, *4633* **51** E2
Kingfisher Co. OK, *15034* **51** E2
King George VA, *4457* **103** E4
King George Co. VA, *23584* **103** E4
Kingman AZ, *28068* **46** B3
Kingman IN, *511* **99** E1
Kingman KS, *3177* **43** E4
Kingman Co. KS, *7858* **43** E4
King of Prussia PA, *19936* **146** C2
King Salmon AK, *374* **154** B3
Kings Beach CA, *3796* **37** D2
Kingsburg CA, *11382* **45** D3
Kingsbury TX, *782* **61** E2
Kingsbury Co. SD, *5148* **27** E3
Kings Co. CA, *152982* **44** C3
Kings Co. NY, *2504700* **147** F1
Kingsford MI, *5133* **68** C2
Kingsford Hts. IN, *1435* **89** E2
Kingsland AR, *447* **117** E4
Kingsland GA, *15946* **139** D1
Kingsland TX, *6030* **61** D1
Kingsley IA, *1411* **35** F1
Kingsley MI, *1480* **69** F4
Kings Mtn. NC, *10296* **122** A1
Kings Park NY, *17282* **149** D3
Kings Pt. NY, *5005* **148** B4
Kingsport TN, *48205* **111** E3
Kingston GA, *637* **120** B3
Kingston ID, *650* **14** B3
Kingston IL, *1164* **88** C1
Kingston KY, *600* **110** C1
Kingston MA, *5591* **151** E2
Kingston MI, *440* **76** C2
Kingston MO, *348* **96** C1
Kingston NH, *6025* **95** E1
Kingston NJ, *1493* **147** D1
Kingston NY, *23893* **94** B2
Kingston OH, *1032* **101** D2
Kingston OK, *1601* **59** F1
Kingston PA, *13182* **93** E2
Kingston RI, *6974* **150** C4
Kingston TN, *5934* **110** B4
Kingston WA, *2099* **12** C3

Key West FL

Key West

Entries in **bold black** indicate counties or parishes.
Entries in **bold color** indicate cities with detailed inset maps.

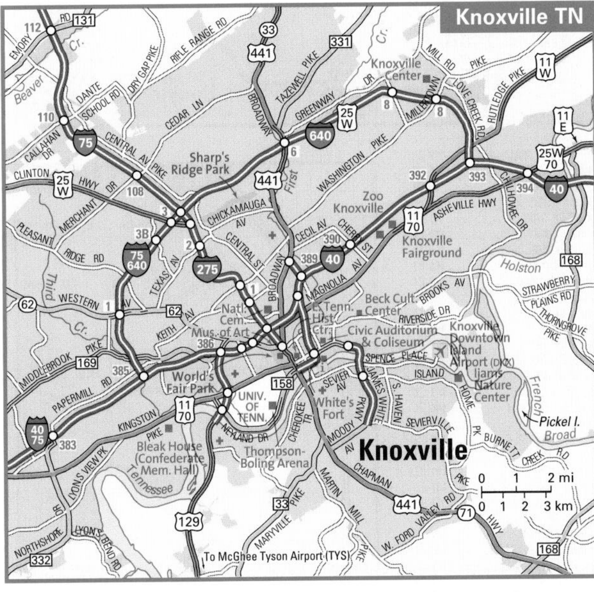

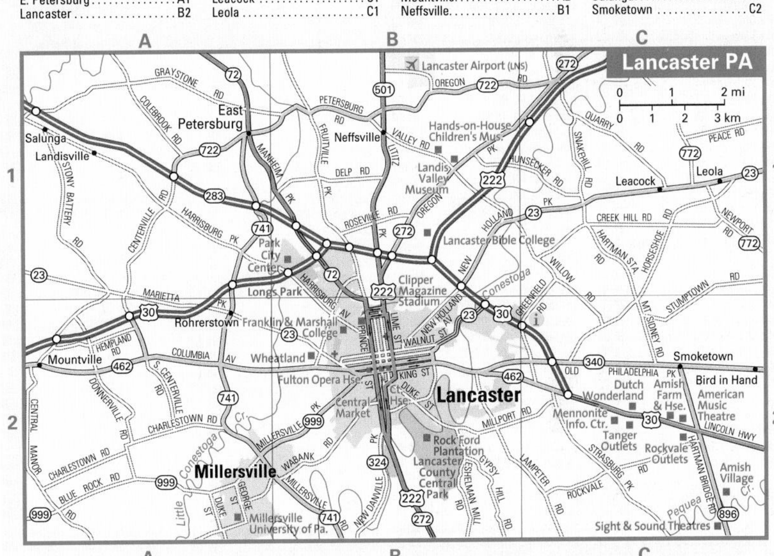

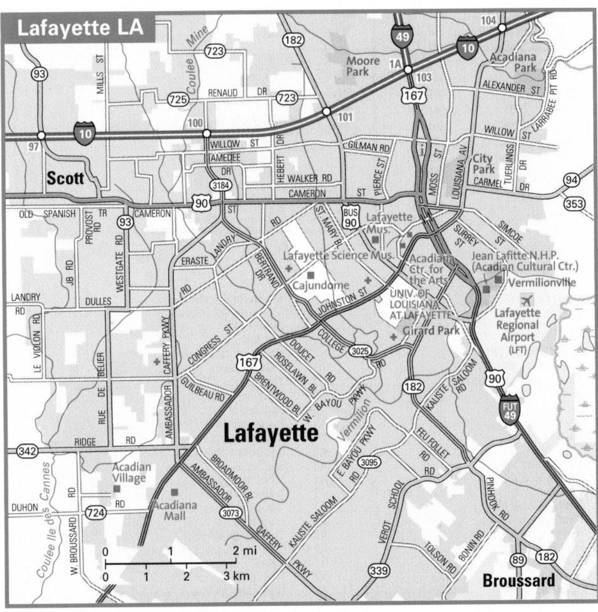

Figures after entries indicate population, page number, and grid reference.

Las Vegas NV

Las Cruces NM

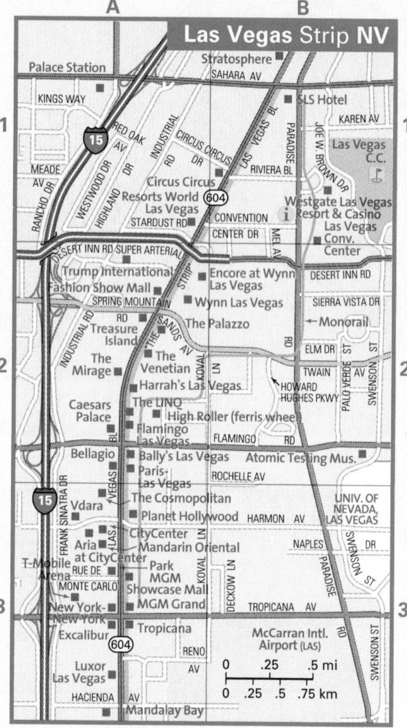

POINTS OF INTEREST

Entries in **bold black** indicate counties or parishes.
Entries in **bold color** indicate cities with detailed inset maps.

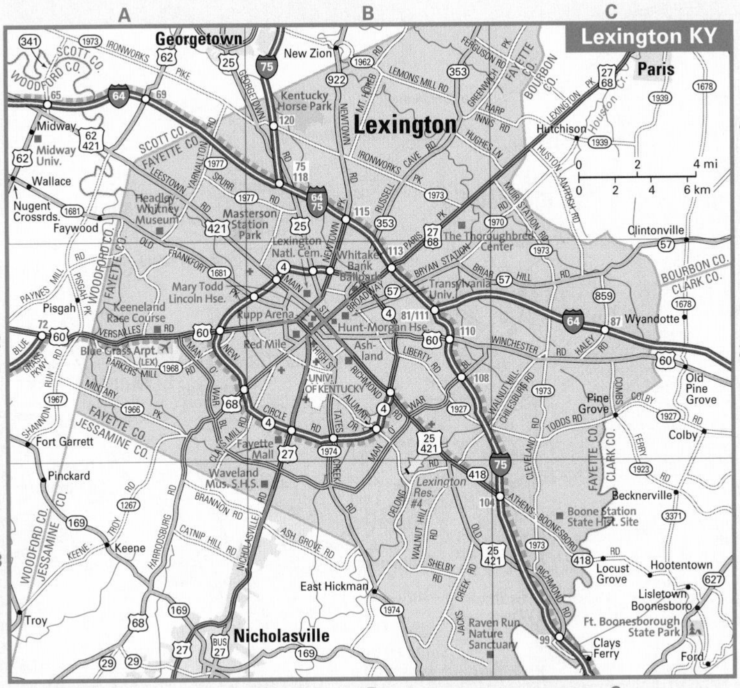

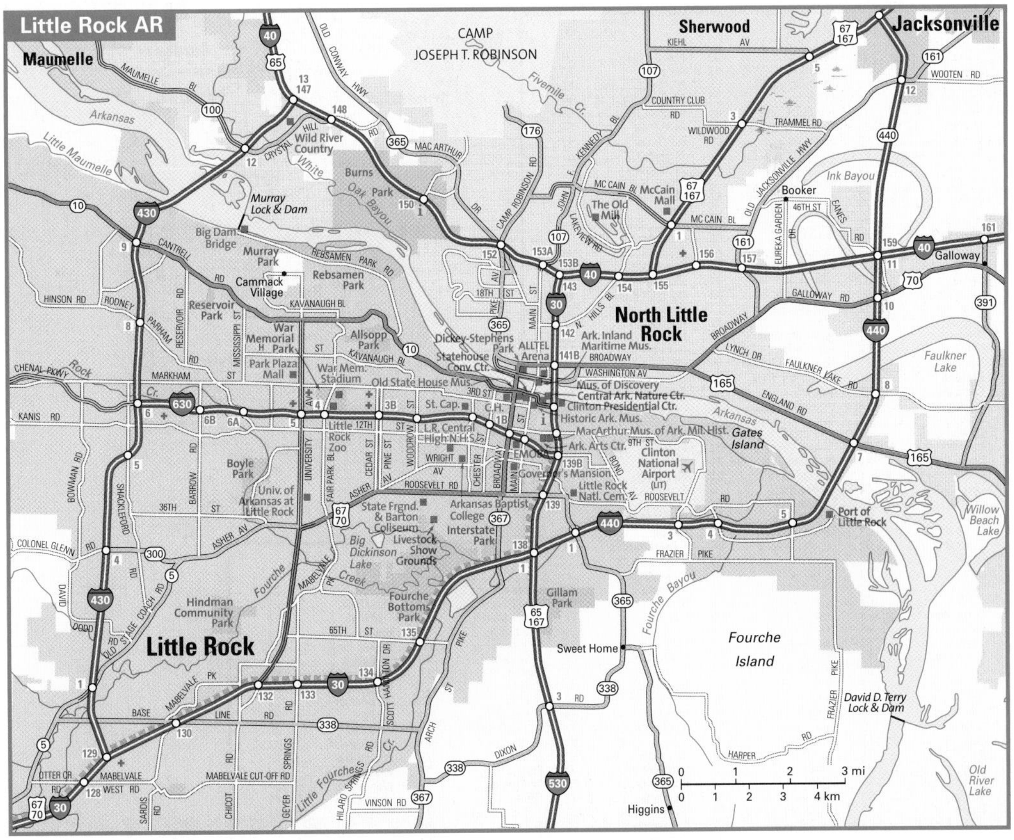

Lexington KY

Lincoln NE

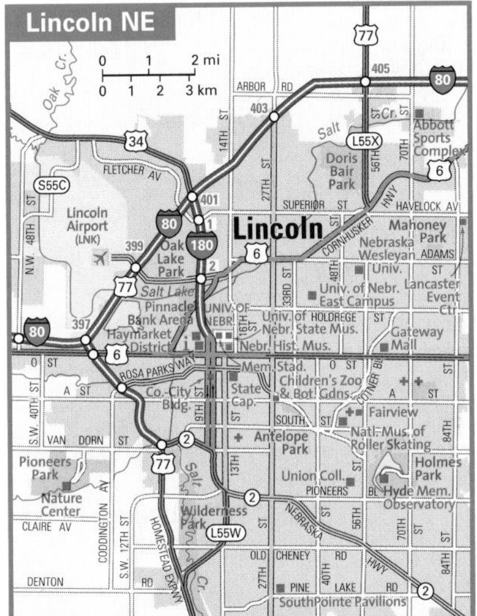

Little Rock AR

Figures after entries indicate population, page number, and grid reference.

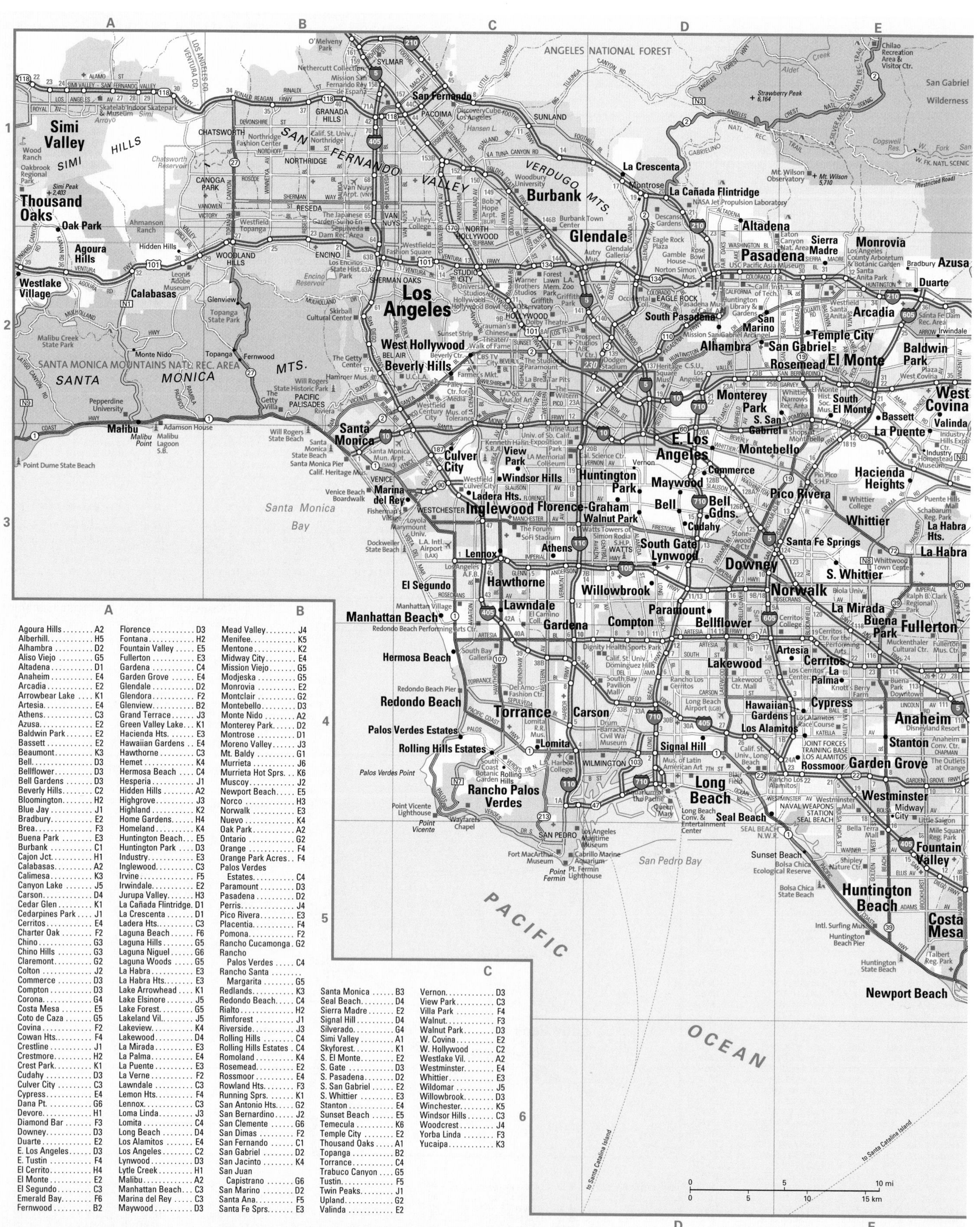

Entries in **bold black** indicate counties or parishes.
Entries in **bold color** indicate cities with detailed inset maps.

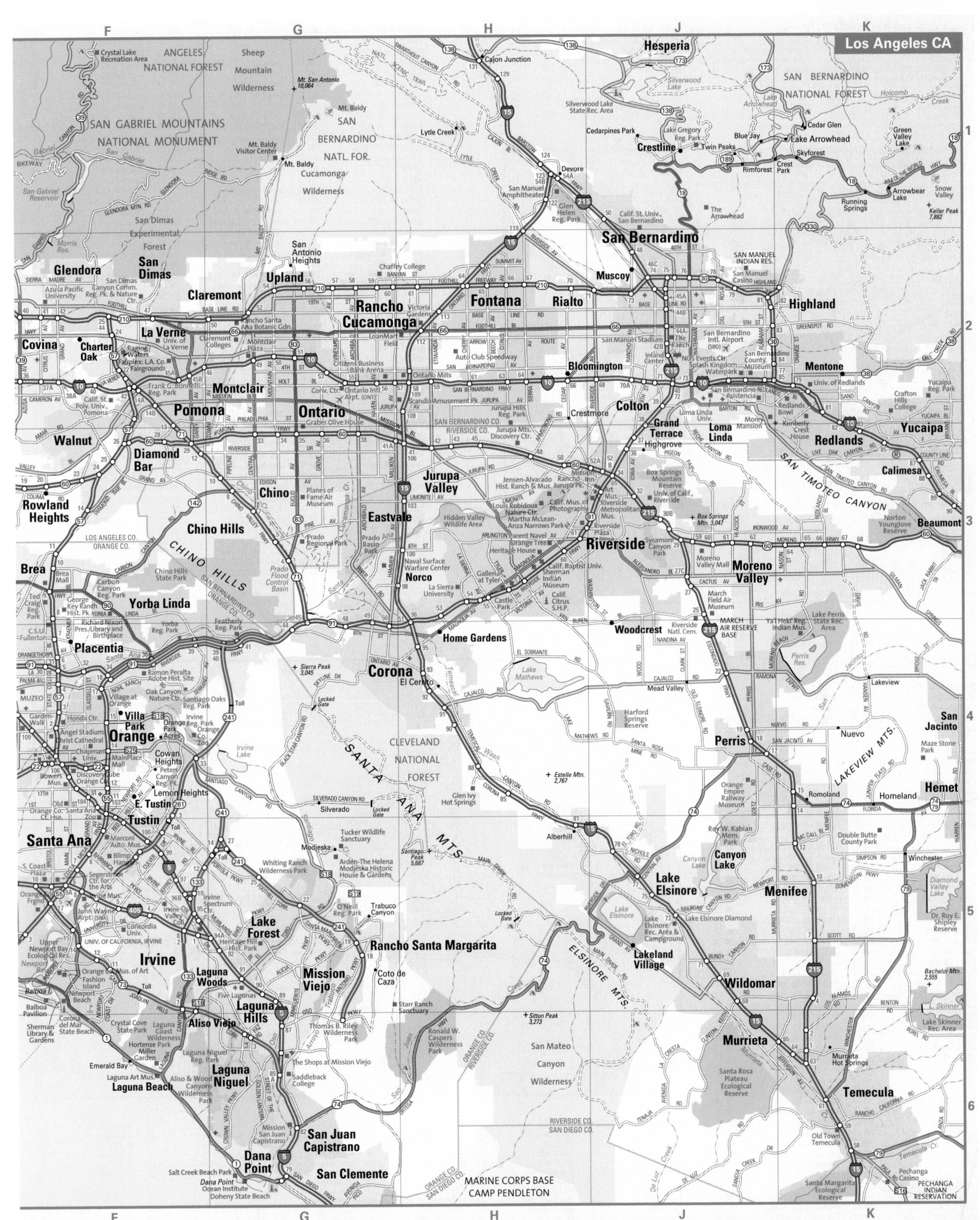

Figures after entries indicate population, page number, and grid reference.

POINTS OF INTEREST

Downtown Los Angeles CA

Louisville KY

Entries in **bold black** indicate counties or parishes.
Entries in **bold color** indicate cities with detailed inset maps.

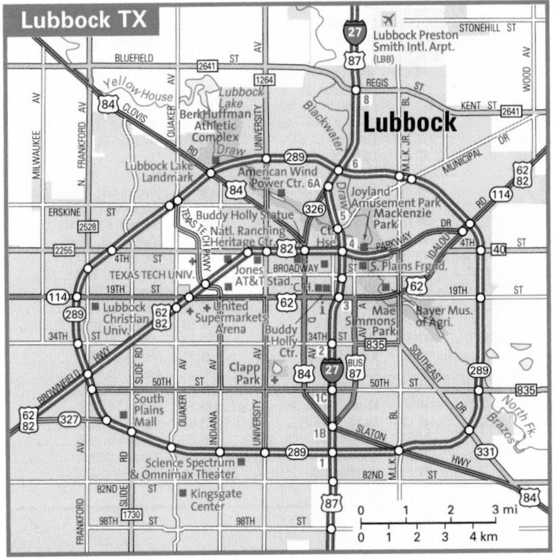

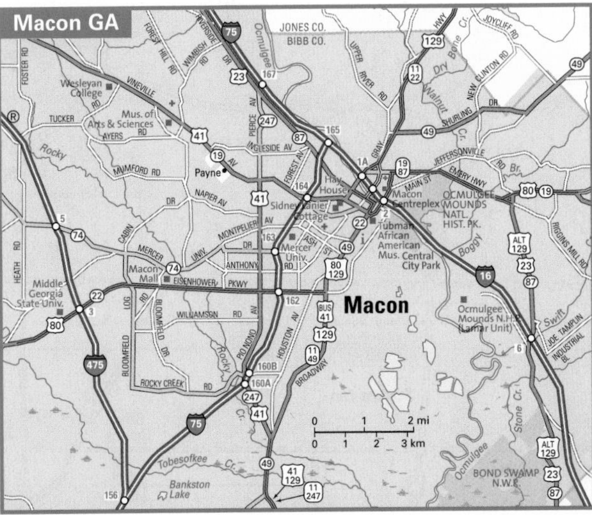

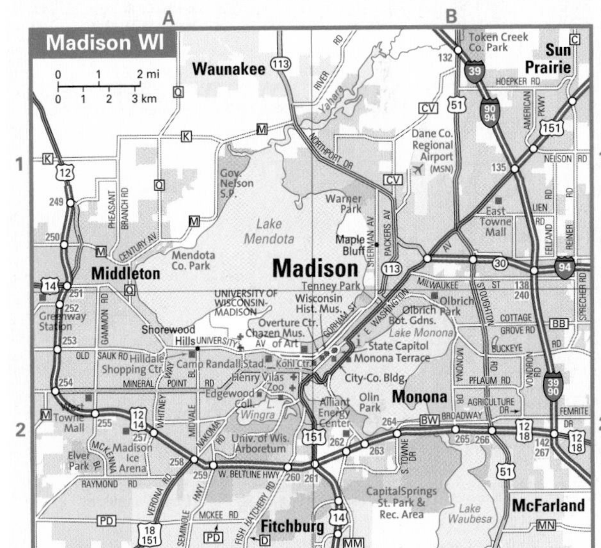

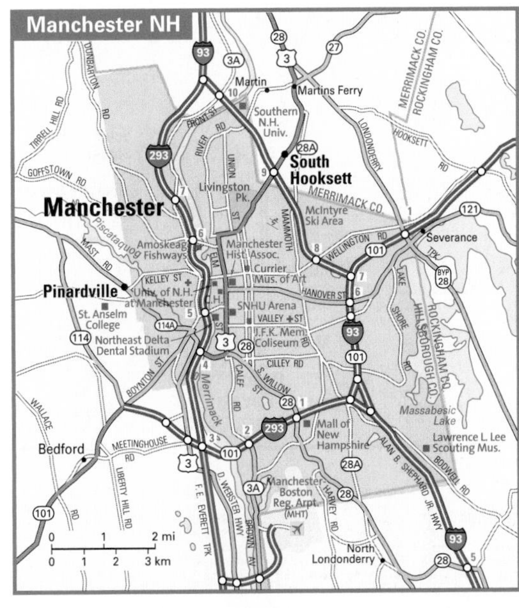

Figures after entries indicate population, page number, and grid reference.

Macon Co. AL, *21452* 128 B3
Macon Co. GA, *14740* 129 D2
Macon Co. IL, *110768* 98 C1
Macon Co. MO, *15566* 97 D1
Macon Co. NC, *33922* 121 D1
Macon Co. TN, *22248* 110 A3
Macoupin Co. IL, *47765* 98 B2
Macungie PA, *3074* 146 B1
Macy NE, *1023* 35 F2
Madawaska ME, *2967* 85 D1
Maddock ND, *382* 19 D2
Madeira OH, *8726* 204 C2
Madeira Beach FL, *4263* 140 B3
Madelia MN, *2308* 72 B1
Madera CA, *61416* 44 C2
Madera Co. CA, *150865* 44 C2

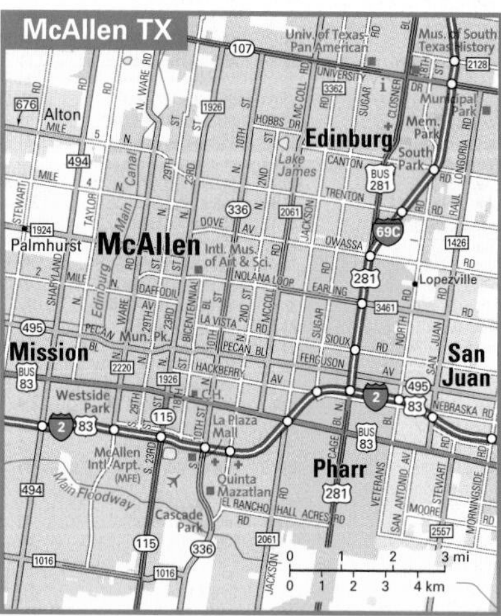

Madill OK, *3770* 51 F4
Madison AL, *42938* 119 F2
Madison AR, *769* 118 A2
Madison CT, *18812* 149 E2
Madison FL, *2843* 137 F2
Madison GA, *3979* 121 D4
Madison IL, *3891* 98 A3
Madison IN, *11967* 100 A3
Madison KS, *701* 43 F3
Madison ME, *2630* 82 B1
Madison MN, *1551* 27 F2
Madison MS, *24149* 126 B2
Madison MO, *554* 97 E2
Madison NE, *2438* 35 E2
Madison NJ, *15845* 148 A4
Madison NC, *2246* 112 B3
Madison OH, *3184* 91 F1
Madison SD, *6474* 27 F3
Madison VA, *229* 102 C4
Madison WV, *3076* 101 E4
Madison WI, *233209* 74 B3
Madison Co. AL, *334811* 119 F2
Madison Co. AR, *15717* 106 C4
Madison Co. FL, *19224* 137 F2
Madison Co. GA, *28120* 121 E3
Madison Co. ID, *37536* 23 F4
Madison Co. IL, *269282* 98 B3
Madison Co. IN, *131636* 89 F4
Madison Co. IA, *15679* 86 C2
Madison Co. KY, *82916* 110 C1
Madison Co. MS, *95203* 126 B2
Madison Co. MO, *12226* 108 A1
Madison Co. MT, *7691* 23 E2
Madison Co. NE, *34876* 35 E2
Madison Co. NY, *73442* 79 E4
Madison Co. NC, *20764* 111 E4
Madison Co. OH, *43435* 100 C1
Madison Co. TN, *98294* 108 C4
Madison Co. TX, *13664* 61 F1

Madison Co. VA, *13308* 102 C3
Madison Hts. MI, *29694* 210 C2
Madison Hts. VA, *11285* 112 C1
Madison Lake MN, *1017* 72 C1
Madison Par. LA, *12093* 126 A3
Madisonville KY, *19591* 109 E1
Madisonville LA, *748* 134 B2
Madisonville TN, *4577* 120 C1
Madisonville TX, *4396* 61 F1
Madras OR, *6046* 21 D3
Madrid IA, *2543* 86 C1
Madrid NY, *757* 80 B1
Maeser UT, *3601* 32 A4
Magalia CA, *11310* 36 C1
Magazine AR, *847* 116 C1
Magdalena NM, *938* 48 B4
Magee MS, *4408* 126 C3
Maggie Valley NC, *1150* 121 E1
Magna UT, *26505* 257 A2
Magnolia AR, *11577* 125 D1
Magnolia DE, *225* 145 E2
Magnolia MS, *2420* 134 B1
Magnolia NJ, *4341* 248 D4
Magnolia NC, *939* 123 E2
Magnolia OH, *978* 91 E3
Magnolia TX, *1393* 132 A2
Magoffin Co. KY, *13333* 111 D1
Mahanoy City PA, *4162* 93 E3
Mahaska Co. IA, *22381* 87 D2
Mahnomen MN, *1214* 19 F3
Mahnomen Co. MN, *5413* 19 F3
Mahomet IL, *7258* 88 C4
Mahoning Co. OH, *238823* 91 F3
Mahopac NY, *8369* 148 C2
Mahtomedi MN, *7676* 235 E1
Mahwah NJ, *25890* 148 B3
Maiden NC, *3310* 122 A1
Maili HI, *9488* 152 A3
Maine NY, *1000* 93 E1
Maineville OH, *975* 100 B2
Maitland FL, *15751* 141 D1
Maize KS, *3420* 43 E4
Majestic KY, *600* 111 E1
Major Co. OK, *7527* 51 D2
Makaha HI, *8278* 152 A3
Makakilo City HI, *18248* 152 A3

Makawao HI, *7184* 153 D1
Makena HI, *99* 153 D1
Malabar FL, *2757* 141 E2
Malad City ID, *2095* 31 E2
Malaga CA, *947* 44 C3
Malaga NJ, *1700* 145 F1
Malakoff TX, *2324* 59 F3
Malcolm NE, *382* 35 F4
Malden MA, *59450* 151 D1
Malden MO, *4275* 108 B3
Malden WV, *750* 200 B2
Malheur Co. OR, *31313* 22 A4
Malibu CA, *12645* 52 B2
Malin OR, *805* 29 D2
Mallory WV, *1654* 111 F1
Malone FL, *2088* 137 D1
Malone NY, *5911* 80 C1
Malone WA, *475* 12 B4
Malta ID, *193* 31 D2
Malta IL, *1164* 88 C1
Malta MT, *1997* 16 C2
Malta NY, *2100* 94 B1
Malta OH, *671* 101 E1
Maltby WA, *10830* 262 B2
Malvern AL, *1448* 136 C1
Malvern AR, *10318* 117 D3
Malvern IA, *1142* 86 A3
Malvern OH, *1189* 91 E3
Malvern PA, *2998* 146 B3
Malverne NY, *8514* 241 G4
Mamaroneck NY, *18929* 148 C3
Mammoth AZ, *1426* 55 D2
Mammoth Hot Sprs. WY, *263* 23 F2
Mammoth Lakes CA, *8234* 37 E4
Mammoth Spr. AR, *977* 107 F3
Mamou LA, *3242* 133 E2
Man WV, *759* 111 F1
Manahawkin NJ, *2303* 147 E4
Manasquan NJ, *5897* 147 E2
Manassa CO, *991* 41 D4
Manassas VA, *37821* 144 A4
Manassas Park VA, *14273* 144 A3
Manatee Co. FL, *322833* 140 C3
Manawa WI, *1371* 74 B1
Mancelona MI, *1390* 70 B4
Manchaca TX, *1133* 61 E2

Manchaug MA, *850* 150 C2
Manchester CT, *30577* 150 A3
Manchester GA, *4230* 128 C2
Manchester IA, *5179* 73 F4
Manchester KY, *1255* 110 C2
Manchester ME, *2465* 82 B2
Manchester MD, *4808* 103 E1
Manchester MI, *2091* 90 B1
Manchester MO, *18094* 256 A3
Manchester NH, *109565* 81 F4
Manchester NY, *1709* 78 C3
Manchester OH, *2023* 100 C3
Manchester PA, *2763* 93 E4
Manchester TN, *10102* 120 A1
Manchester VT, *749* 81 D4
Manchester WA, *5413* 262 A3
Manchester-by-the-Sea MA, *5228* 151 F1
Manchester Ctr. VT, *2120* 81 D4
Mancos CO, *1336* 40 B4
Mandan ND, *18331* 18 C4
Mandaree ND, *596* 18 A3
Manderson SD, *626* 26 A4
Mandeville AR, *700* 116 C4
Mandeville LA, *11560* 134 B2
Mangham LA, *672* 125 F2
Mango FL, *11313* 266 C2
Mangonia Park FL, *1888* 141 F4
Mangum OK, *3010* 50 C3
Manhasset NY, *8080* 148 C4
Manhasset Hills NY, *3592* 241 G3
Manhattan IL, *7051* 89 D2
Manhattan KS, *52281* 43 F2
Manhattan MT, *1520* 23 F1
Manhattan Beach CA, *35135* 228 C3
Manheim PA, *4858* 93 E4
Manila AR, *3342* 108 B4
Manila UT, *310* 32 A3
Manilla IA, *776* 86 A1
Manistee MI, *6226* 75 E1
Manistee Co. MI, *24733* 70 A4
Manistique MI, *3097* 69 E2
Manito IL, *1642* 88 B4
Manitou Beach MI, *2019* 90 B1
Manitou Sprs. CO, *4992* 41 E2
Manitowoc WI, *33736* 75 D1

Manitowoc Co. WI, *81442* 75 D1
Mankato KS, *869* 43 E1
Mankato MN, *39309* 72 C1
Manlius NY, *4704* 79 E3
Manly IA, *1323* 73 D3
Mannford OK, *3076* 51 F2
Manning IA, *1500* 86 B1
Manning ND, *74* 18 A3
Manning SC, *4108* 122 B4
Mannington WV, *2063* 102 A1
Mannsville OK, *863* 51 F4
Manokotak AK, *442* 154 B3
Manomet MA, *2900* 151 E3
Manor PA, *3239* 92 A4
Manor TX, *5037* 61 E1
Manorhaven NY, *6556* 241 G2
Manorville NY, *14314* 149 D3
Mansfield AR, *1139* 116 C2
Mansfield IL, *906* 88 C4
Mansfield LA, *5001* 124 C3
Mansfield MA, *7360* 151 D2
Mansfield MO, *1296* 107 E2
Mansfield OH, *47821* 91 D3
Mansfield PA, *3625* 93 D1
Mansfield TX, *56368* 59 E3
Mansfield Ctr. CT, *947* 150 B3
Mansfield Four Corners CT, *700* 150 B3
Manson IA, *1690* 72 B4
Manson WA, *1468* 13 E2
Mansura LA, *1419* 133 F1
Mantachie MS, *1144* 119 D3
Manteca CA, *67096* 36 C4
Manteno IL, *9204* 89 D2
Manteo NC, *1434* 115 F2
Manti UT, *3276* 39 E2
Manton MI, *1287* 75 F1
Mantorville MN, *1197* 73 D1
Mantua OH, *1043* 91 E2
Mantua UT, *687* 31 E3
Mantua VA, *7135* 270 A4
Manvel ND, *360* 19 E2
Manvel TX, *5179* 132 A4
Manville NJ, *10344* 147 D1
Manville RI, *3800* 150 C2
Many LA, *2853* 125 D4
Many Farms AZ, *1348* 47 F2

Melbourne / Titusville FL

Bellwood A1
Bonaventure B2
Cape Canaveral B2
Cocoa B2
Cocoa Beach B2
Cocoa West A2
Frontenac A1
Georgiana B2
Indialantic B3
Indian Harbour Beach B3
La Grange A1
Malabar B3
Melbourne A3
Melbourne Beach B3
Melbourne Vil. B3
Merritt Island B2
Mims A1
Palm Bay B3
Palm Shores B3
Pineda B2
Port St. John A1
Rockledge A2
Satellite Beach B3
Sharpes A2
S. Patrick Shores B3
Titusville A1
Viera A2
W. Melbourne B3

Entries in **bold black** indicate counties or parishes.
Entries in **bold color** indicate cities with detailed inset maps.

Miami / Fort Lauderdale FL

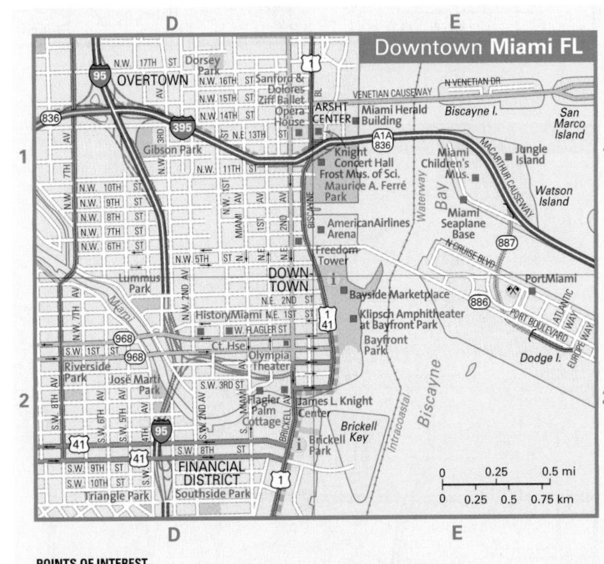

POINTS OF INTEREST

Figures after entries indicate population, page number, and grid reference.

Marysvale UT, *408* ... 39 E3
Marysville CA, *12072* ... 36 C2
Marysville KS, *3294* ... 43 F1
Marysville MI, *9959* ... 76 C3
Marysville OH, *22094* ... 90 C4
Marysville PA, *2534* ... 93 D4
Marysville WA, *60020* ... 12 C2
Maryville IL, *7487* ... 256 D1
Maryville MO, *11972* ... 86 B4
Maryville TN, *27465* ... 110 C4
Marywood MD, *6000* ... 145 D1
Masaryktown FL, *1040* ... 140 B1
Mascot TN, *2411* ... 110 C4
Mascotte FL, *5101* ... 140 C1
Mascoutah IL, *7483* ... 98 B3
Mashpee MA, *1000* ... 151 E3
Mason MI, *8252* ... 76 A4
Mason NV, *500* ... 37 E2
Mason NH, *1382* ... 95 D1
Mason OH, *30712* ... 100 B2
Mason TN, *1609* ... 118 C1
Mason TX, *2114* ... 60 C1
Mason WV, *968* ... 101 E2
Masonboro NC, *11812* ... 123 E3
Mason City IL, *2343* ... 88 B4
Mason City IA, *28079* ... 73 D3
Mason Co. IL, *14666* ... 88 A4
Mason Co. KY, *17490* ... 100 C3
Mason Co. MI, *28705* ... 75 E1
Mason Co. TX, *4012* ... 60 C1
Mason Co. WA, *60699* ... 12 B3
Mason Co. WV, *27324* ... 101 E3
Masontown PA, *3450* ... 102 B1
Masontown WV, *546* ... 102 B1
Masonville KY, *1014* ... 109 E1
Masonville NJ, *7300* ... 147 D3
Massac Co. IL, *15429* ... 108 C2
Massapequa NY, *21685* ... 148 C4
Massapequa Park NY, *17008* ... 148 C4
Massena NY, *10936* ... 80 B1
Massillon OH, *32149* ... 91 E3
Mastic NY, *15481* ... 149 D4
Mastic Beach NY, *12930* ... 149 D4
Masury OH, *2064* ... 91 F2
Matador TX, *607* ... 58 B1
Matagorda Co. TX, *36702* ... 132 A4
Matamoras PA, *2469* ... 94 A3
Matawan NJ, *8810* ... 147 E1
Matewan WV, *499* ... 111 E1
Matherville IL, *723* ... 88 A2
Mathews LA, *2209* ... 134 B3
Mathews VA, *555* ... 113 F1
Mathews Co. VA, *8978* ... 113 F1
Mathis TX, *4942* ... 61 E4
Mathiston MS, *698* ... 118 C4
Matlacha FL, *677* ... 142 C1
Mattapoisett MA, *2915* ... 151 E3
Mattawa WA, *4437* ... 13 E4
Mattawamkeag ME, *825* ... 85 D4
Mattawan MI, *1997* ... 89 F1
Mattawoman MD, *3100* ... 144 B4
Matteson IL, *19009* ... 89 D2
Matthews IN, *596* ... 89 F4
Matthews MO, *628* ... 108 B2
Matthews NC, *27198* ... 122 B1
Mattituck NY, *4219* ... 149 E3
Mattoon IL, *18555* ... 98 C2
Mattydale NY, *6446* ... 79 D3
Matunuck RI, *750* ... 150 C4
Maud OH, *4800* ... 100 B2
Maud OK, *1048* ... 51 F3
Maud TX, *1056* ... 124 C1
Maugansville MD, *3071* ... 103 D1
Maui Co. HI, *154834* ... 153 D1
Mauldin SC, *22889* ... 121 F2
Maumee OH, *14286* ... 90 C2
Maumelle AR, *17163* ... 117 E2
Maunawili HI, *2040* ... 152 B3
Maupin OR, *418* ... 21 D2
Maurertown VA, *770* ... 102 C3
Maurice LA, *964* ... 133 F2
Mauriceville TX, *3252* ... 132 C2
Maury City TN, *674* ... 108 C4
Maury Co. TN, *80956* ... 109 E4
Mauston WI, *4423* ... 74 A2
Maverick Co. TX, *54258* ... 60 B3
Mavisdale VA, *550* ... 111 E2
Max ND, *334* ... 18 B3
Max Meadows VA, *562* ... 112 A2
Maxton NC, *2426* ... 122 C2
Maxwell CA, *1103* ... 36 B2
Maxwell IA, *920* ... 86 C1
Maxwell NM, *254* ... 49 E1
Maybee MI, *562* ... 90 C1
Maybeury WV, *234* ... 111 F1
Maybrook NY, *2958* ... 148 B1
Mayer AZ, *1497* ... 47 D4
Mayer MN, *1749* ... 66 C4
Mayersville MS, *547* ... 126 A1
Mayes Co. OK, *41259* ... 106 A3
Mayesville SC, *731* ... 122 B3
Mayfield KY, *10024* ... 108 C3
Mayfield NY, *832* ... 80 C4
Mayfield OH, *3460* ... 204 G1
Mayfield PA, *1807* ... 93 F2
Mayfield UT, *496* ... 39 E2
Mayfield Hts. OH, *19155* ... 91 E2
Mayflower AR, *2234* ... 117 E2
Maynard IA, *518* ... 73 E4
Maynard MA, *10106* ... 150 C1
Maynardville TN, *2413* ... 110 C3
Mayo FL, *1237* ... 137 F3
Mayo MD, *8298* ... 144 C3
Mayo SC, *1592* ... 121 F1
Mayodan NC, *2478* ... 112 B3
Maypearl TX, *934* ... 59 F3
Mays Chapel MD, *11420* ... 193 C1
Mays Landing NJ, *2135* ... 105 D3
Maysville GA, *1798* ... 121 D3
Maysville KY, *9011* ... 100 C3
Maysville MO, *1114* ... 96 B1
Maysville NC, *1019* ... 115 D4
Maysville OK, *1232* ... 51 E4
Maytown AL, *385* ... 195 D1
Mayville MI, *950* ... 76 C3
Mayville NY, *1711* ... 78 A4
Mayville ND, *1858* ... 19 E3
Mayville WI, *5154* ... 74 C2
Maywood CA, *27395* ... 228 D3
Maywood IL, *24090* ... 203 C4
Maywood NJ, *9555* ... 240 C1
Maywood NY, *4200* ... 188 D2
Maywood Park OR, *752* ... 251 D2
Mazeppa MN, *842* ... 73 D1
Mazomanie WI, *1652* ... 74 A3
Mazon IL, *1015* ... 88 C2
McAdoo PA, *2300* ... 93 E3
McAfee NJ, *2600* ... 148 A2
McAlester OK, *18383* ... 116 A2
McAlisterville PA, *971* ... 93 D3
McAllen TX, *129877* ... 63 E4
McArthur OH, *1701* ... 101 D2
McBain MI, *656* ... 75 F1
McBee SC, *867* ... 122 B3
McCall ID, *2991* ... 22 B2
McCamey TX, *1887* ... 58 A4
McCammon ID, *809* ... 31 E1
McCandless PA, *28457* ... 92 A4
McCaysville GA, *1056* ... 120 C2
McClain Co. OK, *34506* ... 51 E3
McCleary WA, *1653* ... 12 B4
McClellandville DE, *2400* ... 146 B4
McClellanville SC, *499* ... 131 E1
McCloud CA, *1101* ... 28 C3
McClure OH, *725* ... 90 B2
McClure PA, *941* ... 93 D3
McClusky ND, *380* ... 18 C3
McColl SC, *2174* ... 122 C2
McComb MS, *12790* ... 126 B4
McComb OH, *1648* ... 90 B3
McCone Co. MT, *1734* ... 17 E3
McConnellsburg PA, *1220* ... 103 D1
McConnelsville OH, *1784* ... 101 E1
McCook NE, *7698* ... 42 C1
McCook Co. SD, *5618* ... 27 E4
McCordsville IN, *4797* ... 99 F1
McCormack Corners NY, *2300* ... 188 C2
McCormick SC, *2783* ... 121 F4
McCormick Co. SC, *10233* ... 121 F4
McCracken Co. KY, *65565* ... 108 C2
McCreary Co. KY, *18306* ... 110 C2
McCrory AR, *1729* ... 117 F1
McCulloch Co. TX, *8283* ... 58 C4
McCune KS, *405* ... 106 B1
McCurtain OK, *516* ... 116 B1
McCurtain Co. OK, *33151* ... 116 B3
McDermitt NV, *172* ... 30 A2
McDonald OH, *3263* ... 276 B2
McDonald PA, *2149* ... 92 A4
McDonald Co. MO, *23083* ... 106 C3
McDonough GA, *22084* ... 120 C4
McDonough Co. IL, *32612* ... 87 F3
McDowell Co. NC, *44996* ... 111 E4
McDowell Co. WV, *22113* ... 111 F1
McDuffie Co. GA, *21875* ... 129 F1
McEwen TN, *1750* ... 109 E4
McFarland CA, *12707* ... 45 D4
McFarland WI, *7808* ... 74 B3
McGaheysville VA, *500* ... 102 C4
McGehee AR, *4219* ... 117 F4
McGill NV, *1148* ... 38 B2
McGrath AK, *346* ... 154 C2
McGraw NY, *1053* ... 79 E4
McGregor IA, *871* ... 73 F3
McGregor TX, *4987* ... 59 E4
McHenry IL, *26992* ... 74 C4
McHenry KY, *388* ... 109 E1
McHenry Co. IL, *308760* ... 74 C4
McHenry Co. ND, *5395* ... 18 C2
McIntosh FL, *452* ... 138 C4
McIntosh MN, *625* ... 19 F3
McIntosh SD, *173* ... 26 B1
McIntosh Co. GA, *14333* ... 130 B4
McIntosh Co. ND, *2809* ... 27 D1
McIntosh Co. OK, *20252* ... 116 A1
McIntyre GA, *650* ... 129 E2
McKean Co. PA, *43450* ... 92 B1
McKee KY, *800* ... 110 C1
McKee City NJ, *2800* ... 147 F4
McKeesport PA, *19731* ... 92 A4
McKees Rocks PA, *6104* ... 250 B1
McKenna WA, *716* ... 12 C4
McKenney VA, *483* ... 113 E2
McKenzie AL, *530* ... 127 F4
McKenzie TN, *5310* ... 109 D4
McKenzie Co. ND, *6360* ... 17 F2
McKinley Co. NM, *71492* ... 48 A2
McKinleyville CA, *15177* ... 28 A4
McKinney TX, *131117* ... 59 F2
McKownville NY, *2600* ... 188 D3
McLain MS, *441* ... 135 D1
McLaughlin SD, *663* ... 26 C1
McLean IL, *830* ... 88 B4
McLean TX, *778* ... 50 B3
McLean VA, *48115* ... 144 B3
McLean Co. IL, *169572* ... 88 C4
McLean Co. KY, *9531* ... 109 E1
McLean Co. ND, *8962* ... 18 B3
McLeansboro IL, *2883* ... 98 C4
McLennan Co. TX, *234906* ... 59 F4
McLeod Co. MN, *36651* ... 66 C4
McLoud OK, *4044* ... 51 E3
McLouth KS, *880* ... 96 A2
McMechen WV, *1926* ... 101 F1
McMinn Co. TN, *52266* ... 120 C1
McMinnville OR, *32187* ... 20 B2
McMinnville TN, *13605* ... 110 A4
McMullen Co. TX, *707* ... 61 D4
McMurray PA, *4647* ... 92 A4
McNairy Co. TN, *26075* ... 119 D1
McNary AZ, *528* ... 47 F4
McNeil AR, *516* ... 125 D1
McPherson KS, *13155* ... 43 E3
McPherson Co. KS, *29180* ... 43 E3
McPherson Co. NE, *539* ... 34 B3
McPherson Co. SD, *2459* ... 27 D1
McQueeney TX, *2545* ... 61 D2
McRae AR, *682* ... 117 F1
McRae GA, *5740* ... 129 E3
McRoberts KY, *784* ... 111 E2
McSherrystown PA, *3038* ... 103 E1
McVeigh KY, *550* ... 111 E1
McVille ND, *349* ... 19 E3
Mead CO, *3405* ... 33 E4
Mead NE, *569* ... 35 F3
Mead WA, *7275* ... 14 A3
Meade KS, *1721* ... 42 C4
Meade Co. KS, *4575* ... 42 C4
Meade Co. KY, *28602* ... 99 F4
Meade Co. SD, *25434* ... 26 A3
Meadow TX, *593* ... 58 A1
Meadowlakes TX, *1777* ... 61 D1
Meadows Place TX, *4660* ... 132 A3
Meadow Vale KY, *736* ... 230 F1
Meadow Valley CA, *464* ... 36 C1
Meadowview VA, *967* ... 111 F2
Meadville MS, *449* ... 126 A4
Meadville PA, *13388* ... 92 A2
Meagher Co. MT, *1891* ... 15 F4
Mebane NC, *11393* ... 112 C4
Mecca CA, *8577* ... 53 E3
Mechanic Falls ME, *2237* ... 82 B2
Mechanicsburg OH, *1644* ... 90 C4
Mechanicsburg PA, *8981* ... 93 D4
Mechanicsville IA, *1146* ... 87 F1
Mechanicsville MD, *1508* ... 103 E3
Mechanicsville VA, *36348* ... 113 E1
Mechanicville NY, *5196* ... 94 B1
Mecklenburg Co. NC, *919628* ... 122 B1
Mecklenburg Co. VA, *32727* ... 113 D2
Mecosta Co. MI, *42798* ... 75 F2
Medanales NM, *450* ... 48 C2
Medaryville IN, *614* ... 89 E3
Medfield MA, *6483* ... 151 D2
Medford MA, *56173* ... 151 D1
Medford MN, *1239* ... 73 D1
Medford NJ, *22858* ... 147 D3
Medford NY, *24142* ... 149 D4
Medford OK, *996* ... 51 E1
Medford OR, *74907* ... 28 B2
Medford WI, *4326* ... 68 A3
Medford Lakes NJ, *4146* ... 147 D3
Media PA, *5327* ... 146 C3
Mediapolis IA, *1560* ... 87 F3
Medical Lake WA, *5060* ... 13 F3
Medicine Bow WY, *284* ... 33 D2
Medicine Lake MT, *225* ... 17 F2
Medicine Lodge KS, *2009* ... 43 D4
Medina MN, *4892* ... 66 C3
Medina NY, *6065* ... 78 B3
Medina ND, *308* ... 19 D4
Medina OH, *26678* ... 91 E3
Medina TN, *3479* ... 108 C4
Medina WA, *2969* ... 262 B3
Medina Co. OH, *172332* ... 91 E3
Medina Co. TX, *46006* ... 60 C3

Bayside ... D1
Brookfield ... B2
Brown Deer ... C1
Butler ... B1
Cudahy ... D3
Elm Grove ... B2
Fox Pt. ... D1
Glendale ... C1
Greendale ... C3
Greenfield ... C3
Hales Corners ... B3
Lannon ... A1
Menomonee Falls ... B1
Milwaukee ... C2
New Berlin ... B3
Pewaukee (city) ... A2
Pewaukee (village) ... A2
River Hills ... D1
St. Francis ... D3
Shorewood ... D2
Sussex ... A1
Waukesha ... A2
Wauwatosa ... C2
W. Allis ... C3
W. Milwaukee ... C3
Whitefish Bay ... D1

Milwaukee WI

Downtown Milwaukee WI

POINTS OF INTEREST

Amtrak/Intermodal Station ... F2
Betty Brinn Children's Museum ... G2
Broadway Theatre Center ... F2
Court House ... E1
Cudahy Gardens ... G2
Discovery World at Pier Wisconsin ... G2
Federal Plaza ... F2
Fiserv Forum ... F1
Grain Exchange ... F2
Haggerty Museum of Art ... E2
Harley-Davidson Museum ... F2
Helfaer Theatre ... E2
Historic Third Ward ... F2
Lakeshore State Park ... G2
Maier Festival Park ... G2
Marcus Ctr. for the Performing Arts ... F1
Marquette University ... E2
Miller High Life Theatre ... F1
Milwaukee Art Museum & War Memorial Center ... G1
Milwaukee County Hist. Society ... F1
Milwaukee Institute of Art & Design ... F2
Milwaukee Public Market ... F2
Milwaukee Public Museum ... E1
Milwaukee School of Engineering ... F1
Pabst Theater ... F1
Post Office ... F2
Potawatomi Hotel & Casino ... E2
St. Joan of Arc Chapel ... E2
State Office Building ... F1
UW-Milwaukee Panther Arena ... F1
Wisconsin Center ... F2
Wisconsin Conservatory of Music ... G1

Entries in **bold black** indicate counties or parishes.
Entries in **bold color** indicate cities with detailed inset maps.

Minneapolis / St Paul MN

Figures after entries indicate population, page number, and grid reference.

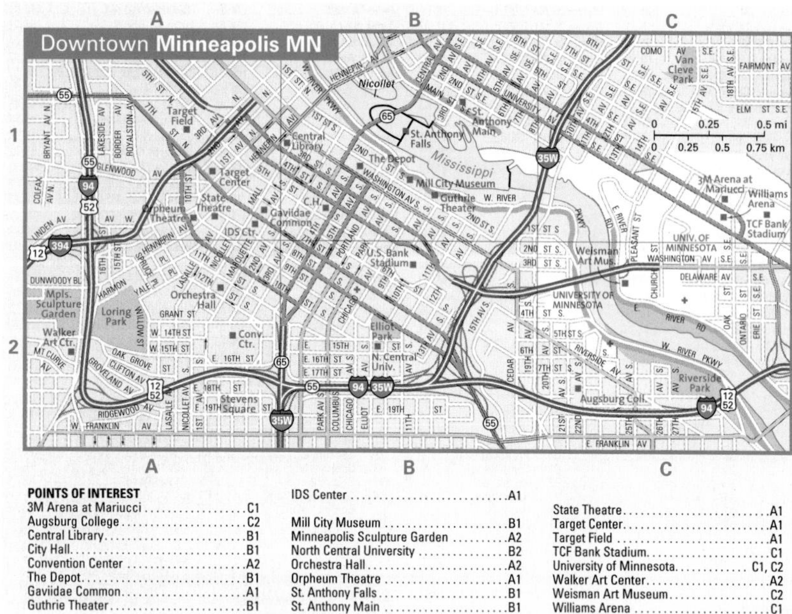

POINTS OF INTEREST

3M Arena at Mariucci C1
Augsburg College C2
Central Library B1
City Hall B1
Convention Center A2
The Depot B1
Gaviidae Common A1
Guthrie Theater B1
IDS Center A1
Mill City Museum B1
Minneapolis Sculpture Garden A2
North Central University B2
Orchestra Hall A2
Orpheum Theatre A1
St. Anthony Falls B1
St. Anthony Main B1
State Theatre A1
Target Center A1
Target Field A1
TCF Bank Stadium C1
University of Minnesota C1, C2
Walker Art Center A2
Weisman Art Museum C2
Williams Arena C1

Mexia TX, *7459* **59** F4
Mexico IN, *836* **89** F3
Mexico ME, *1743* **82** B2
Mexico MO, *11543* **97** E2
Mexico NY, *1624* **79** D2
Mexico Beach FL, *1072* **136** C3
Meyersdale PA, *2184* **102** C1
Meyers Lake OH, *569* **199** B2
Miami AZ, *1837* **55** D1
Miami FL, *399457* **143** F2
Miami OK, *13570* **106** B2
Miami TX, *597* **50** B2
Miami Beach FL, *87779* **143** F2
Miami Co. IN, *36903* **89** F3
Miami Co. KS, *32787* **96** B3
Miami Co. OH, *102506* **90** B4
Miami-Dade Co. FL, *2496435* **143** E2
Miami Gardens FL, *107167* **143** E2
Miami Lakes FL, *29361* **233** A3
Miamisburg OH, *20181* **100** B1
Miami Shores FL, *10493* **143** F2
Miami Sprs. FL, *13809* **143** E2
Micanopy FL, *600* **138** C4
Micaville NC, *750* **111** E4
Micco FL, *9052* **141** E2
Michie TN, *591* **119** D2
Michigan ND, *294* **19** E2
Michigan Ctr. MI, *4672* **90** B1
Michigan City IN, *31479* **89** E1
Middleboro MA, *7319* **151** D3
Middlebourne WV, *815* **101** F2
Middleburg FL, *13008* **139** D3
Middleburg PA, *1309* **93** D3
Middleburg VA, *673* **144** A3
Middleburgh NY, *1500* **79** F4
Middleburg Hts. OH, *15946* **204** E3
Middlebury CT, *6974* **149** D1
Middlebury IN, *3420* **89** F2
Middlebury VT, *6588* **81** D3
Middle Falls NY, *750* **81** D4
Middlefield CT, *4281* **149** E1
Middlefield OH, *2694* **91** F2
Middle Haddam CT, *900* **149** E1
Middle Island NY, *10483* **149** D3
Middle Pt. OH, *593* **90** B3
Middleport NY, *1840* **78** B3
Middleport OH, *2530* **101** E2
Middle River MD, *25191* **144** C2
Middlesboro KY, *10334* **110** C3
Middlesex NJ, *13635* **147** D1
Middlesex NC, *822* **113** D4
Middlesex Co. CT, *165676* **149** E1
Middlesex Co. MA, *1503085* **151** D1
Middlesex Co. NJ, *809858* **147** E2
Middlesex Co. VA, *10959* **113** F1
Middleton ID, *5524* **22** B4
Middleton MA, *7744* **151** F1
Middleton TN, *706* **118** C2
Middleton WI, *17442* **74** B3
Middletown CA, *1323* **36** B2
Middletown CT, *47648* **149** E1
Middletown DE, *18871* **145** E1
Middletown IN, *2322* **89** F4
Middletown IA, *318* **87** F3
Middletown KY, *7218* **100** A4
Middletown MD, *4136* **144** A1
Middletown NY, *28086* **148** A1
Middletown OH, *48694* **100** B1
Middletown PA, *8901* **93** E4
Middletown PA, *7378* **189** B1
Middletown RI, *16150* **151** D4
Middletown VA, *1265* **102** C2
Middle Valley TN, *12684* **120** B1
Middleville MI, *3319* **75** F4
Middleville NY, *512* **79** F3
Midfield AL, *5365* **119** F4
Midland MI, *41863* **76** B2
Midland NC, *3073* **122** B1
Midland PA, *2635* **91** F3
Midland TX, *111147* **58** A3
Midland WA, *8962* **262** A5
Midland City AL, *2344* **128** B4
Midland Co. MI, *83629* **76** A2
Midland Co. TX, *136872* **58** A3
Midlothian IL, *14819* **203** D6
Midlothian TX, *18037* **59** F3
Midlothian VA, *3300* **113** E1
Midtown TN, *1360* **110** B4
Midvale UT, *27964* **257** B3
Midway AL, *499* **128** B3
Midway DE, *1500* **145** F4
Midway FL, *3004* **137** E2
Midway GA, *2121* **130** B3
Midway KY, *1641* **100** B4
Midway LA, *1291* **125** E4
Midway NM, *971* **57** E2
Midway NC, *4679* **112** B4
Midway PA, *2125* **91** F4
Midway TN, *2491* **111** D4
Midway UT, *3845* **31** F4
Midwest WY, *404* **25** D4
Midwest City OK, *54371* **51** E3
Mifflin PA, *642* **93** D4
Mifflinburg PA, *3540* **93** D3
Mifflin Co. PA, *46682* **93** D3
Mifflintown PA, *936* **93** D4
Mifflinville PA, *1253* **93** E3
Milaca MN, *2946* **66** C2
Milam TX, *1480* **124** C4
Milam Co. TX, *24757* **61** F1
Milan GA, *700* **129** E3
Milan IL, *5099* **88** A2
Milan IN, *1899* **100** A2
Milan MI, *5836* **90** C1
Milan MO, *1960* **87** D4
Milan NM, *3245* **48** B3
Milan OH, *1367* **91** D2
Milan TN, *7851* **108** C4
Milbank SD, *3353* **27** F2
Milbridge ME, *1279* **83** E2

Aptos D1
Aromas E2
Ben Lomond D1
Bolsa Knolls E2
Capitola D1
Carmel-by-the-Sea D3
Carmel Highlands D3
Carmel Valley E3
Castroville E2
Corralitos E1
Del Rey Oaks E3
Elkhorn E2
Felton D1
Freedom E1
Gabilan Acres E2
Gilroy E1
La Selva Beach D1
Las Lomas E2
Live Oak D1
Marina E2
Monterey D3
Moss Landing E2
Mt. Hermon D1
Opal Cliffs D1
Pacific Grove D3
Pajaro E1
Paradise Park D1
Pebble Beach D3
Prunedale E2
Rio del Mar D1
Salinas E3
Sand City E3
Santa Cruz D1
Scotts Valley D1
Seaside E3
Soquel D1
Spreckels E3
Twin Lakes D1
Watsonville E1
Zayante D1

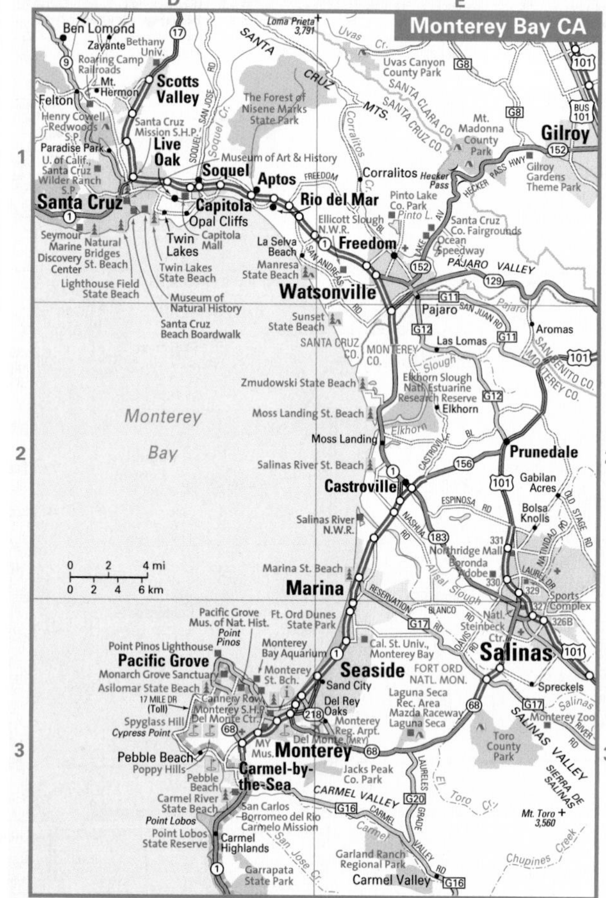

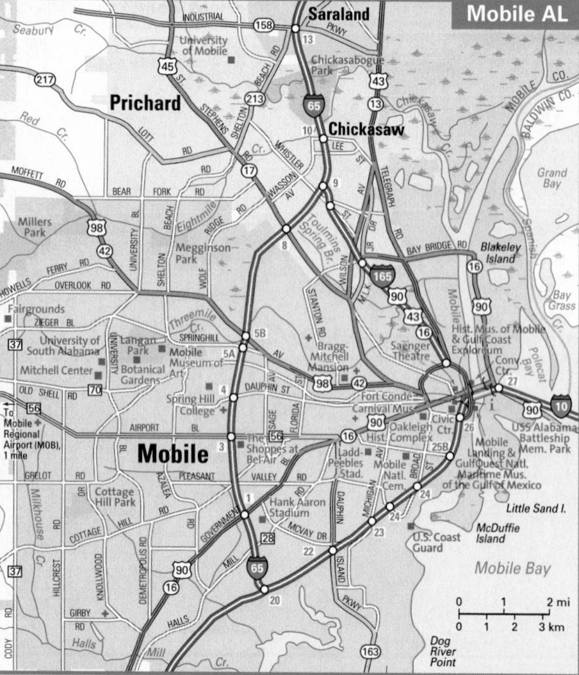

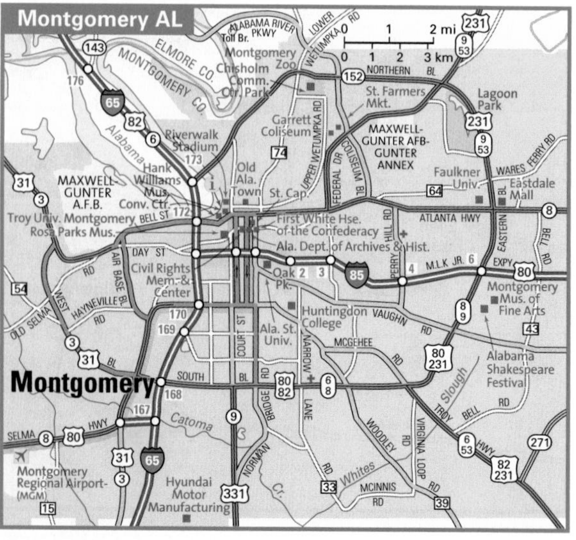

Entries in **bold black** indicate counties or parishes.
Entries in **bold color** indicate cities with detailed inset maps.

Montpelier VT

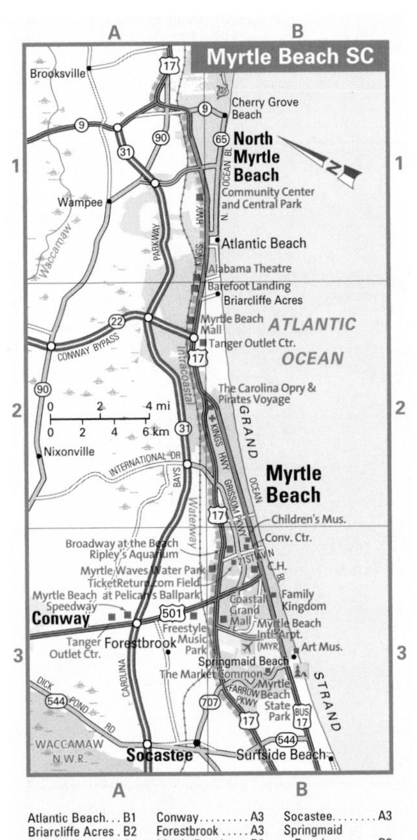

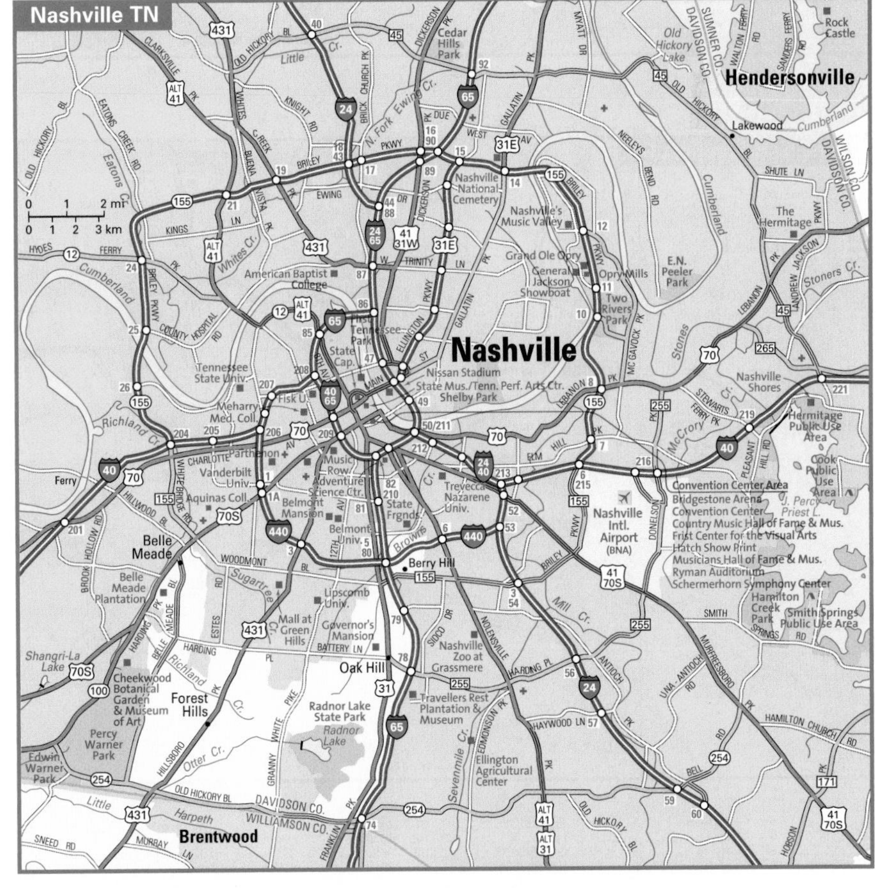

Figures after entries indicate population, page number, and grid reference.

Montello WI, *1495* **74** B2
Monterey CA, *27810* **44** B3
Monterey TN, *2850* **110** B4
Monterey VA, *147* **102** B3
Monterey Co. CA, *415057* **44** B3
Monterey Park CA, *60269* **228** D2
Monte Rio CA, *1152* **36** A3
Montesano WA, *3976* **12** B4
Montevallo AL, *6323* **127** F1
Montevideo MN, *5383* **66** A4
Monte Vista CO, *4444* **41** D4
Montezuma GA, *3460* **129** D3
Montezuma IN, *1022* **99** E1
Montezuma IA, *1462* **87** D2
Montezuma KS, *966* **42** C4
Montezuma Co. CO, *25535* **48** A1
Montezuma Creek UT, *335* **40** A4
Montfort WI, *718* **74** A3
Montgomery AL, *205764* **128** A2
Montgomery IL, *18438* **203** A5
Montgomery LA, *730* **125** D4
Montgomery MN, *2956* **72** C1
Montgomery NY, *3814* **148** A1
Montgomery OH, *10251* **204** C1
Montgomery PA, *1579* **93** D2
Montgomery WV, *1638* **101** F4
Montgomery City MO, *2834* **97** F2
Montgomery Co. AL, *229363* **128** A3
Montgomery Co. AR, *9487* **116** C3
Montgomery Co. GA, *9123* **129** F3
Montgomery Co. IL, *30104* **98** B2
Montgomery Co. IN, *38124* **89** E4
Montgomery Co. IA, *10740* **86** B3
Montgomery Co. KS, *35471* **106** A1
Montgomery Co. KY, *26499* **100** C4
Montgomery Co. MD, *971777* **144** B2
Montgomery Co. MS, *10925* **118** B4
Montgomery Co. MO, *12236* **97** F2
Montgomery Co. NY, *50219* **94** A1
Montgomery Co. NC, *27798* **122** C1
Montgomery Co. OH, *535153* **100** B1
Montgomery Co. PA, *799874* **146** B2
Montgomery Co. TN, *172331* **109** E3
Montgomery Co. TX, *455746* **132** A2
Montgomery Co. VA, *94392* **112** A2
Montgomery Vil. MD, *32032* **144** B2
Montgomeryville PA, *12624* **146** C2
Monticello AR, *9467* **117** F4
Monticello FL, *2506* **137** E2
Monticello GA, *2657* **129** D1
Monticello IL, *5548* **98** C1
Monticello IN, *5378* **89** E3
Monticello IA, *3796* **87** F1
Monticello KY, *6188* **110** B2
Monticello MN, *12759* **66** C3
Monticello MS, *1571* **126** B4
Monticello MO, *98* **87** E4
Monticello NY, *6726* **148** A1
Monticello UT, *1972* **40** A4
Monticello WI, *1217* **74** B4
Montmorency Co. MI, *9765* **70** C4
Montour Co. PA, *18267* **93** E3
Montour Falls NY, *1711* **79** D4
Montoursville PA, *4615* **93** D2
Montpelier ID, *2597* **31** F2
Montpelier IN, *1805* **90** A4
Montpelier OH, *4072* **90** B2
Montpelier VT, *7855* **81** E2
Montreal WI, *807* **65** E4
Montreat NC, *723* **111** E4
Montrose AR, *354* **125** F1
Montrose CA, *18532* **228** D1
Montrose CO, *19132* **40** B3
Montrose IA, *898* **87** F4
Montrose MI, *1657* **76** B3
Montrose MN, *2847* **66** C3
Montrose NY, *2731* **148** B2
Montrose OH, *5177* **188** A1
Montrose PA, *1617* **93** E1
Montrose SD, *472* **27** F4
Montrose Co. CO, *41276* **40** B3
Montross VA, *384* **103** E4
Montvale NJ, *7844* **148** B3
Montverde FL, *1463* **140** C1
Mont Vernon NH, *2409* **95** D1
Montville NJ, *21150* **148** A3
Montz LA, *1918* **239** A1
Monument CO, *5530* **41** E2
Monument Beach MA, *2790* **151** E3
Moodus CT, *1413* **149** E1
Moody AL, *11726* **119** F4
Moody ME, *1000* **82** B4
Moody TX, *1371* **59** E4
Moody Co. SD, *6486* **27** F3
Moonachie NJ, *2708* **240** C2
Moorcroft WY, *1009* **25** E3
Moore ID, *189* **23** D4
Moore MT, *193* **16** B4
Moore OK, *55081* **51** E3
Moore TX, *475* **61** D3
Moore Co. NC, *88247* **122** C1
Moore Co. TN, *6362* **120** A1
Moore Co. TX, *21904* **50** A2
Moorefield WV, *2544* **102** C2
Moore Haven FL, *1680* **141** D4
Mooreland OK, *1190* **51** D1
Moores Hill IN, *597* **100** A2
Moorestown NJ, *19487* **147** D3
Mooresville IN, *9326* **99** F1
Mooresville NC, *32711* **122** B1
Moorhead MN, *38065* **19** F4
Moorhead MS, *2405* **118** A4
Mooringsport LA, *793* **124** C2
Moorland KY, *431* **230** F1
Moorpark CA, *34421* **52** B2
Moose Lake MN, *2751* **64** C4
Moosic PA, *5719* **261** D2
Moosup CT, *3231* **150** B3
Mora MN, *3571* **67** D2
Mora NM, *656* **49** D2
Mora Co. NM, *4881* **49** D2
Morada CA, *3828* **36** C3
Moraga CA, *16016* **259** D2
Moraine OH, *6307* **100** B1
Moran KS, *558* **96** A4
Moravia IA, *665* **87** D3
Moravia NY, *1282* **79** D4
Moravian Falls NC, *1901* **111** F4
Moreauville LA, *929* **133** F1
Morehead KY, *6845* **100** C4
Morehead City NC, *8661* **115** E4
Morehouse MO, *973* **108** B2
Morehouse Par. LA, *27979* **125** F1
Moreland KY, *550* **110** B1
Moreland Hills OH, *3320* **204** G2
Morenci AZ, *1489* **55** E2
Morenci MI, *2220* **90** B1
Moreno Valley CA, *193365* **53** D3
Morgan GA, *240* **128** C4
Morgan MN, *896* **72** B1
Morgan UT, *3687* **31** F3
Morgan City LA, *12404* **134** A3
Morgan Co. AL, *119490* **119** F3
Morgan Co. CO, *28159* **33** F4
Morgan Co. GA, *17868* **121** D4
Morgan Co. IL, *35547* **98** A1
Morgan Co. IN, *68894* **99** F2
Morgan Co. KY, *13923* **100** C4
Morgan Co. MO, *20565* **97** D3
Morgan Co. OH, *15054* **101** E1
Morgan Co. TN, *21987* **110** B3
Morgan Co. UT, *9469* **31** F3
Morgan Co. WV, *17541* **102** C1
Morganfield KY, *3285* **109** D1
Morgan Hill CA, *37882* **44** B2
Morgan's Pt. Resort TX, *4170* **59** E4
Morganton NC, *16918* **111** F4
Morgantown IN, *986* **99** F2
Morgantown KY, *2394* **109** F2
Morgantown PA, *826* **146** B2
Morgantown WV, *29660* **102** A1
Morganville NJ, *5040* **147** E1
Morganza LA, *610* **133** F1
Moriarty NM, *1910* **49** D3
Moriches NY, *2838* **149** D4
Morley MI, *493* **75** F2
Morley MO, *697* **108** B2
Morningdale MA, *2500* **275** D1
Morningside MD, *2015* **271** F4
Morning Sun IA, *836* **87** F3
Moro OR, *324* **21** D2
Morocco IN, *1129* **89** D3
Morongo Valley CA, *3552* **53** D2
Moroni UT, *1423* **39** E1
Morrice MI, *927* **76** B3
Morrill NE, *921* **33** F2
Morrill Co. NE, *5042* **34** A2
Morrilton AR, *6767* **117** E1
Morris AL, *1859* **119** F4
Morris IL, *13636* **88** C2
Morris MN, *5286* **27** F1
Morris NY, *583* **79** E4
Morris OK, *1479* **116** A1
Morris Co. KS, *5923* **43** F3
Morris Co. NJ, *492276* **94** A4
Morris Co. TX, *12934* **124** B1

New Bedford / Fall River MA

Acushnet C1
Bliss Corner C2
Braleys C1
Coury Hts. C1
Eagleville A2
Fairhaven C2
Fall River B1
Faunce Corner C1
Head of Westport B2
Hixville B1
Idlewood C2
Island Park A2
Lakeside B2
Long Plain C1
New Bedford C2
N. Dartmouth C2
N. Fairhaven C2
N. Tiverton A2
Ocean Grove A1
Sherwood Forest C1
Somerset A1
S. Dartmouth C2
S. Swansea A1
Summit Grove B2
Swansea A1
The Hummocks A2
Tiverton A2
Westport Factory B2

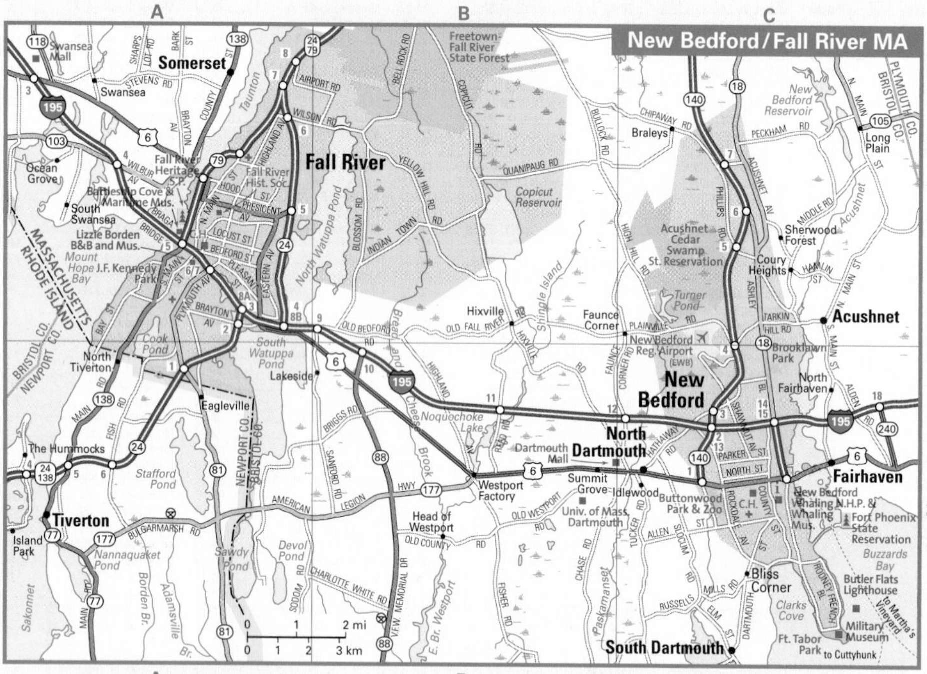

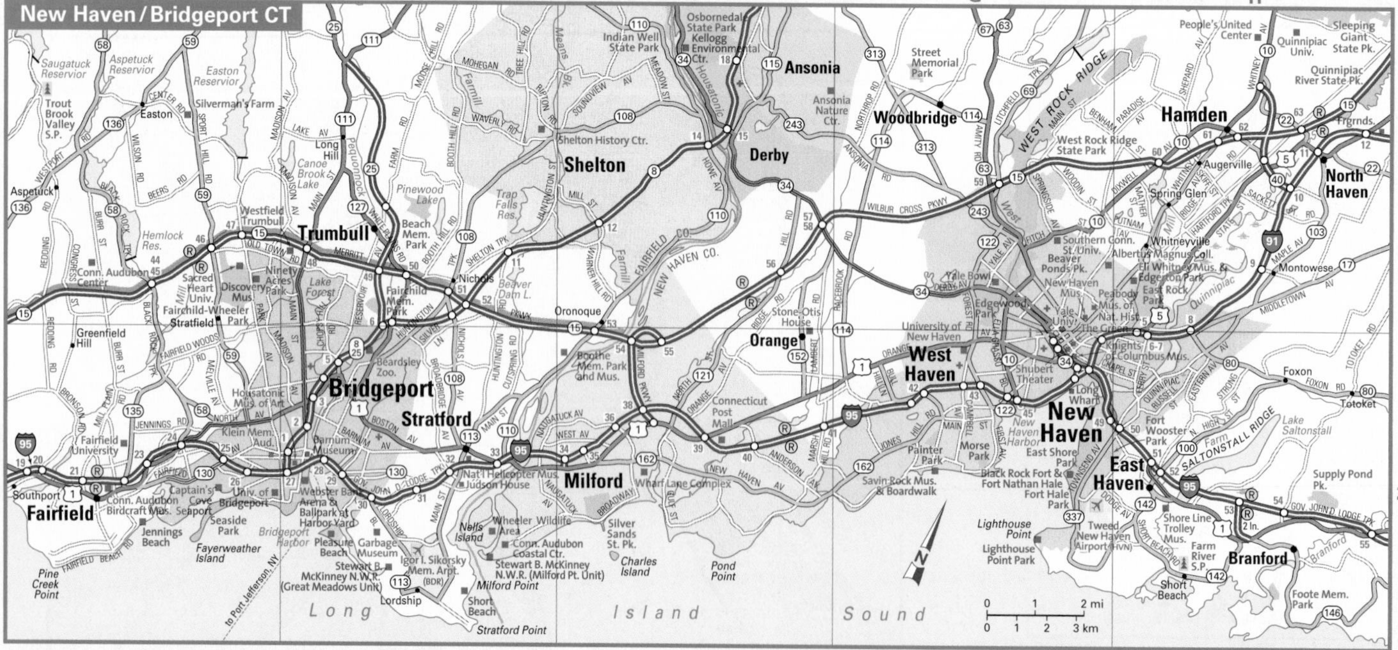

New Haven / Bridgeport CT

Ansonia F1
Aspetuck D1
Augerville H1
Branford H2
Bridgeport E2
Derby F1
E. Haven H2
Easton D1
Fairfield D2
Foxon H2
Greenfield Hill D2
Hamden H1
Long Hill E1
Lordship E2
Milford F2
Montowese H1
New Haven G2
Nichols E1
N. Haven H1
Orange F2
Oronoque F1
Shelton F1
Short Beach H2
Southport D2
Spring Glen H1
Stratfield D1
Stratford E2
Totoket H2
Trumbull E1
W. Haven G2
Whitneyville H1
Woodbridge G1

Entries in **bold black** indicate counties or parishes.
Entries in **bold color** indicate cities with detailed inset maps.

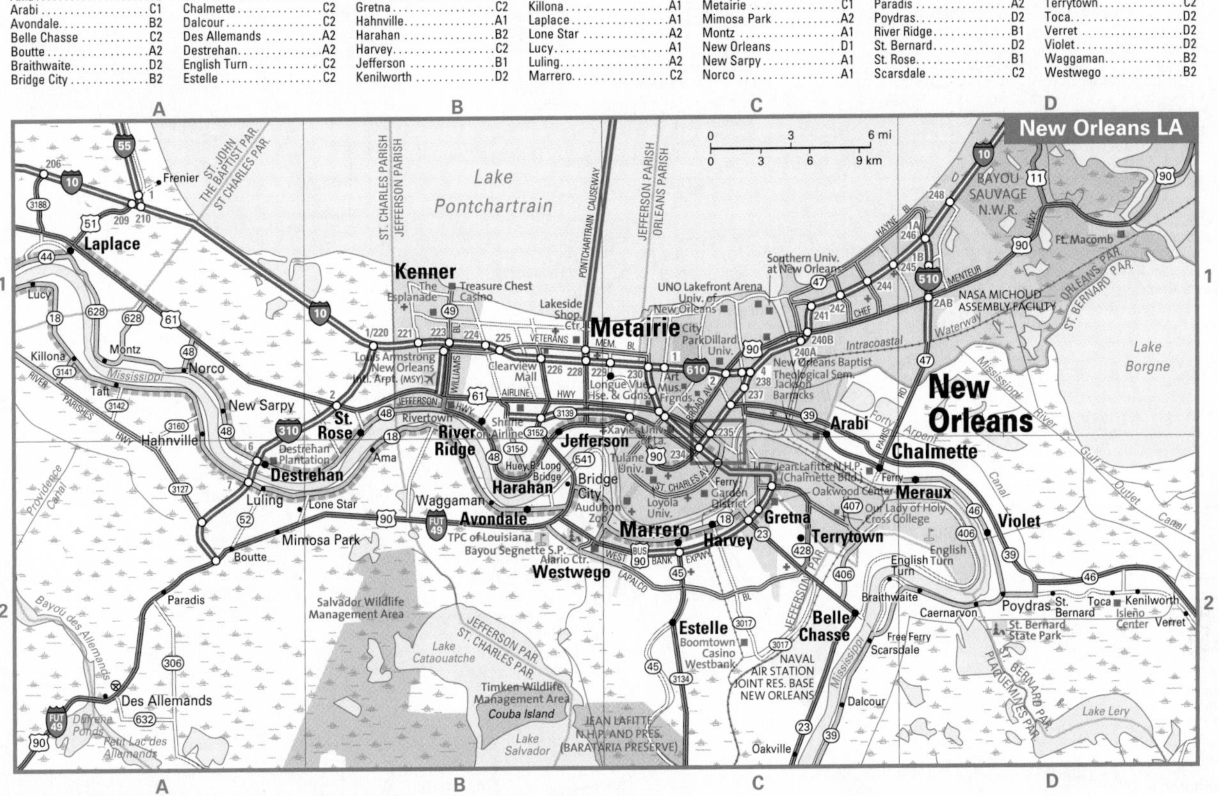

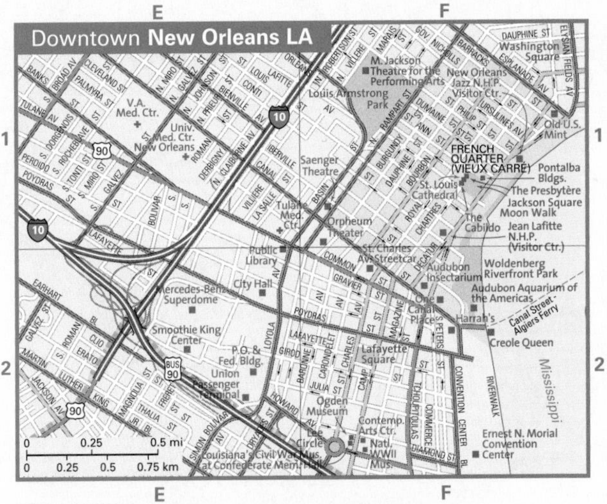

POINTS OF INTEREST

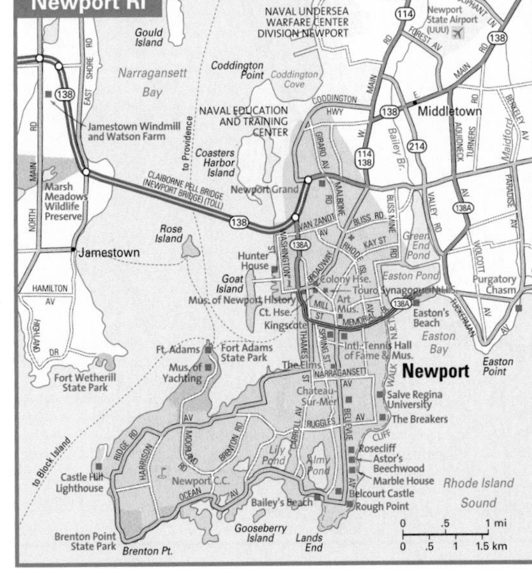

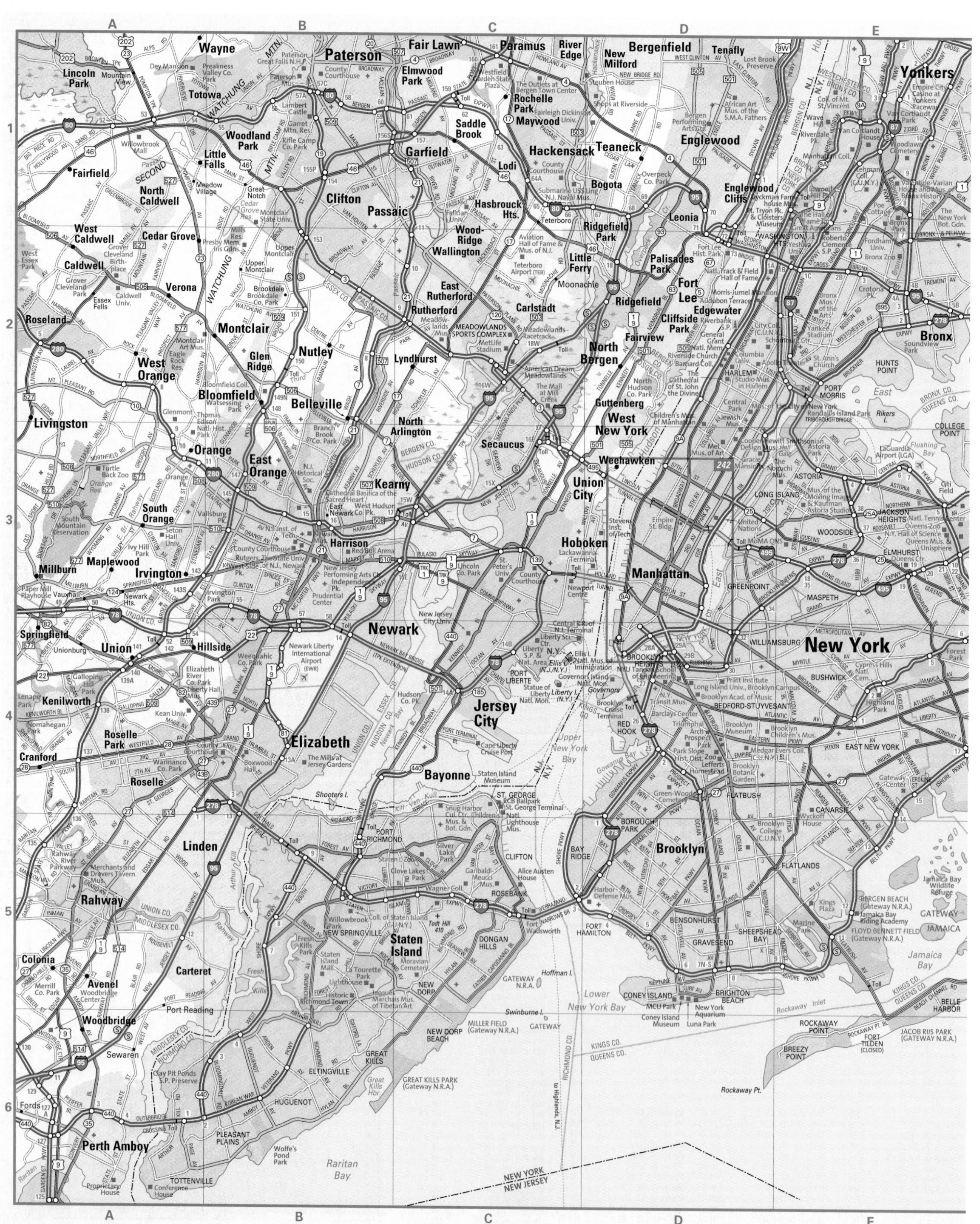
A
B
C
D
E
1
2
3
4
5
6
Wayne
Paterson
Fair Lawn
Paramus
River Edge
New Milford
Bergenfield
Tenafly
Yonkers
Lincoln Park
Totowa
Elmwood Park
Rochelle Park
Maywood
Saddle Brook
Woodland Park
Little Falls
Garfield
Hackensack
Teaneck
Englewood
Fairfield
North Caldwell
Clifton
Passaic
Lodi
Bogota
Hasbrouck Hts.
Englewood Cliffs
Leonia
West Caldwell
Cedar Grove
Wood-Ridge
Wallington
Ridgefield Park
Caldwell
Little Ferry
Palisades Park
Verona
East Rutherford
Rutherford
Moonachie
Fort Lee
Carlstadt
Ridgefield
Edgewater
Roseland
Montclair
Cliffside Park
Fairview
Nutley
Glen Ridge
Lyndhurst
North Bergen
West Orange
Bloomfield
Belleville
Guttenberg
West New York
Livingston
North Arlington
Secaucus
Orange
East Orange
Weehawken
Kearny
Union City
South Orange
Harrison
Hoboken
Maplewood
Millburn
Irvington
Manhattan
Bronx
Newark
Springfield
Union
Hillside
New York
Kenilworth
Jersey City
Roselle Park
Elizabeth
Cranford
Roselle
Bayonne
Linden
Brooklyn
Rahway
Staten Island
Colonia
Carteret
Avenel
Woodbridge
Sewaren
Fords
Perth Amboy
Lower New York Bay
Upper New York Bay
Raritan Bay
Jamaica Bay
NEW YORK
NEW JERSEY
242

Entries in **bold black** indicate counties or parishes.
Entries in **bold color** indicate cities with detailed inset maps.

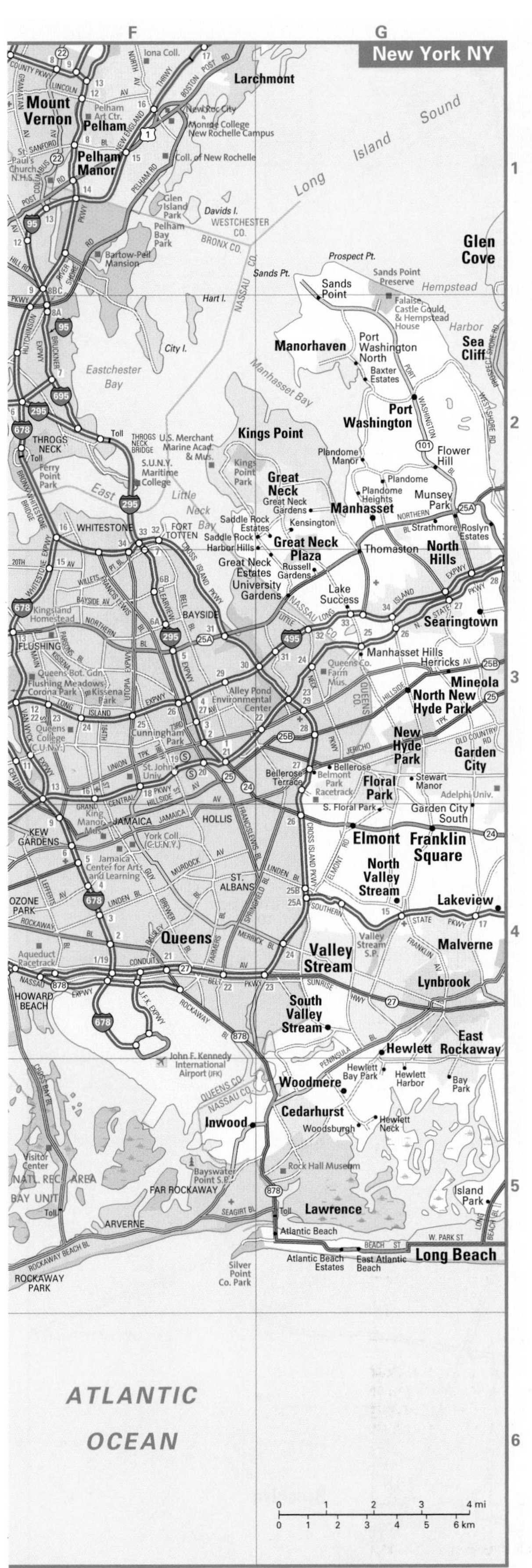

Figures after entries indicate population, page number, and grid reference.

POINTS OF INTEREST

Entries in **bold black** indicate counties or parishes.
Entries in **bold color** indicate cities with detailed inset maps.

Norfolk VA/Hampton Roads

Figures after entries indicate population, page number, and grid reference.

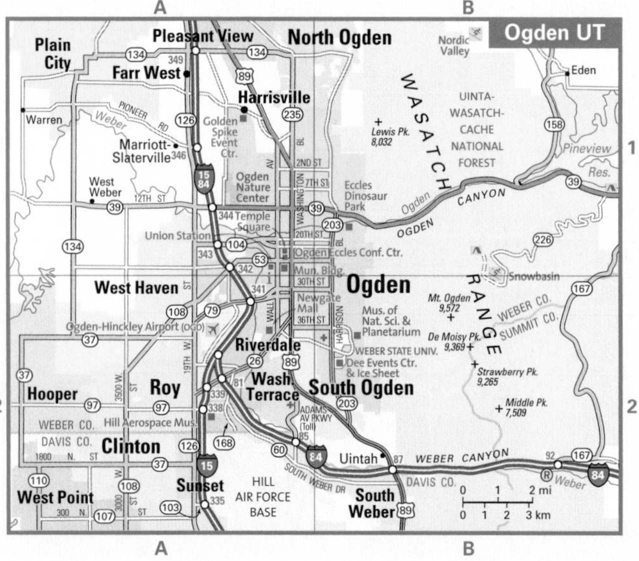

Entries in **bold black** indicate counties or parishes.
Entries in **bold color** indicate cities with detailed inset maps.

Olympia WA

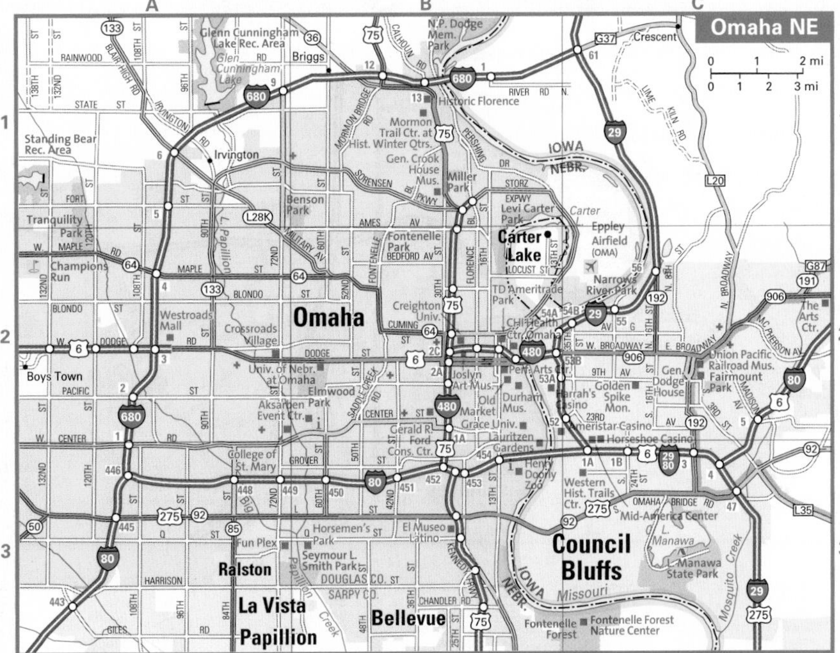

Bellevue ... B3
Boys Town ... A2
Briggs ... B1
Carter Lake ... B2
Council Bluffs ... C3
Crescent ... C1
Irvington ... A1
La Vista ... A3
Omaha ... B2
Papillion ... A3
Ralston ... A3

Figures after entries indicate population, page number, and grid reference.

P

Orlando FL

0 1 2 3 mi
0 1 2 3 4 km

Entries in **bold black** indicate counties or parishes.
Entries in **bold color** indicate cities with detailed inset maps.

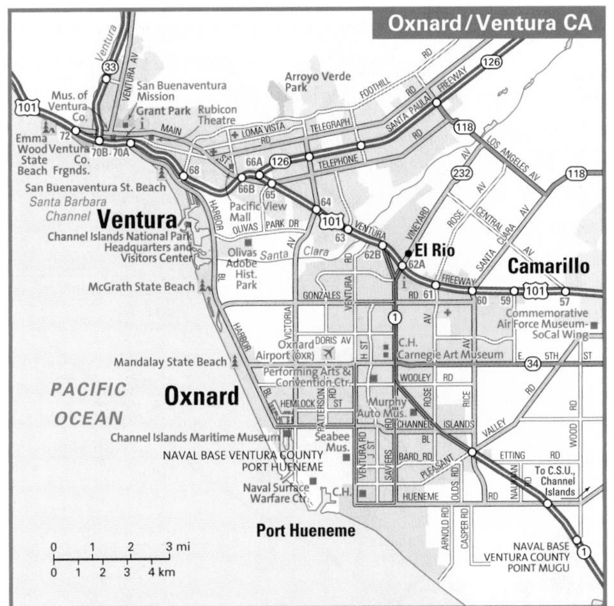

Palm Springs CA

Pensacola FL

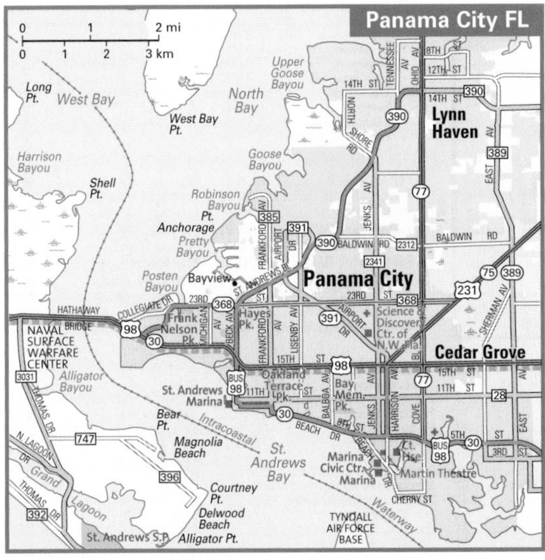

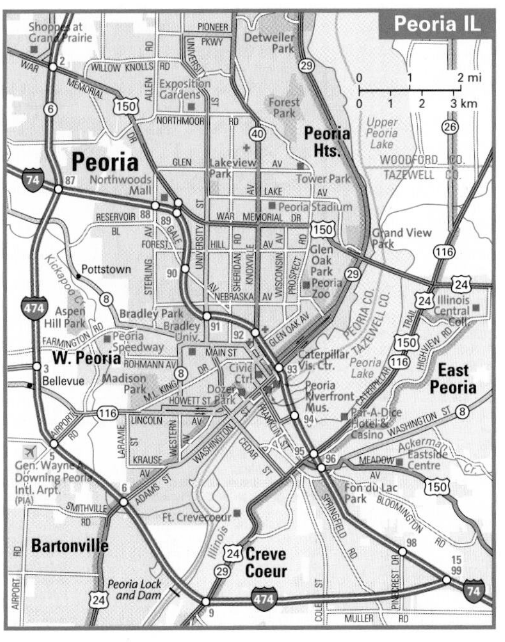

Figures after entries indicate population, page number, and grid reference.

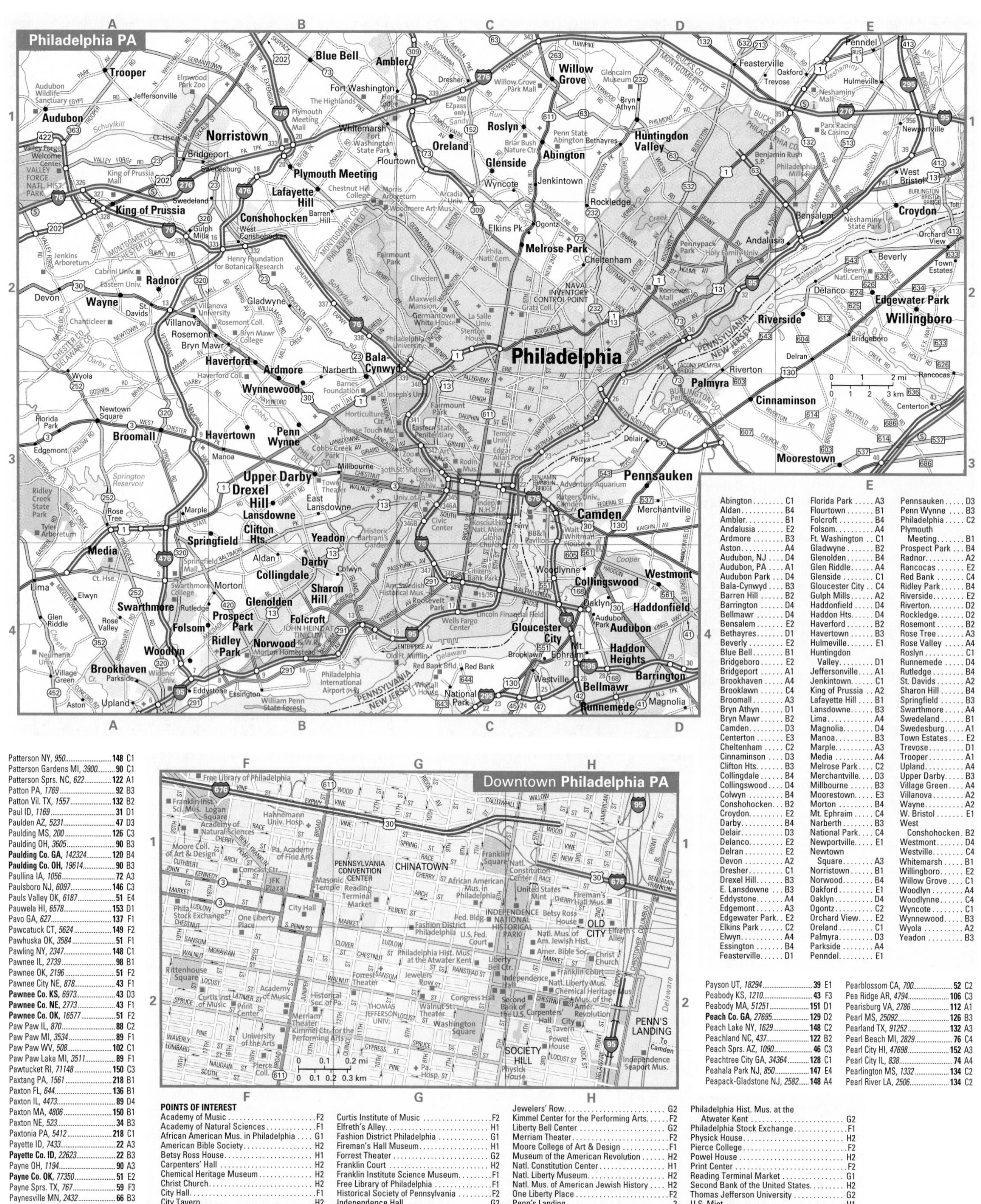

Place	Code
Abington	C1
Aldan	B4
Ambler	B1
Andalusia	E2
Ardmore	B3
Aston	A4
Audubon, NJ	D4
Audubon, PA	A1
Audubon Park	D4
Bala-Cynwyd	B3
Barren Hill	B2
Barrington	D4
Bellmawr	D4
Bensalem	E2
Bethayres	D1
Beverly	E2
Blue Bell	B1
Bridgeboro	E2
Bridgeport	A1
Brookhaven	A4
Brooklawn	C4
Broomall	A3
Bryn Athyn	D1
Bryn Mawr	B2
Camden	D3
Centerton	E3
Cheltenham	C2
Cinnaminson	D3
Clifton Hts.	B3
Collingdale	B4
Collingswood	D4
Colwyn	B4
Conshohocken	B2
Croydon	E2
Darby	B4
Delair	D3
Delanco	E2
Delran	E2
Devon	A2
Dresher	C1
Drexel Hill	B3
E. Lansdowne	B3
Eddystone	A4
Edgemont	A3
Edgewater Park	E2
Elkins Park	C2
Elwyn	A4
Essington	B4
Feasterville	D1
Florida Park	A3
Flourtown	B1
Folcroft	B4
Folsom	A4
Ft. Washington	C1
Gladwyne	B2
Glenolden	B4
Glen Riddle	A4
Glenside	C1
Gloucester City	C4
Gulph Mills	A2
Haddonfield	D4
Haddon Hts.	D4
Haverford	B2
Havertown	B3
Hulmeville	E1
Huntingdon Valley	D1
Jeffersonville	A1
Jenkintown	C1
King of Prussia	A2
Lafayette Hill	B1
Lansdowne	B3
Lima	A4
Magnolia	D4
Manoa	B3
Marple	A3
Media	A4
Melrose Park	C2
Merchantville	D3
Millbourne	B3
Moorestown	E3
Morton	B4
Mt. Ephraim	C4
Narberth	B3
National Park	C4
Newportville	E1
Newtown Square	A3
Norristown	B1
Norwood	B4
Oakford	E1
Oaklyn	D4
Ogontz	C2
Orchard View	E2
Oreland	C1
Palmyra	D3
Parkside	A4
Penndel	E1
Pennsauken	D3
Penn Wynne	B3
Philadelphia	C2
Plymouth Meeting	B1
Prospect Park	B4
Radnor	A2
Rancocas	E2
Red Bank	C4
Ridley Park	B4
Riverside	E2
Riverton	D2
Rockledge	D2
Rosemont	B2
Rose Tree	A3
Rose Valley	A4
Roslyn	C1
Runnemede	D4
Rutledge	B4
St. Davids	A2
Sharon Hill	B4
Springfield	B3
Swarthmore	A4
Swedeland	B1
Swedesburg	A1
Town Estates	E2
Trevose	D1
Trooper	A1
Upland	A4
Upper Darby	B3
Village Green	A4
Villanova	A2
Wayne	A2
W. Bristol	E1
West Conshohocken	B2
Westmont	D4
Westville	C4
Whitemarsh	B1
Willingboro	E2
Willow Grove	C1
Woodlyn	A4
Woodlynne	C4
Wyncote	C1
Wynnewood	B3
Wyola	A2
Yeadon	B3

Place	Page	Grid
Patterson NY, *950*	**148**	C1
Patterson Gardens MI, *3900*	**90**	C1
Patterson Sprs. NC, *622*	**122**	A1
Patton PA, *1769*	**92**	B3
Patton Vil. TX, *1557*	**132**	B2
Paul ID, *1169*	**31**	D1
Paulden AZ, *5231*	**47**	D3
Paulding MS, *200*	**126**	C3
Paulding OH, *3605*	**90**	B3
Paulding Co. GA, *142324*	**120**	B4
Paulding Co. OH, *19614*	**90**	B3
Paullina IA, *1056*	**72**	A3
Paulsboro NJ, *6097*	**146**	C3
Pauls Valley OK, *6187*	**51**	E4
Pauwela HI, *6578*	**153**	D1
Pavo GA, *627*	**137**	F1
Pawcatuck CT, *5624*	**149**	F2
Pawhuska OK, *3584*	**51**	F1
Pawling NY, *2347*	**148**	C1
Pawnee IL, *2739*	**98**	B1
Pawnee OK, *2196*	**51**	F2
Pawnee City NE, *878*	**43**	F1
Pawnee Co. KS, *6973*	**43**	D3
Pawnee Co. NE, *2773*	**43**	F1
Pawnee Co. OK, *16577*	**51**	F2
Paw Paw IL, *870*	**88**	C2
Paw Paw MI, *3534*	**89**	F1
Paw Paw WV, *508*	**102**	C1
Paw Paw Lake MI, *3511*	**89**	F1
Pawtucket RI, *71148*	**150**	C3
Paxtang PA, *1561*	**218**	B1
Paxton FL, *644*	**136**	B1
Paxton IL, *4473*	**89**	D4
Paxton MA, *4806*	**150**	B1
Paxton NE, *523*	**34**	B3
Paxtonia PA, *5412*	**218**	C1
Payette ID, *7433*	**22**	A3
Payette Co. ID, *22623*	**22**	B3
Payne OH, *1194*	**90**	A3
Payne Co. OK, *77350*	**51**	E2
Payne Sprs. TX, *767*	**59**	F3
Paynesville MN, *2432*	**66**	B3
Payson AZ, *15301*	**47**	E4
Payson IL, *1026*	**97**	F1
Payson UT, *18294*	**39**	E1
Peabody KS, *1210*	**43**	F3
Peabody MA, *51251*	**151**	D1
Peach Co. GA, *27695*	**129**	D2
Peach Lake NY, *1629*	**148**	C2
Peachland NC, *437*	**122**	B2
Peach Sprs. AZ, *1090*	**46**	C3
Peachtree City GA, *34364*	**128**	C1
Peahala Park NJ, *850*	**147**	E4
Peapack-Gladstone NJ, *2582*	**148**	A4
Pearblossom CA, *700*	**52**	C2
Pea Ridge AR, *4794*	**106**	C3
Pearisburg VA, *2786*	**112**	A1
Pearl MS, *25092*	**126**	B3
Pearland TX, *91252*	**132**	A3
Pearl Beach MI, *2829*	**76**	C4
Pearl City HI, *47698*	**152**	A3
Pearl City IL, *838*	**74**	A4
Pearlington MS, *1332*	**134**	C2
Pearl River LA, *2506*	**134**	C2

POINTS OF INTEREST

Point of interest	Grid
Academy of Music	F2
Academy of Natural Sciences	F1
African American Mus. in Philadelphia	G1
American Bible Society	H2
Betsy Ross House	H1
Carpenters' Hall	H2
Chemical Heritage Museum	H2
Christ Church	H2
City Hall	F1
City Tavern	H2
Comcast Center	F1
Congress Hall	G2
Curtis Institute of Music	F2
Elfreth's Alley	H1
Fashion District Philadelphia	G1
Fireman's Hall Museum	H1
Forrest Theater	G2
Franklin Court	H2
Franklin Institute Science Museum	F1
Free Library of Philadelphia	F1
Historical Society of Pennsylvania	F2
Independence Hall	G2
Independence Natl. Hist. Park	H1
Independence Seaport Museum	H2
Jewelers' Row	G2
Kimmel Center for the Performing Arts	F2
Liberty Bell Center	G2
Merriam Theater	F2
Moore College of Art & Design	F1
Museum of the American Revolution	H2
Natl. Constitution Center	H1
Natl. Liberty Museum	H2
Natl. Mus. of American Jewish History	H2
One Liberty Place	F2
Penn's Landing	2
Pennsylvania Academy of Fine Arts	F1
Pennsylvania Convention Center	G1
Philadelphia Hist. Mus. at the Atwater Kent	G2
Philadelphia Stock Exchange	F1
Physick House	H2
Pierce College	F2
Powel House	H2
Print Center	F2
Reading Terminal Market	G1
Second Bank of the United States	H2
Thomas Jefferson University	G2
U.S. Mint	H1
University of the Arts	F2
Walnut Street Theater	G2

Entries in **bold black** indicate counties or parishes.
Entries in **bold color** indicate cities with detailed inset maps.

Avondale ... A2	Gilbert ... D3	Litchfield Park ... A2	Phoenix ... B1	Sun City ... A1	Youngtown ... A1
Chandler ... C3	Glendale ... A2	Maricopa Vil. ... A3	Queen Creek ... D3	Sun City West ... A1	
El Mirage ... A1	Goodyear ... A2	Mesa ... D2	Rio Verde ... D1	Surprise ... A1	
Ft. McDowell ... D1	Guadalupe ... C3	Paradise Valley ... C2	Santa Cruz ... B3	Tempe ... C3	
Fountain Hills ... D1	Komatke ... B3	Peoria ... A1	Scottsdale ... C1	Tolleson ... A2	

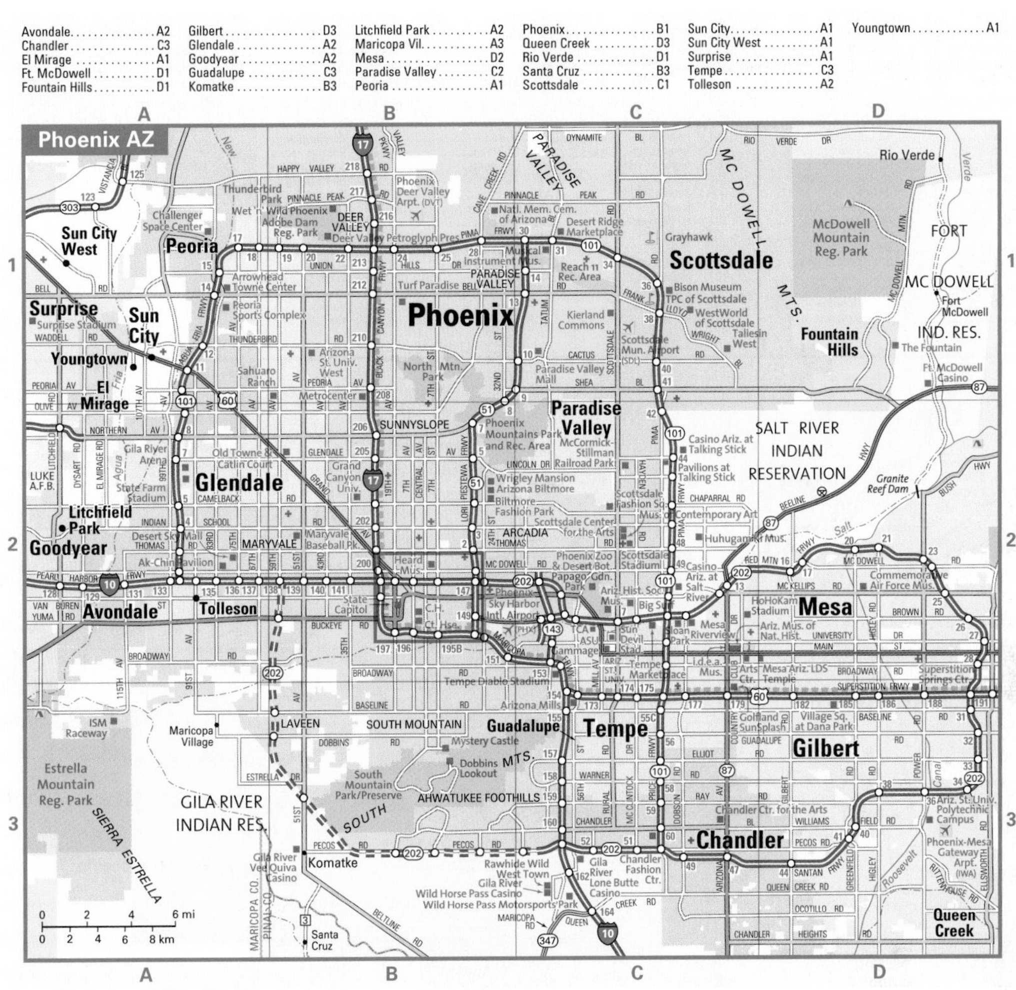

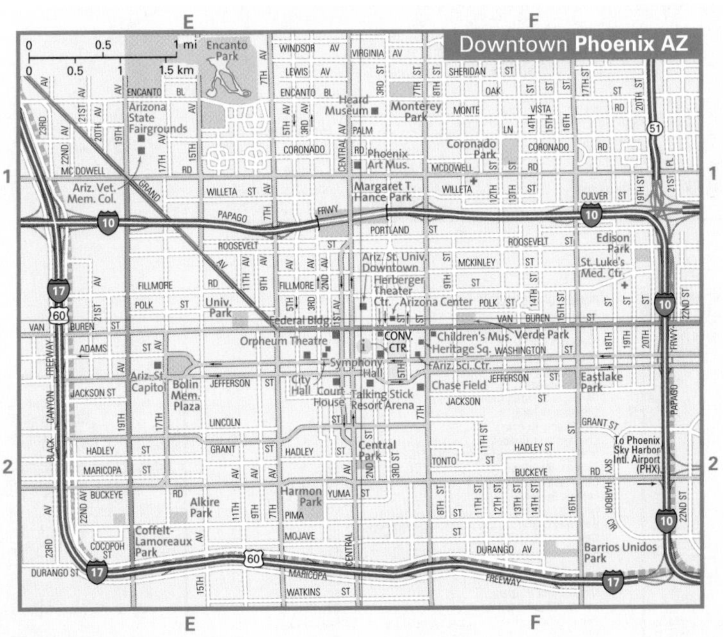

POINTS OF INTEREST

Arizona Center ... F1	Heard Museum ... F1
Arizona Science Center ... F2	Herberger Theater Center ... F2
Arizona State Capitol ... E2	Heritage Square ... F2
Arizona State Fairgrounds ... E1	Orpheum Theatre ... E2
Arizona Veterans Memorial Coliseum ... E1	Phoenix Art Museum ... E1
Chase Field ... F2	Symphony Hall ... F2
Children's Museum ... F2	Talking Stick Resort Arena ... F2
City Hall ... E2	
Convention Center ... F2	

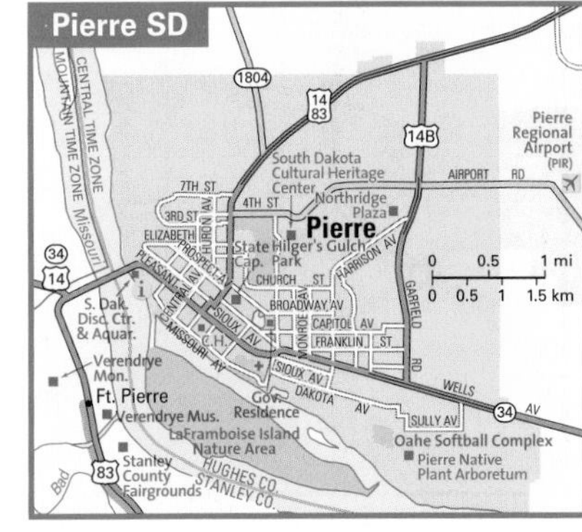

Figures after entries indicate population, page number, and grid reference.

Pickensville AL, *608* **127** D1
Pickerington OH, *18291* **101** D1
Pickett Co. TN, *5077* **110** B3
Pico Rivera CA, *62942* **228** E3
Picture Rocks PA, *678* **93** E2
Piedmont AL, *4878* **120** A4
Piedmont CA, *10667* **259** C2
Piedmont MO, *1977* **108** A2
Piedmont OK, *5720* **51** E2
Piedmont SC, *5103* **121** E2
Piedmont SD, *222* **25** F3
Piedmont WV, *876* **102** B2
Pierce CO, *834* **33** E4
Pierce ID, *508* **14** C4
Pierce NE, *1767* **35** E2
Pierce City MO, *1292* **106** C2
Pierce Co. GA, *18758* **129** F4
Pierce Co. NE, *7266* **35** E2
Pierce Co. ND, *4357* **18** C2
Pierce Co. WA, *795225* **12** C4
Pierce Co. WI, *41019* **67** E4
Pierceton IN, *1015* **89** F2
Pierre SD, *13646* 26 C3
Pierre Part LA, *3169* **134** A3
Pierron IL, *600* **98** B3
Pierson FL, *1736* **139** D4
Pierz MN, *1393* **66** C2
Pigeon LA, *600* **134** A2
Pigeon MI, *1208* **76** C2
Pigeon Cove MA, *1700* **151** F1
Pigeon Forge TN, *5875* **111** D4
Piggott AR, *3849* **108** B3
Pike Co. AL, *32899* **128** A4
Pike Co. AR, *11291* **117** D3
Pike Co. GA, *17869* **128** C1
Pike Co. IL, *16430* **98** A1
Pike Co. IN, *12845* **99** E3
Pike Co. KY, *65024* **111** E1
Pike Co. MS, *40404* **126** B4
Pike Co. MO, *18516* **97** F2
Pike Co. OH, *28709* **101** D2
Pike Co. PA, *57369* **93** F2
Pikesville MD, *30764* **144** C1
Piketon OH, *2181* **101** D2
Pikeville KY, *6903* **111** E1
Pikeville NC, *678* **123** E1
Pikeville TN, *1608* **120** B1
Pilot Grove MO, *768* **97** D3
Pilot Knob MO, *746* **108** A1
Pilot Mtn. NC, *1477* **112** A3
Pilot Pt. TX, *3856* **59** F1
Pilot Rock OR, *1502* **21** F2
Pilot Sta. AK, *568* **154** B3
Pima AZ, *2387* **55** E2
Pima Co. AZ, *980263* **54** C3
Pimmit Hills VA, *6094* **270** B3
Pinal Co. AZ, *375770* **55** D2
Pinardville NH, *4780* **81** F4
Pinch WV, *3262* **101** F3
Pinckard AL, *647* **128** B4
Pinckney MI, *2427* **76** B4
Pinckneyville IL, *5648* **98** B4
Pinconning MI, *1307* **76** B2
Pine AZ, *1963* **47** E4
Pine Beach NJ, *2127* **147** E3
Pine Bluff AR, *49083* **117** E3
Pinebluff NC, *1337* **122** C1
Pine Bluffs WY, *1129* **33** F3
Pine Bush NY, *1780* **148** A1
Pine Castle FL, *10805* **141** D1
Pine City MN, *3123* **67** D2
Pine Co. MN, *29750* **64** C4
Pinecrest FL, *600* **140** C3
Pinecrest FL, *18223* **233** A5
Pineda FL, *1100* **141** E2
Pinedale WY, *2030* **32** A1
Pine Forest TX, *487* **132** C2
Pine Grove CA, *2219* **36** C3
Pine Grove PA, *2186* **146** A1
Pine Grove WV, *552* **101** F1
Pine Grove Mills PA, *1502* **92** C3
Pine Haven WY, *490* **25** E3
Pine Hill AL, *975* **127** E3
Pine Hill NJ, *10233* **146** C3
Pine Hills FL, *60076* **246** B2
Pinehurst ID, *1619* **14** B3
Pinehurst MA, *7152* **151** D1
Pinehurst NC, *13124* **122** C1
Pinehurst TX, *4624* **132** A2
Pinehurst TX, *2274* **132** C2
Pine Island MN, *3263* **73** D1
Pine Island NY, *700* **148** A2
Pine Island TX, *988* **61** F2
Pine Island Ctr. FL, *1854* **214** A1
Pine Knoll Shores NC, *1339* **115** D4
Pine Knot KY, *1621* **110** C3
Pineland FL, *407* **142** C1
Pineland TX, *850* **124** C4
Pine Lawn MO, *3275* **256** B2
Pine Level NC, *1700* **123** E1
Pinellas Co. FL, *916542* **140** B2
Pinellas Park FL, *49079* **140** B3
Pine Mtn. GA, *1304* **128** C2
Pine Plains NY, *1353* **94** B2
Pine Pt. ME, *600* **82** B3
Pine Prairie LA, *1610* **133** E1
Pine Ridge SC, *2064* **122** A4
Pine Ridge SD, *3308* **34** A1
Pine River MN, *944* **64** A4
Pinesdale MT, *917* **15** D4
Pinetop-Lakeside AZ, *4282* **47** F4
Pinetops NC, *1374* **113** E4
Pinetown DE, *1100* **145** F4
Pine Valley CA, *1510* **53** D4
Pine Valley NY, *813* **93** D1

Pittsburgh PA

Acmetonia D1
Aspinwall C1
Avalon A1
Baldwin C3
Bellevue B1
Ben Avon A1
Ben Avon Hts. A1
Bethel Park B3
Blawnox C1
Braddock C2
Braddock Hills C2
Brentwood B3
Bridgeville A3
Broughton B3
Carnegie A2
Castle Shannon B3
Chalfant D2
Cheswick D1
Churchill D2
Coraopolis A1
Crafton A2
Cuddy A3
Dormont B3
Dravosburg C3
Duquesne D3
E. McKeesport D3
E. Pittsburgh D2
Edgewood C2
Emsworth A1
Etna C1
Evergreen B1
Ewingsville A2
Forest Grove A1
Forest Hills C2
Fox Chapel C1
Glassport C3
Glenfield A1
Glen Osborne A1
Glenshaw C1
Green Tree B2
Groveton A1
Haysville A1
Heidelberg A3
Homestead C2
Ingram A2
Kenmawr A1
Kirwan Hts. A3
Liberty C3
McKeesport D3
McKees Rocks B1
Millvale B1
Monroeville D2
Moon Run A2
Morgan A3
Mt. Lebanon B3
Mt. Oliver B2
Munhall C3
N. Braddock C2
Oakmont D1
Penn Hills D2
Pennsbury Vil. A2
Perrysville B1
Pitcairn D2
Pittock A1
Pittsburgh B2
Pleasant Hills C3
Plum D1
Port Vue C3
Presto A3
Rankin C2
Rennerdale A2
Rosslyn Farms A2
Sandy Creek D1
Sharpsburg C1
Springdale D1
Stewartsville D3
Swissvale C2
Sygan A3
Thornburg A2
Trafford D3
Turtle Creek D2
Upper St. Clair A3
Verona D1
Wall D3
W. Homestead C2
W. Mifflin C3
W. Park A1
W. View B1
Whitaker C2
Whitehall B3
White Oak D3
Wilkinsburg C2
Wilmerding D3

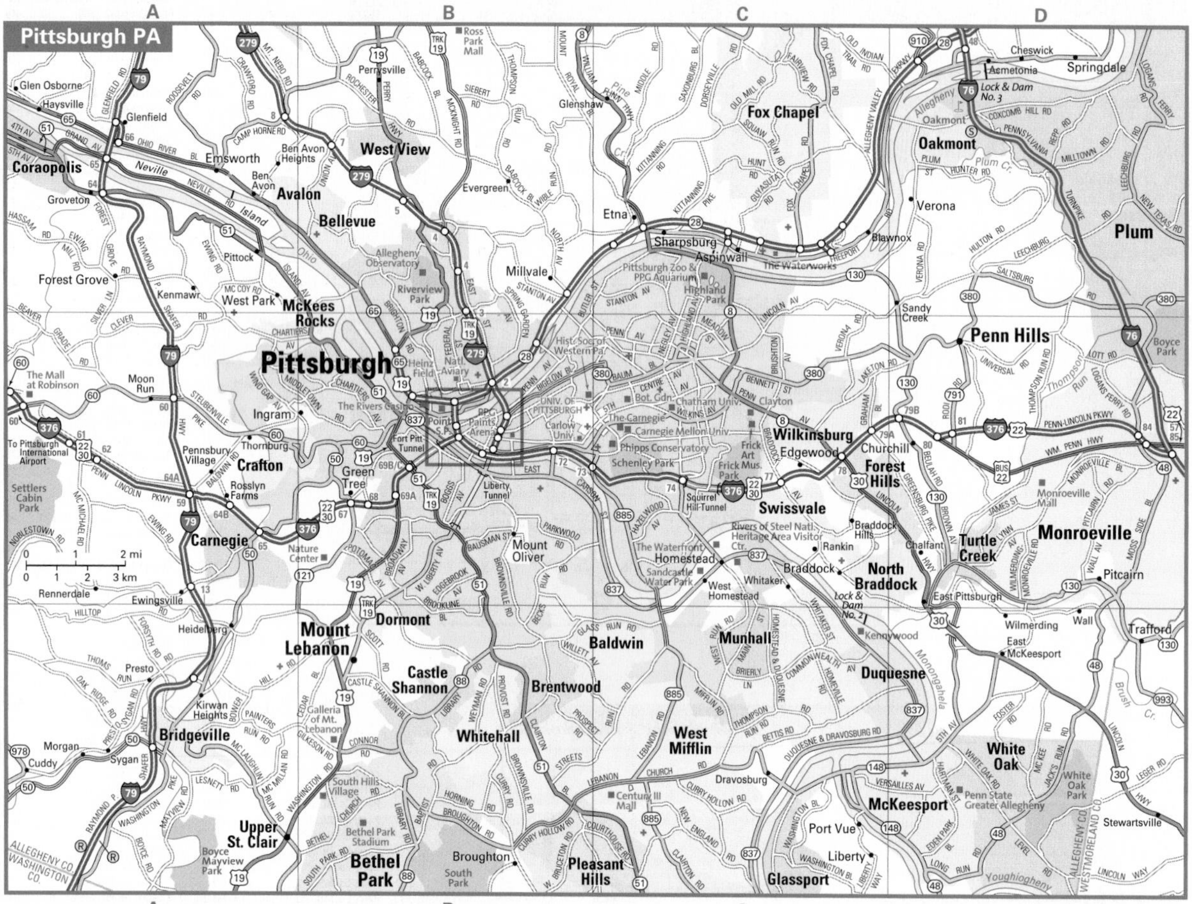

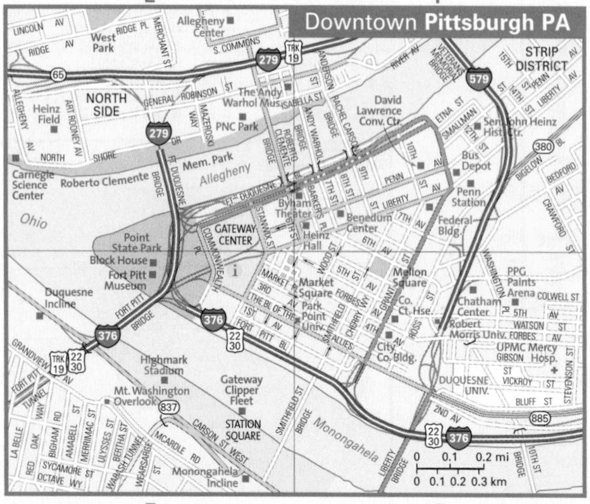

Downtown Pittsburgh PA

POINTS OF INTEREST

Allegheny Center E1
The Andy Warhol Museum E1
Benedum Center F1
Block House E2
Bus Depot F1
Byham Theater F1
Carnegie Science Center E1
Chatham Center F2
City County Building F2
County Court House F2
David Lawrence Convention Center F1
Duquesne Incline E2
Duquesne University F2
Federal Building F1
Fort Pitt Museum E2
Gateway Center E1
Gateway Clipper Fleet E2
Heinz Field E1
Heinz Hall F1
Highmark Stadium E2
Monongahela Incline E2
Mt. Washington Overlook E2
Penn Station F1
PNC Park E1
Point Park University F2
Point State Park E1
PPG Paints Arena F2
Robert Morris University F2
Senator John Heinz Hist. Center F1
Station Square E2

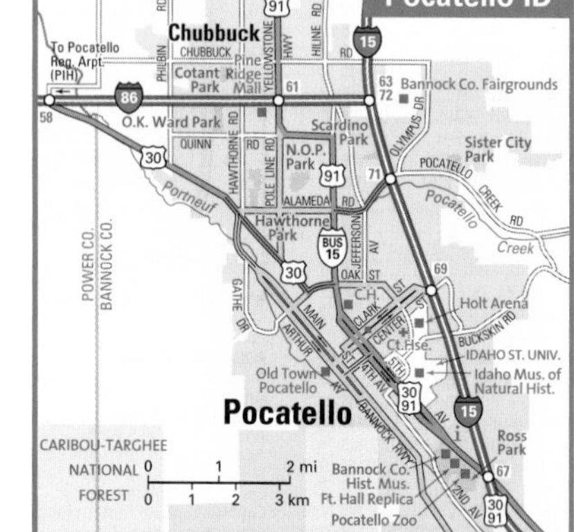

Entries in **bold black** indicate counties or parishes.
Entries in **bold color** indicate cities with detailed inset maps.

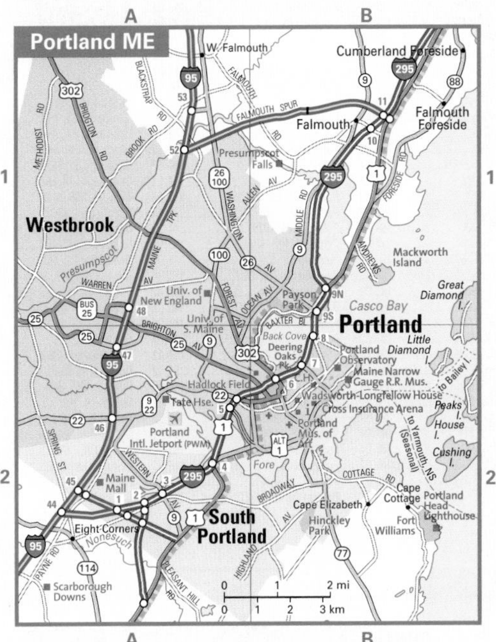

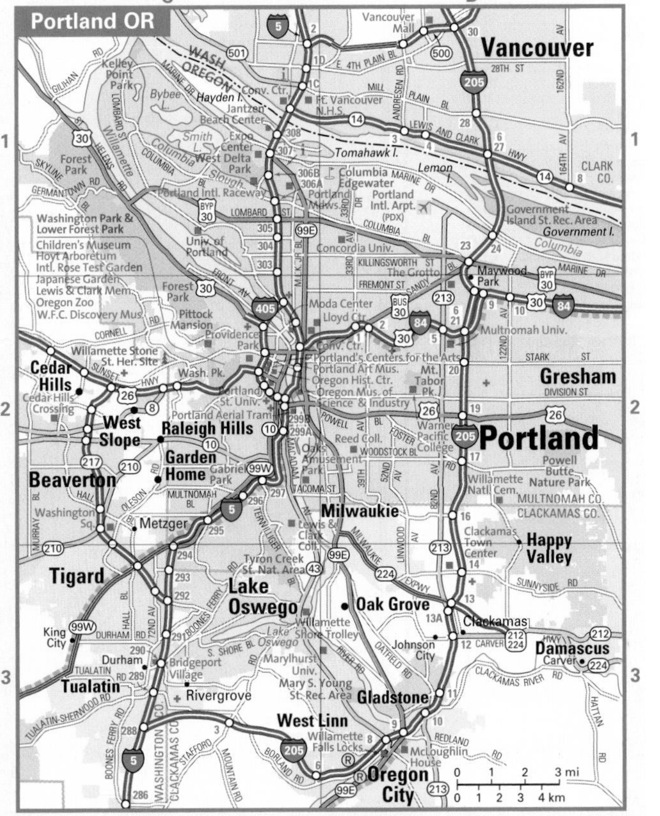

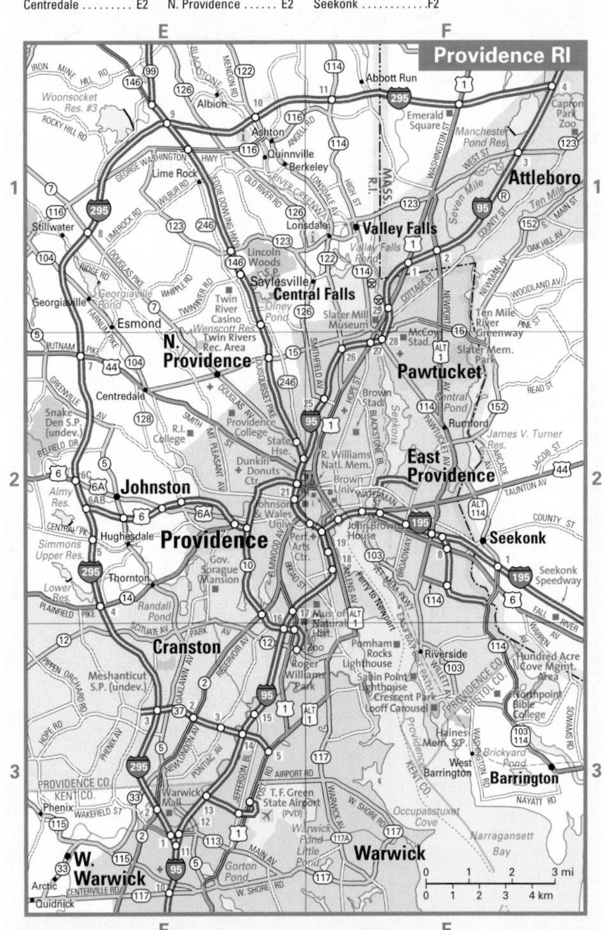

Figures after entries indicate population, page number, and grid reference.

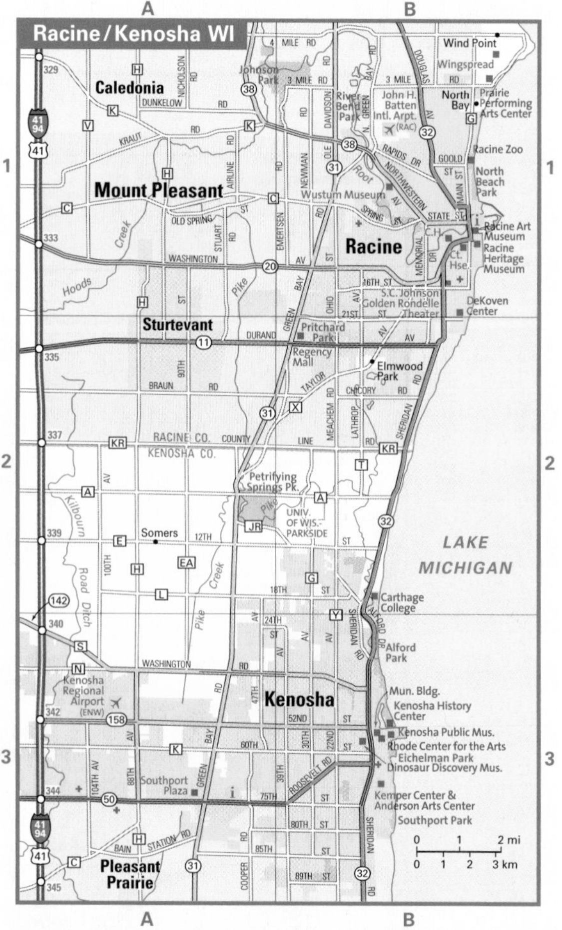

Elmwood Park . . . B2	Mount Pleasant . . . A1	Racine . . . B1
Franksville . . . A1	N. Bay . . . B1	Sturtevant . . . A2
Kenosha . . . A3	Pleasant Prairie . . . A3	Wind Pt. . . . B1

Entries in **bold black** indicate counties or parishes.
Entries in **bold color** indicate cities with detailed inset maps.

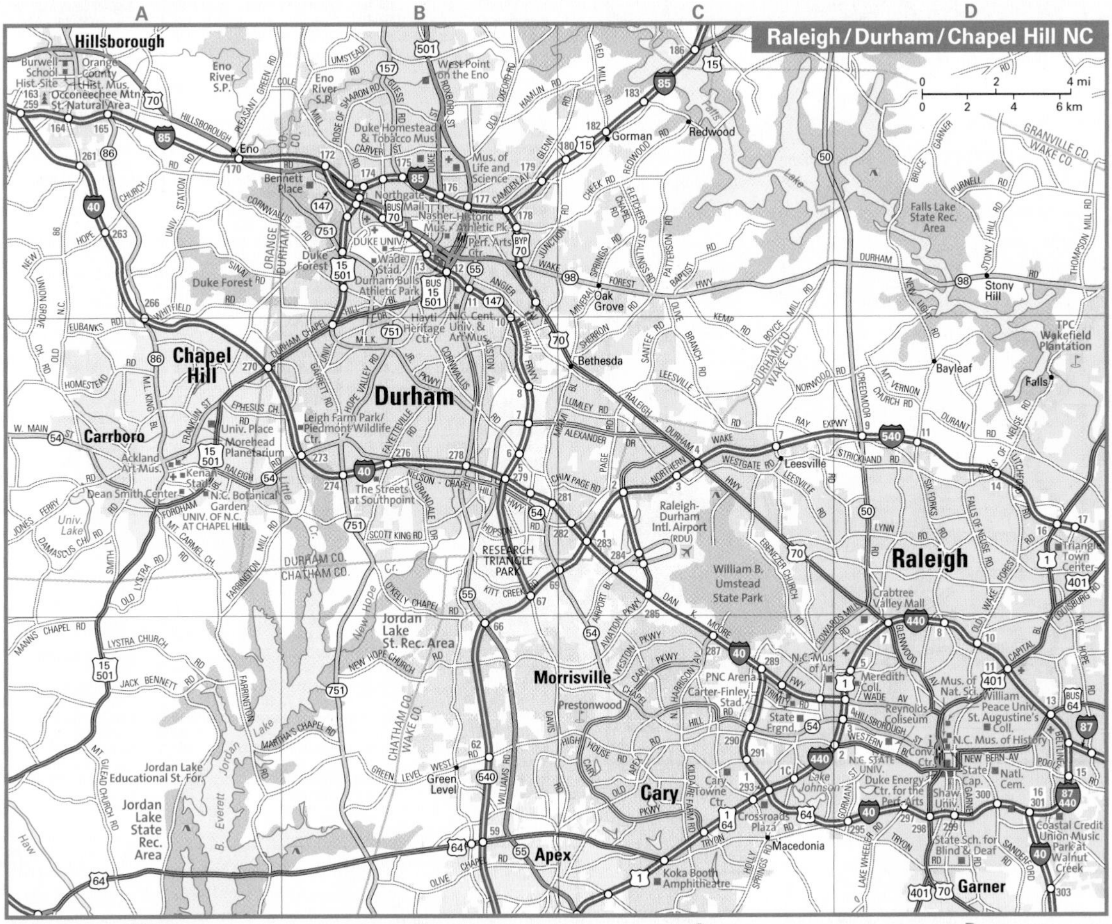

Raleigh/Durham/Chapel Hill NC

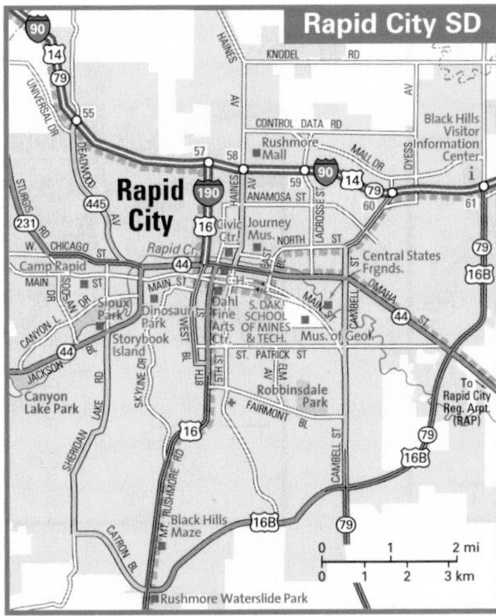

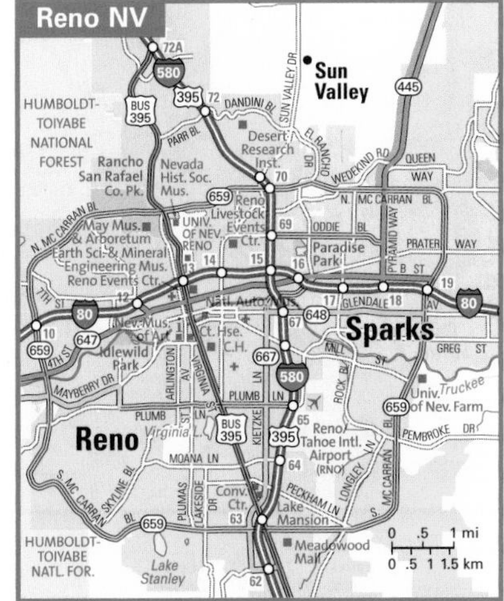

Figures after entries indicate population, page number, and grid reference.

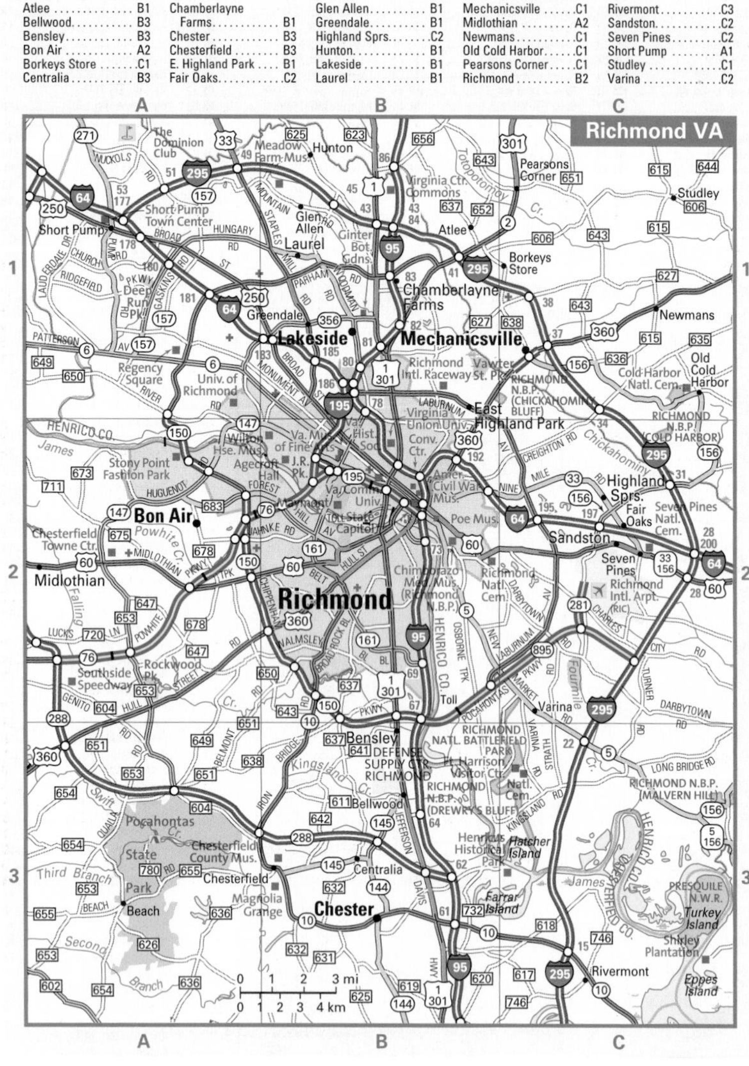

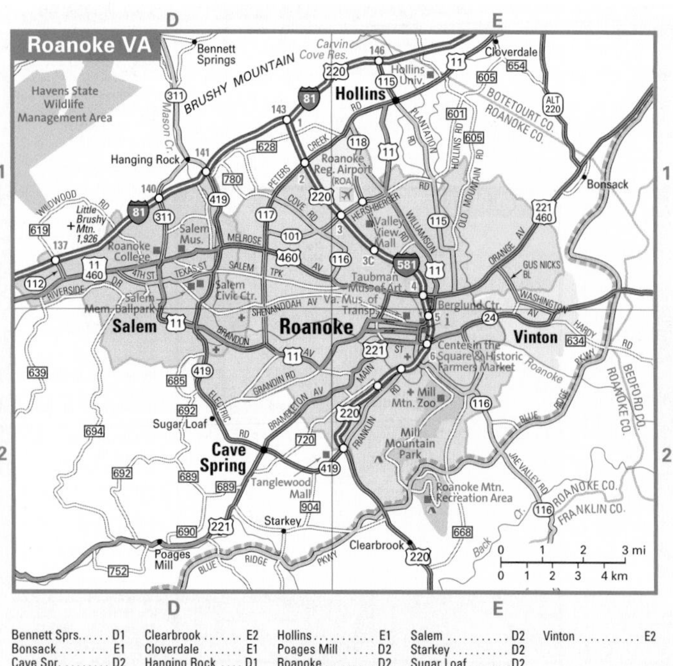

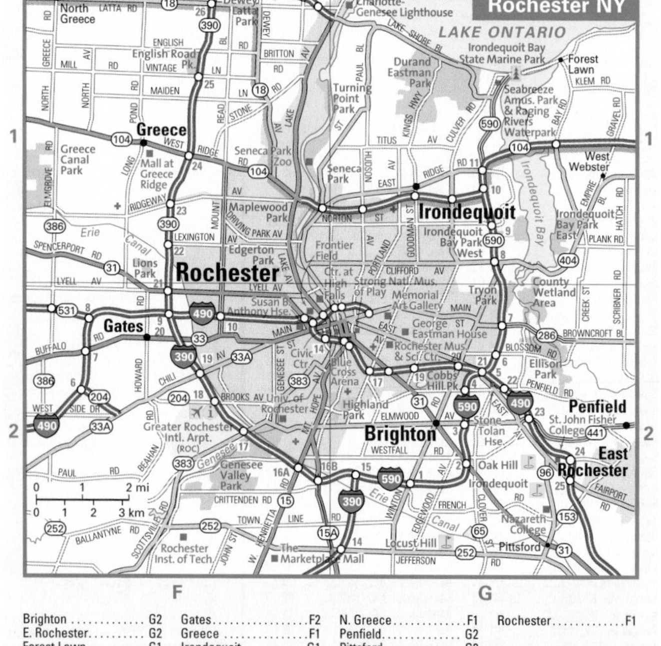

Entries in **bold black** indicate counties or parishes.
Entries in **bold color** indicate cities with detailed inset maps.

Rockford IL

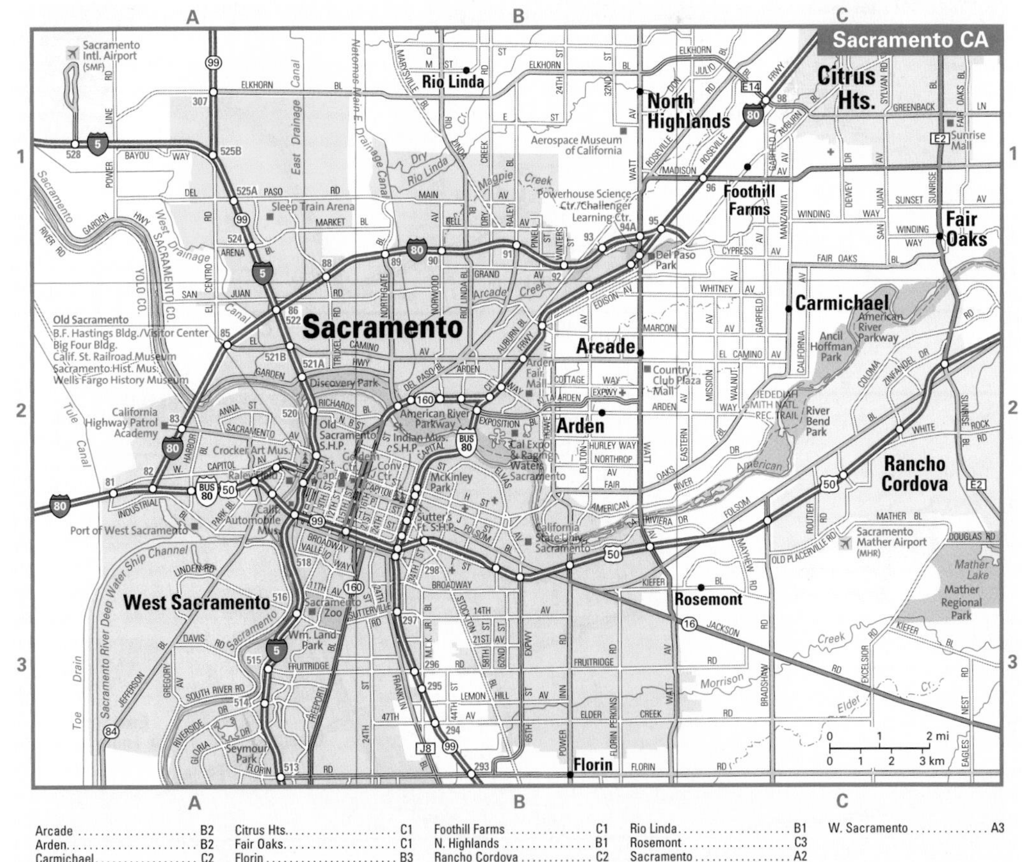

Arcade B2	Citrus Hts. C1	Foothill Farms C1	Rio Linda B1	W. Sacramento A3
Arden B2	Fair Oaks C1	N. Highlands B1	Rosemont C3	
Carmichael C2	Florin B3	Rancho Cordova C2	Sacramento A2	

Figures after entries indicate population, page number, and grid reference.

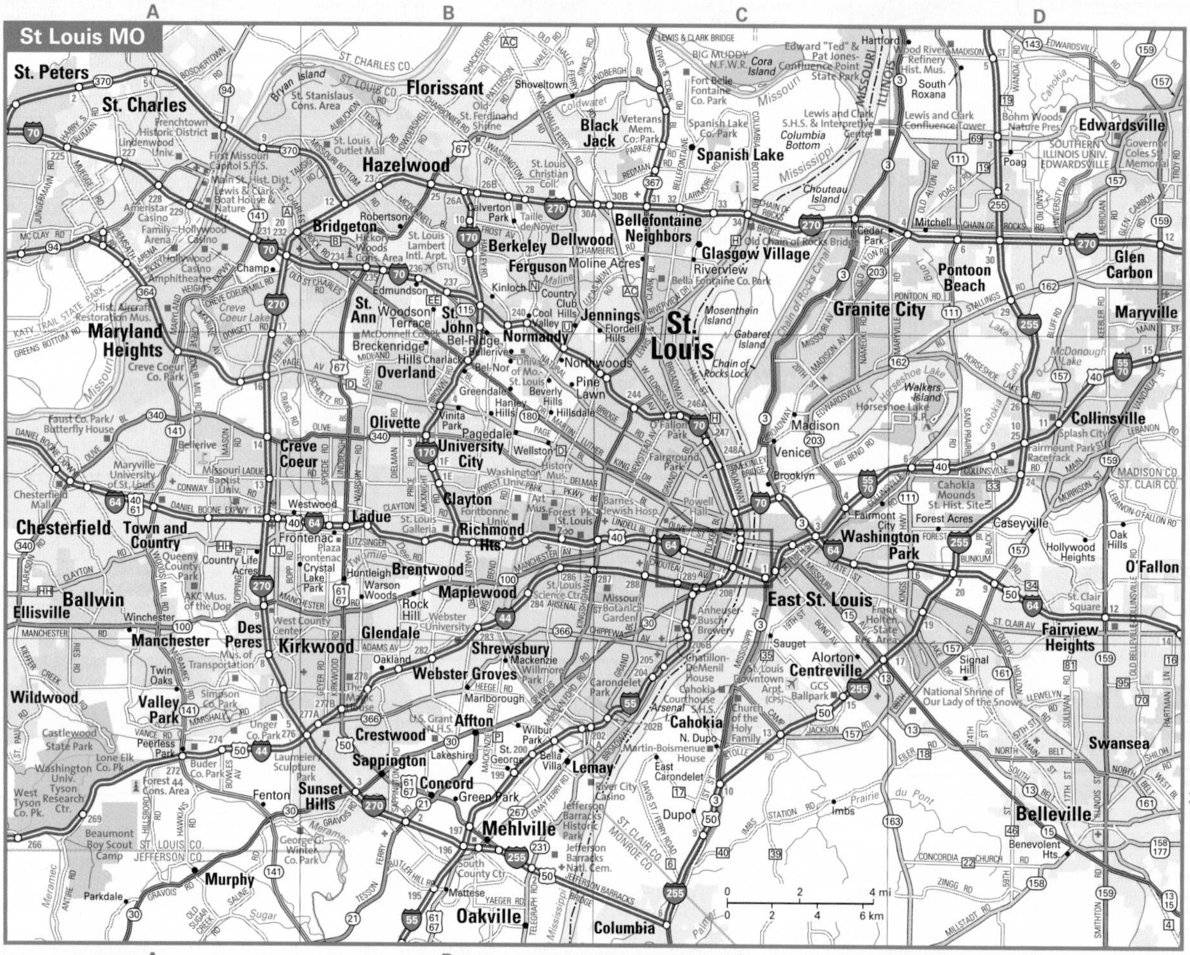

St Louis MO

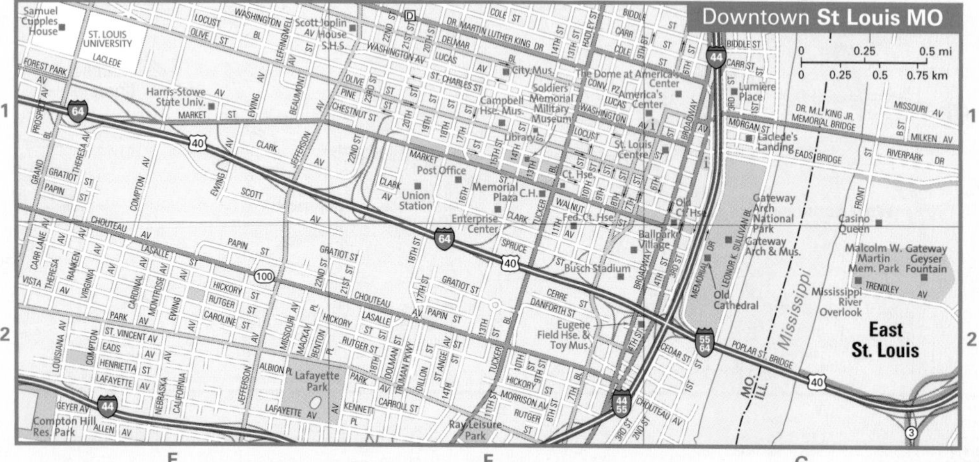

POINTS OF INTEREST

Entries in **bold black** indicate counties or parishes.
Entries in **bold color** indicate cities with detailed inset maps.

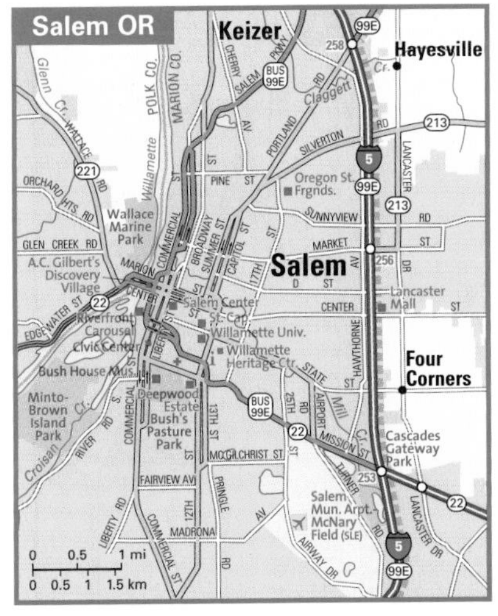

San Antonio TX

Alamo Hts. E2
Balcones Hts. E2
Bracken F1
Buena Vista E3
Castle Hills E2
China Grove F3
Cibolo F1
Converse F2
Garden Ridge F1
Grey Forest D1
Helotes D1
Hill Country Vil. E1
Hollywood Park E1
Kirby F2
Leon Valley D2
Live Oak F2
Macdona D3
Olmos Park E2
San Antonio F3
Sayers F3
Schertz F1
Selma F1
Shavano Park E1
Southton E3
Terrell Hills E2
Universal City F1
Von Ormy D3
Windcrest F2

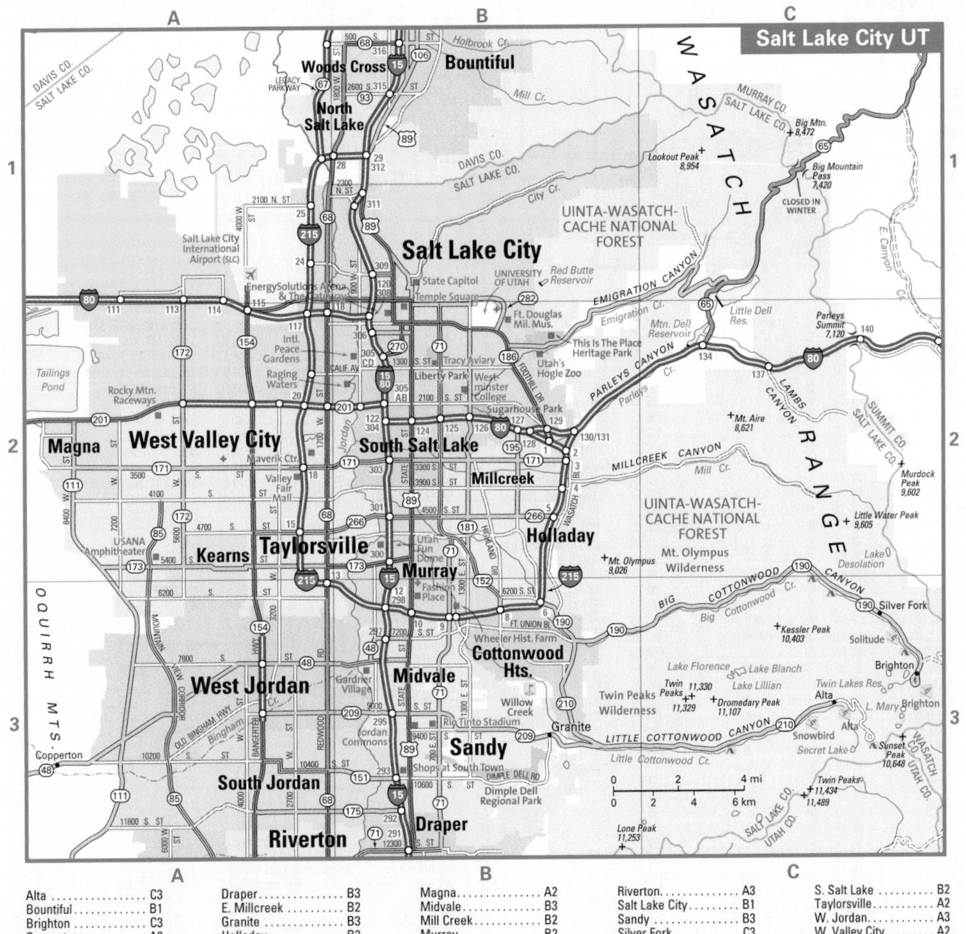

Alta C3
Bountiful B1
Brighton C3
Copperton A3
Cottonwood Hts. B3
Draper B3
E. Millcreek B2
Granite B3
Holladay B2
Kearns A2
Magna A2
Midvale B3
Mill Creek B2
Murray B2
N. Salt Lake B1
Riverton A3
Salt Lake City B1
Sandy B3
Silver Fork C3
S. Jordan A3
S. Salt Lake B2
Taylorsville A2
W. Jordan A3
W. Valley City A2
Woods Cross B1

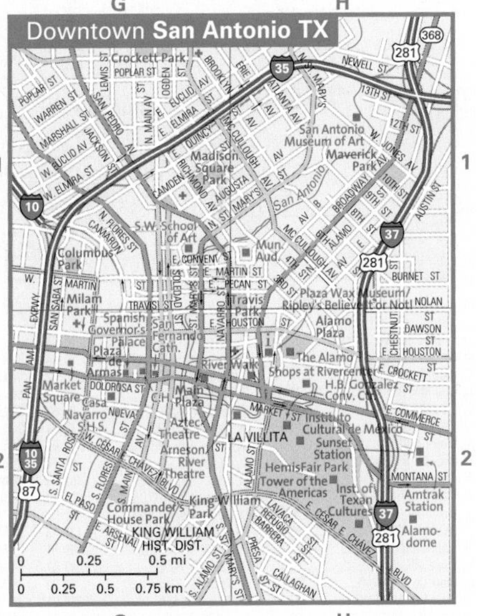

POINTS OF INTEREST

The Alamo H2
Alamodome H2
Amtrak Station H2
Arneson River Theater H2
Aztec Theatre G2
Casa Navarro State Historic Site G2
H.B. Gonzalez Convention Center H2
HemisFair Park H2
Institute of Texan Cultures H2
Instituto Cultural de México H2
Market Square G2
Municipal Auditorium H1
Plaza Wax Museum/Ripley's Believe It or Not! H2
River Walk H2
San Antonio Museum of Art H1
San Fernando Cathedral G2
Shops at Rivercenter H2
Spanish Governor's Palace G2
Sunset Station H2
Southwest School of Art G1
Tower of the Americas H2

Figures after entries indicate population, page number, and grid reference.

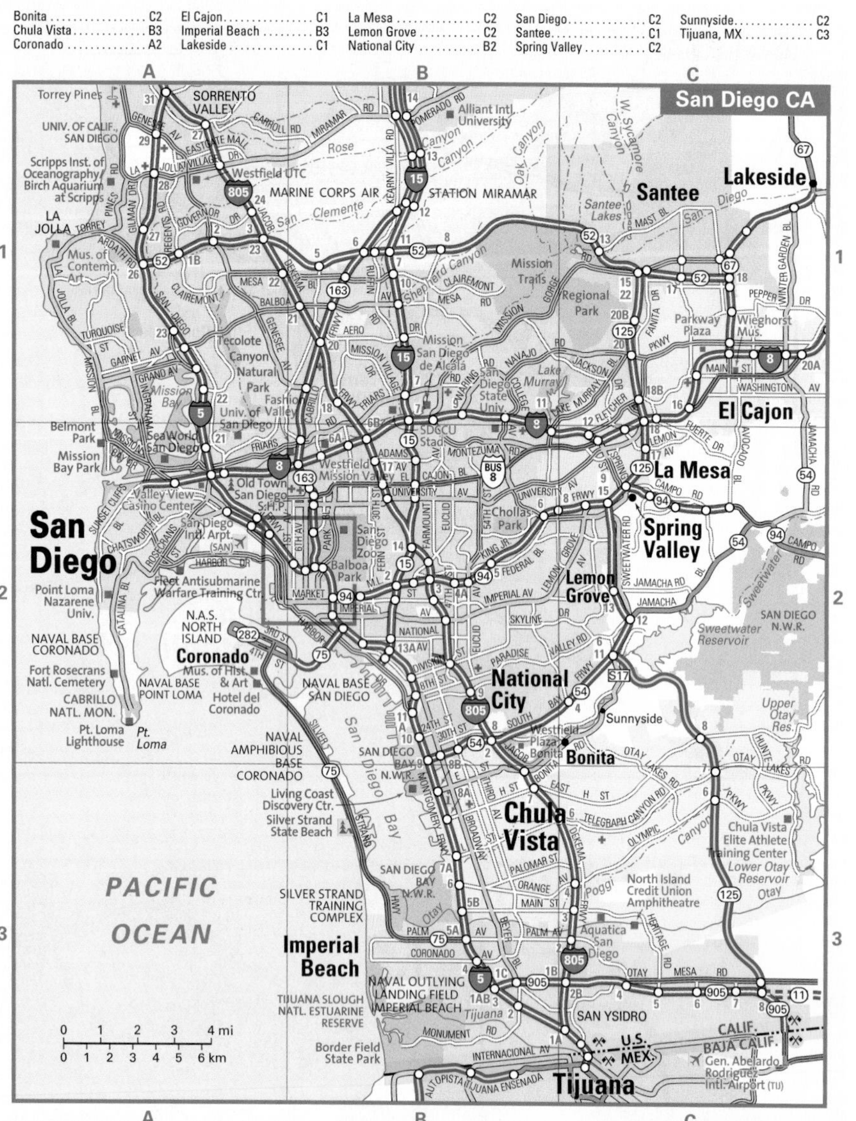

Downtown San Diego CA

POINTS OF INTEREST

SAN FRANCISCO BAY MAP INDEX

Entries in **bold black** indicate counties or parishes.
Entries in **bold color** indicate cities with detailed inset maps.

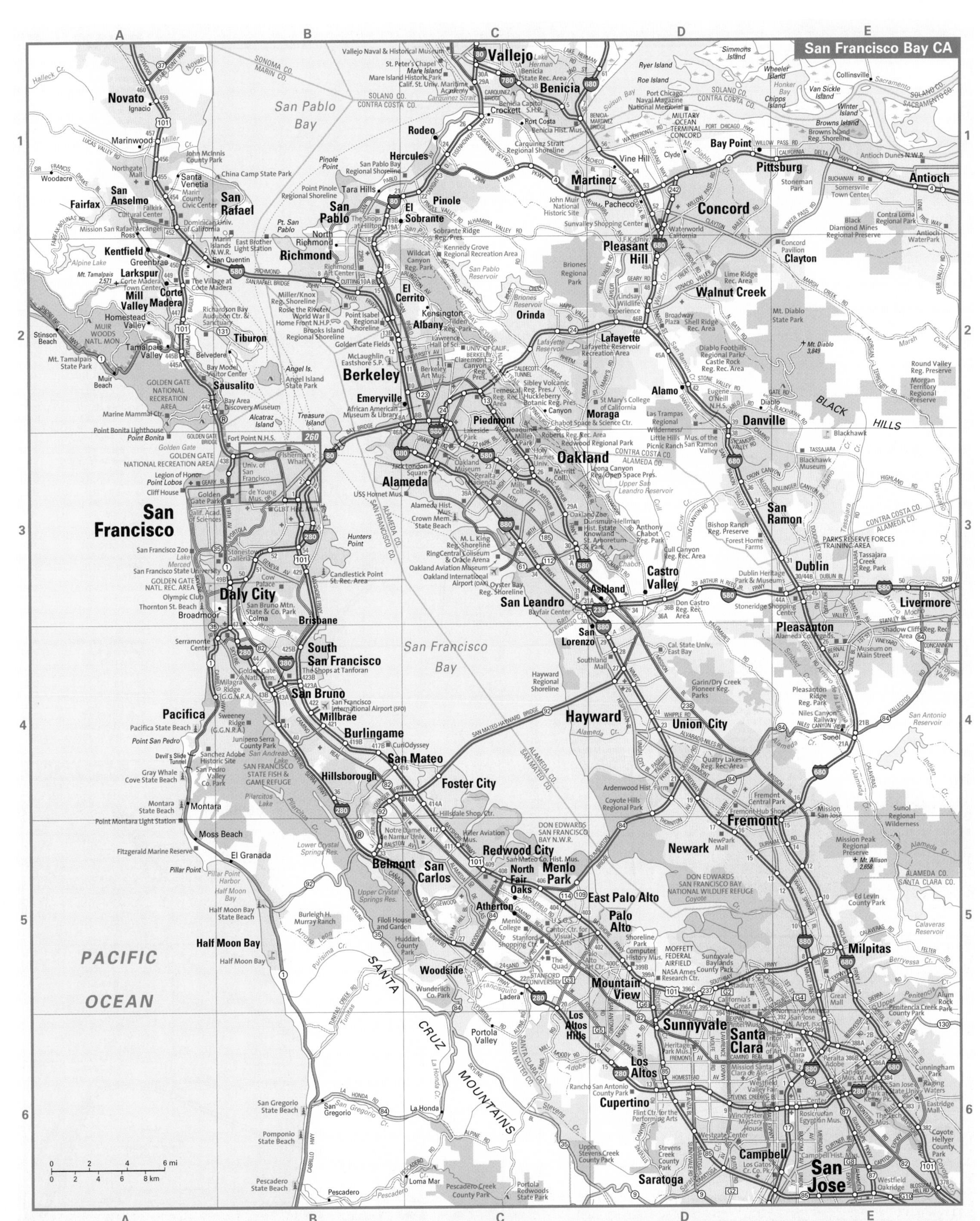

Figures after entries indicate population, page number, and grid reference.

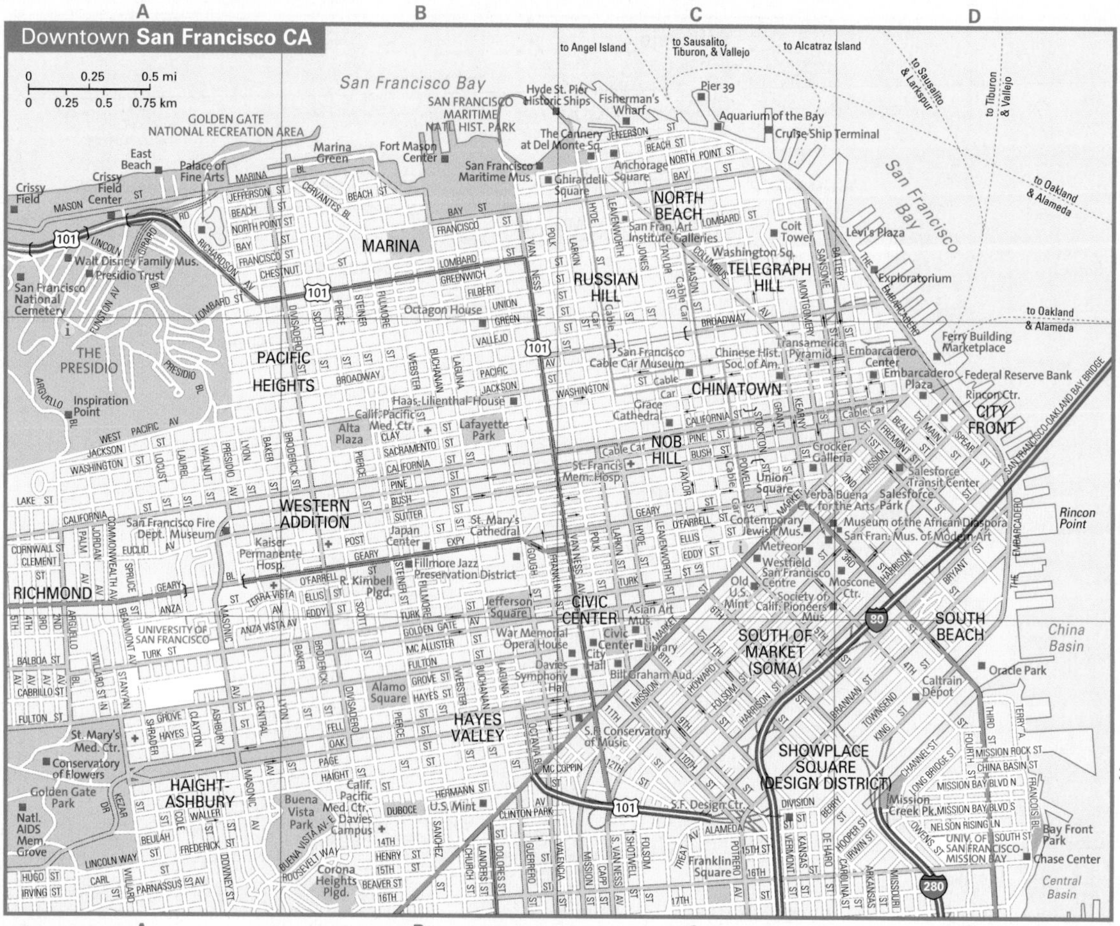

Downtown San Francisco CA

POINTS OF INTEREST

Anchorage Square C1
Aquarium of the Bay. C1
Asian Art Museum C3
Bill Graham Auditorium C3
Caltrain Depot D3
The Cannery at Del Monte Square C1
Chase Center. D3
Chinese Historical Society of America. C2
City Hall. C3
Coit Tower C1
Conservatory of Flowers A3
Contemporary Jewish Mus. C2
Crissy Field. A1
Crissy Field Center A1
Crocker Galleria C2
Cruise Ship Terminal C1
Davies Symphony Hall C3
East Beach. A1
Embarcadero Center D2
Exploratorium. D1
Federal Reserve Bank D2
Fillmore Jazz Preservation District B2
Ferry Building Marketplace D2
Fisherman's Wharf C1
Fort Mason Center B1
Ghirardelli Square. B1
Golden Gate Natl. Rec. Area. . . . A1
Golden Gate Park A3
Grace Cathedral C2
Haas-Lilienthal House B2
Hyde Street Pier Historic Ships . C1
Inspiration Point A2
Japan Center. B2
Levi's Plaza D1
Library. C3
Metreon C2
Moscone Center. D2
Museum of the African Diaspora. D2
National AIDS Memorial Grove . A3
Octagon House B2
Old U.S. Mint C2
Oracle Park D3
Palace of Fine Arts. A1
Pier 39. C1
The Presidio. A2
Presidio Trust A1
Rincon Center D2
St. Mary's Cathedral. B2
San Francisco Art Institute Galleries. C1
San Francisco Cable Car Mus. . . C2
San Francisco Cons. of Music . . C3
San Francisco Design Center. . . . C3
San Francisco Fire Dept. Mus. . . A2
San Francisco Maritime Mus. . . B1
San Francisco Maritime Natl. Hist. Park B1
San Francisco Museum of Modern Art D2
San Francisco Natl. Cemetery . . A1
Soc. of Calif. Pioneers Mus. C2
Transamerica Pyramid. C2
Transbay Transit Center D2
U.S. Mint. B3
Univ. of San Francisco. A3
Univ. of San Francisco-Mission Bay. D3
Walt Disney Family Mus. A1
War Memorial Opera House. . . . C3
Westfield San Francisco Centre. C2
Yerba Buena Center for the Arts. C2

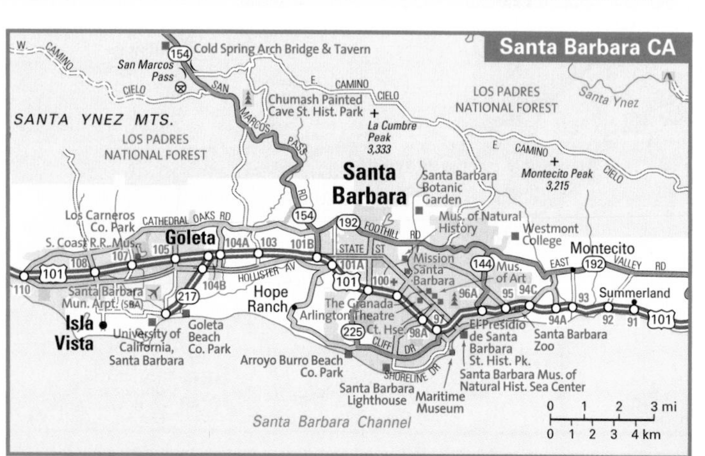

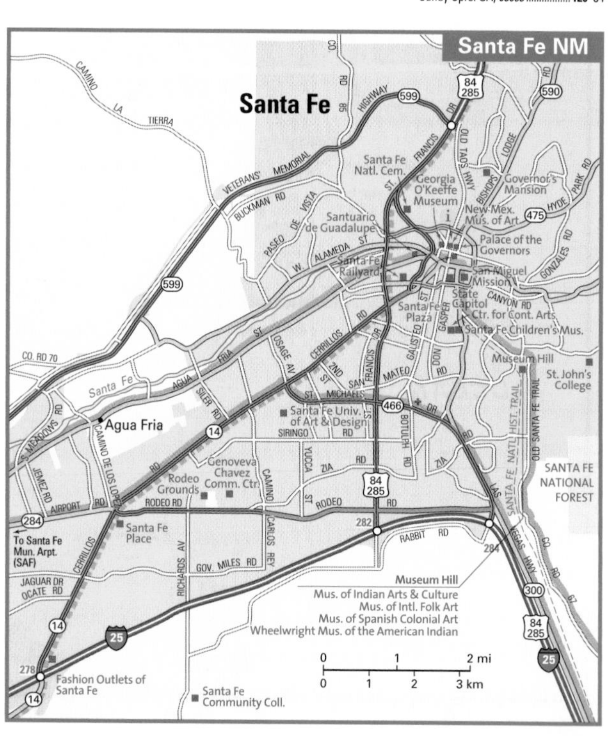

Entries in **bold black** indicate counties or parishes.
Entries in **bold color** indicate cities with detailed inset maps.

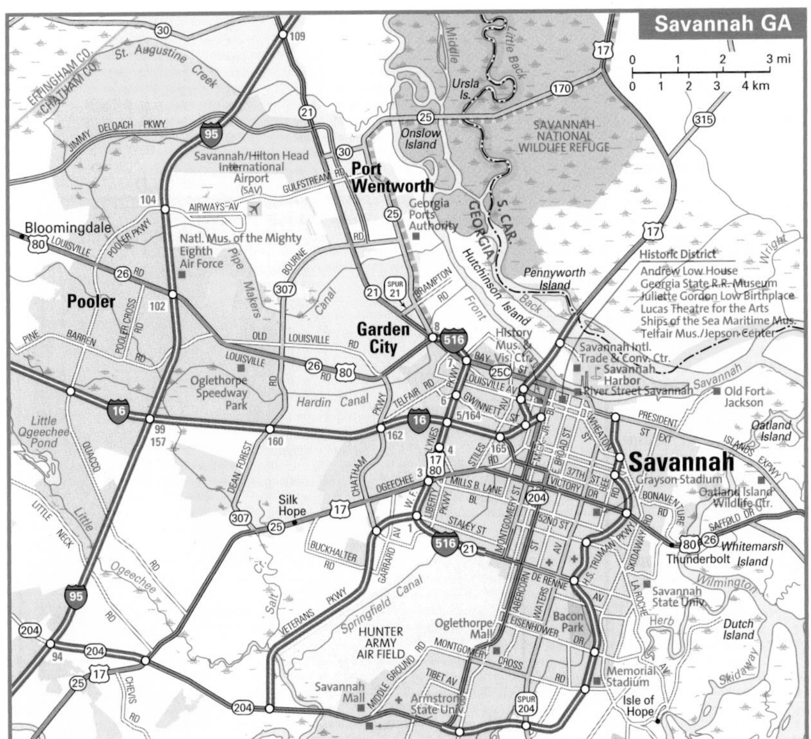

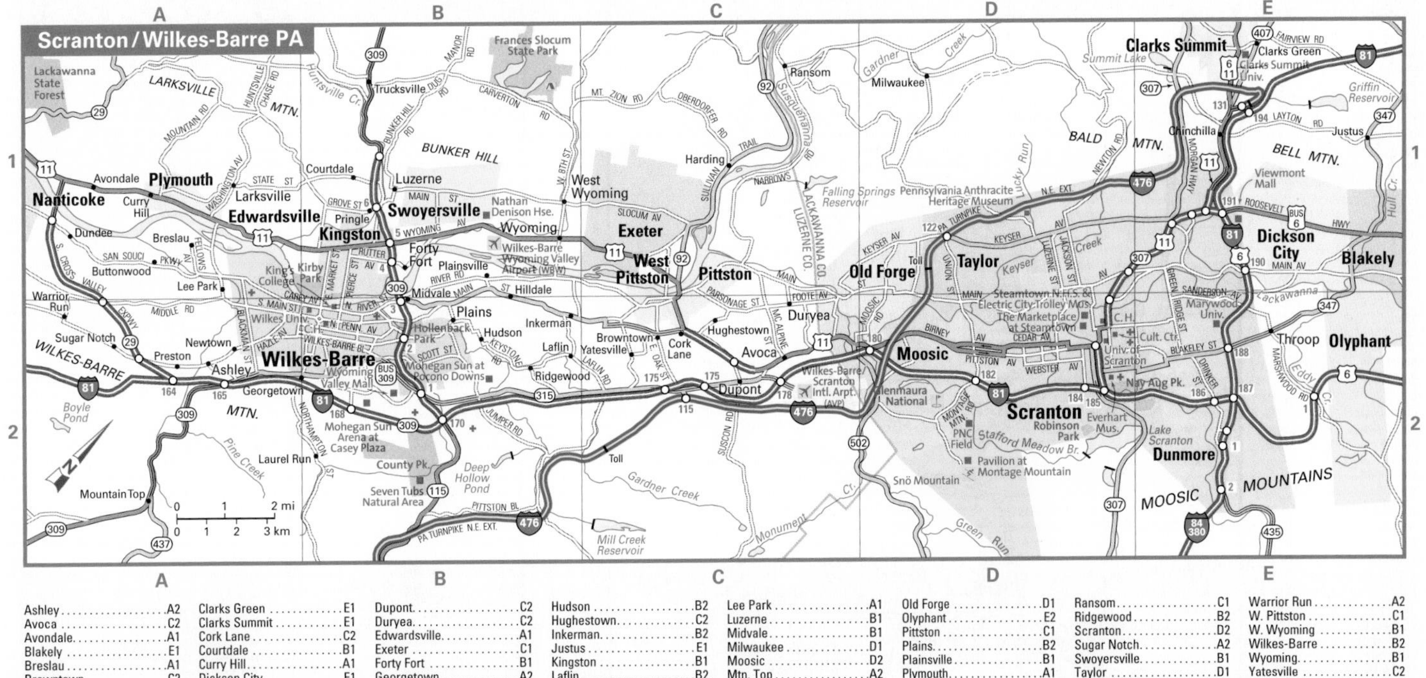

Figures after entries indicate population, page number, and grid reference.

Scranton KS, *710* **96** A3
Scranton ND, *281* **26** A1
Scranton PA, *76089* 93 F2
Scranton SC, *932* **122** C4
Scraper OK, *191* **106** B4
Screven GA, *766* **129** F4
Screven Co. GA, *14593* **130** B2
Scribner NE, *857* **35** F3
Scurry Co. TX, *16921* **58** B2
Seaboard NC, *632* **113** E3
Sea Breeze NC, *1969* **123** E3
Sea Bright NJ, *1412* **147** F2
Seabrook MD, *17287* **271** F2
Seabrook NH, *8693* **95** E1
Seabrook NJ, *1719* **145** F1
Seabrook TX, *11952* **132** B3
Seabrook Island SC, *1714* **131** D2
Sea Cliff NY, *4995* **148** C3
Seadrift TX, *1364* **61** F4
Seaford DE, *6928* **145** E4
Seaford VA, *2000* **113** F2
Seagate NC, *4590* **123** E3
Sea Girt NJ, *1828* **147** F2
Seagoville TX, *14835* **59** F2
Seagraves TX, *2417* **57** F2
Sea Isle City NJ, *2114* **105** D4
Seal Beach CA, *24168* **228** D4
Sealy TX, *6019* **61** F2
Seaman OH, *944* **100** C3
Sea Ranch Lakes FL, *670* **233** C2
Searchlight NV, *539* **46** B3
Searcy AR, *22858* **117** F1
Searcy Co. AR, *8195* **107** E4
Searingtown NY, *4915* **241** G3
Searsport ME, *992* **83** D2
Seaside CA, *33025* **44** B3
Seaside OR, *6457* **20** B1
Seaside Hts. NJ, *2887* **147** E3
Seaside Park NJ, *1579* **147** E3
SeaTac WA, *26909* **12** C3
Seat Pleasant MD, *4542* **271** F3
Seattle WA, *608660* 12 C3
Sebago Lake ME, *550* **82** B3
Sebastian FL, *21929* **141** E3
Sebastian TX, *1917* **63** F4
Sebastian Co. AR, *125744* **116** C1
Sebastopol CA, *7379* **36** B3
Sebeka MN, *711* **64** A4
Sebewaing MI, *1759* **76** B2
Sebree KY, *1603* **109** E1
Sebring FL, *10491* **141** D3
Sebring OH, *4420* **91** F3
Secaucus NJ, *16264* **240** C3
Second Mesa AZ, *962* **47** F2
Secretary MD, *535* **145** D4
Section AL, *770* **120** A2
Security CO, *29845* **41** E2
Sedalia MO, *21387* **97** D3
Sedalia NC, *623* **112** B4
Sedan KS, *1124* **43** F4
Sedgefield NC, *1100* **112** B4
Sedgwick KS, *1695* **43** E3
Sedgwick Co. CO, *2379* **34** A4
Sedgwick Co. KS, *498365* **43** E4
Sedley VA, *470* **113** F2
Sedona AZ, *10031* **47** D3
Sedro-Woolley WA, *10540* **12** C2
Seeley CA, *1739* **53** E4
Seeley Lake MT, *1659* **15** D3
Seelyville IN, *1029* **99** E2
Seffner FL, *7579* **266** D2
Seguin TX, *25175* **61** E2
Seiling OK, *860* **51** D2
Seisholtzville PA, *1400* **146** B1
Selah WA, *7147* **13** D4
Selawik AK, *829* **154** B2
Selby SD, *642* **26** C2
Selbyville DE, *2167* **114** C1
Selden NY, *19851* **149** D3
Selfridge ND, *160* **26** C1
Seligman AZ, *445* **46** C3
Seligman MO, *851* **106** C3
Selinsgrove PA, *5654* **93** D3
Selkirk NY, *1400* **94** B1
Sellersburg IN, *6128* **100** A3
Sellersville PA, *4249* **146** C2
Sells AZ, *2495* **54** C3
Selma AL, *20756* **127** F2
Selma CA, *23219* **45** D3
Selma IN, *866* **90** A4
Selma NC, *6073* **123** E1
Selma TX, *5540* **257** F1
Selma VA, *529* **112** B1
Selmer TN, *4396* **119** D1
Selmont AL, *3502* **127** F2
Seminole FL, *17233* **140** B2
Seminole OK, *7488* **51** F3
Seminole TX, *6430* **57** F2
Seminole Co. FL, *422718* **141** D1
Seminole Co. GA, *8729* **137** D1
Seminole Co. OK, *25482* **51** F3
Senath MO, *1767* **108** B4
Senatobia MS, *8165* **118** B2
Seneca IL, *2371* **88** C2
Seneca KS, *1991* **43** F1
Seneca MO, *2336* **106** B2
Seneca PA, *1065* **92** A2
Seneca SC, *8102* **121** E2
Seneca Co. NY, *35251* **79** D4
Seneca Co. OH, *56745* **90** C3
Seneca Falls NY, *6681* **79** D3

Seattle/Tacoma WA

Alderwood Manor B2
Algona B5
Arletta A5
Auburn B4
Bainbridge Island A3
Bay View A1
Beaux Arts B3
Bellevue B3
Bethel A4
Bonney Lake B5
Bothell B2
Bremerton A3
Brier B2
Brownsville A3
Burien B4
Burley A4
Burton A4
Cathcart B2
Clinton B1
Clyde Hill B3
Colby A3
Covington B4
Des Moines B4
Dockton A4
Eastgate B3
Edgewood B5
Edmonds B2
Ellisport A4
Everett B1
Federal Way B4
Fife B5
Fircrest A5
Fox Island A5
Freeland A1
Gig Harbor A4
Glendale B1
Hansville A1
Hunts Pt. B3
Indianola A2
Kenmore B2
Kent B4
Keyport A2
Kingston A2
Kirkland B2
Lake Forest Park B2
Lake Stevens B1
Lakewood A5
Langley A1
Lofall A2
Lynnwood B2
Maltby B2
Manchester A3
Martha Lake B2
Marysville B1
Maxwelton A1
McMillan B5
Medina B3
Mercer Island B3
Midland A5
Mill Creek B2
Milton B5
Mountlake Terrace B2
Mukilteo B1
Newcastle B3
Normandy Park B4
Olalla A4
Pacific B5
Parkland A5
Portage A4
Port Gamble A2
Port Orchard A3
Poulsbo A2
Purdy A4
Puyallup B5
Redmond B3
Redondo B4
Renton B4
Retsil A3
Rollingbay A3
Rosedale A4
Ruston A5
SeaTac B4
Seattle B2
Shine A2
Shoreline B2
Skyway B4
Snohomish B1
S. Colby A3
S. Hill B5
S. Prairie B5
Southworth A3
Steilacoom A5
Summit B5
Sumner B5
Suquamish A2
Tacoma A5
Tahlequah A4
Tracyton A3
Tukwila B4
Tulalip B1
University Place A5
Vashon A4
Vashon Hts. A3
Wauna A4
White Ctr. B4
Wollochet A5
Woodinville B2
Woodway A2
Yarrow Pt. B3

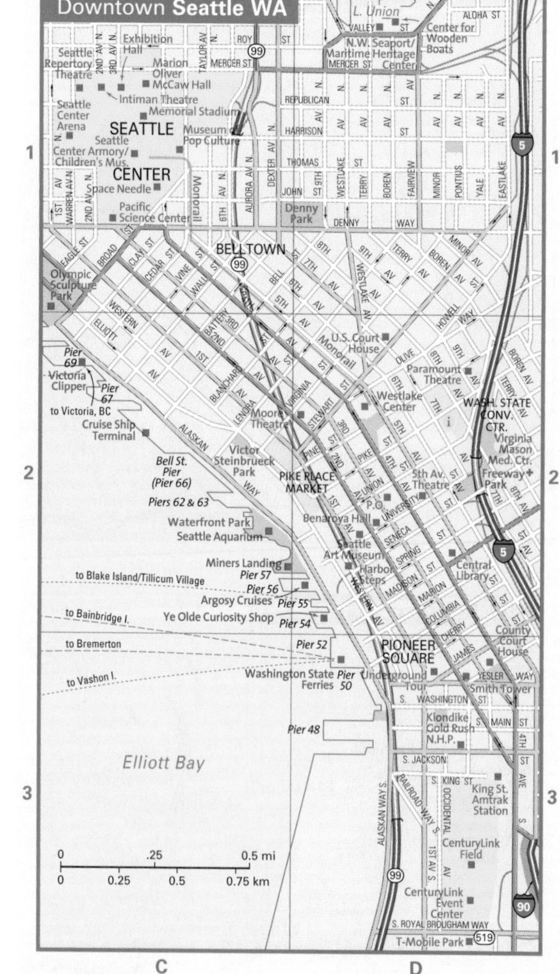

POINTS OF INTEREST

5th Avenue Theatre D2
Argosy Cruises D2
Benaroya Hall D2
Center for Wooden Boats D1
Central Library D2
CenturyLink Event Center D3
CenturyLink Field D3
Cruise Ship Terminal C2
Exhibition Hall C1
Harbor Steps D2
King Street Amtrak Station D3
Klondike Gold Rush Natl. Hist. Park D3
Marion Oliver McCaw Hall C1
Memorial Stadium C1
Miners Landing C2
Monorail C1, D2
Moore Theatre D2
Museum of Pop Culture C1
Northwest Seaport/ Maritime Heritage Center D1
Pacific Science Center C1
Paramount Theatre D2
Pike Place Market D2
Post Office D2
The Seattle Aquarium C2
Seattle Art Museum D2
Seattle Center C1
Seattle Center Arena C1
Seattle Center Armory/Childrens Museum . . C1
Seattle Repertory Theatre C1
Smith Tower D3
Space Needle C1
T-Mobile Park D3
Underground Tour D3
Victoria Clipper C2
Washington State Convention Center D2
Washington State Ferries D3
Westlake Center D2
Ye Old Curiosity Shop D2

Entries in **bold black** indicate counties or parishes.
Entries in **bold color** indicate cities with detailed inset maps.

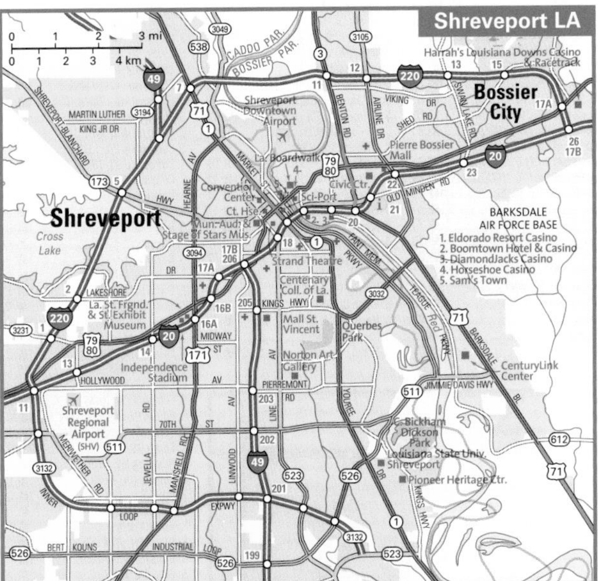

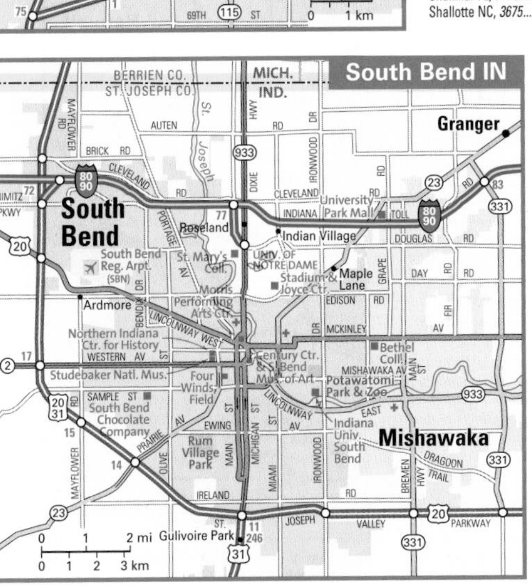

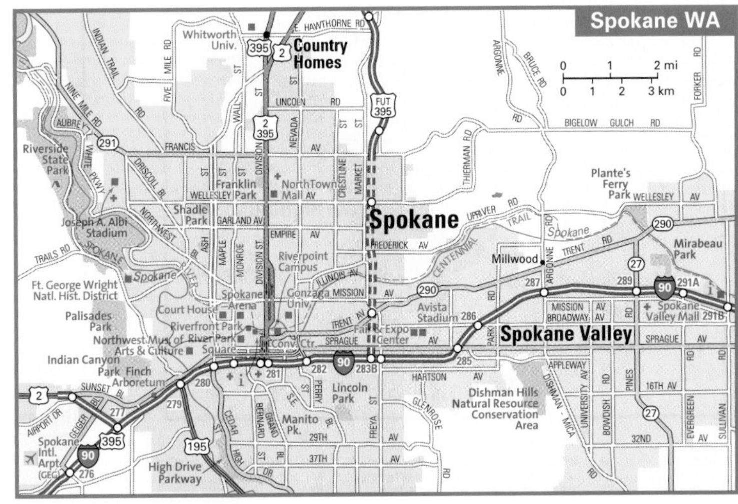

Figures after entries indicate population, page number, and grid reference.

Springfield IL

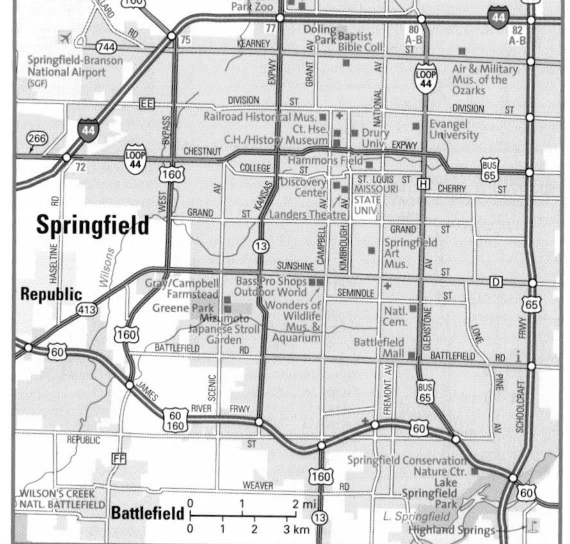

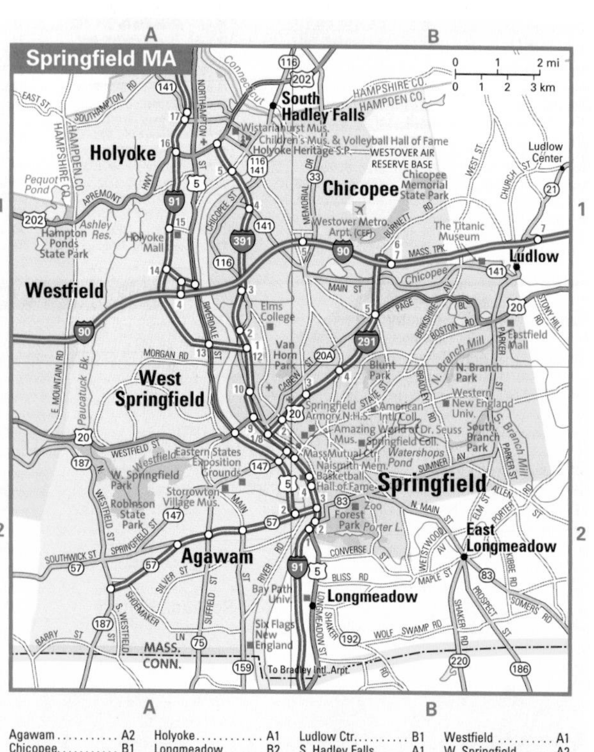

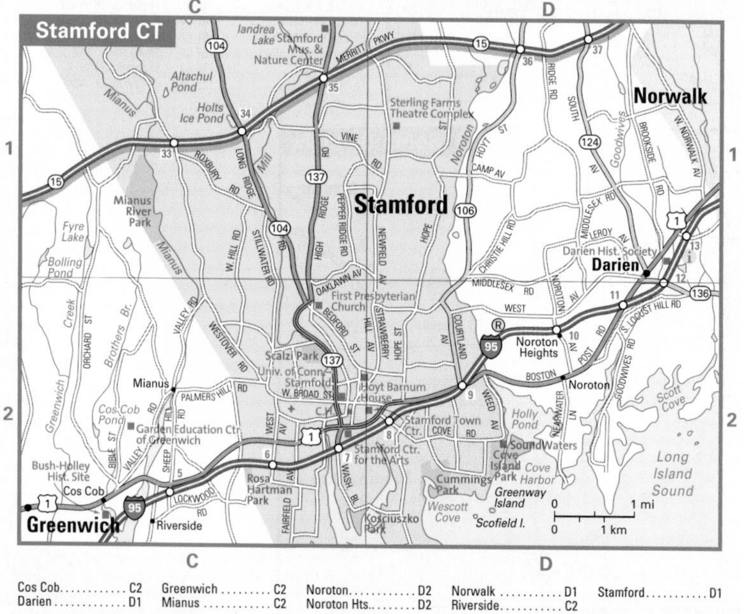

Entries in **bold black** indicate counties or parishes.
Entries in **bold color** indicate cities with detailed inset maps.

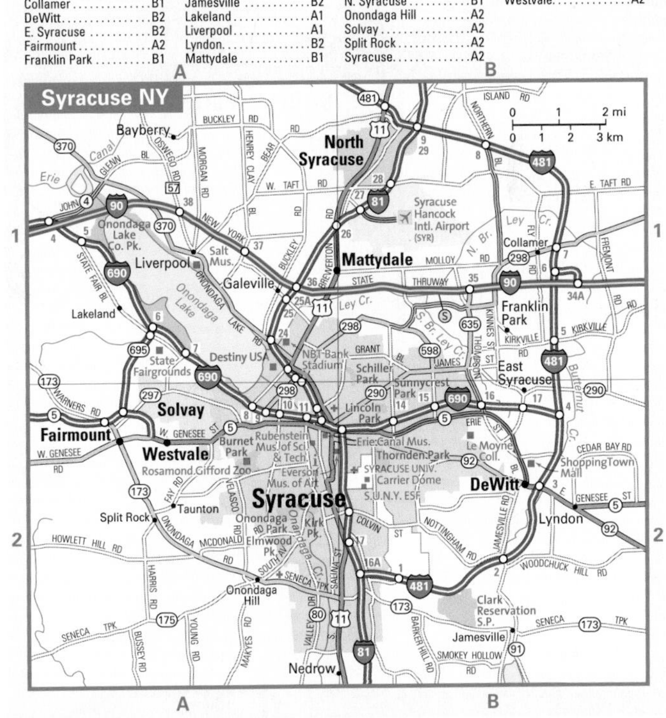

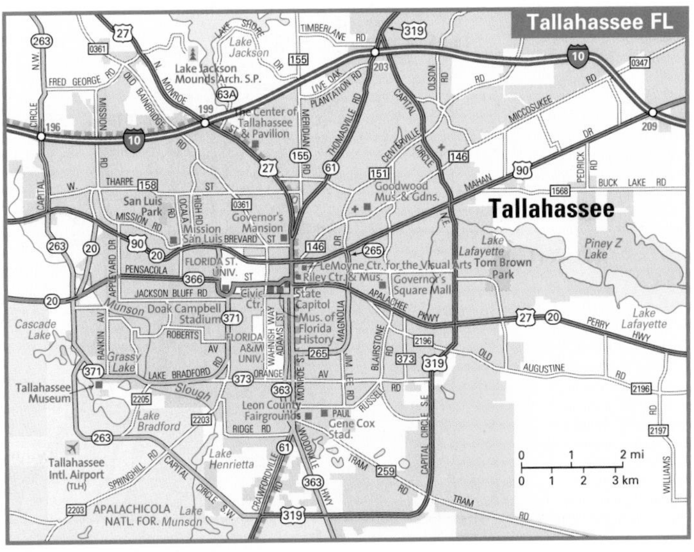

Stockton CA

Figures after entries indicate population, page number, and grid reference.

Tampa / St Petersburg FL

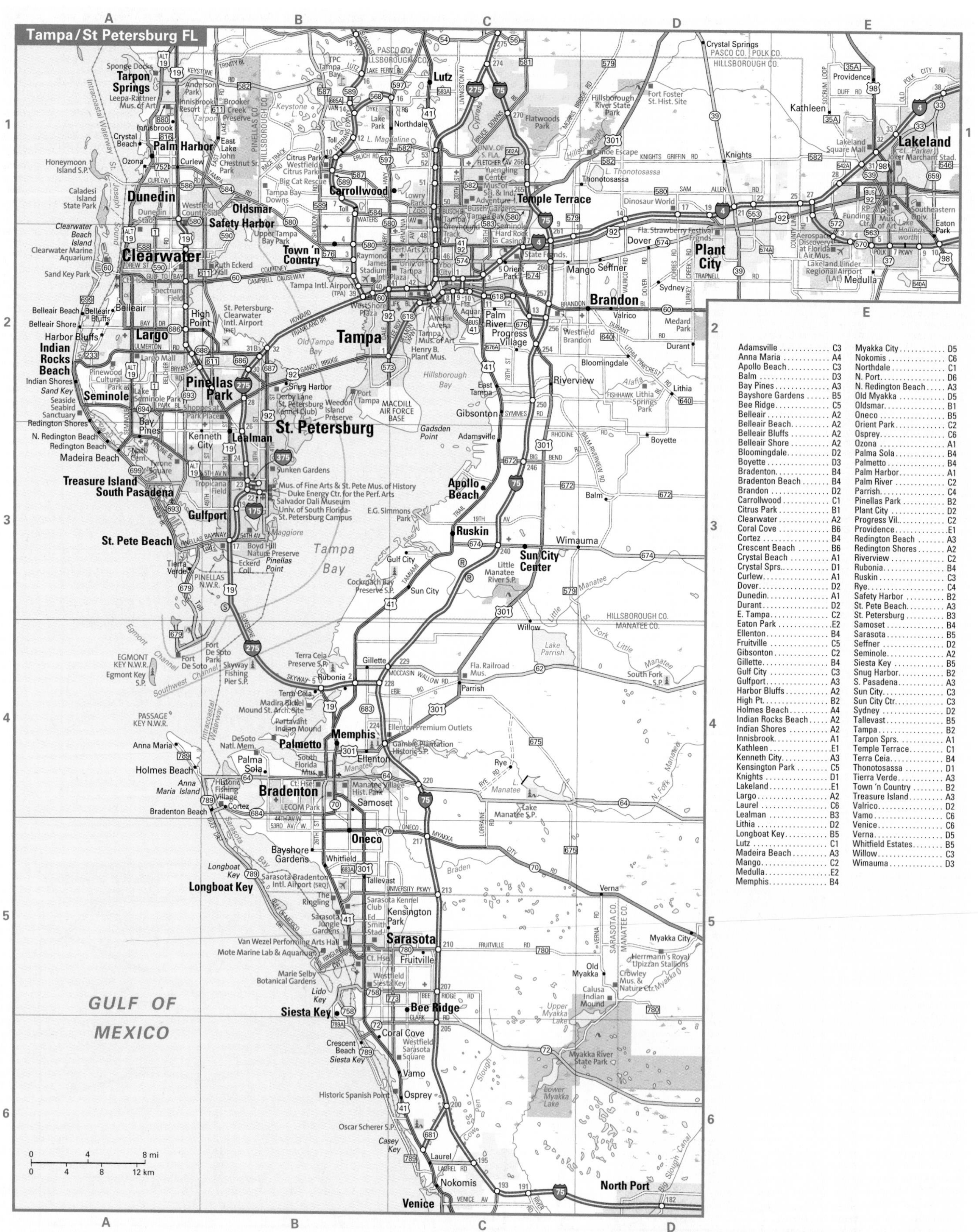

Entries in **bold black** indicate counties or parishes.
Entries in **bold color** indicate cities with detailed inset maps.

Harbor View B1
Holland A2
Lime City B2
Maumee A2
Moline B2
Northwood B2
Oregon B1
Ottawa Hills A1
Perrysburg A2
Rossford B2
Stony Ridge B2
Sylvania A1
Toledo A1
Walbridge B2

Toledo OH

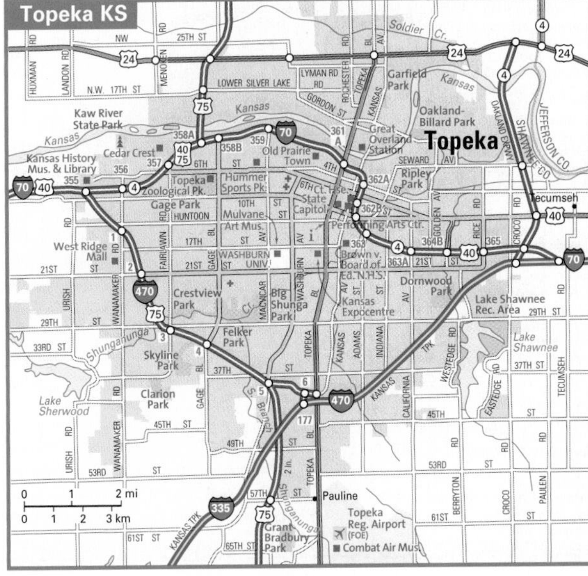

Figures after entries indicate population, page number, and grid reference.

Bakersville	B1	Fallsington	A2	Mercerville	B1	Trenton	B2
Ewing	A1	Lawrenceville	B1	Morrisville	A2	W. Trenton	A1
Ewingville	A1	Lewisville	B1	Slackwood	B1	White Horse	B2

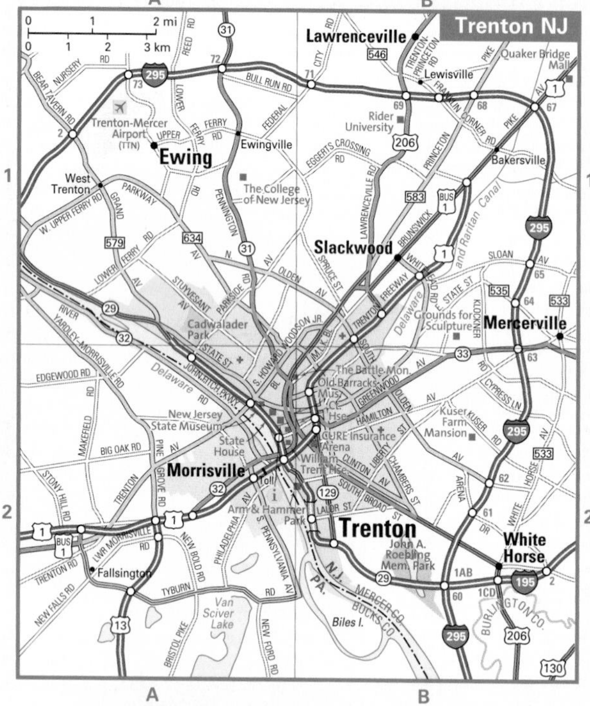

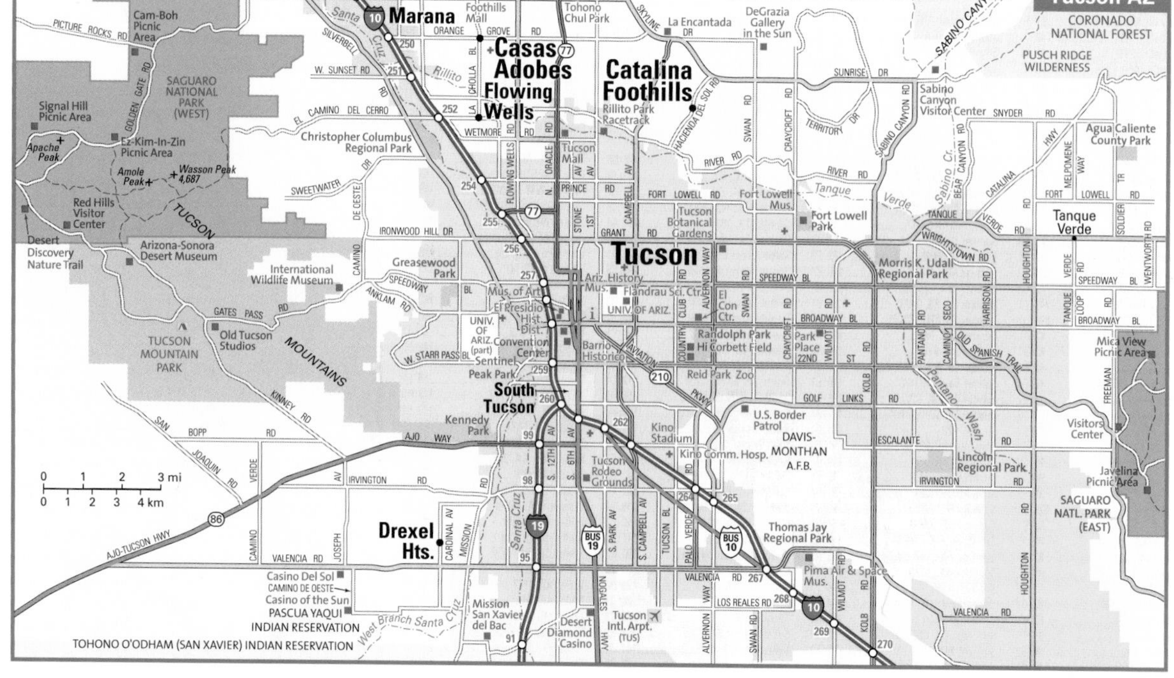

Entries in **bold black** indicate counties or parishes.
Entries in **bold color** indicate cities with detailed inset maps.

Bixby C3 · Bowden A3 · Broken Arrow C3 · Catoosa C1 · Jenks B3 · Oakhurst A3 · Sand Sprs. A2 · Sapulpa A3 · Tiger C1 · Tulsa B2

Tulsa OK

Vicksburg MS

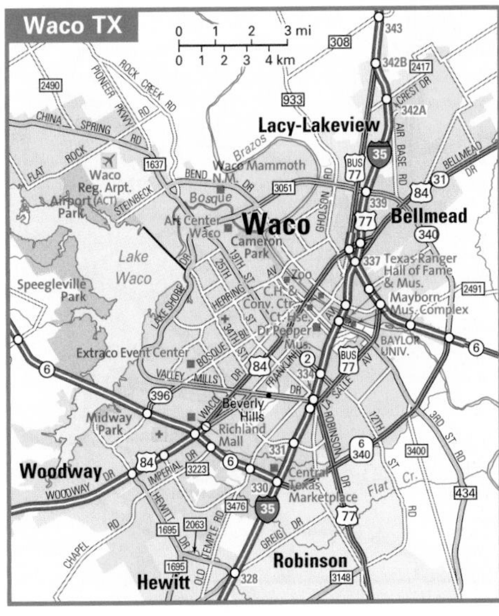

Figures after entries indicate population, page number, and grid reference.

Washington DC

Entries in **bold black** indicate counties or parishes.
Entries in **bold color** indicate cities with detailed inset maps.

Figures after entries indicate population, page number, and grid reference.

POINTS OF INTEREST

Entries in **bold black** indicate counties or parishes.
Entries in **bold color** indicate cities with detailed inset maps.

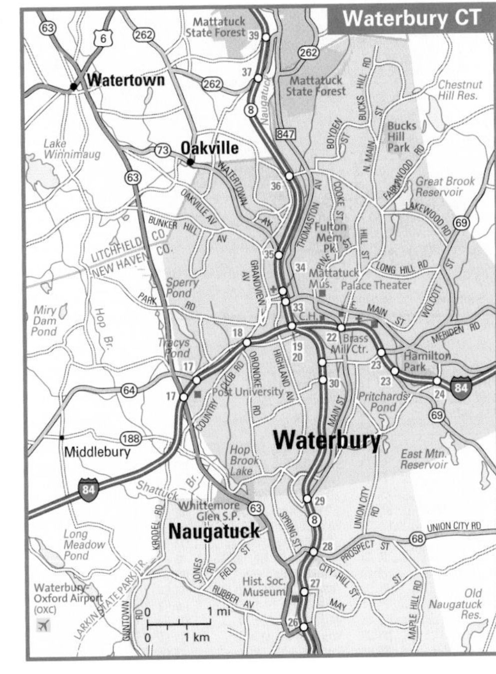

Downtown Washington DC

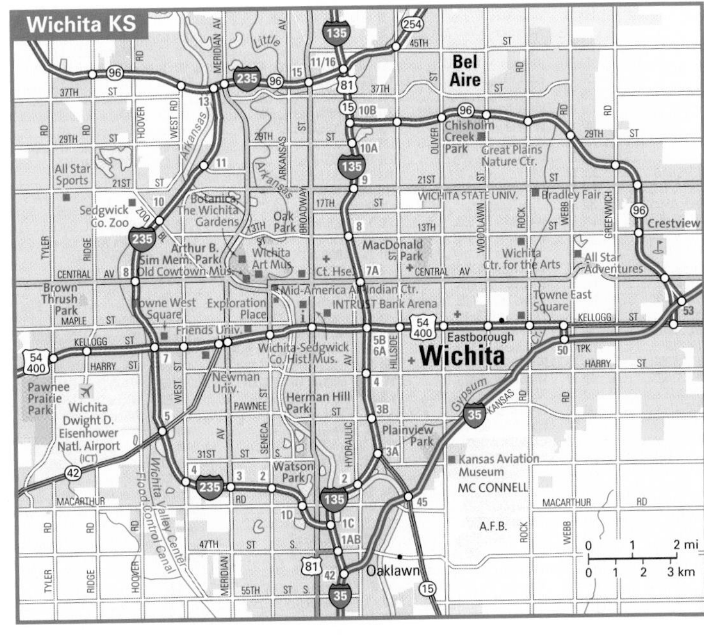

Figures after entries indicate population, page number, and grid reference.

Williamsburg VA

Wilmington DE

Entries in **bold black** indicate counties or parishes.
Entries in **bold color** indicate cities with detailed inset maps.

Worcester MA

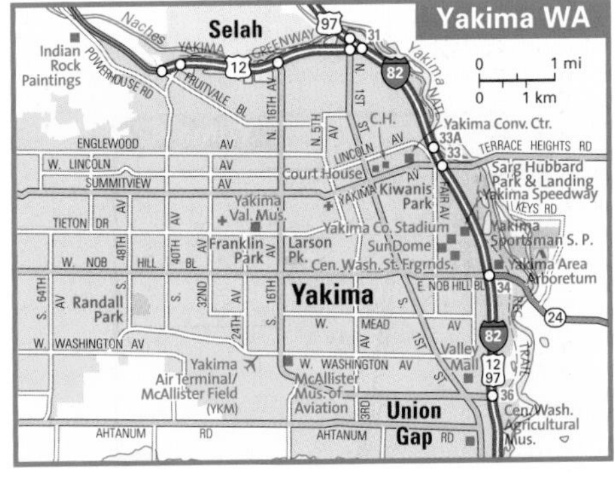

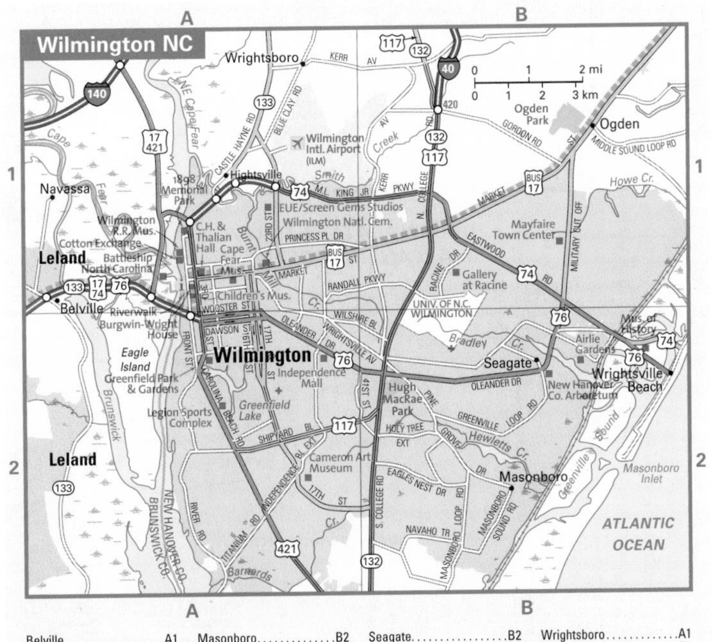

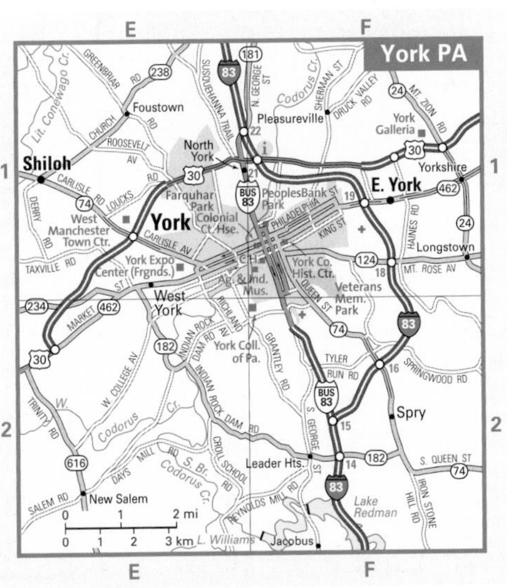

Figures after entries indicate population, page number, and grid reference.

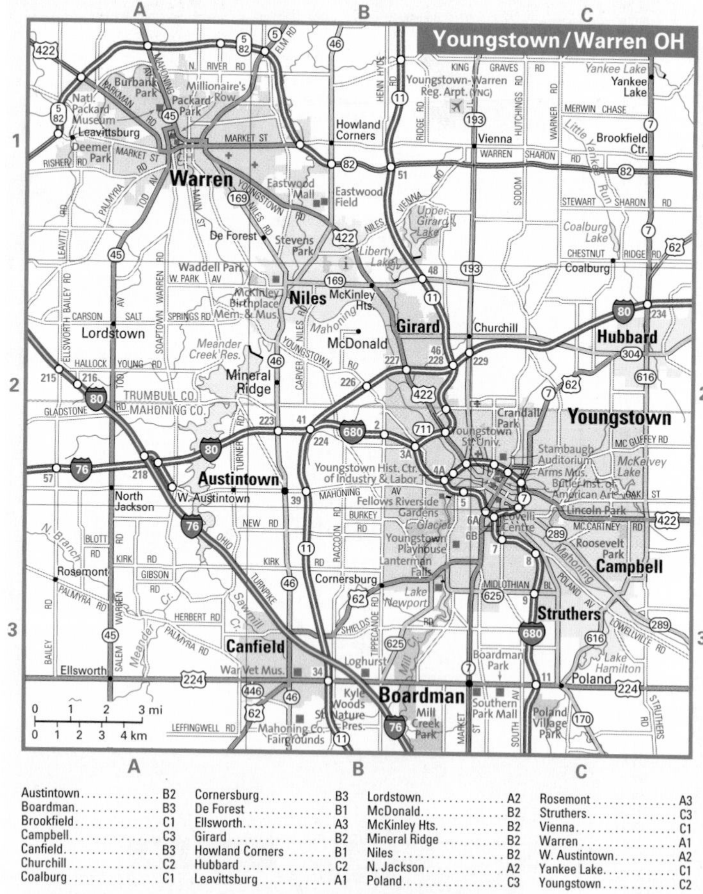

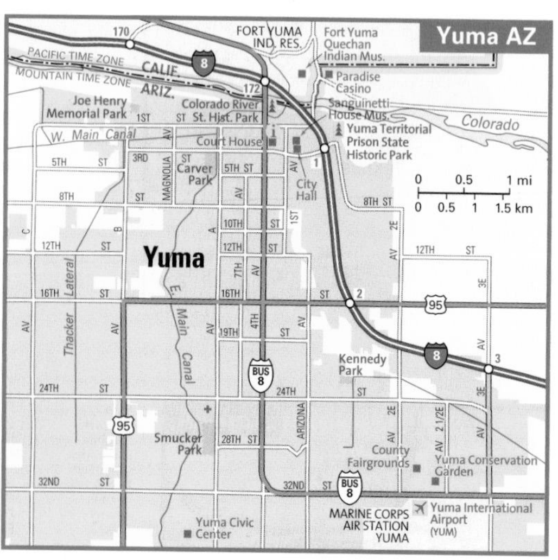

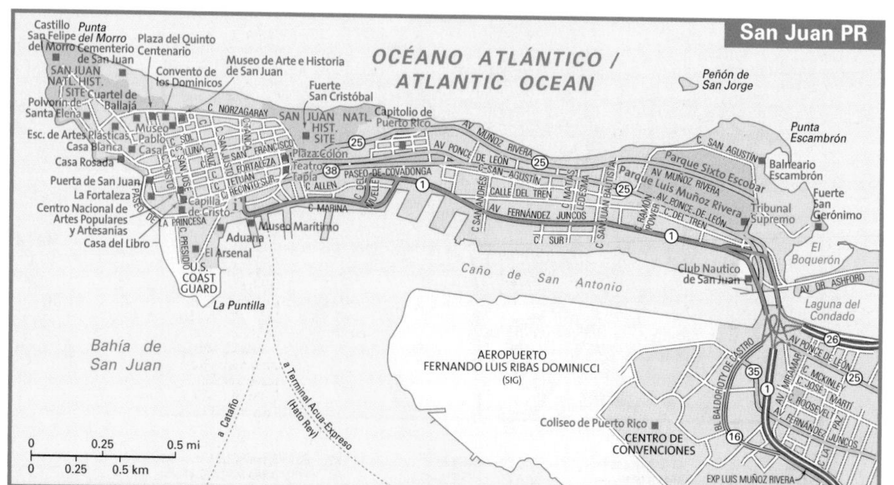

Entries in **bold color** indicate cities with detailed inset maps.

CANADA

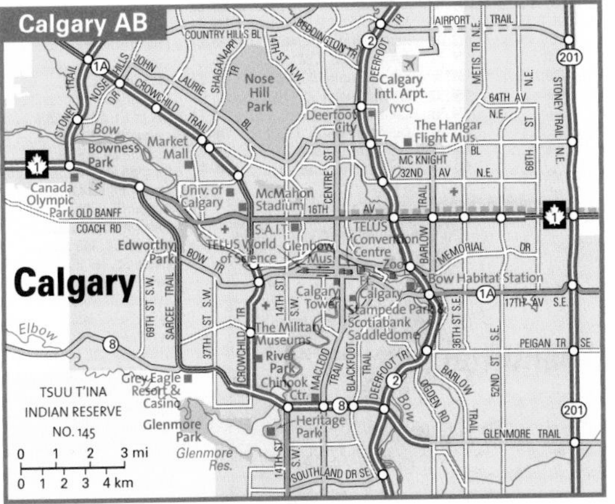

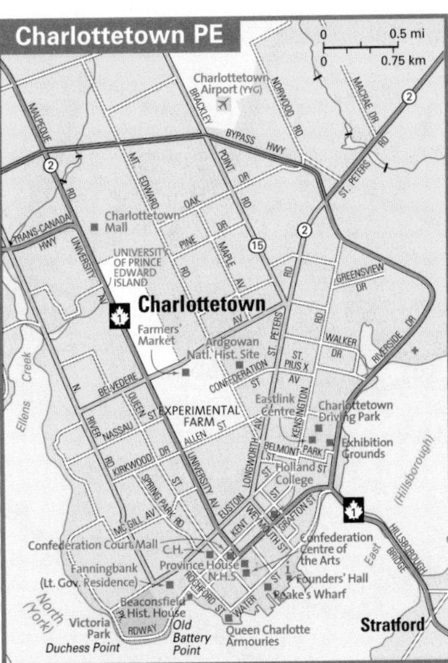

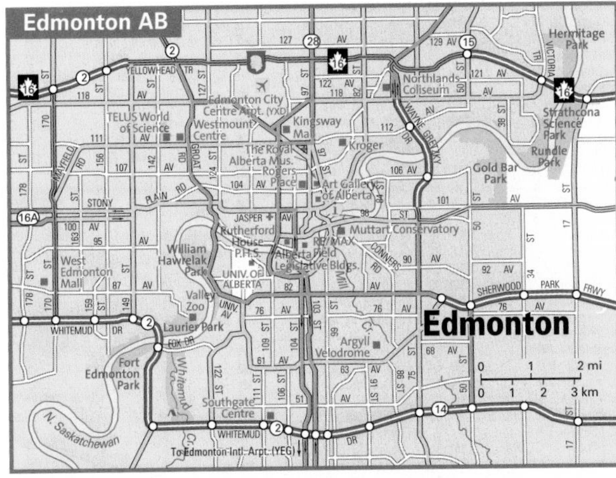

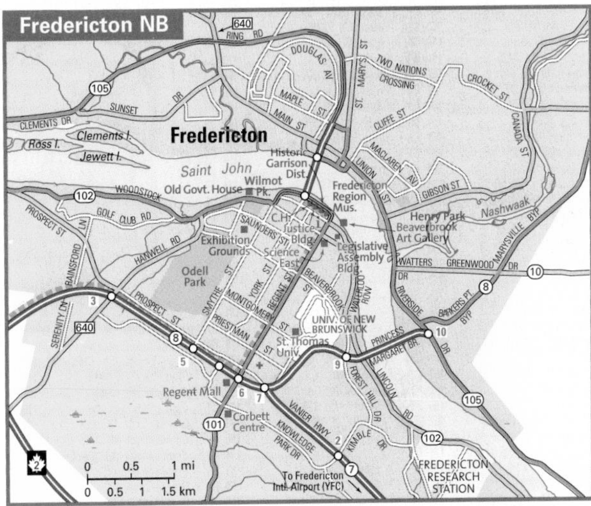

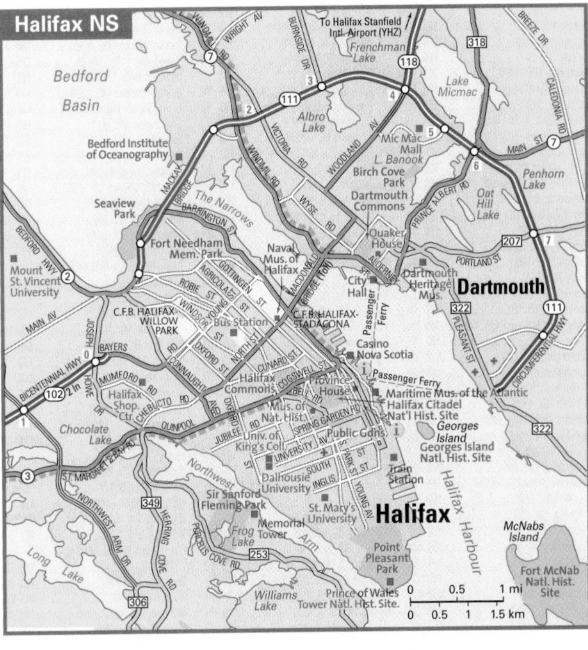

Figures after entries indicate population, page number, and grid reference.

Hamilton ON

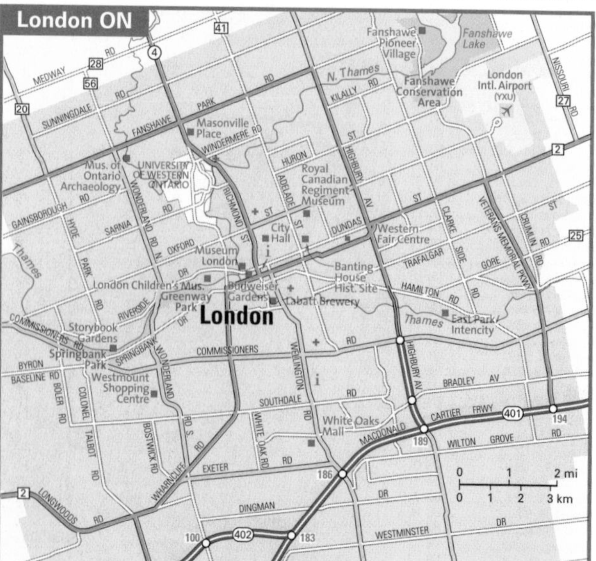

Entries in **bold color** indicate cities with detailed inset maps.

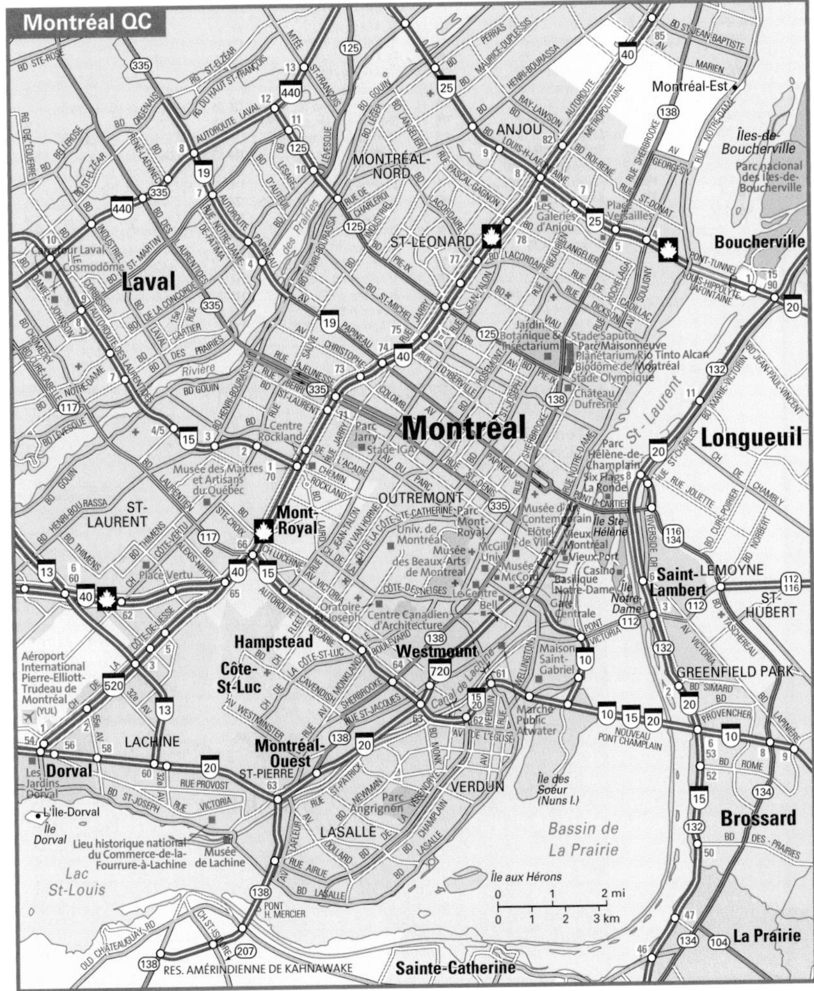

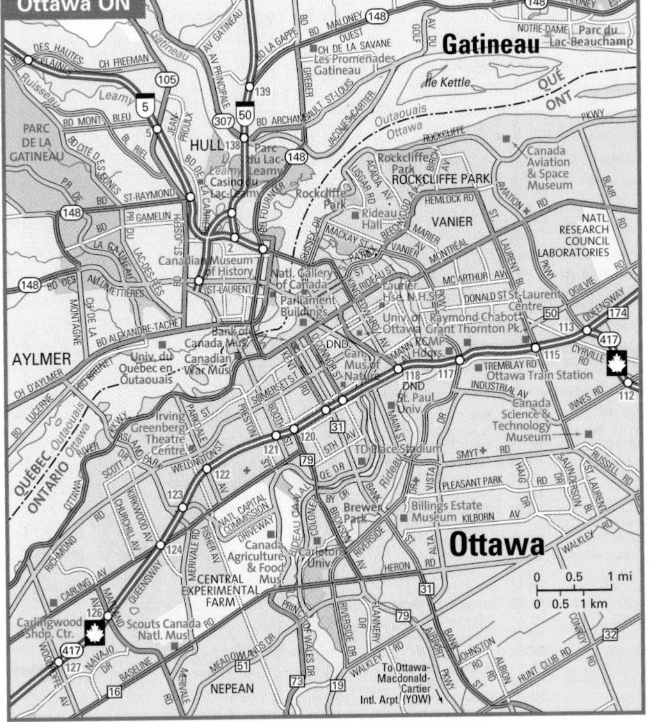

Figures after entries indicate population, page number, and grid reference.

Québec QC

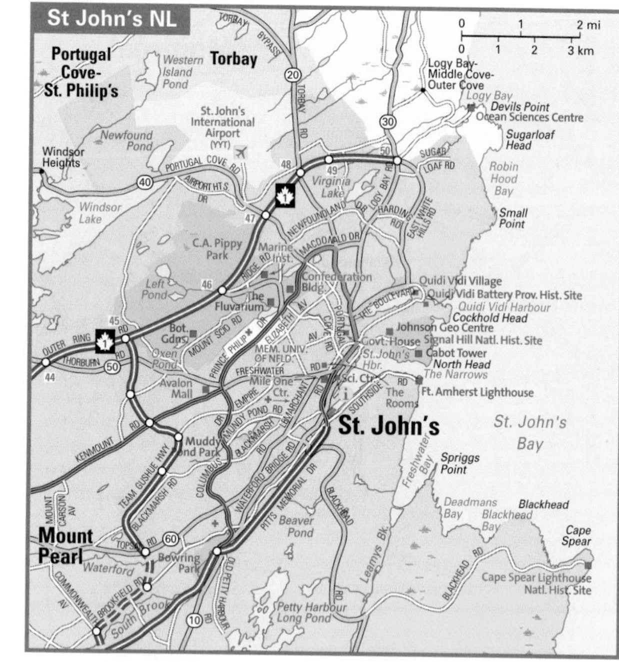

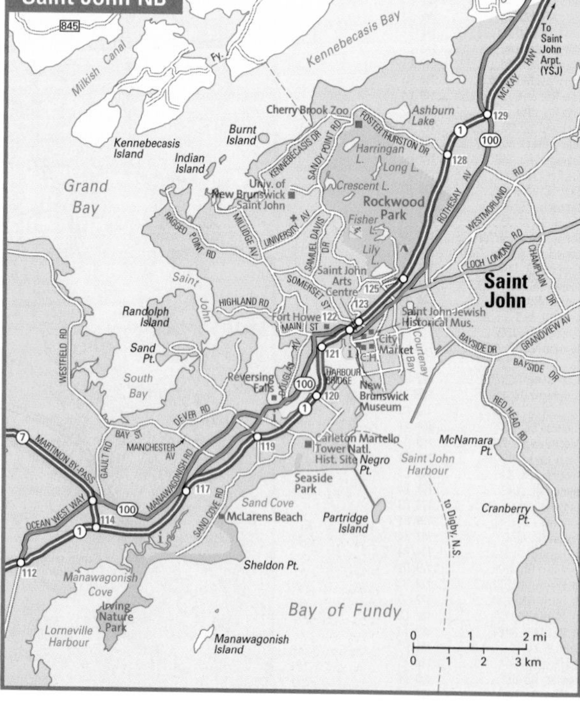

Saskatoon SK

Entries in **bold color** indicate cities with detailed inset maps.

Toronto ON

Downtown Toronto ON

POINTS OF INTEREST

Art Gallery of Ontario ... A1
Canadian Broadcasting Center ... A2
CN Tower ... A2
Design Exchange ... B2
Eaton Centre ... B1
Ed Mirvish Theatre ... B1
Four Seasons Centre for the Performing Arts ... A1
The Grange ... A1
Harbourfront Centre ... A2
Hockey Hall of Fame ... B2
Jack Layton Ferry Terminal ... B2
MacKenzie House ... B1
Massey Hall ... B1
Metro Toronto Convention Ctr. ... A2
Old City Hall ... B1
Princess of Wales Theatre ... A1
Queen's Quay Terminal ... A2
Redpath Sugar Museum ... B2
Ripley's Aquarium ... A2
Rogers Centre ... A2
Royal Alexandra Theatre ... A1
Royerson University ... B1
Roy Thomson Hall ... A2
Saint Lawrence Centre ... B2
Saint Lawrence Market ... B2
Scotiabank Arena ... B2
Sony Centre for the Perf. Arts ... B2
Textile Museum of Canada ... A1
Toronto Stock Exchange ... A1
Union Station ... B2
Yonge-Dundas Square ... B1

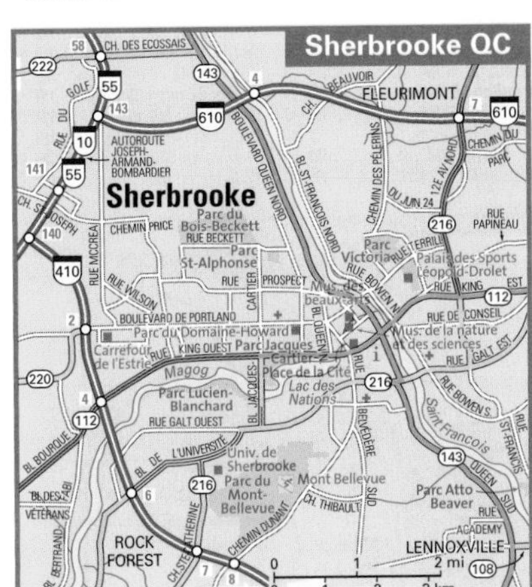

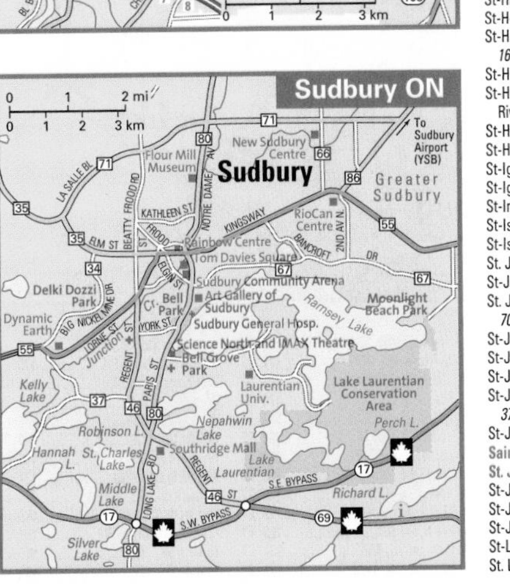

Figures after entries indicate population, page number, and grid reference.

Vancouver BC

Victoria BC

Winnipeg MB

Entries in **bold color** indicate cities with detailed inset maps.

MEXICO

Cancún MX
Isla Mujeres
Laguna Chakmochuk
Isla Mujeres
Ruinas El Cerrito
El Meco
Aeropista
Punta Sam
Punta Sam
Ruinas El Meco
Bahía Mujeres
Playa Garrafón
Punta Sur
Puerto Juárez
Cancún
Carretera Puerto Juárez - Mérida
Plaza de Toros
Palacio de Gobierno
180
Punta Cancún
Centro de Convenciones
Laguna Nichupté
ZONA HOTELERA
Alfredo V. Bonfil
307
Aeropuerto Internacional de Cancún (CUN)
Ruinas El Rey
Canal Nizuc
Ruinas San Miguelito
Playa El Rey
MAR CARIBE / CARIBBEAN SEA
Punta Nizuc
Ventura Park
0 2 4 mi
0 2 4 6 km

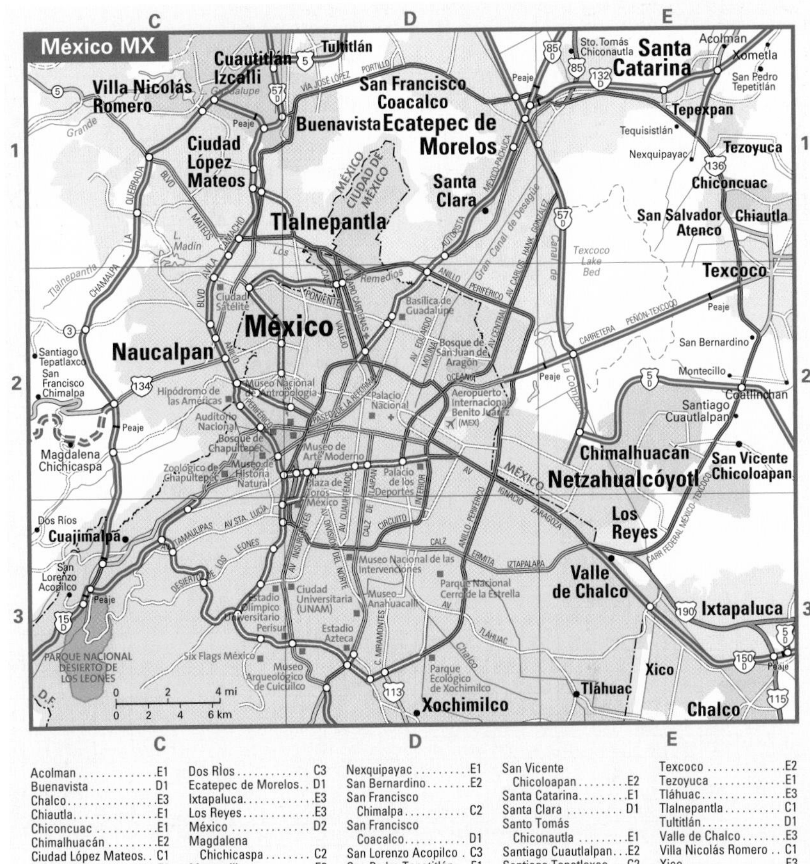

Acolman .E1
Buenavista D1
Chalco .E3
Chiautla .E1
Chiconcuac .E1
Chimalhuacán .E2
Ciudad López Mateos C1
Coatlinchan .E2
Cuajimalpa C3
Cuautitlán Izcalli C1
Dos Rìos C3
Ecatepec de Morelos D1
Ixtapaluca .E3
Los Reyes .E3
México D2
Magdalena Chichicaspa C2
Montecillo .E2
Naucalpan C2
Netzahualcóyotl .E2
Nexquipayac .E1
San Bernardino .E2
San Francisco Chimalpa C2
San Francisco Coacalco D1
San Lorenzo Acopilco C3
San Pedro Tepetitlán .E1
San Salvador Atenco .E1
San Vicente Chicoloapan .E2
Santa Catarina .E1
Santa Clara D1
Santo Tomás Chiconautla .E1
Santiago Cuautlalpan .E2
Santiago Tepatlaxco C2
Tepexpan .E1
Tequisistlán .E1
Texcoco .E2
Tezoyuca .E1
Tláhuac .E3
Tlalnepantla C1
Tultitlán D1
Valle de Chalco .E3
Villa Nicolás Romero C1
Xico .E3
Xochimilco D3
Xometla .E1

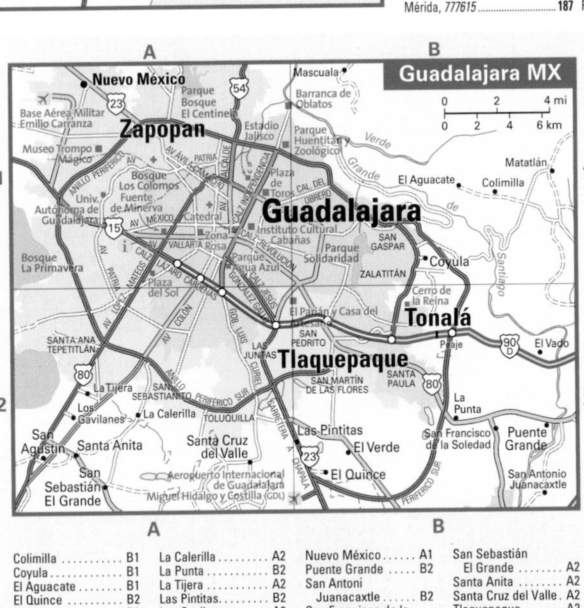

Colimilla B1
Coyula B1
El Aguacate B1
El Quince B2
El Vado B2
El Verde B2
Guadalajara A1
La Calerilla A2
La Punta B2
La Tijera A2
Las Pintitas B2
Los Gavilanes A2
Mascuala B1
Matatlán B1
Nuevo México A1
Puente Grande B2
San Antoni Juanacaxtle B2
San Francisco de la Soledad B2
San Agustín A2
San Sebastián El Grande A2
Santa Anita A2
Santa Cruz del Valle A2
Tlaquepaque A2
Tonalá B2
Zapopan .A1

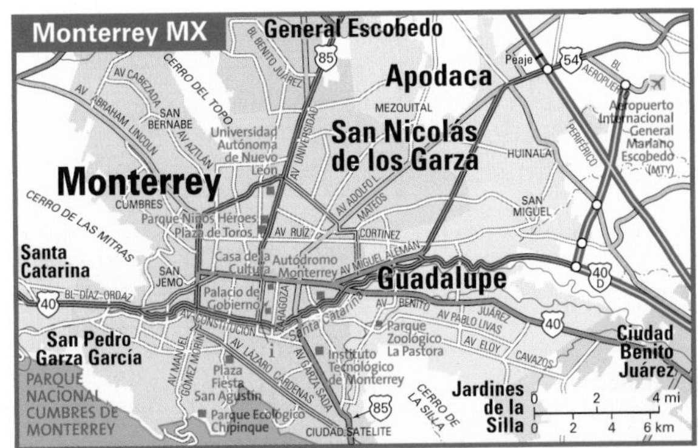

Miles

City	Albany, NY	Albuquerque, NM	Amarillo, TX	Anchorage, AK	Atlanta, GA	Baltimore, MD	Billings, MT	Birmingham, AL	Bismarck, ND	Boise, ID	Boston, MA	Buffalo, NY	Calgary, AB	Charleston, SC	Charleston, WV	Charlotte, NC	Cheyenne, WY	Chicago, IL	Cincinnati, OH	Cleveland, OH	Columbus, OH	Dallas, TX	Denver, CO	Des Moines, IA	Detroit, MI	El Paso, TX	Halifax, NS	Houston, TX	Indianapolis, IN	Jackson, MS	Jacksonville, FL	Kansas City, MO	Las Vegas, NV	Little Rock, AR	Los Angeles, CA	Louisville, KY
Albany, NY		2095	1811	4421	1010	333	2083	1093	1675	2526	172	292	2512	913	634	771	1789	832	730	484	621	1680	1833	1155	571	2326	877	1768	795	1331	1094	1282	2586	1354	2859	832
Albuquerque, NM	3371		286	3563	1490	1902	991	1274	1333	966	2240	1808	1498	1793	1568	1649	538	1352	1409	1619	1476	754	438	1091	1608	263	2945	994	1298	1157	1837	894	578	900	806	1320
Amarillo, TX	2914	460		3734	1206	1618	988	991	1398	1266	1957	1524	1669	1510	1285	1365	534	1069	1126	1335	1192	470	434	808	1324	438	2662	711	1014	874	1517	610	864	617	1092	1036
Anchorage, AK	7113	5733	6008		4304	4297	2601	4253	2724	2745	4592	4133	2065	4495	4093	4348	3056	3584	3890	3935	3946	4087	3300	3421	3872	4002	4821	4328	3771	4294	4652	3547	3356	3929	3403	3886
Atlanta, GA	1625	2397	1940	6925		679	1889	150	1559	2218	1100	910	2395	317	503	238	1482	717	476	726	577	792	1403	967	735	1437	1805	800	531	386	344	801	2067	528	2237	419
Baltimore, MD	536	3060	2603	6914	1093		1959	795	1551	2401	422	370	2388	583	352	441	1665	708	521	377	420	1399	1690	1031	532	2045	1128	1470	600	1032	763	1087	2445	1072	2705	602
Billings, MT	3352	1595	1590	4185	3039	3152		1839	413	626	2254	1796	536	2157	1755	2012	455	1246	1552	1597	1608	1433	554	1007	1534	1255	2806	1673	1432	1836	2237	1088	965	1530	1239	1547
Birmingham, AL	1759	2050	1595	6843	241	1279	2959		1509	2170	1215	909	2346	466	578	389	1434	667	475	725	576	647	1356	919	734	1292	1921	678	481	241	494	753	1852	381	2092	369
Bismarck, ND	2695	2145	2249	4383	2508	2496	665	2428		1039	1846	1388	794	1749	1347	1604	594	838	1144	1189	1200	1342	693	675	1126	1597	2398	1582	1024	1548	1906	801	1378	1183	1702	1139
Boise, ID	4064	1554	2037	4417	3569	3863	1007	3492	1672		2697	2239	735	2520	2182	2375	737	1708	1969	2040	2036	1711	833	1369	1977	1206	3249	1952	1852	2115	2566	1376	760	1808	1033	1933
Boston, MA	277	3604	3149	7389	1770	679	3627	1955	2970	4339		462	2683	1003	741	861	1961	1003	862	654	760	1819	2004	1326	741	2465	714	1890	940	1453	1184	1427	2757	1493	3046	964
Buffalo, NY	470	2909	2452	6650	1464	595	2890	1463	2233	3603	743		2224	899	431	695	1502	545	442	197	333	1393	1546	868	277	2039	1167	1513	508	1134	1080	995	2299	1066	2572	545
Calgary, AB	4042	2410	2685	3323	3854	3842	862	3775	1278	1183	4317	3578		2586	2184	2441	991	1675	1981	2026	2037	2114	1234	1512	1963	1936	2912	2355	1862	2385	2743	1638	1291	2020	1565	1977
Charleston, SC	1469	2885	2430	7232	510	938	3471	750	2814	4055	1614	1446	4161		468	204	1783	907	622	724	637	1109	1705	1204	879	1754	1708	1110	721	703	238	1102	2371	900	2554	610
Charleston, WV	1020	2523	2068	6586	809	566	2824	930	2167	3511	1192	693	3514	753		265	1445	506	209	255	168	1072	1367	802	410	1718	1446	1192	320	816	649	764	2122	745	2374	251
Charlotte, NC	1241	2653	2196	6996	383	710	3237	626	2581	3821	1385	1118	3928	328	426		1637	761	476	520	433	1031	1559	1057	675	1677	1566	1041	575	625	385	956	2225	754	2453	464
Cheyenne, WY	2879	866	859	4917	2385	2679	732	2307	956	1186	3155	2417	1595	2869	2325	2634		972	1233	1304	1300	979	100	633	1241	801	2513	1220	1115	1382	1829	640	843	1076	1116	1197
Chicago, IL	1339	2175	1720	5767	1154	1139	2005	1073	1348	2748	1614	877	2695	1459	814	1224	1564		302	346	359	936	1015	337	283	1543	1555	1108	184	750	1065	532	1768	662	2042	299
Cincinnati, OH	1175	2267	1812	6259	766	838	2497	764	1841	3168	1387	711	3187	1001	336	766	1984	486		253	105	958	1200	599	261	1605	1567	1079	116	700	803	597	1955	632	2215	106
Cleveland, OH	779	2605	2148	6331	1168	607	2570	1167	1913	3282	1052	317	3260	1165	410	837	2098	557	407		144	1208	1347	669	171	1854	1359	1328	319	950	904	806	2100	882	2374	356
Columbus, OH	999	2375	1918	6349	928	676	2587	927	1931	3276	1223	536	3278	1025	270	697	2092	578	169	232		1059	1266	665	192	1706	1465	1179	176	801	818	663	2021	733	2281	207
Dallas, TX	2703	1213	756	6576	1274	2251	2306	1041	2159	2753	2927	2241	3401	1784	1725	1659	1575	1506	1541	1944	1704		887	752	1218	647	2524	241	913	406	1049	554	1331	327	1446	852
Denver, CO	2949	705	698	5310	2257	2719	891	2182	1115	1340	3224	2488	1986	2743	2200	2508	161	1633	1931	2167	2037	1427		676	1284	701	2556	1127	1088	1290	1751	603	756	984	1029	1118
Des Moines, IA	1858	1755	1300	5504	1556	1659	1620	1479	1086	2203	2134	1397	2433	1937	1290	1701	1018	542	964	1076	1070	1210	1088		606	1283	1878	992	481	931	1315	194	1429	567	1703	595
Detroit, MI	919	2587	2130	6230	1183	856	2468	1181	1812	3181	1192	446	3158	1414	660	1086	1997	455	420	275	309	1960	2066	975		1799	1278	1338	318	960	1060	795	2037	891	2310	366
El Paso, TX	3743	423	705	6439	2312	3290	2019	2079	2570	1940	3966	3281	3115	2822	2764	2698	1289	2483	2582	2983	2745	1041	1128	2064	2895		3171	758	1489	1051	1642	1085	717	974	801	1499
Halifax, NS	1411	4739	4283	7757	2904	1815	4515	3091	3858	5228	1149	1878	4685	2748	2327	2520	4043	2502	2521	2187	2357	4061	4113	3022	2056	5102		2595	1646	2158	1889	2133	3309	2198	3583	1669
Houston, TX	2845	1599	1144	6964	1287	2365	2692	1091	2545	3141	3041	2434	3789	1786	1918	1675	1963	1783	1736	2137	1897	388	1813	1596	2153	1220	4175		839	445	884	795	1474	447	1558	972
Indianapolis, IN	1279	2088	1632	6068	854	965	2304	774	1648	2980	1512	817	2996	1160	515	925	1794	296	187	513	283	1469	1751	774	512	2396	2648	1350		675	879	485	1843	587	2104	112
Jackson, MS	2142	1862	1406	6909	621	1660	2954	388	2491	3403	2338	1825	3837	1131	1313	1006	2224	1207	1126	1529	1289	653	2076	1498	1545	1691	3472	716	1086		598	747	1735	269	1851	594
Jacksonville, FL	1760	2956	2441	7485	553	1228	3599	795	3067	4129	1905	1738	4413	383	1044	619	2943	1714	1292	1455	1316	1688	2817	2116	1706	2642	3039	1422	1414	962		1148	2415	873	2441	766
Kansas City, MO	2063	1438	981	5707	1289	1749	1751	1212	1289	2214	2296	1601	2636	1773	1229	1538	1030	856	961	1297	1067	891	970	312	1279	1746	3432	1279	780	1202	1847		1358	382	1632	516
Las Vegas, NV	4161	930	1390	5400	3326	3934	1553	2980	2217	1223	4436	3699	2077	3815	3414	3580	1356	2845	3146	3379	3252	2142	1216	2299	3278	1154	5324	2372	2965	2792	3886	2185		1478	274	1874
Little Rock, AR	2179	1448	993	6322	850	1725	2462	613	1903	2909	2402	1715	3250	1448	1199	1213	1731	1065	1017	1419	1179	526	1583	912	1434	1567	3537	719	944	433	1405	615	2378		1706	526
Los Angeles, CA	4600	1297	1757	5475	3599	4352	1994	3366	2739	1662	4901	4138	2518	4109	3820	3947	1796	3286	3564	3820	3670	2327	1656	2740	3717	1289	5765	2507	3385	2978	3928	2626	441	2745		2126
Louisville, KY	1339	2124	1667	6253	674	969	2489	594	1833	3110	1551	877	3181	981	404	747	1926	481	171	573	333	1371	1799	957	589	2412	2685	1564	180	956	1232	830	3015	846	3421	
Memphis, TN	1953	1662	1207	6570	626	1501	2615	388	2151	3144	2177	1492	3498	1223	975	988	1958	867	793	1194	956	750	1796	1158	1210	1789	3311	943	747	339	1179	862	2592	225	2959	621
México, MX	4520	2352	2051	8061	2821	3899	3641	2624	3952	3985	4574	4058	4737	3319	3541	3208	2911	3421	3360	3760	3522	1815	2750	3002	3776	1926	5709	1535	3287	2249	2956	2684	2846	2344	2981	3187
Miami, FL	2315	3467	2951	7997	1064	1784	4109	1307	3578	4639	2460	2293	4925	938	1599	1175	3455	2224	1836	2011	1871	2200	3329	2626	2254	3152	3595	1932	1924	1472	555	2359	4397	1915	4439	1744
Milwaukee, WI	1495	2294	1837	5651	1308	1295	1891	1228	1234	2813	1770	1033	2579	1614	967	1379	1628	143	640	713	730	1625	1697	608	611	2602	2658	1920	449	1344	1866	922	2909	1202	3350	634
Minneapolis, MN	2003	2154	1697	5110	1817	1804	1350	1736	693	2357	2280	1541	2039	2122	1477	1887	1418	658	1149	1223	1241	1607	1487	396	1121	2462	3168	1995	959	1852	2376	710	2698	1310	3139	1144
Mobile, AL	2162	2162	1780	7258	534	1630	3249	415	2840	3704	2306	1874	4187	1033	1347	920	2526	1485	1176	1578	1339	1028	2378	1794	1595	1981	1981	761	1186	301	660	1496	3092	735	3268	1006
Montréal, QC	370	3495	3038	6607	1997	907	3368	2074	2711	4079	504	639	3535	1842	1323	1614	2895	1353	1311	946	1167	2851	2965	1874	907	3802	1150	3044	1403	2436	2132	2187	4177	2327	4616	1480
Nashville, TN	1614	2008	1553	6534	389	1152	2652	312	2116	3179	1828	1152	3463	874	636	639	1995	763	452	854	615	1096	1870	1167	870	2137	2962	1289	462	681	948	899	2938	571	3305	282
New Orleans, LA	2317	2053	1598	7207	761	1837	3146	565	2790	3595	2515	2018	4135	1260	1490	1147	2417	1504	1319	1722	1482	845	2267	1797	1736	1799	3649	579	1329	298	895	1500	2983	732	3084	1149
New York, NY	243	3242	2785	7062	1398	309	3297	1585	2640	4008	346	644	3990	1244	829	1015	2824	1282	1023	750	861	2557	2895	1804	1001	3596	1480	2671	1150	1968	1533	1934	4106	2031	4537	1189
Oklahoma City, OK	2492	879	422	6245	1519	2179	1974	1173	1828	2423	2726	2031	3070	2008	1644	1773	1244	1298	1389	1726	1496	336	1096	879	1709	1186	3862	722	1210	985	2077	560	1809	571	2175	1245
Omaha, NE	2079	1566	1168	5409	1591	1879	1455	1514	991	1986	2354	1617	2338	2076	1532	1841	800	763	1184	1297	1290	1076	870	219	1195	1989	3242	1464	994	1504	2150	302	2082	917	2521	1133
Orlando, FL	1987	3112	2595	7641	708	1455	3754	951	3223	4283	2130	1965	4570	610	1271	845	3099	1868	1480	1681	1541	1844	2972	2270	1899	2796	3266	1577	1569	1117	227	2003	4042	1559	4084	1389
Ottawa, ON	486	3392	2936	6455	1866	842	3265	1971	2608	3977	665	536	3384	1780	1221	1483	2793	1252	1208	845	1064	2748	2862	1772	805	3701	1324	2941	1302	2333	2069	2085	4074	2224	4515	1377
Philadelphia, PA	359	3144	2689	7010	1258	167	3249	1443	2592	3961	516	666	3939	1102	730	874	2776	1236	927	703	763	2415	2806	1755	953	3455	1651	2529	1054	1826	1393	1836	4023	1891	4441	1091
Phoenix, AZ	4121	750	1212	5776	3006	3807	1929	2772	2674	1598	4354	3659	2454	3514	3274	3390	1615	2927	3018	3355	3125	1733	1455	2507	3337	695	5490	1911	2838	2385	3334	2188	459	2200	594	2874
Pittsburgh, PA	780	2687	2230	6526	1088	396	2766	1228	2109	3477	953	349	3455	1033	349	705	2293	751	470	219	306	2005	2349	1273	470	3046	2087	2198	595	1590	1323	1379	3564	1480	3984	634
Portland, ME	434	3762	3305	7546	1926	837	3784	2113	3128	4497	172	901	4475	1772	1350	1543	3313	1772	1545	1208	1381	3084	3382	2291	1348	4124	872	3199	1670	2494	2061	2454	4594	2558	5059	1709
Portland, OR	4753	2245	2727	3902	4259	4553	1430	4182	2093	695	5030	4291	1371	4743	4199	4508	1876	3438	3858	3973	3965	3443	2029	2893	3870	2843	5918	3831	3669	4093	4817	2904	1911	3599	1562	3800
Québec, QC	582	3734	3279	6846	2209	1120	3607	2314	2951	4320	624	879	3775	2055	1564	1826	3136	1595	1564	1187	1406	3091	3205	2114	1147	4043	940	3284	1644	2676	2344	2428	4417	2566	4858	1720
Raleigh, NC	1028	2867	2412	7157	637	497	3395	880	2739	4014	1173	1033	4085	449	504	254	2829	1385	840	914	776	1913	2703	1862	1165	2951	2307	1928	1028	1260	740	1733	3797	1430	4164	907
Rapid City, SD	2816	1353	1347	4795	2431	2616	610	2354	515	1496	3091	2354	1472	2935	2288	2700	491	1469	1961	2034	2051	1733	650	1012	1932	1778	3979	2121	1772	2346	2991	1142	1665	1759	2106	1955
Reno, NV	4420	1641	2101	4843	3926	4220	1545	3849	2208	692	4697	3958	2069	4410	3866	4175	1543	3105	3525	3640	3632	3110	1696	2560	3537	2116	5585	3334	3335	3760	4484	2571	711	3266	835	3467
Richmond, VA	776	3018	2563	7065	848	245	3303	1091	2647	4016	920	780	3994	689	518	465	2832	1290	853	758	832	2106	2716	1812	1009	3146	2055	2140	1031	1471	980	1746	3932	1582	4315	920
St. Louis, MO	1667	1691	1234	6113	883	1353	2158	806	1694	2619	1900	1205	3041	1368	824	1133	1435	473	563	901	671	1022	1376	702	883	1998	3036	1389	385	813	1442	405	2590	669	2986	425
Salt Lake City, UT	3578	1004	1551	4729	3083	3379	882	3006	1545	550	3854	3115	1406	3569	3025	3334	702	2262	2682	2796	2790	2269	854	1717	2695	1390	4742	2655	2492	2917	3643	1728	671	2425	1112	2624
San Antonio, TX	3142	1316	825	6833	1609	2689	2414	1413	2573	2833	3366	2679	3511	2108	2162	1997	1683	2043	1981	2383	2143	436	1522	1623	2397	895	4500	322	1908	1036	1744	1307	2047	965	2182	1810
San Diego, CA	4697	1327	1788	5673	3485	4383	2095	3252	2840	1763	4932	4235	2619	3995	3850	3870	1897	3387	3595	3921	3701	2212	1757	2841	3818	1175	5866	2393	3414	2864	3813	2727	542	2740	200	3450
San Francisco, CA	4769	1788	2248	4940	4212	4570	1892	3977	2814	1039	5044	4307	2409	4721	4216	4439	1892	3453	3873	3987	3981	2940	2045	2907	3886	1900	5932	3118	3685	3591	4541	2919	925	3237	619	3817
Seattle, WA	4664	2354	2837	3623	4352	4465	1313	4275	1977	805	4940	4203	1093	4784	4137	4549	1986	3318	3810	3883	3900	3553	2138	2932	3781	3128	5828	3940	3619	4203	4911	3012	2021	3709	1847	3804
Tampa, FL	2076	3136	2619	7664	732	1545	3778	975	3247	4307	2220	2053	4592	698	1360	935	3123	1892	1504	1772	1667	1868	2996	2294	1921	2821	3355	1601	1593	1141	315	2026	4064	1583	4108	1413
Toronto, ON	644	2962	2505	6595	1541	909	2835	1541	2179	3546	917	171	3524	1619	864	1290	2362	821	779	488	708	2319	2433	1342	375	3269	1681	2512	870	1903	1910	1654	3644	1794	4084	948
Vancouver, BC	4878	2570	3052	3430	4566	4679	1527	4491	2191	1018	5155	4417	899	4998	4352	4763	2201	3533	4024	4098	4116	3768	2354	3147	3995	3358	6043	4156	3834	4418	5126	3229	2237	3924	2077	4018
Washington, DC	594	3051	2594	6903	1023	61	3142	1220	2486	3854	737	618	3831	867	557	639	2669	1128	832	595	669	2191	2713	1649	846	3231	1873	2306	959	1603	1158	1743	3928	1667	4348	959
Wichita, KS	2367	1138	681	5921	1591	2053	1717	1348	1503	2166	2600	1905	2814	2077	1533	1842	986	1171	1263	1601	1371	591	838	628	1583	1445	3736	978	1084	1241	2151	309	2053	747	2434	1134
Winnipeg, MB	2730	2587	2285	4385	2542	2531	1324	2463	668	2336	3006	2269	1313	2850	2203	2615	1821	1384	1876	1948	1966	2193	1892	1121	1847	3010	3361	2581	1685	2526	3102	1324	3012	1939	3453	1870

Kilometers

Milles

	Memphis, TN	México, MX	Miami, FL	Milwaukee, WI	Minneapolis, MN	Mobile, AL	Montréal, QC	Nashville, TN	New Orleans, LA	New York, NY	Oklahoma City, OK	Omaha, NE	Orlando, FL	Ottawa, ON	Philadelphia, PA	Phoenix, AZ	Pittsburgh, PA	Portland, ME	Portland, OR	Québec, QC	Raleigh, NC	Rapid City, SD	Reno, NV	Richmond, VA	St. Louis, MO	Salt Lake City, UT	San Antonio, TX	San Diego, CA	San Francisco, CA	Seattle, WA	Tampa, FL	Toronto, ON	Vancouver, BC	Washington, DC	Wichita, KS	Winnipeg, MB
Albany, NY	1214	2809	1439	929	1245	1344	230	1003	1440	151	1549	1292	1235	302	223	2561	485	270	2954	362	639	1750	2747	482	1036	2224	1953	2919	2964	2899	1290	400	3032	369	1471	1697
Albuquerque, NM	1033	1462	2155	1426	1339	1344	2172	1248	1276	2015	546	973	1934	2108	1954	466	1670	2338	1395	2321	1782	841	1020	1876	1051	624	818	825	1111	1463	1949	1841	1597	1896	707	1608
Amarillo, TX	750	1275	1834	1142	1055	1106	1888	965	993	1731	262	726	1613	1825	1671	753	1386	2054	1695	2038	1499	837	1306	1593	767	964	513	1111	1397	1763	1628	1557	1897	1612	423	1420
Anchorage, AK	4083	5010	4970	3512	3176	4511	4106	4061	4479	4389	3881	3362	4749	4012	4357	3590	4056	4690	2425	4255	4448	2980	3010	4391	3799	2939	4247	3526	3070	2252	4763	4099	2132	4290	3680	2725
Atlanta, GA	389	1753	661	813	1129	332	1241	242	473	869	944	989	440	1160	782	1868	676	1197	2647	1373	396	1511	2440	527	549	1916	1000	2166	2618	2705	455	958	2838	636	989	1580
Baltimore, MD	933	2423	1109	805	1121	1013	564	716	1142	192	1354	1168	904	523	104	2366	246	520	2830	696	309	1626	2623	152	841	2100	1671	2724	2840	2775	960	565	2908	38	1276	1573
Billings, MT	1625	2263	2554	1175	839	2019	2093	1648	1955	2049	1227	904	2333	2029	2019	1199	1719	2352	889	2242	2110	379	960	2053	1341	548	1500	1302	1176	816	2348	1762	949	1953	1067	823
Birmingham, AL	241	1631	812	763	1079	258	1289	194	351	985	729	941	591	1225	897	1723	763	1313	2599	1438	547	1463	2392	678	501	1868	878	2021	2472	2657	606	958	2791	758	838	1531
Bismarck, ND	1337	2456	2224	767	431	1765	1685	1315	1734	1641	1136	616	2003	1621	1611	1662	1311	1944	1301	1834	1702	320	1372	1645	1053	960	1599	1765	1749	1229	2018	1354	1362	1545	934	415
Boise, ID	1954	2477	2883	1748	1465	2302	2535	1976	2234	2491	1506	1234	2662	2472	2462	993	2161	2795	432	2685	2495	930	430	2496	1628	342	1761	1096	646	500	2677	2204	633	2395	1346	1452
Boston, MA	1353	2843	1529	1100	1417	1433	313	1136	1563	215	1694	1463	1324	413	321	2706	592	107	3126	388	729	1921	2919	572	1181	2395	2092	3065	3135	3070	1380	570	3204	458	1616	1868
Buffalo, NY	927	2522	1425	642	958	1165	397	716	1254	400	1262	1005	1221	333	414	2274	217	560	2667	546	642	1463	2460	485	749	1936	1665	2632	2677	2612	1276	106	2745	384	1184	1410
Calgary, AB	2174	2944	3061	1603	1267	2602	2197	2152	2570	2480	1908	1453	2840	2103	2448	1525	2147	2781	852	2346	2539	915	1286	2482	1890	874	2182	1628	1497	679	2854	2190	559	2381	1749	816
Charleston, SC	760	2063	583	1003	1319	642	1145	543	783	773	1248	1290	379	1106	685	2184	642	1101	2948	1277	279	1824	2741	428	850	2218	1310	2483	2934	2973	434	1006	3106	539	1291	1771
Charleston, WV	606	2201	994	601	918	837	822	395	926	515	1022	952	790	759	454	2035	217	839	2610	972	313	1422	2403	322	512	1880	1344	2393	2620	2571	845	537	2705	346	953	1369
Charlotte, NC	614	1994	730	857	1173	572	1003	397	713	631	1102	1144	525	922	543	2107	438	959	2802	1135	158	1678	2595	289	704	2072	1241	2405	2759	2827	581	802	2960	397	1145	1625
Cheyenne, WY	1217	1809	2147	1012	881	1570	1799	1240	1502	1755	773	497	1926	1736	1725	1004	1425	2059	1166	1949	1758	305	959	1760	892	436	1046	1179	1176	1234	1941	1468	1368	1659	613	1132
Chicago, IL	539	2126	1382	89	409	923	841	474	935	797	807	474	1161	778	768	1819	467	1101	2137	991	861	913	1930	802	294	1406	1270	2105	2146	2062	1176	510	2196	701	728	860
Cincinnati, OH	493	2088	1141	398	714	731	815	281	820	636	863	736	920	751	576	1876	292	960	2398	972	522	1219	2191	530	350	1667	1231	2234	2407	2368	935	484	2501	517	785	1166
Cleveland, OH	742	2337	1250	443	760	981	588	531	1070	466	1073	806	1045	525	437	2085	136	751	2469	738	568	1264	2262	471	560	1738	1481	2437	2478	2413	1101	303	2547	370	995	1211
Columbus, OH	594	2189	1163	454	771	832	725	382	921	535	930	802	958	661	474	1942	190	858	2464	874	482	1275	2257	517	417	1734	1332	2300	2474	2424	1036	440	2558	416	852	1222
Dallas, TX	466	1128	1367	1010	999	639	1772	681	525	1589	209	669	1146	1708	1501	1077	1246	1917	2140	1921	1189	1077	1933	1309	635	1410	271	1375	1827	2208	1161	1441	2342	1362	367	1363
Denver, CO	1116	1709	2069	1055	924	1478	1843	1162	1409	1799	681	541	1847	1779	1744	904	1460	2102	1261	1992	1680	404	1054	1688	855	531	946	1092	1271	1329	1862	1512	1463	1686	521	1176
Des Moines, IA	720	1866	1632	378	246	1115	1165	725	1117	1121	546	136	1411	1101	1091	1558	791	1424	1798	1314	1157	629	1591	1126	436	1067	1009	1766	1807	1822	1426	834	1956	1025	390	697
Detroit, MI	752	2347	1401	380	697	991	564	541	1079	622	1062	743	1180	500	592	2074	292	838	2405	713	724	1201	2198	627	549	1675	1490	2373	2415	2350	1194	233	2483	526	984	1148
El Paso, TX	1112	1197	1959	1617	1530	1231	2363	1328	1118	2235	737	1236	1738	2300	2147	432	1893	2563	1767	2513	1834	1105	1315	1955	1242	864	556	730	1181	1944	1753	2032	2087	2008	898	1871
Halifax, NS	2058	3548	2234	1652	1969	1231	715	1841	2268	920	2400	2015	2030	823	1026	3412	1297	542	3678	584	1434	2473	3471	1277	1887	2947	2797	3646	3687	3622	2085	1045	3756	1164	2322	2089
Houston, TX	586	954	1201	1193	1240	473	1892	801	360	1660	449	910	980	1828	1572	1188	1366	1988	2381	2041	1198	1318	2072	1330	863	1650	200	1487	1938	2449	995	1561	2583	1433	608	1604
Indianapolis, IN	464	2043	1196	279	596	737	872	287	826	715	752	618	975	809	655	1764	370	1038	2280	1022	639	1101	2073	641	239	1549	1186	2122	2290	2249	990	541	2383	596	674	1047
Jackson, MS	211	1398	915	835	1151	187	1514	423	185	1223	612	935	694	1450	1135	1482	988	1550	2544	1663	783	1458	2337	914	505	1813	644	1780	2232	2612	709	1183	2746	996	771	1570
Jacksonville, FL	733	1837	345	1160	1477	410	1325	589	556	953	1291	1336	141	1286	866	2072	822	1281	2994	1457	460	1859	2787	609	896	2264	1084	2370	2822	3052	196	1187	3186	720	1337	1928
Kansas City, MO	536	1668	1466	573	441	930	1359	559	932	1202	348	188	1245	1296	1141	1360	857	1525	1805	1509	1077	710	1598	1085	252	1074	812	1695	1814	1872	1259	1028	2007	1083	192	823
Las Vegas, NV	1611	1769	2733	1808	1677	1922	2596	1826	1854	2552	1124	1294	2512	2532	2500	285	2215	2855	1188	2745	2360	1035	442	2444	1610	417	1272	337	575	1256	2526	2265	1390	2441	1276	1872
Little Rock, AR	140	1457	1190	747	814	457	1446	355	455	1262	355	570	969	1382	1175	1367	920	1590	2237	1595	889	1093	2030	983	416	1507	600	1703	2012	2305	984	1115	2439	1036	464	1205
Los Angeles, CA	1839	1853	2759	2082	1951	2031	2869	2054	1917	2820	1352	1567	2538	2806	2760	369	2476	3144	971	3019	2588	1309	519	2682	1856	691	1356	124	385	1148	2553	2538	1291	2702	1513	2146
Louisville, KY	386	1981	1084	394	711	625	920	175	714	739	774	704	863	856	678	1786	394	1062	2362	1069	564	1215	2155	572	264	1631	1125	2144	2372	2364	878	589	2497	596	705	1162
Memphis, TN		1595	1051	624	940	395	1306	215	396	1123	487	724	830	1243	1035	1500	780	1451	2382	1456	749	1247	2175	843	294	1652	739	1841	2144	2440	845	975	2574	896	597	1359
México, MX			2154	2200	2113	1426	2900	1810	1313	2619	1323	1783	1933	2838	2525	1484	2375	2941	2819	3051	2151	2365	2367	2283	1825	2135	853	1683	2233	2996	1948	2570	3139	2386	1481	2477
Miami, FL				1478	1794	727	1671	907	874	1299	1609	1654	232	1631	1211	2390	1167	1627	3312	1803	805	2176	3105	954	1214	2581	1401	2688	3140	3370	274	1532	3504	1065	1655	2246
Milwaukee, WI					337	1019	939	569	1020	894	880	514	1257	875	865	1892	564	1198	2063	1088	956	842	1970	899	367	1446	1343	2145	2186	1991	1272	607	2124	799	769	789
Minneapolis, MN						1335	1255	886	1337	1211	793	383	1573	1192	1181	1805	881	1515	1727	1405	1273	606	1839	1216	621	1315	1257	2014	2055	1654	1588	924	1788	1115	637	452
Mobile, AL							1575	450	146	1203	799	1119	506	1481	1115	1662	1019	1531	2731	1707	730	1641	2545	861	688	2000	673	1960	2411	2799	521	1214	2933	970	958	1787
Montréal, QC								1094	1632	383	1625	1300	1466	121	454	2637	607	282	2963	155	871	1758	2756	714	1112	2232	2043	2931	2972	2907	1522	330	3041	600	1547	1374
Nashville, TN									539	906	703	747	686	1031	818	1715	569	1234	2405	1244	532	1269	2198	626	307	1675	954	2056	2360	2463	701	764	2597	679	748	1337
New Orleans, LA										1332	731	1121	653	1570	1245	1548	1108	1660	2663	1783	871	1643	2431	1002	690	1932	560	1846	2298	2731	668	1302	2865	1106	890	1755
New York, NY											1469	1258	1094	439	91	2481	367	313	2920	515	499	1716	2713	342	956	2189	1861	2839	2929	2864	1150	507	2998	228	1391	1665
Oklahoma City, OK												463	1388	1563	1408	1012	1124	1792	1934	1776	1237	871	1727	1331	505	1204	466	1370	1657	2002	1403	1295	2136	1350	161	1158
Omaha, NE													1433	1238	1228	1440	928	1561	1662	1451	1265	525	1455	1263	440	932	927	1630	1672	1719	1448	971	1853	1162	307	638
Orlando, FL														1427	1006	2169	963	1422	3091	1598	601	1955	2884	750	993	2360	1180	2467	2918	3149	82	1327	3283	860	1434	2025
Ottawa, ON															451	2575	545	382	2901	257	831	1696	2694	675	1050	2170	1981	2869	2910	2845	1483	268	2978	562	1485	1280
Philadelphia, PA																2420	306	419	2890	586	411	1686	2683	254	895	2160	1774	2779	2900	2835	1062	522	2968	140	1330	1633
Phoenix, AZ																	2136	2804	1335	2788	2249	1308	883	2343	1517	651	987	358	750	1513	2184	2307	1655	2362	1173	2075
Pittsburgh, PA																		690	2590	758	497	1386	2383	341	611	1859	1519	2494	2599	2534	1019	321	2668	240	1046	1332
Portland, ME																			3223	264	827	2019	3016	670	1279	2493	2189	3162	3233	3168	1478	668	3301	556	1714	1966
Portland, OR																				3114	2923	1268	578	2925	2057	771	2322	1093	638	170	3106	2633	313	2824	1775	1463
Québec, QC																					1003	1908	2905	846	1261	2381	2193	3080	3122	3057	1654	479	3190	732	1696	1523
Raleigh, NC																						1777	2716	157	825	2193	1398	2563	2894	2926	656	820	3060	265	1266	1724
Rapid City, SD																							1151	1720	963	628	1335	1372	1368	1195	1970	1429	1328	1620	712	792
Reno, NV																								2718	1850	524	1870	642	217	755	2899	2426	898	2617	1568	1867
Richmond, VA																									834	2194	1530	2684	2934	2869	805	660	3003	108	1274	1667
St. Louis, MO																										1326	968	1875	2066	2125	1008	782	2259	837	441	1075
Salt Lake City, UT																											1419	754	740	839	2375	1902	973	2094	1044	1455
San Antonio, TX																												1285	1737	2275	1195	1714	2410	1635	624	1621
San Diego, CA																													508	1271	2481	2601	1414	2720	1531	2209
San Francisco, CA																														816	2933	2643	958	2834	1784	2193
Seattle, WA																															3164	2577	140	2769	1843	1390
Tampa, FL																																1383	3297	916	1448	2039
Toronto, ON																																	2711	563	1217	1375
Vancouver, BC																																		2902	1977	1375
Washington, DC																																			1272	1566
Wichita, KS																																				956

Kilomètres

	Memphis, TN	México, MX	Miami, FL	Milwaukee, WI	Minneapolis, MN	Mobile, AL	Montréal, QC	Nashville, TN	New Orleans, LA	New York, NY	Oklahoma City, OK	Omaha, NE	Orlando, FL	Ottawa, ON	Philadelphia, PA	Phoenix, AZ	Pittsburgh, PA	Portland, ME	Portland, OR	Québec, QC	Raleigh, NC	Rapid City, SD	Reno, NV	Richmond, VA	St. Louis, MO	Salt Lake City, UT	San Antonio, TX	San Diego, CA	San Francisco, CA	Seattle, WA	Tampa, FL	Toronto, ON	Vancouver, BC	Washington, DC	Wichita, KS
México, MX	2566																																		
Miami, FL	1691	3466																																	
Milwaukee, WI	1004	3540	2378																																
Minneapolis, MN	1512	3400	2887	542																															
Mobile, AL	636	2294	1170	1640	2148																														
Montréal, QC	2101	4666	2689	1511	2019	2534																													
Nashville, TN	346	2912	1459	916	1426	724	1760																												
New Orleans, LA	637	2113	1406	1641	2151	235	2626	867																											
New York, NY	1807	4214	2090	1438	1948	1936	616	1458	2143																										
Oklahoma City, OK	784	2129	2589	1416	1276	1286	2615	1131	1176	2364																									
Omaha, NE	1165	2869	2661	827	616	1800	2092	1202	1804	2024	745																								
Orlando, FL	1335	3110	373	2023	2531	814	2359	1104	1051	1760	2233	2306																							
Ottawa, ON	2000	4566	2624	1408	1918	2383	194	1659	2526	706	2515	1992	2296																						
Philadelphia, PA	1665	4063	1948	1392	1900	1794	730	1316	2003	146	2265	1976	1619	726																					
Phoenix, AZ	2414	2388	3846	3044	2904	2674	4243	2759	2491	3992	1628	2317	3490	4143	3894																				
Pittsburgh, PA	1255	3821	1878	907	1418	1640	977	916	1783	591	1809	1493	1549	877	492	3437																			
Portland, ME	2335	4732	2618	1928	2438	2463	454	1986	2671	504	2883	2512	2288	615	674	4512	1110																		
Portland, OR	3833	4536	5329	3319	2779	4394	4767	3870	4285	4698	3112	2674	4973	4668	4650	2148	4167	5186																	
Québec, QC	2343	4909	2901	1751	2261	2747	249	2002	2869	829	2858	2335	2571	414	943	4486	1220	425	5010																
Raleigh, NC	1205	3461	1295	1538	2048	1175	1401	856	1401	803	1990	2035	967	1337	661	3619	800	1331	4703	1614															
Rapid City, SD	2006	3805	3501	1355	975	2640	2829	2042	2644	2761	1401	845	3146	2729	2713	2105	2230	3249	2040	3070	2859														
Reno, NV	3500	3809	4996	3170	2959	4095	4434	3537	3911	4365	2779	2341	4640	4335	4317	1421	3834	4853	930	4674	4370	1852													
Richmond, VA	1356	3673	1535	1446	1957	1385	1149	1007	1612	550	2142	2032	1207	1086	409	3770	549	1078	4706	1361	253	2767	4373												
St. Louis, MO	473	2936	1953	591	999	1107	1789	494	1110	1538	813	708	1598	1689	1440	2441	983	2058	3310	2029	1327	1549	2977	1342											
Salt Lake City, UT	2658	3435	4153	2327	2116	3218	3591	2695	3109	3522	1937	1500	3797	3492	3475	1047	2991	4011	1241	3831	3529	1010	843	3530	2134										
San Antonio, TX	1189	1372	2254	2161	2023	1083	3287	1535	901	2994	750	1492	1899	3187	2854	1588	2444	3522	3736	3529	2249	2148	3009	2462	1558	2283									
San Diego, CA	2962	2708	4325	3451	3241	3154	4716	3308	2970	4568	2204	2623	3969	4616	4471	576	4013	5088	1759	4956	4124	2208	1033	4319	3017	1213	2068								
San Francisco, CA	3450	3593	5052	3517	3306	3879	4782	3797	3697	4713	2666	2690	4695	4682	4666	1207	4182	5202	1027	5023	4656	2201	349	4721	3324	1191	2795	817							
Seattle, WA	3926	4821	5422	3204	2661	4504	4677	3963	4394	4608	3221	2766	5067	4578	4562	2434	4077	5097	274	4919	4708	1923	1215	4616	3419	1350	3660	2045	1313						
Tampa, FL	1360	3134	441	2047	2555	838	2449	1128	1075	1850	2257	2330	132	2386	1709	3514	1640	2378	4998	2661	1056	3170	4664	1295	1622	3821	1923	3992	4719	5091					
Toronto, ON	1569	4135	2465	977	1487	1953	531	1229	2095	816	2084	1562	2135	431	840	3712	516	1075	4236	771	1319	2299	3903	1062	1258	3060	2758	4185	4253	4146	2225				
Vancouver, BC	4142	5051	5638	3418	2877	4719	4893	4179	4610	4824	3437	2981	5282	4792	4776	2663	4293	5311	504	5133	4924	2137	1445	4832	3635	1566	3878	2275	1541	225	5305	4362			
Washington, DC	1442	3839	1714	1286	1794	1561	965	1093	1780	367	2172	1870	1384	904	225	3800	386	895	4544	1178	426	2607	4211	174	1347	3369	2631	4376	4560	4455	1474	906	4669		
Wichita, KS	961	2383	2663	1237	1025	1541	2489	1204	1432	2238	259	494	2307	2389	2140	1887	1683	2758	2856	2729	2037	1146	2523	2050	710	1680	1004	2463	2870	2965	2330	1958	3181	2047	
Winnipeg, MB	2187	3985	3614	1270	727	2875	2211	2151	2824	2679	1863	1027	3258	2060	2627	3339	2143	3163	2354	2451	2774	1274	3004	2682	1730	2341	2608	3554	3529	2237	3281	2212	2212	2520	1538

Distances and Driving Times across North America

TEMPERATURE CONVERSIONS

°F	°C	°C	°F
110	43.3	40	104
100	37.8	35	95
90	32.2	30	86
80	26.7	25	77
70	21.1	20	68
60	15.6	15	59
50	10.0	10	50
40	4.4	5	41
32	0	0	32
30	-1.1	-5	23
20	-6.7	-10	14
10	-12.2	-15	5
0	-17.8	-20	-4
-10	-23.3	-25	-13
-20	-28.9	-30	-22
-30	-34.4	-35	-31
-40	-40.0	-40	-40
-50	-45.6	-45	-49

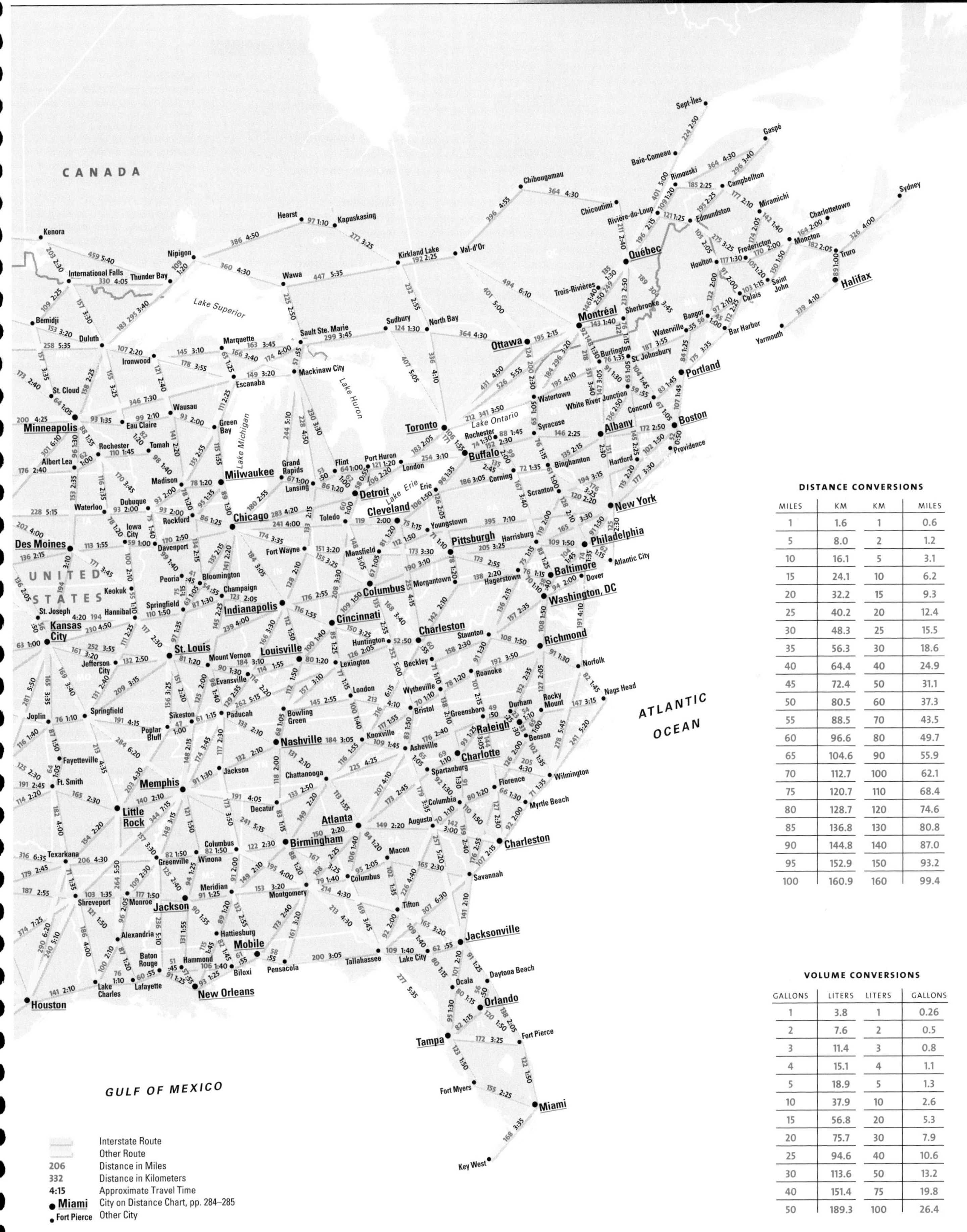

DISTANCE CONVERSIONS

MILES	KM	KM	MILES
1	1.6	1	0.6
5	8.0	2	1.2
10	16.1	5	3.1
15	24.1	10	6.2
20	32.2	15	9.3
25	40.2	20	12.4
30	48.3	25	15.5
35	56.3	30	18.6
40	64.4	40	24.9
45	72.4	50	31.1
50	80.5	60	37.3
55	88.5	70	43.5
60	96.6	80	49.7
65	104.6	90	55.9
70	112.7	100	62.1
75	120.7	110	68.4
80	128.7	120	74.6
85	136.8	130	80.8
90	144.8	140	87.0
95	152.9	150	93.2
100	160.9	160	99.4

VOLUME CONVERSIONS

GALLONS	LITERS	LITERS	GALLONS
1	3.8	1	0.26
2	7.6	2	0.5
3	11.4	3	0.8
4	15.1	4	1.1
5	18.9	5	1.3
10	37.9	10	2.6
15	56.8	20	5.3
20	75.7	30	7.9
25	94.6	40	10.6
30	113.6	50	13.2
40	151.4	75	19.8
50	189.3	100	26.4

TOURISM INFORMATION

UNITED STATES

Alabama
@TweetHomeAla
www.alabama.travel

Alaska
@TravelAlaska
www.travelalaska.com

Arizona
@ArizonaTourism
www.visitarizona.com

Arkansas
@artourism
www.arkansas.com

California
@VisitCA
www.visitcalifornia.com

Colorado
@Colorado
www.colorado.com

Connecticut
@CTvisit
www.ctvisit.com

Delaware
@DelawareTourism
www.visitdelaware.com

District of Columbia
@washingtondc
www.washington.org

Florida
@VisitFlorida
www.visitflorida.com

Georgia
@ExploreGeorgia
www.exploregeorgia.org

Hawai'i
@gohawaii
www.gohawaii.com

Idaho
@visitidaho
www.visitidaho.org

Illinois
@enjoyillinois
www.enjoyillinois.com

Indiana
@visitindiana
www.visitindiana.com

Iowa
@Travel_Iowa
www.traveliowa.com

Kansas
@TravelKS
www.travelks.com

Kentucky
@KentuckyTourism
www.kentuckytourism.com

Louisiana
@LouisianaTravel
www.louisianatravel.com

Maine
@visitmaine
www.visitmaine.com

Maryland
@TravelMD
www.visitmaryland.org

Massachusetts
@VisitMA
www.massvacation.com

Michigan
@PureMichigan
www.michigan.org

Minnesota
@ExploreMinn
www.exploreminnesota.com

Mississippi
@visitms
www.visitmississippi.org

Missouri
@VisitMO
www.visitmo.com

Montana
@visitmontana
www.visitmt.com

Nebraska
@NebraskaTourism
www.visitnebraska.com

Nevada
@TravelNevada
www.travelnevada.com

New Hampshire
@VisitNH
www.visitnh.gov

New Jersey
@Visit_NJ
www.visitnj.org

New Mexico
@NewMexico
www.newmexico.org

New York
@I_LOVE_NY
www.iloveny.com

North Carolina
@VisitNC
www.visitnc.com

North Dakota
@NorthDakota
www.ndtourism.com

Ohio
@OhioFindItHere
www.ohio.org

Oklahoma
@TravelOK
www.travelok.com

Oregon
@TravelOregon
www.traveloregon.com

Pennsylvania
@visitPA
www.visitpa.com

Rhode Island
@RITourism
www.visitrhodeisland.com

South Carolina
@Discover_SC
www.discoversouthcarolina.com

South Dakota
@southdakota
www.travelsouthdakota.com

Tennessee
@TNVacation
www.tnvacation.com

Texas
@TravelTexas
www.traveltexas.com

Utah
@VisitUtah
www.visitutah.com

Vermont
@VermontTourism
www.vermontvacation.com

Virginia
@VisitVirginia
www.virginia.org

Washington
@ExperienceWA
www.experiencewa.com

West Virginia
@WVtourism
www.wvtourism.com

Wisconsin
@TravelWI
www.travelwisconsin.com

Wyoming
@visitwyoming
www.wyomingtourism.org

Puerto Rico
@discover_PR
www.discoverpuertorico.com

CANADA

Alberta
@TravelAlberta
www.travelalberta.com

British Columbia
@HelloBC
www.hellobc.com

Manitoba
@TravelManitoba
www.travelmanitoba.com

New Brunswick
@DestinationNB
www.tourismnewbrunswick.ca

Newfoundland & Labrador
@NLtweets
www.newfoundlandlabrador.com

Northwest Territories
@spectacularNWT
www.spectacularnwt.com

Nova Scotia
@VisitNovaScotia
www.novascotia.com

Nunavut
@NunavutTourism
www.travelnunavut.ca

Ontario
@OntarioTravel
www.ontariotravel.net

Prince Edward Island
@tourismpei
www.tourismpei.com

Québec
@TourismQuebec
www.quebecoriginal.com

Saskatchewan
@Saskatchewan
www.tourismsaskatchewan.com

Yukon
@TravelYukon
www.travelyukon.com

MEXICO

@VisitMex
www.visitmexico.com

BORDER CROSSING INFORMATION

TRAVEL ADVISORY

All U.S. citizens are now required to present a passport, passport card, or WHTI (Western Hemisphere Travel Initiative)-compliant document when entering the United States by air, sea or land. U.S. citizens traveling directly to or from Puerto Rico and the U.S. Virgin Islands are not required to have a passport. For more detailed information and updated schedules, please see http://travel.state.gov.

CANADA

All persons entering Canada must carry both proof of citizenship and proof of identity. A valid U.S. passport, passport card or other WHTI-compliant document satisfies these requirements for U.S. citizens. U.S. citizens entering Canada from a third country must have a valid U.S. passport. A visa is not required for U.S. citizens to visit Canada for up to 180 days.

U.S. driver's licenses are valid in Canada; individual provinces and territories specify the length of time. Drivers should be prepared to present proof of their vehicle's registration, ownership, and insurance. International visitors to Canada who are not U.S. citizens must present a valid passport and visa (if required). Citizens of Mexico require a visa to enter Canada.

UNITED STATES (FROM CANADA)

Canadian driver's licenses are valid in the U.S.; lengths of time vary depending on state. Drivers should be prepared to present proof of their vehicle's registration, ownership, and insurance.

MEXICO

All persons entering Mexico must carry proof of citizenship, either a valid passport or their original birth certificate (U.S. citizens should bear in mind the requirements set by the U.S. government for re-entry to the U.S.). Visas are not required for stays of up to 180 days. Naturalized citizens and alien permanent residents should carry the appropriate official documentation. Individuals under the age of 18 traveling alone, with one parent, or with other adults must carry notarized parental/legal guardian authorization. All U.S. citizens visiting for up to 180 days must also procure a tourist permit, obtainable from Mexican consulates, tourism offices, border crossing points, and airlines serving Mexico. However, tourist cards are not needed for visits shorter than 72 hours to areas within the Border Zone (extending approximately 25 km into Mexico).

U.S. driver's licenses are valid in Mexico. Visitors who wish to drive beyond the Baja California Peninsula or the Border Zone must obtain a temporary import permit for their vehicles. To acquire a permit, one must submit evidence of citizenship and of the vehicle's title and registration, as well as a valid driver's license. A processing fee must be paid. Permits are available at border crossings or selected Mexican consulates. Mexican law also requires the posting of a refundable bond to guarantee the departure of the vehicle.

All visitors driving in Mexico should be aware that U.S. auto insurance policies are not valid and that full-coverage insurance from a Mexican insurance company is mandatory. Many U.S. insurance companies sell short-term tourist auto insurance for travel in Mexico.

IMPORTANT WEB SITES

U.S. State Department,
www.travel.state.gov
U.S. Customs and Border Protection,
www.cbp.gov
Canada Border Services Agency,
www.cbsa-asfc.gc.ca
Citizenship and Immigration Canada,
www.cic.gc.ca
Mexican Ministry of Foreign Affairs,
www.gob.mx/sre
Mexican National Institute of Migration,
www.gob.mx/inm

COMMON ABBREVIATIONS

Arch.	Archaeological
Bfld.	Battlefield
Cons.	Conservation
Ent.	Entrance
Hist.	Historic(al)
Mem.	Memorial
Mon.	Monument
Mtn.	Mountain
Mts.	Mountains
Mus.	Museum
Natl.	National
Nat.	Natural
N.H.S.	National Historic Site
N.H.P.	National Historical Park
N.M.P.	National Military Park
N.R.A.	National Recreation Area
Pk. Hqtrs.	Park Headquarters
Pres.	Preserve
Prov.	Provincial
Rec.	Recreation(al)
Res.	Reservation–Reserve
S.H.S.	State Historic Site
S.P.	State Park
Sta.	Station
Vis. Ctr.	Visitor Center

ALABAMA

ALABAMA	PAGE	GRID	LATITUDE LONGITUDE
National Park & Rec. Areas			
Freedom Riders Natl. Mon.	120	A4	33.635108 -85.908448
Horseshoe Bend N.M.P.-Vis. Ctr.	128	B1	32.977130 -85.739600
Russell Cave Natl. Mon.-Main Road	120	A2	34.980220 -85.809650
Russell Cave Natl. Mon.-Vis. Ctr.	120	A2	34.980400 -85.809800
Tuskegee Airmen N.H.S.	128	B2	32.424942 -85.691052
Tuskegee Airmen N.H.S.-Pk. Hqtrs.	128	B2	32.428600 -85.708500
Tuskegee Institute N.H.S.	128	B2	32.428751 -85.704120
Tuskegee Institute N.H.S.-Pk. Hqtrs.	128	B2	32.428600 -85.708500
State Park & Rec. Areas			
Bladon Springs S.P.	127	E4	31.730920 -88.195580
Blue Springs S.P.	128	B4	31.661990 -85.508150
Bucks Pocket S.P.	120	A3	34.469560 -86.049080
Cathedral Caverns S.P.	120	A2	34.572299 -86.221499
Cheaha S.P.	120	A4	33.474490 -85.807260
Chewacla S.P.	128	B2	32.554520 -85.481920
Desoto S.P.	120	A3	34.495460 -85.618860
Frank Jackson S.P.	128	A4	31.291400 -86.255900
Gulf S.P.	135	F2	30.270490 -87.582130
Joe Wheeler S.P.	119	E2	34.793020 -87.379950
Lake Guntersville S.P.	120	A3	34.367530 -86.222850
Lake Jackson RV Park at Florala	136	B1	30.998590 -86.329980
Lake Lurleen S.P.	127	E1	33.295880 -87.676870
Lakepoint S.P.	128	C3	31.990320 -85.114970
Meaher S.P.	135	E1	30.669720 -87.936030
Monte Sano S.P.	119	F2	34.745220 -86.511650
Oak Mtn. S.P.	127	F1	33.324710 -86.758740
Paul M. Grist S.P.	127	F2	32.595380 -86.996080
Rickwood Caverns S.P.	119	F4	33.876870 -86.867230
Roland Cooper S.P.	127	F3	32.055350 -87.245330
Wind Creek S.P.	128	A1	32.856820 -85.946540

ALASKA

ALASKA	PAGE	GRID	LATITUDE LONGITUDE
National Park & Rec. Areas			
Admiralty Island Natl. Mon.	155	E4	57.618060 -134.161110
Aleutian WWII Natl. Hist. Area	154	A4	53.888889 -166.527222
Aniakchak Natl. Mon. & Pres.	154	B4	56.833333 -158.250556
Bering Land Bridge Natl. Pres.	154	B2	65.595320 -164.301800
Cape Krusenstern Natl. Mon.	154	B1	67.471630 -163.312300
Denali Natl. Park & Pres.-Denali Vis. Ctr.	154	C2	63.737000 -148.895000
Denali Natl. Park & Pres.-Eielson Vis. Ctr.	154	C2	63.440900 -150.239000
Gates of the Arctic Natl. Park & Pres.-Anaktuvuk Pass Ranger Sta.	154	C1	68.139900 -151.735400
Gates of the Arctic Natl. Park & Pres.-Arctic Interagency Vis. Ctr.	154	C1	67.253700 -150.187000
Gates of the Arctic Natl. Park & Pres.-Bettles Ranger Sta.	154	C1	66.912500 -151.667100
Gates of the Arctic Natl. Park & Pres.-Coldfoot Ranger Sta.	154	C1	67.253700 -150.187000
Glacier Bay Natl. Park & Pres.-Glacier Bay Lodge & Vis. Ctr.	155	D3	58.454900 -135.882600
Katmai Natl. Park & Pres.	154	C3	58.667030 -156.524600
Kenai Fjords Natl. Park-Vis. Ctr.	154	C3	60.105300 -149.435000
Klondike Gold Rush N.H.P.	155	D3	60.113550 -149.441342
Kobuk Valley Natl. Park	154	B1	67.073230 -159.839500
Lake Clark Natl. Park & Pres.	154	C3	60.471450 -154.576390
Misty Fiords Natl. Mon.	155	E4	55.472600 -130.429700
Noatak Natl. Pres.	154	C1	67.320740 -162.646370
White Mts. N.R.A.	154	C2	65.524300 -147.156400
Wrangell-Saint Elias Natl. Park & Pres.-Kennecott Vis. Ctr.	155	D3	61.485600 -142.881100
Wrangell-Saint Elias Natl. Park & Pres.-Wrangell-Saint Elias Vis. Ctr.	155	D3	61.964300 -145.317900
Yukon-Charley Rivers Natl. Pres.	155	D2	65.341680 -143.120650
State Park & Rec. Areas			
Afognak Island S.P.	154	C4	58.227100 -152.067300
Chilkat S.P.	155	D3	59.211111 -135.398056
Chugach S.P.	154	C3	61.037440 -149.780830
Denali S.P.	154	C3	62.734600 -150.199600
Point Bridget S.P.	155	E3	58.671225 -134.958801
Shuyak Island S.P.	154	C4	58.533100 -152.486100
Wood-Tikchik S.P.	154	B3	59.909600 -158.672000

ARIZONA

ARIZONA	PAGE	GRID	LATITUDE LONGITUDE
National Park & Rec. Areas			
Agua Fria Natl. Mon.	47	D4	34.276490 -112.114350
Canyon de Chelly Natl. Mon.-Vis. Ctr.	48	A2	36.153200 -109.539000
Casa Grande Ruins Natl. Mon.-Ent. Sta.	54	C2	32.994700 -111.537000
Chiricahua Natl. Mon.-Main Road	55	E3	32.009250 -109.382230
Chiricahua Natl. Mon.-Ent. Sta.	55	E3	32.007500 -109.388900
Coronado Natl. Mem.-Vis. Ctr.	55	E4	31.346300 -110.254000
Fort Bowie N.H.S.-Vis. Ctr.	55	E3	32.146600 -109.435000
Glen Canyon N.R.A.-Ent. Sta.	47	E1	36.943300 -111.493600
Grand Canyon Natl. Park-East Ent.	47	D2	36.038800 -111.828000
Grand Canyon Natl. Park-North Ent.	47	D2	36.334900 -112.116000
Grand Canyon Natl. Park-South Ent.	47	D2	36.000100 -112.121600
Grand Canyon-Parashant Natl. Mon.	46	C2	36.452170 -113.724367
Ironwood Forest Natl. Mon.	54	C3	32.478380 -111.530220
Lake Mead N.R.A.-Boulder City Ent.	46	C2	36.020800 -114.796000
Lake Mead N.R.A.-Henderson Ent.	46	C2	36.105400 -114.901200
Lake Mead N.R.A.-Las Vegas–Rt 147 Ent.	46	C2	36.161000 -114.905100
Lake Mead N.R.A.-South Ent.	46	C2	35.225600 -114.551000
Montezuma Castle Natl. Mon.-Vis. Ctr.	47	D4	34.611600 -111.839000
Navajo Natl. Mon.-Betatakin Ruin	47	E1	36.683500 -110.541470
Navajo Natl. Mon.-Inscription House Ruin-Closed To Public	47	E1	36.661250 -110.775940
Navajo Natl. Mon.-Keet Seel Ruin	47	E1	36.683500 -110.541470
Navajo Natl. Mon.-Vis. Ctr.	47	E1	36.678200 -110.541000
Organ Pipe Cactus Natl. Mon.-Vis. Ctr.	54	B3	31.954800 -112.801000
Petrified Forest Natl. Park-North Ent.	47	F3	35.069600 -109.778000
Petrified Forest Natl. Park-South Ent.	47	F3	34.799600 -109.885000
Pipe Spring Natl. Mon.-Vis. Ctr.	47	D1	36.862500 -112.737000
Saguaro Natl. Park-East	55	D3	32.178430 -110.737990
Saguaro Natl. Park-Vis. Ctr.	55	D3	32.180200 -110.736000
Saguaro Natl. Park-West	55	D3	32.251660 -111.191660
Sonoran Desert Natl. Mon.	54	C2	33.001730 -112.421220
Sunset Crater Volcano Natl. Mon.-Vis. Ctr.	47	E3	35.368800 -111.543000
Tonto Natl. Mon.-Vis. Ctr.	55	D1	33.645200 -111.113000
Tumacácori N.H.P.-Vis. Ctr.	55	D4	31.567800 -111.051000
Tuzigoot Natl. Mon.-Pk. Hqtrs.	47	D4	34.561000 -111.853000
Vermilion Cliffs Natl. Mon.	47	D1	36.806389 -111.741111
Walnut Canyon Natl. Mon.-Walnut Canyon Vis. Ctr.	47	E3	35.171700 -111.509000
Wupatki Natl. Mon.-Vis. Ctr.	47	E3	35.520300 -111.372000
State Park & Rec. Areas			
Alamo Lake S.P.	46	C4	34.234270 -113.553220
Boyce Thmpson Arbrtum S.P.	55	D2	33.311150 -111.055790
Buckskin Mtn. S.P.	46	B4	34.255000 -114.134070
Catalina S.P.	55	D3	32.416760 -110.937500
Cattail Cove S.P.	46	B4	34.355075 -114.165877
Dead Horse Ranch S.P.	47	D4	34.748490 -112.022930
Homolovi S.P.	47	E3	35.023940 -110.630120
Kartchner Caverns S.P.	55	D3	31.840770 -110.342710
Lake Havasu S.P.	46	B4	34.473970 -114.345850
Lost Dutchman S.P.	54	C1	33.464920 -111.481350
Lyman Lake S.P.	48	A4	34.362870 -109.375370
Oracle S.P.	55	D2	32.610239 -110.740619
Patagonia Lake S.P.	55	D4	31.488970 -110.853790
Picacho Peak S.P.	54	C2	32.646340 -111.398090
Red Rock S.P.	47	D4	34.818920 -111.836700
Roper Lake S.P.	55	E2	32.758710 -109.709520
Slide Rock S.P.	47	D3	34.944340 -111.752810
Tonto Nat. Bridge S.P.	47	E4	34.323400 -111.449460

ARKANSAS

ARKANSAS	PAGE	GRID	LATITUDE LONGITUDE
National Park & Rec. Areas			
Fort Smith N.H.S.-Main Road	116	B1	35.387480 -94.429660
Fort Smith N.H.S.-Vis. Ctr.	116	B1	35.385800 -94.429800
Hot Springs Natl. Park-Main Road	117	D2	34.511660 -93.053980
Hot Springs Natl. Park-Vis. Ctr.	117	D2	34.513800 -93.053400
Pea Ridge N.M.P.-Main Road	106	C3	36.442600 -94.025980
Pea Ridge N.M.P.-Vis. Ctr.	106	C3	36.443800 -94.025900
State Park & Rec. Areas			
Bull Shoals-White River S.P.	107	E3	36.365590 -92.557490
Conway Cemetery S.P.	124	C1	33.101909 -93.683161
Crater of Diamonds S.P.	116	C3	34.038610 -93.667630
Crowley's Ridge S.P.	108	A4	36.044840 -90.666770
Degray Lake Resort S.P.-North Ent.	117	D3	34.248870 -93.116880
Degray Lake Resort S.P.-South Ent.	117	D3	34.217390 -93.085820
Hampson Arch. Mus. S.P.	118	B1	35.568990 -90.041060
Historic Washington S.P.	116	C4	33.774005 -93.683235
Hobbs S.P.-Cons. Area	106	C3	36.244880 -93.972640
Jacksonport S.P.	107	F4	35.641440 -91.305350
Jenkins Ferry Bfld. S.P.	117	E3	34.212070 -92.547490
Lake Charles S.P.	107	F4	36.066870 -91.132700
Lake Chicot S.P.	126	A1	33.373070 -91.194940
Lake Dardanelle S.P.	117	D1	35.251690 -93.213380
Lake Fort Smith S.P.	106	C4	35.654040 -94.150140
Lake Frierson S.P.	108	A4	35.988570 -90.717540
Lake Ouachita S.P.	117	D2	34.610990 -93.165520
Lake Poinsett S.P.	118	A1	35.535510 -90.688700
Louisiana Purchase S.P.	118	A2	35.150340 -90.734990
Lower White River Mus. S.P.	117	F2	34.977035 -91.495131
Mammoth Spring S.P.	107	F3	36.496010 -91.535960
Marks' Mills Battleground S.P.	117	E4	33.781085 -92.256427
Moro Bay S.P.	125	E1	33.298890 -92.348940
Mount Magazine S.P.	116	C1	35.149900 -93.563600
Mount Nebo S.P.	117	D1	35.224870 -93.229930
Ozark Folk Center S.P.	107	E4	35.883480 -92.116340
Parkin Arch. S.P.	118	A1	35.268607 -90.554809
Petit Jean S.P.	117	D1	35.128320 -92.898530
Poison Springs Battleground S.P.	117	D4	33.638340 -93.005250
Powhatan Hist. S.P.	107	F4	36.083234 -91.117858
Prairie Grove Bfld. S.P.	106	C4	35.983120 -94.305590
Toltec Mounds Arch. S.P.	117	E2	34.647370 -92.058510
Village Creek S.P.	118	A1	35.199650 -90.724540
White Oak Lake S.P.	117	D4	33.687490 -93.117240
Withrow Springs S.P.	106	C4	36.203800 -93.578200
Woolly Hollow S.P.	117	E1	35.286402 -92.285646

CALIFORNIA

CALIFORNIA	PAGE	GRID	LATITUDE LONGITUDE
National Park & Rec. Areas			
Amboy Crater Natl. Nat. Landmark	53	E2	34.542196 -115.790920
Berryessa Snow Mountain Natl. Mon.	36	B2	38.902521 -123.411455
Carrizo Plain Natl. Mon.	52	B1	35.191000 -119.792000
Castle Mountains Natl. Mon.	53	F1	35.250563 -115.116773
Channel Islands Natl. Park	52	B2	34.248500 -119.267000
Death Valley Natl. Park-Furnace Creek Vis. Ctr.	45	F3	36.461800 -116.867000
Devils Postpile Natl. Mon.	37	E4	37.630330 -119.084300
Giant Sequoia Natl. Mon.-North Unit	45	D2	36.705501 -118.824821
Giant Sequoia Natl. Mon.-South Unit	45	E3	36.062389 -118.317784
Golden Gate N.R.A.-Marin Headlands	36	B4	37.830900 -122.525000
Golden Gate N.R.A.-Mott Vis. Ctr.	36	B4	37.799800 -122.460000
Joshua Tree Natl. Park-Indian Cove	53	E3	34.120000 -116.156000
Joshua Tree Natl. Park-North Ent.	53	E3	34.078300 -116.037000
Joshua Tree Natl. Park-West Ent.	53	E3	34.093600 -116.266000
Kings Canyon Natl. Park-East Ent.	45	D2	36.715870 -118.940420
Kings Canyon Natl. Park-West Ent.	45	D2	36.723720 -118.956490
Lassen Volcanic Natl. Park-Ent.	29	D4	40.537900 -121.571000
Lava Beds Natl. Mon.-Vis. Ctr.	29	D2	41.713900 -121.509000
Manzanar N.H.S.	45	E3	36.732260 -118.148500
Mojave Trails Natl. Mon.	53	E2	34.169528 -115.788162
Pinnacles Natl. Park-East Ent.	44	B3	36.483200 -121.162000
Pinnacles Natl. Park-West Ent.	44	B3	36.473300 -121.224400
Point Reyes Natl. Seashore-Bear Valley Vis. Ctr.	36	A3	38.043100 -122.799000
Point Reyes Natl. Seashore-Kenneth C. Patrick Vis. Ctr.	36	A3	38.027800 -122.961000
Point Reyes Natl. Seashore-Vis. Ctr.	36	A3	37.996500 -123.021000
Redwood Natl. Park-Kuchel Vis. Ctr.	28	A3	41.286800 -124.090900
Redwood Natl. Park-Prairie Creek Vis. Ctr.	28	A3	41.365300 -124.022000
Sand to Snow Natl. Mon.	53	D2	34.045197 -117.054096
San Gabriel Mountains Natl. Mon.	52	C2	34.286213 -117.884488
Santa Monica Mts. N.R.A.-Vis. Ctr.	52	B2	34.188600 -118.887000
Santa Rosa & San Jacinto Mts. Natl. Mon.	53	E3	33.755173 -116.729736
Sequoia Natl. Park-North Ent.	45	D3	36.647900 -118.826370
Sequoia Natl. Park-South Ent.	45	D3	36.487130 -118.836810
Shasta-Trinity N.R.A.	28	C4	40.633204 -122.601127
Trona Pinnacles Natl. Nature Landmark	45	F4	35.611944 -117.369444
Whiskeytown-N.R.A.	28	C4	40.751500 -122.320580
Yosemite Natl. Park-Arch Rock Ent.	37	D3	37.687500 -119.730000
Yosemite Natl. Park-Big Oak Flat Ent.	37	D3	37.800800 -119.874000
Yosemite Natl. Park-Hetch Hetchy Ent.	37	D3	37.893500 -119.842000
Yosemite Natl. Park-South Ent.	37	D3	37.507000 -119.632000
Yosemite Natl. Park-Tioga Pass Ent.	37	D3	37.910700 -119.258000
State Park & Rec. Areas			
Ahjumawi Lava Springs S.P.	29	D3	41.107140 -121.468600
Anza-Borrego Desert S.P.	53	E4	33.256550 -116.399340
Big Basin Redwoods S.P.	44	A2	37.168380 -122.221530
Bothe-Napa Valley S.P.	36	B3	38.553410 -122.525640
Butano S.P.	44	A2	37.200660 -122.344140
Carlsbad State Beach	53	D3	33.147530 -117.345280
Castle Crags S.P.	28	C3	41.149280 -122.317480
China Camp S.P.	36	B3	38.003990 -122.466480
Clear Lake S.P.	36	B2	39.009780 -122.805400
Cuyamaca Rancho S.P.	53	D4	32.933790 -116.562560
Del Norte Coast Redwoods S.P.	28	A3	41.603280 -124.100130
Doheny State Beach	52	C3	33.463820 -117.688830
Donner Mem. S.P.	37	D2	39.323880 -120.228370
Ed Z'Berg Sugar Pine Point S.P.	37	D2	39.056290 -120.119200
Emerald Bay S.P.	37	D2	38.956710 -120.108850
Fremont Peak S.P.	44	B3	36.760340 -121.502670
Garrapata S.P.	44	B3	36.475310 -121.936280
Gaviota S.P.	52	A2	34.475250 -120.228590
Grizzly Creek Redwoods S.P.	28	B4	40.486630 -123.903520
Grover Hot Springs S.P.	37	D3	38.695230 -119.836760
Henry Cowell Redwoods S.P.	44	A2	37.044020 -122.070990
Henry W. Coe S.P.	44	B2	37.085600 -121.467340
Humboldt Lagoons S.P.	28	A3	41.284330 -124.089720
Humboldt Redwoods S.P.	28	A4	40.284740 -124.056950
Jedediah Smith Redwoods S.P.	28	A2	41.798190 -124.084030
Julia Pfeiffer Burns S.P.	44	B3	36.160700 -121.668210
Manchester S.P.	36	A2	38.980450 -123.703020
Marina State Beach	44	B3	36.683030 -121.809440
McGrath State Beach	52	B2	34.227270 -119.256460
Mendocino Headlands S.P.	36	A2	39.307570 -123.798910
Morro Bay S.P.	44	B4	35.354020 -120.843800
Morro Strand State Beach	44	B4	35.435390 -120.888060
Mount Diablo S.P.	36	B4	37.844210 -121.950200
Mount Tamalpais S.P.	36	B3	37.904290 -122.604040
Navarro River Redwoods S.P.	36	A2	39.175000 -123.676390

CALIFORNIA (cont.)	PAGE	GRID	LATITUDE LONGITUDE
Pacheco S.P.	44	B2	37.055650 -121.016250
Palomar Mtn. S.P.	53	D3	33.325340 -116.893330
Patrick's Point S.P.	28	A3	41.135690 -124.150500
Pfeiffer Big Sur S.P.	44	B3	36.250930 -121.786550
Placerita Canyon S.P.	52	C2	34.377530 -118.470290
Plumas-Eureka S.P.	36	C1	39.758360 -120.695360
Point Dume State Beach	52	B2	34.003110 -118.807250
Point Sal State Beach	52	A1	34.897760 -120.642760
Prairie Creek Redwoods S.P.	28	A3	41.355490 -124.073670
Red Rock Canyon S.P.	52	C1	35.359734 -117.978351
Russian Gulch S.P.	36	A2	39.330990 -123.805050
Saddleback Butte S.P.	52	C2	34.689820 -117.824340
Samuel P. Taylor S.P.	36	B3	38.004660 -122.708400
San Gregorio State Beach	36	B4	37.321490 -122.401640
San Onofre State Beach	53	D3	33.383380 -117.580790
Sonoma Coast State Beach	36	A3	38.441060 -123.122970
Sunset State Beach	44	B2	36.897780 -121.835450
The Forest of Nisene Marks S.P.	44	B2	37.042024 -121.856231
Tolowa Dunes S.P.	28	A2	41.825800 -124.187500
Trinidad State Beach	28	A3	41.061090 -124.142290
Van Damme S.P.	36	A2	39.273990 -123.790490
Westport-Union Landing State Beach	36	A1	39.658350 -123.784930
Wilder Ranch S.P.	44	A2	36.962160 -122.080850
Zmudowski State Beach	44	B2	36.845580 -121.804300

COLORADO	PAGE	GRID	LATITUDE LONGITUDE
National Park & Rec. Areas			
Arapaho N.R.A.	41	D1	40.197870 -105.869440
Bent's Old Fort N.H.S.	41	F3	38.045980 -103.431440
Black Canyon-Gunnison Natl. Park-North Ent.	40	C3	38.586890 -107.695940
Black Canyon-Gunnison Natl. Park-South Ent.	40	C3	38.553980 -107.686390
Browns Canyon Natl. Mon.	41	D2	38.753093 -105.973528
Canyons of the Ancients Natl. Mon.	40	A4	37.587880 -108.916890
Colorado Natl. Mon.-Northwest Ent.	40	B2	39.117620 -108.730910
Colorado Natl. Mon.-Southeast Ent.	40	B2	39.032860 -108.631460
Colorado Natl. Mon.-South Ent.	40	B2	39.021100 -108.659540
Colorado Natl. Mon.-Southwest Ent.	40	B2	39.055070 -108.742500
Curecanti N.R.A.-East Ent.	40	C3	38.515010 -107.020560
Curecanti N.R.A.-North Ent.	40	C3	38.463380 -107.419580
Curecanti N.R.A.-South Ent.	40	C3	38.473160 -107.076450
Curecanti N.R.A.-West Ent.	40	C3	38.444680 -107.341980
Dinosaur Natl. Mon.-East Ent.	32	B4	40.443120 -108.517790
Dinosaur Natl. Mon.-South Ent.	32	B4	40.243920 -108.973750
Florissant Fossil Beds Natl. Mon.	41	E2	38.937440 -105.283400
Great Sand Dunes Natl. Park-Ent. Sta.	41	D4	37.725000 -105.519000
Hovenweep Natl. Mon.-Cutthroat	40	A4	37.413000 -108.720240
Hovenweep Natl. Mon.-Hackberry	40	A4	37.398890 -109.036680
Hovenweep Natl. Mon.-Holly	40	A4	37.398890 -109.036680
Hovenweep Natl. Mon.-Horseshoe	40	A4	37.464610 -108.974680
Mesa Verde Natl. Park-Ent. Sta.	40	B4	37.331100 -108.416000
Rocky Mtn. Natl. Park-Beaver Meadows Ent.	33	E4	40.367300 -105.578000
Rocky Mtn. Natl. Park-Fall River Ent.	33	E4	40.404000 -105.590000
Rocky Mtn. Natl. Park-Grand Lake Ent.	33	E4	40.267300 -105.833000
Rocky Mtn. Natl. Park-Wild Basin Ent.	33	E4	40.219000 -105.534000
Sand Creek Massacre N.H.S.	42	A3	38.541250 -102.505910
Yucca House Natl. Mon.	40	B4	37.251678 -108.684911
State Park & Rec. Areas			
Barr Lake S.P.	41	E1	39.938160 -104.733470
Boyd Lake S.P.	33	E4	40.428990 -105.045400
Castlewood Canyon S.P.	41	E2	39.325860 -104.737640
Crawford S.P.	40	C3	38.708000 -107.617550
Eleven Mile S.P.	41	D2	38.948570 -105.526450
Golden Gate Canyon S.P.	41	D1	39.875560 -105.453650
Harvey Gap S.P.	40	C1	39.606210 -107.659010
Highline Lake S.P.	40	B2	39.270910 -108.835930
Jackson Lake S.P.	33	F4	40.409110 -104.070130
James M. Robb-Colorado River S.P.-Corn Lake	40	B2	39.062709 -108.455110
James M. Robb-Colorado River S.P.-Island Acres	40	B2	39.165709 -108.300610
John Martin Reservoir S.P.	42	A3	38.065390 -102.927110
Lake Pueblo S.P.	41	E3	38.258130 -104.719160
Lathrop S.P.	41	E4	37.602830 -104.833740
Lory S.P.	33	E4	40.593143 -105.185413
Mancos S.P.	40	B4	37.399890 -108.266750
Mueller S.P.	41	E2	38.884940 -105.157710
Navajo S.P.	48	B1	37.067800 -107.407599
North Sterling S.P.	34	A4	40.787740 -103.264990
Paonia S.P.	40	C2	38.980440 -107.342900
Pearl Lake S.P.	33	D4	40.790160 -106.894610
Ridgway S.P.	40	B3	38.229710 -107.729410
Rifle Falls S.P.	40	B1	39.695290 -107.701090
Rifle Gap S.P.	40	B1	39.627460 -107.762520
Roxborough S.P.	41	E2	39.451300 -105.070200
San Luis S.W.A.	41	D4	37.663130 -105.734480
Spinney Mtn. S.P.	41	D2	39.014760 -105.625880
Stagecoach S.P.	33	D4	40.286100 -106.866920
Staunton S.P.	41	D1	39.509959 -105.394411
Steamboat Lake S.P.	32	C4	40.805240 -106.943600
Sweitzer Lake S.P.	40	B2	38.712050 -108.042640
Sylvan Lake S.P.	40	C1	39.516710 -106.753170
Trinidad Lake S.P.	49	E1	37.149700 -104.563650
Vega S.P.	40	B2	39.226890 -107.810250
Yampa River S.P.	32	C4	40.533190 -107.444483

CONNECTICUT	PAGE	GRID	LATITUDE LONGITUDE
National Park & Rec. Areas			
Weir Farm N.H.S.	148	C2	41.255890 -73.455980
State Park & Rec. Areas			
Bigelow Hollow S.P.	150	B2	41.991600 -72.134840
Bluff Point S.P.	149	F2	41.335800 -72.033520
Chatfield Hollow S.P.	150	A4	41.361400 -72.580190
Day Pond S.P.	150	A4	41.553432 -72.418419
Devils Hopyard S.P.	150	A4	41.486529 -72.342462
Gay City S.P.	150	A3	41.716100 -72.434470
Gillette Castle S.P.	150	A4	41.430670 -72.427990
Hammonasset Beach S.P.	149	E2	41.273640 -72.562350
Haystack Mtn. S.P.	94	C2	42.002010 -73.209960
Hurd S.P.	150	A4	41.530650 -72.537650
John A. Minetto S.P.	94	C2	41.884020 -73.170280
Lake Waramaug S.P.	148	C1	41.706290 -73.382460
Mashamoquet Brook S.P.	150	B3	41.860320 -71.987230
Mount Riga S.P.	94	B2	42.028830 -73.428620
Putnam Mem. S.P.	148	C2	41.344200 -73.381500
Rocky Neck S.P.	149	F2	41.316920 -72.242690
Selden Neck S.P.	150	A4	41.287500 -72.331100
Silver Sands S.P.	149	D2	41.198410 -73.076180
Southford Falls S.P.	149	D1	41.455700 -73.166150
Squantz Pond S.P.	148	C1	41.508580 -73.471040
Stoddard Hill S.P.	150	B4	41.461900 -72.065500
Sunrise S.P.	149	E1	41.502642 -72.477201
Wadsworth Falls S.P.	150	A4	41.536080 -72.687380
West Rock Ridge S.P.	149	D2	41.347810 -72.968260

DELAWARE	PAGE	GRID	LATITUDE LONGITUDE
State Park & Rec. Areas			
Cape Henlopen S.P.	145	F3	38.782360 -75.103010
Delaware Seashore S.P.	145	F4	38.614420 -75.071540
Fenwick Island S.P.	145	F4	38.469740 -75.051550
Fort Delaware S.P.	145	E1	39.578700 -75.588320
Fort Dupont S.P.	145	E1	39.568930 -75.588590
Holts Landing S.P.	145	F4	38.584080 -75.128380
Killens Pond S.P.	145	E3	38.990320 -75.544920
Lums Pond S.P.	145	E1	39.570520 -75.733490
Trap Pond S.P.	145	E4	38.525860 -75.483170
White Clay Creek S.P.	146	B4	39.709810 -75.776560

FLORIDA	PAGE	GRID	LATITUDE LONGITUDE
National Park & Rec. Areas			
Biscayne Natl. Park-Dante Fascell Vis. Ctr.	143	F3	25.464400 -80.334900
Canaveral Natl. Seashore	141	E1	28.611410 -80.808390
Castillo de San Marcos Natl. Mon.	139	D3	29.897747 -81.311461
Dry Tortugas Natl. Park-Vis. Ctr.	142	B4	24.628500 -82.873400
Everglades Natl. Park-Ent.	143	E3	25.394400 -80.589300
Fort Matanzas Natl. Mon.	139	E3	29.715660 -81.234190
Gulf Islands Natl. Seashore	135	F2	30.362880 -87.139630
State Park & Rec. Areas			
Alafia River S.P.	140	C3	27.789920 -82.120830
Amelia Island S.P.	139	D2	30.543900 -81.449700
Anastasia S.P.	139	E3	29.874740 -81.285030
Anclote Key Pres. S.P.	140	B2	28.193070 -82.850660
Avalon S.P.	141	E3	27.542840 -80.318060
Bahia Honda S.P.	143	D4	24.659540 -81.277810
Bald Point S.P.	138	A3	29.902700 -84.408600
Big Lagoon S.P.	135	F2	30.322290 -87.401170
Big Shoals S.P.	138	C2	30.339115 -82.683182
Big Talbot Island S.P.	139	D2	30.460500 -81.421950
Blue Spring S.P.	141	D1	28.952270 -81.331300
Bulow Creek S.P.	139	E4	29.388000 -81.132399
Bulow Plantation Ruins Hist. S.P.	139	E4	29.433590 -81.144590
Caladesi Island S.P.	140	B2	28.059890 -82.813780
Cedar Key Mus. S.P.	138	B4	29.151172 -83.048299
Charlotte Harbor Pres. S.P.	140	C4	26.850691 -82.022026
Collier-Seminole S.P.	143	D2	25.991630 -81.591700
Crystal River Pres. S.P. & Arch. S.P.	140	B1	28.909530 -82.628680
Curry Hammock S.P.	143	E4	24.742640 -80.984793
Dade Bfld. Hist. S.P.	140	C1	28.654430 -82.124970
Deleon Springs S.P.	139	D4	29.131920 -81.360400
Delnor-Wiggins Pass S.P.	142	C1	26.272500 -81.826900
Dudley Farm Hist. S.P.	138	C3	29.649617 -82.630738
Eden Gardens S.P.	136	B2	30.361530 -86.125010
Egmont Key S.P.	140	B3	27.723490 -82.679390
Fakahatchee Strand Pres. S.P.	143	D2	25.961900 -81.364600
Faver-Dykes S.P.	139	E3	29.668050 -81.268030
Florida Caverns S.P.	137	D1	30.809160 -85.212270
Fort Clinch S.P.	139	D1	30.668010 -81.434300
Fort Cooper S.P.	140	C1	28.801300 -82.309200
Fort Pierce Inlet S.P.-East Ent.	141	E3	27.485160 -80.299430
Fort Pierce Inlet S.P.-West Ent.	141	E3	27.475930 -80.316980
Gasparilla Island S.P.	140	C4	26.718200 -82.261400
Grayton Beach S.P.	136	B2	30.328930 -86.155790
Henderson Beach S.P.	136	B2	30.387000 -86.447499
Highlands Hammock S.P.	141	D3	27.476554 -81.557148
Hontoon Island S.P.	141	D1	28.976680 -81.357690
Hugh Taylor Birch S.P.	143	F1	26.138220 -80.104450
Indian Key Hist. S.P.	143	E4	24.888056 -80.678056
John Gorrie Mus. S.P.	137	D3	29.725768 -84.983244
John Pennekamp Coral Reef S.P.	143	E3	25.127620 -80.409650
Jonathan Dickinson S.P.	141	F4	27.002920 -80.099980
Kissimmee Prairie Pres. S.P.	141	D3	27.538826 -81.022945
Lafayette Blue Springs S.P.	138	B2	30.115136 -83.229417
Lake Griffin S.P.	140	C1	28.857450 -81.902240
Lake Kissimmee S.P.	141	D2	27.971930 -81.380220
Lake Louisa S.P.	140	C1	28.460070 -81.751620
Lake Manatee S.P.	140	C3	27.475140 -82.336800
Little Talbot Island S.P.	139	D2	30.460500 -81.421950
Long Key S.P.	143	E4	24.821580 -80.819510
Lovers Key S.P.	142	C1	26.391000 -81.877800
Manatee Springs S.P.	138	B4	29.496230 -82.958630
Myakka River S.P.	140	C4	27.242670 -82.332240
Natural Bridge Bfld. Hist. S.P.	138	A2	30.284730 -84.152260
O'Leno S.P.	138	C3	29.809100 -82.550700
Olustee Bfld. Hist. S.P.	138	C2	30.214650 -82.428960
Oscar Scherer S.P.	140	B4	27.168840 -82.477360
Paynes Prairie Pres. S.P.	138	C3	29.520720 -82.300400
Perdido Key S.P.	135	F2	30.291480 -87.465360
Ponce De Leon Springs S.P.	136	C1	30.713260 -85.922490
Rainbow Springs S.P.	138	C4	29.103818 -82.438782
Ravine Gardens S.P.	139	D3	29.637490 -81.646830
River Rise Pres. S.P.	138	C3	29.859961 -82.605395
Saint Sebastian River Pres. S.P.	141	E3	27.815241 -80.513820
San Marcos de Apalache Hist. S.P.	138	A2	30.152890 -84.210030
Savannas Pres. S.P.	141	E3	27.245960 -80.250270
Sebastian Inlet S.P.	141	E2	27.870200 -80.453599
Silver River S.P.	139	D4	29.202550 -82.053610
Suwannee River S.P.	138	B2	30.389610 -83.157850
Three Rivers S.P.	137	D1	30.736800 -84.936500
Tomoka S.P.	139	E4	29.342210 -81.086200
Torreya S.P.	137	D2	30.553530 -84.946740
Troy Spring S.P.	138	B3	29.918000 -82.893300
Waccasassa Bay Pres. S.P.	138	B4	29.188100 -82.925500
Washington Oaks Gardens S.P.	139	E3	29.634670 -81.205500
Wekiwa Springs S.P.	141	D1	28.710490 -81.462810
Windley Key Fossil Reef Geological S.P.	143	E4	24.914100 -80.642800
Yulee Sugar Mill Ruins Hist. S.P.	140	B1	28.784730 -82.607370

GEORGIA	PAGE	GRID	LATITUDE LONGITUDE
National Park & Rec. Areas			
Chattahoochee River N.R.A.	120	C3	34.002910 -84.349180
Chickamauga & Chattanooga N.M.P.	120	B2	34.941430 -85.258790
Cumberland Island Natl. Seashore	139	D1	30.720300 -81.548760
Ed Jenkins N.R.A.	120	C2	34.682900 -84.198200
Fort Frederica Natl. Mon.	130	B4	31.219790 -81.386570
Fort Pulaski Natl. Mon.	130	C3	32.016520 -80.891680
Jimmy Carter N.H.S.	128	C3	32.034090 -84.401600
Kennesaw Mtn. Natl. Battlefied Park-Vis. Ctr.	120	C3	33.983000 -84.577900
Ocmulgee Natl. Mon.	129	D2	32.848560 -83.602140
State Park & Rec. Areas			
Amicalola Falls S.P.	120	C2	34.558940 -84.248890
Black Rock Mtn. S.P.	121	D2	34.918150 -83.400310
Cloudland Canyon S.P.	120	B2	34.830430 -85.482040
Crooked River S.P.	139	D1	30.844840 -81.559350
Dames Ferry S.P.	129	D1	33.043709 -83.758201
Don Carter S.P.	121	D3	34.387622 -83.746462
Elijah Clark S.P.	121	E4	33.854210 -82.391913
Florence Marina S.P.	128	C3	32.090988 -85.043263
Fort Mtn. S.P.	120	C2	34.763090 -84.689330
Fort Yargo S.P.	121	D4	33.984940 -83.733580
Franklin D. Roosevelt S.P.	128	C2	32.848670 -84.793230
General Coffee S.P.	129	E4	31.511490 -82.745360
George L. Smith S.P.	130	A2	32.570310 -82.103760
George T. Bagby S.P.	128	C4	31.739940 -85.074820
Georgia Veterans S.P.	129	D3	31.957951 -83.903787
Gordonia-Alatamaha S.P.	130	A3	32.081900 -82.123550
Hamburg S.P.	129	E1	33.208800 -82.774870
Hard Labor Creek S.P.	121	D4	33.677820 -83.593840
Hart State Outdoor Rec. Area	121	E3	34.376040 -82.910260
High Falls S.P.	129	D1	33.176590 -84.020280
Indian Springs S.P.	129	D1	33.247480 -83.921190
James H. "Sloppy" Floyd S.P.	120	B3	34.440260 -85.347580
Kolomoki Mounds S.P.	128	C4	31.468633 -84.9485331
Laura S. Walker S.P.	138	C1	31.143130 -82.212920
Little Ocmulgee S.P.	129	E3	32.100590 -82.886360
Magnolia Springs S.P.	130	A1	32.875760 -81.962560
Mistletoe S.P.	121	E4	33.638770 -82.390540
Moccasin Creek S.P.	121	D2	34.845160 -83.589140
Panola Mtn. S.P.	120	C4	33.622042 -84.173078
Providence Canyon S.P.	128	C3	32.068270 -84.929150
Red Top Mtn. S.P.	120	C3	34.145950 -84.720190
Reed Bingham S.P.	137	F1	31.161310 -83.538880
Richard B. Russell S.P.	121	E3	34.166778 -82.745691
Seminole S.P.	137	D1	30.811420 -84.873570
Skidaway Island S.P.	130	C3	31.947720 -81.052550
Stephen C. Foster S.P.	138	C1	30.827020 -82.361310

	PAGE	GRID	LATITUDE LONGITUDE
Tallulah Gorge S.P.	121	D2	34.736350 -83.391950
Tugaloo S.P.	121	E3	34.501940 -83.082320
Unicoi S.P.	121	D2	34.724620 -83.728170
Victoria Bryant S.P.	121	E3	34.299380 -83.158770
Vogel S.P.	121	D2	34.766190 -83.922000
Watson Mill Bridge S.P.	121	E3	34.041140 -83.126990

HAWAII	PAGE	GRID	LATITUDE LONGITUDE
National Park & Rec. Areas			
Haleakala Natl. Park-Main Road	153	D1	20.769130 -156.242850
Haleakala Natl. Park-Kipahulu Ent.	153	D1	20.662000 -156.045600
Haleakala Natl. Park-North Ent.	153	D1	20.769000 -156.243000
Hawaii Volcanoes Natl. Park-Ent.	153	F4	19.428700 -155.254500
Honouliuli Natl. Mon.	152	A3	21.354145 -158.090528
Kalaupapa N.H.P.	152	C3	21.174110 -157.002830
State Park & Rec. Areas			
Ahupua'a 'O Kahana S.P.	152	A2	21.555210 -157.873260
Haena S.P.	152	B1	22.220930 -159.579600
Kaena Point S.P.	152	A2	21.551270 -158.244180
Kaumahina State Wayside Park	153	D1	20.871610 -156.170310
Kokee S.P.	152	B1	22.112580 -159.671050
Makena S.P.	153	D1	20.634030 -156.444180
Palaau S.P.	152	C3	21.174110 -157.002830
Polihale S.P.	152	B1	22.084480 -159.756700
Puaa Kaa State Wayside	153	D1	20.817560 -156.125800
Waianapanapa S.P.	153	E1	20.786230 -156.003010
Wailua River S.P.	152	B1	22.044180 -159.337250
Wailua Valley State Wayside	153	D1	20.840110 -156.139980
Wailuku River S.P.	153	F3	19.713340 -155.130490
Waimea Canyon S.P.	152	B1	22.031990 -159.671100

IDAHO	PAGE	GRID	LATITUDE LONGITUDE
National Park & Rec. Areas			
City of Rocks Natl. Res.	31	D2	42.078950 -113.677650
Craters of the Moon Natl. Mon. & Pres.	23	D4	43.462030 -113.559930
Hagerman Fossil Beds Natl. Mon.	30	C1	42.760980 -114.928220
Minidoka Natl. Hist. Site	31	D1	42.636944 -114.232222
Nez Perce N.H.P.-Clearwater Bfld.	22	B1	46.072600 -115.975400
Nez Perce N.H.P.-East Kamiah Site	22	B1	46.216600 -115.992400
Nez Perce N.H.P.-Vis. Ctr.	22	B1	46.446500 -116.817000
Nez Perce N.H.P.-White Bird Bfld.	22	B1	45.794400 -116.282000
Sawtooth N.R.A.	22	C3	44.211000 -114.946000
State Park & Rec. Areas			
Bear Lake S.P.	31	F2	42.026180 -111.257690
Bruneau Dunes S.P.	30	B1	42.910940 -115.713890
Castle Rocks S.P.	31	D2	42.135400 -113.670000
Dworshak S.P.	14	B4	46.577610 -116.327310
Eagle Island S.P.	22	B4	43.684510 -116.400300
Farragut S.P.	14	B2	47.952790 -116.602170
Harriman S.P.	23	F3	44.321000 -111.471200
Hells Gate S.P.	14	B4	46.380500 -117.044780
Henrys Lake S.P.	23	F3	44.620000 -111.370300
Heyburn S.P.	14	B3	47.353840 -116.748770
Lake Cascade S.P.	22	B3	44.520686 -116.046685
Lake Walcott S.P.	31	D1	42.674850 -113.482570
Land of the Yankee Fork S.P.	22	C3	44.475190 -114.208860
Lucky Peak S.P.	22	B4	43.530880 -116.055160
Massacre Rocks S.P.	31	D1	42.672200 -112.990800
McCroskey S.P.	14	B4	47.721080 -116.826310
Old Mission S.P.	14	B3	47.549420 -116.356940
Ponderosa S.P.	22	B2	44.926810 -116.083860
Priest Lake S.P.	14	B1	48.622082 -116.827798
Round Lake S.P.	14	B2	48.166110 -116.634230
Thousand Springs S.P.-Box Canyon	30	C1	42.709800 -114.791900
Thousand Springs S.P.-Malad Gorge	30	C1	42.864400 -114.854600
Thousand Springs S.P.-Niagara Springs	30	C1	42.662800 -114.672400
Three Island Crossing S.P.	30	C1	42.945280 -115.314850
Winchester Lake S.P.	22	B1	46.232280 -116.635570

ILLINOIS	PAGE	GRID	LATITUDE LONGITUDE
National Park & Rec. Areas			
Lincoln Home N.H.S.	98	B1	39.798120 -89.645150
Ronald Reagan Boyhood Home N.H.S.	88	B1	41.836700 -89.481100
State Park & Rec. Areas			
Apple River Canyon S.P.	74	A4	42.443990 -90.053280
Argyle Lake S.P.	87	F4	40.450680 -90.805080
Banner Marsh State Fish & Wildlife Area	88	B4	40.539600 -89.864500
Beall Woods S.P.	99	D4	38.351540 -87.836380
Beaver Dam S.P.	98	B2	39.214390 -89.959390
Big Bend State Fish & Wildlife Area	88	A2	41.634900 -90.044600
Buffalo Rock S.P.	88	C2	41.329720 -88.913090
Carlyle Lake State Fish & Wildlife Area	98	C3	38.768500 -89.193900
Castle Rock S.P.	88	B1	41.978230 -89.357040
Cave-In-Rock S.P.	109	D1	37.468010 -88.159950
Chain O'Lakes S.P.	74	C4	42.458390 -88.211950
Channahon S.P.	88	C2	41.415826 -88.223133
Coffeen Lake State Fish & Wildlife Area	98	B2	39.057000 -89.412400
Crawford County State Fish & Wildlife Area	99	D2	39.099800 -87.713100
Delabar S.P.	87	F3	40.957830 -90.939460
Des Plaines State Fish & Wildlife Area	88	C2	41.376600 -88.207400
Dixon Springs S.P.	108	C1	37.383600 -88.672830
Donnelley–Depue State Fish & Wildlife Area	88	B2	41.324000 -89.314100
Edward R. Madigan State Fish & Wildlife Area	88	B4	40.115280 -89.402240
Eldon Hazlet State Rec. Area	98	B3	38.667610 -89.327200
Ferne Clyffe S.P.	108	C1	37.532550 -88.966430
Fort Massac S.P.	108	C2	37.161720 -88.693850
Fox Ridge S.P.	99	D2	39.406020 -88.134810
Gebhard Woods S.P.	88	C2	41.357350 -88.440210
Giant City S.P.	108	C1	37.612250 -89.181790
Green River State Wildlife Area	88	B2	41.631600 -89.516500
Hamilton County State Fish & Wildlife Area	98	C4	38.065100 -88.404700
Hazel & Bill Rutherford Wildlife Prairie S.P.	88	B3	40.734180 -89.747270
Henderson County Cons. Area	87	F3	40.857505 -90.975005
Horseshoe Lake State Fish & Wildlife Area	108	C2	37.130465 -89.338505
Illini S.P.	88	C2	41.318770 -88.711070
Illinois Beach S.P.	75	D4	42.429920 -87.820150
Iroquois County State Wildlife Area	89	D3	40.994300 -87.598700
Jim Edgar Panther Creek State Fish & Wildlife Area	98	B1	40.011700 -90.177005
Johnson-Sauk Trail S.P.	88	A2	41.327510 -89.904850
Jubilee College S.P.	88	B3	40.844580 -89.827260
Kankakee River S.P.	89	D2	41.203400 -88.001880
Kaskaskia River State Fish & Wildlife Area	98	B4	38.229700 -89.879500
Kickapoo State Rec. Area	89	D4	40.138290 -87.737770
Lake Le Aqua-Na State Rec. Area	74	A4	42.422800 -89.823900
Lake Murphysboro S.P.	108	C1	37.771800 -89.382670
Lasalle Lake State Fish & Wildlife Area	88	C2	41.238400 -88.655500
Lincoln Trail S.P.	99	D2	39.346480 -87.696460
Lowden S.P.	88	B1	42.034860 -89.324950
Mackinaw River State Fish & Wildlife Area	88	B4	40.545801 -89.294301
Marshall State Fish & Wildlife Area	88	B3	41.007900 -89.410100
Matthiessen S.P.	88	C2	41.285010 -89.010050
Mautino State Fish & Wildlife Area	88	B2	41.323100 -89.718900
Middle Fork State Fish & Wildlife Area	89	D4	40.258300 -87.795900
Mississippi Palisades S.P.	88	A1	42.135820 -90.163300
Mississippi River State Fish & Wildlife Area	98	A2	38.991900 -90.542100
Morrison-Rockwood S.P.	88	A1	41.856350 -89.950120
Nauvoo S.P.	87	F4	40.543590 -91.386650
Newton Lake State Fish & Wildlife Area	99	D2	38.922400 -88.306700
Pere Marquette S.P.	98	A2	38.968110 -90.497430
Prophetstown S.P.	88	B2	41.672090 -89.920310
Pyramid S.P.	98	B4	38.004110 -89.425680
Ray Norbut State Fish & Wildlife Area	98	A1	39.685000 -90.648500
Red Hills S.P.	99	D3	38.728850 -87.838660
Rend Lake State Fish & Wildlife Area	98	C4	38.043800 -88.988900
Rice Lake State Fish & Wildlife Area	88	A4	40.476785 -89.949205
Saline County State Fish & Wildlife Area	109	D1	37.691300 -88.379100
Sam Dale Lake State Fish & Wildlife Area	98	C3	38.536005 -88.565605
Sam Parr State Fish & Wildlife Area	99	D2	39.011022 -88.126955
Sanganois State Fish & Wildlife Area	88	A4	40.091605 -90.283205
Sangchris Lake State Rec. Area	98	B1	39.656830 -89.487940
Shabbona Lake S.P.	88	C1	41.732250 -88.864930
Shelbyville State Fish & Wildlife Area	98	C2	39.566300 -88.566200
Siloam Springs S.P.	97	F1	39.899340 -90.955050
Silver Springs State Fish & Wildlife Area.	88	C2	41.627500 -88.518550
Snakeden Hollow State Fish & Wildlife Area	88	A3	41.030200 -90.080100
South Shore S.P.	98	B3	38.610250 -89.314570
Starved Rock S.P.	88	C2	41.321750 -89.010850
Stephen A. Forbes State Rec. Area	98	C3	38.718140 -88.743250
Ten Mile Creek State Fish & Wildlife Area	98	C4	38.081200 -88.594200
Turkey Bluffs State Fish & Wildlife Area	98	B4	37.877200 -89.771100
Walnut Point S.P.	99	D1	39.705150 -88.030390
Wayne Fitzgerrell S.P.	98	C4	38.089250 -88.937010
Weinberg-King S.P.	87	F4	40.226830 -90.899700
Weldon Springs S.P.	88	C4	40.125080 -88.921400
White Pines Forest S.P.	88	B1	41.988730 -89.461590
Wolf Creek S.P.	98	C2	39.488310 -88.680370
Woodford State Fish & Wildlife Area	88	B3	40.878900 -89.444800

INDIANA	PAGE	GRID	LATITUDE LONGITUDE
National Park & Rec. Areas			
George Rodgers Clark N.H.P.	99	D3	38.677880 -87.535350
Indiana Dunes Natl. Park	89	D1	41.653160 -87.062630
Lincoln Boyhood Natl. Mem.	99	E4	38.116800 -86.997860
State Park & Rec. Areas			
Bass Lake State Beach	89	E2	41.220100 -86.580200
Brown County S.P.	99	F2	39.197170 -86.215830
Chain O' Lakes S.P.	90	A2	41.336000 -85.422950
Charlestown S.P.	100	A3	38.448300 -85.644700
Clifty Falls S.P.	100	A3	38.761220 -85.420720
Fort Harrison S.P.	99	F1	39.871921 -86.018859
Harmonie S.P.	99	D4	38.089210 -87.934080
Indiana Dunes S.P.	89	E2	41.651470 -87.062620
Lincoln S.P.	99	E4	38.118370 -86.980080
McCormick's Creek S.P.	99	E2	39.283340 -86.726680
O'Bannon Woods S.P.	99	F4	38.200600 -86.254678
Ouabache S.P.	90	A3	40.728090 -85.111060
Pokagon S.P.	90	A1	41.707960 -85.029320
Potato Creek S.P.	89	E2	41.534950 -86.360290
Prophetstown S.P.	89	E4	40.500211 -86.829548
Shades S.P.	99	E1	39.941630 -87.057670
Shakamak S.P.	99	E2	39.181800 -87.232200
Spring Mill S.P.	99	F3	38.723330 -86.418460
Summit Lake S.P.	100	A1	40.018680 -85.302720
Tippecanoe River S.P.	89	E3	41.117330 -86.602750
Turkey Run S.P.	99	E1	39.882010 -87.200550
Versailles S.P.	100	A2	39.063900 -85.205330
Whitewater Mem. S.P.	100	B1	39.611300 -84.942300

IOWA	PAGE	GRID	LATITUDE LONGITUDE
National Park & Rec. Areas			
Effigy Mounds Natl. Mon.	73	F3	43.089310 -91.192350
Herbert Hoover N.H.S.	87	F1	41.671390 -91.346640
State Park & Rec. Areas			
Ambrose A. Call S.P.	72	B3	43.049650 -94.243430
Backbone S.P.	73	E4	42.600730 -91.532700
Beed's Lake S.P.	73	D4	42.767209 -93.241705
Bellevue S.P.	88	A1	42.247870 -90.416920
Black Hawk S.P.	72	B4	42.302700 -95.048680
Bobwhite S.P.	86	C3	40.710200 -93.393850
Clear Lake S.P.	72	C3	43.110281 -93.394441
Cold Springs S.P.	86	B2	41.289540 -95.083810
Echo Valley S.P.	73	E3	42.944040 -91.776880
Elk Rock S.P.	87	D2	41.400470 -93.063050
Fort Defiance S.P.	72	B2	43.393260 -94.851290
Geode S.P.	87	F3	40.832500 -91.385000
George Wyth Mem. S.P.	73	E4	42.536980 -92.394210
Green Valley S.P.	86	B3	41.114490 -94.377270
Heery Woods S.P.	73	D4	42.766450 -92.675250
Honey Creek S.P.	87	D3	40.863940 -92.939050
Lake Ahquabi S.P.	86	C2	41.286710 -93.572690
Lake Anita S.P.	86	B2	41.434150 -94.762470
Lake Keomah S.P.	87	D2	41.286570 -92.541660
Lake Macbride S.P.	87	F1	41.803090 -91.570950
Lake of Three Fires S.P.	86	B3	40.716391 -94.691671
Lake Wapello S.P.	87	D3	40.824890 -92.570530
Ledges S.P.	86	C1	41.998970 -93.896110
Maquoketa Caves S.P.	87	F1	42.119890 -90.770950
McIntosh Woods S.P.	72	C3	43.132580 -93.457580
Mini-Wakan S.P.	72	B2	43.498460 -95.102320
Nine Eagles S.P.	86	C3	40.591250 -93.765130
Palisades-Kepler S.P.	87	F1	41.916880 -91.497050
Pammel S.P.	86	C2	41.295590 -94.073150
Pikes Point S.P.	72	A2	43.415320 -95.162860
Pilot Knob S.P.	72	C3	43.255470 -93.574840
Prairie Rose S.P.	86	A2	41.601590 -95.210660
Preparation Canyon S.P.	86	A1	41.901570 -95.911670
Rice Lake S.P.	72	C2	43.401350 -93.502490
Rock Creek S.P.	87	D1	41.760580 -92.835410
Springbrook S.P.	86	B1	41.776390 -94.459440
Stone S.P.	35	F1	42.555460 -96.476050
Trappers Bay S.P.	72	A2	43.453630 -95.335510
Twin Lakes S.P.	72	B4	42.480180 -94.629860
Viking Lake S.P.	86	B3	40.973170 -95.053710
Wanata S.P.	72	A3	42.911340 -95.338080
Waubonsie S.P.	86	A3	40.677770 -95.683680
Wildcat Den S.P.	87	F2	41.467700 -90.869330

KANSAS	PAGE	GRID	LATITUDE LONGITUDE
National Park & Rec. Areas			
Fort Larned N.H.S.	43	D3	38.188740 -99.220620
Fort Scott N.H.S.	106	B1	37.843350 -94.704840
Monument Rocks Natl. Landmark	42	B2	38.790569 -100.762366
Nicodemus N.H.S.	42	C2	39.390833 -99.617500
State Park & Rec. Areas			
Atchison State Fishing Lake	96	B1	39.639010 -95.171830
Black Kettle State Fishing Lake	43	E3	38.229240 -97.509390
Bourbon State Fishing Lake	106	B1	37.793450 -95.069690
Brown State Fishing Lake	96	A1	39.847030 -95.373860
Cedar Bluff S.P.	42	C2	38.798230 -99.715060
Chase State Fishing Lake	43	F3	38.368480 -96.588000
Cheney S.P.	43	E4	37.732700 -97.844350
Clark State Fishing Lake	42	C4	37.391670 -99.784720
Clinton S.P.	96	A3	38.941970 -95.353960
Cowley State Fishing Lake	51	F1	37.104040 -96.795000
Crawford S.P.	106	B1	37.634320 -94.809820
Cross Timbers S.P.	106	A1	37.774514 -95.943431
Douglas State Fishing Lake	96	B3	38.796030 -95.165150
Eisenhower S.P.	96	A3	38.535720 -95.744270
El Dorado S.P.	43	F4	37.861420 -96.749460
Elk City S.P.	106	A2	37.251130 -95.774090
Fallriver S.P.	43	F4	37.653550 -96.043600
Glen Elder S.P.	43	D1	39.512160 -98.339140
Hain State Fishing Lake	42	C4	37.854250 -99.858020
Hamilton State Fishing Lake	42	B3	38.039090 -101.816940
Hillsdale S.P.	96	B3	38.660700 -94.894000
Kanopolis S.P.	43	E3	38.600340 -97.979500
Kingman State Fishing Lake	43	E4	37.651390 -98.306940
Kiowa State Fishing Lake	43	D4	37.612570 -99.299000
Leavenworth State Fishing Lake	96	B2	39.126970 -95.141700
Logan State Fishing Lake	42	B2	38.940280 -101.236940
Lovewell S.P.	43	E1	39.903310 -98.043090
Lyon State Fishing Lake	43	F3	38.546520 -96.058050
McPherson State Fishing Lake	43	E3	38.478667 -97.468267
Meade S.P.	42	C4	37.172220 -100.450000

Park	Page	Grid	Latitude Longitude
Miami State Fishing Lake	96	B3	38.422220 -94.785280
Milford S.P.	43	F2	39.104290 -96.895520
Mushroom Rock S.P.	43	E2	38.722222 -98.032222
Nebo State Fishing Lake	96	A2	39.447220 -95.595830
Neosho State Fishing Lake	106	B1	37.430570 -95.202550
Ottawa State Fishing Lake	43	E2	39.103040 -97.573060
Perry S.P.	96	A2	39.140210 -95.492480
Pomona S.P.	96	A3	38.652400 -95.600800
Pottawatomie State Fishing Lake No. 1	43	F1	39.470370 -96.407510
Pottawatomie State Fishing Lake No. 2	43	F2	39.228100 -96.533660
Prairie Dog S.P.	42	C1	39.811810 -99.963920
Prairie Spirit Trail S.P.	96	A4	38.280278 -95.242222
Rooks State Fishing Lake	43	D2	39.398290 -99.315020
Saline State Fishing Lake	43	E2	38.903159 -97.657510
Sand Hills S.P.	43	E3	38.116667 -97.833333
Scott S.P.	42	B2	38.684867 -100.922500
Shawnee State Fishing Lake	96	A2	39.206940 -95.804170
Tuttle Creek S.P.	43	F2	39.255560 -96.583330
Washington State Fishing Lake	43	E1	39.929780 -97.118830
Webster S.P.	43	D2	39.407840 -99.454550
Wilson State Fishing Lake	106	A1	38.910450 -98.497950
Wilson S.P.	43	D2	38.915000 -98.500000

KENTUCKY	PAGE	GRID	LATITUDE LONGITUDE
National Park & Rec. Areas			
Abraham Lincoln Birthplace N.H.P.	110	A1	37.532280 -85.733570
Land Between the Lakes N.R.A.	109	D2	36.776912 -88.059988
Mammoth Cave Natl. Park-Vis. Ctr.	109	F2	37.186800 -86.101300
State Park & Rec. Areas			
Barren River Lake State Resort Park	110	A2	36.853220 -86.053850
Blue Licks Bfld. State Resort Park	100	C3	38.434960 -83.991340
Buckhorn Lake State Resort Park	111	D1	37.312890 -83.423040
Carter Caves State Resort Park	101	D4	38.371470 -83.108510
Columbus-Belmont S.P.	108	C2	36.761990 -89.107000
Cumberland Falls State Resort Park	110	C2	36.834390 -84.350170
Fishtrap Lake S.P.	111	E1	37.432048 -82.417926
Fort Boonesborough S.P.	110	C1	37.899345 -84.270040
General Butler State Resort Park	100	A3	38.669950 -85.146050
Grayson Lake S.P.	101	D4	38.208630 -83.014910
Greenbo Lake State Resort Park	101	D3	38.479130 -82.867630
Green River Lake S.P.	110	A2	37.277440 -85.338730
Jenny Wiley State Resort Park-East Ent.	111	E1	37.730120 -82.740990
Jenny Wiley State Resort Park-South Ent.	111	E1	37.687680 -82.725690
Jenny Wiley State Resort Park-West Ent.	111	E1	37.727250 -82.745880
John James Audubon S.P.	99	D4	37.889250 -87.556510
Kentucky Dam Village State Resort Park	109	D2	36.996880 -88.285716
Kingdom Come S.P.	111	D2	36.981850 -82.982210
Lake Barkley State Resort Park	109	D2	36.809190 -87.928310
Lake Cumberland State Resort Park	110	B2	36.930320 -85.040960
Lake Malone S.P.	109	E2	37.076110 -87.038060
Levi Jackson Wilderness Road S.P.	110	C2	37.085250 -84.059250
Lincoln Homestead S.P.	110	B1	37.760080 -85.215930
My Old Kentucky Home S.P.	110	A1	37.808140 -85.458840
Natural Bridge State Resort Park	110	C1	37.777470 -83.676310
Nolin Lake S.P.	109	F1	37.297641 -86.212624
Old Fort Harrod S.P.	110	B1	37.762130 -84.845670
Pennyrile Forest State Resort Park	109	E2	37.057410 -87.649390
Pine Mtn. State Resort Park	110	C3	36.735270 -83.700790
Rough River State Resort Park	109	F1	37.615410 -86.504410
Taylorsville Lake S.P.	100	A4	37.993990 -85.227813
Yatesville Lake S.P.	101	D4	38.093300 -82.617800

LOUISIANA	PAGE	GRID	LATITUDE LONGITUDE
National Park & Rec. Areas			
Cane River Creole N.H.P.	125	D4	31.739690 -93.083080
Jean Lafitte N.H.P. & Pres.-Chalmette Vis. Ctr.	134	A3	29.942100 -89.994400
Jean Lafitte N.H.P. & Pres.-French Quarter Vis. Ctr.	134	A3	29.954600 -90.065100
Jean Lafitte N.H.P.-Wetlands Acadian Cultural Center	134	A3	29.795969 -90.824480
Poverty Point Natl. Mon. & S.H.S.	125	F2	32.633370 -91.403880
State Park & Rec. Areas			
Bayou Segnette S.P.	134	B3	29.902720 -90.153800
Chemin-A-Haut S.P.	125	F1	32.913460 -91.847550
Chicot S.P.	133	E1	30.829870 -92.276180
Cypremort Point S.P.	133	F3	29.731960 -91.840740
Fairview-Riverside S.P.	134	B2	30.408730 -90.140360
Fontainebleau S.P.	134	B2	30.345470 -90.022850
Grand Isle S.P.-Temp. Closed	134	B4	29.256640 -89.958480
Hodges Gardens S.P.	125	D4	31.369280 -93.424860
Jimmie Davis S.P.	125	E3	32.265000 -92.540300
Lake Bistineau S.P.	125	D2	32.440250 -93.395910
Lake Bruin S.P.	126	A3	31.955370 -91.198080
Lake Claiborne S.P.	125	D2	32.713000 -92.923360
Lake D'Arbonne S.P.	125	E2	32.784850 -92.490310
Lake Fausse Pointe S.P.	133	F3	30.067820 -91.615790
North Toledo Bend S.P.	124	C4	31.558910 -93.732060
Palmetto Island S.P.	133	F3	29.862877 -92.144165
Poverty Point Reservoir S.P.	125	F2	32.540446 -91.421356
Saint Bernard S.P.	134	C3	29.864460 -89.899190
South Toledo Bend S.P.	125	D4	31.213889 -93.575000
Tickfaw S.P.	134	B2	30.382180 -90.631150

MAINE	PAGE	GRID	LATITUDE LONGITUDE
National Park & Rec. Areas			
Acadia Natl. Park-Park Loop Road	83	D2	44.338700 -68.183200
Acadia Natl. Park-Sieur de Monts Ent.	83	D2	44.360000 -68.205200
Acadia Natl. Park-Stanley Brook Ent.	83	D2	44.296300 -68.242000
Katahdin Woods & Waters Natl. Mon.	85	D3	45.883549 -68.737849
State Park & Rec. Areas			
Aroostook S.P.	85	E2	46.612720 -68.005840
Baxter S.P.	84	C3	45.950290 -69.049080
Camden Hills S.P.	82	C2	44.232050 -69.046530
Cobscook Bay S.P.	83	E1	44.855290 -67.171680
Damariscotta Lake S.P.	82	C2	44.200070 -69.452900
Ferry Beach S.P.	82	B4	43.482410 -70.391520
Lake Saint George S.P.	82	C2	44.398950 -69.345710
Lamoine S.P.	83	D2	44.456000 -68.298520
Mount Blue S.P.	82	B1	44.721780 -70.417080
Peaks-Kenny S.P.	84	C4	45.256680 -69.254600
Popham Beach S.P.	82	C3	43.738740 -69.795830
Rangeley Lake S.P.	82	B1	44.919550 -70.696950
Range Ponds S.P.	82	B3	44.033540 -70.345080
Roque Bluffs S.P.	83	E2	44.614680 -67.479300
Saint Croix Island International Hist. Site	83	E1	45.128333 -67.133333
Sebago Lake S.P.	82	B3	43.916590 -70.570190
Shackford Head S.P.	83	F1	44.906191 -66.989979
Swan Lake S.P.	82	C2	44.568860 -68.981070
Vaughan Woods Mem. S.P.	82	A4	43.212680 -70.809320
Warren Island S.P.	82	C2	44.260445 -68.952255
Wolfe's Neck Woods S.P.	82	B3	43.827190 -70.084460

MARYLAND	PAGE	GRID	LATITUDE LONGITUDE
National Park & Rec. Areas			
Assateague Island Natl. Seashore	114	C2	38.239580 -75.140410
Harriet Tubman Underground RR N.H.P.	103	F3	38.322307 -76.176243
Thomas Stone N.H.S.	144	B4	38.529700 -77.032370
State Park & Rec. Areas			
Assateague S.P.	114	C2	38.250170 -75.156270
Big Run S.P.	102	B1	39.545090 -79.137254
Catoctin Mtn. Park-Vis. Ctr.	144	A1	39.633100 -77.449700
Cunningham Falls S.P.	144	A1	39.625040 -77.458130
Deep Creek Lake S.P.	102	B1	39.512110 -79.300150
Elk Neck S.P.	145	D1	39.482890 -75.983630
Fort Frederick S.P.	103	D1	39.616050 -78.007060
Gambrill S.P.	144	A1	39.468330 -77.495730
Greenwell S.P.	103	E4	38.364930 -76.525260
Gunpowder Falls S.P.	144	C1	39.536710 -76.502800
Hart-Miller Island S.P.	144	C2	39.251219 -76.376903
Janes Island S.P.	103	F4	38.009810 -75.846380
Martinak S.P.	145	E3	38.862920 -75.837790
North Point S.P.	144	C2	39.221910 -76.431600
Patapsco Valley S.P.	144	B2	39.296580 -76.781500
Patuxent River S.P.	144	B1	39.280790 -77.129620
Pocomoke River S.P.	114	C2	38.135410 -75.494870
Point Lookout S.P.	103	F4	38.066190 -76.336550
Rocks S.P.	144	C1	39.630140 -76.418120
Rocky Gap S.P.	102	C1	39.698430 -78.651150
Rosaryville S.P.	144	C3	38.778450 -76.799260
Saint Clement's Island S.P.	103	E4	38.225200 -76.749690
Saint Mary's River S.P.	103	E4	38.262940 -76.525640
Sandy Point S.P.	144	C3	39.021750 -76.420280
Seneca Creek S.P.	144	A2	39.152200 -77.247710
Smallwood S.P.	144	B4	38.556509 -77.185257
South Mtn. S.P.	144	A1	39.540058 -77.607422
Susquehanna S.P.	145	D1	39.599840 -76.154590
Swallow Falls S.P.	102	B1	39.506550 -79.448750
Tuckahoe S.P.	145	D3	38.967120 -75.943410
Washington Mon. S.P.	144	A1	39.499810 -77.631890
Wye Oak S.P.	145	D3	38.939150 -76.080230

MASSACHUSETTS	PAGE	GRID	LATITUDE LONGITUDE
National Park & Rec. Areas			
Adams N.H.P.-Vis. Ctr.	151	D1	42.257000 -71.011200
Boston Harbor Island N.R.A.	151	D1	42.319705 -70.928555
Cape Cod Natl. Seashore	151	F2	41.835890 -69.973730
Lowell N.H.P.-Market Mills Vis. Ctr.	95	E1	42.644400 -71.312800
Minute Man N.H.P.-Minute Man Vis. Ctr.	151	D1	42.449000 -71.268700
Minute Man N.H.P.-North Bridge Vis. Ctr.	151	D1	42.470800 -71.352600
New Bedford Whaling N.H.P.	151	D4	41.635570 -70.924250
Salem Maritime N.H.S.	151	D1	42.521490 -70.886980
Saugus Iron Works N.H.S.	151	D1	42.468230 -71.009110
Waquoit Bay Natl. Estuarine Research Res.	151	E4	41.581300 -70.524800
State Park & Rec. Areas			
Ames-Nowell S.P.	151	D2	42.113140 -70.975230
Ashland S.P.	150	C2	42.246380 -71.475560
Blackstone River & Canal Heritage S.P.	150	C2	42.099500 -71.618780
Borderland S.P.	151	D2	42.058560 -71.166330
Bradley Palmer S.P.	151	F1	42.652180 -70.911000
Callahan S.P.	150	C1	42.315140 -71.372410
Demarest Lloyd S.P.	151	D4	41.525790 -70.990530
Dighton Rock S.P.	151	D3	41.811230 -71.098440
Halibut Point S.P.	151	F1	42.686100 -70.631070
Hampton Ponds S.P.	150	A2	42.178350 -72.690030
Joseph Sylvia State Beach	151	E4	41.424140 -70.553870
Lake Wyola S.P.-Carroll Holmes Rec. Area	150	A1	42.500366 -72.430642
Moore S.P.	150	B1	42.312354 -71.954269
Mount Holyoke Range S.P.	150	A1	42.297270 -72.530890
Nickerson S.P.	151	F3	41.775550 -70.028290
Pilgrim Mem. (Plymouth Rock) S.P.	151	E2	41.958850 -70.662870
Red Bridge S.P.	150	A2	42.175500 -72.406600
Robinson S.P.	150	A2	42.081680 -72.658650
Rutland S.P.	150	B1	42.371470 -71.997680
Savoy Mtn. State Forest	94	C1	42.626540 -73.015580
Skinner S.P.	150	A1	42.304220 -72.598790
South Cape Beach S.P.	151	E4	41.554582 -70.508194
Wahconah Falls S.P.	94	C1	42.491430 -73.120790
Watson Pond S.P.	151	D2	41.956260 -71.116090
Wells S.P.	150	B2	42.142290 -72.042400
Whitehall S.P.	150	C2	42.227210 -71.584330
Wompatuck S.P.	151	D2	42.218770 -70.866600

MICHIGAN	PAGE	GRID	LATITUDE LONGITUDE
National Park & Rec. Areas			
Father Marquette Natl. Mem.	70	C2	45.853912 -84.728874
Grand Island N.R.A.	70	A1	46.500405 -86.657605
Isle Royale Natl. Park-Rock Harbor Vis. Ctr.	65	F2	48.145530 -88.482220
Isle Royale Natl. Park-Windigo Vis. Ctr.	65	F2	47.912700 -89.156990
Keweenaw N.H.P.	65	F3	47.242160 -88.448020
Pictured Rocks Natl. Lakeshore-East Ent.	70	A1	46.657450 -86.021160
Pictured Rocks Natl. Lakeshore-West Ent.	70	A1	46.474000 -86.553000
Sleeping Bear Dunes Natl. Lakeshore	70	A4	44.785210 -86.049690
State Park & Rec. Areas			
Albert E. Sleeper S.P.	76	C2	43.972880 -83.205530
Algonac S.P.	76	C4	42.654760 -82.514510
Aloha S.P.	70	C3	45.525850 -84.464390
Baraga S.P.	65	F4	46.762070 -88.499320
Bewabic S.P.	68	C2	46.094260 -88.422290
Brimley S.P.	70	C1	46.412970 -84.555040
Burt Lake S.P.	70	C3	45.401305 -84.619505
Cambridge Junction Hist. S.P.	90	B1	42.066990 -84.225550
Charles Mears S.P.	75	E2	43.781980 -86.439670
Cheboygan S.P.	70	C2	45.644860 -84.420440
Clear Lake S.P.	70	C3	45.127390 -84.173910
Coldwater Lake S.P.	90	A1	43.665975 -84.948703
Craig Lake S.P.	68	C1	46.538810 -88.127700
Duck Lake S.P.	75	E3	43.354880 -86.397560
F.J. Mclain S.P.	65	F3	47.239400 -88.587190
Fayette Hist. S.P.	70	A2	45.717200 -86.664600
Fisherman's Island S.P.	70	B3	45.307550 -85.301540
Fort Wilkins Hist. S.P.	65	F3	47.466780 -87.878240
Fred Meijer White Pine Trail S.P.	75	F2	44.222900 -85.426700
Grand Haven S.P.	75	E3	43.056100 -86.245990
Grand Mere S.P.	89	E1	41.995190 -86.538790
Harrisville S.P.	71	D4	44.649800 -83.293920
Hart-Montague Trail S.P.	75	E2	43.688800 -86.371900
Hartwick Pines S.P.	70	C4	44.744180 -84.648340
Holland S.P.	75	E4	42.780310 -86.201410
Indian Lake S.P.	70	A2	45.960420 -86.364400
Interlochen S.P.	70	B4	44.631370 -85.766630
J.W. Wells S.P.	69	D3	45.389070 -87.371360
Kal-Haven Trail S.P.	75	E4	42.324698 -85.667739
Keith J. Charters Traverse City S.P.	70	B4	44.748050 -85.553800
Lake Gogebic S.P.	68	B1	46.459950 -89.573110
Lakeport S.P.	76	C3	43.129120 -82.501820
Leelanau S.P.	70	B3	45.209320 -85.546220
Ludington S.P.	75	E1	44.031100 -86.505460
Mackinac Island S.P.	70	C2	45.849880 -84.617650
Mike Levine Lakelands Trail S.P.	76	B4	42.408249 -83.964043
Muskallonge Lake S.P.	70	B1	46.677100 -85.625210
Muskegon S.P.	75	E3	43.247900 -86.341480
Negwegon S.P.	71	D4	44.855020 -83.329240
Newaygo S.P.	75	F2	43.500600 -85.582260
North Higgins Lake S.P.	70	C4	44.515030 -84.753980
Onaway S.P.	70	C3	45.430530 -84.229020
Orchard Beach S.P.	75	E1	44.278860 -86.314480
Otsego Lake S.P.	70	C4	44.927770 -84.688980
P.H. Hoeft S.P.	70	C3	45.463700 -83.883560
P.J. Hoffmaster S.P.	75	E3	43.132870 -86.265460
Palms Book S.P.	70	A2	46.003280 -86.385130
Petoskey S.P.	70	B3	45.407950 -84.902160
Porcupine Mts. Wilderness S.P.	65	E4	46.816070 -89.621850
Port Crescent S.P.	76	C1	44.007570 -83.051290
Sanilac Petroglyphs Hist. S.P.	76	C2	43.649367 -83.018016
Saugatuck Dunes S.P.	75	E4	42.695990 -86.186840
Seven Lakes S.P.	76	B3	42.816750 -83.648120
Silver Lake S.P.	75	E2	43.663650 -86.492660
Sleepy Hollow S.P.	76	A3	42.925020 -84.408620
South Higgins Lake S.P.	76	A1	44.432818 -84.670299
Sterling S.P.	90	C1	41.921490 -83.342680
Straits S.P.	70	C2	45.858090 -84.720200
Tahquamenon Falls S.P.-East Ent.	70	B1	46.598030 -85.147890
Tahquamenon Falls S.P.-West Ent.	70	B1	46.564190 -85.292530
Tawas Point S.P.	76	B1	44.255820 -83.443050
Thompson's Harbor S.P.	71	D3	45.346705 -83.567431
Twin Lakes S.P.	65	E4	46.892210 -88.856560

Name	Page	Grid	Latitude Longitude
Van Buren S.P.	75	E4	42.333830 -86.304830
Van Buren Trail S.P.	89	F1	42.211405 -86.171105
Van Riper S.P.	68	C1	46.525260 -87.991150
Walter J. Hayes S.P.	90	B1	42.072830 -84.137820
Warren Dunes S.P.	89	E1	41.900980 -86.595260
Warren Woods S.P.	89	E1	41.840680 -86.631290
Wetzel Rec. Area	76	C4	42.596720 -82.825140
Wilderness S.P.-East Ent.	70	B2	45.748160 -84.853500
Wilderness S.P.-West Ent.	70	B2	45.679360 -84.964170
William Mitchell S.P.	75	F1	44.236880 -85.453990
Wilson S.P.	76	A1	44.029620 -84.806070
Young S.P.	70	B3	45.235240 -85.041450

MINNESOTA

MINNESOTA	PAGE	GRID	LATITUDE LONGITUDE
National Park & Rec. Areas			
Grand Portage Natl. Mon.	65	E2	47.996274 -89.734256
Pipestone Natl. Mon.	27	F3	44.013150 -96.325360
Voyageurs Natl. Park-Ash River Vis. Ctr.	64	C2	48.435600 -92.850300
Voyageurs Natl. Park-Kabetogama Lake Vis. Ctr.	64	C2	48.446100 -93.030100
Voyageurs Natl. Park-Rainy Lake Vis. Ctr.	64	C2	48.584400 -93.161500
State Park & Rec. Areas			
Afton S.P.	67	D4	44.847930 -92.791020
Banning S.P.	67	D2	46.179730 -92.855170
Bear Head Lake S.P.	64	C3	47.792720 -92.083720
Beaver Creek Valley S.P.	73	E2	43.636790 -91.573190
Blue Mounds S.P.	27	F4	43.714340 -96.183100
Buffalo River S.P.	19	F4	46.866260 -96.469980
Camden S.P.	27	F3	44.362880 -95.917480
Caribou Falls State Wayside	65	D3	47.463890 -91.030660
Carley S.P.	73	E1	44.116790 -92.169320
Cascade River S.P.	65	D3	47.712950 -90.497930
Charles A. Lindbergh S.P.	66	C2	45.959410 -94.387640
Cross River State Wayside	65	D3	47.543420 -90.897770
Crow Wing S.P.	66	C1	46.272630 -94.316400
Father Hennepin S.P.	66	C1	46.144520 -93.484260
Flandrau S.P.	72	B1	44.294360 -94.482020
Flood Bay State Wayside	64	C4	47.038500 -91.642540
Forestville Mystery Cave S.P.	73	E2	43.637520 -92.220270
Fort Ridgely S.P.	72	B1	44.454810 -94.718310
Franz Jevne S.P.	64	B2	48.641140 -94.058260
Frontenac S.P.	67	E4	44.525200 -92.338730
George H. Crosby Manitou S.P.	65	D3	47.478990 -91.123070
Glacial Lakes S.P.	66	A3	45.540550 -95.529600
Glendalough S.P.	19	F4	46.313314 -95.679290
Gooseberry Falls S.P.	65	D3	47.145430 -91.462380
Grand Portage S.P.	65	E2	47.999150 -89.596690
Great River Bluffs S.P.	73	E1	43.939100 -91.430050
Hayes Lake S.P.	19	F1	48.641070 -95.570600
Hill Annex Mine S.P.	64	B3	47.327490 -93.277520
Inspiration Peak State Wayside	66	A1	46.136880 -95.578650
Itasca S.P.	64	A3	47.194490 -95.166740
Jay Cooke S.P.	64	C4	46.658790 -92.349200
John A. Latsch S.P.	73	E1	44.164720 -91.823860
Joseph R. Brown State Wayside	66	B4	44.750328 -95.324425
Judge C.R. Magney S.P.	65	E3	47.818090 -90.051230
Kilen Woods S.P.	72	B2	43.732140 -95.072220
Kodonce River State Wayside	65	E3	47.793930 -90.154140
Lac Qui Parle S.P.	27	F2	45.024680 -95.896580
Lake Bemidji S.P.	64	A3	47.536890 -94.832320
Lake Bronson S.P.	19	F1	48.730940 -96.630720
Lake Carlos S.P.	66	B2	46.000540 -95.334430
Lake Louise S.P.	73	D2	43.532620 -92.509250
Lake Maria S.P.	66	C3	45.304810 -93.935570
Lake Shetek S.P.	72	A1	44.105740 -95.699730
L.Vermilion-Soudan Underground Mine S.P.	64	C2	47.818130 -92.246090
Maplewood S.P.	19	F4	46.549910 -95.966720
McCarthy Beach S.P.	64	B3	47.674110 -93.027350
Mille Lacs Kathio S.P.	66	C2	46.160740 -93.758020
Minneopa S.P.	72	C1	44.162190 -94.110310
Monson Lake S.P.	66	B3	45.321300 -95.270470
Moose Lake S.P.	64	C4	46.436360 -92.743090
Myre-Big Island S.P.	73	D2	43.623847 -93.289096
Nerstrand Big Woods S.P.	73	D1	44.327040 -93.111210
Old Mill S.P.	19	F2	48.369790 -96.569420
Ray Berglund State Wayside	65	D3	47.608200 -90.771930
Rice Lake S.P.	73	D1	44.095380 -93.063940
Rush River State Wayside	66	C4	44.507240 -93.931409
Saint Croix S.P.	67	D2	45.960615 -92.611630
Sakatah Lake S.P.	72	C1	44.218000 -93.509970
Sam Brown Mem. State Wayside	27	F1	45.596160 -96.841410
Savanna Portage S.P.	64	B4	46.819130 -93.176040
Scenic S.P.	64	B3	47.702450 -93.564710
Schoolcraft S.P.	64	B3	47.223040 -93.805320
Sibley S.P.	66	B3	45.318990 -95.011930
Split Rock Creek S.P.	27	F4	43.907240 -96.367970
Split Rock Lighthouse S.P.	65	D3	47.189800 -91.395010
Temperance River S.P.	65	D3	47.558780 -90.867930
Tettegouche S.P.	65	D3	47.337210 -91.200670
Upper Sioux Agency S.P.	66	B4	44.734540 -95.456460
Whitewater S.P.	73	E1	44.068880 -92.040100
Wild River S.P.	67	D3	45.524100 -92.754500
William O'Brien S.P.	67	D3	45.223900 -92.763500
Zippel Bay S.P.	64	A1	48.840630 -94.849950

MISSISSIPPI

MISSISSIPPI	PAGE	GRID	LATITUDE LONGITUDE
National Park & Rec. Areas			
Gulf Islands Natl. Seashore	135	D2	30.407200 -88.749220
Natchez N.H.P.-Vis. Reception Ctr.	125	F4	31.553900 -91.412400
State Park & Rec. Areas			
Bogue Homa State Fishing Lake	127	D4	31.703200 -89.026400
Calling Panther State Fishing Lake	126	B3	32.197100 -90.265100
Clarkco S.P.	127	D3	32.108500 -88.693970
Columbia State Fishing Lake	134	C1	31.183500 -89.738400
Florewood S.P.	118	B4	33.525120 -90.250362
George Payne Cossar S.P.	118	B3	34.122710 -89.882100
Golden Mem. S.P.	126	C2	32.568560 -89.407640
Great River Road S.P.	118	A4	33.851733 -91.027574
Hugh White S.P.	118	B4	33.796080 -89.743010
J.P. Coleman S.P.	119	D2	34.924254 -88.171706
Jeff Davis State Fishing Lake	126	B4	31.567700 -89.839800
John W. Kyle S.P.	118	B3	34.438060 -89.807500
Kemper County State Fishing Lake	127	D2	32.804167 -88.730556
Lake Lincoln S.P.	126	B4	31.684354 -90.337142
Legion S.P.	127	D1	33.148690 -89.042460
Leroy Percy S.P.	126	A1	33.160500 -90.938250
Mary Crawford State Fishing Lake	126	B4	31.574900 -90.154000
Monroe State Fishing Lake	119	D4	33.941500 -88.568700
Natchez S.P.	126	A4	31.589580 -91.220350
Neshoba County State Fishing Lake	126	C2	32.706200 -89.010500
Paul B. Johnson S.P.	134	C1	31.133800 -89.233910
Percy Quin S.P.	134	B1	31.189020 -90.510660
Perry State Fishing Lake	135	D1	31.132400 -88.899800
Prentiss Walker State Fishing Lake	126	C3	31.833200 -89.589500
Roosevelt S.P.	126	C2	32.321920 -89.664980
Simpson County State Fishing Lake	126	C3	31.913500 -89.794500
Tippah County State Fishing Lake	118	C2	34.794290 -88.950660
Tishomingo S.P.	119	D2	34.615670 -88.183390
Tom Bailey State Fishing Lake	127	D2	32.425030 -88.523069
Tombigbee S.P.	119	D3	34.231870 -88.628870
Trace S.P.	118	C3	34.260020 -88.886560
Wall Doxey S.P.	118	C2	34.660270 -89.459290
Walthall State Fishing Lake	134	B1	31.059184 -90.133939

MISSOURI

MISSOURI	PAGE	GRID	LATITUDE LONGITUDE
National Park & Rec. Areas			
George Washington Carver Natl. Mon.	106	C2	36.986160 -94.351890
Ozark Natl. Scenic Riverways	107	F2	37.281400 -91.408000
State Park & Rec. Areas			
Bennett Spring S.P.	107	D1	37.725440 -92.856390
Big Lake S.P.	86	A4	40.092090 -95.347300
Big Oak Tree S.P.	108	C3	36.641990 -89.290180
Big Sugar Creek S.P.	106	C3	36.584106 -93.819122
Crowder S.P.	86	C4	40.082140 -93.669310
Cuivre River S.P.	97	F2	39.062380 -90.938640
Echo Bluff S.P.	107	F1	37.315893 -91.411322
Elephant Rocks S.P.	108	A1	37.652150 -90.690810
Finger Lakes S.P.	97	E2	39.075400 -92.314750
Graham Cave S.P.	97	F3	38.908850 -91.576090
Grand Gulf S.P.	107	F3	36.544100 -91.636370
Ha Ha Tonka S.P.	97	D4	37.975410 -92.762230
Harry S. Truman S.P.	97	D4	38.274650 -93.442390
Hawn S.P.	108	B1	37.833660 -90.241610
Johnson's Shut-Ins S.P.	108	A1	37.547920 -90.853020
Katy Trail S.P.	97	E3	38.975190 -92.750160
Knob Noster S.P.	96	C3	38.753020 -93.577440
Lake of the Ozarks S.P.	97	E4	38.133990 -92.564260
Lake Wappapello S.P.	108	A2	36.942210 -90.344400
Lewis & Clark S.P.	96	B1	39.538900 -95.052900
Long Branch S.P.	97	E1	39.767610 -92.526480
Mark Twain S.P.	97	E2	39.485270 -91.795340
Meramec S.P.	97	F4	38.215350 -91.123070
Montauk S.P.	107	F1	37.454710 -91.690970
Morris S.P.	108	B3	36.554166 -90.043220
Onondaga Cave S.P.	97	F4	38.064310 -91.230140
Pershing S.P.	97	D1	39.776270 -93.211130
Pomme de Terre S.P.	107	D1	37.874380 -93.318700
Roaring River S.P.	106	C3	36.590110 -93.834420
Robertsville S.P.	98	A3	38.429120 -90.818110
Rock Bridge Mem. S.P.	97	E3	38.883350 -92.331890
Saint Francois S.P.	98	A4	37.972900 -90.536210
Saint Joe S.P.	108	A1	37.824990 -90.537480
Sam A. Baker S.P.	108	A2	37.254530 -90.505080
Stockton S.P.	106	C1	37.622470 -93.753070
Table Rock S.P.	107	D3	36.583440 -93.309150
Taum Sauk Mtn. S.P.	108	A1	37.669500 -90.673400
Thousand Hills S.P.	87	D4	40.185160 -92.643070
Trail of Tears S.P.	108	B1	37.452880 -89.490760
Van Meter S.P.	97	D2	39.262590 -93.267210
Wakonda S.P.	97	F1	40.004250 -91.526060
Wallace S.P.	96	C1	39.660760 -94.213290
Washington S.P.	98	A4	38.085600 -90.685650
Watkins Mill S.P.	96	C2	39.393920 -94.265130
Weston Bend S.P.	96	B2	39.392960 -94.863430

MONTANA

MONTANA	PAGE	GRID	LATITUDE LONGITUDE
National Park & Rec. Areas			
Bighorn Canyon N.R.A.	24	C2	45.330090 -107.871650
Fort Benton Natl. Hist. Landmark	16	A2	47.823210 -110.661910
Glacier Natl. Park-Many Glacier Ent.	15	D1	48.827150 -113.551540
Glacier Natl. Park-St Mary Ent.	15	D1	48.747120 -113.439650
Glacier Natl. Park-Two Medicine Ent.	15	D1	48.494210 -113.262250
Glacier Natl. Park-West Ent.	15	D1	48.499890 -113.987190
Grant-Kohrs Ranch N.H.S.	15	E4	46.398900 -112.736680
Little Bighorn Bfld. Natl. Mon.	24	C1	45.570080 -107.434710
Natl. Bison Range	15	D3	47.371674 -114.262066
Rattlesnake N.R.A.	15	D4	47.040775 -113.933333
State Park & Rec. Areas			
Ackley Lake S.P.	16	B4	46.947220 -109.936110
Anaconda Smoke Stack S.P.	23	D1	46.111037 -112.969599
Bannack S.P.	23	D2	45.159170 -112.997780
Beaverhead Rock S.P.	23	E2	45.383330 -112.458330
Beavertail Hill S.P.	15	D4	46.721660 -113.576420
Big Arm S.P.	15	D3	47.815360 -114.307930
Black Sandy S.P.	15	E4	46.756940 -111.888890
Chief Plenty Coups S.P.	24	B2	45.429700 -108.532500
Clark's Lookout S.P.	23	E2	45.236110 -112.630560
Cooney S.P.	24	B2	45.435050 -109.225330
Council Grove S.P.	15	D4	46.912500 -114.150000
Finley Point S.P.	15	D3	47.763830 -114.078723
First Peoples Buffalo Jump S.P.	16	A3	47.494887 -111.525201
Fish Creek S.P.	14	C4	46.990214 -114.715914
Fort Owen S.P.	15	D4	46.519440 -114.095830
Frenchtown Pond S.P.	15	D3	47.039530 -114.259220
Granite Ghost Town S.P.	23	D1	46.319000 -113.257000
Greycliff Prairie Dog Town S.P.	24	B1	45.767600 -109.794180
Hell Creek S.P.	17	D3	47.620290 -106.884510
Lake Elmo S.P.	24	C1	45.845280 -108.481310
Lake Mary Ronan S.P.	15	D2	48.204020 -114.330340
Lewis & Clark Caverns S.P.	23	E1	45.821840 -111.848510
Logan S.P.	14	C2	48.204020 -114.330340
Lone Pine S.P.	15	D2	48.175580 -114.339560
Lost Creek S.P.	23	D1	46.203020 -112.993810
Madison Buffalo Jump S.P.	23	F1	45.665140 -111.062770
Makoshika S.P.	17	F4	47.090240 -104.709970
Medicine Rocks S.P.	25	F1	46.046460 -104.456740
Missouri Headwaters S.P.	23	F1	45.909129 -111.497411
Painted Rocks S.P.	22	C1	45.706650 -114.282530
Pictograph Cave S.P.	24	C1	45.737500 -108.430830
Pirogue Island S.P.	17	E4	46.440560 -105.816670
Placid Lake S.P.	15	D3	47.138040 -113.524960
Rosebud Bfld. S.P.	25	D2	45.208270 -106.944460
Salmon Lake S.P.	15	D4	47.042270 -113.390390
Sluice Boxes S.P.	16	A3	47.211400 -110.939660
Smith River S.P.	16	A4	46.721219 -111.173819
Spring Meadow Lake S.P.	15	E4	46.612220 -112.075000
Thompson Falls S.P.	14	C3	47.618060 -115.387500
Tongue River Reservoir S.P.	25	D2	45.093520 -106.804670
Tower Rock S.P.	15	E3	47.181000 -111.816000
Travelers' Rest S.P.	15	D4	46.751000 -114.089000
Wayfarers S.P.	15	D2	48.057400 -114.079550
West Shore S.P.	15	D2	47.948780 -114.189160
Whitefish Lake S.P.	15	D2	48.204020 -114.330340
Wild Horse Island S.P.	15	D3	47.844640 -114.279970
Yellow Bay S.P.	15	D2	47.874500 -114.027080

NEBRASKA

NEBRASKA	PAGE	GRID	LATITUDE LONGITUDE
National Park & Rec. Areas			
Agate Fossil Beds Natl. Mon.	33	F2	42.423860 -103.791120
Chimney Rock N.H.S.	33	F3	41.719650 -103.336070
Pine Ridge N.R.A.	33	F1	42.625880 -103.205570
Scotts Bluff Natl. Mon.	33	F2	41.832380 -103.717550
State Park & Rec. Areas			
Chadron S.P.	34	A1	42.711540 -103.008500
Eugene T. Mahoney S.P.	35	F3	41.026387 -96.314180
Fort Robinson S.P.	33	F1	42.654050 -103.492100
Indian Cave S.P.	86	A4	40.263280 -95.586630
Niobrara S.P.	35	E1	42.747450 -98.051850
Platte River S.P.	35	F3	40.986840 -96.219290
Ponca S.P.	35	F1	42.600360 -96.714940
Smith Falls S.P.	34	C1	42.891670 -100.316670

NEVADA

NEVADA	PAGE	GRID	LATITUDE LONGITUDE
National Park & Rec. Areas			
Basin & Range Natl. Mon.	38	B3	37.931620 -115.350935
Devils Hole (Death Valley Natl. Park)	45	F3	36.423889 -116.305833
Gold Butte Natl. Mon.	46	B1	36.390553 -114.170000
Great Basin Natl. Park-Vis. Ctr.	38	C2	39.005600 -114.220000
Lake Mead N.R.A.-North Ent.	46	B2	36.161180 -114.905200
Lake Mead N.R.A.-South Ent.	46	B2	36.021230 -114.796340
Lake Mead N.R.A.-West Ent.	46	B2	36.105980 -114.900940
Spring Mts. N.R.A.	46	A1	36.245200 -115.233910
Tule Springs Fossil Beds Natl. Mon.	46	A1	36.324457 -115.293643
State Park & Rec. Areas			
Berlin-Ichthyosaur S.H.P.	37	F2	38.880300 -117.607930
Big Bend of the Colorado State Rec. Area	53	F1	35.116730 -114.640820

	PAGE	GRID	LATITUDE LONGITUDE
Cathedral Gorge S.P.	38	C4	37.820280 -114.407890
Dayton S.P.-North Ent.	37	D2	39.253540 -119.587190
Echo Canyon S.P.	38	C4	38.195000 -114.512900
Kershaw-Ryan S.P.	38	C4	37.586380 -114.533260
Lake Tahoe-Nevada S.P.	37	D2	39.213670 -119.928300
Spring Mtn. Ranch S.P.	46	A2	36.073830 -115.443710
Spring Valley S.P.	38	C3	38.003920 -114.207570
Valley of Fire S.P.	46	B1	36.429710 -114.513590
Wild Horse State Rec. Area	30	B3	41.670739 -115.799805

NEW HAMPSHIRE	PAGE	GRID	LATITUDE LONGITUDE
National Park & Rec. Areas			
Saint-Gaudens N.H.S.	81	E4	43.501570 -72.362510
State Park & Rec. Areas			
Bear Brook S.P.	81	F4	43.133800 -71.366040
Cardigan S.P.	81	E3	43.647990 -71.949570
Crawford Notch S.P.	81	F2	44.181760 -71.398780
Echo Lake S.P.	81	F3	44.067430 -71.166000
Forest Lake S.P.	81	F2	44.354490 -71.673180
Hampton Beach S.P.	95	E1	42.898333 -70.812778
Kingston S.P.	95	E1	42.929020 -71.054680
Lake Tarleton S.P.	81	E3	43.975833 -71.963333
Miller S.P.	95	D1	42.861630 -71.878750
Monadnock S.P.	95	D1	42.845440 -72.086590
Mount Sunapee S.P.	81	E4	43.332120 -72.079800
Pawtuckaway S.P.	81	F4	43.082150 -71.152130
Pillsbury S.P.	81	E4	43.236860 -72.122830
Pisgah S.P.	94	C1	42.810310 -72.408340
Umbagog Lake S.P.	81	F1	44.712990 -71.072700
Wellington S.P.	81	F3	43.641280 -71.782980
Wentworth S.P.	81	F3	43.603056 -71.136389
White Lake S.P.	81	F3	43.830880 -71.218220
Winslow S.P.	81	E4	43.391730 -71.869540

NEW JERSEY	PAGE	GRID	LATITUDE LONGITUDE
National Park & Rec. Areas			
Delaware Water Gap N.R.A.	94	A4	40.970390 -75.128100
Gateway N.R.A.	147	F1	40.396420 -73.981160
Morristown N.H.P.	148	A4	40.744670 -74.565290
Thomas Edison N.H.P.	148	A4	40.787188 -74.256497
State Park & Rec. Areas			
Allaire S.P.	147	E2	40.153470 -74.111390
Allamuchy Mtn. S.P.	104	C1	40.921244 -74.782222
Barnegat Lighthouse S.P.	147	E4	39.762750 -74.107950
Cape May Point S.P.	104	C4	38.932950 -74.961010
Corson's Inlet S.P.	105	D4	39.216340 -74.647070
Delaware & Raritan Canal S.P.	147	D1	40.473230 -74.571100
Double Trouble S.P.	147	E3	39.900550 -74.225120
Farny S.P.	148	A3	40.997170 -74.459060
Fortescue State Marina	145	F2	39.243178 -75.176636
Fort Mott S.P.	146	B4	39.612100 -75.543430
Hacklebarney S.P.	105	D1	40.751170 -74.736590
High Point S.P.	148	A2	41.304800 -74.669650
Hopatcong S.P.	148	A3	40.911780 -74.667000
Island Beach S.P.	147	E3	39.905240 -74.081510
Liberty S.P.	148	B4	40.697330 -74.063870
Long Pond Ironworks S.P.	148	A2	41.140986 -74.309228
Monmouth Bfld. S.P.	147	E2	40.269340 -74.302800
Parvin S.P.	146	C4	39.524490 -75.160460
Pigeon Swamp S.P.	147	E1	40.394420 -74.487150
Princeton Bfld. S.P.	147	D2	40.332490 -74.675650
Rancocas S.P.	147	D3	39.990420 -74.837480
Ringwood S.P.	148	A2	41.127600 -74.260130
Swartswood S.P.	94	A4	41.081680 -74.813620
Voorhees S.P.	104	C1	40.695060 -74.887030
Washington Crossing S.P.	147	D2	40.296920 -74.866420
Washington Rock S.P.	148	A4	40.613580 -74.472860
Wawayanda S.P.	148	A2	41.199240 -74.392440

NEW MEXICO	PAGE	GRID	LATITUDE LONGITUDE
National Park & Rec. Areas			
Aztec Ruins Natl. Mon.	48	B1	36.833920 -108.000570
Bandelier Natl. Mon.	48	C2	35.780130 -106.264830
Capulin Mtn. Natl. Mon.	49	E1	36.781990 -103.986110
Carlsbad Caverns Natl. Park-Vis. Ctr.	57	E3	32.175400 -104.444000
Chaco Culture N.H.P.	48	B2	36.016190 -107.924060
Datil Well N.R.A.	48	B4	34.154130 -107.852610
El Malpais Natl. Cons. Area	48	B4	35.059720 -107.876400
El Morro Natl. Mon.	48	B3	35.043480 -108.346250
Fort Union Natl. Mon.	49	D2	35.904230 -105.010740
Gila Cliff Dwellings Natl. Mon.	56	A2	33.229540 -108.264630
Kasha-Katuwe Tent Rocks Natl. Mon.	48	C2	35.663200 -106.410800
Manhattan Project N.H.P.	48	C2	35.882455 -106.304212
Pecos N.H.P.	49	D3	35.578750 -105.762400
Petroglyph Natl. Mon.	48	C3	35.139490 -106.709670
Río Grande Del Norte Natl. Mon.	49	D1	36.640260 -105.877033
Salinas Pueblo Missions Natl. Mon.	48	C4	34.520370 -106.241250
Salinas Pueblo Missions Natl. Mon.-Gran Quivira	49	D4	34.260000 -106.091000
White Sands Natl. Mon.	56	C2	32.820130 -106.272980
State Park & Rec. Areas			
Bluewater Lake S.P.	48	B3	35.302730 -108.106930
Bottomless Lakes S.P.	57	E2	33.316630 -104.332880
Brantley Lake S.P.	57	E3	32.571390 -104.366210
Caballo Lake S.P.	56	B2	32.911370 -107.313580
Cerrillos Hills S.P.	49	D3	35.446413 -106.098498
Cimarron Canyon S.P.	49	D1	36.537600 -105.221130
City of Rocks S.P.	56	A2	32.594860 -107.973850
Clayton Lake S.P.	49	F1	36.573070 -103.300690
Conchas Lake S.P.	49	E3	35.394760 -104.181790
Coronado S.P.	48	C3	35.329130 -106.557870
Coyote Creek S.P.	49	D2	36.188020 -105.233260
Eagle Nest S.P.	49	D1	36.542100 -105.261300
Elephant Butte Res. S.P.-South Ent.	56	B1	33.176180 -107.207460
El Vado Lake S.P.	48	C1	36.593710 -106.735790
Fenton Lake S.P.	48	C2	35.887230 -106.723170
Heron Lake S.P.	48	C1	36.693840 -106.654230
Hyde Mem. S.P.	49	D2	35.737890 -105.836540
Leasburg Dam S.P.	56	B3	32.492680 -106.922380
Living Desert Zoo & Gardens S.P.	57	E3	32.449839 -104.286341
Manzano Mtn. S.P.	48	C4	34.603880 -106.360960
Morphy Lake S.P.	49	D2	35.968660 -105.366600
Navajo Lake S.P.	48	B1	36.831950 -107.586950
Oasis S.P.	49	F4	34.259740 -103.334280
Oliver Lee Mem. S.P.	56	C2	32.744640 -105.934520
Pancho Villa S.P.	56	B4	31.828050 -107.641200
Percha Dam S.P.	56	B2	32.873610 -107.308100
Rockhound S.P.	56	B3	32.185550 -107.613090
Santa Rosa Lake S.P.	49	E3	34.987930 -104.658750
Smokey Bear Hist. S.P.	57	D1	33.545620 -105.573170
Storrie Lake S.P.	49	D2	35.655720 -105.231840
Sugarite Canyon S.P.	49	E1	36.944191 -104.381651
Sumner Lake S.P.	49	E4	34.607520 -104.389050
Ute Lake S.P.	49	F3	35.340630 -103.442500
Villanueva S.P.	49	D3	35.259530 -105.368970

NEW YORK	PAGE	GRID	LATITUDE LONGITUDE
National Park & Rec. Areas			
Eleanor Roosevelt N.H.S.	94	B3	41.763170 -73.902960
Fire Island Natl. Seashore	149	D4	40.735320 -72.866620
Fort Stanwix Natl. Mon.	79	E3	43.211930 -75.454740
Gateway N.R.A.	148	B4	40.581100 -73.887790
Home of F.D.R. N.H.S.	94	B3	41.767038 -73.938193
Sagamore Hill N.H.S.	148	C3	40.882480 -73.505550
Saratoga N.H.P.	81	D4	43.002690 -73.612110
Statue of Liberty Natl. Mon.	148	B4	40.689547 -74.044029
Thomas Cole N.H.S.	94	B2	42.225900 -73.861600
Van Buren N.H.S.	94	B2	42.370610 -73.701010
Vanderbilt Mansion N.H.S.	94	B3	41.796482 -73.942359
Women's Rights N.H.P.	79	D3	42.910580 -76.800260
State Park & Rec. Areas			
Adirondack Park	80	C2	43.455590 -73.695930
Allegany S.P.	92	B1	42.106480 -78.765940
Battle Island S.P.	79	D3	43.362780 -76.442150
Bear Mtn. S.P.	148	B2	41.278350 -73.970290
Beaver Island S.P.	78	A3	42.968170 -78.969560
Bowman Lake S.P.	79	E4	42.516970 -75.670400
Buttermilk Falls S.P.	79	D4	42.347410 -76.489130
Caleb Smith S.P. Pres.	149	D3	40.854190 -73.221190
Canandaigua Lake State Marine Park	78	C3	42.875964 -77.275600
Captree S.P.	149	D4	40.636640 -73.263210
Catskill Park	94	A2	42.050290 -74.288840
Cedar Point S.P.	79	D1	44.200670 -76.191000
Chenango Valley S.P.	93	E1	42.215040 -75.818020
Chittenango Falls S.P.	79	E3	42.981520 -75.845030
Clarence Fahnestock S.P.	148	B1	41.423620 -73.799560
Cold Spring Harbor S.P.	148	C3	40.867450 -73.461900
Connetquot River S.P. Pres.	149	D4	40.748070 -73.153510
Cumberland Bay S.P.	81	D1	44.725090 -73.421450
Darien Lakes S.P.	78	B3	42.908460 -78.433300
Delta Lake S.P.	79	E3	43.290030 -75.414910
Evangola S.P.	78	A4	42.604460 -79.105610
Fair Haven Beach S.P.	79	D3	43.320570 -76.696210
Fort Niagara S.P.	78	A3	43.261790 -79.061460
Four Mile Creek S.P.	78	A3	43.272530 -78.996270
Franny Reese S.P.	148	B1	41.704118 -73.956553
Gilbert Lake S.P.	79	F4	42.572720 -75.128170
Golden Hill S.P.	78	B2	43.365250 -78.489310
Goosepond Mtn. S.P.	148	A2	41.354460 -74.254470
Gov. Alfred E. Smith/Sunken Meadow S.P.	149	D3	40.911970 -73.262940
Green Lakes S.P.	79	E3	43.060000 -75.969030
Hamlin Beach S.P.	78	C2	43.361130 -77.944460
Harriman S.P.	148	B2	41.293010 -74.026560
Heckscher S.P.	149	D4	40.712860 -73.168480
Highland Lakes S.P.	148	A1	41.489806 -74.325085
Hither Hills S.P.	149	F3	41.007700 -72.014500
Hudson Highlands S.P.	148	B2	41.428060 -73.966740
Hudson River Islands S.P.	94	B2	42.318574 -73.778343
James Baird S.P.	148	B1	41.689100 -73.799390
Jones Beach S.P.	148	C4	40.595000 -73.521070
Keewaydin S.P.	79	E1	44.322390 -75.925740
Keuka Lake S.P.	78	C4	42.594280 -77.130360
Lake Erie S.P.	78	A4	42.419070 -79.434430
Lakeside Beach S.P.	78	B2	43.367090 -78.236040
Lake Superior S.P.	94	A3	41.658590 -74.869280
Letchworth S.P.	78	B4	42.693530 -77.961210
Lodi Point S.P.	79	D4	42.619210 -76.863980
Long Point S.P.	79	D1	44.026130 -76.219650
Mark Twain S.P.	93	D1	42.205200 -76.823799
Mary Island S.P.	79	E1	44.350460 -75.930400
Max V. Shaul S.P.	79	F4	42.546790 -74.410370
Minnewaska S.P. Pres.	148	A1	41.745910 -74.268370
Montauk Point S.P.	149	F3	41.065020 -71.886700
Moreau Lake S.P.	80	C4	43.226370 -73.707710
Oquaga Creek S.P.	93	F1	42.172320 -75.442840
Orient Beach S.P.	149	F2	41.154580 -72.245600
Pixley Falls S.P.	79	E2	43.401100 -75.345960
Point Au Roche S.P.	81	D1	44.779990 -73.411090
Robert Moses S.P.	148	C4	40.624930 -73.261900
Saratoga Spa S.P.	80	C4	43.056950 -73.801490
Selkirk Shores S.P.	79	D2	43.544300 -76.191510
Seneca Lake S.P.	79	D3	42.873410 -76.960940
Southwick Beach S.P.	79	D2	43.767270 -76.196230
Sterling Forest S.P.	148	A2	41.220200 -74.187210
Storm King S.P.	148	B2	41.432560 -73.987020
Taconic S.P.	94	B2	42.007680 -73.508400
Tallman Mtn. S.P.	148	B3	41.037270 -73.915920
Verona Beach S.P.	79	E3	43.179070 -75.725090
Waterson Point S.P.	79	E1	44.339030 -76.010580
Watkins Glen S.P.	79	D4	42.375896 -76.871078
Wellesley Island S.P.	79	E1	44.315970 -76.019480
Whetstone Gulf S.P.	79	E2	43.702310 -75.459120
Wildwood S.P.	149	D3	40.954230 -72.788470
Wilson-Tuscarora S.P.	78	B3	43.307080 -78.854500

NORTH CAROLINA	PAGE	GRID	LATITUDE LONGITUDE
National Park & Rec. Areas			
Cape Hatteras Natl. Seashore	115	F3	35.766700 -75.526640
Cape Lookout Natl. Seashore	115	E4	34.886110 -76.331220
Carl Sandburg Home N.H.S.	121	E1	35.270000 -82.450000
Fort Raleigh N.H.S.	115	F2	35.932360 -75.708500
Great Smoky Mts. Natl. Park-Cades Cove Vis. Ctr.	121	D1	35.585300 -83.842900
Great Smoky Mts. Natl. Park-Oconaluftee Vis. Ctr.	121	D1	35.515300 -83.305300
Great Smoky Mts. Natl. Park-Sugarlands Vis. Ctr.	121	D1	35.685600 -83.536700
State Park & Rec. Areas			
Carolina Beach S.P.	123	E3	34.045240 -77.903430
Cliffs of the Neuse S.P.	123	E1	35.232900 -77.898390
Crowders Mtn. S.P.	122	A1	35.212350 -81.292920
Dismal Swamp S.P.	113	F3	36.517470 -76.360720
Fort Macon S.P.	115	E4	34.697750 -76.699580
Goose Creek S.P.	123	F1	35.483140 -76.902290
Gorges S.P.	121	E1	35.108400 -82.943900
Hammocks Beach S.P.	123	F2	34.671810 -77.138720
Hanging Rock S.P.	112	B3	36.413030 -80.253950
Haw River S.P.	112	B3	36.249719 -79.755971
Jockey's Ridge S.P.	115	F2	35.961820 -75.626970
Jones Lake S.P.	123	D2	34.698900 -78.624990
Lake James S.P.	111	F4	35.728064 -81.901980
Lake Norman S.P.	112	A4	35.665780 -80.938410
Lake Waccamaw S.P.	123	D3	34.272650 -78.466040
Lumber River S.P.	123	D3	34.390831 -79.004145
Medoc Mtn. S.P.	113	D3	36.280410 -77.877820
Merchants Millpond S.P.	113	F3	36.450601 -76.692978
Morrow Mtn. S.P.	122	B1	35.370390 -80.102410
Mount Mitchell S.P.	111	E4	35.814600 -82.146100
Pettigrew S.P.	113	F4	35.789580 -76.406980
Pilot Mtn. S.P.	112	A3	36.345530 -80.478390
Raven Rock S.P.	123	D1	35.461520 -78.912660
Singletary Lake S.P.	123	D2	34.581570 -78.452070
South Mts. S.P.	121	F1	35.601190 -81.626700
Stone Mtn. S.P.	112	A3	36.374390 -81.018010

NORTH DAKOTA	PAGE	GRID	LATITUDE LONGITUDE
National Park & Rec. Areas			
Fort Union N.H.S.	17	F2	48.002390 -104.043560
Knife River N.H.S.	18	B3	47.336680 -101.387450
Theodore Roosevelt Natl. Park-Elkhorn Site	17	F3	47.226950 -103.622310
Theodore Roosevelt Natl. Park-North Unit	18	A3	47.600300 -103.261000
Theodore Roosevelt Natl. Park-South Unit	18	A4	46.915500 -103.527000
State Park & Rec. Areas			
Beaver Lake S.P.	18	C4	46.401260 -99.615860
Cross Ranch S.P.	18	B3	47.213530 -101.000180
Doyle Mem. S.P.	27	D1	46.204880 -99.482150
Fort Abercrombie S.P.	19	F4	46.444530 -96.718800
Fort Lincoln S.P.	18	B4	46.769420 -100.847860
Fort Ransom S.P.	19	E4	46.544100 -97.925570
Fort Stevenson S.P.	18	B3	47.596890 -101.420530
Grahams Island S.P.	19	D2	48.052500 -99.068300
Icelandic S.P.	19	E1	48.772620 -97.736990
Lake Metigoshe S.P.	18	C1	48.980640 -100.326710
Lake Sakakawea S.P.	18	B3	47.511020 -101.449350
Lewis & Clark S.P.	18	A2	48.115350 -103.241490
Little Missouri Bay S.P.	18	A3	47.550030 -102.738240
Pembina S.P.	19	E1	48.964720 -97.240500

	PAGE	GRID	LATITUDE LONGITUDE
Turtle River S.P.	19	E2	47.931660 -97.505390
Whitestone Bfld. S.P.	27	D1	46.169190 -98.857330

OHIO	PAGE	GRID	LATITUDE LONGITUDE
National Park & Rec. Areas			
Charles Young Buffalo Soldiers Natl. Mon.	100	C1	39.689722,-83.891111
Cuyahoga Valley Natl. Park-Canal Vis. Ctr.	91	E2	41.372600 -81.613700
Cuyahoga Valley Natl. Park-Hunt Farm Vis. Info. Ctr.	91	E2	41.200900 -81.573100
Hopewell Culture N.H.P.	101	D2	39.298360 -82.917810
James A. Garfield N.H.S.	91	E2	41.663600 -81.351260
State Park & Rec. Areas			
A.W. Marion S.P.	101	D1	39.633730 -82.885720
Adams Lake S.P.	100	C3	38.812900 -83.519400
Alum Creek S.P.	90	C4	40.226870 -82.981320
Barkcamp S.P.	101	F1	40.047030 -81.031710
Beaver Creek S.P.	91	F3	40.726220 -80.613590
Blue Rock S.P.	101	E1	39.832780 -81.858370
Buck Creek S.P.	100	C1	39.946410 -83.729550
Buckeye Lake S.P.	101	D1	39.906540 -82.526270
Burr Oak S.P.	101	E1	39.527740 -82.023260
Caesar Creek S.P.	100	C1	39.515730 -84.041070
Catawba Island S.P.	91	D2	41.573530 -82.855780
Cowan Lake S.P.	100	C2	39.387600 -83.882970
Crane Creek S.P.	90	C2	41.603770 -83.192910
Deer Creek S.P.	101	D1	39.649260 -83.246340
Delaware S.P.	90	C4	40.377690 -83.071590
Dillon S.P.	101	E1	40.023600 -82.111910
East Fork S.P.	100	C2	39.002050 -84.151210
East Harbor S.P.	91	D2	41.540930 -82.820830
Findley S.P.	91	D3	41.122990 -82.219390
Forked Run S.P.	101	E2	39.085000 -81.770460
Geneva S.P.	91	F1	41.852760 -80.963280
Grand Lake Saint Marys S.P.	90	B4	40.549240 -84.436500
Guilford Lake S.P.	91	F3	40.796100 -80.893760
Harrison Lake S.P.	90	B2	41.637190 -84.361760
Headlands Beach S.P.	91	E1	41.752140 -81.294480
Hocking Hills S.P.	101	D2	39.494180 -82.611910
Hueston Woods S.P.	100	B1	39.573820 -84.715380
Independence Dam S.P.	90	B2	41.282470 -84.313500
Indian Lake S.P.	90	B4	40.510360 -83.842980
Jackson Lake S.P.	101	D3	38.902850 -82.596780
Jefferson Lake S.P.	91	F4	40.472050 -80.808930
John Bryan S.P.	100	C1	39.791020 -83.867790
Kelleys Island S.P.	91	D2	41.614080 -82.712110
Kiser Lake S.P.	90	B4	40.197650 -83.981740
Lake Alma S.P.	101	D2	39.153450 -82.516810
Lake Hope S.P.	101	E2	39.318500 -82.354920
Lake Logan S.P.	101	D1	39.536400 -82.460590
Lake Loramie S.P.	90	B4	40.359750 -84.359730
Lake White S.P.	101	D2	39.109160 -83.040330
Madison Lake S.P.	100	C1	39.866250 -83.374930
Malabar Farm S.P.	91	D3	40.649590 -82.398390
Mary Jane Thurston S.P.	90	B2	41.409630 -83.881320
Maumee Bay S.P.	90	C2	41.678020 -83.353360
Mohican S.P.	91	D4	40.609510 -82.257600
Mosquito Lake S.P.	91	F2	41.301940 -80.767990
Mount Gilead S.P.	91	D4	40.547820 -82.816770
Muskingum River S.P.	101	E1	40.044140 -81.978260
Nelson-Kennedy Ledges S.P.	91	F2	41.330090 -81.040190
Paint Creek S.P.	100	C2	39.228360 -83.374450
Pike Lake S.P.	101	D2	39.158270 -83.220950
Portage Lakes S.P.	91	E3	40.966260 -81.565190
Punderson S.P.	91	E2	41.461540 -81.219590
Pymatuning S.P.	91	F2	41.580110 -80.541530
Quail Hollow S.P.	91	E3	40.970200 -81.325100
Rocky Fork S.P.	100	C2	39.188310 -83.529730
Salt Fork S.P.	91	E4	40.081830 -81.460400
Scioto Trail S.P.	101	D2	39.223620 -82.931210
Shawnee S.P.	101	D3	38.747670 -83.211220
South Bass Island S.P.	91	D2	41.644690 -82.835950
Stonelick S.P.	100	C2	39.226160 -84.057210
Strouds Run S.P.	101	E2	39.334320 -82.017690
Sycamore S.P.	100	B1	39.803410 -84.374370
Tar Hollow S.P.	101	D2	39.353790 -82.780200
Tinkers Creek S.P.	91	E2	41.276180 -81.368910
Van Buren S.P.	90	C3	41.138290 -83.644940
West Branch S.P.	91	E3	41.133310 -81.189660
Wolf Run S.P.	101	F1	39.789770 -81.540180

OKLAHOMA	PAGE	GRID	LATITUDE LONGITUDE
National Park & Rec. Areas			
Chickasaw N.R.A.	51	F4	34.497390 -96.970110
Winding Stair Mtn. N.R.A.	116	B2	34.749705 -94.793055
State Park & Rec. Areas			
Adair S.P.	106	B4	35.832230 -94.624100
Alabaster Caverns S.P.	51	D1	36.697490 -99.149430
Arrowhead S.P.	116	A1	35.168240 -95.639970
Beaver Dunes S.P.	50	B1	36.841129 -100.514988
Bernice S.P.	106	B3	36.626670 -94.901670
Black Mesa S.P.	49	F1	36.855620 -102.885680
Boggy Depot S.P.	51	F4	34.321747 -96.311302
Boiling Springs S.P.	51	D1	36.452950 -99.298900
Brushy Lake S.P.	116	B1	35.543680 -94.817676
Cherokee Landing S.P.	106	B4	35.758890 -94.908610
Cherokee S.P.	106	B3	36.480280 -95.050560
Clayton Lake S.P.	116	A2	34.549420 -95.308330
Dripping Springs S.P.	51	F3	35.611437 -96.068911
Fort Cobb S.P.	51	D3	35.203720 -98.464990
Foss S.P.	51	D3	35.578510 -99.186830
Gloss Mtn. S.P.	51	D2	36.367190 -98.576460
Great Plains S.P.	51	D4	34.730340 -98.985690
Great Salt Plains S.P.	51	E1	36.753170 -98.149930
Greenleaf S.P.	106	A4	35.623260 -95.180950
Hochatown S.P.	116	B3	34.197390 -94.766300
Honey Creek S.P.	106	B3	36.574060 -94.784370
Hugo Lake S.P.	116	A3	34.016384 -95.375061
Keystone S.P.	51	F2	36.137440 -96.264340
Lake Eucha S.P.	106	B3	36.353930 -94.824000
Lake Eufaula S.P.	116	A1	35.427900 -95.546100
Lake Murray S.P.	51	F4	34.154880 -97.120950
Lake Texoma S.P.	59	F1	33.997590 -96.651310
Lake Thunderbird S.P.	51	E3	35.232320 -97.247550
Lake Wister S.P.	116	B2	34.948700 -94.710400
Little Blue-Disney S.P.	106	B3	36.480260 -95.009130
Little Sahara S.P.	51	D1	36.532900 -98.882870
McGee Creek S.P.	116	A3	34.302927 -95.875467
Natural Falls S.P.	106	B4	36.151900 -94.673300
Okmulgee S.P.	51	F2	35.621900 -96.067700
Osage Hills S.P.	51	F1	36.757360 -96.176220
Raymond Gary S.P.	116	A3	33.997580 -95.253860
Red Rock Canyon S.P.	51	D3	35.456350 -98.358310
Sequoyah Bay S.P.	106	A4	35.886000 -95.276000
Sequoyah S.P.	106	A4	35.932960 -95.230650
Snowdale S.P.	106	A3	36.307710 -95.199040
Spavinaw S.P.	106	B3	36.385890 -95.053290
Talimena S.P.	116	B2	34.788290 -94.950690
Tenkiller S.P.	116	B1	35.598000 -95.031100
Twin Bridges S.P.	106	B2	36.804320 -94.757920
Wah-Sha-She S.P.	51	F1	36.926000 -96.091000
Walnut Creek S.P.	51	F2	36.251210 -96.280130

OREGON	PAGE	GRID	LATITUDE LONGITUDE
National Park & Rec. Areas			
Cascade-Siskiyou Natl. Mon.	28	C2	42.068300 -122.399940
Crater Lake Natl. Park-Annie Spring Ent. Sta.	28	C1	42.868700 -122.169000
Crater Lake Natl. Park-North Ent. Sta.	28	C1	43.086900 -122.116000
Hells Canyon N.R.A.-East Ent.	22	B1	45.500680 -116.806560
Hells Canyon N.R.A.-South Ent.	22	B1	44.903300 -116.957080
Hells Canyon N.R.A.-West Ent.	22	B1	45.176360 -117.040740
John Day Fossil Beds Natl. Mon.-Clarno Unit	21	D2	44.911250 -120.431780
John Day Fossil Beds Natl. Mon.-Painted Hills Unit	21	D3	44.661170 -120.254750
John Day Fossil Beds Natl. Mon.-Sheep Rock Unit	21	E3	44.555480 -119.645010
Lewis & Clark N.H.P.-Fort Clatsop	20	B1	46.138260 -123.876670
Lewis & Clark N.H.P.-Salt Works	20	B1	46.134551 -123.880420
Lewis & Clark N.H.P.-Sunset Beach	20	B1	46.099430 -123.936390
Newberry Natl. Volcanic Mon.	21	D4	43.716800 -121.376960
Oregon Caves Natl. Mon. & Pres.	28	B2	42.103910 -123.414300
Oregon Dunes N.R.A.-North Ent.	20	A4	43.885610 -124.120860
Oregon Dunes N.R.A.-South Ent.	20	A4	43.579470 -124.186490
State Park & Rec. Areas			
Ainsworth S.P.	20	C2	45.595720 -122.052980
Alfred A. Loeb S.P.	28	A2	42.113180 -124.188520
Beverly Beach S.P.	20	B3	44.726250 -124.057290
Bob Straub S.P.	20	B2	45.183160 -123.965116
Bullards Beach S.P.	28	A1	43.150990 -124.395480
Cape Arago S.P.	20	A4	43.326140 -124.381770
Cape Blanco S.P.	28	A1	42.826660 -124.524640
Cape Lookout S.P.	20	B2	45.367667 -123.961127
Carl G. Washburne Mem. S.P.	20	A3	44.141990 -124.117490
Cascadia S.P.	20	C3	44.397100 -122.477480
Catherine Creek S.P.	22	A2	45.148890 -117.733990
Collier Mem. S.P.	28	C1	42.641810 -121.880630
Ecola S.P.	20	B1	45.916550 -123.967430
Elijah Bristow S.P.	20	C4	43.935470 -122.844270
Fort Columbia S.P.	20	B1	46.252580 -123.921500
Fort Stevens S.P.	20	B1	46.183200 -123.959940
Harris Beach S.P.	28	A2	42.067930 -124.305860
Hat Rock S.P.	21	E1	45.908260 -119.164510
Hilgard Junction S.P.	21	F2	45.342060 -118.236470
Humbug Mtn. S.P.	28	A1	42.686870 -124.445970
Illinois River Forks S.P.	28	B2	42.154870 -123.649870
Jessie M. Honeyman Mem. S.P.	20	A4	43.933440 -124.106440
L.L. Stub Stewart S.P.	20	B1	45.739050 -123.199461
Lake Owyhee S.P.	22	A4	43.638380 -117.229090
Lapine S.P.	21	D4	43.768452 -121.513399
Maryhill S.P.	21	D1	45.683060 -120.825830
Mayer S.P.	21	D1	45.682780 -121.301080
Milo Mciver S.P.	20	C2	45.306110 -122.372220
Molalla River S.P.	20	C2	45.294840 -122.696400
Nehalem Bay S.P.	20	B1	45.710000 -123.931470
Ona Beach S.P.	20	B3	44.518060 -124.075960
Oswald West S.P.	20	B1	45.770000 -123.958610
Port Orford Heads S.P.	28	A1	42.739470 -124.509730
Prineville Reservoir S.P.	21	D3	44.144660 -120.737770
Rooster Rock S.P.	20	C2	45.546320 -122.236500
Shore Acres S.P.	20	A4	43.329940 -124.376510
Silver Falls S.P.	20	C2	44.853752 -122.662258
Smith Rock S.P.	21	D3	44.360540 -121.138400
South Beach S.P.	20	B3	44.598450 -124.059350
Starvation Creek S.P.	20	C1	45.688550 -121.690180
Sunset Bay S.P.	20	A4	43.339010 -124.353990
The Cove Palisades S.P.	21	D3	44.557460 -121.262110
Tumalo S.P.	21	D3	44.086760 -121.308730
Umpqua Lighthouse S.P.	20	A4	43.669610 -124.182830
Valley of the Rogue S.P.	28	B1	42.410770 -123.129310
Viento S.P.	20	C1	45.697240 -121.668310
Wallowa Lake S.P.	22	A2	45.280690 -117.208230
White River Falls S.P.	21	D2	45.166870 -121.087420
Willamette Mission S.P.	20	B2	45.080740 -123.031510
William M. Tugman S.P.	20	A4	43.623640 -124.181910

PENNSYLVANIA	PAGE	GRID	LATITUDE LONGITUDE
National Park & Rec. Areas			
Allegheny N.R.A	92	B1	41.943055 -78.867025
Allegheny Portage Railroad N.H.S.	92	B4	40.377020 -78.835870
Eisenhower N.H.S.	103	E1	39.818000 -77.232610
Flight 93 Natl. Mem.	92	B4	40.055200 -78.900900
Fort Necessity Natl. Bfld.	102	B1	39.816340 -79.584310
Friendship Hill N.H.S.	102	B1	39.777778 -79.929167
Gettysburg N.M.P.	103	E1	39.811600 -77.226100
Grey Towers N.H.S.	94	A3	41.325224 -74.871113
Hopewell Furnace N.H.S.	146	B2	40.206760 -75.773570
Johnstown Flood Natl. Mem.	92	B4	40.350710 -78.772480
Valley Forge N.H.P.	146	C2	40.102240 -75.422960
State Park & Rec. Areas			
Bald Eagle S.P.	92	C3	41.041960 -77.642780
Big Spring S.P.	92	C4	40.266850 -77.654410
Black Moshannon S.P.	92	C3	40.915190 -78.058570
Blue Knob S.P.	92	B4	40.265800 -78.584480
Buchanan's Birthplace S.P.	103	D1	39.872660 -77.953190
Caledonia S.P.	103	D1	39.905610 -77.478880
Chapman S.P.	92	B1	41.757850 -79.170350
Cherry Springs S.P.	92	C2	41.662778 -77.823056
Codorus S.P.	103	E1	39.783180 -76.908920
Colonel Denning S.P.	93	D4	40.281820 -77.416630
Colton Point S.P.	93	D2	41.711180 -77.465430
Cook Forest S.P.	92	B2	41.333790 -79.210440
Cowans Gap S.P.	103	D1	39.997980 -77.921530
Delaware Canal S.P.	146	C1	40.545565 -75.087831
Elk S.P.	92	B2	41.606100 -78.564780
Erie Bluffs S.P.	91	F1	42.008333 -80.410833
Evansburg S.P.	146	C2	40.197510 -75.407080
Frances Slocum S.P.	93	E2	41.347380 -75.893760
French Creek S.P.	146	B2	40.236580 -75.795660
Gouldsboro S.P.	93	F2	41.232250 -75.495730
Greenwood Furnace S.P.	92	C3	40.649610 -77.756090
Hickory Run S.P.	93	F3	41.035170 -75.736220
Hills Creek S.P.	93	D1	41.805190 -77.187600
Hyner Run S.P.	92	C2	41.359150 -77.623850
Kettle Creek S.P.	92	C2	41.377120 -77.930130
Keystone S.P.	92	A4	40.374250 -79.377830
Lackawanna S.P.	93	F2	41.575030 -75.711520
Laurel Hill S.P.	102	B1	39.984470 -79.234840
Laurel Mtn. S.P.	92	B4	40.179670 -79.131530
Laurel Ridge S.P.	92	B4	39.958400 -79.360160
Lehigh Gorge S.P.	93	F3	40.971900 -75.761840
Leonard Harrison S.P.	93	D2	41.698420 -77.450810
Little Buffalo S.P.	93	D4	40.454420 -77.169170
Little Pine S.P.	93	D2	41.371240 -77.360310
Lyman Run S.P.	92	C1	41.723650 -77.768470
Marsh Creek S.P.	146	B3	40.069360 -75.717320
Maurice K. Goddard S.P.	92	A2	41.428380 -80.145140
McConnells Mill S.P.	92	A3	40.963530 -80.168810
Memorial Lake S.P.	93	E4	40.424760 -76.590540
Mont Alto S.P.	103	D1	39.839130 -77.540630
Moraine S.P.	92	A3	40.940280 -80.098520
Nescopeck S.P.	93	E3	41.067100 -75.925300
Nockamixon S.P.	146	C1	40.463630 -75.242010
Ohiopyle S.P.	102	B1	39.865030 -79.504310
Oil Creek S.P.-East Ent.	92	A2	41.512130 -79.661810
Ole Bull S.P.	92	C2	41.543590 -77.709430
Parker Dam S.P.	92	C2	41.205140 -78.504310
Penn-Roosevelt S.P.	92	C3	40.726389 -77.702500
Pine Grove Furnace S.P.	103	D1	40.032910 -77.305070
Poe Paddy S.P.	93	D3	40.834150 -77.417380
Presque Isle S.P.	92	A1	42.114200 -80.153590
Prince Gallitzin S.P.	92	B3	40.669760 -78.575650
Promised Land S.P.	93	F2	41.313560 -75.210370
Pymatuning S.P.	91	F2	41.605440 -80.387840
Raccoon Creek S.P.	91	F4	40.503160 -80.424460
Ralph Stover S.P.	146	C1	40.440420 -75.106050
Raymond B. Winter S.P.	93	D3	40.992340 -77.200450

Ricketts Glen S.P.	93	E2	41.336190 -76.300420
Ryerson Station S.P.	102	A1	39.892310 -80.450030
S.B. Elliott S.P.	92	C3	41.112740 -78.526100
Salt Springs S.P.	93	E1	41.911090 -75.868720
Samuel S. Lewis S.P.	103	E1	39.996580 -76.550410
Shawnee S.P.	102	C1	40.038060 -78.645850
Shikellamy S.P.	93	D3	40.879390 -76.802950
Sinnemahoning S.P.	92	C2	41.450650 -78.055090
Susquehannock S.P.	146	A3	39.805770 -76.283410
Swatara S.P.	93	E4	40.481480 -76.551350
Tobyhanna S.P.	93	F2	41.214130 -75.384030
Trough Creek S.P.	92	C4	40.311620 -78.131820
Tyler S.P.	146	C2	40.233330 -74.951170
Warriors Path S.P.	92	C4	40.193330 -78.249880
Washington Crossing Hist. Park	104	C2	40.312256 -74.859711
Whipple Dam S.P.	92	C3	40.682250 -77.868410
Worlds End S.P.	93	E2	41.471880 -76.587060
Yellow Creek S.P.	92	B4	40.575830 -79.004420

RHODE ISLAND	PAGE	GRID	LATITUDE LONGITUDE
State Park & Rec. Areas			
Beavertail S.P.	150	C4	41.457030 -71.396950
Block Island State Beach	95	D4	41.180850 -71.566460
Brenton Point S.P.	150	C4	41.450430 -71.355870
Burlingame S.P.	150	C4	41.361610 -71.701370
Casimir Pulaski Mem. S.P.	150	C3	41.950000 -71.766670
Colt S.P.	151	D3	41.684590 -71.288860
East Matunuck State Beach	150	C4	41.378350 -71.525630
Fishermen's Mem. S.P.	150	C4	41.380630 -71.488000
Fort Adams S.P.	150	C4	41.469150 -71.339990
Goddard Mem. S.P.	150	C3	41.651030 -71.442040
Haines Mem. S.P.	150	C3	41.752960 -71.348600
Misquamicut State Beach	95	D4	41.324510 -71.800670
Rocky Point S.P.	150	C3	41.691482 -71.363654
R.W. Wheeler State Beach	150	C4	41.372620 -71.495530
Scarborough State Beach	150	C4	41.389770 -71.474260

SOUTH CAROLINA	PAGE	GRID	LATITUDE LONGITUDE
National Park & Rec. Areas			
Charles Pinckney N.H.S.	131	D2	32.847150 -79.824090
Congaree Natl. Park	122	A4	33.836100 -80.827660
Kings Mtn. N.M.P.	122	A1	35.140120 -81.386890
Ninety Six N.H.S.	121	F3	34.162740 -82.010980
Reconstruction Era Natl. Mon.	130	C2	32.432790 -80.670458
State Park & Rec. Areas			
Andrew Jackson S.P.	122	B2	34.839560 -80.810110
Barnwell S.P.	130	B1	33.329250 -81.300400
Calhoun Falls S.P.	121	E3	34.106792 -82.604200
Cheraw S.P.	122	C2	34.642370 -79.927640
Devils Fork S.P.	121	E2	34.952527 -82.946085
Edisto Beach S.P.	130	C2	32.505410 -80.310310
Givhans Ferry S.P.	130	C1	33.031640 -80.382150
Hickory Knob State Resort Park	121	E4	33.884250 -82.416010
Huntington Beach S.P.	123	D4	33.502650 -79.081200
Jones Gap S.P.	121	E1	35.126360 -82.558350
Kings Mtn. S.P.	122	A1	35.113030 -81.394040
Lake Warren S.P.	130	B2	32.844830 -81.165070
Little Pee Dee S.P.	122	C3	34.331020 -79.282170
Myrtle Beach S.P.	123	D4	33.649210 -78.938600
N.R. Goodale S.P.	122	B3	34.281580 -80.525150
Oconee S.P.	121	E2	34.867297 -83.106098
Paris Mtn. S.P.	121	E2	34.924970 -82.365540
Poinsett S.P.	122	B4	33.804360 -80.544920
Santee S.P.	122	B4	33.500200 -80.489820
Table Rock S.P.	121	E2	35.022050 -82.710700

SOUTH DAKOTA	PAGE	GRID	LATITUDE LONGITUDE
National Park & Rec. Areas			
Badlands Natl. Park-Interior Ent.	26	B4	43.741900 -101.957000
Badlands Natl. Park-Northeast Ent.	26	B4	43.792400 -101.906000
Badlands Natl. Park-Pinnacles Ent.	26	B4	43.885500 -102.238000
Jewel Cave Natl. Mon.	25	F4	43.736500 -103.819940
Minuteman Missile N.H.S.	26	B4	43.833931 -101.899685
Mount Rushmore Natl. Mem.	26	A4	43.886730 -103.440610
Wind Cave Natl. Park-Vis. Ctr.	26	A4	43.556100 -103.478000
State Park & Rec. Areas			
Bear Butte S.P.	26	A3	44.460580 -103.433750
Custer S.P.	26	A4	43.770310 -103.440130
Fisher Grove S.P.	27	E2	44.883340 -98.356640
Hartford Beach S.P.	27	F2	45.398870 -96.665260
Lake Herman S.P.	27	F4	43.993120 -97.159790
Newton Hills S.P.	35	F1	43.218860 -96.569700
Oakwood Lakes S.P.	27	F3	44.454310 -96.989490
Palisades S.P.	27	F4	43.687970 -96.511470
Roy Lake S.P.	27	E1	45.703360 -97.419650
Sica Hollow S.P.	27	E1	45.740690 -97.229150
Union Grove S.P.	35	F1	42.922630 -96.785530

TENNESSEE	PAGE	GRID	LATITUDE LONGITUDE
National Park & Rec. Areas			
Andrew Johnson N.H.S.	111	D4	36.157710 -82.836880
Big South Fork Natl. River & Rec. Area	110	B3	36.475400 -84.752100
Manhattan Project N.H.P.	37	D2	35.928419 -85.350923
State Park & Rec. Areas			
Big Hill Pond S.P.	119	D1	35.078890 -88.718860
Big Ridge S.P.	110	C3	36.241600 -83.929280
Bledsoe Creek S.P.	109	F3	36.378050 -86.356660
Cedars of Lebanon S.P. & Forest	109	F4	36.093930 -86.335620
Chickasaw S.P.	119	D1	35.393241 -88.772298
Cove Lake S.P.	110	C3	36.305830 -84.210750
Cumberland Mtn. S.P.	110	B4	35.898460 -84.995130
David Crockett S.P.	119	E1	35.242690 -87.354850
Davy Crockett Birthplace S.P.	111	E3	36.221980 -82.662770
Edgar Evins S.P.	110	A4	36.086050 -85.812460
Fall Creek Falls S.P.	120	B1	35.622200 -85.208000
Frozen Head S.P. & Nat. Area-North Ent.	110	B4	36.122550 -84.433320
Frozen Head S.P. & Nat. Area-South Ent.	110	B4	36.102180 -84.446970
Harpeth River S.P.	109	E4	36.079240 -86.956920
Harrison Bay S.P.	120	B1	35.175850 -85.115350
Henry Horton S.P.	119	F1	35.596510 -86.698690
Hiwassee–Ocoee Scenic Rivers S.P.	120	C1	35.224557 -84.504269
Indian Mtn. S.P.	110	C3	36.583050 -84.139900
Long Hunter S.P.	109	F4	36.094340 -86.557330
Meeman-Shelby Forest S.P.	118	B1	35.336800 -90.029010
Montgomery Bell S.P.	109	E4	36.106750 -87.268690
Mousetail Landing S.P.	109	D4	35.581900 -87.859100
Natchez Trace S.P.	109	D4	35.839580 -88.252820
Nathan Bedford Forrest S.P.	109	D4	36.087900 -87.979750
Norris Dam S.P.	110	C3	36.234560 -84.127020
Old Stone Fort State Arch. Park	120	A1	35.487270 -86.101330
Panther Creek S.P.	111	D3	36.212760 -83.412420
Paris Landing State Resort Park	109	D3	36.441760 -88.090180
Pickett S.P.	110	B3	36.537374 -84.802126
Pickwick Landing S.P.	119	D2	35.051790 -88.242650
Pinson Mounds State Arch. Park	119	D1	35.504130 -88.683020
Reelfoot Lake S.P.	108	B3	36.414410 -89.426880
Roan Mtn. S.P.	111	E4	36.161110 -82.097000
Rock Island S.P.	110	A4	35.810000 -85.641550
Standing Stone S.P.	110	A3	36.458910 -85.437690
T.O. Fuller S.P.	118	B2	35.057810 -90.113650
Tims Ford S.P.	120	A1	35.220999 -86.255889
Warriors Path S.P.	111	E5	36.504610 -82.481090

TEXAS	PAGE	GRID	LATITUDE LONGITUDE
National Park & Rec. Areas			
Alibates Flint Quarries Natl. Mon.	50	A3	35.571900 -101.633880
Amistad N.R.A.	60	B2	29.449920 -101.053170
Big Bend Natl. Park-North Ent.	62	C4	29.680900 -103.167000
Big Bend Natl. Park-West Ent.	62	C4	29.306600 -103.523000
Fort Davis N.H.S.	62	B2	30.604120 -103.886010
Guadalupe Mts. Natl. Park-Vis. Ctr.	57	D3	31.894300 -104.822000
Lyndon B. Johnson N.H.P.	61	D2	30.276020 -98.411990
Padre Island Natl. Seashore	63	F3	27.553470 -97.248370
Palo Alto Btld. N.H.P.	63	F4	26.011630 -97.481570
State Park & Rec. Areas			
Abilene S.P.	58	C3	32.241360 -99.879230
Atlanta S.P.	124	C1	33.229500 -94.249300
Balmorhea S.P.	62	B2	30.946270 -103.784890
Bastrop S.P.	61	E2	30.098960 -97.229090
Bentsen-Rio Grande Valley S.P.	63	E4	26.182530 -98.382360
Big Bend Ranch S.P.	62	B4	29.265070 -103.791910
Big Spring S.P.	58	A3	32.229650 -101.483090
Blanco S.P.	61	D2	30.093240 -98.423420
Bonham S.P.	59	F1	33.543100 -96.149640
Brazos Bend S.P.	132	A4	29.371480 -95.631890
Buescher S.P.	61	E2	30.073570 -97.176140
Caddo Lake S.P.	124	C2	32.684230 -94.177070
Caprock Canyons S.P. & Trailway	50	B4	34.406440 -101.048830
Choke Canyon S.P.-Calliham Unit	61	D4	28.460970 -98.356380
Choke Canyon S.P.-South Shore Unit	61	D4	28.467610 -98.239550
Cleburne S.P.	59	E3	32.265180 -97.560680
Colorado Bend S.P.	61	D1	31.062510 -98.504250
Cooper Lake S.P.	124	A1	33.305282 -95.648346
Copper Breaks S.P.	50	C4	34.113660 -99.747800
Daingerfield S.P.	124	B1	33.028720 -94.714510
Davis Mts. S.P.	62	B2	30.599520 -103.929220
Dinosaur Valley S.P.	59	E3	32.250020 -97.814620
Eisenhower S.P.	59	F1	33.822670 -96.616120
Fairfield Lake S.P.	59	F3	31.765910 -96.076220
Falcon S.P.	63	D3	26.583500 -99.144790
Fort Boggy S.P.	124	A4	31.189627 -95.986069
Fort Griffin S.H.S.	58	C2	32.924690 -99.219370
Fort Parker S.P.	59	F4	31.592650 -96.524370
Fort Richardson S.P. & Hist. Site	59	D2	33.206060 -98.164810
Franklin Mts. S.P.	56	C3	31.912060 -106.517140
Galveston Island S.P.	132	B4	29.196240 -94.956210
Garner S.P.	60	C2	29.600900 -99.744220
Goliad S.P.	61	E4	28.655190 -97.383580
Goose Island S.P.	61	F4	28.134060 -96.984350
Guadalupe River S.P.	61	D2	29.849890 -98.509590
Hueco Tanks S.H.S.	56	C3	31.926453 -106.042437
Huntsville S.P.	132	A2	30.638130 -95.511370
Inks Lake S.P.	61	D1	30.738290 -98.366450
Kerrville-Schreiner S.P.	60	C2	30.007930 -99.117640
Lake Arrowhead S.P.	59	D1	33.759300 -98.396610
Lake Bob Sandlin S.P.	124	B1	33.054090 -95.101250
Lake Brownwood S.P.	59	D3	31.857370 -99.021280
Lake Casa Blanca International S.P.	63	D2	27.536739 -99.432449
Lake Colorado City S.P.	58	B3	32.313460 -100.924800
Lake Corpus Christi S.P.	61	E4	28.060360 -97.867690
Lake Livingston S.P.	132	B1	30.671300 -95.008200
Lake Mineral Wells S.P.	59	E2	32.814570 -98.042270
Lake Somerville S.P. & Trailway	61	F1	30.315760 -96.625080
Lake Tawakoni S.P.	59	F2	32.841610 -95.990710
Lake Whitney S.P.	59	E3	31.924780 -97.356280
Lockhart S.P.	61	E2	29.857610 -97.697400
Longhorn Cavern S.P.	61	D1	30.686610 -98.351380
Lyndon B. Johnson S.P. & Hist. Site-Ranch Unit	61	D2	30.235180 -98.629100
Martin Creek Lake S.P.	124	B3	32.283090 -94.583470
Martin Dies Junior S.P.	132	C1	30.848980 -94.164720
Meridian S.P.	59	E3	31.892440 -97.695670
Mission Tejas S.P.	124	A4	31.546110 -95.234720
Monahans Sandhills S.P.	57	F4	31.634940 -102.814850
Mother Neff S.P.	59	E4	31.319150 -97.474210
Mustang Island S.P.	63	F2	27.677020 -97.173730
Palmetto S.P.	61	E2	29.597280 -97.584640
Palo Duro Canyon S.P.	50	B3	34.985710 -101.703190
Pedernales Falls S.P.	61	D1	30.273110 -98.256830
Possum Kingdom S.P.	59	D2	32.878970 -98.561740
Purtis Creek S.P.	124	A2	32.373340 -95.974530
Ray Roberts Lake S.P.	59	F1	33.444050 -96.925860
Rusk–Palestine S.P.-East	124	B3	31.803560 -95.194880
Rusk–Palestine S.P.-West	124	A4	31.739260 -95.570450
Sabine Pass Battleground S.H.S.	132	C3	29.726520 -93.878280
San Angelo S.P.	58	B4	31.491919 -100.547148
Sea Rim S.P.	132	C3	29.677900 -94.039900
Seminole Canyon S.P. & Hist. Site	60	A2	29.709000 -101.298480
South Llano River S.P.	60	C1	30.445430 -99.804610
Stephen F. Austin S.P.	61	F2	29.812030 -96.108200
Tyler S.P.	124	A2	32.481750 -95.281760

UTAH	PAGE	GRID	LATITUDE LONGITUDE
National Park & Rec. Areas			
Arches Natl. Park	40	A2	38.615570 -109.616920
Bears Ears Natl. Mon.	41	A3	37.703318 -109.919962
Bryce Canyon Natl. Park	39	E4	37.641700 -112.168000
Canyonlands Natl. Park-East Ent.	40	A3	38.168510 -109.750980
Canyonlands Natl. Park-Horseshoe Canyon Unit	39	F3	38.497740 -110.205960
Canyonlands Natl. Park-North Ent.	40	A3	38.490150 -109.807930
Canyonlands Natl. Park-West Ent.	40	A3	38.255440 -110.180050
Capitol Reef Natl. Park	39	E3	38.291020 -111.261410
Cedar Breaks Natl. Mon.-East Ent.	39	D4	37.655230 -112.811350
Cedar Breaks Natl. Mon.-North Ent.	39	D4	37.665730 -112.838130
Cedar Breaks Natl. Mon.-South Ent.	39	D4	37.598730 -112.850080
Glen Canyon N.R.A.	39	F4	38.255440 -110.180050
Golden Spike N.H.S.	31	E3	41.620482 -112.547471
Grand Staircase-Escalante Natl. Mon.	39	E4	37.420000 -111.550000
Natural Bridges Natl. Mon.	39	F4	37.608120 -109.966280
Rainbow Bridge Natl. Mon.	47	E1	37.110810 -110.406050
Zion Natl. Park-East Ent.	39	D4	37.235370 -112.864470
Zion Natl. Park-Main Ent.	39	D4	37.201970 -112.988380
State Park & Rec. Areas			
Anasazi S.P. Mus.	39	E3	37.922399 -111.425743
Antelope Island S.P.	31	E4	41.089290 -112.116490
Bear Lake (Rendezvous Beach) S.P.	31	F2	41.962200 -111.400320
Bear Lake S.P.	31	F2	41.965360 -111.399480
Camp Floyd– Stagecoach Inn S.P.	31	E4	40.258360 -112.097270
Coral Pink Sand Dunes S.P.	47	D1	37.036964 -112.731196
Dead Horse Point S.P.	40	A3	38.510220 -109.729460
Deer Creek S.P.	31	F4	40.452620 -111.477820
Edge of the Cedars S.P.	40	A4	37.629760 -109.491730
Escalante Petrified Forest S.P.	39	E4	37.783820 -111.630220
Fred Hayes S.P. at Starvation	32	A4	40.104100 -110.330900
Fremont Indian S.P.	39	D3	38.579537 -112.314773
Frontier Homestead S.P.	39	D4	37.688349 -113.061896
Goblin Valley S.P.	39	F3	38.580620 -110.712580
Goosenecks S.P.	40	A4	37.174730 -109.926950
Green River S.P.	39	F2	38.995500 -110.156910
Gunlock S.P.-North Ent.	38	C4	37.275970 -113.768780
Gunlock S.P.-South Ent.	38	C4	37.251490 -113.772820
Huntington S.P.	39	F2	39.315200 -110.977100
Hyrum S.P.	31	E3	41.626220 -111.872170
Kodachrome Basin S.P.	39	E4	37.501670 -111.993610
Millsite S.P.	39	E2	39.099020 -111.184240
Otter Creek S.P.	39	E3	38.167430 -112.021570
Palisade S.P.	39	E2	39.195800 -111.691600
Piute S.P.	39	E3	38.322530 -112.204200
Quail Creek S.P.	39	D4	37.105000 -113.576600
Red Fleet S.P.	32	B4	40.553300 -109.518472
Rockport S.P.	31	F4	40.751890 -111.367410
Sand Hollow S.P.	46	C1	37.144830 -113.382139
Scofield S.P.	39	E1	39.708600 -110.921000
Snow Canyon S.P.-East Ent.	38	C4	37.212120 -113.630870
Snow Canyon S.P.-North Ent.	38	C4	37.256790 -113.632990
Snow Canyon S.P.-South Ent.	38	C4	37.183380 -113.645010

Name	Page	Grid	Latitude Longitude
Steinaker S.P.-North Ent.	32	A4	40.534870 -109.522440
Steinaker S.P.-South Ent.	32	A4	40.504850 -109.528870
Territorial Statehouse S.P.	39	D2	38.985880 -112.353530
Wasatch Mtn. S.P.	31	F4	40.477770 -111.519990
Willard Bay S.P.-North Ent.	31	E3	41.418810 -112.052390
Willard Bay S.P.-South Ent.	31	E3	41.350610 -112.069060
Yuba S.P.	39	E2	39.381240 -112.028360

VERMONT

VERMONT	PAGE	GRID	LATITUDE LONGITUDE
National Park & Rec. Areas			
Marsh-Billings-Rockefeller N.H.P.	81	E3	43.635833 -72.538333
Moosalamoo Natl. Rec. Area	81	D3	43.879457 -73.098532
State Park & Rec. Areas			
Allis S.P.	81	E3	44.051150 -72.626440
Branbury S.P.	81	D3	43.904250 -73.065370
Burton Island S.P.	81	D1	44.779660 -73.180050
Camp Plymouth S.P.	81	E4	43.475810 -72.694987
D.A.R. S.P.	81	D3	44.058850 -73.409210
Emerald Lake S.P.	81	D4	43.283790 -73.002250
Half Moon S.P.	81	D3	43.699720 -73.223220
Kingsland Bay S.P.	81	D2	44.226230 -73.277660
Lake Saint Catherine S.P.	81	D4	43.483000 -73.202580
Little River S.P.	81	D2	44.388940 -72.768360
Molly Stark S.P.	94	C1	42.854920 -72.813790
North Hero S.P.	81	D1	44.908210 -73.235110
Ricker Pond S.P.	81	E2	44.251467 -72.247550
Stillwater S.P.	81	E2	44.280200 -72.275060
Townshend S.P.	81	E4	43.041920 -72.691600
Underhill S.P.	81	D2	44.528880 -72.843920
Woodford S.P.	94	C1	42.894450 -73.037790
Woods Island S.P.	81	D1	44.802500 -73.209283

VIRGINIA

VIRGINIA	PAGE	GRID	LATITUDE LONGITUDE
National Park & Rec. Areas			
Appomattox Court House N.H.P.	112	C1	37.377367 -78.795290
Booker T. Washington Natl. Mon.	112	B2	37.120500 -79.733340
Cedar Creek & Belle Grove N.H.P.	102	C2	39.023500 -78.289000
Colonial N.H.P.	114	A4	37.211390 -76.776730
Cumberland Gap N.H.P.-Vis. Ctr.	111	D3	36.602600 -83.695400
Fredericksburg & Spotsylvania Co. Bflds. Mem. N.M.P.	103	D4	38.254300 -77.451890
George Washington Birthplace Natl. Mon.	114	A2	38.192353 -76.927192
Manassas Natl. Bfld. Park	144	A3	38.806030 -77.572810
Mount Rogers N.R.A.	111	F2	36.811360 -81.420130
Shenandoah Natl. Park-Front Royal North Ent.	102	C3	38.903300 -78.192400
Shenandoah Natl. Park-Rockfish Gap South Ent.	102	C3	38.033900 -78.858900
Shenandoah Natl. Park-Swift Run Gap Ent.	102	C3	38.359100 -78.546700
Shenandoah Natl. Park-Thornton Gap Ent.	102	C3	38.662300 -78.320600
State Park & Rec. Areas			
Bear Creek Lake S.P.	113	D1	37.532970 -78.274890
Belle Isle S.P.	114	B2	37.774526 -76.599222
Chippokes Plantation S.P.	114	A4	37.140400 -76.748590
Claytor Lake S.P.	112	A2	37.057620 -80.622140
Douthat S.P.	102	B4	37.914520 -79.796740
Fairy Stone S.P.	112	B2	36.791790 -80.117890
False Cape S.P.	115	F1	36.691370 -75.924410
First Landing S.P.	114	B4	36.915601 -76.057000
Grayson Highlands S.P.	111	F3	36.611920 -81.489900
Holliday Lake S.P.	113	D1	37.404610 -78.644920
Hungry Mother S.P.	111	F2	36.880860 -81.525750
James River S.P.	112	C1	37.540400 -78.839300
Kiptopeke S.P.	114	B4	37.169292 -75.982919
Lake Anna S.P.	103	D4	38.125850 -77.821690
Mason Neck S.P.	103	E3	38.640740 -77.194400
Natural Bridge S.P.	112	C1	37.633038 -79.543034
Natural Tunnel S.P.	111	E3	36.707520 -82.744090
New River Trail S.P.	112	A2	36.870180 -80.868550
Occoneechee S.P.	113	D3	36.633330 -78.525420
Pocahontas S.P.	113	E1	37.366240 -77.573870
Powhatan S.P.	113	D1	37.678066 -77.925997
Sailor's Creek Bfld. Hist. S.P.	113	D1	37.298470 -78.229470
Sky Meadows S.P.	103	D2	38.988703 -77.968913
Smith Mtn. Lake S.P.	112	B2	37.091110 -79.592110
Twin Lakes S.P.	113	D2	37.336900 -77.934100
Westmoreland S.P.	103	E4	38.158690 -76.870120
York River S.P.	113	F1	37.414190 -76.713650

WASHINGTON

WASHINGTON	PAGE	GRID	LATITUDE LONGITUDE
National Park & Rec. Areas			
Columbia River Gorge Natl. Scenic Area	21	D1	45.715322 -121.818667
Fort Vancouver N.H.S.	20	C1	45.626940 -122.656310
Hanford Reach Natl. Mon.	13	E4	46.483333 -119.533333
Lake Chelan N.R.A.	13	D2	48.309080 -120.657730
Lake Roosevelt N.R.A.	13	F2	47.972680 -118.970580
Lewis & Clark N.H.P.-Discovery Trail	12	B4	46.370033 -124.053503
Lewis & Clark N.H.P.-Dismal Nitch	20	B1	46.249033 -123.862903
Lewis & Clark N.H.P.-Sta. Camp	20	B1	46.263111 -123.932571
Manhattan Project N. H.P.	13	E4	46.316332 -119.301848
Mount Baker N.R.A.	12	C1	48.714167 -121.805900
Mount Rainier Natl. Park-Nisqually Ent.	12	C5	46.741400 -121.919040
Mount Rainier Natl. Park-Stevens Can. Ent.	12	C7	46.754730 -121.557010
Mount Rainier Natl. Park-White River Ent.	12	C8	46.902040 -121.554340
Mount Saint Helens Natl. Mon.	12	C4	46.277590 -122.218820
North Cascades Natl. Park-Golden West	13	D1	48.308200 -120.655000
North Cascades Natl. Park-Northern Cascades Vis. Ctr.	13	D1	48.666100 -121.264000
Olympic Natl. Park-Vis. Ctr.	12	B2	48.096700 -123.428000
Olympic Natl. Park-Vis. Ctr.-Hoh Rain Forest	12	B2	47.860700 -123.935000
Olympic Natl. Park-Vis. Ctr.-Hurricane Ridge	12	B2	47.969200 -123.498000
Ross Lake N.R.A.	13	D1	48.674250 -121.244730
San Juan Island N.H.P.	12	B2	48.534580 -123.016250
San Juan Islands Natl. Mon.	12	C2	48.531944,-123.029167
Whitman Mission N.H.S.	21	F1	46.040910 -118.468110
State Park & Rec. Areas			
Alta Lake S.P.	13	E2	48.031990 -119.934710
Anderson Lake S.P.	12	C2	48.014590 -122.810680
Belfair S.P.	12	C3	47.430630 -122.881400
Birch Bay S.P.	12	C1	48.903210 -122.757880
Bogachiel S.P.	12	A2	47.894790 -124.362820
Bridgeport S.P.	13	E2	48.012549 -119.618571
Brooks Mem. S.P.	21	D1	45.950590 -120.664200
Camano Island S.P.	12	C2	48.131680 -122.503240
Cape Disappointment S.P.	20	B1	46.294210 -124.053610
Columbia Hills S.P.	21	D1	45.643030 -121.106410
Crawford S.P.	14	A1	48.992070 -117.370370
Curlew Lake S.P.	13	F1	48.719280 -118.661740
Deception Pass S.P.	12	C2	48.390970 -122.646880
Dosewallips S.P.	12	C3	47.687570 -122.899860
Fields Spring S.P.	22	A1	46.087520 -117.173650
Flaming Geyser S.P.	12	C3	47.280230 -122.041870
Fort Casey S.P.	12	C2	48.159760 -122.672410
Fort Okanogan S.P.	13	E2	48.102370 -119.678720
Fort Simcoe S.P.	13	D4	46.345340 -120.823460
Fort Townsend S.P.	12	C2	48.078260 -122.805690
Ginkgo Petrified Forest S.P.	13	E4	46.949010 -119.997490
Goldendale Observatory S.P.	21	D1	45.837090 -120.815890
Grayland Beach S.P.	12	B4	46.792382 -124.097802
Ike Kinswa S.P.	12	C4	46.555780 -122.536570
Jarrell Cove S.P.	12	B3	47.285940 -122.881080
Joseph Whidbey S.P.	12	C2	48.308370 -122.713170
Kitsap Mem. S.P.	12	C3	47.816580 -122.646840
Lake Chelan S.P.	13	D2	47.869430 -120.191110
Lake Easton S.P.	13	D3	47.249380 -121.190920
Lake Wenatchee S.P.	13	D3	47.816340 -120.729780
Larrabee S.P.	12	C2	48.650620 -122.489810
Lewis & Clark S.P.	12	C4	46.525850 -122.817910
Lewis & Clark Trail S.P.	13	F4	46.287600 -118.073340
Lincoln Rock S.P.	13	D3	47.535490 -120.282280
Millersylvania S.P.	12	B4	46.909610 -122.905950
Moran S.P.	12	C1	48.657700 -122.859630
Mount Spokane S.P.	14	B2	47.899290 -117.124350
Nolte S.P.	12	C3	47.267320 -121.943420
Ocean City S.P.	12	B4	47.038520 -124.158130
Pacific Beach S.P.	12	A3	47.205980 -124.202220
Pacific Pines S.P.	12	B4	46.507610 -124.049150
Palouse Falls S.P.	13	F4	46.664030 -118.228660
Peace Arch S.P.	12	C1	49.000980 -122.751580
Pearrygin Lake S.P.	13	E2	48.496720 -120.146950
Peshastin Pinnacles S.P.	13	D3	47.578810 -120.613860
Potholes S.P.	13	E4	46.970780 -119.351180
Potlatch S.P.	12	B3	47.363000 -123.158140
Rainbow Falls S.P.	12	B4	46.631010 -123.237350
Rockport S.P.	12	C2	48.487920 -121.601870
Sacajawea S.P.	21	F1	46.210140 -119.046050
Scenic Beach S.P.	12	C3	47.649250 -122.845470
Seaquest S.P.	12	C4	46.295880 -122.820860
Sequim Bay S.P.	12	B2	48.040750 -123.030920
Shine Tidelands S.P.	12	C2	47.867990 -122.638700
Steamboat Rock S.P.	13	E2	47.828650 -119.134340
Sun Lakes S.P.	13	E3	47.596540 -119.387760
Triton Cove S.P.	12	B3	47.609112 -122.986526
Twenty-Five Mile Creek S.P.	13	D2	47.992520 -120.263610
Twin Harbors S.P.	12	B4	46.858850 -124.104210
Wallace Falls S.P.	12	C2	47.865610 -121.680050
Wanapum S.P.	13	E4	46.924760 -119.991690
Westport Light S.P.	12	B4	46.891700 -124.111630

WEST VIRGINIA

WEST VIRGINIA	PAGE	GRID	LATITUDE LONGITUDE
National Park & Rec. Areas			
Bluestone Natl. Scenic River	112	A1	37.584300 -80.957900
Gauley River N.R.A.	101	F4	38.191800 -81.001920
Harpers Ferry N.H.P.	103	D2	39.318820 -77.759060
New River Gorge Natl. River	101	F4	37.875670 -81.077598
Spruce Knob Seneca Rocks N.R.A.	102	B3	38.681180 -79.544480
State Park & Rec. Areas			
Audra S.P.	102	A2	39.041110 -80.067500
Beartown S.P.	102	A4	38.051750 -80.275420
Blennerhassett Island Hist. S.P.	101	E2	39.273300 -81.644800
Bluestone S.P.	112	A1	37.623050 -80.934710
Cacapon Resort S.P.	102	C1	39.502980 -78.291330
Camp Creek S.P.	111	F1	37.508173 -81.132873
Carnifex Ferry Bfld. S.P.	101	F4	38.211290 -80.941850
Cass Scenic Railroad S.P.	102	A3	38.396520 -79.914280
Cedar Creek S.P.	101	F3	38.880780 -80.849420
Droop Mtn. Bfld. S.P.	102	A4	38.113200 -80.271670
Holly River S.P.	102	A3	38.653140 -80.382620
Little Beaver S.P.	112	A1	37.756570 -81.079780
Moncove Lake S.P.	112	B1	37.616950 -80.354730
Pinnacle Rock S.P.	111	F1	37.308190 -81.291430
Prickett's Fort S.P.	102	A1	39.514090 -80.099960
Tomlinson Run S.P.	91	F4	40.550660 -80.595950
Tygart Lake S.P.	102	A2	39.248160 -80.021060
Valley Falls S.P.	102	A2	39.392900 -80.070480
Watoga S.P.	102	A4	38.122510 -80.155660
Watters Smith Mem. S.P.	102	A2	39.174520 -80.414260

WISCONSIN

WISCONSIN	PAGE	GRID	LATITUDE LONGITUDE
National Park & Rec. Areas			
Apostle Islands Natl. Lakeshore	65	D4	46.812210 -90.820780
Saint Croix Natl. Scenic Riverway	67	E2	45.415700 -92.646270
State Park & Rec. Areas			
Amnicon Falls S.P.	64	C4	46.608210 -91.887850
Aztalan S.P.	74	B3	43.068310 -88.863750
Belmont Mound S.P.	74	A4	42.768611 -90.349444
Big Bay S.P.	65	D4	46.811030 -90.696960
Big Foot Beach S.P.	74	C4	42.567330 -88.436790
Blue Mound S.P.	74	A3	43.026990 -89.840740
Brunet Island S.P.	67	F3	45.176220 -91.161610
Buckhorn S.P.	74	A1	43.948280 -90.002130
Copper Culture S.P.	68	C4	44.887440 -87.897940
Copper Falls S.P.	65	D4	46.351710 -90.643670
Council Grounds S.P.	68	A3	45.184840 -89.734290
Devil's Lake S.P.	74	A2	43.429010 -89.734900
Governor Dodge S.P.	74	A3	43.019560 -90.141950
Governor Thompson S.P.	68	C3	45.326309 -88.219205
Harrington Beach S.P.	75	D2	43.499430 -87.811890
Hartman Creek S.P.	74	B1	44.318070 -89.194320
High Cliff S.P.	74	C1	44.166680 -88.291760
Interstate S.P.	67	D3	45.396410 -92.636580
Kinnickinnic S.P.	67	D4	44.837280 -92.733190
Kohler-Andrae S.P.	75	D2	43.672740 -87.719320
Lake Kegonsa S.P.	74	B3	42.978005 -89.230300
Lake Wissota S.P.	67	F4	44.980950 -91.313740
Merrick S.P.	73	E1	44.152740 -91.744120
Mill Bluff S.P.	74	A1	43.961610 -90.317980
Mirror Lake S.P.	74	A2	43.568770 -89.834930
Natural Bridge S.P.	74	A2	43.344930 -89.928290
Nelson Dewey S.P.	73	F4	42.743740 -91.037860
New Glarus Woods S.P.	74	B4	42.786830 -89.631980
Newport S.P.	69	D3	45.241470 -86.998830
Pattison S.P.	64	C4	46.535290 -92.121410
Peninsula S.P.	69	D3	45.133080 -87.213280
Perrot S.P.	73	F1	44.016350 -91.479670
Potawatomi S.P.	69	D4	44.849990 -87.407640
Rib Mtn. S.P.	68	B4	44.915800 -89.669360
Roche-A-Cri S.P.	74	A1	43.996120 -89.812370
Rock Island S.P.	69	E3	45.398990 -86.855970
Rocky Arbor S.P.	74	A2	43.647890 -89.808240
Straight Lake S.P.	67	E2	45.597399 -92.406609
Tower Hill S.P.	74	A3	43.147090 -90.043750
Whitefish Dunes S.P.	69	D4	44.928910 -87.182150
Wildcat Mtn. S.P.	74	A2	43.688870 -90.566800
Willow River S.P.	67	D3	45.017610 -92.672610
Wyalusing S.P.	73	F3	42.978770 -91.118560
Yellowstone Lake S.P.	74	A4	42.777360 -89.993540

WYOMING

WYOMING	PAGE	GRID	LATITUDE LONGITUDE
National Park & Rec. Areas			
Devils Tower Natl. Mon.	25	E3	44.586870 -104.706710
Flaming Gorge N.R.A.	32	A3	41.254860 -109.611400
Fort Laramie N.H.S.	33	E2	42.202530 -104.558590
Fossil Butte Natl. Mon.	31	F2	41.855370 -110.782340
Grand Teton Natl. Park-Granite Canyon Ent.	23	F4	43.597990 -110.801640
Grand Teton Natl. Park-Moose Ent.	23	F4	43.655860 -110.718350
Grand Teton Natl. Park-Moran Ent.	23	F4	43.843640 -110.511950
John D. Rockefeller Jr. Mem. Parkway	24	A3	44.108800 -110.685508
Medicine Wheel Natl. Hist. Landmark	24	C2	44.826200 -107.921717
Yellowstone Natl. Park-East Ent.	23	F3	44.489540 -110.001560
Yellowstone Natl. Park-North East Ent.	23	F3	45.006120 -109.991550
Yellowstone Natl. Park-North Ent.	23	F3	45.030110 -110.705460
Yellowstone Natl. Park-South Ent.	23	F3	44.134730 -110.666170
Yellowstone Natl. Park-West Ent.	23	F3	44.658720 -111.098970
State Park & Rec. Areas			
Bear River S.P.	31	F3	41.267257 -110.938030
Boysen S.P.	32	C1	43.270160 -108.115260
Buffalo Bill S.P.	24	B3	44.505020 -109.249540
Curt Gowdy S.P.	33	E3	41.175380 -105.243640
Edness K. Wilkins S.P.	33	D1	42.857220 -106.177370
Glendo S.P.	33	E1	42.476060 -104.998910
Guernsey S.P.	33	E2	42.287400 -104.763460
Hot Springs S.P.	24	C4	43.653980 -108.201790
Keyhole S.P.	25	E3	44.356490 -104.825810
Seminoe S.P.	33	D2	42.150350 -106.905870
Sinks Canyon S.P.	32	B1	42.752600 -108.804770

CANADA

ALBERTA

ALBERTA	PAGE	GRID	LATITUDE LONGITUDE
National Park & Rec. Areas			
Banff Natl. Park-Banff Vis. Ctr.	164	B2	51.177400 -115.570900
Banff Natl. Park-Lake Louise Vis. Ctr.	164	B2	51.425200 -116.178400
Banff Park Mus. N.H.S.	164	B3	51.174300 -115.571100
Bar U Ranch N.H.S.	164	C3	50.420300 -114.244400
Cave and Basin N.H.S.	164	B3	51.168300 -115.591400
Elk Island Natl. Park	159	D4	53.572500 -112.841900
Jasper Natl. Park-Icefield Center	164	A1	52.233500 -117.234800
Jasper Natl. Park-Jasper Information Center	164	A1	52.877300 -118.080900
Rocky Mtn. House N.H.S.	164	C2	52.377590 -114.931237
Waterton Lakes Natl. Park-Waterton Vis. Ctr.	164	C4	49.051400 -113.906300
Wood Buffalo Natl. Park-Fort Chipewyan Vis. Ctr.	155	F2	48.714100 -111.154300
Provincial Park & Rec. Areas			
Aspen Beach Prov. Park	164	C2	52.454530 -113.975750
Beauvais Lake Prov. Park	164	C4	49.409500 -114.117000
Big Hill Springs Prov. Park	164	C3	51.251670 -114.386940
Big Knife Prov. Park	165	D2	52.489720 -112.210560
Birch Mts. Wildland Prov. Park	159	D1	57.509400 -112.957000
Bluerock Wildland Prov. Park	164	C3	50.642300 -114.654000
Bob Creek Wildland Prov. Park	164	C4	49.973700 -114.286000
Bow Valley Prov. Park	164	C3	51.040400 -115.077000
Bow Valley Wildland Prov. Park	164	B3	51.032600 -115.259000
Brown-Lowery Prov. Park	164	C3	50.813900 -114.430600
Calling Lake Prov. Park	159	D3	55.179720 -113.272500
Caribou Mts. Wildland Prov. Park	155	F3	59.205600 -114.897000
Carson-Pegasus Prov. Park	158	C3	54.295800 -115.645000
Castle Wildland Prov. Park	164	C4	49.306456 -114.299287
Chain Lakes Prov. Park	164	C3	50.200000 -114.183330
Chinchaga Wildland Prov. Park	158	B1	57.163400 -119.582000
Cold Lake Prov. Park	159	E3	54.602400 -110.072000
Cold Lake Prov. Park-North Shore	159	E3	54.644800 -110.103600
Crimson Lake Prov. Park	164	C2	52.466900 -115.048000
Cross Lake Prov. Park	159	D3	54.649300 -113.791000
Crow Lake Prov. Park	159	D2	55.800456 -112.152014
Dillberry Lake Prov. Park	165	E1	52.570200 -110.030000
Dinosaur Prov. Park	165	D3	50.770100 -111.480000
Don Getty Wildland Prov. Park	164	B2	50.893000 -114.993000
Dry Island Buffalo Jump Prov. Park	164	C2	51.929500 -112.975000
Dunvegan Prov. Park	158	B2	55.923600 -118.594400
Dunvegan West Wildland Prov. Park	158	B2	56.088900 -119.297000
Elbow Sheep Wildland Prov. Park	164	C3	50.703500 -114.939000
Fort Assiniboine Sandhills Wildland Prov. Park	158	C3	54.387100 -114.608000
Garner Lake Prov. Park	159	D3	54.183420 -111.741000
Gipsy Lake Wildland Prov. Park	159	E2	56.493500 -110.386000
Gooseberry Lake Prov. Park	165	D2	52.116940 -110.759170
Grand Rapids Wildland Prov. Park	159	D1	56.484200 -112.343000
Greene Valley Prov. Park	158	B2	56.140900 -117.242000
Gregoire Lake Prov. Park	159	E1	56.485000 -111.182780
Grizzly Ridge Wildland Prov. Park	158	C3	55.137700 -115.049000
Hay-Zama Lakes Wildland Prov. Park	155	F3	58.774100 -119.016000
Hilliard's Bay Prov. Park	158	C2	55.502900 -116.001000
Hubert Lake Wildland Prov. Park	158	C3	54.554100 -114.244000
Kakwa Wildland Prov. Park	158	A3	54.034600 -119.810000
Kinbrook Island Prov. Park	165	D3	50.437189 -111.910595
La Biche River Wildland Prov. Park	159	D3	54.987000 -112.626000
Lakeland Prov. Park	159	E3	54.759300 -111.557000
Lakeland Prov. Rec. Area	159	E3	54.721800 -111.398000
Lesser Slave Lake Prov. Park	158	C2	55.448000 -114.817000
Lesser Slave Lake Wildland Prov. Park	158	C2	55.497700 -115.567000
Little Bow Prov. Park	164	C3	50.227930 -112.926590
Little Fish Lake Prov. Park	165	D2	51.374246 -112.200944
Long Lake Prov. Park	159	D3	54.439986 -112.763465
Marguerite River Wildland Prov. Park	159	E1	57.638400 -110.266000
Midland Prov. Park	165	D2	51.478295 -112.771085
Miquelon Lake Prov. Park	159	D4	53.246900 -112.874000
Moonshine Lake Prov. Park	158	B2	55.883800 -119.216000
Moose Lake Prov. Park	159	E3	54.272986 -110.931143
Notikewin Prov. Park	158	C1	57.218300 -117.148000
Obed Lake Prov. Park	158	B4	53.558200 -117.101000
O'Brien Prov. Park	158	B3	55.065242 -118.822285
Otter-Orloff Lakes Wildland Prov. Park	159	D2	55.364200 -113.551000
Park Lake Prov. Park	164	C4	49.806621 -112.924681
Peace River Wildland Prov. Park	158	B2	55.983200 -117.765000
Pembina River Prov. Park	158	C4	53.611859 -114.985313
Peter Lougheed Prov. Park	164	B3	50.684100 -115.184000
Pigeon Lake Prov. Park	164	C1	53.029547 -114.150507
Police Outpost Prov. Park	164	C4	49.004503 -113.464980
Queen Elizabeth Prov. Park	158	B2	56.219128 -117.693540
Red Lodge Prov. Park	164	C2	51.947917 -114.243862
Rochon Sands Prov. Park	165	D2	52.461755 -112.892373
Rock Lake Solomon Creek Wildland Prov. Park	158	B4	53.413700 -118.118000
Saskatoon Island Prov. Park	158	B2	55.205201 -119.085401
Sheep River Prov. Park	164	C3	50.647300 -114.660000
Sir Winston Churchill Prov. Park	159	D3	54.832050 -111.976109
Spray Valley Prov. Park	164	B3	50.888700 -115.293000
Stony Mtn. Wildland Prov. Park	159	E2	56.211500 -111.244000
Sundance Prov. Park	158	B4	53.668700 -116.926000
Sylvan Lake Prov. Park	164	C2	52.315760 -114.092272
Thunder Lake Prov. Park	158	C3	54.131941 -114.725882
Tillebrook Prov. Park	165	D3	50.538593 -111.812268
Vermilion Prov. Park	159	E4	53.367679 -110.909771
Wabamun Lake Prov. Park	158	C4	53.565029 -114.441575
Whitehorse Wildland Prov. Park	164	B1	52.957900 -117.395000
Whitemud Falls Wildland Prov. Park	159	E1	56.703400 -110.084000
Whitney Lakes Prov. Park	159	E4	53.847100 -110.537000
William A. Switzer Prov. Park	158	B4	53.492000 -117.804000
Williamson Prov. Park	158	B3	55.081821 -117.560174
Willow Creek Prov. Park	164	C3	50.118067 -113.776021
Winagami Lake Prov. Park	158	C2	55.627500 -116.738000
Winagami Wildland Prov. Park	158	C2	55.611900 -116.635000
Woolford Prov. Park	164	C4	49.178498 -113.190438
Writing-On-Stone Prov. Park	165	D4	49.061400 -111.639000
Wyndham-Carseland Prov. Park	164	C3	50.827750 -113.436542
Young's Point Prov. Park	158	B3	55.148000 -117.572000

BRITISH COLUMBIA

BRITISH COLUMBIA	PAGE	GRID	LATITUDE LONGITUDE
National Park & Rec. Areas			
Chilkoot Trail N.H.S.	155	D3	59.756667 -134.960833
Fort Langley N.H.S.	163	D3	49.168056 -122.569167
Fort McLeod N.H.S.	157	E1	54.992384 -123.039629
Fort Saint James N.H.S.	157	D2	54.440278 -124.255556
Gitwangak Battle Hill N.H.S.	156	C1	55.119444 -128.018056
Glacier Natl. Park-Eastern Welcome Sta.	164	A2	51.511700 -117.442000
Glacier Natl. Park-Rogers Pass Discovery Center	164	A2	51.300600 -117.521500
Gulf Islands Natl. Park Res.	163	D4	48.769400 -123.210000
Gulf of Georgia Cannery N.H.S.	163	D3	49.124722 -123.199722
Gwaii Haanas Natl. Park Res. & Haida Heritage Site	156	A3	52.349722 -131.433056
Kootenay Natl. Park-Radium Hot Springs Vis. Ctr.	164	B3	50.619500 -116.069800
Kootenay Natl. Park-Vermilion Crossing Vis. Ctr.	164	B3	51.000000 -115.966000
Mount Revelstoke Natl. Park-Western Welcome Sta.	164	A2	51.042000 -117.983900
Pacific Rim Natl. Park Res.-Broken Group Islands	162	B3	48.891100 -125.300800
Pacific Rim Natl. Park Res.-Pacific Rim Vis. Ctr.	162	B3	48.992000 -125.587200
Pacific Rim Natl. Park Res.-West Coast Trail	162	C4	48.704800 -124.866100
Pacific Rim Natl. Park Res.-Wickaninnish Interpretive Center	162	B3	49.012700 -125.674200
Yoho Natl. Park-Field Vis. Ctr.	164	B2	51.397800 -116.492000
Provincial Park & Rec. Areas			
Akamina-Kishinena Prov. Park	164	C4	49.032700 -114.178000
Alexandra Bridge Prov. Park	163	E2	49.700000 -121.399722
Alice Lake Prov. Park	163	D2	49.783056 -123.116667
Allison Lake Prov. Park	163	F2	49.683056 -120.599722
Anstey Hunakwa Prov. Park	164	A2	51.140600 -118.924300
Arctic Pacific Lakes Prov. Park	157	E2	54.384400 -121.553000
Arrow Lakes Prov. Park	164	A3	49.883056 -118.065667
Arrowstone Prov. Park	163	E1	50.879900 -121.273000
Atlin Prov. Park	155	E3	59.165400 -133.914000
Babine Lake-Pendleton Bay Marine Prov. Park	157	D2	54.533000 -125.724800
Babine Lake-Smithers Landing Marine Prov. Park	156	C1	55.098400 -126.600000
Babine Mountains Prov. Park	156	C1	54.913100 -126.928000
Babine River Corridor Prov. Park	156	C1	55.577400 -127.032000
Barkerville Prov. Park	157	E3	53.088889 -121.510833
Bear Creek Prov. Park	163	F2	49.930556 -119.520556
Bearhole Lake Prov. Park	158	A3	55.043400 -120.568000
Beatton Prov. Park	158	A1	56.333056 -120.933056
Beaumont Prov. Park	157	D2	54.050000 -124.616667
Beaver Creek Prov. Park	164	A4	49.066667 -117.600000
Big Bar Lake Prov. Park	157	E4	51.316667 -121.816667
Big Bunsby Marine Prov. Park	162	A2	50.120800 -127.504200
Big Creek Prov. Park	157	E4	51.301500 -123.158000
Bijoux Falls Prov. Park	157	E1	55.300000 -122.666667
Birkenhead Lake Prov. Park	163	D1	50.577900 -122.737000
Bishop River Prov. Park	162	C1	50.912500 -124.038000
Blanket Creek Prov. Park	164	A3	50.833056 -118.083056
Bligh Island Marine Prov. Park	162	A2	49.633300 -126.553000
Bowron Lake Prov. Park	157	F3	53.174100 -121.012000
Boya Lake Prov. Park	155	E3	59.380500 -129.090000
Brandywine Falls Prov. Park	163	D2	50.033056 -123.116667
Bridal Veil Falls Prov. Park	163	E3	49.183056 -121.733056
Bridge Lake Prov. Park	157	F4	51.483056 -120.700000
Bromley Rock Prov. Park	163	F3	49.416667 -120.258056
Brooks Peninsula Prov. Park	162	A2	50.180300 -127.657000
Broughton Archipelago Marine Prov. Park	162	A1	50.687100 -126.663000
Bugaboo Prov. Park	164	B3	50.794700 -116.808000
Callaghan Lake Prov. Park	163	D2	50.206900 -123.189000
Bull Canyon Prov. Park	157	E4	52.091667 -123.374722
Canal Flats Prov. Park	164	B3	50.183056 -115.816667
Canim Beach Prov. Park	157	F4	51.816667 -120.872667
Cape Scott Prov. Park	162	A1	50.765900 -128.246000
Cariboo Mts. Prov. Park	157	F3	52.852600 -120.538000
Cariboo River Prov. Park	157	F3	52.873600 -121.222000
Carmanah Walbran Prov. Park	162	C4	48.654500 -124.628000
Carp Lake Prov. Park	157	E2	54.769400 -123.387000
Catala Island Marine Prov. Park	162	A2	49.835833 -127.054167
Cathedral Prov. Park	163	F3	49.069800 -120.174000
Champion Lakes Prov. Park	164	A4	49.184100 -117.624000
Charlie Lake Prov. Park	158	A1	56.316667 -120.999722
Chasm Prov. Park	157	F4	51.178900 -121.438000
Chilliwack Lake Prov. Park	163	E3	49.072200 -121.436000
Clayoquot Arm Prov. Park	162	B3	49.172800 -125.560000
Clayoquot Plateau Prov. Park	162	B3	49.225100 -125.428000
Clendinning Prov. Park	162	C1	50.429700 -123.733000
Codville Lagoon Marine Prov. Park	156	C4	52.060833 -127.855556
Conkle Lake Prov. Park	164	A4	49.166667 -119.100000
Coquihalla Canyon Prov. Park	163	E3	49.371944 -121.366667
Cormorant Channel Marine Prov. Park	162	A1	50.593500 -126.850900
Cowichan River Prov. Park	162	C4	48.780800 -123.920000
Crooked River Prov. Park	157	E2	54.466667 -122.666667
Crowsnest Prov. Park	164	C4	49.649722 -114.699722
Cummins Lakes Prov. Park	164	A2	52.104100 -118.066000
Cypress Prov. Park	163	D3	49.425800 -123.209000
Dahl Lake Prov. Park	157	E2	53.769900 -123.293000
Desolation Sound Marine Prov. Park	162	C2	50.101100 -124.710000
Diana Lake Prov. Park	156	B2	54.216667 -130.166667
Downing Prov. Park	163	E1	51.000000 -121.783056
Dry Gulch Prov. Park	164	B3	50.583056 -116.033056
Duffey Lake Prov. Park	163	D1	50.407500 -122.337000
Dune Za Keyih Prov. Park	155	E3	58.323000 -126.355000
Echo Lake Prov. Park	164	A3	50.199722 -118.700000
Edge Hills Prov. Park	163	E1	51.035900 -121.871000
Elk Falls Prov. Park	162	B2	50.041000 -125.324000
Elk Lakes Prov. Park	164	C3	50.480800 -115.088000
Ellison Prov. Park	164	A3	50.173333 -119.433056
Emory Creek Prov. Park	163	E3	49.516667 -121.416667
Eneas Lakes Prov. Park	163	F2	49.752400 -119.936000
Entiako Prov. Park	157	D3	53.221500 -125.443000
Epper Passage Prov. Park	162	B3	49.219167 -125.949722
Eskers Prov. Park	157	E2	54.081300 -123.205000
Ethel F. Wilson Mem. Prov. Park	157	D2	54.416667 -125.683056
Fillongley Prov. Park	162	C3	49.534100 -124.755200
Finger-Tatuk Prov. Park	157	D2	53.515600 -124.226000
Flat Lake Prov. Park	157	F4	51.499400 -121.521000
Flores Island Prov. Park	162	B3	49.291000 -126.173000
Francois Lake Prov. Park	157	D2	53.966667 -125.166667
French Beach Prov. Park	162	C4	48.383056 -123.933056
Garibaldi Prov. Park	163	D2	49.943200 -122.751000
Gibson Marine Prov. Park	162	B3	49.266667 -126.066667
Gitnadoiks River Prov. Park	156	B2	54.161700 -129.162000
Gladstone Prov. Park	164	A4	49.268900 -118.269000
God's Pocket Marine Prov. Park	162	A1	50.837200 -127.562000
Goldpan Prov. Park	163	E2	50.350000 -121.383056
Gordon Bay Prov. Park	162	C4	48.833056 -124.199722
Graham-Laurier Prov. Park	155	F4	56.594900 -123.466000
Graystokes Prov. Park	164	A3	49.986200 -118.850000
Green Inlet Marine Prov. Park	156	C3	52.918167 -128.485944
Green Lake Prov. Park	157	F4	51.400000 -121.199722
Hamber Prov. Park	164	A2	52.380300 -117.882000
Harmony Islands Marine Prov. Park	162	C2	49.862222 -124.012222
Ha'thayim Marine Prov. Park	162	C2	50.169400 -124.955000
Heather-Dina Lakes Prov. Park	157	E1	55.508300 -123.285000
Height of the Rockies Prov. Park	164	B3	50.488900 -115.228000
Herald Prov. Park	164	A3	50.788056 -119.201000
Hesquiat Lake Prov. Park	162	B3	49.500000 -126.385833
Hitchie Creek Prov. Park	162	C4	48.795556 -124.737500
Horne Lake Caves Prov. Park	162	C3	49.344167 -124.755556
Horsefly Lake Prov. Park	157	F3	52.383056 -121.300000
Inkaneep Prov. Park	163	F3	49.233056 -119.533056
Inland Lake Prov. Park	162	C2	49.953800 -124.481000
Itcha Ilgachuz Prov. Park	157	D3	52.711500 -124.974000
Jackman Flats Prov. Park	164	A1	52.950000 -119.416667
Jedediah Island Marine Prov. Park	162	C3	49.500000 -124.199722
Jewel Lake Prov. Park	164	A4	49.183056 -118.599722
Jimsmith Lake Prov. Park	164	B4	49.483056 -115.833056
Joffre Lakes Prov. Park	163	D2	50.344100 -122.477000
Johnstone Creek Prov. Park	164	A4	49.050000 -119.049722
Juan De Fuca Prov. Park	162	C4	48.489800 -124.290000
Junction Sheep Range Prov. Park	157	E4	51.801000 -122.435000
Juniper Beach Prov. Park	163	E1	50.785833 -121.083056
Kakwa Prov. Park & Protected Area	158	A3	54.057200 -120.296000
Kekuli Bay Prov. Park	164	A3	50.183056 -119.340278
Kentucky-Alleyne Prov. Park	163	F2	49.916667 -120.566667
Kianuko Prov. Park	164	B4	49.421600 -116.456000
Kikomun Creek Prov. Park	164	B4	49.233056 -115.250000
Kilby Prov. Park	163	E3	49.237500 -121.960833
Kinaskan Lake Prov. Park	155	E4	57.496100 -130.234000
Kiskatinaw Prov. Park	158	A2	55.950000 -120.566667
Kleanza Creek Prov. Park	156	C2	54.599722 -128.399722
Klewnuggit Inlet Marine Prov. Park	156	B2	53.688500 -129.697000
Kluskoil Lake Prov. Park	157	D3	53.202900 -123.892000
Kokanee Creek Prov. Park	164	B4	49.605722 -117.133056
Kokanee Glacier Prov. Park	164	B4	49.781800 -117.136000
Kootenay Lake Prov. Park	164	B3	50.085000 -116.931189

Park	Page	Grid	Latitude Longitude
Kwadacha Wilderness Prov. Park	155	E3	57.820400 -125.058000
Lac Le Jeune Prov. Park	163	F1	50.483056 -120.483056
Lakelse Lake Prov. Park	156	C2	54.398900 -128.533000
Lawn Point Prov. Park	162	A1	50.333056 -127.966667
Lockhart Beach Prov. Park	164	B4	49.516667 -116.783056
Lockhart Creek Prov. Park	164	B4	49.497300 -116.705000
Loveland Bay Prov. Park	162	B2	50.049722 -125.450000
Lowe Inlet Marine Prov. Park	156	B2	53.555556 -129.580278
MacMillan Prov. Park	162	C3	49.283056 -124.666667
Main Lake Prov. Park	162	B2	50.210000 -125.215000
Mansons Landing Prov. Park	162	C2	50.121500 -124.928300
Maquinna Marine Prov. Park	162	B3	49.390500 -126.342000
Marble River Prov. Park	162	A1	50.544300 -127.526000
Martha Creek Prov. Park	164	A3	51.141667 -118.198122
McConnell Lake Prov. Park	163	F1	50.521944 -120.456667
McDonald Creek Prov. Park	164	A3	50.131056 -117.813667
Mehatl Creek Prov. Park	163	E2	50.036100 -122.054000
Moberly Lake Prov. Park	158	A2	55.800000 -121.700000
Momich Lakes Prov. Park	164	A2	51.327200 -119.353000
Monck Prov. Park	163	F2	50.178667 -120.533056
Moose Valley Prov. Park	157	E4	51.649800 -121.648000
Morton Lake Prov. Park	162	B2	50.116667 -125.483056
Mount Assiniboine Prov. Park	164	B3	50.937400 -115.761000
Mount Blanchet Prov. Park	157	D1	55.275500 -125.863000
Mount Fernie Prov. Park	164	C4	49.483056 -115.099722
Mount Pope Prov. Park	157	D2	54.490700 -124.331000
Mount Robson Prov. Park	164	A1	52.927000 -118.831000
Mount Seymour Prov. Park	163	D3	49.392400 -122.926000
Mount Terry Fox Prov. Park	164	A1	52.940800 -119.254000
Moyie Lake Prov. Park	164	B4	49.373333 -115.837222
Myra-Bellevue Prov. Park	164	A4	49.752100 -119.374000
Nahatlatch Prov. Park	163	E2	49.980200 -121.780000
Naikoon Prov. Park	156	A2	53.863400 -131.889000
Nairn Falls Prov. Park	163	D2	50.283056 -122.833056
Nancy Greene Prov. Park	164	A4	49.250000 -117.933056
Nickel Plate Prov. Park	163	F3	49.399722 -119.949722
Nicolum River Prov. Park	163	E3	49.366667 -121.341667
Nimpkish Lake Prov. Park	162	A2	50.337700 -127.005000
Niskonlith Lake Prov. Park	163	F1	50.795556 -119.777778
Norbury Lake Prov. Park	164	B4	49.533056 -115.483056
Nuchatlitz Prov. Park	162	A2	49.815700 -126.981000
Octopus Island Marine Prov. Park	162	B2	50.278400 -125.242100
Okanagan Lake Prov. Park	163	F2	49.683056 -119.719867
Okanagan Mtn. Prov. Park	163	F2	49.724600 -119.629000
Okeover Arm Prov. Park	162	C2	49.999722 -124.726667
One Island Lake Prov. Park	158	A2	55.300000 -120.266667
Paarens Beach Prov. Park	157	D2	54.416667 -124.399722
Paul Lake Prov. Park	163	F1	50.741667 -120.120556
Pinecone Burke Prov. Park	163	D3	49.526200 -122.721000
Porpoise Bay Prov. Park	162	C3	49.516667 -123.749722
Porteau Cove Prov. Park	163	D3	49.549722 -123.233056
Premier Lake Prov. Park	164	B4	49.900000 -115.650000
Princess Louisa Marine Prov. Park	162	C2	50.203722 -123.766667
Ptarmigan Creek Prov. Park	157	F2	53.487600 -120.880000
Puntchesakut Lake Prov. Park	157	E3	52.983056 -122.933056
Purden Lake Prov. Park	157	E2	53.928000 -121.912000
Quatsino Prov. Park	162	A1	50.491667 -127.816667
Rearguard Falls Prov. Park	157	F3	52.973333 -119.366667
Redfern-Keily Prov. Park	155	F3	57.405600 -123.878000
Roberts Creek Prov. Park	162	C3	49.433056 -123.666667
Rolley Lake Prov. Park	163	D3	49.250000 -122.400000
Rosebery Prov. Park	164	B3	50.033056 -117.400000
Rubyrock Lake Prov. Park	157	D2	54.677100 -125.348000
Ruckle Prov. Park	163	D4	48.766667 -123.383056
Rugged Point Marine Prov. Park	162	A2	49.963889 -127.238889
Saint Mary's Alpine Prov. Park	164	B4	49.877000 -116.348000
Sandy Island Marine Prov. Park	162	C3	49.616667 -124.849722
Schoen Lake Prov. Park	162	B2	50.176500 -126.245000
Schoolhouse Lake Prov. Park	157	F4	51.883600 -120.993000
Seeley Lake Prov. Park	156	C1	55.199722 -127.683056
Seven Sisters Prov. Park	156	C1	54.946900 -128.150000
Silver Beach Prov. Park	164	A2	51.240278 -118.955556
Silver Lake Prov. Park	163	E3	49.316667 -121.399722
Silver Star Prov. Park	164	A3	50.376900 -119.082000
Simson Prov. Park	162	C3	49.479700 -123.962900
Skihist Prov. Park	163	E2	50.249722 -121.500000
Skookumchuck Narrows Prov. Park	162	C2	49.744700 -123.915500
Smelt Bay Prov. Park	162	C2	50.033056 -124.983056
Sowchea Bay Prov. Park	157	D2	54.419167 -124.448333
Sproat Lake Prov. Park	162	C3	49.300000 -124.916667
Squitty Bay Prov. Park	162	C3	49.454167 -124.166667
Stagleap Prov. Park	164	B4	49.058700 -117.048000
Steelhead Prov. Park	163	E1	50.752778 -120.868056
Stemwinder Prov. Park	163	F3	49.366667 -120.133056
Stone Mtn. Prov. Park	155	E3	58.588600 -124.757000
Strathcona Prov. Park	162	B2	49.629300 -125.710000
Stuart Lake Marine Prov. Park	157	D2	54.650000 -125.000000
Sugarbowl Prov. Park	157	E2	53.801200 -121.589000
Sukunka Falls Prov. Park	157	E1	55.316667 -121.700000
Sulphur Passage Prov. Park	162	B3	49.412000 -126.094000
Summit Lake Prov. Park	164	A3	50.150000 -117.666667
Surge Narrows Prov. Park	162	B2	50.233056 -125.149722
Sutherland River Prov. Park	157	D2	54.338300 -124.818000
Sydney Inlet Prov. Park	162	B3	49.480000 -126.283000
Syringa Prov. Park	164	A4	49.378000 -117.906000
Tahsish-Kwois Prov. Park	162	A2	50.189100 -127.161000
Tatlatui Prov. Park	155	E4	56.996200 -127.386000
Tatshenshini-Alsek Prov. Park	155	D3	59.595900 -137.443000
Taylor Arm Prov. Park	162	B3	49.283056 -125.049722
Ten Mile Lake Prov. Park	157	E3	53.066667 -122.450000
Thurston Bay Marine Prov. Park	162	B2	50.383056 -125.316667
Ts'il-os Prov. Park	157	D4	51.191700 -123.971000
Tudyah Lake Prov. Park	157	E1	55.066667 -123.033056
Tunkwa Prov. Park	163	E1	50.615200 -120.887000
Tyhee Lake Prov. Park	156	C2	54.700000 -127.033056
Union Passage Marine Prov. Park	156	B3	53.410900 -129.436000
Upper Adams River Prov. Park	164	A2	51.682700 -119.228000
Valhalla Prov. Park	164	A4	49.873700 -117.567000
Vargas Island Prov. Park	162	B3	49.174000 -126.031000
Vaseux Lake Prov. Park	164	A4	49.268200 -119.474000
Walsh Cove Prov. Park	162	C2	50.268056 -124.800000
Wasa Lake Prov. Park	164	B4	49.793056 -115.738056
West Arm Prov. Park	164	B4	49.507000 -117.118000
West Lake Prov. Park	157	E2	53.733056 -122.866667
Whiskers Point Prov. Park	157	E1	54.900000 -122.933056
White Pelican Prov. Park	157	E3	52.284000 -123.031000
Whiteswan Lake Prov. Park	164	B3	50.145300 -115.487000
Woss Lake Prov. Park	162	A2	50.060400 -126.626000
Yahk Provincial Park	164	B4	49.083056 -116.083056
Yard Creek Prov. Park	164	A3	50.899722 -118.799722

MANITOBA	PAGE	GRID	LATITUDE LONGITUDE
National Park & Rec. Areas			
Lower Fort Garry N.H.S.	167	E3	50.136850 -96.940569
Riding Mtn. Natl. Park-Deep Lake Ranger Sta.	167	D3	50.860300 -100.836600
Riding Mtn. Natl. Park-Lake Audy Ranger Sta.	167	D3	50.712900 -100.230600
Riding Mtn. Natl. Park-McKinnon Creek Ranger Sta.	167	D3	50.787100 -99.579500
Riding Mtn. Natl. Park-Moon Lake Ranger Sta.	167	D3	50.995900 -100.067200
Riding Mtn. Natl. Park-South Lake Ranger Sta.	167	D3	50.655200 -100.061600
Riding Mtn. Natl. Park-Sugarloaf Ranger Sta.	167	D3	50.985300 -100.742100
Riding Mtn. Natl. Park-Whirlpool Ranger Sta.	167	D3	50.683300 -99.553500
Provincial Park & Rec. Areas			
Asessippi Prov. Park	166	C3	50.966400 -101.379700
Atikaki Prov. Wilderness Park	167	F2	51.532200 -95.547000
Bakers Narrows Prov. Park	161	D3	54.671100 -101.675000
Beaudry Prov. Park	167	E4	49.853900 -97.473300
Bell Lake Prov. Park	166	C1	52.541700 -101.241400
Birds Hill Prov. Park	167	E3	50.028800 -96.893200
Camp Morton Prov. Park	167	E3	50.710000 -96.990300
Clearwater Lake Prov. Park	161	D3	54.096200 -101.162000
Criddle–Vane Homestead Prov. Park	167	D4	49.707600 -99.596600
Duck Mtn. Prov. Park	167	D2	51.715600 -101.112000
Elk Island Prov. Park	167	E3	50.758300 -96.536500
Grand Beach Prov. Park	167	E3	50.567900 -96.554900
Grass River Prov. Park	161	D3	54.655500 -101.092000
Hecla–Grindstone Prov. Park	167	E2	51.198300 -96.660200
Hnausa Beach Prov. Park	167	E3	50.900300 -96.992200
Kettle Stones Prov. Park	167	D2	52.359200 -100.595300
Lake Saint George Prov. Park	167	E2	51.719703 -97.406772
Lundar Beach Prov. Park	167	E3	50.724000 -98.273000
Manipogo Prov. Park	167	D2	51.517000 -99.550000
Nopiming Prov. Park	167	F3	50.665200 -95.305600
North Steeprock Lake Prov. Park	166	C1	52.611800 -101.380000
Paint Lake Prov. Park	161	E2	55.492100 -98.018000
Patricia Beach Prov. Park	167	E3	50.467300 -96.575300
Pembina Valley Prov. Park	167	E4	49.038500 -98.296400
Pinawa Dam Prov. Park	167	F3	50.145200 -95.945700
Rainbow Beach Prov. Park	167	D3	51.099400 -99.718400
Saint Ambroise Beach Prov. Park	167	E3	50.275500 -98.074300
Saint Malo Prov. Park	167	E4	49.321400 -96.930490
South Atikaki Prov. Park	167	F3	51.041400 -95.417600
Spruce Woods Prov. Park	167	D4	49.703100 -99.141900
Stephenfield Prov. Park	167	E4	49.523400 -98.300500
Turtle Mtn. Prov. Park	167	D4	49.041500 -100.216000
Watchorn Prov. Park	167	E2	51.293100 -98.598500
Whitefish Lake Prov. Park	166	C2	52.333900 -101.587100
Whiteshell Prov. Park	167	F3	50.140900 -95.584400
William Lake Prov. Park	167	D4	49.055000 -100.038800
Winnipeg Beach Prov. Park	167	E3	50.512300 -96.967000

NEW BRUNSWICK	PAGE	GRID	LATITUDE LONGITUDE
National Park & Rec. Areas			
Beaubears Island N.H.S.	179	D3	46.972778 -65.569444
Fort Beauséjour N.H.S.	180	C1	45.865278 -64.290278
Fort Gaspareaux N.H.S.	180	C1	46.040833 -64.072778
Fundy Natl. Park-Vis. Ctr.	180	C1	45.659500 -65.132600
Kouchibouguac Natl. Park-Vis. Ctr.	179	D3	46.773200 -65.004900
Monument Lefebvre N.H.S.	180	C1	45.979167 -64.567222
Roosevelt Campobello International Park	180	A2	44.849722 -66.949722
Saint Andrews Blockhouse N.H.S.	180	A2	45.076389 -67.063889
Saint Croix Island International Hist. Site	180	A2	45.127778 -67.133333
Provincial Park & Rec. Areas			
De la République Prov. Park	178	B3	47.442778 -68.395556
Herring Cove Prov. Park	180	A2	44.866667 -66.933056
Mactaquac Prov. Park	180	A1	45.959025 -66.892556
Mount Carleton Prov. Park	178	C3	47.392300 -66.835500
Murray Beach Prov. Park	180	C1	46.016667 -63.983056
New River Beach Prov. Park	180	A2	45.133056 -66.533056
Parlee Beach Prov. Park	180	C1	46.233056 -64.499722
Sugarloaf Prov. Park	178	C2	47.974000 -66.671900
The Anchorage Prov. Park	180	A3	44.649722 -66.800000

NEWFOUNDLAND & LABRADOR	PAGE	GRID	LATITUDE LONGITUDE
National Park & Rec. Areas			
Castle Hill N.H.S.	183	E4	47.251389 -53.971111
Gros Morne Natl. Park-Vis. Ctr.	182	C2	49.571500 -57.877900
Hawthorne Cottage N.H.S.	183	E4	47.543333 -53.210833
L'Anse aux Meadows N.H.S.	183	F1	51.595000 -55.532778
Port au Choix N.H.S.	182	C1	50.712222 -57.375278
Red Bay N.H.S.	183	F1	51.733056 -56.415556
Ryan Premises N.H.S.	183	E3	48.648056 -53.112500
Terra Nova Natl. Park-Information Center	183	E3	48.394900 -54.204000
Terra Nova Natl. Park-Saltons Vis. Ctr.	183	E3	48.580600 -53.958900
Provincial Park & Rec. Areas			
Barachois Pond Prov. Park	182	C3	48.477100 -58.256600
Blow Me Down Prov. Park	182	C2	49.090833 -58.364444
Butter Pot Prov. Park	183	F4	47.390900 -53.071300
Chance Cove Prov. Park	183	F4	46.776900 -53.045400
Codroy Valley Prov. Park	182	C4	47.833333 -59.337778
Deadman's Bay Prov. Park	183	E2	49.331389 -53.692500
Dildo Run Prov. Park	183	E2	49.535556 -54.721667
Dungeon Prov. Park	183	E3	48.666667 -53.083611
Frenchman's Cove Prov. Park	183	D4	47.209444 -55.401667
Gooseberry Cove Prov. Park	183	E4	47.068056 -54.087778
J.T. Cheeseman Prov. Park	182	C4	47.631111 -59.249444
La Manche Prov. Park	183	F4	47.175200 -52.901200
Lockston Path Prov. Park	183	E3	48.437778 -53.379722
Notre Dame Prov. Park	183	E2	49.115833 -55.086389
Pinware River Prov. Park	183	F1	51.631667 -56.704167
Sandbanks Prov. Park	182	C4	47.607222 -57.646944
Sir Richard Squires Mem. Prov. Park	183	D2	49.354000 -57.213400
The Arches Prov. Park	182	C2	50.113333 -57.663056

NORTHWEST TERRITORIES	PAGE	GRID	LATITUDE LONGITUDE
National Park & Rec. Areas			
Nááts'ihch'oh Natl. Park Res.	155	E2	62.617399 -128.787113
Nahanni Natl. Park Res.	155	E3	61.083333 -123.600000
Tuktut Nogait Natl. Park	155	E1	69.283333 -123.016667

NOVA SCOTIA	PAGE	GRID	LATITUDE LONGITUDE
National Park & Rec. Areas			
Alexander Graham Bell N.H.S.	181	F1	46.102778 -60.745556
Cape Breton Highlands Natl. Park-East Ent.	182	B4	46.642800 -60.404200
Cape Breton Highlands Natl. Park-West Ent.	182	B4	46.647300 -60.950200
Fort Anne N.H.S.	180	B3	44.741667 -65.519167
Fort Edward N.H.S.	180	C2	44.995556 -64.135278
Fortress of Louisbourg N.H.S.	181	F1	45.900300 -59.995100
Grand-Pré N.H.S.	180	C2	45.108889 -64.311944
Grassy Island N.H.S.	181	F2	45.336667 -60.973611
Kejimkujik Natl. Park (Seaside Adjunct)	180	C4	43.865800 -64.836900
Kejimkujik Natl. Park and N.H.S.	180	B3	44.336700 -65.268200
Marconi N.H.S.	181	F4	46.211111 -59.952778
Port-Royal N.H.S.	180	B3	44.712500 -65.610556
Saint Peters Canal N.H.S.	181	F1	45.655556 -60.870556
York Redoubt N.H.S.	181	D3	44.596583 -63.552439
Provincial Park & Rec. Areas			
Amherst Shore Prov. Park	180	C1	45.961181 -63.879025
Battery Prov. Park	181	F1	45.657022 -60.866764
Beaver Mtn. Prov. Park	181	E2	45.567556 -62.153583
Blomidon Prov. Park	180	C2	45.255869 -64.352056
Boylston Prov. Park	181	E2	45.426839 -61.510603
Cape Chignecto Prov. Park	180	C2	45.375800 -64.891300
Caribou–Munroes Island Prov. Park	181	D1	45.721800 -62.656914
Ellenwood Lake Prov. Park	180	B4	43.929481 -66.005700
Five Islands Prov. Park	180	C2	45.407781 -64.021500
Graves Island Prov. Park	180	C3	44.565550 -64.218642
Laurie Prov. Park	181	D2	44.878175 -63.602194
Martinique Beach Prov. Park	181	D3	44.689911 -63.147567
Mira River Prov. Park	181	F1	46.026006 -60.037433
Porters Prov. Park	181	D3	44.691106 -63.308892
Rissers Beach Prov. Park	180	C3	44.232397 -64.423919
Salsman Prov. Park	181	E2	45.236856 -61.767150
Salt Springs Prov. Park	181	D2	45.545280 -62.878890
Shubenacadie Prov. Wildlife Park	181	D2	45.087222 -63.387500
Smileys Prov. Park	180	C2	45.013925 -63.961247
The Islands Prov. Park	180	B4	43.765503 -65.340347
Thomas Raddall Prov. Park	180	C4	43.844783 -64.919694
Valleyview Prov. Park	180	B2	44.875200 -65.316064
Wentworth Prov. Park	181	D2	45.622222 -63.567222
Whycocomagh Prov. Park	181	F1	45.968094 -61.109908

ONTARIO	PAGE	GRID	LATITUDE LONGITUDE
National Park & Rec. Areas			
Battle of the Windmill N.H.S.	174	B4	44.722778 -75.486944
Bell Homestead N.H.P.	172	C3	43.107946 -80.273060
Bellevue House N.H.S.	173	F1	44.220556 -76.506667
Bruce Peninsula Natl. Park	170	C4	45.189100 -81.485500
Fathom Five Natl. Marine Park	170	C4	45.304800 -81.727600
Fort George N.H.S.	173	D3	43.252778 -79.051111
Fort Henry N.H.S.	173	F1	44.230833 -76.459444
Fort Malden N.H.S.	172	A4	42.108056 -83.113889
Fort Mississauga N.H.S.	173	D3	43.260833 -79.076667
Fort Saint Joseph N.H.S.	170	B3	46.063889 -83.944167
Fort Wellington N.H.S.	174	B4	44.713889 -75.510833
Georgian Bay Islands Natl. Park-Welcome Center	171	D4	44.803900 -79.720400
Glengarry Cairn N.H.S.	174	C3	45.121667 -74.490278
Merrickville Blockhouse N.H.S.	174	B4	44.916667 -75.837500
Peterborough Lift Lock N.H.S.	173	E1	44.308056 -78.300556
Point Clark Lighthouse N.H.S.	172	B2	44.073056 -81.756667
Point Pelee Natl. Park-Park Ent. Kiosk	172	A4	41.987700 -82.549900
Point Pelee Natl. Park-Vis. Ctr.	172	A4	41.931700 -82.513500
Pukaskwa Natl. Park-Information Center	170	A2	48.700400 -86.197200
Queenston Heights N.H.S.	173	D3	43.158056 -79.052778
Sault Ste. Marie Canal N.H.S.	170	B3	46.511667 -84.355556
Sir John Johnson House N.H.S.	174	C4	45.144444 -74.580000
Southwold Earthworks N.H.S.	172	B3	42.677778 -81.351389
Thousand Islands Natl. Park-Vis. Ctr.	174	A4	44.452300 -75.860300
Trent-Severn Waterway N.H.S.	173	E1	44.137500 -77.590100
Woodside N.H.S.	172	C2	43.466667 -80.499722
Provincial Park & Rec. Areas			
Abitibi-De-Troyes Prov. Park	171	D1	48.786500 -80.066300
Albany River Prov. Park	169	E1	51.358200 -88.134000
Algonquin Prov. Park	171	E4	45.605300 -78.323900
Arrowhead Prov. Park	171	D4	45.391700 -79.197200
Awenda Prov. Park	172	C1	44.854400 -79.989800
Balsam Lake Prov. Park	173	D1	44.642000 -78.864000
Bass Lake Prov. Park	173	D1	44.602000 -79.475000
Batchawana Prov. Park	170	B3	46.941900 -84.587010
Blue Lake Prov. Park	168	B3	49.904200 -93.525600
Bon Echo Prov. Park	171	E4	44.905600 -77.246600
Bonnechere Prov. Park	171	E4	45.658400 -77.570800
Bonnechere River Prov. Park	171	E4	45.674400 -77.661500
Brightsand River Prov. Park	169	D3	49.936700 -90.265400
Bronte Creek Prov. Park	173	D2	43.410490 -79.767830
Caliper Lake Prov. Park	168	B3	49.061670 -93.912780
Carson Lake Prov. Park	171	E4	45.502780 -77.746390
Chapleau-Nemegosenda River Prov. Park	170	B2	48.262300 -83.035300
Charleston Lake Prov. Park	174	A4	44.515400 -76.013600
Chutes Prov. Park	170	C3	46.219510 -82.071480
Craigleith Prov. Park	172	C1	44.535000 -80.367000
Darlington Prov. Park	173	D2	43.875480 -78.778300
Devil's Glen Prov. Park	172	C1	44.361000 -80.207800
Driftwood Prov. Park	171	E3	46.179000 -77.843000
Earl Rowe Prov. Park	172	C1	44.150000 -79.898000
Emily Prov. Park	173	D1	44.340530 -78.532860
Esker Lakes Prov. Park	171	D2	48.290100 -79.906100
Fairbank Prov. Park	170	C3	46.468070 -81.440410
Ferris Prov. Park	173	E1	44.293000 -77.788000
Finlayson Point Prov. Park	171	D3	47.055000 -79.797000
Fitzroy Prov. Park	174	A3	45.482680 -76.209400
French River Prov. Park	171	D3	46.008600 -80.620900
Frontenac Prov. Park	174	A4	44.540500 -76.512700
Fushimi Lake Prov. Park	169	F3	49.824800 -83.913800
Greenwater Prov. Park	170	C1	49.215900 -81.291000
Grundy Lake Prov. Park	171	D4	45.939800 -80.530400
Halfway Lake Prov. Park	170	C3	46.905700 -81.650500
Inverhuron Prov. Park	172	B1	44.298000 -81.580000
Ivanhoe Lake Prov. Park	170	C2	47.957600 -82.742600
John E. Pearce Prov. Park	172	B4	42.617000 -81.444000
Kakabeka Falls Prov. Park	169	D4	48.403290 -89.624130
Kap-Kig-Iwan Prov. Park	171	D2	47.789960 -79.884990
Kettle Lakes Prov. Park	170	C1	48.569400 -80.865400
Killarney Prov. Park	170	C3	46.099400 -81.386900
Killbear Prov. Park	171	D4	45.346200 -80.191200
Kopka River Prov. Park	169	D2	50.006300 -89.493000
Lady Evelyn-Smoothwater Prov. Park	171	D2	47.368500 -80.489300
Lake of the Woods Prov. Park	168	B3	49.221200 -94.606000
Lake on the Mtn. Prov. Park	173	F1	44.039940 -77.056080
Lake Saint Peter Prov. Park	171	E4	45.322000 -78.024000
Lake Superior Prov. Park	170	A2	47.595200 -84.756500
Larder River Prov. Park	171	D2	47.936300 -79.642800
La Verendrye Prov. Park	169	D4	48.138300 -90.431300
Little Abitibi Prov. Park	170	C1	49.637900 -80.922900
Little Current River Prov. Park	169	E2	50.724100 -86.211000
Long Point Prov. Park	172	C4	42.565000 -80.306000
Lower Madawaska River Prov. Park	171	E4	45.236200 -77.289300
MacGregor Point Prov. Park	172	B1	44.403700 -81.465600
Macleod Prov. Park	169	E3	49.676190 -86.931000
Makobe-Grays River Prov. Park	171	D2	47.617200 -80.376300
Mara Prov. Park	173	D1	44.589000 -79.349000
Mark S. Burnham Prov. Park	173	E1	44.299900 -78.257000
Marten River Prov. Park	171	D3	46.729000 -79.807000
Mattawa River Prov. Park	171	D3	46.315000 -79.108400
McRae Point Prov. Park	173	D1	44.569000 -79.320000
Mikisew Prov. Park	171	D4	45.820000 -79.512000
Missinaibi River Prov. Park	170	B1	49.101400 -83.234700
Mississagi Prov. Park	170	C3	46.596500 -82.682500
Mississagi River Prov. Park	170	C3	47.012600 -82.632700
Murphys Point Prov. Park	174	A4	44.774300 -76.240700
Nagagamisis Prov. Park	169	F3	49.475700 -84.771000
Neys Prov. Park	169	E4	48.750500 -86.591900
North Beach Prov. Park	173	E2	43.951050 -77.522660
Oastler Lake Prov. Park	171	D4	45.309000 -79.964800
Obabika River Prov. Park	171	D3	47.221200 -80.262600
Obatanga Prov. Park	170	A2	48.323000 -85.093700
Ojibway Prov. Park	168	C3	49.990900 -92.144400
Opeongo River Prov. Park	171	E4	45.576256 -77.887363
Otoskwin-Attawapiskat River Prov. Park	169	D1	52.235700 -87.491300
Ottawa River Prov. Park	174	A3	45.741700 -76.779800
Ouimet Canyon Prov. Park	169	D4	48.773350 -88.667400
Oxtongue River-Ragged Falls Prov. Park	171	D4	45.366900 -78.914100
Pakwash Prov. Park	168	B2	50.749800 -93.551400
Pancake Bay Prov. Park	170	B3	46.967200 -84.661100
Petroglyphs Prov. Park	173	E1	44.618300 -78.041700
Pigeon River Prov. Park	169	D4	48.025041 -89.572294
Pinery Prov. Park	172	B3	43.257200 -81.834000
Pipestone River Prov. Park	169	D1	52.244300 -90.313500
Point Farms Prov. Park	172	B2	43.804000 -81.700000
Port Bruce Prov. Park	172	B3	42.664000 -81.027000
Port Burwell Prov. Park	172	C3	42.646000 -80.816000
Potholes Prov. Park	170	B2	47.958700 -84.294020
Presqu'Ile Prov. Park	173	E2	44.007000 -77.735000
Quetico Prov. Park	168	C4	48.404500 -91.498700
Rainbow Falls Prov. Park	169	E4	48.830090 -87.389580
Renè Brunelle Prov. Park	170	C1	49.453700 -82.147900
Restoule Prov. Park	171	D3	46.080400 -79.839800
Rideau River Prov. Park	174	B4	45.060000 -75.672000
Rock Point Prov. Park	173	D3	42.854000 -79.552000
Rondeau Prov. Park	172	B4	42.278200 -81.865100
Rushing River Prov. Park	168	B3	49.681850 -94.234890
Samuel de Champlain Prov. Park	171	D3	46.301900 -78.864100
Sandbanks Prov. Park	173	F2	43.910200 -77.267200
Sandbar Lake Prov. Park	168	C3	49.491000 -91.555700
Sauble Falls Prov. Park	172	B1	44.673170 -81.257350
Selkirk Prov. Park	172	C3	42.824000 -79.961000
Sharbot Lake Prov. Park	174	A4	44.775500 -76.724600
Sibbald Point Prov. Park	173	D1	44.322160 -79.325570
Silent Lake Prov. Park	171	E4	44.907500 -78.047200
Silver Lake Prov. Park	174	A4	44.829770 -76.574680
Sioux Narrows Prov. Park	168	B3	49.429570 -94.037260
Six Mile Lake Prov. Park	171	D4	44.819500 -79.733500
Sleeping Giant Prov. Park	169	D4	48.419300 -88.795500
Solace Prov. Park	170	C3	47.189200 -80.683500
Springwater Prov. Park	173	D1	44.443500 -79.748500
Steel River Prov. Park	169	E3	49.161900 -86.812600
Sturgeon Bay Prov. Park	171	D4	45.623400 -80.414100
Sturgeon River Prov. Park	170	C3	46.949800 -80.523900
The Massasauga Prov. Park	171	D4	45.203400 -80.044300
The Shoals Prov. Park	170	B2	47.884800 -83.808000
Turkey Point Prov. Park	172	C3	42.694000 -80.333150
Turtle River-White Otter Lake Prov. Park	168	C3	49.129700 -92.042300
Upper Madawaska River Prov. Park	171	E4	45.513700 -78.078700
Wabakimi Prov. Park	169	D2	50.719100 -89.448500
Wakami Lake Prov. Park	170	C2	47.489700 -82.842000
Wasaga Beach Prov. Park	172	C1	44.494000 -80.027100
Wheatley Prov. Park	172	A4	42.098000 -82.448800
White Lake Prov. Park	170	A1	48.603500 -85.880900
Windy Lake Prov. Park	170	C3	46.619820 -81.455980
Woodland Caribou Prov. Park	168	B2	51.096900 -94.744900

PRINCE EDWARD ISLAND	PAGE	GRID	LATITUDE LONGITUDE
National Park & Rec. Areas			
Port-la-Joye–Fort Amherst N.H.S.	179	E4	46.195278 -63.133611
Prince Edward Island Natl. Park-Brackley Vis. Ctr.	179	E4	46.406200 -63.196600
Prince Edward Island Natl. Park-Cavendish Vis. Ctr.	179	E4	46.492300 -63.379700
Provincial Park & Rec. Areas			
Brudenell River Prov. Park	179	F4	46.209583 -62.588556
Buffaloland Prov. Park	179	F4	46.092500 -62.617778
Cabot Beach Prov. Park	179	E4	46.557250 -63.704250
Cedar Dunes Prov. Park	177	F4	46.622222 -64.381944
Chelton Beach Prov. Park	179	E4	46.303944 -63.747167
Green Park Prov. Park	177	F4	46.590972 -63.890333
Jacques Cartier Prov. Park	177	F4	46.851222 -64.013000
Kings Castle Prov. Park	179	F4	46.019167 -62.567389
Linkletter Prov. Park	179	E4	46.402694 -63.853061
Lord Selkirk Prov. Park	179	F4	46.091889 -62.906000
Mill River Prov. Park	177	F4	46.749722 -64.166667
Northumberland Prov. Park	179	F4	45.966667 -62.716667
Panmure Island Prov. Park	179	F4	46.133056 -62.466667
Red Point Prov. Park	179	F4	46.366667 -62.133056
Wood Islands Prov. Park	181	D1	45.949722 -62.749722

QUÉBEC	PAGE	GRID	LATITUDE LONGITUDE
National Park & Rec. Areas			
Lieu Historique Natl. du Fort-Lennox	175	D4	45.120556 -73.268056
Lieu Historique Natl. du Fort-Témiscamingue	171	D2	47.295000 -79.456667
Parc Natl. de Forillon	179	D1	48.854300 -64.396300
Parc Natl. de la Mauricie-East Ent.	175	D1	46.752600 -72.792600
Parc Natl. de la Mauricie-South Ent.	175	D1	46.650000 -72.969200
Parc Natl. d'Opémican	171	D3	46.884041 -79.096604
Réserve de Parc Natl. de l'Archipel-de-Mingan	177	F1	50.237100 -63.606900
Provincial Park & Rec. Areas			
Parc d'Aiguebelle	171	D1	48.510300 -78.745800
Parc d'Anticosti	182	A2	49.463200 -62.819000
Parc de Frontenac	175	E3	45.848600 -71.184600
Parc de la Gaspésie	178	C1	48.941500 -66.214400
Parc de la Gatineau	174	A3	45.566667 -75.949722
Parc de la Jacques-Cartier	175	E1	47.317300 -71.347000
Parc de la Pointe-Taillon	176	C3	48.717300 -71.993600
Parc de la Yamaska	175	D3	45.429400 -72.601800
Parc de l'Île-Bonaventure-et-du-Rocher-Percé	179	E1	48.496389 -64.161944
Parc de Miguasha	178	C2	48.110556 -66.369444
Parc de Plaisance	174	B3	45.597900 -75.123600
Parc de Récréation du Mont-Orford	175	D3	45.344700 -72.212900
Parc des Grands-Jardins	176	C4	47.681300 -70.836900
Parc des Hautes-Gorges-de-la-Rivière-Malbaie	176	C3	47.918700 -70.498700
Parc des Monts-Valin	176	C3	48.598600 -70.825300
Parc du Bic	178	A1	48.355300 -68.797600
Parc du Mont-Mégantic	175	E3	45.450700 -71.167300
Parc du Mont-Saint-Bruno	175	D3	45.555278 -73.309722
Parc du Mont-Tremblant	174	C2	46.443000 -74.344600
Parc du Saguenay	176	C3	48.289900 -70.243400
Parc Marin du Saguenay-Saint-Laurent	178	A2	48.133056 -69.733056
Parc Régional du Massif du Sud	175	F2	46.581389 -70.467778

SASKATCHEWAN	PAGE	GRID	LATITUDE LONGITUDE
National Park & Rec. Areas			
Batoche N.H.S.	165	F1	52.752800 -106.116700
Battle of Fish Creek N.H.S.	165	F1	52.550000 -106.180300
Fort Battleford N.H.S.	165	E1	52.713800 -108.259600
Fort Espérance N.H.S.	166	C3	50.451400 -101.712800
Fort Livingstone N.H.S.	166	C2	51.903880 -101.960620
Fort Pelly N.H.S.	166	C2	51.795900 -101.951800
Fort Walsh N.H.S.	165	E4	49.559100 -109.901700
Grasslands Natl. Park-East Block Vis. Ctr.	166	A4	49.370800 -106.384800
Grasslands Natl. Park-West Block Vis. Reception Ctr.	166	A4	49.203800 -107.732700
Prince Albert Natl. Park-Waskesiu Vis. Ctr.	160	B3	53.922500 -106.081800
Provincial Park & Rec. Areas			
Blackstrap Prov. Park	166	A2	51.755600 -106.458300
Buffalo Pound Prov. Park	166	B3	50.576200 -105.361000
Candle Lake Prov. Park	160	B4	53.845000 -105.252000
Cannington Manor Prov. Hist. Park	166	C4	49.712900 -102.027300
Clearwater River Prov. Park	159	E1	56.929300 -109.043000
Crooked Lake Prov. Park	166	C3	50.592200 -102.741400
Cumberland House Prov. Hist. Park	160	C4	53.948000 -102.421400
Cypress Hills Interprovincial Park	165	E4	49.632400 -109.809000
Danielson Prov. Park	166	A2	51.252200 -106.866000
Douglas Prov. Park	166	A3	51.025300 -106.480000
Echo Valley Prov. Park	166	B3	50.808500 -103.891900
Fort Carlton Prov. Park	166	A1	52.867100 -106.542700
Fort Pitt Prov. Park	165	E1	53.577000 -109.806300
Good Spirit Lake Prov. Park	166	C2	51.543500 -102.707000
Greenwater Lake Prov. Park	166	C1	52.532000 -103.448000
Katepwa Point Prov. Park	166	B3	50.693165 -103.626025
Lac La Ronge Prov. Park	160	C3	55.249200 -104.769000
Last Mtn. House Prov. Park	166	B3	50.722800 -104.823300
Makwa Lake Prov. Park	159	E3	54.016800 -109.234000
Meadow Lake Prov. Park	159	E3	54.501400 -109.076000
Moose Mtn. Prov. Park	166	C4	49.821300 -102.424000
Narrow Hills Prov. Park	160	C3	54.091300 -104.643000
Pike Lake Prov. Park	166	A2	51.893200 -106.819000
Rowan's Ravine Prov. Park	166	B3	50.995600 -105.179700
Saint Victor Prov. Park	166	A4	49.395300 -105.873200
Saskatchewan Landing Prov. Park	165	F3	50.664600 -107.997000
Steele Narrows Prov. Park	159	E3	54.025900 -109.318400
The Battlefords Prov. Park	165	E1	53.132500 -108.381300
Touchwood Hills Prov. Park	166	B2	51.306400 -104.014100
Wildcat Hill Prov. Park	166	C1	53.273946 -102.492828
Wood Mtn. Post Prov. Hist. Park	166	A4	49.320833 -106.379167

YUKON	PAGE	GRID	LATITUDE LONGITUDE
National Park & Rec. Areas			
Dawson Hist. Complex N.H.S.	155	D2	64.050000 -139.433330
Ivvavik Natl. Park	155	D1	69.519722 -139.525000
Kluane Natl. Park and Res.-North Vis. Ctr.	155	D3	60.991800 -138.520800
Kluane Natl. Park and Res.-South Vis. Ctr.	155	D3	60.752900 -137.510100
Vuntut Natl. Park	155	D1	68.306944 -140.047500
Provincial Park & Rec. Areas			
Herschel Island-Qikiqtaruk Territorial Park	155	D1	69.592100 -139.092400

Continued from page 11

SOUTHEAST

Blue Ridge Parkway★★

574 miles/924 kilometers
Maps 102, 112, 111, 190, 121

From **Front Royal**, take US-340 S to begin **Skyline Drive★★**, the best-known feature of **Shenandoah NP★★**. The drive follows former Indian trails along the **Blue Ridge Parkway★★**. **Marys Rock Tunnel** to **Rockfish Entrance Station★★** passes the oldest rock in the park and **Big Meadows★**. The Drive ends at **Rockfish Gap** at I-64, but continue S on the Parkway. From Terrapin Hill Overlook, detour 16mi W on Rte. 130 to see **Natural Bridge★★**. Enter NC at **Cumberland Knob**, then pass **Blowing Rock★**, **Grandfather Mountain★★** and **Linville Falls★★**. Detour 4.8mi to **Mount Mitchell SP★** to drive to the top of the tallest mountain (6,684ft) E of the Mississippi. At mile 382, the **Folk Art Center** stocks high-quality regional crafts. Popular **Biltmore Estate★★** in **Asheville★** (North Exit of US-25, then 4mi N) includes formal **gardens★★**. The rugged stretch from French Broad River to Cherokee courses 17 tunnels within two national forests. **Looking Glass Rock★★** is breathtaking. The Parkway ends at **Cherokee**, gateway to **Great Smoky Mountains NP★★★** and home of Cherokee tribe members.

Skyline Drive, Shenandoah NP, Blue Ridge Parkway

Central Kentucky★★

379 miles/610 kilometers
Maps 230, 100, 214, 2 27, 110

From **Louisville★★**, home of the **Kentucky Derby★★★**, take I-64 E to **Frankfort**, the state capital. Continue E to **Lexington★★**, heart of **Bluegrass Country★★** with its rolling meadows and white-fenced horse farms. Stop at the **Kentucky Horse Park★★★** for the daily **Parade of Breeds**. Then head S on I-75 through Richmond to the craft center/college town of **Berea**. Return to Lexington and follow the Blue Grass Parkway SW to Exit 25. There, US-150 W leads to Bardstown, site of **My Old Kentucky Home SP★**, immortalized by Stephen Foster in what is now the state song. Drive S from Bardstown on US-31E past **Abraham Lincoln Birthplace NHS★**. Turn right onto Rte. 70 to Cave City, then take US-31W to Park City, gateway to **Mammoth Cave NP★★★**, which features the world's longest cave system. Return to Louisville via I-65 to end the tour.

Florida's Northeast Coast★★

174 miles/280 kilometers
Maps 222, 139, 141, 232

From **Jacksonville★**, drive E on Rte. 10 to **Atlantic Beach**, the most affluent of Jacksonville's beach towns. Head S on Rte. A1A through residential **Neptune Beach**, blue-collar **Jacksonville Beach** and upscale **Ponte Vedra Beach** to reach **St. Augustine★★★**, the oldest city in the US and former capital of Spanish Florida. Farther S, car-racing mecca **Daytona Beach** is known for its **international speedway**. Take US-92 across the Intracoastal Waterway to US-1, heading S to **Titusville**. Take Rte. 402 across the Indian River to **Merritt Island NWR★★** to begin **Black Point Wildlife Drive★**. Return to Titusville and follow Rte. 405 to **Kennedy Space Center★★★**, one of Florida's top attractions, to end the tour.

Castillo de San Marcos, St. Augustine, Florida's Northeast Coast

Florida Keys★★

168 miles/270 kilometers Maps 143, 142

*Note: Green **mile-marker** (MM) posts, sometimes difficult to see, line US-1 (Overseas Hwy.), showing distances from Key West (MM 0). Much of the route is two-lane, and traffic can be heavy in December to April and on weekends. Allow 3hrs for the drive. Crossing 43 bridges and causeways (only one over land), the highway offers fine views of the Atlantic Ocean (E) and Florida Bay (W).*

Drive S from **Miami★★★** on US-1. Near **Key Largo★**, **John Pennekamp Coral Reef SP★★** habors tropical fish, coral and fine snorkeling waters. To the SW, **Islamorada** is known for **charter fishing**. At **Marathon** (MM 50), **Sombrero Beach** is a good swimming spot,

Bahia Honda SP, Florida Keys

but **Bahia Honda SP★★** (MM 36.8) is considered the best **beach★★** in the Keys. Pass **National Key Deer Refuge★** (MM 30.5), haven to the 2ft-tall deer unique to the lower Keys. End at **Key West★★★**, joining others at **Mallory Square Dock** to view the **sunset★★**.

The Ozarks★

343 miles/552 kilometers
Maps 227, 117, 219, 107, 106

From the state capital of **Little Rock**, take I-30 SW to Exit 111, then US-70 W to Hot Springs. Drive N on Rte. 7/Central Ave. to **Hot Springs NP★★** to enjoy the therapeutic waters. Travel N on Rte. 7 across the Arkansas River to Russellville. Continue on **Scenic Highway 7★** N through **Ozark National Forest** and across the **Buffalo National River** to Harrison. Take US-62/65 NW to Bear Creek Springs, continuing W on US-62 through **Eureka Springs★**, with its historic district, to **Pea Ridge NMP★**, a Civil War site. Return E on US-62 to the junction of Rte. 21 at Berryville. Travel N on Rte. 21 to Blue Eye, taking Rte. 86 E to US-65, which leads N to the entertainment hub of **Branson**, Missouri, to end the tour.

River Road Plantations★★

200 miles/323 kilometers
Maps 239, 134, 194

From **New Orleans★★★**, take US-90 W to Rte. 48 along the Mississippi River to Destrehan (note that due to the levees, the river isn't visible). At no. 13034, **Destrehan★★** is considered the oldest plantation house in the Mississippi Valley. Continue NW on Rte. 48 to US-61 to Laplace to connect to Rte. 44. Head N past **San Francisco Plantation★**, built in 1856. At Burnside, take Rte. 75 N to St. Gabriel. En route, watch for **Houmas H ouse★**. Take Rte. 30 to **Baton Rouge★**, the state capital. Then drive S along the **West Bank★★** on Rte. 1 to White Castle, site of **Nottoway★**, the largest plantation home in the South. Continue to Donaldsonville, then turn onto Rte. 18. Travel E to Gretna, passing **Oak Alley★** (no. 3645) and **Laura Plantation★★** (no. 2247) along the way. From Gretna, take US-90 to New Orleans, where the tour ends.

CANADA

Gaspésie, Québec★★★

933 kilometers/578 miles (loop)
Maps 178, 179

Leave **Sainte-Flavie** via Rte. 132 NE, stopping to visit **Reford Gardens★★★** en route to **Matane**. After Cap-Chat, take Rte. 299 S to

Percé Rock, Gaspésie, Québec
© Sime/Photononstop

Gaspésie Park★ for expansive **views★★**. Back on Rte. 132, follow the Scenic Route from **La Martre to Rivière-au-Renard★★**. Continue to **Cap-des-Rosiers**, entrance to majestic **Forillon NP★★**. Follow Rte. 132 along the coast through **Gaspé★**, the administrative center of the peninsula, to **Percé★★★**, a coastal village known for **Percé Rock★★**, a mammoth offshore rock wall. Drive SW on Rt. 132 through **Paspébiac** to **Carleton**, which offers a **panorama★★** from the summit of **Mont Saint-Joseph**. Farther SW, detour 6km/4mi S to see an array of fossils at **Parc de Miguasha★**. Back on Rte. 132, travel W to **Matapédia**, then follow Rte. 132 N, passing **Causapscal**—a departure point for salmon fishing expeditions—to end the tour at Sainte-Flavie.

North Shore Lake Superior★★

275 kilometers/171 miles Map 169

From the port city of **Thunder Bay★★**—and nearby **Old Fort William★★**—drive the Trans-Canada Hwy. (Rte. 11/17) E to Rte. 587. Detour to **Sleeping Giant PP★**, which offers fine **views★** of the lake. Back along the Trans-Canada Hwy., **Amethyst Mine** (take E. Loon Rd.) is a rock hound's delight (fee).
Farther NE, located 12km/8mi off the highway, **Ouimet Canyon★★** is a startling environment for the area. Just after the highway's Red Rock turnoff, watch for **Red Rock Cuesta**, a natural formation 210m/690ft high. Cross the Nipigon River and continue along **Nipigon Bay★★**, enjoying **views★★** of the rocky, conifer-covered islands. The **view★★** of **Kama Bay** through **Kama Rock Cut** is striking. Continue to **Schreiber** to end the tour.

Nova Scotia's Cabot Trail★★

338 kilometers/210 miles Map 181

From **Baddeck★**, follow Hwy. 105 S to the junction with **Cabot Trail** to **North East Margaree★** in salmon-fishing country. Take this road NW to Margaree Harbour, then N to **Chéticamp**, an enclave of Acadian culture. Heading inland, the route enters **Cape Breton Highlands NP★★**, combining seashore and mountains. At Cape North, detour N around Aspy Bay to **Bay St. Lawrence★★**. Then head W to tiny **Capstick** for **shoreline views★**. Return S to Cape North, then drive E to South Harbour. Take the coast road, traveling S through the fishing villages of **New Haven** and **Neils Harbour★**. Rejoin Cabot Trail S, passing the resort area of the **Ingonishs**. Take the right fork after Indian Brook to reach St. Ann's, home of **Gaelic College★**, specializing in bagpipe and Highland dance classes. Rejoin Hwy. 105 to return to Baddeck.

Cabot Trail, Cape Breton Highlands NP
© Jerry Whaley/age fotostock

Canadian Rockies★★★

467 kilometers/290 miles Map 164

Note: Some roads in Yoho NP are closed to cars mid-Oct to June due to snow, but are open for skiing.

Leave Banff★★ by Hwy. 1, traveling W. After 5.5km/3.5mi, take **Bow Valley Parkway★** (Hwy. 1A) NW within **Banff NP★★★**. At Lake Louise Village, detour W to find **Lake Louise★★★**. Back on Hwy. 1, head N to the junction of Hwy. 93, turn W and follow Hwy. 1 past Kicking Horse Pass into **Yoho NP★★**. Continue through Field, and turn right onto the road N to **Emerald Lake★★★**. Return to the junction of Rte. 93 and Hwy. 1, heading N on Rte. 93 along the Icefields **Parkway★★★**. Pass **Crowfoot Glacier★★** and **Bow Lake★★** on the left. Peyto Lake★★★ is reached by spur road. After **Parker Ridge★★**, massive **Athabasca Glacier★★★** looms on the left. Continue to Jasper★ and Jasper NP★★★. From Jasper, turn left onto Hwy. 16 and head into **Mount Robson PP★★**, home to **Mount Robson★★★** (3,954m/12,972ft.). End the tour at Tête Jaune Cache.

Moraine Lake, Banff NP, Canadian Rockies
© Robert Harding/hemis.fr

Vancouver Island★★★

337 kilometers/209 miles

Maps 282, 163, 162

To enjoy a scenic drive that begins 11mi N of **Victoria★★★**, take Douglas St. N from Victoria to the Trans-Canada Highway (Hwy. 1) and follow **Malahat Drive★** (between Goldstream PP and Mill Bay Rd.) for 12mi. Continue N on Hwy. 1 past Duncan, **Chemainus★**—

Tofino harbor, Vancouver Island
© Eric P. Lucas/Michelin

known for its murals—and Nanaimo to Parksville. Take winding Rte. 4 W (Pacific Rim Hwy.) passing **Englishman River Falls PP★** and Cameron Lake. Just beyond the lake, **Cathedral Grove★★** holds endangered 800-year-old Douglas firs. The road descends to **Port Alberni**, departure point for cruises on Barkley Sound, and follows Sproat Lake before climbing Klitsa Mountain. The route leads to the Pacific along the Kennedy River. At the coast, turn left and drive SE to Ucluelet. Then head N to enter **Pacific Rim NPR★★★**. Continue to road's end at **Tofino★** to end the tour.

Yukon Circuit★★

1,485 kilometers/921 miles Map 155

Note: Top of the World Highway is closed mid-Oct to mid-May due to snow.

From **Whitehorse★**, capital of Yukon Territory, drive N on the **Klondike Hwy**. (Rte. 2), crossing the Yukon River at **Carmacks**. After 196km/122mi, small islands divide the river into fast-flowing channels at **Five Finger Rapids★**. From Stewart Crossing, continue NW on Rte. 2 to **Dawson★★**, a historic frontier town. Ferry across the river and drive the **Top of the World Hwy.★★** (Rte. 9), with its **views★★★**, to the Alaska border. Rte. 9 joins Rte. 5, passing tiny Chicken, Alaska. At Tetlin Junction, head SE on Rte. 2, paralleling Tetlin NWR. Enter Canada and follow the **Alaska Highway★★** (Rte. 1) SE along **Kluane Lake★★** to **Haines Junction**, gateway to **Kluane NPR★★**, home of **Mount Logan**, Canada's highest peak (5,959m/19,550ft). Continue E to Rte. 2 to return to Whitehorse.

Kluane NP, Yukon Circuit
© Aflo/hemis.fr

travelguide.michelin.com
www.viamichelin.com

Notes

Notes

Developed using Globe Turner, LLC data. The information contained herein is for informational purposes only. No representation is made or warranty given as to its content, road conditions or route usability or expeditiousness. User assumes all risk of use. Globe Turner, LLC, its parents and affiliates, and Michelin North America, Inc. and their respective suppliers assume no responsibility for any loss or delay resulting from such use.

MICHELIN NORTH AMERICA, INC.
Michelin Travel & Lifestyle North America
One Parkway South
Greenville, SC 29615 U.S.A.